50: *Afro-American Writers Before the Harlem Renaissance,* edited by Trudier Harris (1986)

51: *Afro-American Writers from the Harlem Renaissance to 1940,* edited by Trudier Harris (1987)

52: *American Writers for Children Since 1960: Fiction,* edited by Glenn E. Estes (1986)

53: *Canadian Writers Since 1960,* First Series, edited by W. H. New (1986)

54: *American Poets, 1880-1945,* Third Series, 2 parts, edited by Peter Quartermain (1987)

55: *Victorian Prose Writers Before 1867,* edited by William B. Thesing (1987)

56: *German Fiction Writers, 1914-1945,* edited by James Hardin (1987)

57: *Victorian Prose Writers After 1867,* edited by William B. Thesing (1987)

58: *Jacobean and Caroline Dramatists,* edited by Fredson Bowers (1987)

59: *American Literary Critics and Scholars, 1800-1850,* edited by John W. Rathbun and Monica M. Grecu (1987)

60: *Canadian Writers Since 1960,* Second Series, edited by W. H. New (1987)

61: *American Writers for Children Since 1960: Poets, Illustrators, and Nonfiction Authors,* edited by Glenn E. Estes (1987)

62: *Elizabethan Dramatists,* edited by Fredson Bowers (1987)

63: *Modern American Critics, 1920-1955,* edited by Gregory S. Jay (1988)

64: *American Literary Critics and Scholars, 1850-1880,* edited by John W. Rathbun and Monica M. Grecu (1988)

65: *French Novelists, 1900-1930,* edited by Catharine Savage Brosman (1988)

66: *German Fiction Writers, 1885-1913,* 2 parts, edited by James Hardin (1988)

67: *Modern American Critics Since 1955,* edited by Gregory S. Jay (1988)

68: *Canadian Writers, 1920-1959,* First Series, edited by W. H. New (1988)

69: *Contemporary German Fiction Writers,* First Series, edited by Wolfgang D. Elfe and James Hardin (1988)

70: *British Mystery Writers, 1860-1919,* edited by Bernard Benstock and Thomas F. Staley (1988)

71: *American Literary Critics and Scholars, 1880-1900,* edited by John W. Rathbun and Monica M. Grecu (1988)

72: *French Novelists, 1930-1960,* edited by Catharine Savage Brosman (1988)

73: *American Magazine Journalists, 1741-1850,* edited by Sam G. Riley (1988)

74: *American Short-Story Writers Before 1880,* edited by Bobby Ellen Kimbel, with the assistance of William E. Grant (1988)

75: *Contemporary German Fiction Writers,* Second Series, edited by Wolfgang D. Elfe and James Hardin (1988)

76: *Afro-American Writers, 1940-1955,* edited by Trudier Harris (1988)

77: *British Mystery Writers, 1920-1939,* edited by Bernard Benstock and Thomas F. Staley (1989)

78: *American Short-Story Writers, 1880-1910,* edited by Bobby Ellen Kimbel, with the assistance of William E. Grant (1989)

Documentary Series

1: *Sherwood Anderson, Willa Cather, John Dos Passos, Theodore Dreiser, F. Scott Fitzgerald, Ernest Hemingway, Sinclair Lewis,* edited by Margaret A. Van Antwerp (1982)

2: *James Gould Cozzens, James T. Farrell, William Faulkner, John O'Hara, John Steinbeck, Thomas Wolfe, Richard Wright,* edited by Margaret A. Van Antwerp (1982)

3: *Saul Bellow, Jack Kerouac, Norman Mailer, Vladimir Nabokov, John Updike, Kurt Vonnegut,* edited by Mary Bruccoli (1983)

4: *Tennessee Williams,* edited by Margaret A. Van Antwerp and Sally Johns (1984)

5: *American Transcendentalists,* edited by Joel Myerson (1988)

Yearbooks

1980, edited by Karen L. Rood, Jean W. Ross, and Richard Ziegfeld (1981)

1981, edited by Karen L. Rood, Jean W. Ross, and Richard Ziegfeld (1982)

1982, edited by Richard Ziegfeld; associate editors: Jean W. Ross and Lynne C. Zeigler (1983)

1983, edited by Mary Bruccoli and Jean W. Ross; associate editor: Richard Ziegfeld (1984)

1984, edited by Jean W. Ross (1985)

1985, edited by Jean W. Ross (1986)

1986, edited by J. M. Brook (1987)

1987, edited by J. M. Brook (1988)

Concise Series

The New Consciousness, 1941-1968 (1987)

Colonization to the American Renaissance, 1640-1865 (1988)

Realism, Naturalism, and Local Color, 1865-1917 (1988)

Dictionary of Literary Biography • Volume Seventy-eight

American Short-Story Writers, 1880-1910

Dictionary of Literary Biography • Volume Seventy-eight

American Short-Story Writers, 1880-1910

Edited by
Bobby Ellen Kimbel
Pennsylvania State University, Ogontz Campus

with the assistance of
William E. Grant
Bowling Green State University

A Bruccoli Clark Layman Book
Gale Research Inc. • Book Tower • Detroit, Michigan 48226

Manufactured by Edward Brothers, Inc.
Ann Arbor, Michigan
Printed in the United States of America

Copyright © 1989
GALE RESEARCH INC.

Library of Congress Cataloging-in-Publication Data

American short-story writers, 1880-1910.
   p. cm.–(Dictionary of literary biography; v. 78)
"A Bruccoli Clark Layman book."
Bibliography: p.
Includes index.
   1. Short stories, American–History and criticism.
2. Short stories, American–Bio-bibliography. 3. Authors,
American–Biography–Dictionaries. I. Kimbel, Bobby
Ellen. II. Grant, William E. (William Earl), 1933-
PS374.S5A39   1988   813'.01'09   88-30994

ISBN 0-8103-4556-0

for Selma K. Roomberg,
who taught me the love of literature

Contents

Plan of the Series

. . . Almost the most prodigious asset of a country, and perhaps its most precious possession, is its native literary product—when that product is fine and noble and enduring.

Mark Twain*

The advisory board, the editors, and the publisher of the *Dictionary of Literary Biography* are joined in endorsing Mark Twain's declaration. The literature of a nation provides an inexhaustible resource of permanent worth. We intend to make literature and its creators better understood and more accessible to students and the reading public, while satisfying the standards of teachers and scholars.

To meet these requirements, *literary biography* has been construed in terms of the author's achievement. The most important thing about a writer is his writing. Accordingly, the entries in *DLB* are career biographies, tracing the development of the author's canon and the evolution of his reputation.

The purpose of *DLB* is not only to provide reliable information in a convenient format but also to place the figures in the larger perspective of literary history and to offer appraisals of their accomplishments by qualified scholars.

The publication plan for *DLB* resulted from two years of preparation. The project was proposed to Bruccoli Clark by Frederick G. Ruffner, president of the Gale Research Company, in November 1975. After specimen entries were prepared and typeset, an advisory board was formed to refine the entry format and develop the series rationale. In meetings held during 1976, the publisher, series editors, and advisory board approved the scheme for a comprehensive biographical dictionary of persons who contributed to North American literature. Editorial work on the first volume began in January 1977, and it was published in 1978. In order to make *DLB* more than a reference tool and to compile volumes that individually have claim to status as lit-

erary history, it was decided to organize volumes by topic, period, or genre. Each of these freestanding volumes provides a biographical-bibliographical guide and overview for a particular area of literature. We are convinced that this organization—as opposed to a single alphabet method—constitutes a valuable innovation in the presentation of reference material. The volume plan necessarily requires many decisions for the placement and treatment of authors who might properly be included in two or three volumes. In some instances a major figure will be included in separate volumes, but with different entries emphasizing the aspect of his career appropriate to each volume. Ernest Hemingway, for example, is represented in *American Writers in Paris, 1920-1939* by an entry focusing on his expatriate apprenticeship; he is also in *American Novelists, 1910-1945* with an entry surveying his entire career. Each volume includes a cumulative index of subject authors and articles. Comprehensive indexes to the entire series are planned.

With volume ten in 1982 it was decided to enlarge the scope of *DLB*. By the end of 1986 twenty-one volumes treating British literature had been published, and volumes for Commonwealth and Modern European literature were in progress. The series has been further augmented by the *DLB Yearbooks* (since 1981) which update published entries and add new entries to keep the *DLB* current with contemporary activity. There have also been *DLB Documentary Series* volumes which provide biographical and critical source materials for figures whose work is judged to have particular interest for students. One of these companion volumes is entirely devoted to Tennessee Williams.

We define literature as the *intellectual commerce of a nation:* not merely as belles lettres but as that ample and complex process by which ideas are generated, shaped, and transmitted. *DLB* entries are not limited to "creative writers" but extend to other figures who in their time and in their way influenced the mind of a people. Thus the series encompasses historians, journalists, publishers, and screenwriters. By this means readers of *DLB* may be aided to perceive litera-

*From an unpublished section of Mark Twain's autobiography, copyright © by the Mark Twain Company.

ture not as cult scripture in the keeping of intellectual high priests but firmly positioned at the center of a nation's life.

DLB includes the major writers appropriate to each volume and those standing in the ranks immediately behind them. Scholarly and critical counsel has been sought in deciding which minor figures to include and how full their entries should be. Wherever possible, useful references are made to figures who do not warrant separate entries.

Each *DLB* volume has a volume editor responsible for planning the volume, selecting the figures for inclusion, and assigning the entries. Volume editors are also responsible for preparing, where appropriate, appendices surveying the major periodicals and literary and intellectual movements for their volumes, as well as lists of further readings. Work on the series as a whole is coordinated at the Bruccoli Clark Layman editorial center in Columbia, South Carolina, where the editorial staff is responsible for accuracy of the published volumes.

One feature that distinguishes *DLB* is the illustration policy—its concern with the iconography of literature. Just as an author is influenced by his surroundings, so is the reader's understanding of the author enhanced by a knowledge of his environment. Therefore *DLB* volumes include not only drawings, paintings, and photographs of authors, often depicting them at various stages in their careers, but also illustrations of their families and places where they lived. Title pages are regularly reproduced in facsimile along with dust jackets for modern authors. The dust jackets are a special feature of *DLB* because they often document better than anything else the way in which an author's work was perceived in its own time. Specimens of the writers' manuscripts are included when feasible.

Samuel Johnson rightly decreed that "The chief glory of every people arises from its authors." The purpose of the *Dictionary of Literary Biography* is to compile literary history in the surest way available to us—by accurate and comprehensive treatment of the lives and work of those who contributed to it.

The *DLB* Advisory Board

Foreword

The period covered by this volume (the second on American short-story writers in the *Dictionary of Literary Biography* series) is 1880-1910, a short span of time as historical periods go, but one demonstrating dramatic changes in the conception of the short-story form in America. In 1880 Henry James had entered only his "middle phase"; Bret Harte and Mark Twain were at the apex of their illustrious but stylistically traditional careers. The literary movements called "realism" and "naturalism" (these terms are employed in the sense that they have traditionally been used although many contemporary critics find them inexact) were dominant during this period, and, although the changes in rhetorical strategies and thematic focus they embodied were in many ways startlingly new, the worlds they created were, even for the most unsophisticated reader, identifiable. At the end of the period Gertrude Stein's *Three Lives* (1909) was published, its innovations in language and in narrative technique so extreme that the short-story form, up to then comfortably defined by nineteenth-century models, was thrust, suddenly, into the twentieth century. (For an extended discussion of Stein's short fiction, see the next *DLB* volume on American short-story writers.) As with any dramatic shift in vision and technique in the world of art, the phenomenon that *Three Lives* represented was the culmination of a series of responses to powerful currents in the larger world beyond the writer's study.

From 1880 to 1910 extraordinary upheavals took place in the Western world, radical shifts in culture, in its very idea of itself, its beliefs, its values, its modes of production, its look, its possibilities, its expectations for the future. The speed at which the Industrial Revolution transformed society between the last years of the nineteenth century and the early years of the twentieth is dizzying. Thomas A. Edison invented the phonograph in 1877 and the first incandescent-filament light bulbs in 1879. The first synthetic fiber was produced in 1883; the Parsons steam turbine in 1884; the electric motor and the Kodak box camera in 1888; the kinetoscope in 1894. In 1895 Diesel developed his engine; Roentgen discovered X rays; Marconi invented the radio telegraph; and the Lumière brothers developed the movie camera. In 1896 Ford tested his first car; in 1903 at Kitty Hawk the Wright brothers demonstrated to the world that human beings could in fact fly.

The intellectual advances that were permanently to alter our views of the essential nature of human life and of the physical world had only recently appeared; they shattered fundamental and cherished assumptions. Charles Darwin's *The Origin of the Species* was published in 1859; Herbert Spencer's *First Principles*, with its view of human nature as fundamentally ruthless (the "survival of the fittest"), in 1862 and 1863; Charles Lyell's *The Geological Evidences of the Antiquity of Man* in 1863. These treatises worked to expand, by millions of years, the estimated age of the earth and to shrink, immutably, the place and the stature of human life in the larger scheme of things. The discovery of the cave paintings at Altamira in 1879 led to the recognition that those creatures existing thirty-five thousand years ago were not mindless brutes but possessed an intelligent culture and were capable of imaginatively recording it, and thus, they joined their modern counterparts in the species Homo sapiens in the annals of recorded human history. In 1867 the first volume of Karl Marx's *Das Kapital* was published; 1895 saw Sigmund Freud's first major psychoanalytical work, *Studies in Hysteria*. Together, they subverted previously held notions of the structure of society and the structure of mind. In a 1914 Harvard lecture Bertrand Russell caught the sense of things adrift in the cultural arena, teeming with theories, facts, discoveries: "The immense extension of our knowledge of facts in recent times has made men distrustful of the truth of wide, ambitious systems: theories come and go swiftly, each serving, for a moment, to classify known facts and promote the search for new ones, but each in turn proving inadequate to deal with the new facts when they have been found. Even those who invent the theories do not, in science, regard them as anything but a temporary makeshift. The ideal of an all-embracing synthesis, such as the Middle Ages believed themselves to have attained, recedes further and further beyond the limits of what seems feasible. In such a world, as in the world of Montaigne, nothing seems worthwhile except the discovery of more and more facts, each in turn the deathblow to some cherished theory; the ordering intellect grows weary, and becomes slovenly through despair."

The texture of daily life for the middle class, a distinct, rapidly expanding, and increasingly powerful group, mirrored these changes. During the second half of the nineteenth century museum visitors saw paintings such as *Whistler's Mother*, John Singer Sargent's limpid portraits, or Winslow Homer's seascapes; by 1910 they had become familiar with (even if they had not adjusted to) the increasingly nonrepresentational works of impressionists such as Claude Monet, Edouard Manet, and Paul Cézanne, and–through the exhibition of paintings by Les Fauves at the 1905 Autumn Salon in Paris and the 1907 cubist exhibition in Paris–they were beginning to become aware of avant-garde works of artists such as Henri Matisse and Pablo Picasso (though most Americans were not to discover modern nonrealistic art until the New York Armory Show of 1913). The airy operettas of Gilbert and Sullivan and the light operas of Jacques Offenbach represent the prevailing musical taste of the 1880s; thirty years later the musical status quo was challenged by the dark and somber postromantic musical compositions of Gustav Mahler and Arnold Schönberg, and in 1913 Parisians, outraged by the strangeness of the new musical sound, rioted at the first performance of Igor Stravinsky's ballet *The Rite of Spring*. Between 1880 and 1910 immigration swelled the population of New York City from one to four million; street lighting made night travel possible; movie theaters provided a new kind of entertainment. The "weekend" as a vacation concept evolved; and the comic strip began to be a regular feature in newspapers. In 1880 people moved from place to place in horse-drawn buggies; in 1910, 458,377 automobiles were registered in the United States. Most revealing about this era–aptly named, after Mark Twain and Charles Dudley Warner's novel, *The Gilded Age* (1873)–never in American history had there been so huge a gap between the very rich and the very poor.

One of the byproducts of the great technological imperative of the late 1800s was the creation of a peculiarly American aristocracy–the cap-tains of industry and finance. There were only three millionaires in 1860; by the turn of the century there were four thousand. The Carnegies, Goulds, Astors, Vanderbilts, Huntingtons, Cookes, Morgans, and Armours exemplified the much vaunted "rugged individualism" of the age; nearly all had begun as have-nots–farm boys, office boys, clerks–and through tough-mindedness, shrewdness, hard work, and, just as often, unscrupulousness, amassed huge fortunes. Vernon L. Parrington described these business titans as "blackguards for the most part, railway wreckers, cheaters and swindlers . . . who fought their way encased in rhinoceros hides." Their fortunes were often assured and augmented by ubiquitous corruption in government–vote selling, embezzlement of public funds, and political chicanery of every kind.

The grand architectural symbols of wealth and power accumulated in clusters on New York's Fifth Avenue and in Newport, Rhode Island, exemplifying as neither before nor since in American history Thorstein Veblen's theory of "conspicuous consumption." Seventy-room mansions were decorated with artifacts from palaces and churches all over Europe and the Orient. To assemble them thousands of skilled artisans were imported. Meanwhile, the poor, largely an immigrant class, lived and worked under abysmal conditions. Labor unions were in their infancy, and workers were without power or protection; wages were often a dollar a day; the ten-hour workday was common. In the steel industry a twelve-hour day and a seven-day week prevailed. Big business, optimistic and exuberant, remained above it all, unrestrained by either the authority of government or a sense of social responsibility.

The new age, defined by technological marvels, fervent scientism, and monstrous social inequities, gave rise to a new literature reflecting its impulses. Although the process was gradual and there were reactionary currents, there was a steady movement after the Civil War away from the exotic, idealized, and visionary and toward the local and familiar, the carefully observed, and the coolly sociological and psychological. This new literature described and evaluated the very real tensions and complexities of American life and American character, and with the rapid growth of literacy, higher education, and libraries, it found a large, receptive readership. "Realism"–a term derived from William Dean Howells's appeal to his colleagues to commit themselves to "nothing more and nothing less than the truthful treatment of material"–was to determine the direction of American fiction for the next half-century.

Many of the popular magazines that had flourished since mid century helped to effect the transition from romance to realism in the short-story form, often by publishing the work of regionalist writers. *Harper's New Monthly, Lippincott's,* and the *Atlantic Monthly* competed actively for fiction pieces that could capture the dialect and idiom of the newly developing regions across the country. By 1880 Harriet Beecher Stowe and Rose Terry Cooke had written about life in New England, Sarah Orne Jewett about the Maine coast, Rebecca Harding Davis about the iron mills of Pennsylvania and West Virginia, George Washington Cable about New Orleans, Helen Hunt Jackson and Bret Harte about the Far West. After 1880 Mary E. Wilkins Freeman and Kate Chopin depicted life as they witnessed it first-hand in New England and in Louisiana, demonstrating, beyond the authentic sense of place for which they were applauded, real sensitivity to social injustice and great skill at capturing the significance of the ordinary–the truthful treatment of the commonplace that Howells had advocated.

In October 1885 Brander Matthews, the first short-story theorist since Edgar Allan Poe, announced the requirements for the form in a *Lippincott's* magazine essay, "The Philosophy of the Short-Story." The short story should have, he said, originality, unity, compression, brilliancy of style, action, substance, and, if possible, fantasy. Authors have long since abandoned such strictures, but the effect of this carefully reasoned critical theory–that is, description, interpretation, assessment–was to give validity and respectability to the form. In fact the short story, codified and formally named by Matthews, had before then been considered any fictional prose work that was less than the traditional length of the novel. The essay, the first serious, extended genre study, was republished three years later in *Pen and Ink*, a collection of Matthews's essays, and it was revised for publication as a separate volume in 1901. The importance of Matthews's essay cannot be overstated. Here are the distinctions he makes between the short story and the novel: "the Short Story–in spite of the fact that in our language it has no name of its own–is one of the few sharply defined literary forms. It is a *genre*, as M. Bruetière terms it, a species, as a naturalist might call it, as individual as the Lyric itself and as various. It is as distinct an entity as the Epic,

as Tragedy, as Comedy. Now the Novel is not a form of the same sharply defined individuality; it is–or at least it may be anything. It is the child of the Epic and the heir of the Drama; but it is a hybrid. . . . In the history of literature the Short-story was developed long before the Novel, which indeed is but a creature of yesterday, and which was not really established in popular esteem as a worthy rival of the drama until after the widespread success of the Waverly Novels in the early years of the nineteenth century. The Short-story also seems much easier of accomplishment than the Novel, if only because it is briefer. And yet the list of the masters of the Short-story is far less crowded than the list of the masters of the longer form. There are a score or more of very great novelists recorded in the history of fiction; but there are scarcely more than half a score of Short-story writers of an equal eminence."

Matthews offered this prescription: "A good Short-story should have one fresh, central incident, two or three well conceived and sharply drawn characters, a certain symmetrical unity in construction, a deep significance in the catastrophe or climax–not necessarily a moral, as ordinarily understood, but as nothing should be purposeless, the Short-story should illustrate some defect or virtue in human character, or portray some special experience whereby the imagination of the reader may be gratified, his sympathies awakened, or his knowledge of the world increased. It is not easy to fix the limitations of the Short-story. Its construction is an art, far more so than is generally believed." Matthews's enthusiasm for the short story as separate and unique–a form very different from a story that is short–and his dedicated promotion of skilled short-story writers gave an enormous boost to the reputation of a form that had been regarded, when it was regarded at all, as apprentice work or the exercise of fiction writers honing their skills for the longer, more respectable novel.

Matthews's essay, together with critical writings by William Dean Howells, lectures of Walter Besant, articles by Robert Louis Stevenson, and Henry James's prefaces for the New York Edition of his works, established a growing body of critical theory on fiction, which in turn created an acute self-consciousness in fiction writers about the requirements of their craft, with the consequent gradual elevation of the novel and short story to the realms of high art. Fiction, in all its forms, was to become the authentic voice of the twentieth century.

After 1880 the full force of pessimistic determinism inherent in the writings of Darwin, Lyell, Spencer, and Marx could be felt in the larger world, and the growing spiritual unrest was expressed by philosophers such as William James, John Dewey, and George Santayana; by social critics such as Thorstein Veblen and Lincoln Steffens; by historians such as Henry Adams; and by the later realist and naturalist fiction writers, influenced by the pessimism of Fyodor Dostoyevski, Ivan Turgenev, and Leo Tolstoy in Russia and by Gustave Flaubert, Guy de Maupassant, and Émile Zola in France.

In 1891 Hamlin Garland's *Main-Travelled Roads*, a collection of somber tales, described the collapse of expectations about life on the American frontier. The stories caught the texture of daily existence in the West: the awful degradation, the grinding work, and the bone-crushing weariness of the settlers, a world Garland knew well having experienced it. In his review of the collection Howells described the stories as "full of those gaunt, grim, sordid, pathetic, ferocious figures, whom our satirists find so easy to caricature as Hayseeds, and whose blind groping for fairer conditions is so grotesque to the newspapers and so menacing to the politicians." Garland's bitter, convincingly realized stories are one of the earliest American responses to Émile Zola's demand that "a novelist must be only a scientist, an analyst, an anatomist, and his work must have the certainty, the solidity and the practical application of a work of science." Not until Theodore Dreiser was there a writer who followed Zola's prescription precisely; but strains of naturalism are evident in Garland's stories, as they were to be in the fiction of Stephen Crane, Frank Norris, and Jack London.

While Easterners could read about the bleak lives of Garland's frontier people at a comfortable remove, they could not have been prepared for Crane's *Maggie: A Girl of the Streets* (1893), which depicted degeneration in their midst. This spare, brutal novel and the works by Crane which followed–among them *The Red Badge of Courage* (1895), "The Open Boat" (1897), and "The Blue Hotel" (1898)–were, in theme, tone, technique, and intent, a far cry from the realism of William Dean Howells and the moral probings of Henry James. Crane's understanding of the effect of environment on an individual's behavior, his acute depictions of fear,

and his astounding ability to seize a moment pictorially are the hallmarks of his style. He had been trained as a reporter, but, as one critic said, "Life came to him in its primary colors, blue, red, and yellow, and he asked its meaning. The newspaper is not interested in such notions."

Such writers as Willa Cather, Richard Harding Davis, Zona Gale, Lafcadio Hearn, Irvin S. Cobb, Edna Ferber, Damon Runyon, Theodore Dreiser, and Ernest Hemingway also began as journalists. The daily disciplining of the imagination and the awareness of the editor's prerogative to blue-pencil must have engendered a precision inherent, then as now, in the best short-story writing. As reporters they were trained to catch the vivid details of the physical world and the subtle nuances of human experience that might serve as material for stories.

By the end of the nineteenth century short stories had become popular commodities and were frequently syndicated. The fifteen-cent magazine and the Sunday supplement paid handsomely for short fiction by distinguished writers (as well as hacks). One could find in mass-circulation magazines some of the most memorable fiction of the period–the late work of Henry James, for example, or the remarkable stories of Willa Cather, Stephen Crane, Jack London, Mary E. Wilkins Freeman, and O. Henry (whose "snapper" endings are formulaic but whose adroitness at capturing the experience of the modern metropolis is considerable). Cheek by jowl with these masterpieces sat slick, meretricious stories, whose banality, inflated language, acceptance of sexual taboos, and reliance on neatly packaged happy endings combine to create the very antithesis of life as it is lived.

The writers who were struggling to discover their individual voices and the rhetorical means to convey the "truths" of the world around them were dismayed to find their stories competing for placement in magazines with such debased examples of short fiction. No one expressed the bewilderment and exasperation of these fine writers more convincingly than Theodore Dreiser, telling of his beginnings as a serious writer in *A Book About Myself* (1922): "I set to examining the current magazines and the fiction and articles to be found therein: *Century, Scribner's, Harper's*. I was never more confounded than by the discrepancy existing between my own observations and those displayed here, the beauty and peace and charm to be found in everything, the almost complete absence of any reference to the coarse and the vulgar and the cruel and the terrible. . . . Love was almost invariably rewarded in these tales. Almost invariably one's dreams came true, in the magazines. Most of these bits of fiction, delicately phrased, flowed so easily, with such an air of assurance, omniscience and condescension, that I was quite put out by my own lacks and defects. . . . I read and I read, but all I could gather was that I had no such tales to tell, and, however much I tried, I could not think of any."

Two other writers who attempted to stem the tide of pulp fiction, insisting on the highest aesthetic standards for their work, were Edith Wharton and Willa Cather. It was once fashionable, until recent feminist scholars provided a new perspective, to place these two women inalterably in the shadow of Henry James. Cather in this or that story was Jamesian or un-Jamesian; Wharton was described variously as a disciple of James, a lesser James, or a female James. Indeed, the man who was both friend and mentor to her was to become, finally, her albatross—the titan to whom she was inevitably compared and usually found wanting. The literary characteristics these three share are those that define most traditionalist literature: a deliberately unhurried narrative; a consecutive chronology; and a recognizable social world in which time-honored institutions—the bonds of family and community, the strength, dignity, and endurance of the human spirit form a moral nexus. But Wharton and Cather worked from impulses of a very different kind from those that drove Henry James. To say that they had no interest in imitating his long, circuitous sentences, qualifiers piled up one after another in search of the perfect moral equivalent, is to address only the most arresting stylistic distinction between his writing and their own. Wharton and Cather consistently expressed a longing to escape the restrictions imposed on women of their time, a concern that distinguishes them from James. In their work one can see an underlying weariness, predictive, perhaps, of the catastrophic events that came in the second decade of the twentieth century. ("The world broke in two in 1912 or thereabouts," Cather remarked with characteristic terseness.)

While, like James, Wharton and Cather are more often regarded as novelists, the remarkable quality of their short fiction makes it clear that they regarded the story not as an exercise, a re-

prieve from the more taxing demands of novel writing, but as a separate vehicle, perfect for the creation of fictional constructs wholly inappropriate to the longer form. Indeed, Wharton devoted one full chapter of *The Writing of Fiction* (1925) to a discussion of the short story, which she called not a "loose web spread over the surface of life," but rather a "shaft driven straight into the heart of human experience." This statement and Brander Matthews's prescription for the "special experience that increases the reader's knowledge of the world" are perhaps all we need of definition.

In 1880 America was still recovering from the agonies of that long, impossible battle, the Civil War; in 1910 the country was rapidly approaching an even more unthinkable one, the Great War. It is a compelling bracketing. American literature, which in 1880 was largely, if not wholly, determined to witness affirmation in the mirror held up to life—represented, for example, by the pastoral ideal, the warmly rustic, or the sweetly sentimental—metamorphosed in just three decades to a literature of dark, brooding pessimism, whether in the comfortable drawing rooms of the wealthy, where very bad behavior is accompanied by very fine wine, or the dark streets of decaying cities, where drunks and whores and orphans wait for a redemption that will never come. These desperate, lonely people, described by Frank O'Connor in *The Lonely Voice* (1963) as a "submerged population group," first appear in the stories of Crane, and then swell in numbers through the twentieth century—in the work of Gertrude Stein, Sherwood Anderson, William Faulkner, Carson McCullers, Flannery O'Connor, Bobbie Ann Mason, Raymond Carver, Joyce Carol Oates—until they become not the isolated, but the representative figures in American fiction. "Never such innocence again," reads a line in a Phillip Larkin poem, which might serve as a poignant epitaph for the early years of the period covered in this volume. At its close we find in our literature an altered sensibility, whose lineaments would soon be projected in images of darkness or the bottomless pit or the wasteland or the valley of ashes and conveying—in poetry, drama, novel, and story—the inexorable collapse of the American dream.

—Bobby Ellen Kimbel

Acknowledgments

This book was produced by Bruccoli Clark Layman, Inc. Karen L. Rood senior editor for the *Dictionary of Literary Biography* series and J. M. Brook were the in-house editors.

Production coordinator is Kimberly Casey. Art supervisor is Cheryl A. Crombie. Copyediting supervisor is Joan M. Prince. Typesetting supervisor is Kathleen M. Flanagan. William Adams, Laura Ingram, and Michael D. Senecal are editorial associates. The production staff includes Rowena Betts, Charles D. Brower, Amanda Caulley, Patricia Coate, Sarah A. Estes, Cynthia Hallman, Judith K. Ingle, Warren McInnis, Kathy S. Merlette, Sheri Beckett Neal, Virginia Smith, and Mark Van Gunten. Jean W. Ross is permissions editor. Susan Todd is photography editor. Penney L. Haughton did photographic copy work for the volume.

Walter W. Ross and Rhonda Marshall did the library research with the assistance of the reference staff at the Thomas Cooper Library of the University of South Carolina: Daniel Boice, Cathy Eckman, Gary Geer, Cathie Gottlieb, David L. Haggard, Jens Holley, Dennis Isbell, Jackie Kinder, Marcia Martin, Jean Rhyne, Beverly Steele, Ellen Tillett, Carol Tobin, and Virginia Weathers.

Vesta Lee Gordon helped to procure illustrations for the volume.

Dictionary of Literary Biography • Volume Seventy-eight

American Short-Story Writers, 1880-1910

Dictionary of Literary Biography

Gertrude Atherton
(30 October 1857-15 June 1948)

Charlotte S. McClure
Georgia State University

See also the Atherton entry in *DLB 9: American Novelists, 1910-1945*.

BOOKS: *What Dreams May Come, A Romance,* as Frank Lin (Chicago & New York: Belford, Clarke, 1888; London, Glasgow, Manchester & New York: Routledge, 1889);

Hermia Suydam (New York: Current Literature, 1889); republished as *Hermia, An American Woman* (London: Routledge, 1889);

Los Cerritos, A Romance of the Modern Time (New York: Lovell, 1890; London: Heinemann, 1891);

A Question of Time (New York: Lovell, 1891; London: Gay & Bird, 1892);

The Doomswoman (New York: Tait, 1893; London: Hutchinson, 1895);

Before the Gringo Came (New York: Tait, 1894); revised and enlarged as *The Splendid Idle Forties, Stories of Old California* (New York & London: Macmillan, 1902);

A Whirl Asunder (New York & London: Stokes, 1895; London: Cassell, 1895);

Patience Sparhawk and Her Times, A Novel (London & New York: John Lane/Bodley Head, 1897);

His Fortunate Grace (New York: Appleton, 1897; London: Bliss, Sands, 1897);

The Californians (London: John Lane, 1898; New York: Grosset & Dunlap, 1898);

American Wives and English Husbands, A Novel (London: Service & Paton, 1898; New York: Dodd, Mead, 1898);

The Valiant Runaways (New York: Dodd, Mead, 1898; London: Nisbet, 1899);

Gertrude Atherton

A Daughter of the Vine (London & New York: John Lane/Bodley Head, 1899);

Senator North (New York & London: John Lane/Bodley Head, 1900);

The Aristocrats, Being the Impression of the Lady Helen Pole During Her Sojourn in the Great North Woods as Spontaneously Recorded in Her

Letters to Her Friend in North Britain, the Countess of Edge and Ross (London & New York: Lane, 1901);

The Conqueror, Being the True and Romantic Story of Alexander Hamilton (New York & London: Macmillan, 1902); revised as *The Conqueror, A Dramatized Biography of Alexander Hamilton* (New York: Stokes, 1916);

Heart of Hyacinth (New York: Harper, 1903);

Mrs. Pendleton's Four-in-Hand (New York & London: Macmillan, 1903);

Rulers of Kings, A Novel (New York & London: Harper, 1904);

The Bell in the Fog and Other Stories (New York & London: Harper, 1905);

The Traveling Thirds (New York & London: Harper, 1905);

Rezánov (New York & London: Authors and Newspapers Association, 1906; London: Murray, 1906);

Ancestors, A Novel (New York & London: Harper, 1907; London: Murray, 1907);

The Gorgeous Isle, A Romance, Scene, Nevis, B. W. I., 1842 (New York: Doubleday, Page, 1908; London: Murray, 1908);

Tower of Ivory, A Novel (New York: Macmillan, 1910; London: Murray, 1910);

Julia France and Her Times, A Novel (New York: Macmillan, 1912; London: Murray, 1912);

Perch of the Devil (New York: Stokes, 1914; London: Murray, 1914);

California, An Intimate History (New York & London: Harper, 1914);

Mrs. Balfame, A Novel (New York: Stokes, 1916; London: Murray, 1916);

Life in the War Zone (New York: Systems Printing Company, 1916);

The Living Present (New York: Stokes, 1917; London: Murray, 1917);

The White Morning, A Novel of the Power of the German Women in Wartime (New York: Stokes, 1918);

The Avalanche, A Mystery Story (New York: Stokes, 1919);

Transplanted, A Novel (New York: Dodd, Mead, 1919);

The Sisters-in-Law, A Novel of Our Time (New York: Stokes, 1921; London: Murray, 1921);

Sleeping Fires, A Novel (New York: Stokes, 1922); republished as *Dormant Fires* (London: Murray, 1922);

Black Oxen (New York: Boni & Liveright, 1923; London: Murray, 1923);

The Crystal Cup (New York: Boni & Liveright, 1925; London: Murray, 1925);

The Immortal Marriage (New York: Boni & Liveright, 1927; London: Murray, 1927);

The Jealous Gods, A Processional Novel of the Fifth Century B.C. (Concerning One Alcibiades) (New York: Liveright, 1928); republished as *Vengeful Gods* (London: Murray, 1928);

Dido, Queen of Hearts (New York: Liveright, 1929; London: Chapman & Hall, 1929);

The Sophisticates (New York: Liveright, 1931; London: Chapman & Hall, 1931);

Adventures of a Novelist (New York: Liveright, 1932; London: Cape, 1932);

The Foghorn, Stories (Boston & New York: Houghton Mifflin, 1934; London: Jarrolds, 1935);

Golden Peacock (Boston & New York: Houghton Mifflin, 1936; London: Butterworth, 1937);

Rezánov and Doña Concha (New York: Stokes, 1937);

Can Women Be Gentlemen? (Boston: Houghton Mifflin, 1938);

The House of Lee (New York & London: Appleton-Century, 1940; London: Eyre & Spottiswoode, 1942);

The Horn of Life (New York: Appleton-Century, 1942);

Golden Gate Country (New York: Duell, Sloan & Pearce, 1945);

My San Francisco, A Wayward Biography (Indianapolis & New York: Bobbs-Merrill, 1946).

OTHER: *A Few of Hamilton's Letters, Including His Description of the Great West Indian Hurricane of 1772*, edited by Atherton (New York & London: Macmillan, 1903);

"Concha Arguëllo, Sister Dominica," in *The Spinsters' Book of Fiction* (San Francisco & New York: Elder, 1907);

"Wanted: Imagination," in *What Is a Book? Thoughts About Writing*, edited by Dale Warren (Boston: Houghton Mifflin, 1935).

PERIODICAL PUBLICATIONS:
FICTION
"Mrs. Pendleton's Four-in-Hand," *Cosmopolitan*, 10 (December 1890): 186-204;

"The Doomswoman," *Lippincott's*, 50 (August 1892): 261-365;

"Andreo's Love: The Vengeance of Padre Arroyo," *Current Literature*, 16 (September 1894): 196-197;

"Death," *Anti-Philistine*, 4 (15 September 1897): 220-227;

"Sylvia's Last Story," *Pocket Magazine*, 6 (May 1898): 1-33;

"Modern Primitives," *Good Housekeeping*, 77 (October 1923): 12-16, 214-220;

"Flotsam," *Regionalism and the Female Imagination*, 4 (Winter 1979): 60-91;

"Deep Collar," *New Orleans Review*, 7, no. 1 (1980): 69-81.

NONFICTION

"The Literary Development of California," *Cosmopolitan*, 10 (January 1891): 269-278;

"The Novel and the Short Story," *Bookman* (New York), 17 (March 1903): 36-37;

"Some Truths About American Readers," *Bookman* (New York), 18 (February 1904): 658-660;

"Why Is American Literature Bourgeois?," *North American Review*, 175 (May 1904): 771-781.

Gertrude Atherton's literary reputation may rest as much on her severe criticism in the early 1900s of William Dean Howells's leadership of the "littleistic" school of American literature as on her story chronicle of California that appeared in her novels and short fiction from 1892 to 1942. An admirer of Bret Harte and Mark Twain as original, imaginative writers expressing the energy and unique spirit of the relatively new American nation, California-born Atherton confronted the eastern literary establishment and British literary circles with her provocative personality and literary rendering of what she called the most "original and audacious country the world has ever known" ("Why Is American Literature Bourgeois?," *North American Review*, May 1904). In contrast to Harte's and Twain's characterizations of western miners and other adventurers, Atherton in the 1890s began to depict realistically the daily life and romantic aspirations of the early Californians—Spanish-Mexican landowners—and the inhabitants of San Francisco. Her characters, women and men, were prototypes of the new American that she transformed out of western, European, and some eastern cloth.

Atherton, whose father, Thomas Ludovich Horn, was a New England businessman and whose mother, Gertrude Franklin Horn, was a southern belle, grew up in the area around San Francisco. The fortunes and misfortunes of the first thirty years of her life nurtured the "rotten spot" in her brain, which she claimed was the source of her fiction. Her childhood made erratic by continually changing family circumstances, she attended public and private schools but received the best impetus for a classical education from her Presbyterian grandfather, Stephen Franklin, who insisted that she be well-read. After her romantic elopement at eighteen to marry George Atherton (14 February 1876), son of Dean Faxon Atherton, a New England businessman, and Dominga de Goñi, of Valparaiso, Chile, Atherton gained social acceptance and stability within this Catholic family as well as acquaintance with customs of Spanish-Americans. Fulfilling her desire to be a writer, she secretly submitted stories to periodicals. She experienced two early tragedies: one of her two children, George, died, and her husband perished at sea. Thus, at the age of thirty Gertrude Atherton had to create a new life that would support her daughter, Muriel, and herself. As her first literary attempt at depicting life in San Francisco society in "The Randolphs of Redwood: A Romance" (*Argonaut*, 31 March 1883-5 May 1883) caused her to be ostracized by that society, she decided in 1888 to go to New York and London to carve out her writing career. When Atherton returned to New York and then to California in the early 1890s, she had established the pattern of her writing career—getting a story idea in one place and traveling to another place to write it. When she read in a weekly magazine the question "Why do California writers neglect the old Spanish life of that State?" Atherton reacted by exploring the history and culture of Spanish California in the environs of Monterey, San Luis Obispo, and Santa Barbara, out of which came her first short-story collection, *Before the Gringo Came* (1894), which was revised and expanded as *The Splendid Idle Forties* (1902). She also wrote "Concha Arguëllo, Sister Dominica" specifically for a collection of stories, *The Spinsters' Book of Fiction* (1907), which was produced by California writers to aid the ailing California poet laureate Ina Coolbrith. Her assimilation of this cultural history of old California and her own early life in San Francisco she later transformed into novels of her story-chronicle of California, which Atherton claimed began with *The Doomswoman* (1893).

Until 1907 Gertrude Atherton continued to write short stories portraying the Spanish-Mexican aristocracy in California while she produced several of her best novels of California: *Patience Sparhawk and Her Times* (1897), *The Californians* (1898), and *Ancestors* (1907). The British

Pages from the manuscript for Atherton's 1897 novel His Fortunate Grace *(Gertrude Atherton Collection #6780-c, Clifton Waller Barrett Library, Special Collections Department, University of Virginia Library)*

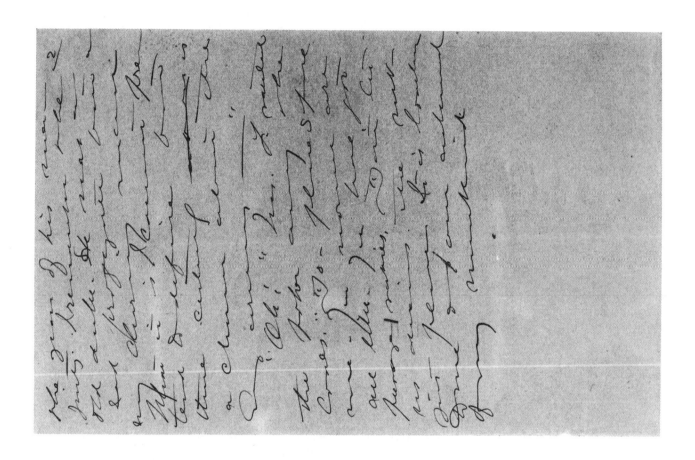

reading public in part satisfied its curiosity about America through her stories of the West. She gathered several tales, reflecting her experiences in the literary and social milieu of London and New York, in a volume entitled *The Bell in the Fog and Other Stories* (1905), dedicated to Henry James, and in *The Foghorn, Stories* (1934). Unpublished manuscripts in Atherton's papers in the Atherton Collection, Bancroft Library, University of California, Berkeley, indicate she continued to write short stories after she achieved success as a novelist. Two of these manuscripts, both treating a new type of woman and apparently written in the early 1930s, have been recently published: "Flotsam" (*Regionalism and the Female Imagination*, Winter 1979) and "Deep Collar" (*New Orleans Review*, 1980).

Atherton's importance as a short-story writer rests on her depiction, both romantic and realistic, of different types of characters in episodes rendered with two elements she thought necessary for the short story—"brilliancy of phrase and lightning strokes from the observing brain" ("The Novel and the Short Story," *Bookman*, March 1903). This strategy fulfilled her attack on her definition of Howells's literary realism as "littleism" and on other writers' formulaic conformity to the so-called magazine school of writing that she believed caused the lack of vitality and originality in American literature. Desiring as a writer to extend her readers' experience of the world, especially that of women, beyond their bourgeois perceptions, Atherton in short stories and novels lifted various types of men and women out of their commonplace conditions to which they were apparently doomed (realism) and transferred them to an environment replete with change and opportunity where any latent potentialities and purpose in life could be developed (romance). She joined this technique of characterization with her discovery of similar types of characters in different social levels, countries, and races: for example, a Spanish mother aspiring to select a husband for her daughter, a young man in Harlem aspiring to higher social status, a Russian countess searching for her exiled lover in California. Atherton believed that perceived differences in human motives were actually universal, the differences originating in universal motives such as love, power, and aspiration rather than in national conditions. As a result, her characters and fictional world expressed a larger universe than that of the United States alone. Frequently her male and female characters

had similar traits that appeared different because of their socially determined roles. Furthermore, her selection of varied types of characters and her placement of them without prejudging them in their true environment generated a similar variety of themes: the individual's quest for happiness; the passions of love, ambition, greed, and revenge among Spanish Californians; the conflict between old Spanish customs and Americans' pursuit of money and progress; arranged international marriage; and supernatural vision. Atherton's rendering of her themes, interesting because of their different cultural setting and the author's detached attitude toward them and unusual because they were frequently related from a woman's point of view, sometimes caused her stories to reach a climactic ending rather abruptly; a sudden death of the main character, the fulfillment of a curse, or a last-minute recognition of the gruesome result of ambition—all stretched the readers' experience beyond their own worlds. In these ways she considered herself along with Edgar Allan Poe, Mary Wilkins Freeman, Bret Harte, Mark Twain, and Ambrose Bierce as "real creators" of, as distinguished from "intellectually manufactured" writers of, short stories.

The eleven stories of *Before the Gringo Came* are primarily romances, vividly re-creating the lost California arcadia of the 1840s, especially told from the point of view of the Spanish women's reactions to their customs and by their comparison with English and American mores. Atherton depicts several different types of characters in that milieu crossing over boundaries of sex, traditional social role, class, and national origin. She captures variances in the speech of the Spanish at different social levels and of Americans trying to speak Spanish. Though her characters often declaim their romantic aspirations in monologues and stilted conversation, Atherton is able to make their story compelling as well as melodramatic. Examination of the themes and characterizations in the stories collected in *Before the Gringo Came* support Atherton's claim of the universal origin of emotion and the uncertainty of the outcome of human choice and diverse motives.

The first three stories, "The Pearls of Loreto" (*Harper's Weekly*, 1 April 1893), "The Ears of Twenty Americans," and "The Wash-Tub Mail" (both previously unpublished), relate episodes in Monterey in 1846 and 1847 when the threat of war between the United States and Mexico resulted in a divided loyalty among Californians. These three romances, concerned with the choice of the beautiful heroine, *la favorita*, of a mate and with the happy or sorrowful outcome of that choice, also add realistic details of Spanish social events and ritual and descriptions of the natural beauty of California. In "The Ears of Twenty Americans" the struggle of a California mother and daughter to choose between their loyalty to their Spanish heritage and the men they love, who, because they belong to the United States Navy, will conquer and alter the Spanish way of life, is told through the viewpoint of the aristocratic mother, Doña Eustaquia. By contrast, in "The Wash-Tub Mail" the servants of California women, gossiping on domestic, social, and political matters around their washtubs, reveal the bittersweet romance of Tulita, *la favorita*, who spurned her Spanish lover in favor of an ambitious American lieutenant, who she learns years later from the "wash-tub mail" will never return to claim her as his bride.

In other stories in *Before the Gringo Came* Atherton adds social history to fiction as she portrays the stresses of familial relationships in the early California families where intermarriage was commonplace. In these stories Atherton experimented with her technique of associating human characteristics with a national or regional origin, a technique she employed frequently in her novels. Out of these conflicts between husband and wife, parents and children, mother and daughter, motives and choices become confusing and cultural values change. Several characters show up in additional stories so that the reader sees not only a whole changing society but also the prolonged result of the character's choice of conformity or rebellion against parental or social authority. In "The Conquest of Doña Jacoba" (*Blackwood's Magazine*, April 1892) Doña Jacoba is as sternly authoritative as her patriarchal Scots husband, Don Roberto Duncan. Elena, their youngest, most passive daughter, unexpectedly conquers her mother's authority by insisting on marrying a Spanish-Indian rancher. In the next story, "A Ramble with Eulogia" (previously unpublished), the reader learns that Elena died of tuberculosis after bearing three children and from the neglect of her indifferent husband, Dario. In contrast, Eulogia, aware of romantic perils from reading the novels of Alexandre Dumas, plans to be as independent as men appear to be.

Atherton experimented with various points of view in several sketches or vignettes in this collection. In "Lukari's Story" (previously unpub-

lished) the first-person narrator, a servant of the Carlos Ybarra family, tells a new master of the 1837 tragedy in which unconverted Indians attacked the Ybarra rancho. In "Perdida" (previously unpublished) religious law and justice in California before the Americans came is explored through the eyes of Perdida, forced at fourteen to marry an old man, loved at sixteen by an ardent young man, and punished with shorn hair and forced public labor. An Indian viewpoint is presented in "The Vengeance of Padre Arroyo" (first published as "Andreo's Love: The Vengeance of Padre Arroyo," *Current Literature*, September 1894), while in "The Bells of San Gabriel" (previously unpublished) the building and protection of a church by Spanish soldiers and converted Indians are seen through the eyes of the Spanish captain until his death at the hands of marauding Indians.

Reviewers of *Before the Gringo Came* described the stories as passionate, intense tales and as tragic episodes, particularly in the lives of women, but the volume did not sell well, perhaps because New York and the eastern United States held more interest for the publishing world and the reading public than historical tales of a bygone era in the West. In 1902 Atherton captured critical acclaim by both American and British reviewers for *The Conqueror, Being the True and Romantic Story of Alexander Hamilton*, in which she applied the method of fiction to biographical fact. To capitalize on the popularity as well as the acclaim of *The Conqueror*, Atherton added two California stories to the eleven in *Before the Gringo Came* and had the thirteen published under the title *The Splendid Idle Forties, Stories of Old California*. And in 1905, still drawing on this critical attention and taking advantage of Henry James's first visit to the United States in twenty years, with an itinerary that included California, Atherton collected ten stories under the title *The Bell in the Fog*, a volume dedicated "To the Master Henry James." The two new stories in *The Splendid Idle Forties* treat the effect of ambitious Catholic priests on the heathen and on the faithful in early California. In a larger sense Atherton's stories in this expanded volume deal with the theme of the relationship between human nature and nature and civilization which she developed more fully in her novels.

Only two of the ten stories in Atherton's 1905 collection, *The Bell in the Fog*, have early California setting and characters. In the eleven years since the publication of *Before the Gringo Came* Atherton had lived in France, England, and New York and had written novels with a Jamesian international theme, comparing the civilizations of the United States and England through romances between her typical California heroine and an upper-class Englishman. "Crowned with One Crest" (previously unpublished) exemplifies this theme. The other six stories in this volume treat, sometimes satirically, various types of characters in Harlem, New York, England, and France. One is a prologue to a play she apparently intended to write on the unwed parents of Alexander Hamilton. In the two California stories, "Talbot of Ursula" (*Anglo-Saxon Review*, December 1899) and "A Monarch of a Small Survey" (previously unpublished), Atherton depicts an Anglo-Saxon character who purchases land once owned by the Spanish and shows how he reacts to the change in his circumstance and environment; Talbot serves his people as a legislator, but Webster, of the latter tale, becomes a stingy monarch of his holdings. In "The Tragedy of a Snob" (previously unpublished) Atherton employs the omniscient narrator for her satirical portrayal of Andrew Webb, a young clerk in Harlem who finds disillusionment when his dream of being accepted as an aristocratic New Yorker in posh Newport collapses. Then in "The Greatest Good of the Greatest Number" (previously unpublished) she dared to show the logical and compelling conclusion of the struggles of a doctor, Morton Blaine, in his attempts to provide treatment for a morphine addict.

The two most acclaimed stories in this 1905 volume are the title story and "The Striding Place," both previously unpublished and both showing Atherton's intent to affect the reader's response by exploring the inner life and the extraneous circumstances and reactions of her characters. "The Striding Place," Atherton's favorite among her own stories, a tale with a gruesome air that was inspired by a William Wordsworth poem and an actual "striding place" over a whirlpool in the Wharfe River, concerns a young man who attempts to rescue a friend caught in the vortex of the whirlpool and discovers that the body he pulls from the water is faceless. The story actually is an episode about two men's deep friendship and their intellectual curiosity about the notion that the soul, which has no face, returns to the body after death. In the title story, "The Bell in the Fog," Ralph Orth, a successful American writer who expatriated himself to an English country estate, is obsessed with the portrait of a lovely girl. He convinces himself that she is a reincarna-

Photograph of Atherton used as the frontispiece for The Bell in the Fog and Other Stories *(1905)*

tion of the daughter of a middle-class American woman visiting nearby and befriends the American child named Blanche. However, inevitably Blanche has to return to the United States, preferring to be with her American family than to stay in England with her benefactor. Though the story abounds in mysterious, even occult, suggestiveness, B. R. McElderry, Jr., has argued that Ralph Orth is Henry James, whom Atherton may be chiding for staying away too long from his American roots and losing touch with his own kind.

Reviewers of *The Bell in the Fog* remarked on the varying merit of the stories, but one critic, writing in the *New York Times Saturday Supplement* (25 February 1905), singled out the title story as "a charming tale with a touch of occult, . . . a faraway suggestion of Poe's 'Lady Ligeia.' " A few reviewers cited Atherton's ability to deal with the supernatural and to lift the veil which divides the commonplace and the extraordinary.

Nearly thirty years after the publication of *The Bell in the Fog*, Gertrude Atherton settled permanently in San Francisco. During this period she wrote nineteen novels, including several crime mysteries, as well as journalistic pieces, and her memoir, *Adventures of a Novelist* (1932). Responsive to social and psychological undercurrents in the public's consciousness, she continued to experiment with new types of characters and to rework themes of reincarnation and mystery in short stories, two of them unpublished until recently. In 1934 she collected four stories under the title *The Foghorn*. This volume included two new stories, "The Foghorn" (*Good Housekeeping*, November 1933) and "The Eternal Now" (previously unpublished), as well as "The Striding Place" from *The Bell in the Fog* and "The Sacrificial Altar" (*Harper's*, August 1916), a crime tale. Atherton wrote this last story, about a San Francisco author who commits a crime as part of his struggle to keep his "rotten spot" alive, at about the same time that she published her first novel with a crime theme, *Mrs. Balfame* (1916). The senseless murder of a young Frenchwoman in "The Sacrificial Altar" and the mystically faceless victim of the whirlpool in "The Striding Place" are psychologically based episodes that perpetuate Atherton's emphasis on stretching her readers' imaginations beyond their commonplace existence. In "The Foghorn" and "The Eternal Now" Atherton abandoned her usual straightforward development of character and gave her protagonists a moment of consciousness, an epiphany, that depends upon their recall of the past to make sense of the present. The protagonist of "The Foghorn," an old woman, reviews her youth in a few minutes of lucidity before death, while Simon de Brienne in "The Eternal Now" dashes from being host to a party at his Long Island estate to its fourteenth-century prototype in France, where he reenacts his namesake ancestor's last days as the beloved of Jeanne de Valois, wife of the king of Navarre.

A few reviewers of the collection praised Atherton's ability to thrill or horrify her readers, and others claimed her talent for characterization was not realized in the short-story form. "The Foghorn" was reprinted several times, most importantly by W. Somerset Maugham in his collection *Great Modern Reading* (1943), in which he called this story a "powerful" one.

In two short stories found in her papers collected in Bancroft Library, University of California, Berkeley, and apparently written in the early 1930s, Atherton portrayed a type of ordinary city woman, many of whom she must have come to recognize in her civic activities after her return to San Francisco in 1932. Both Sadie Parkins in "Flotsam" and Doris Brand in "Deep Collar" have lived in a narrow but respectable environment and have to work to support themselves and their ailing mothers. Atherton placed each one in different circumstances. On her mother's death Sadie is free to explore the world around her but remains lonely, while Doris trades dependence on her mother's way of life for dependence on Matt Biggs's mysterious life of gambling. As in "The Foghorn," Atherton in "Deep Collar" employed the frame technique to allow Doris Brand to review how her aspiration for a gold necklace became in her role as wife of a violent gambler the same kind of restriction that her earlier narrow but respectable life afforded her. Neither story was published, perhaps because in the depression years tales of diminished aspirations and violence and crime did not appeal to magazine editors or to romantic-minded readers.

From the middle 1930s to her death in 1948 Atherton wrote novels that updated her California story-chronicle to the eve of World War II as well as two books on her beloved San Francisco, which she regarded as a wayward character striving to fulfill potential in a chaotic world. Although Atherton's literary achievement in writing the short story is overshadowed by her greater reputation as a novelist and by the acclaim earned by other writers of the short story whose work she admired, her short-story collections were always reviewed and her tales now deserve critical attention. She began to write short stories in the local-color era, recording dialect, local customs, and women's daily life in the West, as if she were writing history as Gustave Flaubert advised, but she moved beyond her region to explore the universal motives and emotions of characters wherever and whenever they lived. Although the short-story form restricted her talent for the gradual development of her characters, she respected it as an art form and experimented with it, not always successfully, to find other ways within the form to mold her characters and to test, sometimes with awkwardness, modern modes of narration, notions of the occult, and multiple levels of consciousness.

Interviews:
"Gertrude Atherton Assails 'The Powers,'" *New York Times*, 29 December 1907, VI: 2;

Pendennis, "My Types–Gertrude Atherton," *Forum*, 58 (November 1917): 585-594.

References:
Joseph Henry Jackson, *Gertrude Atherton* (New York: Appleton-Century, [1940]);

Charlotte S. McClure, "A Checklist of the Writings of and About Gertrude Atherton," *American Literary Realism*, 9 (Spring 1976): 103-162;

McClure, *Gertrude Atherton* (Boise: Boise State University, 1976);

McClure, *Gertrude Atherton* (Boston: G. K. Hall, 1979);

McClure, "Gertrude Atherton (1857-1948)," *American Literary Realism*, 9 (Spring 1976): 95-101;

B. R. McElderry, Jr., "Gertrude Atherton and Henry James," *Colby Library Quarterly*, 3 (November 1954): 269-272;

Kevin Starr, *Americans and the California Dream, 1850-1915* (New York: Oxford University Press, 1973), pp. 345-364;

Lionel Stevenson, "Atherton Versus Grundy: The Forty-Years' War," *Bookman* (New York), 69 (July 1929): 464-472.

Papers:
The Atherton Collection, Bancroft Library, University of California, Berkeley, contains short stories by Atherton, a typescript of "The Foghorn," and drafts of fiction and nonfictional prose as well as poetry.

Mary Austin

(9 September 1868-13 August 1934)

Melody Graulich
University of New Hampshire

See also the Austin entry in *DLB 9: American Novelists, 1910-1945*.

BOOKS: *The Land of Little Rain* (Boston & New York: Houghton, Mifflin, 1903);

The Basket Woman: A Book of Fanciful Tales for Children (Boston & New York: Houghton, Mifflin, 1904);.

Isidro (Boston & New York: Houghton, Mifflin, 1905; London: Constable, 1905);

The Flock (Boston & New York: Houghton, Mifflin, 1906; London: Constable, 1906);

Santa Lucia: A Common Story (New York & London: Harper, 1908);

Lost Borders (New York & London: Harper, 1909);

Outland, as Gordon Stairs (London: Murray, 1910); as Mary Austin (New York: Boni & Liveright, 1919);

The Arrow-Maker: A Drama in Three Acts (New York: Duffield, 1911; revised edition, Boston & New York: Houghton Mifflin, 1915);

Christ in Italy: Being the Adventures of a Maverick Among Masterpieces (New York: Duffield, 1912);

A Woman of Genius (Garden City, N.Y.: Doubleday, Page, 1912; revised edition, Boston: Houghton Mifflin, 1917);

The Lovely Lady (Garden City, N.Y.: Doubleday, Page, 1913);

Love and the Soul Maker (New York & London: Appleton, 1914);

California: The Land of the Sun, text by Austin and paintings by Palmer Sutton (New York: Macmillan, 1914; London: A. & C. Black, 1914); revised as *The Lands of the Sun* (Boston & New York: Houghton Mifflin, 1927);

The Man Jesus: Being a Brief Account of the Life and Teaching of the Prophet of Nazareth (New York & London: Harper, 1915); revised and enlarged as *A Small Town Man* (New York & London: Harper, 1925);

The Ford (Boston & New York: Houghton Mifflin, 1917);

Mary Austin, circa 1900 (photograph by Charles Lummis)

The Trail Book (Boston & New York: Houghton Mifflin, 1918);

The Young Woman Citizen (New York: Woman's Press, 1918);

No. 26 Jayne Street (Boston & New York: Houghton Mifflin, 1920);

The American Rhythm (New York: Harcourt, Brace, 1923); revised and enlarged as *The American Rhythm: Studies and Reexpressions of Amerindian Songs* (Boston & New York: Houghton Mifflin, 1930);

The Land of Journeys' Ending (New York & London: Century, 1924);

Everyman's Genius (Indianapolis: Bobbs-Merrill, 1925);

The Children Sing in the Far West (Boston & New York: Houghton Mifflin, 1928);

Taos Pueblo, text by Austin and photographs by Ansel Adams (San Francisco: Grabhorn Press, 1930);

Starry Adventure (Boston & New York: Houghton Mifflin, 1931);

Experiences Facing Death (Indianapolis: Bobbs-Merrill, 1931; London: Rider, 1931);

Earth Horizon: Autobiography (Boston & New York: Houghton Mifflin, 1932);

One-Smoke Stories (Boston & New York: Houghton Mifflin, 1934);

Can Prayer Be Answered? (New York: Farrar & Rinehart, 1934);

Mother of Felipe and Other Early Stories, edited by Franklin Walker (San Francisco: Book Club of California, 1950).

PLAY PRODUCTIONS: *The Arrow-Maker,* New York City, New Theatre, 27 February 1911;

Fire, Carmel, California, Forest Theatre, 1912;

The Man Who Didn't Believe in Christmas, New York City, Cohan and Harris Theatre, 1916.

PERIODICAL PUBLICATIONS:
FICTION
"Shepherd of the Sierras," *Atlantic Monthly,* 86 (July 1900): 54-58;

"Spring O' the Year," *Century Magazine,* 75 (April 1908): 923-928;

"Christmas Fiddle," *Century Magazine,* 81 (December 1910): 239-247;

"Frustrate," *Century Magazine,* 83 (January 1912): 467-471;

"White Cockatoo," *Century Magazine,* 83 (February 1912): 549-560.

NONFICTION
"The American Form of the Novel," *New Republic,* 30 (12 April 1922): 3-5;

"Regionalism in American Fiction," *English Journal,* 21 (February 1932): 97-107;

"The Folk Story in America," *South Atlantic Quarterly,* 32 (January 1934): 10-19.

Born in Carlinsville, Illinois, to George and Susanna Savilla Hunter, Mary Hunter graduated from Blackburn College before homesteading with her family in California in 1888. Her years in the desert there led to her first and most successful book, *The Land of Little Rain* (1903), mystical nature sketches in the Emersonian tradition. After leaving her husband, Stafford Wallace Austin, in 1905 (the couple had married on 19 May 1891), Austin briefly joined artist communities in Carmel, Greenwich Village, and London; but she devoted most of her life and her art to the Southwest, particularly to her beloved New Mexico. The native people of the desert region, their traditions, and their spiritual kinship to the land are her major subjects. She says in her autobiography, *Earth Horizon* (1932), "I would write imaginatively not only of people, but of the scene, the totality which is called Nature, and ... I would give myself intransigently to the quality of experience called Folk, and to the frame of behavior known as Mystical."

Contemporaries of Austin such as Willa Cather, Van Wyck Brooks, and Carl Van Doren praised her work. At Austin's death, Elizabeth Shepley Sergeant wrote in the *Saturday Review of Literature* (8 September 1934) that she was among the most important American women writers. She was better known as an essayist, novelist, poet, and "personality," than as a short-story writer, though she published in such popular periodicals as *Overland Monthly, Atlantic, Harper's,* and *Century.* Four collections contain most of her stories, many of them previously unpublished: *The Basket Woman: A Book of Fanciful Tales for Children* (1904); *Lost Borders* (1909); *The Trail Book* (1918); and *One-Smoke Stories* (1934). After her death, Franklin Walker collected her first fiction in *Mother of Felipe and Other Early Stories* (1950).

Like the American expatriates of the 1920s, Austin criticized the conventionality of small town life, but she believed that America possessed great riches in its regional cultures. In "Regionalism in American Fiction" (*English Journal,* February 1932), she argued that art is generated through the writer's relationship to a region and its history, and she became a leader in the movement to preserve southwestern art. Based on local legends, often merging history and myth, Austin's stories are imagistic and often brief. In them she explores the art of storytelling and its nurturance of the imagination. Believing that landscape shapes the American spirit and art, she sought to express "the continuity of natural forces and their relationship to the life of man," the subject of *The American Rhythm* (1923), her cultural declaration of independence, in which she showed how Indian poems reflect the rhythmic cycles of nature. Like many American writers, she experimented with form in search of a uniquely American style, attempting to convey "that intui-

Austin, circa 1895

tive access to the collective consciousness, which it is the dream and probably the mission of democracy to achieve" ("The American Form of the Novel," *New Republic*, 12 April 1922). In "The Folk Story in America" (*South Atlantic Quarterly*, January 1934), she claimed that folktales provide such a form. Her stories successfully achieve her intentions. They are suggestive and highly original, and her collections are well unified, structurally and thematically.

Austin unifies *The Basket Woman: A Book of Fanciful Tales for Children* by creating a single storyteller, a compassionate and insightful Indian Basket Maker who weaves "western myths" for a little boy, Alan. She tells him tales about the history of her tribe, transporting him into the past through her vision, and personifies the natural world to emphasize that it is alive with spiritual meaning. Her stories become so much a part of him that he believes he has dreamed them. Austin thus conveys that they speak to his unconscious inner needs and lend shape to his experience.

Austin frequently creates farseeing women like the Basket Woman, Seyavi, a Basket Maker from *The Land of Little Rain,* or the Chisera, a Medicine Woman with special powers and vision in her play, *The Arrow-Maker* (1911). One of her finest stories, "The Coyote-Spirit and the Weaving Woman" (previously unpublished), is about such

a woman, "different from other people" because her vision is larger. She lives alone in the wilderness, "weaving patterns in her baskets of all she saw or thought." Her art reveals the richness of her imagination and experience, causing others "as they stroked the perfect curves of her bowls or traced out the patterns" to think "how fine life would be if it were so rich and bright as she made it seem, instead of the dull occasion they had found it." The Weaving Woman sees more than others because she is responsive to nature and its mysteries: "the wild things showed her many a wonder hid from those who have not rainbow fringes to their eyes; and because she was not afraid of anything, she went farther and farther into the silent places until . . . she met the Coyote-Spirit."

Half-man, half-coyote, the Coyote-Spirit's two natures are at odds. The Weaving Woman manages to "throw the veil of her mind" over her friend, thereby helping him affirm his humanity. But her insight and power lead to her rejection, for he turns away from her. Like the Chisera, the Weaving Woman is denied love, but she remains content in her artistic self-expression and her solitude in nature. This mystical story is a parable about the isolated, misunderstood, but satisfied artist, and it is a mirror which reflects the artistry of the Basket Woman and of Austin herself. These farseeing women are among her most original and fully realized creations.

Austin unifies *Lost Borders,* her second collection, with a previously unpublished sketch, "The Land," in which she likens the desert, the subject or "mood" of her book, to a strong, maternal woman who possesses "largeness to her mind" and spiritual ease and confidence, a woman so mysterious and primal that she is like a sphinx. The land gives these same qualities to those souls "marked" by her, as is the Walking Woman, the central character in the collection's most interesting story.

"The Walking Woman" (*Atlantic*, August 1907) is told by an unnamed narrator whose responses to her experience help shape those of the reader. She has heard many stories about the Walking Woman, a desert wanderer who "had begun by walking off an illness" and "was healed at last by the large soundness of nature." Having "lost her name," she is a mysterious and universal figure, rumored to be "cracked," but she talks wondrously and with wisdom of all that she has seen.

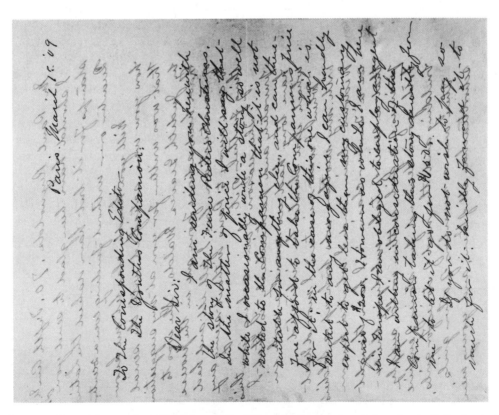

Letter from Austin to an editor of the popular children's periodical Youth's Companion *(Mary Austin Collection [#7472], Clifton Waller Barrett Library, Special Collections Department, University of Virginia Library)*

this, in our neighborhood, and we had some interesting times among ourselves as well as in struggle with shepherders, grass fires, cloud-burgers and drouth.

I thought if a series of separate tales involving the same character and I sufficient consistency to make up a book, but the truth is I have not the time to take from more profitable novel writing to do this. What I think is that if the lady known to you as Miss Webb proves of the right competency, she might do them under my direction. I should be glad to hear from you in this matter. What you have to say I course will be strictly between us two.

Sincerely yours
Mary Austin

(51 rue d'Assas,
Paris.)

George Sterling, Mary Austin, Jack London, and Jimmy Hopper on the beach at Carmel (Bancroft Library, University of California, Berkeley)

The narrator finally meets her at a desert spring, a symbol of her inner depth and fertility, and the two begin to discuss those experiences which are "indispensable" to their understanding of their selfhood. The Walking Woman tells of finding herself through working well, experiencing love, and having a child. Her self-knowledge and ability to express the soul's deepest needs impress the narrator, who realizes, "She was the Walking Woman. That was it. She had walked off all sense of society-made values, and, knowing the best when the best came to her, was able to take it." Austin stresses the Walking Woman's role as spiritual leader in the story's final image. Remembering the rumors that she walks "twisted," the narrator looks at her footsteps and sees that "the track of her feet bore evenly and white."

Lost Borders contains several other stories which explore basic human relationships like marriage or motherhood, important themes in Austin's work. She undercuts the familiar folk story that is the basis for Washington Irving's "Rip Van Winkle" in "The Return of Mr. Wills" (*Century*, April 1908) by presenting the plot from a woman's point of view. When Mr. Wills abandons his family to search for a lost mine, Mrs. Wills discovers that "she not only did not need

Mr. Wills, but got on better without him." When he returns, he settles "on his family like a blight," stealing from his wife her newfound strength and independence. Relationships between men and women and their different inner beings are major themes in Austin's fiction.

Like *The Basket Woman*, *The Trail Book* is intended for children, but Austin's fables, which present a mythic history of the American continent, speak on many levels for adults as well. A young brother and sister follow the "trails" of their guides, the Indians and animals who make up the exhibits of a natural history museum and who magically come alive to tell them stories. The unifying trail metaphor teaches the children the connections between landscape and human experience. They learn that "like the trails . . . every word is an expression of a need" and that "there is a story about everything." The trails lead them through myths about friendships between humans and talking animals into more recent times, "to the place in the Story of the Trails, which is known in the schoolbooks as 'History.'" The trails show them the interrelationships between myth, history, nature, and human culture and identity when they discover that "all the stories of that country, like the trails, seemed to run into one another."

Austin's "wickiup" in Carmel, California, where she wrote each morning (Henry E. Huntington Library, San Marino, California)

The trail metaphor, so rich in suggestion, connects several excellent stories, the best of which is "How the Corn Came" (previously unpublished). It is told by the Corn Woman, a follower of another Chisera-figure, "Giver-of-the-Corn who died giving." A "wise woman" and shaman, she leads her followers in tribute to the "God of the Seed, a woman god who was served by women." She sacrifices herself to save her adopted tribe from starvation, uniting her people with the cyclical rhythms of growth and cultivation. Her gift to them is her offspring, the kernels of corn which give life and die each year only to be reborn the next. Through her story, Austin explains women's fertility, for Giver-of-the-Corn makes her women followers "keepers of the seed."

In her introduction to *One-Smoke Stories*, considered by some to be her best volume, Austin presents her most succinct description of her art. Each story is told, ritually, in the time it takes its teller's cigarette to burn, remaining brief and allusive, "located somewhere in the inner sense of the audience, unencumbered by . . . background."

Your true desert dweller travels light. He makes even of his experience a handy package with the finished neatness that distinguishes his artifacts. How else could they be passed intact from tribe to tribe, from generation to generation? Just before the end, like the rattle that warns that the story is about to strike, comes the fang of experience, most often in the shape of a wise saying. Then the speaker resumes the soul-consoling smoke while another takes up the dropped stitch of narrative and weaves it into the pattern of the talk.

For Austin, such stories are the basis of culture, expressing the shared experience of humankind.

Her one-smoke stories *are* wise. They contain her oft-repeated themes of relations between whites and Indians and women and men; folk experience; ecological awareness; mysticism. Once again there is a Chisera, this time a "foreknowing" mother in "White Wisdom" (previously unpublished). Many stories are humorous, ending with an ironic twist. Two such stories are "Papago Wedding" (first published in "Three Tales of Love," *American Mercury*, September 1925), where an Indian woman outwits her white common-law husband, who is trying to take her children from her, when she testifies that they are not his, and the ribald "Stewed Beans" (previously unpublished), in which an Indian feeds his wife's lover beans so that he will "go in his insides r-r-r-ru, phutt-phutt!" and loudly expose himself.

Austin repeated in *One-Smoke Stories* one of her earliest and probably best-known story, "The Last Antelope" (*Atlantic*, July 1903; also included in *Lost Borders*). A lonely shepherd follows the cycles of the seasons to rendezvous each summer with the last antelope to inhabit a mountain meadow. The two share a "reciprocal friendliness" and a mutual interdependence. Slightly late one year, Pete comes to the mountaintop only to see the antelope shot. He mourns the death of his kindred soul, having "been breathed on by that spirit which goes before cities like an exhalation. . . ." This powerful ecological statement presents the theme Austin explored most faithfully throughout her long career: the human response to nature, which nourishes the lonely soul and expands the consciousness.

Austin is a fine and original writer in many genres, but her work has been largely ignored. Her outspoken feminism probably contributed to her reputation as a humorless egotist, a stereotype which has overshadowed her literary reputation. Her short stories, almost uniformly of high quality, have received almost no critical attention, nor have they been influential outside southwestern or Indian literature, areas largely unexplored by eastern literati. Perhaps readers have considered her a transcriber of folk legend rather than a creative artist, though her style is clearly her own. T. M. Pearce argues that her short stories are among her strongest work. She is best remembered for her sympathetic treatment of Indians and her efforts to save their cultures. Like Robert Frost, William Carlos Williams, Cather, and others with faith in the American grain, Austin

proves that America possesses regional cultures and historical riches which nourish the artistic imagination and contribute to a native literature. Like the Weaving Woman, this unique and undervalued artist deserves a far wider audience.

Letters:

Literary America, 1903-1934: The Mary Austin Letters, selected and edited by T. M. Pearce (Westport, Conn. & London: Greenwood Press, 1979).

Bibliography:

Joseph Gaer, *Mary Austin, Bibliography and Biographical Data, California Literary Research Project Digest, Monograph II*, no. 1 (Berkeley, 1934).

References:

Van Wyck Brooks, *The Confident Years: 1885-1915* (New York: Dutton, 1932);

Helen McKnight Doyle, *Mary Austin: Woman of Genius* (New York: Gotham House, 1939);

Arthur Dubois, "Mary Hunter Austin, 1868-1934," *Southwest Review*, 20 (April 1935): 321-364;

Jo W. Lyday, *Mary Austin: The Southwest Works* (Austin, Tex.: Steck-Vaughn, 1968);

Mary Austin: A Memorial, edited by William Hoagland (Santa Fe, N.M.: The Laboratory of Anthropology, 1944);

T. M. Pearce, *Mary Hunter Austin* (New York: Twayne, 1965);

Carl Van Doren, "American Rhythm: Mary Austin," in his *Many Minds* (New York: Knopf, 1924).

Papers:

Austin's papers are located at the Huntington Library, San Marino, California.

Alice Brown

(5 December 1856-21 June 1948)

Deborah G. Lambert
Merrimack Valley College

BOOKS: *Stratford-by-the-Sea, A Novel* (New York: Holt, 1884);

Fools of Nature: A Novel (Boston: Ticknor, 1887);

Robert Louis Stevenson: A Study, by Brown, with a prelude and a postlude by Louise Imogen Guiney (Boston: Copeland & Day, 1895);

Meadow-grass: Tales of New England Life (Boston: Copeland & Day, 1895; London: Dent, 1897);

The Road to Castaly (Boston: Copeland & Day, 1896);

By Oak and Thorn: A Record of English Days (Boston & New York: Houghton, Mifflin, 1896; London: Gay & Bird, 1896);

Mercy Warren (New York: Scribners, 1896; London: Murray, 1896);

The Rose of Hope (Cambridge, Mass., 1896);

The Day of His Youth (Boston & New York: Houghton, Mifflin, 1897; London: Watt, 1897);

Tiverton Tales (Boston & New York: Houghton, Mifflin, 1899);

King's End (Boston & New York: Houghton, Mifflin, 1901; Westminster: Constable, 1901);

Margaret Warrener (Boston & New York: Houghton, Mifflin, 1901);

The Mannerings (Boston & New York: Houghton, Mifflin, 1903; London: Nash, 1903);

Judgment (New York & London: Harper, 1903);

The Merrylinks (New York: McClure, Phillips, 1903);

High Noon (Boston & New York: Houghton, Mifflin, 1904; London: Nash, 1904);

Paradise (Boston & New York: Houghton, Mifflin, 1905; London: Constable, 1905);

The Court of Love (Boston & New York: Houghton, Mifflin, 1906);

The Country Road (Boston & New York: Houghton, Mifflin, 1906; London: Constable, 1906);

Rose MacLeod (Boston & New York: Houghton, Mifflin, 1908; London: Constable, 1908);

The Story of Thyrza (Boston & New York:

Alice Brown

Houghton Mifflin, 1909; London: Constable, 1909);

Country Neighbors (Boston & New York: Houghton Mifflin, 1910; London: Constable, 1910);

John Winterbourne's Family (Boston & New York: Houghton Mifflin, 1910; London: Constable, 1910);

The One-Footed Fairy and Other Stories (Boston & New York: Houghton Mifflin, 1911; London: Constable, 1912);

My Love and I, as Martin Redfield (New York: Macmillan, 1912; London: Constable, 1912);

The Secret of the Clan (New York: Macmillan, 1912; London: Constable, 1913);

Vanishing Points (New York: Macmillan, 1913; London: Constable, 1913);

Robin Hood's Barn (New York: Macmillan, 1913);

Joint Owners in Spain: A Comedy in One Act (Chicago: Chicago Little Theatre, 1914);

Children of Earth, A Play of New England (New York: Macmillan, 1915);

The Prisoner (New York: Macmillan, 1916);

The Road to Castaly, and Later Poems (New York: Macmillan, 1917);

Bromley Neighborhood (New York: Macmillan, 1917);

The Flying Teuton and Other Stories (New York: Macmillan, 1918);

The Loving Cup: A Play in One Act (Boston: Baker, 1918);

The Black Drop (New York: Macmillan, 1919);

The Buckets in the Sea (Boston: Massachusetts Eye and Ear Infirmary, 1920);

The Wind Between the Worlds (New York: Macmillan, 1920; London: Nash, 1921);

Homespun and Gold (New York: Macmillan, 1920);

Louise Imogen Guiney (New York: Macmillan, 1921);

One Act Plays (New York: Macmillan, 1921);

Old Crow (New York: Macmillan, 1922; London: Nash & Grayson, 1923);

Louise Imogen Guiney: Appreciations by Alice Brown and Robert Haven Schauffler, Written in Connection with E. M. Tenison's New Biography of Louise Imogen Guiney (London: Macmillan, 1923);

Ellen Prior (New York: Macmillan, 1923);

Charles Lamb: A Play (New York: Macmillan, 1924);

The Mysteries of Ann (New York: Macmillan, 1925);

Dear Old Templeton (New York: Macmillan, 1927; London: Nash & Grayson, 1927);

The Golden Ball (New York: Macmillan, 1929);

The Marriage Feast: A Fantasy (New York: Macmillan, 1931);

The Kingdom in the Sky (New York: Macmillan, 1932);

The Diary of a Dryad (Boston: Todd, 1932);

Jeremy Hamlin (New York & London: Appleton-Century, 1934);

The Willoughbys (New York & London: Appleton-Century, 1935);

Fable and Song (Boston, 1939);

Pilgrim's Progress: A Play (Boston: Privately printed, 1944).

PLAY PRODUCTION: *Children of Earth*, New York, Booth Theatre, 12 January 1915.

OTHER: *A Summer in England. A Hand-Book for the Use of American Women*, edited by Brown and Louise Imogen Guiney (Boston: Women's Rest Tour Association, 1891);

"Agnes Surriage," in *Three Heroines of New England Romance, Their True Stories Herein Set Forth by Mrs. Harriet Prescott Spofford, Miss Louise Imogen Guiney, and Miss Alice Brown* (Boston: Little, Brown, 1894), pp. 63-105;

"Peggy," in *The Whole Family: A Novel by Twelve Authors* (New York & London: Harper, 1908).

Usually associated with Sarah Orne Jewett and Mary E. Wilkins Freeman, Alice Brown is known as a regional writer. Although not all of her work employs rural settings and rustic dialect, the early stories that made her reputation are written in that vein. Her first two collections of short stories, *Meadow-grass: Tales of New England Life* (1895) and *Tiverton Tales* (1899), were well received by critics and by the public, and they remain her most impressive contributions to American literature.

Alice Brown was born on a farm in Hampton Falls, New Hampshire, the second child and only daughter of Levi and Elizabeth Lucas Robinson Brown. Though the year of her birth is frequently listed as 1857, the Hampton Falls town records list her birth date as 5 December 1856. She attended the district school in Hampton Falls and graduated in 1876 from the Robinson Seminary in Exeter, New Hampshire, four miles from her home. Brown taught school for five years, first in New Hampshire and then in Boston, but found that she disliked teaching and turned to editing. She worked first on the staff of the *Christian Register*, and by 1884—when her first novel, *Stratford-by-the-Sea*, was published—she had begun her long career as a writer of short stories, novels, and plays. In 1885 she went to work for *Youth's Companion*. For the rest of her life she lived in Boston, but until the 1940s she spent summers in Newburyport, Massachusetts, and at her farm in Hill, New Hampshire. Brown quickly became part of the Boston literary world, and in the course of her long life she knew many of the writers and editors, including William Dean Howells, Thomas Wentworth Higginson, Annie Fields, and Robert Frost. She continued to have books published into the 1940s, but when she died on 21 June

1948 at the age of ninety-one she had outlived her reputation by several decades.

At the start of her literary career, Brown met poet Louise Imogen Guiney, who became–and remained–her close friend, and their friendship seems to have been a spur to Brown's creative efforts. Like Brown, who first visited England in 1886, Guiney loved the English countryside, and the two women founded the Women's Rest Tour Association and its magazine, *Pilgrim Scrip*. This Boston-based organization, which still exists, supplies women with lists of inexpensive and safe lodgings and is designed to encourage women to travel abroad. Brown recorded her impressions of a summer 1895 English walking tour with Guiney in *By Oak and Thorn* (1896). Brown, Guiney, and Harriet Prescott Spofford each wrote a section of *Three Heroines of New England Romance* (1894), and Guiney wrote a prelude and a postlude for Brown's appreciative study of Robert Louis Stevenson's work (1895). Their friendship continued after Guiney went to live in England in 1901, and when Guiney died in 1920, Brown wrote a sympathetic account of her life and writing (1921). Unfortunately, Brown burned all of her friends' letters to her, including Guiney's, making it almost impossible to reconstruct the story of this important relationship.

Of the nine volumes of short stories that Brown published between 1895 and 1920, five collect her New England tales. In these Brown expresses her pantheistic, even mystical, feelings about the natural world; employs her firsthand knowledge of life on New Hampshire farms in the late nineteenth century; and demonstrates an acute understanding of the people who live in her somewhat idealized small towns.

Her first collection, *Meadow-grass: Tales of New England Life*, introduces the country village of Tiverton and the typical Brown protagonist, who is middle-aged or elderly. In Brown's stories characters' desires to live life more fully frequently come into conflict with the expectations of the community. The resolution is usually positive: her characters assert themselves and yet remain valued members of their communities. Deeply attached to the New Hampshire countryside, they take pleasure in caring for their animals and their homes and in maintaining harmony with nature. Brown's narrator sets the nostalgic and commemorative tone of the volume: "We who are Tiverton born, though false ambition may have ridden us to market, or the world's voice incited us to kindred clamoring,

have a way of shutting our eyes, now and then, to present changes, and seeing things as they were once, as they are still, in a certain sleepy, yet altogether individual corner of country life." The narrator views Tiverton life from a perspective both affectionate and insightful.

As Jewett did in *Deephaven* (1877), Brown attempted to make *Meadow-grass* more than a collection of separate short stories. The presence of a single narrator throughout *Meadow-grass* unifies the stories. Brown also employs the same characters in more than one story, and the introductory and concluding sketches focus on the community as a whole, rather than on individuals. The opening sketch describes the boys and girls who attended the Tiverton country schoolhouse and reveals what becomes of them as adults. The conclusion, "Strollers in Tiverton," portrays the townsfolk of Tiverton as they gather for a circus. Despite these attempts, *Meadow-grass* is only loosely unified. As in her later work Brown's interest seems to be in the emotional lives of her characters, not in narrative structure.

At their best Brown's stories depict powerful feelings in the simplest of images. In one of her best short stories, "Farmer Eli's Vacation" (*Century*, August 1893), an old farmer, who has wanted all of his life to see the ocean only six miles away, finally makes a trip to the seashore with his family. Leaving his buggy, Eli "turned and looked at the sea. He faced it as a soul might face Almighty Greatness, only to be stricken blind thereafter; for his eyes filled painfully with slow, hot tears." That night Eli cannot sleep. In the morning he returns to his farm, where he leaps "from the wagon as if twenty years had been taken from his bones." The story concludes with his remark to the hired man, "I guess I'm too old for such jaunts. I hope you didn't forgit them cats." Eli's return home is a victory, not a defeat: in his acceptance of the shape and meaning of his life, he expresses integrity of heroic proportion. At the same time Brown leaves ambiguous the implications of his choice.

Like Freeman and Jewett, Brown often writes of middle-aged women who demonstrate their courage in quiet ways. Similar to Jewett's country people, Brown's women typically struggle through doubt to self-assertion and greater autonomy. Against a tranquil background of home and community, they face the conflict between societal expectations and their own deepest urgings. Not so typically, they make richer lives through unconventional choices. In "After All"

Alice Brown prop to
67 Pinckney St,
Boston.

Sept. Atlantic

HIS ENEMY

Doctor St.John was travelling down to Hartsdale by the express. A man of world-wide mark,he had also a ~~strong~~ local
following,and wherever he might go,within a day's journey from *home,*
~~his native city~~,some one was sure to name him as St.John,the
oculist. A stranger even might have guessed out part of his
profession from the keen glance,the considered movements of a
man used to meeting emergencies. The doctor's face wore a veil
of reserve; friendly to the present,it indicated a guarded
past: and the iron-grey hair,the sunken temples,showed,with some
likelihood of exactness,how remote a past it had been. On that
journey,memory gripped him hard. He was retracing twenty-odd
years,and wondering how,in all that time,he could have been so
sure God would deliver his enemy into his hand. He put it so,
not from any belief in God's immediate justice,but because a
formulated saying was easily remembered,and stood by him when
he scorned to recall the poor old drama which had at once
impoverished and enriched him.

In that past,so far removed now that childhood seemed the
nearer,he was a young man with a good deal of money,some knowledge of medicine,and a beautiful wife. ~~later,as~~ *Now, with* his perceptions quickened under the lash,he realized how dull he must
have been in those old days: not so much with the facile dull-
ness of youth,articulate because it has so little to say,but
from that inertia born of prosperity and a belief in the
permanence of tangible things. His practice lay among a class

First and last pages from the typescript for a story collected in Brown's 1904 book, High Noon *(Alice Brown Collection
[#7553-b], Clifton Waller Barrett Library, Special Collections Department, University of Virginia Library)*

29

go back. We must begin now. Mildred,won't you take it -
what I have to offer you? Wont you come?"

   Her face softened into something pathetic and yet grateful.

   "Yes," she said quietly, "I will come."

She ~~put~~ held out her hand,and he gave it a little pressure.
But instead of putting it to his lips,he drew her gently up
from her chair and led her to the window.

   "Come," he said, "let us take a look at the eyes."

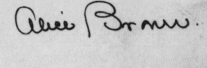

(first published in *Meadow-grass*), a story reminiscent of Freeman's "One Good Time," an elderly woman decides, after the death of her tyrannical father, to live the life she has been denied. The narrator first presents Lucindy from the point of view of her conventional sister-in-law. From this perspective Lucindy appears deprived and pathetic but also threatening in her determination to have something for herself. Slowly, however, the narrator leads the reader toward admiration for Lucindy's courage and generosity of spirit. She adopts the orphaned daughter of a wandering musician, and, calmly defying her neighbors, Lucindy brings the girl, who shares her love of gaiety, into her home. The two constitute a natural and joyous family, in which Lucindy finds the renewal and purpose she has sought. At the story's conclusion the reader can no longer view Lucindy as a pitiable figure; she is heroic in her ability to recreate herself.

Brown accords a similar dignity to the old women of "Joint Owners in Spain" (*Atlantic Monthly*, January 1895), one of her better-known short stories. Here two old women living in a home for old people cannot live peacefully with any of the other inhabitants of the home. Nearly despairing, the director asks the two difficult ones to share a room. After days of bitter remonstrance on the one hand, and aggressive passivity on the other, the two old women agree to divide the room in half. Within the imaginary boundaries they create, the women discover solitude and regain control of their lives. They become neighbors, and then friends. The property lines they establish are fictitious, but their mutual respect is life-giving. When Brown rewrote "Joint Owners in Spain" as a one-act play, it was performed frequently and with great success. It was published separately in 1914 and collected in *One Act Plays* (1921).

In "Heartsease" (*Atlantic Monthly*, October 1894), collected in *Tiverton Tales*, Brown approaches the problem of aging from another perspective. When Mrs. Lamson's son and daughter-in-law are called away because of illness, she delights in escaping the idleness that the well-meaning couple has forced upon her by baking her favorite cream-of-tartar biscuits, washing and ironing her dead husband's shirts, and spending the long summer night wandering through the fields. When her son returns early in the morning with the news that his wife will be away all week, Mrs. Lamson wryly asserts that she guesses she can manage the house for a week. The narrator emphasizes the joy of her liberation from idleness, obscuring the fact that nothing really has changed. Frequently, the Brown narrator does not acknowledge the darker undertones of the plot, nor does the story suggest a resolution to the protagonist's dilemma.

Tiverton Tales, Brown's second collection, was well received by readers and critics. Like *Meadow-grass*, it begins and ends with framing sketches, and the reappearance of Brad Freeman, also a character in *Meadow-grass*, who functions here as the communal voice of the town, also testifies to Brown's intention to unify her work. Finally, however, Brown's stories come across as individual pieces rich in humor, dialect, and shrewd comment.

Brown's predecessors in the New England tradition most often portrayed spinsters and widows whose romantic lives were far in the past; Brown's fiction describes women at the moment they refuse marriage in favor of the solitary life. In *Tiverton Tales* the question of marriage versus the single life becomes a significant theme. In "A Second Marriage" (*Atlantic Monthly*, September 1897) Amelia's much-older husband dies, leaving her free to marry her childhood sweetheart. Yet, when her former lover appears at her door one year and one day after her husband's funeral, Amelia realizes that she cannot marry again. She believes that her husband's traditions have become part of her and that to marry would be to abandon them. Amelia's desire to remain alone is expressed by the narrator in tones of passionate conviction. Similarly, in "The Last Assembling" (*New England Magazine*, September 1898) Dilly Joyce, who has never married, rejects the suitor to whom she has been pledged for fifteen years when she is finally freed of the family responsibilities that have prevented their marriage earlier. Her commitment is to her ancestors and to their home. Summoning the strength to elect this path, she remembers her courageously unconventional ancestors: for example, one relative committed suicide at the beginning of the Revolutionary War rather than risk killing another man in battle. For the narrator this choice and Dilly's are heroic.

Another story in *Tiverton Tales* explicitly asserts the individual's right to solitude. "A Way of Peace" (*Outlook*, 19 November 1898) concerns a middle-aged woman who refuses to live with relatives when she is left alone after her mother's death. Lucy Ann slowly transforms herself into an image of her mother, whom she resembles, by wearing her mother's clothes and arranging her hair as her mother did. As she turns herself into a replica of her mother, Lucy Ann feels that she is "dwelling in a sacred isolation, yet not altogether alone, but with her mother and all their bygone years." Brown portrays Lucy Ann's obsession as eccentric, but not as pathological, and even gives Lucy Ann's plight a more general significance: "Was she always to be subject to the tyranny of those who had set up their hearthstones in a more enduring form? Was her home not a home because there were no men and children in it?" Lucy Ann asserts herself and wins the right to live alone. Just as her desire for reunion with her mother underlies her attachment to the past, the avoidance of marriage by other Brown protagonists has similar motivation.

On occasion, Brown's female protagonists are figures of heroic, even mythic, dimension. Delilah Joyce, in "At Sudleigh Fair" (first published in *Tiverton Tales*), is viewed by her neighbors as a good witch and respected for her special powers. In tune with the natural world, Delilah can explain why Farmer Tolman's cows have dried up and why young Elvin Drew is suddenly anxious and irritable. Brown values this sort of natural wisdom, which in this story brings Elvin to confess a past crime, thus gaining redemption and peace of mind. Mary Dunbar of "Horn o' the Moon" (first published in *Tiverton Tales*) is another woman of mythical stature. As the narrator presents her, Mary is goddesslike in appearance, "of great proportions and elemental strength." Spiritually no less extraordinary, she is "the one righteous among many . . . the good nurse whom we all go to seek in our times of trouble . . . who perpetually saves her city from the odium of the world." For all of Mary's mother-goddess qualities, she at least once has an altogether human experience. Nursing a visiting young man back to health, she is moved to something like romantic affection. But the young man returns to his ordinary sweetheart in the village, and Mary remains, despite her all-too-human moment, a transcendent virgin-goddess. Brown is clearly far more interested in the powerful figure of Mary than in the story's subordinate romantic plot.

High Noon (1904) collects stories that depart from Brown's New England subject matter. Set in drawing rooms rather than in farm kitchens, they contain characters who are articulate and educated, and they often deal with romantic love. These stories do not focus on the moment's decisive action that may enrich a life. Instead, they are comparatively static and tend to include long discussions on the nature of love or on the differences in the ways that men and women love. Brown asserts that women's love is higher, purer, and more spiritual. Even when she is not emphasizing the vitality and courage of New Hampshire women, Brown still believes in a kind of female superiority. Her women are heroic in their loving.

A history of the critical reception of *High Noon* would illuminate not only Brown's career but also Americans' changing taste in short fiction. By the time *High Noon* appeared, Brown had established herself as a worthy successor to Freeman and Jewett, Rose Terry Cooke and Harriet Beecher Stowe. Blanche Colton Williams, writing in 1920, saw *High Noon* as inaugurating a significant second period. Having portrayed the world of her childhood in her first two collections, Brown embarked on a more risky creative venture. Thus Williams, in probably the most favorable commentary on the volume, saw these stories as "trials toward a new goal." A more representative view is that of Charles Miner Thompson, who objected in a July 1906 *Atlantic Monthly* article to the ideology of romantic love that dominates the stories of *High Noon*. Although Brown returns to New Hampshire in three later volumes of short stories, her writing from this time on differs from her earlier work in its greater tendency to emphasize her moral and philosophical positions at the expense of character and plot.

"A Meeting in the Market-Place" (first published in *High Noon*) asserts woman's superior gift for love. A dying woman summons to her bedside a man whom she has not seen for six months. As he visits her during these last weeks of her life, Edith becomes the young man's spiritual guide, until he finally acknowledges what she has known all along: that they are spiritually suited to one another and bonded in this life and the next. The narrator occasionally introduces wry social commentary into their spiritual dialogue. For example, Edith says, "I am having . . . a unique experience. I am telling a man the absolute truth, without disguise, knowing I sh'n't' be paid out for it in social flagellation"; and the narrator points out that social convention and emotional realities do not easily coincide this side of the grave.

Brown's mystical belief that the souls of people who love each other are mated for eternity is expressed throughout *High Noon*, in stories such as "The Tryst" and "A Dream in the Morning" (both previously unpublished). "There and Here" (*Harper's New Monthly*, October 1897) applies this notion to two women, describing a supernatural experience in which a dead woman returns to her childhood home to spend one gloriously happy evening with the friend she has not seen for eight years. The woman who awakens the next day to news of her friend's death has learned that a person is only temporarily separated from those she loves. Despite the supernatural theme that is carried by the narrative frame, the central narrative is clearly the story of the friends' joyous reunion.

The *Country Road* (1906), which collects thirteen local-color stories, and Brown's next collection of short stories, *Country Neighbors* (1910), return to the setting, themes, and characters of *Meadow-grass* and *Tiverton Tales*. Most of these stories concern middle-aged or old people. One of the finest stories in *The Country Road* is "A Sea Change" (*Atlantic Monthly*, August 1900), in which Brown portrays a farm wife who is slowly going mad from isolation and overwork. As Susan Allen Toth has noted, this farm wife resembles the woman in Robert Frost's well-known poem "The Hill Wife." No longer able to tolerate life with her husband, a stolid farm man, not cruel but only silent and insensitive, Cynthia abruptly leaves the farm and travels to the coast, to a sister she has not seen in twenty years. Cynthia sums up her years of loneliness and neglect in a single complaint: " 'He greases his boots so much. He leaves 'em by the oven door.' That seemed to be all she could remember, and quite enough. Any woman would know." In "Old Immortality" (*Harper's Monthly*, May 1905) Brown demonstrates her ability to treat the emotional lives of old people effectively and unsentimentally. John Buckham has earned the nickname of Old Immortality because he has lived so long that he almost believes that he will live forever; but, when his wife falls ill, he slowly realizes that if she dies he will not want to live on alone.

The stories in this volume and in *Country Neighbors* differ significantly from those in her earlier collections of regional stories. Her women characters have become conventional, inclining toward self-sacrifice. In their acceptance of traditional values they resemble the characters of *High Noon*, and not the unusual, daring women of Brown's first two collections. In "Rosy Balm" (*Harper's Monthly*, November 1905; collected in *The Country Road*) Arletta, a single, middle-aged woman, finds purpose in a plan to earn money for a foreign mission. Her fantasy of making a large contribution enlarges her sense of her life's value. Yet she finds she cannot sell her home-made lotion and instead gives it away, bottle by bottle. It is no surprise when virtue is rewarded: Arletta's account of her plight moves a tightfisted man to mirth and then to charity. He replaces Arletta's savings and provides a donation to the foreign mission as well. Other stories in *The Country Road*, such as "The Cave of Adullam" (*Atlantic Monthly*, August 1902) and "The Pilgrim Chamber" (*Atlantic Monthly*, August 1905), follow this same pattern of self-sacrifice and virtue rewarded.

Country Neighbors extends the treatment of the themes of *The Country Road* to include questions of faith and affirmation. In "Flowers of Paradise" (*Atlantic Monthly*, December 1905) a widow, Hetty, anguishes over the death of her only child. Desperate for consolation, yet unable to accept the faith of her pious neighbors, she bargains with God: "If the Lord'll send me some flowers afore tomorrer night, I'll believe in Him. If He'll send me one flower or a sprig o' green, I'll believe in Him. . . ." She forgets her proposal, but then she finds the pasture blue with violets. Her faith in life's goodness has been restored. "Masquerade" (*Atlantic Monthly*, January 1910; collected in *Country Neighbors*) deals explicitly with the value of a community's old people while simultaneously satirizing the summer visitors' preoccupation with remaining youthful. In the autumn, after the summer boarders have returned to New York, the townspeople decide to hold a dance at which "They were to offer, in the guise of jesting, their big protest against the folly of sickening over youth." They hold a masquerade at which they appear as the old people they most admire: "It was a loyal and passionate upholding of the state of those who were already old." A deep sense of community grows up among the generations as, remembering their aged and their dead, they share an awakened sense of time's rapid passing.

In *Country Neighbors* Brown's gentle humor becomes more pronounced. Mrs. Dill ("The Other Mrs. Dill," *Atlantic Monthly*, May 1909) stands up to her domineering husband for the first time, in a story reminiscent of Freeman's "The Revolt of Mother." Mrs. Dill wants to remain in her old house and give the new house that her husband has just bought to their son. Unaccustomed to defying her husband, she claims she is suffering from "split personality" and that she, the good Mrs. Dill, has no control over her outspoken counterpart. Like Abigail Bennett ("A Day Off," *Harper's Monthly*, August 1905; collected in *The Country Road*), who enjoys lying about everything once she discovers how easy it is and thereby learns the attraction of sin, Mrs. Dill asserts herself, but there is no change in her marriage; like Mrs. Penn in Freeman's "The Revolt of Mother," she has simply decided to win this time.

An unusual story in *Country Neighbors,* yet one reflecting Brown's continuing concern with autonomy and the single life, is "A Flower of April" (*Harper's Bazar*, 31 March 1900). An innocent girl living with her widowed mother devotes all of her energy to gardening, until she notices that girls of her own age are courting and marrying. When boys notice her she flees to her mother and to her garden. No temporary flight from growing up, Ellen's retreat signals a strong impulse to avoid sexual encounter. Like Lucy Ann in "A Way of Peace," Ellen has chosen to prolong attachment to her mother.

Between *Country Neighbors* and Brown's last collection, *Homespun and Gold* (1920), a final volume of New England tales, Brown produced three volumes of nonregional stories: *The One-Footed Fairy and Other Stories* (1911), *Vanishing Points* (1913), and *The Flying Teuton and Other Stories* (1918). Other stories appeared in magazines but have never been collected. During this same period Brown's *Children of Earth, A Play of New England* won the Winthrop Ames prize of ten thousand dollars and was produced on Broadway in 1915. The play was not a popular success, and Brown said she had learned that "doors are not always to be swung wide and that sometimes, when they seem to be, one is only caught in them disastrously, and that if you write books and plays there is only one happiness you can expect: that of the hourly enchantment of the writing itself. . . ." Despite her disappointment at the reception of *Children of Earth,* Brown published *One Act Plays* in 1921 and *Charles Lamb: A Play* in 1924. She also produced a novel at least every other year. Guiney claimed that Brown published only one-third of what she wrote, but critics still complained that she published too much and edited too little. Certainly by 1915 Brown's reputation was fading, and she never gained the reputation as a playwright for which she had hoped.

The One-Footed Fairy and Other Stories collects a dozen or so moralistic fables about fairies, animals, and imaginary kingdoms. One tale in this collection is "The Unambitious Queen," which concerns a queen who assiduously avoids war, demands politely unaggressive behavior from neighboring kings, and diverts the military to peacetime uses, such as requiring soldiers to teach gymnastics to schoolchildren. Though the stories may be best suited for children, for the adult reader this volume may provide some insight into Brown's political attitudes.

Vanishing Points focuses on temptations facing artists and the discrepancy between real literary worth and reputation. One puzzling fact about these stories is that none presents a woman writer who might embody Brown's own experience. Like many other professional women writers, including Willa Cather, Brown considers writing a male activity and fails to imagine that women can be, like her, both female and creative.

In *Vanishing Points,* which was much admired by reviewers of the time, Brown considers contemporary economic problems. In one story she portrays an idealistic young socialist and in another the machinations of a dishonest financier. Sympathetic to the unemployed and aware of abuses in the American economic system, Brown nevertheless advocates individual rather than governmental solutions. In "The Man in the Cloister" (*Harper's Monthly*, October 1909) a visiting aunt from New Hampshire solves the problem of an unemployed man by the simple expedient of trading him room and board for work around her country place–after a young communist, a wealthy industrialist, and a Christian minister have all been stymied by the problem. In "The Lantern" (*Scribner's Magazine*, February 1909) a young journalist, guided in his work by his self-effacing wife, writes an exposé of a corrupt financier. When the man visits the young couple to ask them to omit evidence about a land swindle, on the grounds that an old woman with an invalid daughter would suffer as a result, the young couple are stunned into respect for the man. Thus in dealing with economic issues Brown is essentially conservative: she emphasizes not only the complexity of each human being but also the need for individual actions and solutions–moral and spiritual, rather than economic or political, cures. While Williams believed that Brown perfected her art in this volume, critical consensus suggests that Brown's efforts to portray the worlds of art and economics never equaled her mastery of the New England tale.

Alice Brown

The Flying Teuton and Other Stories includes four stories related to World War I (including the title story, a version of the Flying Dutchman), four stories concerning writers, four on spiritual and supernatural themes, and one concerning a revolutionary feminist, "The Man and the Militant" (*Atlantic Monthly*, August 1913), that may have been suggested by the suffragist activities of English feminists such as Emmeline Pankhurst. The intense nationalistic and anti-German feelings expressed by the war stories echo the spirit of the time. The "writer" stories have a more enduring interest for their portrayal of the elderly writer who fears the aging process and the loss of creative power. "The Mid-Victorian" (*Scribner's Magazine*, December 1912) captures the situation of the aging writer out of touch with a new, socially conscious generation. No longer able to sell his material to the magazine editors who had formerly pursued him, he graciously reconciles himself to his professional demise, even contributing money saved for a trip to Italy to his nephew's politically radical magazine.

"The Man and the Militant" is an account of a young American woman who joins a group resembling Pankhurst's Women's Social and Political Union in its rather spectacular militant means of furthering its cause. Grace's American fiancé,

who strongly disapproves of her methods, though he claims to approve her goals, abducts her and imprisons her in a cottage in Yorkshire. After Grace's three-day hunger strike, Douglas releases her. Although she professes to understand his brutal treatment of her, she cannot forgive his betrayal of her group's latest plan. Painfully, because they care for each other, they break their engagement, and Grace returns to working with English women for the right to vote. Brown highlights the irony in Douglas's demand that Grace fight for her political goal within the bounds of law, while he has lied to her and tricked her. Yet Douglas is not evil. He and Grace are in love, and they feel like dupes of history.

For *Homespun and Gold* Brown returned to the New England setting and characters that she had begun with more than twenty-five years before. The stories in this volume are often sentimentally romantic and optimistic: eight of them are accounts of young lovers overcoming obstacles to marriage. Yet two of them are among Brown's best regional fiction. "Confessions" (*Harper's Monthly*, October 1912) resembles "A Sea Change" from *The Country Road* in its depiction of a farm wife on the verge of collapse. Exhausted and depressed, Mary confesses to her stolid, unaware husband that she hates their farm, their friends, their life together—hates each aspect of her life because she has given up her strength and energy to each in its turn. The only thing she does not hate is the larkspur that has sprung up unaided near the barn. After months of passivity and withdrawal, Mary begins to mend, in part because Andrew, slowly coming to understand his wife, has transplanted the larkspur into a carefully prepared bed near her window.

Brown's last collected local-color story, "Up on the Mountain" (*Harper's Monthly*, August 1916), is an appropriate climax for her career. It deals with a middle-aged woman's rejecting servitude in marriage (her husband's dirty boots, as in "A Sea Change," symbolize the horrors of married life) and asserting her right to innocent, independent pleasures, even though they are beyond her husband's comprehension. Criticized by her husband and a neighbor for taking solitary mountain walks, Molly replies, "But I felt different up there. 'Twas the wind. And the sun risin' off there in the east, and the way that bird sung. I never heard that bird anywhere's else. I'd get so homesick I'd have to go." Finally realizing that she is alone in her feeling for nature and solitude, Molly leaves for good. The men last see her "hurrying along toward the sunset. She was on a knoll, and her figure looked very tall against the brightening sky." Molly, in her courage and her refusal to barter independent joys for the safety of marriage, is the characteristic hero of Alice Brown's fiction.

In general Brown's novels resemble her short stories. In *Rose MacLeod* (1908) Brown creates vital characters and introduces complex psychological and economic problems into an idyllic rural world. Yet, as in some of her short stories, she seems to lose control of her plot and resolve conflicts rapidly and sentimentally. Jewett was critical of *Margaret Warrener* (1901) perhaps because the title character is a gifted actress who sacrifices her career to marry a mediocre artist. *The Prisoner* (1916) was praised by at least one critic for its attempt at grappling with the problems of rehabilitation, while Hugh Walpole and the *New York Times* selected *Old Crow*, the story of a man's moral and psychological crisis at midlife, as one of the best novels of 1922. A late novel, *Jeremy Hamlin* (1934) is of interest because it moves toward a darker and more complex portrait of life in rural New England. All of Brown's novels are out of print. Many, if not all, of them have value as literature and as cultural documents and should be made available.

From the 1890s until just after World War I, Alice Brown was a popular fiction writer, as well as a well-known figure in the Boston literary world, serving as president of the Boston Authors Club. By the time of her death in 1948, she had been forgotten by readers and critics alike. Until the late 1960s all of her work was out of print. Now, five of her nine volumes of short stories have been reprinted, as has her biography of Revolutionary War writer Mercy Warren (1896).

No doubt the sheer size of Brown's canon has contributed to her neglect, as have her sentimentality, her mid-Victorian optimism, and her apparent rejection of the modern ethos. Yet, now that the tendency to denigrate local-color fiction has somewhat abated, all of Brown's work, like that of Jewett, Freeman, and other regional writers, should be reread and reconsidered. As literary scholars continue to redefine the canon of American literature, they will discover much that is of lasting value in the writing of Alice Brown.

References:

Alice Brown (New York: Macmillan, 1927);

Charles Miner Thompson, "The Short Stories of Alice Brown," *Atlantic Monthly,* 98 (July 1906): 55-65;

Susan Allen Toth, "Alice Brown (1857-1948)," *American Literary Realism 1870-1920,* 2 (Spring 1972): 134-143;

Toth, "A Forgotten View from Beacon Hill: Alice Brown's New England Short Stories," *Colby Library Quarterly,* 10 (March 1973): 1-16;

Toth, "More than Local-color: A Reappraisal of Rose Terry Cooke, Mary Wilkins Freeman and Alice Brown," Ph.D. dissertation, University of Minnesota, 1969;

Dorothea Walker, *Alice Brown* (New York: Twayne, 1974);

Blanche Colton Williams, *Our Short Story Writers* (New York: Moffat, Yard, 1920).

Papers:
The Beinecke Rare Book and Manuscript Library at Yale University is the major repository for Brown's manuscripts, letters, and other miscellaneous materials. There are also collections of letters at the Houghton Library, Harvard University, and the Dinand Library, College of the Holy Cross.

H. C. Bunner

(3 August 1855-11 May 1896)

Samuel I. Bellman

California State Polytechnic University, Pomona

BOOKS: *A Woman of Honor* (Boston: Osgood, 1883);

Airs from Arcady and Elsewhere (New York: Scribners, 1884; London: Hutt, 1885);

In Partnership: Studies in Story-Telling, by Bunner and Brander Matthews (New York: Scribners, 1884; Edinburgh: Douglas / London: Hamilton, Adams, 1885);

The Midge (New York: Scribners, 1886);

The Story of a New York House (New York: Scribners, 1887);

"Short Sixes": Stories to Be Read While the Candle Burns (New York: Keppler & Schwarzmann, 1891; London: Brentano's, 1891);

Zadoc Pine and Other Stories (New York: Scribners, 1891; London: Gay & Bird, 1891);

The Runaway Browns: A Story of Small Stories (New York: Keppler & Schwarzmann, 1892; London: Brentano's, 1892);

Rowen: "Second Crop" Songs (New York: Scribners, 1892);

"Made in France": French Tales Retold with a United States Twist (New York: Keppler & Schwarzmann, 1893);

More "Short Sixes" (New York: Keppler & Schwarzmann, 1894);

Jersey Street and Jersey Lane: Urban and Suburban Sketches (New York: Scribners, 1896);

The Suburban Sage. Stray Notes and Comments on His Simple Life (New York: Keppler & Schwarzmann, 1896);

Love in Old Cloathes and Other Stories (New York: Scribners, 1896; London: Downey, 1897);

The Poems of H. C. Bunner (New York: Scribners, 1896; enlarged, 1897; enlarged again, 1917);

Three Operettas, librettos by Bunner, music by Oscar Weil (New York: Harper, 1897);

Our Girls: Poems in Praise of the American Girl (New York: Moffatt, Yard, 1907).

Collections: *The Stories of H. C. Bunner, First Series* (New York: Scribners, 1916);

The Stories of H. C. Bunner, Second Series (New York: Scribners, 1916);

The Stories of H. C. Bunner: "Short Sixes" (New York: Scribners, 1917);

The Stories of H. C. Bunner: More "Short Sixes," The Runaway Browns (New York: Scribners, 1917).

Among the long-forgotten short-story writers of the later-nineteenth century is Henry Cuyler Bunner, the editor of *Puck: The Comic Weekly*. Writing five years after Bunner's death, W. P. Trent called Bunner "a humorist of a refined and most attractive type" ("A Retrospect of American Humor," *Century Illustrated Monthly Magazine*, November 1901). He was a novelist, essayist, parodist, and writer of light verse, some of it quite sentimental. To celebrate New York City and its environs, the land of his Dutch ancestors, he wrote essays filled with loving details of his city's neighborhoods and byways, landmarks and polyglot population–including "Jersey and Mulberry" (*Scribner's Magazine*, May 1893), "Tiemann's to Tubby Hook" (*Scribner's Magazine*, August 1893), and "The Bowery and Bohemia" (*Scribner's Magazine*, April 1894)–all collected in *Jersey Street and Jersey Lane* (1896)–as well as sketches in *The Suburban Sage. Stray Notes and Comments on His Simple Life* (1896).

Henry Cuyler Bunner was born in Oswego, New York, the second son of Rudolph Bunner and Ruth Keating Tuckerman Bunner, sister of poet and essayist Henry T. Tuckerman. By 1865 the family was living in New York City, and the studious Bunner directed his course toward Columbia College. He went through the rigorous academic preparation of Dr. A. Callisen's School for Young Gentlemen; but because of restricted family finances he left school in 1871 and went to work for the New York wine-importing firm of G. Amsinck & Company. By that time, however, he had read extensively and had a fair command of Latin. He worked as a clerk for the company until he was fired for taking an unauthorized holiday in February 1873. Journalism then drew his attention and he contributed to the *Arcadian*, a

H. C. Bunner, 1885

"short-lived journal," and other periodicals and increased his knowledge of recent French and German literature. In 1877 he became editor of *Puck: The Comic Weekly*, an English-language version of a German comic periodical, holding the post until his death.

In January 1886 Bunner married Alice Trumbull Learned, and later that year their first child was born. In 1887 they settled in Nutley, New Jersey, and their family continued to grow. To support them Bunner maintained a rigorous work schedule. He also drank somewhat immoderately, and before long his health became impaired. He died of pulmonary tuberculosis in Nutley, New Jersey, when he was just forty years old and was buried in New London, Connecticut, his wife's hometown, where the family frequently vacationed.

Bunner's forte as a fiction writer was the well-rounded story of incident, in the manner of the French conte. It includes no real character development, merely a brief, somewhat-suspenseful story line whose conflict is quickly resolved, leaving the reader to smile at what Thomas Hardy called "life's little ironies." Bunner was greatly influenced by Giovanni Boccaccio and Guy de Maupassant. Bunner's friend Brander Matthews, one of the best interpreters of Bunner's fiction, explained at length in his obituary essay on Bunner (*Scribner's Magazine,* September 1896) the relationship between Bunner's literary parodies and the writers who inspired them. In "By Way of Explanation," his preface to *"Made in France"* (1893), a collection of his Americanized Maupassant tales (published originally in *Puck* during the first half of 1893), Bunner wrote, "I have selected a few ethi-

Seven State Street, New York, the setting for Bunner's 1887 book, The Story of a New York House, *which he called "hardly more than a rambling sketch"*

cal situations from among the brightest of Maupassant's inventions, and have tried to reproduce them, not as translations, but as English, or rather American stories based on a Frenchman's inspiration—and I have done this with the sole hope of making that inspiration clear to people who will not or can not read Maupassant in the original." There is also an element of whimsy in Bunner's short fictions that transcends the exact specifications of the well-told tale in the manner of Maupassant. Yet only a very few of his stories are genuinely inventive; possibly because the demands *Puck* made on him sapped his best creative energies, and he tended to parody or remake familiar works of fiction.

By far the greatest number of Bunner's short stories deal with romantic love: courtship, the reuniting of separated lovers, the removal of impediments to marriage. Bunner was ardently patriotic, and one also finds in his stories a stress on American values of his period: hard work, honesty, determination to succeed, national self-awareness. Sometimes these values are presented

in sharp contrast to the crude ways of unassimilated immigrants and vulgar foreigners deficient in ambition and a sense of the dominant cultural mores. Dutch-Americans, long established in the New World, come in for particular praise. In contrast, Bunner was sometimes critical of Anglo-Americans. For example, he wrote in "An Old, Old Story" (*Puck*, January 1888; collected in *"Short Sixes,"* 1891), "I suppose the Tullingworth-Gordons were good Americans at heart; but [they] were of English extraction, and, as somebody once said, the extraction had not been completely successful—a great deal of the English soil clung to the roots of the family tree." Dutch-Americans were not the only ones favored. In his "French for a Fortnight" (*Scribner's Magazine*, August 1894; collected in *Love in Old Cloathes and Other Stories*, 1896) he approvingly describes a large French family in Westchester County.

Another important category of Bunner's stories is concerned with colorful "characters"—eccentric drunks, quaint rustics, and droll "originals," as well as animals with personalities. The animal stories are modest tales: "Zenobia's Infidelity" (*Puck*, 20 August 1890) and "Hector" (*Puck*, 6 August 1890)–collected in *"Short Sixes"*–and "The Cumbersome Horse" (*Puck*, 7 and 14 February 1894; collected in *More "Short Sixes,"* 1894).

A handful of Bunner's romantic-love tales deserve the attention of modern readers. "Love in Old Cloathes" (*Century*, September 1883; first collected in *In Partnership*, 1884) is in the form of a series of journal entries dated 1883, but written in the language of earlier centuries. A lovelorn suitor bemoans his sorry state and the dire threat posed by his rival. His absorbing record of his great tournament ends with his marriage to the object of his desires. "The Love Letters of Smith" (*Puck*, 23 July 1890; collected in *"Short Sixes"*) presents a silent, in fact barely perceptible, courtship involving two dissimilar people in a New York tenement: a poor working girl of refined tastes and a rough-hewn, illiterate rustic of noble character and unbelievable shyness. These tenement neighbors communicate almost entirely through brief notes passed along the ledge outside their adjoining windows. "The Nice People" (*Puck*, 30 July 1890; collected in *"Short Sixes"*), one of Bunner's more-ingeniously constructed stories, is about a young married couple staying in a summer boarding house atop a mountain in a scenic area near the New York-New Jersey border. Apparently ordinary vacationers like the other guests, they are disturbingly inconsistent in their accounts of their personal history–where they have been and how many children they have, for example. Their discrepancies accumulate to the point where the proprietor demands to see their wedding license. They turn out to be honeymooners who were so fearful of being made the object of ribald jokes about newlyweds that they have tried to give the impression of having been married longer. "A Sisterly Scheme" (*Puck*, 24 September 1890; collected in *"Short Sixes"*) perpetuates the stereotype of the designing female and the male whom she manipulates. All through the summer at a Maine resort hotel, a jealous young woman coaches in the arts of love a backward, overly trusting young man who hopes to win the affections of her rudely unresponsive sister. In an uncollected story, "Jasper Ax's Courtship" (*Puck*, 19 and 26 December 1894), a small-town Canadian farmer engages a visiting journalist as his scribe to produce courtship letters extolling his good character and his freedom from vices, for the benefit of a distant correspondent. It is understood that the woman will not answer until she makes

up her mind, and she will be taking her time deciding. Deftly constructed, Bunner's tale reveals that she is a very unusual inspiration for such a campaign since she happens to be the farmer's former wife.

Bunner's remaining romantic-love tales appear now to be carelessly contrived and have little enduring social or literary significance. A short novelette, "The Red Silk Handkerchief" (*Century*, June 1884; collected in *Love in Old Cloathes and Other Stories*) is the sad account of a young lawyer who fails at the crucial moment–through timidity and bad luck–to win his true love, just as years before, his congressman father had failed at a critical moment to convey from the floor of the House of Representatives his great, precedent-shattering message of moderation and conciliation for North and South: he was speaking to a practically empty house. Three variations on Bunner's "Amor Vincit Omnia" formula appeared in *Puck* in 1890 and were collected in *"Short Sixes": Stories to Be Read While the Candle Burns*. (The title derives from the then-common packets of six short candles.) "The Nine Cent-Girls" (13 August) is a trivial rewrite, in cowboy terms, of the Roman legend of the Rape of the Sabine Women. "Mr. Copernicus and the Proletariat" (17 September) is an account of an educated con man's insinuating himself into the bosom of a wealthy family and persuading the daughter to outwit her parents and flee with him by train. (The story ends happily, however.) "A Round-Up" (10 September) focuses on what happens after the death, in a small garrison town, of a high-society lady who has given all for love to a base deceiver, the least deserving of her many suitors, and lost.

Two more stories that fit his "Amor Vincit Omnia" formula appear in *More "Short Sixes."* "'Samantha Boom-de-ay'" (*Puck*, 29 August and 5 September 1894) and "My Dear Mrs. Billington" (*Puck*, 12 September 1894) treat the removal of impediments to marriage. Two uncollected stories that employ the same formula, "The Plain Girl" (*Puck*, 10 October 1894) and "Jack's Wife's Poet" (*Puck*, 21 and 28 November 1894), have to do with jealousy livening up relationships. In "The Plain Girl" (which includes as an authorial aside a special tribute to Dutch women) jealousy works on the overly busy, and thereby neglectful, fiancée of an obtuse, proper young man. In "Jack's Wife's Poet" a husband is obliged to overcome the pernicious influence on his wife of a minor poet, a former suitor, who

Father Anastasius.

In 1862, he said, I was settled in a small village in
New Jersey. It was a sort of surburb of a larger town, also,
I regret to say, in New Jersey. There was a convent in the
place, the convent of the Sacred Cross. I was visiting physician there, though I am not a catholic.

In the middle of the winter--I think it was in December--
there was an epidemic of diphtheria in the poor quarter of the
town. The Sisters threw open the large hospital attached to
the convent, and took in all the indigent sick. For several
weeks my duties kept me at the convent night and day. Thus I
saw a great deal of Father Anastasius, the senior priest res-
i dent in the convent. I was interested in Father Anastasous
from the first moment that I set eyes upon him. Perhaps it
would be better to say that I was fascinated by the man.

He was about forty years old,though he looked fifty at
least. He was over six feet in height, and his frame was simply gigantic. And in spite of his grey hair and his bloodless
dark face, he was the handsomest man I ever saw. His eyes a-
lone would have made him handsome--great dark, deep-sunken eyes
that fairly blazed and burned when he preached, in his wrapt,
wild, ecstatic way, telling of the glories of the Church, of
the demands she made upon her servants, of the promises she
gave them.

But even if his eyes had not possessed that terrible
beauty, he would have been a wonderful man to look at.

Worn with vigils and fasting until the wasted flesh had
shrunk almost to the bone, his face had yet a sensuous, passion
ate strength. I knew when first I looked at him, why he had
made himself a priest. He would have been a devil, else.
I knew also, before long, that he was killing himself, slowly
but surely, with loss of sleep and lack of food.

I remonstrated with Father Anastasius. I had desired to
speak to him on the subject; but, frankly, I had not dared,
until Sister Agatha, the gentlest, sweetest and youngest of all
the sisters--a little dove-like creature with soft grey eyes--
came to me and pleaded with me, almost tearfully, to entreat
the good father to take more care of his perishable mortal
tenement. I went to him, as a physician, and told him that he
must moderate his ascetic exercises if he wished to live and
do his work. He heard me through, turned his great eyes full
on me, and said, with a determination that I knew no words of
mine could shake:

"I thank you, Doctor;but you are wasting your time.
You speak well, according to your light. I obey a higher law--
I have a higher promise. It will not fail me. I shall not ch
change my ways."

There was nothing more to be said.

I left him to his mortification of the flesh; and Sister
Agatha wept when I told her his answer.

"He will die," she said.

Two weeks after Christmas, Father Anastasius was offocia-
ting in the convent chapel. It was the hour of meditation, and
I slipped in, as I sometimes did, in leisure moments, to watch
that strange spectacle of silent devotion. There sat the long
row of novices, their heads bowed, still as so many statues--
still as death. It was absolute silence, if you know what that
is. A footfall would have seemed a desecration.

The chapel was still   1

Opening pages from the typescripts for two of Bunner's stories (Henry Cuyler Bunner Collection, [#6183-a], Clifton Waller Barrett Library, Special Collections Department, University of Virginia Library)

THE SPOOK.

The incidents which I am about to narrate, said Ferguson,
occurred some two years ago. It was towards the close of an
exhausting season. I had striven for some months to perform th
that feat known as 'Keeping ones end up'. I had tried to keep
my end up. There is concurrent and contemporaneous testimony
to the effect that I did keep my end up. Looking back on it
now, it seems to me that I kept two or three ends up. I kept
my end up at afternoon teas. I kept my end up at early morning suppers. I was up before, and after, the lark. I generally managed to see the moon in bed. I do not know whether I
make this clear to you. As I said, prehaps I ought to have
left the subject to a scientific man. Any scientific man could
have explained that this sort of thing is wearing to the most
cast-iron constitution.

One dewy morn in February, I slipped into bed just asthe
first milk-cart rattled beneath my window. I was very tired.
I was very tired indeed. My eyes were just closing when I saw,
seated upon the foot of my bed, what I can nly describe as a
supernatural visitant.

It was a pale gray, mottled spook, about sixteen hands
high. I wasn't afraid of it . I said:

"Hello{ who are you?"

"I'm a spook," it replied.

"All right," I said; "spook when your'e spoken too. Good
night." And then I turned over.

"Where are you going?" inquired the spook.

"Going to sleep." I told him.

"Not now, you're not," said the spook.

"What's to hinder me," I queried, in a scientific spirit.

"I am," the spook said; "that's what I'm here for. I'm
the recording spook. I'm sent here to wait on you every night,
when you go to bed, and to report to you before you go to
sleep, every foolish, conventional or unnecessary thing you
have said during the d y."

I mildly intimated that he had a contract on hand.

"I have," said he, rubbing his hands; "and I'm the boy
that can fill it, too. Come now, young man, roll over so that
I can see you, take your hands out of your ears and listen.
The entertainment is going to begin right now, and the curtain
is up."

I groaned. I might as well have whistled.

"Let's see," said the spook, grinning hideously and rubbing his hands; "let's see. You met Jones at the club this
morning. You hadn't seen Jones in two days, and what did gu
you say to Jones? Why, you said: 'Quite a stranger, ain't you?
Now that was brilliant, wasn't it? The edge hadn't been rubbed
off that observation in fifteen hundred boarding houses, had it
Whay, that was the regulation joke in the ark when Noah happened to miss a breakfast through sitting up too late the night
before inspecting his private stock."

"Go away," said I. "I want to go to sleep."

But he didn't go away. He went--he went on.

"Th n you when to the Turkish bath, didn't you? And you
went into the hot room--temperature 200. And you saw Robinson
there, eh? And what did you say to Robinson?

I said that I didn't remember.

"You do remember," said the spook; "you said: 'Is it hot
enough for you?' that's what you said. You didn't happen to

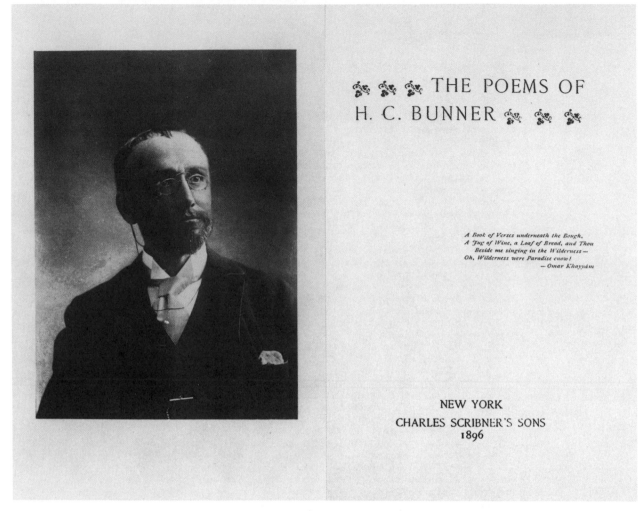

Frontispiece and title page for a posthumously published collection of what Bunner's friend Brander Matthews called the writings for which Bunner was "likely to be longest remembered"

has lost out to Jack but persists in writing about her in his frequently appearing verses.

Bunner had a special fondness for colorful characters. "The Tenor" (*Puck*, 3 September 1890; collected in *"Short Sixes"*) exposes a celebrated French tenor as a crude, unfeeling boor, and two upper-class girls as hysterical ninnies bent on worshipping any popular idol. A person such as the tenor is in sharp contrast to a Bunner hero (worker, entrepreneur, and American): Zadoc Pine. In "The Zadoc Pine Labor Union" (*Scribner's Magazine*, December 1887; collected in *Zadoc Pine and Other Stories*, 1891) this one-man labor force from the North Woods puts to shame slothful workingmen, unenterprising tradesmen, greedy and corrupt labor unions, and small-minded, unproductive types everywhere. Two other pieces in *"Short Sixes"* deal with crusty old codgers involved in a bitter ecclesiastical rivalry

over a hoped-for bequest ("The Two Churches of 'Quawket," *Puck*, 27 August 1890) and a droll astrologer who–through a slapdash, improvisatorial approach to human problems–catalytically unites his benefactor and the hitherto unresponsive object of that man's affections ("Zozo," *Puck*, 1 October 1890).

"A Letter and a Paragraph" (first published in *In Partnership*) provides, through an epistle that cannot be sent, a dying journalist's account of his happy marriage, which proves to be all vain fancy. Several other "short sixes" in *More "Short Sixes"* reveal an even broader base of whimsy and human quirkiness. "The Ghoolah" (*Puck*, 14 and 21 March 1894) tests a belief in oriental spiritualism and personality transfer, with bizarre results and an amusing "back to the drawing board" conclusion. The protagonist in "Cutwater of Seneca" (*Puck*, 28 March 1894) is a district attorney prosecuting an accused murderer who happens to be one of his oldest friends. He is devastated when he proves the man guilty, and then connives to get him a better defense and a new trial. "What Mrs. Fortesque Did" (*Puck*, 6 and 13 June 1894) depicts a lively old woman who, despite her age and her residence in an old ladies' home, draws on her old profession of actress and plays a real-life role drastically different from any she has handled on stage: wife to a millionaire and nominal guardian of his young ward in a boarding school. When she is found out and has to confess her imposture to the millionaire, he turns out to have known about her deception for some time, but he has willingly accepted it because as a boy he had been a secret admirer of her. A malicious revenge seeker in "The Man with the Pink Pants" (*Puck*, 20 June 1894) achieves his purpose through a smear campaign, starting a rumor that his victim has been seen on the street dressed in an odd way. In "Our Aromatic Uncle" (*Scribner's Magazine*, August 1895; collected in *Love in Old Cloathes and Other Stories*), an imposter "returns" home to "his" family after many years of living abroad. Bunner sounds a novel variation on the theme of the convincing double's return and eventual unmasking.

Reading Bunner's light entertainments, "short sixes," and essay-stories about New York neighborhoods does not in the least prepare the reader for Bunner's best short story, one that transcends conventional clichés of black-white relations in the later-nineteenth century. "Col. Brereton's Aunty" (*Puck*, 16 July 1890; collected in "*Short Sixes*") is bold and honest.

The colonel is an unreconstructed Southerner who settles in a small northern town. A onetime lawyer, he ekes out a living by practicing law occasionally; but he spends most of his time in taverns, lamenting to the other drinkers and loafers about his lost plantation in Virginia, the five-hundred slaves that were taken away from him, and his present reduced state. Then he begins complaining about "the whole system of free colored labor" and lets it be known that his knife will redress some of what he considers the injustices done to him. As a token of this pledge he cuts up the Negro coachman of one of the town's leading citizens and makes it clear that he will treat all other former slaves in the same manner.

Apprehended by town leaders, the colonel is given every chance to recant and to promise to behave in the future. When he refuses, the town leaders reluctantly put him in jail. Before long, a huge Negro woman appears with a large amount of money to bail him out. She explains that the colonel himself did not own all the slaves that he claimed to have had; they belonged to his father. The "Aunty" also explains that she is the only family servant left. She has taken care of the colonel since he was a baby; and, so long as she can be there to look after him, she insists, he will not cause any trouble.

The authorities agree to release the colonel to her custody. From time to time he gets away from his "Aunty," but she manages to track him down, until one time when she gets caught in a blizzard and nearly dies in the snow. After a long period he returns to her, but by this time she is too old and weak to pursue him. He continues to give her whatever money he earns, and when he gets out of line with his "Aunty," the colonel is sure to receive the "treatment" his disobedience has always earned from her: it will be rather hard for him to sit down for quite a while afterward.

Bunner is notable for his unusual skill in shaping well-rounded tales of incident—a few of them quite provocative and memorable—and in adapting or parodying the literary expressions of other writers. Along with Thomas Bailey Aldrich and Brander Matthews, he has been credited with formulating the "well-made" short story. Matthews called him an "accomplished craftsman in fiction," and in 1922 one reviewer ranked him among the best American short-story writers of the latter half of the nineteenth century (*Literary Review*, 4 November 1922). While his stories are now largely unread, the best of them deserve rediscovery.

References:

Gerard E. Jensen, *The Life and Letters of Henry Cuyler Bunner* (Durham, N.C.: Duke University Press, 1939);

Albert Parry, *Garrets and Pretenders: A History of Bohemianism in America,* revised edition, with a new chapter by Harry T. Moore (New York: Dover, 1960).

Papers:

The largest collections of Bunner's papers are at the Huntington Library, San Marino, California; Butler Library, Columbia University; and Alderman Library, University of Virginia.

James Branch Cabell
(14 April 1879-5 May 1958)

Ritchie D. Watson
Randolph-Macon College

See also the Cabell entry in *DLB 9: American Novelists, 1910-1945.*

BOOKS: *The Eagle's Shadow* (New York: Doubleday, Page, 1904; London: Heinemann, 1904);

The Line of Love (New York & London: Harper, 1905);

Gallantry (New York & London: Harper, 1907);

The Cords of Vanity (New York: Doubleday, Page, 1909; London: Hutchinson, 1909);

Chivalry (New York & London: Harper, 1909);

The Soul of Melicent (New York: Stokes, 1913); republished as *Domnei* (New York: McBride, 1920; London: John Lane/Bodley Head, 1927);

The Rivet in Grandfather's Neck (New York: McBride, 1915; London: McBride, Nast, 1915);

The Certain Hour (New York: McBride, 1916; London: McBride, Nast, 1917);

From the Hidden Way (New York: McBride, 1916);

The Cream of the Jest (New York: McBride, 1917; London: John Lane/Bodley Head, 1923);

Beyond Life (New York: McBride, 1919; London: John Lane/Bodley Head, 1925);

Jurgen (New York: McBride, 1919; London: John Lane/Bodley Head, 1921);

The Judging of Jurgen (Chicago: Bookfellows, 1920);

Figures of Earth (New York: McBride, 1921; London: John Lane/Bodley Head, 1921);

Taboo (New York: McBride, 1921);

Joseph Hergesheimer (Chicago: Bookfellows, 1921);

The Jewel Merchants (New York: McBride, 1921);

The High Place (New York: McBride, 1923; London: John Lane/Bodley Head, 1923);

Straws and Prayer-Books (New York: McBride, 1924; London: John Lane/Bodley Head, 1926);

The Silver Stallion (New York: McBride, 1926; London: John Lane/Bodley Head, 1926);

The Music from Behind the Moon (New York: Day,

James Branch Cabell, circa 1915 (James Branch Cabell Library of Virginia Commonwealth University)

1926); revised and republished in *The Witch-Woman* (New York: Farrar, Straus, 1948);

Something About Eve (New York: McBride, 1927; London: John Lane/Bodley Head, 1927);

Ballades from the Hidden Way (New York: Crosby Gaige, 1928);

The White Robe (New York: McBride, 1928; London: John Lane/Bodley Head, 1928); revised and republished in *The Witch-Woman* (1948);

Sonnets from Antan (New York: Fountain Press, 1929);

The Way of Ecben (New York: McBride, 1929; London: John Lane/Bodley Head, 1929); revised and republished in *The Witch-Woman* (1948);

Some of Us (New York: McBride, 1930; London: John Lane/Bodley Head, 1930);

Townsend of Lichfield, Storisende Edition, volume 18 (New York: McBride, 1930);

These Restless Heads (New York: McBride, 1932);

Special Delivery (New York: McBride, 1933);

Smirt (New York: McBride, 1934);

Ladies and Gentlemen (New York: McBride, 1934);

Smith (New York: McBride, 1935);

Preface to the Past (New York: McBride, 1936);

Smire (Garden City, N.Y.: Doubleday, Doran, 1937);

The King Was in his Counting House (New York & Toronto: Farrar & Rinehart, 1938; London: John Lanc/Bodley Head, 1939);

Hamlet Had An Uncle (New York & Toronto: Farrar & Rinehart, 1940; London: John Lane/Bodley Head, 1940);

The First Gentleman of America (New York & Toronto: Farrar & Rinehart, 1942); republished as *The First American Gentleman* (London: John Lane/Bodley Head, 1942);

The St. Johns, by Cabell and A. J. Hanna (New York: Farrar & Rinehart, 1943);

There Were Two Pirates (New York: Farrar, Straus, 1946; London: John Lane/Bodley Head, 1947);

Let Me Lie (New York: Farrar, Straus, 1947);

The Witch-Woman: A Trilogy About Her (New York: Farrar, Straus, 1948);

The Devil's Own Dear Son (New York: Farrar, Straus, 1949; London: John Lane/Bodley Head, 1950);

Quiet, Please (Gainesville: University of Florida Press, 1952);

As I Remember It (New York: McBride, 1955).

Collections: *Works*, Kalki Edition, 19 volumes (New York: McBride, 1921-1927);

The Works of James Branch Cabell, Storisende Edition, 18 volumes (New York: McBride, 1927-1930).

Virginia-born James Branch Cabell, along with fellow Richmonder Ellen Glasgow, was one of the first voices of what would later become a rising chorus of modern southern writers. He is recognized today as a pioneering novelist and short-story writer of the southern literary renaissance. Cabell was descended from venerable Virginia stock. His father, Robert Gamble Cabell II, was the scion of a long-established Old Dominion family which had produced one governor, Cabell's great-grandfather. Cabell's mother, Anne Branch Cabell, belonged to a solidly bourgeois family with comfortable fortunes resting on mercantile and banking interests.

Born on 14 April 1879, Cabell grew up in post-Civil War Richmond. He was nourished by children's books, especially Charles Henry Hanson's *Stories of the Days of King Arthur* (1882). Not surprisingly these Arthurian legends became inextricably bound in his youthful imagination with equally romantic tales of the exploits of the South's Confederate heroes. The noble King Arthur was easily identified with the equally illustrious Robert E. Lee, and the uncivilized Yankee hordes which had invaded the South were equivalent to the followers of the hated Mordred.

From his earliest years, then, Cabell's consciousness was imbued with a sense of the mythic dimension in human affairs. This mythic sense remained with him and profoundly influenced his fiction. Of course, by the time Cabell began writing he had formed a more objective and ironic attitude toward his region's cherished myths. For even in Richmond, the spiritual bastion of the Confederacy, it was sometimes difficult for a boy to match the legend with present-day reality. After all, as Cabell observed in a beautifully written essay entitled "Almost Touching the Confederacy" (*Atlantic Monthly*, October 1946; collected in *Let Me Lie*, 1947), "you lived in Richmond; and Richmond was not like Camelot. Richmond was a modern city, with sidewalks and plumbing and gas lights and horse cars. . . . Damsels in green kirtles and fire-breathing dragons and champions in bright armor did not go up and down the streets of Richmond, but only some hacks and surreys, and oxcarts hauling tobacco. . . ." Moreover, as he grew older he slowly began to realize that his elders did not speak as enthusiastically about the Confederacy and its heroes "when they were just talking to one another in your father's drugstore, or in your mother's dining room at Sunday night supper. . . ." Slowly the youth began to see that his elders were not describing the real Confederacy or the real Richmond. They were molding a myth. "They were creating . . . in the same instant that they lamented the Old South's extinction, an Old South which had died proudly at Appomattox without ever having been smirched by the wear and tear of existence."

Cabell's early Richmond years helped to fix his subsequent course as a writer. He never outgrew his love of the chivalric past. Though some of his stories would be set in contemporary Virginia, most of them would hark back to Europe of the medieval and eighteenth-century periods. Cabell was never able to embrace realism–which he defined in a collection of essays entitled *Be-*

Burton Rascoe, literary editor of the Chicago Tribune, *novelist Ellen Glasgow, James Branch Cabell, Priscilla Bradley Cabell, and Elliott White Springs, novelist and aviator, in the dining room of the Cabells' home in Richmond, Virginia*

yond Life (1919) as "the art of being superficial seriously"–or naturalism–which he described in the novel *Smirt* (1934) as "a very lusty bastard begotten upon realism with the phallus of agony." Yet his preference for romantic subject matter was conditioned by marked cynicism and by darker ironies. He did not forget the paradoxical lesson that he learned growing up in Richmond, that man is driven to embrace ideals and myths both in spite of the fact and because of the fact that they distort and falsify reality.

At the age of fifteen Cabell enrolled as a freshman at the College of William and Mary in the sleepy town of Williamsburg. Here he distinguished himself as both a precocious and an outstanding student. He was especially adept at languages, teaching French and Greek classes as an upperclassman. The love of drama and of poetry, particularly medieval French poetry, which he developed at William and Mary, would also strongly influence the development of his fiction.

Cabell's academic career at William and Mary was marred in his senior year by a homosexual scandal in which a middle-aged village intellectual was rumored to have had affairs with several students, including Cabell. No incriminating evi-

dence was ever brought forward, however. And after Cabell's mother descended from Richmond with the family lawyer, he was duly graduated in 1898. The shame that attached to Cabell from this incident was intensified by the 1901 murder of John Scott, a cousin of Cabell's mother with whom she was rumored to be having an affair. Richmond gossip ascribed the deed to Cabell, though years later it was brought to light that the murderers were brothers of a country girl who had been seduced by Scott. These traumatic episodes served to confirm Cabell in his cynicism, and they caused him to fortify himself behind the impenetrable pose of aloof urbanity, the pose of those gallant gentlemen he would later present in his stories.

From 1898 until 1901 Cabell worked on newspapers in Richmond and New York, and from 1901 to 1911 he supported himself primarily through genealogical research. During these years he was mainly concerned with establishing the pedigree of his mother's family, the Branches, in England and Virginia. This interest in genealogy was ultimately reflected in his fiction in the multivolume Storisende Edition of his works, known collectively as "The Biography of the Life of Manuel" (1927-1930), which consists of eighteen individual novels and collections of tales which trace for over six hundred years the descendants of Manuel, medieval swineherd become king, and of Jurgen, poet and pawnbroker, from the mythical Middle Age kingdom of Poictesme down to modern-day Virginia. Many of the tales which were collected and which ultimately became a part of the work were published during the period of 1900-1915 in magazines such as *Argosy, Smart Set, Collier's,* and *Harper's Weekly.* These years also marked the appearance of Cabell's earliest novels, *The Eagle's Shadow* (1904), *The Cords of Vanity* (1909), *The Soul of Melicent* (1913), and *The Rivet in Grandfather's Neck* (1915).

The summer of 1913 found Cabell, after a two-year stint of working in the West Virginia coalfields, vacationing at Rockbridge Alum Springs. This was one of a number of vacations he enjoyed at various Virginia mountain resorts, which in his published reminiscences, *Quiet, Please* (1952) and *As I Remember It* (1955), he described as enlivened by illicit amours carried on behind the staid facade of middle-class respectability. Cabell's carefree bachelor days ended, however, at Rockbridge Alum when he met and eventually married Priscilla Bradley Shepherd, a Richmond widow with five children who was nearly five years his senior. After their marriage the couple moved to Richmond, where they lived in Priscilla's house, Dumbarton Grange, just outside town and where Priscilla took up the competent management of domestic affairs, leaving Cabell free to write.

The period from 1916 to 1926 was a remarkably productive one for Cabell during which he wrote most of his best work. *The Cream of the Jest* (1917) was his first novel accepted by Robert M. McBride for publication, though it was the fourth of Cabell's books to be issued by McBride's company. Cabell's editor at McBride, Guy Holt, subsequently became a close friend and adviser. Out of their conversations and correspondence came a collection of critical essays, *Beyond Life,* which would later serve as a prologue to "The Biography of the Life of Manuel."

Cabell was thrust from a position of relative obscurity to one of instant fame as a result of the controversy over the reputedly salacious subject matter of *Jurgen* (1919). The seizure, by John Sumner, head of the New York Society for the Prevention of Vice, of the publisher's plates and of all copies of this novel set the stage for a famous

trial, which ended on 16 October 1922, with the judge directing the jury to bring a verdict of acquittal. Meanwhile Cabell and his fiction had become a cause célèbre for America's intelligentsia, attracting such disparate admirers as Joseph Hergesheimer, Carl Van Vechten, Sinclair Lewis, and H. L. Mencken.

By the publication of his novel *Figures of Earth* in 1921 Cabell had evolved the central concept of "The Biography of the Life of Manuel" that would link his early tales and novels with the fiction he was now writing. *The High Place* (1923) and *The Silver Stallion* (1926), along with *Jurgen* and *Figures of Earth,* are today recognized as the novels which best dramatize the stories of Manuel and Jurgen and of their descendants. In order to integrate his earlier fiction with this design, Cabell revised it in the early 1920s for the Kalki Edition of his works. The Kalki Edition, in turn, became the precursor of the better-known Storisende Edition. Cabell's prefaces to each volume of this edition were collected in *Preface to the Past* (1936). These prefaces, along with the essays of *Beyond Life,* constitute his most important reflections on literature and on his own work.

The acclamation with which Cabell's work was received in the early and mid 1920s largely vanished in the 1930s. To the socially conscious critics of the depression era his fiction seemed little more than meretricious romances, written primarily to appeal to whimsical tastes and escapist sentiments. Oscar Cargill's judgment in *Intellectual America* (1941) that Cabell was "beyond all shadow of a doubt, the most tedious person who has achieved high repute as a *literatus* in America . . ." expressed the common critical attitude.

Through these oscillations of his reputation Cabell continued to live quietly in Richmond. Repeated attacks of pneumonia required annual winter retreats to St. Augustine, beginning in 1935. Florida would subsequently provide the setting for *The St. Johns* (1943), *There Were Two Pirates* (1946), and *The Devil's Own Dear Son* (1949). Cabell's literary output remained strong. Most notable among his later works were his mock-Freudian "nightmare trilogy," *Smirt, Smith* (1935), and *Smire* (1937), and collections of reflective and autobiographical essays, *Let Me Lie* (1947), *Quiet, Please,* and *As I Remember It.* In spite of his prolific publications, when he died in Richmond in 1958, he had been virtually forgotten by the American critical establishment.

Today the consensus of those who continue to evaluate Cabell's work is that he is far from a te-

Cabell (first row, center) at Joseph Hergesheimer's 1923 Halloween party held at the West Chester, Pennsylvania, country club. Priscilla Cabell is the first woman on the left in the first row, in front of Hergesheimer. On Cabell's left is Elinor Wylie, in front of H. L. Mencken. Blanche and Alfred Knopf are at the far right in the first row. Carl Van Vechten is in the third row, behind the woman in the large white hat (James Branch Cabell Library of Virginia Commonwealth University).

dious romancer. Cabell's worldview is predicated on the conviction that the universe is irrational and incomprehensible to man. In the face of the horrible chaos of matter man has no alternative but to dream and to create and worship his own fictions, which provide, if only for a short period of time, the illusion that the universe is meaningful and that man's existence is purposeful. Cabell's characters obstinately refuse to accept the ultimate reality of the natural world; and this obstinacy exposes them to disillusionment, when their dreams are inevitably smashed by reality, or to failure, when they understand that they can never completely realize their dreams. Yet the price man pays in shattered illusions is essential if he is to sustain the imaginative spark within him which is the quintessential mark of his humanness. No sooner has one network of "dynamic illusions" been ripped apart than man properly employs himself spinning another.

In *Beyond Life* Cabell defines three attitudes which he believes have dominated man's imagination through history. The chivalric attitude cre-

ates the illusion that man is God's special creature and that his purpose on earth consists of striving to accomplish God's will. Manuel himself is such a chivalric figure. The gallant attitude accepts the fact that man can know nothing about the universe and offers the fiction that he can be happy on earth by avoiding speculations about his cosmic fate and concentrating exclusively on the pleasures of day-to-day living. The poetic attitude sees chaotic reality as the raw material for creative vision, to be shaped by the artist into lovely and harmonious fictions that can sustain the illusion of meaning and purpose.

All of these attitudes give man a sense of order and coherence; all of them come to dominate various periods of human history; and all of them eventually fail and are supplanted by newer visions. Yet momentarily they evoke the fullest expression of the human spirit. Cabell's world view is one of kindly and humane skepticism which understands the necessity for imaginative attitudes and for the myths which cluster around them at the same time as it realizes the ultimate inadequacy of these attitudes and myths. A passage from *The Cream of the Jest* nicely captures this ambivalent attitude toward man, the dreamer: "In short, to me this man seemed an inadequate kickworthy creature, who had muddled away the only life he was quite certain of enjoying, in contemplation of a dream; and who had, moreover, despoiled the lives of others, too, for the dream's sake. To him the dream alone could matter—his proud assurance that life was not a blind and aimless business, not all a hopeless waste and confusion; and that he, this gross weak animal, could be strong and excellent and wise, and his existence a pageant of beauty and nobility. To prove this dream was based on a delusion would be no doubt an enjoyable retaliation, for his being so unengaging to the eye and so stupid to talk to; but it would make the dream no whit less lively or less dear to him—or to the rest of us, either."

For the reader who would understand Cabell's work fully, the early stories, composed largely between 1900 and 1915, are an important element in the writer's overall design. They are, as Carl Van Doren metaphorically described them in an early analysis, the "smaller chapels braced against the central structure" of the "towered cathedral" of the late novels. In his short fiction Cabell developed his themes and refined his irony of vision, gradually evolving toward the mature understanding of "The Biography of the Life of Manuel."

Before proceeding to a discussion of specific stories, however, two general observations need to be made about Cabell's short fiction. First, it is important to understand that Cabell was ill at ease with the term "short story." He called the stories of his first published collection, *The Line of Love* (1905), "episodes" and those of his fourth collection, *The Certain Hour* (1916), "sketches." Indeed, Cabell's terminology suggests that he was aware that his tales were not short stories in the modern sense of the word. Although they have scenic substance and developed plots, they lack the realistic style and texture and the sharply individualized characterization, the deep and often morbid introspection, which distinguishes the short fiction of Cabell's contemporaries. Even at this early point in his career Cabell viewed his characters less as individuals than as representatives of three dominant attitudes toward life—the chivalric, the gallant, and the poetic. Thus his characters, without being precisely allegorical, are broadly representative of common and abiding human types. Cabell's broadly

sketched characters, combined with his antique settings and his elaborate and highly polished style, make his stories seem closer in tone and form to Washington Irving than to Sherwood Anderson. His short fiction may therefore be more accurately described as tales than as short stories.

A second important observation about Cabell's short fiction is that the individual stories appear, not in one, but in three different published versions—the original published collection, the revised Kalki Edition, and the final Storisende Edition. Cabell once remarked of his early short-story collections that "were the choice afforded me, not one of these first editions . . . would today exist." However, he retained a greater interest in his early short fiction than this harsh judgment implies. Beginning in 1921 with *The Line of Love* he set about conscientiously revising the stories for the Kalki Edition in order that they might be fully incorporated into the design of "The Biography of the Life of Manuel."

The Line of Love illustrates well the additions and revisions that the author made to his early work. In his introduction to the Storisende Edition Cabell said that he considered this collection the germ of his "The Biography of the Life of Manuel," since the stories in it illustrated all of the attitudes—chivalric, gallant, and poetic—that would later be dramatized in the larger plan of his series. Had not Cabell revised it, however, *The Line of Love* could not have formed a part of the larger work, for there was no connection between the protagonists of the eight original stories and the line of King Manuel. The 1921 Kalki Edition, however, contained two new stories and brought the total number, ten, into accord with the number of stories in his later short-story collections. The two stories also served to tie *The Line of Love* to the saga of Manuel's descendants.

One of these additional stories, "The Wedding Jest" (*Century Magazine*, September 1919), was placed at the beginning of the expanded collection. This story features Florian de Puysange in a variation of the Rip Van Winkle legend in which Florian is enchanted on his wedding night, only to reawaken thirty years later, still young, to confront his corpulent, middle-aged bride, Adalaide, who has remarried in the intervening years and borne a daughter as beautiful as she once was. Though he is appalled by the sight of his former wife, Florian refuses to accept the fact that all things in the physical world—love included—change. The story's end finds him casting his

P O R C E L A I N   C U P S, *by James Branch Cabell*

I

Of Greatness Intimately Viewed

"Oh, but they are beyond all praise," said Cynthia Allonby,

enraptured: "they are unspeakably lovely; and certainly you should

have presented them to the Queen."

"Her majesty already possesses a cup of that ware," replied Lord

Pevensey. "It was one of her New Year's gifts, from Robert Cecil. Hers

is, I *believe,* not quite so fine as *either of* yours; but then, they tell me,

there is not the like of this pair *in England, nor indeed* on the hither side of Cataia."

He sat the two pieces of Chinese pottery upon the shelves in the

south corner of the room.   These cups were of that sea-green tint

called céladon, *Such oddities were the last vogue at Court, in this year of grace 1593;* with a very wonderful glow and radiance, and Cynthia

could not but *speculate as to* what monstrous sum Lord Pevensey had paid for *this, his latest gift to her.*

~~Nobody at Court had two pieces of porcelain finer than these were, not~~

~~even the Queen's~~ ~~Pevensey had procured them for Cynthia~~

~~Allonby~~

~~punished~~

~~George~~

~~them~~

Now he turned, smiling, a really superb creature in his blue and gold. "I had to-day another message from the

Queen." ~~And I confess, I draw~~

~~as you, I slowly approach the end of yours."~~

~~"But I make no~~ "I

~~merely tell you that~~

~~And,~~ "George," ~~she said~~ [Cynthia said,] with fond concern, "it frightens me to see you

thus foolhardy, in tempting alike the Queen's anger and the Plague."

"Eh, as goes the Plague, it spares nine out of ten," [he answered, lightly.] ~~as safe in London as I would be under Margaret's cannon fire.~~ "The Queen,

I grant you, is another pair of sleeves, for an irritated Tudor spares

nobody." ~~Meanwhile,~~

~~"You have lost reason to fear fortune. Money time for—."~~

But [~~Then~~] Cynthia Allonby kept silence, [and did not exactly smile, while she appraised her famous young kinsman.]

She was flattered by, and a little afraid of, the gay self-confidence

which led anybody to take such chances.　Two weeks ago it was the [painted trivial old] Queen

had named Lord Pevensey to go straightway into France, where, rumor had

it, King Henri was preparing to renounce the Reformed Religion, and [making]

his peace with the Pope: and for two weeks Pevensey had lingered, on one

pretence or another, at his house in London, with the Plague creeping

about the city like an invisible/ incalculable flame, and the Queen

asking questions at Windsor.　[Of all the monarchs that had war reigned in England, Elizabeth was the least used to having her orders disregarded. Meanwhile Lord Pevensey came every] ~~Every day Pevensey came to the Marquis of~~

[day to the Marquis of →] Falmouth's lodgings at Deptford: and every day Lord Pevensey pointed out

to the marquis's daughter that Pevensey [whose wife had died in child birth a year back,] did not intend to go into France,

for nobody could foretell how long a stay, as a ~~bachelor.~~ [widower.]　Certainly it

was [all] very flattering....

~~But every day she put it off (for one excellent reason or another), though Cynthia, like everybody else, admired the ... Many said that this young earl was the handsomest and most becoming of the Queen's courtiers; Cynthia ... thought it ... ... simply, as by long odds the handsomest person she ... It was no wonder, she considered, that the haggard painted irascible old dragon at Windsor accorded him indulgences denied to others: nor since ... death had there been much doubt that nobody stood higher in the Queen's favor than Lord Pevensey....~~

eyes on Adalaide's daughter, Sylvie, convinced that she will be as he once believed Adalaide was—the great love of his life.

The skillfully developed illusion-reality theme of "The Wedding Jest" serves as an appropriate introduction to the stories which follow, but the story also serves a second purpose. For Cabell suggests in a brief introduction that Florian is the illegitimate son of Jurgen; and Sylvie is the great-granddaughter of Manuel, descended through Manuel's daughter, Melicent. The eight original stories thus become stories of successive generations of characters descended from Manuel and Jurgen through Florian and Sylvie. "Porcelain Cups" (*Century*, November 1919), which Cabell added to the end of his collection, traces the line of Manuel from England to Virginia through the marriage of Cynthia Allonby and Ned Musgrave. Thus *The Line of Love*, which originally had been unconnected with the legend of Manuel, by the deft additions of the 1921 Kalki Edition had been fully integrated into the "biography."

Cabell did more than simply add stories to *The Line of Love*, however. "In Necessity's Mortar" (*Harper's Monthly*, October 1904) illustrates the stylistic revisions which he incorporated into many of his tales to make his tone firmer and less romantic and to make his irony sharper. Combining the conflict of illusion and reality with the ideas of the loss of innocence through maturity and the attainment of nobility of character through renunciation, "In Necessity's Mortar" brings Cabell's major themes together more successfully than any other story in the collection. The tale contrasts François Villon's youthful ardor for Catherine de Vaucelles with the bitter disillusionment he feels when he returns to her after an absence of seven years. Catherine's willful rejection of him has catapulted Villon into a life of crime and infamy; yet ironically when he presents himself to her—balding and ravaged by time, "rotten and weak and honeycombed with vice"—she realizes that she has always loved him. Villon also loves Catherine; but he realizes that his corruption is irremediable, and he nobly resolves to force her to deny him. He presents her with a litany of his vices and devastates her by boasting that, although the boy who was Villon loved her, the man who is Villon prefers a whore named "Fat Peg." Villon's observation that "necessity pounds us in her mortar to what shape she will" seems only half true. Fate indeed does play a role in the separation of the lovers. Youthful illusions do

seem inevitably shattered. Yet Villon's denial of the willing Catherine is both an act of free will and an authentic act of gallantry.

Although the story line and its themes remain unchanged, Cabell did make significant stylistic revisions in the Kalki Edition of "In Necessity's Mortar." Some of these changes have the effect of making the tone less romantic. For example, in the version that appeared in *The Line of Love* Villon exclaims upon meeting Catherine again: "I love her. Mother of God! Has there been a moment when I have not loved her!" In the Kalki Edition Villon expresses himself this way: "I am still past reason in all that touches this ignorant, hot-headed, Pharisaical, rather stupid wench! That is droll. But love is a resistless tyrant, and, Mother of God! has there been in my life a day, an hour, a moment when I have not loved her!" The original romantic expostulation has been delightfully qualified by a tone of ironic realism.

There is also a significant revision of the story's ending which has the effect of introducing a new and provocative theme. At the end of the original version Villon prays that she will be happy with her noble fiancé: "Mother of God, grant that Noel may be kind to her! Mother of God, grant that she may be happy! Mother of God, grant that I may not live long!" For the Kalki Edition Cabell added an additional paragraph: "And straightway he perceived that triple invocation could be, rather neatly, worked out in ballade form. Yes, with a separate prayer to each verse. So, dismissing for the while his misery, he fell to considering, with undried cheeks, what rhymes he needed." The additional paragraph is not only an ironic counterpoint to the prayer for death which precedes it; it also suggests a theme that Cabell develops more fully in his stories of famous artists, *The Certain Hour*. Poets ironically create great art out of the shame and wreckage and misery of their real lives.

Cabell's revisions, such as those of the stories in *The Line of Love*, do not alter radically the action or the thematic emphasis of his early versions. They do reveal, however, a tone, an ironic understanding, and a style more in keeping with the author's mature work. The slightly revised versions of these Kalki stories—volumes 6, 8, 10, and 12 of the Storisende Edition—represent the final form in which Cabell intended for his tales to be read. Hereafter the dates which follow the discussion of specific titles will be the original dates of

Burton Rascoe, James Branch Cabell, and Elliott White Springs in front of Springs's airplane

publication, but the text used for critical purposes will be the definitive Storisende text.

The Line of Love was followed in 1907 by *Gallantry*, a collection of ten stories set in England of the mid eighteenth century. By this time Cabell's work was beginning to attract a moderate amount of critical attention. A reviewer, writing in the 7 November *Nation*, mildly approved the "cleverness, tact, and invention" with which the stories were wrought. No one seemed aware, however, that the major purpose of the stories was to present the gallant attitude in a century during which it reigned supreme. In Cabell's preface to the 1921 Kalki Edition he defined the gallant gentleman as follows: "He will consider the world with a smile of toleration, and his own doings with a smile of amusement, and Heaven with a smile that is not distrustful." This sort of world-weary toleration is the distinguishing characteristic of the protagonists of *Gallantry*.

"Simon's Hour" (*Ainslee's Magazine*, April 1905) and "In the Second April" (*Harper's Monthly*, April, May 1907) perhaps best exemplify the gallant attitude. "In the Second April" presents the lighter side of gallantry. John Bulmer, the Duke of Ormskirk, having reached the highest level of attainment in England, is seized at mid-

dle age by ennui. Traveling to Poictesme to marry Claire de Puysange, he poses as John Bulmer, the Duke's representative; and he proceeds to court Claire away from the Duke. After saving Claire from brigands, the two are secretly married. But the revelation of this marriage brings Bulmer's arrest and the prospect of the gallows. The timely intervention of noblemen who know his true identity saves the Duke. This last-moment rescue is followed by Claire's astonishing admission that she knew all along that the John Bulmer she married was the Duke of Ormskirk.

Through all the vicissitudes of plot the Duke of Ormskirk handles himself like a true gallant. Regarding the world with bemused detachment, he is stoic in the face of danger. Portly and middle-aged, he courts the youthful Claire with sincerity, always aware of the rather ridiculous figure he cuts. He utters sentiments which might be said to constitute the gallant's credo: "Faith, let us live this life as a gentleman should, and keep our hands and our conscience as clean as may be possible, and for the outcome trust to God's common-sense."

In contrast to "In the Second April," "Simon's Hour" is a dark and tragic tale in which Lord Rokesle traps Lady Allonby on his island es-

James Branch Cabell and Julia Peterkin in New York City (South Caroliniana Library, University of South Carolina)

tate and attempts to force her to marry him. In terror the lady turns to Rokesle's servile cleric, Simon Orts, a former suitor whom Lady Allonby had rejected and who, like François Villon, had descended into a life of drunken wastefulness. The lady's frightened appeal to remember "the man you have been" galvanizes Simon into action. He kills Lord Rokesle in a sword fight and helps Lady Allonby escape from the island. At the end Simon faces certain death as well as the knowledge that he has always loved Lady Allonby, even though she is not worthy of him.

The key to Simon's behavior is that in the last analysis he serves not Lady Allonby, but an idea of himself. Unlike the chivalrous protagonist, Simon has no illusions about his love. He clearly realizes that Lady Allonby is a vain and foolish creature. His action in saving her is taken to preserve the last measure of his own self-respect. Like a true gallant Simon exhibits grace under pressure. He makes the magnificent gesture, even though he understands the ultimate futility of it. He is capable at the end of looking on

his deed "with a smile of amusement."

Cabell moved from the analysis of the gallant attitude to the analysis of the chivalric attitude in a collection of ten stories he published in 1909 under the simple title *Chivalry*. Translated from the medieval French of the fictitious Nicholas de Caen, these tales follow Manuel's line into England through Alianora, wife of Henry III. Each story features a chivalrous gesture and presents a protagonist who, in the words of Cabell, always serves "his God, his honour, and his lady without any reservation." The chivalrous hero, unlike his gallant counterpart, is dull enough not to see the reality behind the illusion. Paradoxically, while in one sense he fails, he succeeds in another.

"The Sestina" (*Harper's Monthly*, January 1906) perhaps best illustrates the code of chivalry as Cabell understood it. This story begins when Queen Alianora presents herself at the house of Osmund Heleigh, a balding knight well past his prime who in youth had created and sung a beautiful sestina for the maiden Alianora. Alianora has returned secretly to England from France, where she has vainly sought aid to free her husband, Henry III, from the captivity of rebellious barons. Now she seeks Osmund's aid in reaching the king's forces in Bristol. Disguised as jongleurs, the two travel through the battle-scarred English countryside until they successfully reach their destination.

Osmund risks his life for the queen in part because he remembers her as she was thirty years before, a "clean-eyed girl, joyous and exceedingly beautiful." Now her eyes are hardened by pride and harsh experience, and Alianora is hated by most of her subjects. Osmund realizes that she has served many of her subjects badly. Yet he says, "I must serve you because you are a woman and helpless. . . ." In the end he dies for the queen in individual combat with a younger and more powerful warrior. Yet even at this point he insists that his deeds are "trivial services . . . such as any gentleman must render a woman in distress."

Unlike Simon Orts or the Duke of Ormskirk, Osmund Heleigh believes in the idea of service to a lady. His understanding of Alianora's weaknesses is not tinctured by irony or tolerant amusement. He is a knight about his chivalrous business, and he takes his allegiances seriously. His last request of the queen is that she "reign wisely . . . that thereafter men may not say I was slain in an evil cause."

"The Sestina" is also interesting because it vividly illustrates the influence of lyric poetry, especially of French medieval forms, in Cabell's fiction. Nearly all of his stories contain poems ranging in form from ballades to sonnets. These poems attest to Cabell's love of the lyric. In "The Sestina" the form of the verse, six stanzas of six unrhymed lines, becomes one with the structure of the story. For the beautiful sestina which Osmund composed for his lovely maiden thirty years before and which saves them when they are commanded by hostile troops to perform is mirrored by the sestina of days during which Osmund shepherds the queen and achieves new life. "Naught else have I afforded you, madame," he says, "save very anciently a Sestina. Ho, a Sestina! And in return you have given me a Sestina of fairer make—a Sestina of days, six days of life."

In 1916 *The Certain Hour*, Cabell's last collection of short fiction, was published. This collection was the only one not republished in the Kalki Edition, though Cabell incorporated slight

Cabell in his study, circa 1955 (James Branch Cabell Library of Virginia Commonwealth University)

revisions into his Storisende Edition. *The Certain Hour* investigates the poetic attitude as it is displayed in a number of historical figures, including William Shakespeare, Robert Herrick, William Wycherley, Alexander Pope, and Richard Sheridan. Cabell wrote that the stories dealt with "the struggle of a special temperament with a fixed form." The "special temperament" is that of the artist who "desires to write perfectly of beautiful happenings." The "fixed form" is the solid matter of life into which the artist must descend and exist. The common theme that runs through these investigations of the poetic attitude is that successful artists are seldom successful as people.

"Judith's Creed" (*Lippincott's Magazine*, July 1915) focuses on one afternoon in the life of William Shakespeare. This year is 1609, and Shakespeare, near the end of a successful career, is visited by the Dark Lady, whom he had loved tempestuously years before. It was she who, through her disdain and rejection, had helped to spark the dark intensity of his sonnets and his tragedies. The relation of Shakespeare and the Dark Lady suggests, of course, the way François Villon converts the misery of his life into art in "In Necessity's Mortar." However, Shakespeare is ultimately blessed with a new muse, his loving daughter Judith. Under her benign influence the tragic vision is supplanted by the comic vision of life as love and reconciliation. This is the vision of the play he writes in his garden after the Dark Lady leaves, *The Tempest*.

In spite of Shakespeare's eventual reconciliation with life, the visit of the Dark Lady serves to remind him ruefully that for the artist it takes "a deal of ruined life . . . to make a little art." This idea is amplified and given an interesting twist in "The Lady of all Our Dreams" (first published as "The Dream," *Argonaut*, 23 November 1912), a story which moves the collection into contemporary times and introduces us to Cabell's fictional Virginia writer, John Charteris. Charteris has returned to Fairhaven (Williamsburg) to deliver the commencement address at his alma mater, King's College (William and Mary). After years of obscurity he finds himself celebrated by the college "now that his colorful tales had risen, from the semi-oblivion of being cherished merely by people who cared seriously for beautiful things, to the distinction of being purchasable in railway stations. . . ."

Strolling on the college lawn the evening after his speech, Charteris meets an old college flame, Pauline Romayne, who seems scarcely to have changed over the years. Seeing the woman he might have married, Charteris realizes that while he has written "brave books that would preserve the glories of the Dream untarnished," the Dream has been "an exacting master." "My books," he observes, "such as they are, have been made what they are at the dear price of never permitting myself to care seriously for anything else." At the moment when Charteris resolves that the dream is not enough and that he must have Pauline, he is awakened by a friend. The meeting with Pauline itself was a dream. This scarcely altered lady was, in reality, "the gray-haired woman in purple who carried out her squalling brat" as Charteris was delivering his address. In this story of the poetic attitude Cabell works with delightful irony on the themes of illusion and reality and of art and life.

After the publication of *The Certain Hour* Cabell turned to the writing of the series of novels which would establish his reputation. Yet even in these longer narratives he did not really abandon the short fiction form. Just as Cabell's tales are ill defined by the term "short story," his Poictesme narratives strain to fit the conventional contemporary definition of the novel. Upon closer examination they present themselves as loosely constructed romances, highly picaresque in form. Cabell, in fact, continued to write his tales; but

he later integrated them, usually by relating them to the adventures of a common protagonist, into a longer narrative.

Cabell's habit of writing shorter tales for publication in magazines and of then incorporating them into novels was one he followed from early in his career. For example, *The Cords of Vanity*, published in 1909, contained six stories spread out over sixteen of the novel's chapters, stories which had appeared as early as 1902 in the *Smart Set*. *Figures of Earth*, the first novel of "The Biography of the Life of Manuel," published in 1921, included six tales which had been published in 1919 and 1920 in the *Century* and in *McClure's* magazines. *Jurgen* contains one of the most interesting examples of this technique of incorporation. For this novel Cabell reached back seventeen years and resurrected his first published story, "An Amateur Ghost," which appeared in *Argosy* magazine in February 1902. Though he changed the names of his characters and invested the story with the amusing double entendre that accounts for much of the appeal of the novel, the action and most of the dialogue of "An Amateur Ghost" are preserved in chapters 16 and 17 of *Jurgen*.

James Branch Cabell was in the most fundamental sense a writer of short fiction. The tales of his early period were followed by novels which were composed to a significant degree of tales which had already been published in magazines. He never really lost interest in the short fiction form, and most of his novels were indeed dependent on this form. The stories of Cabell's early period, published in the collections which appeared from 1905 to 1916, thus indicate the direction of the writer's development in more than one way. They prefigure the loosely picaresque structure of the novels. But they also indicate, through Cabell's analysis of the chivalric, gallant, and poetic attitudes, his principal themes. From the very beginning Cabell was concerned in his writing with the relation of myth and illusion to reality and with the various stratagems men employ to impose meaning in a universe which appears chaotic and meaningless. The early stories begin the analysis of themes which Cabell would develop with even greater force and assurance in his later romances. The key to Cabell's vision, however, is to be found in the early short fiction.

Letters:
Between Friends: Letters of James Branch Cabell and Others, edited by Padraic Colum and Marga-

ret Freeman Cabell (New York: Harcourt, Brace & World, 1962);

The Letters of James Branch Cabell, edited by Edward Wagenknecht (Norman: University of Oklahoma Press, 1975).

Bibliographies:

Frances Joan Brewer, *James Branch Cabell: A Bibliography of His Writings, Biography and Criticism* (Charlottesville: University of Virginia Press, 1957);

Matthew J. Bruccoli, *James Branch Cabell: A Bibliography, Part II: Notes on the Cabell Collections at the University of Virginia* (Charlottesville: University of Virginia Press, 1957).

References:

Joe Lee Davis, *James Branch Cabell* (New York: Twayne, 1962);

Maurice Duke, *James Branch Cabell: A Reference Guide* (Boston: G. K. Hall, 1979);

Paul Spenser, "Jurgen and the 'Ghost,'" *Kalki*, 7, no. 4 (1978): 129-133;

Spenser, " 'Some Ladies' and *Jurgen*," *Kalki*, 7, no. 2 (1976): 51-57;

Desmond Tarrant, *James Branch Cabell: The Dream and the Reality* (Norman: University of Oklahoma Press, 1967);

Carl Van Doren, "Cabell Minor," in *James Branch Cabell*, revised edition (New York: The Literary Guide, 1932), pp. 1-30;

Van Doren, "Irony in Velvet: The Short Stories of James Branch Cabell," *Century Magazine*, 108 (August 1924): 561-566;

Arvin R. Wells, *Jesting Moses: A Study in Cabellian Comedy* (Gainesville: University of Florida Press, 1962), pp. 63-76.

Papers:

The Alderman Library of the University of Virginia holds many of Cabell's manuscripts, scrapbooks, and more than two thousand letters covering the years 1896-1958; the Cabell Collection of Virginia Commonwealth University's James Branch Cabell Library holds scrapbooks, notebooks, and more than six hundred letters.

Willa Cather

(7 December 1873-24 April 1947)

Rosalie Hewitt

Northern Illinois University

See also the Cather entries in *DLB 9: American Novelists, 1910-1945; DLB 54: American Poets, 1880-1945*; and *DLB Documentary Series 1*.

BOOKS: *April Twilights* (Boston: Badger, 1903);

The Troll Garden (New York: McClure, Phillips, 1905);

Alexander's Bridge (Boston & New York: Houghton Mifflin, 1912); republished as *Alexander's Bridges* (London: Heinemann, 1912);

O Pioneers! (Boston & New York: Houghton Mifflin, 1913; London: Heinemann, 1913);

The Song of the Lark (Boston & New York: Houghton Mifflin, 1915; London: Murray, 1916); revised as volume 2 of *The Novels and Stories of Willa Cather* (Boston: Houghton Mifflin, 1937);

My Ántonia (Boston & New York: Houghton Mifflin, 1918; London: Heinemann, 1919);

Youth and the Bright Medusa (New York: Knopf, 1920; London: Heinemann, 1921);

One of Ours (New York: Knopf, 1922; London: Heinemann, 1923);

April Twilights and Other Poems (New York: Knopf, 1923; London: Heinemann, 1924; enlarged edition, New York: Knopf, 1933); abridged in volume 3 of *The Novels and Stories of Willa Cather* (Boston: Houghton Mifflin, 1937);

A Lost Lady (New York: Knopf, 1923; London: Heinemann, 1924);

The Professor's House (New York: Knopf, 1925; London: Heinemann, 1925);

My Mortal Enemy (New York: Knopf, 1926; London: Heinemann, 1928);

Death Comes for the Archbishop (New York: Knopf, 1927; London: Heinemann, 1927);

Shadows on the Rock (New York: Knopf, 1931; London, Toronto, Melbourne & Sydney: Cassell, 1932);

Obscure Destinies (New York: Knopf, 1932; London, Toronto, Melbourne & Sydney: Cassell, 1932);

Lucy Gayheart (New York: Knopf, 1935; London,

Willa Cather in Red Cloud, Nebraska, circa 1922 (Willa Cather Pioneer Memorial and Educational Foundation, Nebraska State Historical Society)

Toronto, Melbourne & Sydney: Cassell, 1935);

Not Under Forty (New York: Knopf, 1936; London, Toronto, Melbourne & Sydney: Cassell, 1936);

Sapphira and the Slave Girl (New York: Knopf, 1940; London, Toronto, Melbourne & Sydney: Cassell, 1941);

The Old Beauty and Others (New York: Knopf, 1948; London: Cassell, 1956);

Willa Cather on Writing (New York: Knopf, 1949);

Writings from Willa Cather's Campus Years, edited by James R. Shively (Lincoln: University of Nebraska Press, 1950);

Willa Cather in Europe, edited by George N. Kates (New York: Knopf, 1956);

Early Stories, edited by Mildred R. Bennett (New York: Dodd, Mead, 1957);

Willa Cather's Collected Short Fiction, 1892-1912 (Lincoln: University of Nebraska Press, 1965);

The Kingdom of Art: Willa Cather's First Principles and Critical Statements, 1893-1896, edited by Bernice Slote (Lincoln: University of Nebraska Press, 1966);

The World and the Parish: Willa Cather's Articles and Reviews, 1893-1902, 2 volumes, edited by William M. Curtin (Lincoln: University of Nebraska Press, 1970);

Uncle Valentine and Other Stories, edited by Slote (Lincoln: University of Nebraska Press, 1973);

Willa Cather in Person: Interviews, Speeches, and Letters, selected and edited by L. Brent Bohlke (Lincoln: University of Nebraska Press, 1986).

Collection: *The Novels and Stories of Willa Cather*, Autograph Edition, 13 volumes (Boston: Houghton Mifflin, 1937-1941).

OTHER: Georgine Milmine, *The Life of Mary G. Baker Eddy*, ghostwritten by Cather (New York: Doubleday, Page, 1909);

S. S. McClure, *My Autobiography*, ghostwritten by Cather (New York: Stokes, 1914; London: Murray, 1914).

The literary reputation of Willa Cather has steadily risen since her first volume of short stories appeared in 1905, but her present stature as an important American writer rests largely on her twelve novels, most particularly *My Ántonia* (1918), *A Lost Lady* (1923), and *Death Comes for the Archbishop* (1927). In recent years, however, Cather has also achieved recognition for a substantial body of short fiction, written over the entire period of her literary activity from her teens to her death. This fiction portrays the lives of a diverse group of characters ranging from midwestern immigrants to middle-class easterners to cosmopolitan singers and artists.

The geographical settings of Willa Cather's fiction reflect her deep attachments to the several areas in the United States which, at one time or another, she called home. Born in Back Creek Valley, Virginia, to Charles F. and Mary Virginia Boak Cather, Cather (who was baptized Wilella) was part of a family that traced its ancestors to colonial America and from there to Ireland. From childhood she had a keen sense of the values of an enduring tradition and the strengths and struggles of pioneer life. In 1883 she and her family moved to Nebraska, settling finally in Red Cloud.

By the time of her graduation from high school and the beginning of her studies at the University of Nebraska in Lincoln in fall 1891, Cather had come to appreciate two sometimes contradictory aspects of life in the Midwest—the simplicity of a stoic people rooted to a harsh existence and the imagination of youths who, like herself, longed for lives of art and beauty. The pioneer strain in Cather kept her tied to the earth and manifested itself in her practical decision to pursue her art while supporting herself as a journalist and drama critic for the *Nebraska State Journal* while at the university. These endeavors earned her statewide recognition, even some renown outside Nebraska, and—after she earned an A.B. degree in 1895—led to her acceptance of a position in June 1896 as editor for the magazine *Home Monthly* in Pittsburgh, Pennsylvania.

Cather's life in Pittsburgh for the next ten years was crucial for her development as a writer. She concentrated her energies on poetry and short fiction. In summer 1897 she resigned her editorship and that fall she began teaching Latin and English in a public high school. Through the friendship of Isabelle McClung, whom she met in 1899, Cather was provided a home in which she could work and a cultural milieu conducive to her interests. While she was living in Pittsburgh her first book, the poetry collection *April Twilights* (1903), and her first collection of fiction, *The Troll Garden* (1905), were published.

In 1906 Cather was hired as an editor of *McClure's* magazine in New York City. Cather's years at the magazine provided her new opportunities for artistic development; yet her duties there restricted the time she could devote to her fiction. In fall 1911, with her first novel, *Alexander's Bridge* (1912; serialized in *McClure's*, February-April 1912), about to be published, Cather relinquished journalism entirely for imaginative writing. Her long apprenticeship was over.

During the next two decades Cather produced her major novels, a second collection of short fiction, *Youth and the Bright Medusa* (1920), and established an international reputation. Her

Cather in Pittsburgh, 1901 or 1902 (Willa Cather Pioneer Memorial and Educational Foundation Collection, Nebraska State Historical Society)

renown rested on her ability to capture the essence of life on the midwestern plains and in the Southwest, a region she first visited in 1912 and came to love for its aesthetic and spiritual qualities. While her novels of this period are set in the Midwest and West, the relatively few short stories she wrote during this time are set in Pittsburgh and New York.

During the 1930s Cather produced three novels and an important collection of short fiction, *Obscure Destinies* (1932), and oversaw the publication of the Autograph Edition of her works (1937-1941). In *Sapphira and the Slave Girl* (1940), her last novel and the last book published in her lifetime, Cather turned to her Virginia roots, recreating her birthplace as it was before the Civil War.

Until her death in 1947 Cather maintained residences in New York City but frequently traveled to the American West and to Europe, developing a deep emotional attachment to France. From her years at *McClure's* until her death at age seventy-three she lived with her close friend

Edith Lewis. In her fiction Cather often reflected on the necessary sacrifices artists must make so that their creations might live, and in choosing a solitary, intensely private life for herself, Cather unwaveringly made such sacrifices.

She was much honored during her lifetime, receiving a Pulitzer Prize (1922) for *One of Ours* (1922), the William Dean Howells Medal of the American Academy of Arts and Letters (1930) for *Death Comes for the Archbishop* (1927), the National Institute of Arts and Letters Gold Medal (1944), and several honorary doctorates.

Twenty-five years after Cather's very first published story, "Peter," appeared in the 21 May 1892 issue of *Mahogany Tree*, Cather reworked it as an episode in *My Ántonia*. Cather frequently drew upon her early stories for later works, and Peter, the old Bohemian who destroys his violin rather than allow it to be sold by his acquisitive son, is a character type that often appears in her fiction. The story expresses her sympathy for the old, her reverence for music and the past, and her rejection of exploitative materialism. "Peter" also employs, in rough form, the narrative technique of time shifting that would become almost a hallmark of her short fiction.

All but one of Cather's undergraduate stories are set on the Nebraska plains and have European immigrants as their major characters. Sometimes the plains demand of their settlers a reluctant admiration, but more often life on the plains provides a cruel lesson in the survival of the fittest. The naturalism of these early stories was to be gradually modified and transformed in Cather's later fiction. "A Night at Greenway Court" (*Nebraska Literary Magazine*, June 1896), which takes place in colonial Virginia, employs an older narrator who looks back on his youth and tells of the rivalry between two aristocrats over the portrait of a beautiful woman. Here is an adolescent, sentimental rendering of a situation that fascinated Cather throughout her life: a male narrator in the act of re-creating his youthful adoration of a beautiful woman.

Cather's interest in human psychology and behavior manifests itself in her Pittsburgh stories. Some of these stories are set in the Midwest, but others have urban settings. The independent, spirited female is introduced in "Tommy, the Unsentimental" (*Home Monthly*, August 1896). An instinctive appreciation for life communicated between the old and the young is the major theme of "Jack-a-Boy" (*Saturday Evening Post*, 30 March 1901). "The Count of Crow's Nest" (*Home Monthly*, September and October 1896) and "The Prodigies" (*Home Monthly*, July 1897) echo a Jamesian theme, the manipulation of young and old by mercenary family members who should be devoted and protective. In "Nanette: An Aside" (*Courier*, 31 July 1897) and "A Singer's Romance" (*Library*, 28 July 1900) Cather introduces artist figures. In each story an opera singer sacrifices a personal relationship for the private, emotionally draining, life of art.

"A Resurrection" (*Home Monthly*, April 1897) prefigures Cather's later use of the shifting center of consciousness, through which she is able to establish reader sympathy for two or more different characters. Cather seems to have been searching for and experimenting with character and theme during 1896-1902, but it was not until she wrote the stories collected in *The Troll Garden* that she could skillfully unite content and technique.

The stories in *The Troll Garden* are written in the clean, graceful prose style that is one of the most distinctive characteristics of Cather's mature fiction, a combination of economy and lyri-

cism. For this collection Cather carefully selected and arranged stories that share a common theme—the intrusion of the insensitive, vulgar, or brutal on beauty and imagination. In each story locale is intricately related to character, and like Nathaniel Hawthorne or Edgar Allan Poe, Cather carefully creates a mood through symbolically suggestive descriptions. Each of the stories concerns in some way an artist figure's effect on, or transformation of, others.

In the opening story, "Flavia and Her Artists" (previously unpublished), the artist is the exploiter; the foreign artist Roux benefits from Flavia's hospitality but eventually betrays her by satirizing her in print. In "The Sculptor's Funeral" (*McClure's*, January 1905), now ranked among Cather's best short stories, the body of artist Harvey Merrick is brought back to his prairie home for burial. Most of the village's citizens and Merrick's family are portrayed in varying degrees as insensitive and hypocritical, unable to appreciate Merrick's character or art. Only his inarticulate father and Jim Laird, a boyhood friend who is now a lawyer, react sympathetically. Now wedded to materialism, Laird can only partially express his appreciation of Merrick's artistic and moral integrity. The person Laird once was seems finally to be buried with Merrick.

The complex characterization in "The Garden Lodge" (previously unpublished) has been largely unrecognized. The story's center of consciousness, Caroline Noble, a woman who rejects her romantic, artistic impulses for a life of restraint and discipline, is masterfully realized, especially in the story's surrealistic evocation of her irrational self in a nightmarish dream.

The last two stories, "A Wagner Matinée" (*Everybody's Magazine*, February 1904; extensively revised for inclusion in *The Troll Garden*) and "Paul's Case" (previously unpublished) are ranked, by common consensus, at the very top of Cather's short fiction, and "Paul's Case," probably the finest story Cather ever wrote, is now considered an American classic. Aunt Georgina, the simple plainswoman of "A Wagner Matinée," is viewed through the eyes of her nephew, who is witness to her transformation from a stoical silence to a joyful, but poignant, self-expression triggered by her sense of communion with the music at a Wagner concert. Aunt Georgina's strength of character belongs to the plains, while her soul belongs to the music.

"Paul's Case" is the thematic and artistic culmination of *The Troll Garden*. Young Paul is not an artist; yet he has an artist's temperament, a yearning for the beauty and intensity of feeling he thinks only a glamorous environment can provide. With stolen money he escapes from the stifling, workaday world of Pittsburgh and goes to New York City. His search is for some inexpressible means of transcendence from his commonplace existence, but, once he has spent the money, he believes he has no way to achieve his desires: "The carnations in his coat were drooping with the cold, he noticed; their red glory all over. It occurred to him that all the flowers he had seen in the glass cases that first night must have gone the same way, long before this." Paul forgets the promise of what still might await him and commits suicide. He fails to realize the power of his own imagination, one of the most urgent themes in Cather's fiction. She believed in the infinite possibilities of the imaginative life, no matter what one's physical environment, and she recognized the tragic poignancy of those who, like Paul, are too impatient to realize that power.

The Cather stories that appeared in periodicals from 1905 through 1912 do not, overall, have the power or artistry of those in *The Troll Garden*. Cather's duties at *McClure's* restricted the time she could spend on writing fiction, and she devoted much of her free time to work on her first novel. Most of her short fiction of this peri-

od, including the Jamesian tale "Eleanor's House" (*McClure's*, October 1907) and the Hawthornesque story "The Profile" (*McClure's*, June 1907), is derivative. Her work at the muckraking *McClure's* doubtless influenced her inclusion of explicit social protest in stories such as "Behind the Singer Tower" (*Collier's*, May 1912), which focuses on capitalist exploitation of immigrant workers. Cather's major fiction eschews blatant social commentary.

Two stories of this period, however, are evidence of Cather's development as a writer. In "The Enchanted Bluff " (*Harper's*, April 1909), which was later revised as a section of her novel *The Professor's House* (1925), Cather employs the rock with an ancient village at its top as a symbol for the eternal verities of the universe. The boys in the story, who sense the supernatural power of the rock, never fulfill their plans to climb it. As they grow older they become more and more immersed in the trivialities of the material world.

"The Bohemian Girl" (*McClure's*, August 1912) foreshadows *My Ántonia*. Nils Ericson, who has gone east to make his fortune, returns to his home on the plains. Having already made his decision to break with the past, he persuades Clara Vavricka, the wife of his older brother, to elope with him. Clara's vitality, her love of music and dancing, and her desire for adventure all work to

Frederick Duneka, Willa Cather, and Edward S. Martin at the dinner celebrating Samuel Clemens's seventieth birthday,
The Delmonico Restaurant, New York, 5 December 1905

A New Book of Stories by the Author of
"My Antonia"

YOUTH·AND·THE BRIGHT·MEDUSA

By WILLA CATHER

THERE are not many living writers from whom a new book commands the mixture of excitement, anticipation, and curious respect with which each successive volume of Miss Cather's is now awaited.

This collection of eight stories is a new exhibition of the writer's power and remarkable artistry. The theme on which all the stories more or less loosely hang—youth's adventure with the many-colored Medusa of art—is in itself fascinating; but it is the writer's quick, bold cutting into the very tissues of

[continued on back of wrapper]

ALFRED A. KNOPF   **PUBLISHER, N.Y.**

Dust jacket for Cather's second collection of short stories. After its publication in 1920, Cather devoted most of her time to writing novels.

turn her away from the lonely life she envisions for herself on the plains. While Cather does not condemn Clara's decision, she also demonstrates clearly that life on the plains has its virtues and that they are perhaps even more compelling than adventures in the East. When Eric, the youngest Ericson brother, is tempted to leave his mother to live with Clara and Nils, he hesitates in midjourney and takes the train back home. As his mother accepts him back, "happiness filled his heart." The tension between the West and the East, between loyalty and liberation, is not simply resolved. The story is an indication of Cather's

move back to a fictional treatment of the Nebraska landscape, which would fuel her creative energies as much as, perhaps more than, the East. Certainly this return to western sources manifests itself in most of the novels Willa Cather wrote over the next twenty years, but her ten published short stories of 1915-1929 (seven of which were uncollected until 1973) have urban settings. Of the stories from 1915-1929 included in *Uncle Valentine and Other Stories* (1973), five are set in New York and two in Pittsburgh.

The New York stories which appeared in periodicals from 1915 to 1920 generally explore the behavior of the business and commercial classes. Cather is clearly drawing upon her experiences in publishing as she continues to present sympathetic portraits of those who resist the superficial rewards of money and power. "Consequences" (*McClure's*, November 1915) is intriguing because of its connection with Henry James's "The Jolly Corner" (1908). Cather's protagonist, Cavenaugh, is not confronted by the ghost of his alter ego, however, but by an actual person who may embody the spirit of Cavenaugh's dead twin brother. Cavenaugh's subsequent suicide seems to be his acceptance of guilt for his material success, perhaps at the cost of his brother's life. In "The Bookkeeper's Wife" (*Century*, May 1916), a rather lightweight story, Bixby steals money from his firm so he may marry a woman who appreciates a more comfortable life than he is able to provide. Ironically, as Bixby fails in both his job and his marriage, his wife aggressively succeeds in the business world.

"Ardessa" (*Century*, May 1918) is a humorous treatment of an ironic situation (indeed many of these stories have comedic touches that are usually not attributed to Willa Cather). The setting is a magazine office run by a self-indulgent secretary who eventually loses her position because of her inattention to her duties. The young, efficient Becky Tietelbaum is willing to do these very tasks that Ardessa shuns, and in the process Becky achieves the power that Ardessa has self-assuredly believed to be her own. The more-serious story "Her Boss" (*Smart Set*, October 1919) also presents a sympathetic portrait of a young woman, Annie Wooley, who sacrifices her own ego for the benefit of her employer. Yet, after his death, his wife and children refuse to acknowledge a bequest he has made to Annie.

The most-interesting and best-known story of these years is "Coming, Aphrodite!," first published in the August 1920 issue of *Smart Set* as "Coming, Eden Bower!" The version of the story that is included in *Youth and the Bright Medusa* is substantially different from the one in *Smart Set*. Since "Coming, Aphrodite!" is the most sexually explicit of Cather's stories, it may be that the story was censored by H. L. Mencken, the *Smart Set* editor.

The beautiful Eden Bower, destined to be a famous opera singer, has a brief summer affair with Don Hedger, a struggling artist who relishes his privacy and believes that his mind and art can be nurtured only away from the public glare.

Cather's narrator agrees with Hedger: Eden "did not guess that her neighbor would have more temptuous adventures sitting in his dark studio than she would find in all the capitals of Europe, or in all the latitude she was prepared to permit herself." Yet, Eden has an independent, spirited quality that Hedger lacks, and her balloon ride at Coney Island demonstrates the risks she is willing to take to fulfill her desires. The story ends rather optimistically, for both Eden and Hedger achieve their goals–her name on a New York marquee, his name on paintings that have earned a quiet, but admiring, notice.

In addition to "Coming, Aphrodite!" and four stories from *The Troll Garden*, *Youth and the Bright Medusa* includes "The Diamond Mine" (*McClure's*, October 1916), "A Gold Slipper" (*Harper's*, January 1917), and "Scandal" (*Century*, August 1919)–all united by the theme of the exploitation of the artist. Cressida Garnet, the opera singer in "The Diamond Mine," and Kitty Ayrshire, also an opera singer and the central figure of "A Gold Slipper" and "Scandal," are beautiful women who maintain their artistry by sheer force of will in the midst of betrayal by family, friends, and acquaintances. Each woman, however, has an admirer who is attentive to her and allows her the freedom to be what she wishes. As in most of Cather's stories of beautiful but vulnerable women, this admirer also acts as narrator.

There is some evidence of a feminist perspective in these stories that was not apparent in Cather's earlier short fiction, although it emerges in novels such as *O Pioneers!* (1913) and *The Song of the Lark* (1915). Kitty Ayrshire, for instance, in defending her choice of independence and a career to a stolid and arrogant businessman protests that men see women primarily in terms of sex and fail to see that when women are confronted with "danger and difficulty" they have "important qualifications" for survival.

Cather's magazine publication in the 1920s included only "Coming, Aphrodite!" and two Pittsburgh stories, "Uncle Valentine" (*Woman's Home Companion*, February 1925) and "Double Birthday" (*Forum*, February 1929). Like "The Diamond Mine," "Uncle Valentine" is one of a very few Cather stories narrated by a woman. It also employs the sort of a story-within-a-story framework that Cather refined in some of her novels. "Uncle Valentine" demonstrates the importance of place for the artist's creativity. Valentine Ramsey composes his finest music during a one-year period when he can wander at leisure on his neighbor's

S. S. McClure, Willa Cather, Ida M. Tarbell, and Will Irwin, 1924 (Lilly Library, Indiana University)

wooded estate. After his former wife purchases that estate, Valentine loses his sense of identity, moves to Paris, and still feeling displaced, is killed as he steps into traffic. In "Double Birthday" an old man and his middle-aged nephew who share the same birthday are spiritually bolstered by renewing their friendship with a woman who was part of their past.

Obscure Destinies (1932), Cather's third collection and the last to be published in her lifetime, contains three thematically linked stories set in the Midwest: "Neighbour Rosicky," "Old Mrs. Harris," and "Two Friends." As the book's title suggests, the protagonists in these stories never know fame or glory; yet they achieve integrity, dignity, and humanity through their enduring devotion to family and friends.

The title character in "Neighbour Rosicky" (*Woman's Home Companion*, April 1930) is a kind and generous Bohemian immigrant who helps his American daughter-in-law to understand the Bohemian's attachment to the land and loyalty to family. The friendship that develops between the two harkens back to such early stories as "Tommy, the Unsentimental," which also dramatizes an instinctive communion between the old and the young.

In contrast, "Old Mrs. Harris" (first published as "Three Women" in the September-November 1932 issues of *Ladies' Home Journal*) emphasizes the isolation and displacement of the aged and dying. The family of Mrs. Harris, the oldest of several women in the story, views her only in terms of her social roles of grandmother and mother. Only two female outsiders, the immigrant neighbor Mrs. Rosen and the maidservant Mandy, see her as an individual with her own needs and desires. The three women to which the original title refers–Mrs. Harris; Victoria, her daughter; and Vickie, her granddaughter–all have loving attachments to one another, but life intrudes upon their expression of this love. While there is some sympathetic communion between Mrs. Harris and Vickie, the young girl's preparation for college often creates a barrier. Victoria is oblivious to both her mother and her daughter, absorbed by her social functions and her unwanted pregnancy.

The stories of the three women create a complex mosaic, but Cather's narrator has most sympathy for the grandmother, whose isolation is starkly dramatized. Only after her death does she become an object of "much attention and excitement." Among Cather's finest short stories,

"Mrs. Harris" deserves to be ranked with "Paul's Case."

"Two Friends" (*Woman's Home Companion*, July 1932), not as strong as the other two stories in the collection, is linked to them by its elegiac tone. Two close friends, both businessmen, separate after an insignificant political quarrel, and the young narrator, who has been witness to their closeness, can only lament a friendship "that was senselessly wasted." It would be too simplistic to describe these stories in *Obscure Destinies*, in their return to an earlier America, as Cather's nostalgic evocation of the past; for they illustrate, and do not easily resolve, the tension between belief in permanent values and the realization that human existence is all too vulnerable and transitory. Cather's nostalgia, if that word is appropriate, is not for a certain period in the past, or for a certain place, but for the experience of sharing, the experience of a mutual joy and understanding.

Cather's last short stories were published posthumously in *The Old Beauty and Others* (1948). None of these is among Cather's best fiction, but "The Old Beauty" (written in 1936) is notable for its structurally intricate narration about the final days of a beautiful woman imprisoned by her past. Her guilt over her indifference to the many men who had admired her is the price that she pays for the "exceptional gift" of beauty. While the characters in this story are similar to others in Cather's fiction, the emphasis on the debilitating effects of memory strikes a fresh note. Lady Longstreet steadfastly, almost irritatingly, refuses to gain any satisfaction from the present; and the story's movement from present to past, from one consciousness to another, illustrates Cather's continuing dexterity with narrative technique. Of her last stories, this one most firmly rejects an illusory nostalgia. Even Lady Longstreet's request to be buried in Père-Lachaise cemetery in Paris is an empty salute to the past, a choice made by other "ladies who had once held a place in the world."

"The Best Years," the last story Cather wrote, is weakened by sentimentality as it returns to the theme of "Neighbour Rosicky." This time the protagonist is a young woman who in her short life has an enduring impact on her family, friends, and students. "Before Breakfast," the last story in the collection, is memorable primarily for its hero's rejection of the business and scientific world for solitude in the natural world, where he can restore his spiritual being. The story reflects Cather's own rejection of public life. To the very end she sought privacy and decried any act that violated the sacredness of the individual self and its expression.

Cather's determination to control the destiny of her reputation led her to include only *Youth and the Bright Medusa* and *Obscure Destinies* in the collected edition of her works. While these two books certainly include her finest short stories, she wrote many other good stories. Now that nearly all her stories have been collected, the variety within her short fiction is more readily apparent, and the expanded canon can only enhance her reputation as a short-story writer.

Bibliographies:

Bernice Slote, "Willa Cather," in *Sixteen Modern American Authors*, edited by J. R. Bryer (Durham: Duke University Press, 1973), pp. 28-73;

Margaret O'Connor, "A Guide to the Letters of Willa Cather," *Resources for American Literary Study*, 4 (Autumn 1974): 145-172;

Joan Crane, *Willa Cather: A Bibliography* (Lincoln & London: University of Nebraska Press, 1982);

Marilyn Arnold, *Willa Cather: A Reference Guide* (Boston: G. K. Hall, 1986).

Biographies:

E. K. Brown, *Willa Cather: A Critical Biography* (New York: Knopf, 1953);

Elizabeth Shepley Sergeant, *Willa Cather: A Memoir* (Philadelphia: Lippincott, 1953);

Edith Lewis, *Willa Cather Living* (New York: Knopf, 1953);

Sharon O'Brien, *Willa Cather: The Emerging Voice* (New York: Oxford University Press, 1987);

James Woodress, *Willa Cather: A Literary Life* (Lincoln: University of Nebraska Press, 1987).

References:

Marilyn Arnold, *Willa Cather's Short Fiction* (Athens: Ohio University Press, 1984);

Mildred Bennett, *The World of Willa Cather* (Lincoln: University of Nebraska Press, 1961);

Edward and Lillian Bloom, *Willa Cather's Gift of Sympathy* (Carbondale: Southern Illinois University Press, 1962);

David Daiches, *Willa Cather: A Critical Introduction* (Ithaca: Cornell University Press, 1951);

Philip Gerber, *Willa Cather* (Boston: Twayne, 1975);

Richard Giannone, *Music in Willa Cather's Fiction* (Lincoln: University of Nebraska Press, 1968);

John Murphy, ed., *Critical Essays on Willa Cather* (Boston: G. K. Hall, 1983);

John H. Randall III, *The Landscape and the Looking Glass: Willa Cather's Search for Value* (Boston: Houghton Mifflin, 1960);

Susan Rosowski, *The Voyage Perilous: Willa Cather's Romanticism* (Lincoln: University of Nebraska Press, 1986);

James Schroeter, ed., *Willa Cather and Her Critics* (Ithaca: Cornell University Press, 1967);

Bernice Slote and Virginia Faulkner, eds., *The Art of Willa Cather* (Lincoln: University of Nebraska Press, 1974);

David Stouck, *Willa Cather's Imagination* (Lincoln: University of Nebraska Press, 1975).

Papers:
Cather's manuscripts and letters are scattered among the Guy W. Bailey Library, University of Vermont; the Clifton Waller Barrett Library, University of Virginia; the Carnegie Library, Pittsburgh; the Colby College Library; the Houghton Library, Harvard University; the Huntington Library, San Marino, California; the Morgan Library, New York City; the University of Nebraska; the Nebraska State Historical Society; the Newberry Library, Chicago; the Willa Cather Pioneer Memorial, Red Cloud, Nebraska; and the Yale University Library.

Mary Hartwell Catherwood

(16 December 1847-26 December 1902)

Kenneth A. Robb
Bowling Green State University

BOOKS: *A Woman in Armor* (New York: Carleton/London: Low, 1875);

The Dogberry Bunch (Boston: Lothrop, 1879);

Craque-O'-Doom. A Story (Philadelphia: Lippincott, 1881);

Rocky Fork (Boston: Lothrop, 1882);

Old Caravan Days (Boston: Lothrop, 1884);

The Secrets at Roseladies (Boston: Lothrop, 1888);

The Romance of Dollard (New York: Century, 1889; London: Unwin, 1889);

The Story of Tonty (Chicago: McClurg, 1890; London: Richards, 1904);

The Lady of Fort St. John (Boston & New York: Houghton, Mifflin, 1891; London: Low, 1892);

Old Kaskasia (Boston & New York: Houghton, Mifflin, 1893);

The White Islander (New York: Century, 1893; London: Unwin, 1893);

The Chase of Saint-Castin and Other Stories of the French in the New World (Boston & New York: Houghton, Mifflin, 1894);

The Spirit of an Illinois Town and The Little Renault:

Two Stories of Illinois at Different Periods (Boston & New York: Houghton, Mifflin, 1897);

The Days of Jeanne d'Arc (New York: Century, 1897; London: Gay & Bird, 1898);

Bony and Ban: The Story of a Printing Venture (Boston: Lothrop, 1898);

Heroes of the Middle West: The French (Boston: Ginn, 1898);

The Queen of the Swamp and Other Plain Americans (Boston & New York: Houghton, Mifflin, 1899);

Mackinac and Other Stories (New York & London: Harper, 1899);

Spanish Peggy : A Story of Young Illinois (Chicago & New York: Stone, 1899);

Lazarre (Indianapolis: Bowen-Merrill, 1901; London: Richards, 1902).

A local-color writer who later turned to romantic fiction, Mary Hartwell Catherwood is now remembered for the part her early stories played in the history of midwestern short fiction.

Mary Hartwell Catherwood, 1899

The daughter of Marcus and Phoebe Thompson Hartwell, Mary Hartwell was born in Luray, Ohio, about thirty miles east of Columbus. When she was nine, her family migrated to Milford, Illinois, and within two years the three Hartwell children were orphaned and returned to Hebron, Ohio, to be raised by their maternal grandparents. Mary Hartwell began teaching at the age of fourteen to earn money for college, and at eighteen she entered Granville Female College. In 1868 she finished a four-year course after only three years. She returned to teaching in Ohio and Illinois briefly, but when her poems and sketches began to be accepted regularly for publication, she became a free-lance writer, moving first to Newburgh, New York, in 1874, then, in 1875, to Cincinnati, and finally, during the economic depression of 1876, back to Illinois, where relatives and friends helped support her. On 27 December 1877 she married James Steele Catherwood of Hoopeston, Illinois, and they settled in Indianapolis, where she became friends with James Whitcomb Riley and other midwestern writers. In 1882 the Catherwoods returned to James

Catherwood's hometown, spending summers on Mackinac Island. Mary Hartwell Catherwood resided in Chicago from 1897 until her death.

Catherwood was a prolific writer of short stories and novels both for children and for adults. Early in her career she wrote local-color stories set in the Great Lakes region, but in the 1890s she turned to romantic historical fiction, focusing on the French in America. In 1893 she defended her current subject matter and treatment of it against Hamlin Garland, who advocated the realism Catherwood had practiced earlier. Although some commentators regret the loss of a local colorist who might have rivaled Mary E. Wilkins Freeman, others consider that her stories of the French and Indians represent, as Robert Price says, "The best integration of Mrs. Catherwood's particular narrative powers."

Some of the early local-color stories collected in *The Queen of the Swamp and Other Plain Americans* (1899) are also historical, their action being set twenty to forty years earlier than when they were written. Nine of the thirteen stories center on courtship and marriage, a central theme of many of Catherwood's stories, realistic or romantic.

"Queen of the Swamp" (*Harper's Christmas*, December 1882), for example, is set in 1846. Its heroine, Priscilla Thompson, although much admired by many young men, is unacceptable to the mother of the most eligible, Martin Macauley, until an accident happens as the young people are on their way to the Macauleys' to celebrate Christmas and the proud Priscilla winds up cold and wet, clinging to Mrs. Macauley's neck for succor. In the course of ministering to Priscilla, Mrs. Macauley's attitude toward her softens, and a marriage between her Martin and Priscilla seems likely at the end of the story. Description of the food and games at the party, the language of the characters, and the sense of community conveyed provide the local-color aspects of this romantic tale, as they do for "The Stirring-Off" (*Lippincott's*, March 1883). In both stories slight plots are given interest by local color and their overall light, comedic tone. The same tone, combined with more extensive description, appears in "Beetrus" (*Harper's Bazar*, 25 December 1886), in which lovely young Beatrice Jenkins completely wins the heart of a handsome but somewhat dissipated drummer.

Less conventional wooings are depicted in other stories. In "Sweetness" (*Living Age*, supplement, 2 September 1899), for example, Lanson

The house at 4852 West Washington Boulevard, Chicago, where Catherwood spent her final years

Bundle finally wins over Wilda Coon, whom he has courted for twelve years, when he shows his devotion to her decrepit mother, the "Sweetness" of the title. In "Rose Day" (*Harper's Bazar,* 3 July 1886) forty-year-old twin sisters, opposites in temperament, head toward the altar by the end of the story. Both stories are rather treacly.

"A Kentucky Princess" (previously unpublished) strikes a darker note. Proud, lovely, wealthy America Poynton, engaged to marry Ross Carr, is confronted by Becky Inchbald, who holds Ross's illegitimate son in her arms. When Becky refuses to care for the child, America accepts him and commands the nervous father-fiancé to show up promptly for their wedding the next Thursday. Later in the day a slave finds Ross lying in remorseful anguish in a cornfield. The son is raised along with the other Carr children. There is no report of America's ever taking any revenge on Ross, but one day someone reveals the boy's true parentage to him, and the bitterest fruit of the father's sin matures as "that child threw himself on the ground to sob in secret agony because the beautiful and tender woman he loved with such devotion was not really his mother." Not all Catherwood's women show the strength of America Poynton, but many

do. Peggy B. Treece calls Catherwood's women characters "heroines who succeeded in combining independence and self-reliance with womanhood," comparing them to Catherwood herself.

Mrs. Harbison of "The Fairfield Poet" (*Harper's Bazar,* 10 January 1885) is a lightning rod for misfortune: her husband's business fails, and the family declines; then her beloved, promising son, Willie, is left deaf and dumb by spotted fever. But Willie writes poems about the woods he haunts and the town he flits through on his bicycle and shares them with his mother. The townspeople love him as he loves them, but only his mother knows what the world has lost when an express train hits him as he is riding his bicycle one evening. The theme is, of course, reminiscent of Thomas Gray's "Elegy Written in a Country Churchyard" (1751), and the story looks forward to Edgar Lee Masters's *Spoon River Anthology* (1915).

Similar to Willie is Jerome Marsh in "The Babe Jerome" (*Harper's Bazar,* 2 September 1882), whom Lilian Brooks meets while she is camping with her engineer brother, Eric, on the banks of the Wabash River, where Eric is overseeing a project. Once a promising boy, Jerome was left retarded by scarlet fever. At twenty-five he

Catherwood's grave in Floral Hill Cemetery, Hoopeston, Illinois

seems to Lilian "a sylvan creature strayed out of pastoral days into the hazy regions of the Wabash," a minstrel of the woods, who plays the violin hauntingly for Lilian and fashions her an aeolian harp. When Lilian realizes that Jerome loves her, she leaves with her fiancé, Jack, who arrives just in time. A year later she and her husband meet Jerome's father in Chicago at the World's Columbian Exposition and learn that Jerome died of tuberculosis not long after she left. The overall tone of pathos is qualified somewhat by the descriptions of the Wabash and of the Marsh homestead, and by the innocent, childlike relationship between Jerome and Lilian. Lilian's closing comment gives the story a near-tragic twist: "Oh Jack! . . . I have killed the Babe Jerome!"

The style of Catherwood's midwestern stories is plain and functional, with only a few short passages describing settings. Catherwood occasionally represents regional dialect in dialogue and uses some dialect terms for objects and customs. In her stories of French America, on the other hand, evocative description is more frequent and lengthier, and Catherwood suggests in English the French dialogue of her characters. The stories of *The Chase of Saint-Castin and Other Stories of the French in the New World* (1894) convey well an impression of a French-American culture about to be changed under the onslaught of the English and the English colonists.

Saint-Castin, seignior of a French settlement on Penobscot Bay, falls in love with the daughter of an Indian chief in "The Chase of Saint-Castin" (*Atlantic Monthly*, July 1893). The woman rejects his advances, however, even after he has cast off his Indian wives, because she has been converted and is preparing to found a convent under the guidance of Father Petit. When the English colonists invade the settlement, she helps Saint-Castin escape and hides with him as the English search for him, experiencing with him the peril of imminent discovery and death. After the danger is past, she consents to marry him. The combination of adventure and romance in an exotic setting seems to have appealed strongly to Catherwood and still holds some interest for the reader today.

The combination is repeated in the melodramatic "Wolfe's Cove" (*Atlantic Monthly*, January 1894), the best of three stories set near Quebec at the time of Gen. James Wolfe's assault in 1759. The heroine is an unlikely one: a mannish, aggressive Jeannette Descheneaux, who falls in love with her captor, Colonel Fraser of the Highlanders. Jeannette escapes from the prison ship in disguise, following Fraser, and witnesses the storming of the Plains of Abraham, but in the confusion she falls in with a group of Canadian and Indian ambushers, and when the Highlanders attack the group, Colonel Fraser plunges his short sword into her breast and moves on, leaving Jeannette to die. The characterization of Jeannette is well done, as is the description of the gathering of British forces at the vulnerable point in the Canadian defenses along the St. Lawrence River. The irony and pathos of Jeannette's death mirror the same qualities found in her countrymen's defeat. "The Kidnapped Bride" (*Atlantic Monthly*, September 1894), on the other hand, is a comedy-romance of tricksters outtricked, set in the Illinois Territory near St. Louis.

The stories of *Mackinac and Other Stories* (1899) are predominantly comic, except for the first, "Marianson" (*Harper's Monthly*, December 1897), which tells of the desertion of a young Canadian from the British forces attacking the Americans on Mackinac in 1812. He takes shelter from his Sioux pursuers in a cave, where he finds a lovely young widow, Marianson Bruelle. Marianson falls in love with him and steals into the village at night to obtain a boat in which he can escape, but when she returns, she discovers that a Sioux has executed him. Marianson is a finely drawn, strong character, and Catherwood expertly depicts her alternating feelings of romantic and maternal love for the deserter.

"The Cobbler in the Devil's Kitchen" (*Harper's Monthly*, August 1897) tells how a Scotsman tricks his cousin into not discarding his Indian wife, Blackbird, to take a French wife. In "The Mothers of Honoré" (*Harper's Monthly*, June 1899) Clethera and Honoré conspire to prevent her Indian grandmother from becoming his father's fifth wife. Of course, they fail and fall in love with each other. *Mackinac and Other Stories* includes a mélange of British, French, Indian, and American characters gradually amalgamating in usually comic stories.

"The King of Beaver" (*Harper's Monthly*, January 1898), one of the stories set on Beaver Island, is particularly interesting. The orphaned Emmeline, who has broken with her love in Detroit, has come to live there with her Mormon uncle. As a Gentile, she is repelled by the Mormons' polygamy, especially by the fact that James Strang, "King and Prophet" of the group, has eight wives, the most recent addition being Mary French, who had been a Gentile herself. Yet Emmeline is also attracted to the King, as he courts her, even sending Mary French to her to "tell you that you will be welcomed into our family." Emmeline pleads with Mary to help her resist his power over her. Mary does, but her motives are as mixed as Emmeline's feelings about the King. Does Mary write Emmeline's Detroit lover to come and rescue Emmeline out of pity for her or out of jealousy? Even as Emmeline sails away, she sees the King on the dock and reaches "her hands toward him in the darkness." Catherwood's portrayal of ambivalent feelings is expertly done, and this story, like "A Kentucky Princess," demonstrates her sure command of psychological insight.

Catherwood's greatest popular success was the historical romance *Lazarre* (1901). Yet critics today, when they discuss her work, focus on her local-color fiction. *The Chase of Saint-Castin, The Queen of the Swamp*, and *Mackinac* all have been reprinted since 1969, suggesting that Catherwood is of some importance in the history of the development of the American short story. In fact, Robert Price sees her stories and novels of the small midwestern town as among the first in a long line leading to Sherwood Anderson's *Winesburg, Ohio* (1919).

References:

Robert Price, "A Critical Biography of Mrs. Mary Hartwell Catherwood: A Study in Middle Western Regional Authorship, 1847-1902," Ph.D. dissertation, Ohio State University, 1943;

Price, "Mary Hartwell Catherwood," in *Ohio Authors and Their Books,* edited by William Coyle (Cleveland: World, 1962), pp. 104-106;

Peggy B. Treece, "The Characterization of the Nineteenth Century Woman in the Selected Works of Mrs. Mary Hartwell Catherwood," M.A. thesis, Bowling Green State University, 1975;

Treece, "A Hidden Woman of Local Color: Mrs. Mary Hartwell Catherwood," *Midwestern Miscellany,* 3 (1975): 24-31;

Treece, "Mary Hartwell Catherwood's Disguised Handbooks of Feminism," *Midwestern Miscellany,* 7 (1979): 7-14.

Papers:

The Newberry Library in Chicago has letters, manuscripts, clippings, and photographs.

Charles Waddell Chesnutt

(20 June 1858-15 November 1932)

Sylvia Lyons Render

See also the Chesnutt entries in *DLB 12: American Realists and Naturalists* and *DLB 50: Afro-American Writers Before the Harlem Renaissance.*

BOOKS: *The Conjure Woman* (Boston & New York: Houghton, Mifflin, 1899; London: Gay & Bird, 1899);

Frederick Douglass (Boston: Small, Maynard, 1899; London: Kegan Paul, Trench & Trübner, 1899);

The Wife of His Youth and Other Stories of the Color Line (Boston & New York: Houghton, Mifflin, 1899);

The House Behind the Cedars (Boston & New York: Houghton, Mifflin, 1900);

The Marrow of Tradition (Boston & New York: Houghton, Mifflin, 1901);

The Colonel's Dream (New York: Doubleday, Page, 1905; London: Constable, 1905);

Baxter's Procrustes (Cleveland: Rowfant Club, 1966);

The Short Fiction of Charles W. Chesnutt, edited by Sylvia Lyons Render (Washington, D.C.: Howard University Press, 1974; revised, 1981).

Charles Waddell Chesnutt, a "voluntary Negro" (one who, though so fair as to be mistaken for white, chooses not to "pass"), was born in Cleveland, Ohio, the eldest child of Andrew Jackson Chesnutt and the former Ann Maria Sampson, free blacks, who in 1856 had fled their native North Carolina to escape the increasing circumscription of their rights as the national controversy over slavery intensified. After the Civil War, however, the family, which eventually included five living children, moved back to Fayetteville, North Carolina, where the father operated a downtown grocery.

The impressionable Charles Chesnutt grew up in this region, which became the setting for much of his short fiction. Until his father's business failed about 1872, he usually helped out in the store after school and paid close attention to the easy exchanges among the customers, black and white. When he had a little free time, he enjoyed browsing in a nearby bookstore or reading in an excellent private library to which he had been granted access. When Charles was about nine years old, curiosity propelled him toward the sound of gunfire; he discovered that a Negro man in custody and about to be arraigned for alleged rape had been shot and killed. The scene became an indelible memory, as did other less violent but nevertheless traumatic encounters with increasingly overt racial prejudice. Worsening conditions impelled him in 1883 to leave the South

Charles Waddell Chesnutt

him had appeared in a local newspaper when he was fourteen). This desire remained constant after Chesnutt returned to Fayetteville in 1877 to serve as first assistant to the principal of the new Colored State Normal School. In 1878 he married a colleague, Susan U. Perry, and began to study shorthand as a means of finding employment in the North. Neither fatherhood, family disapproval, nor Chesnutt's elevation to the school principalship upon the death of Robert Harris in 1880 weakened his resolve to leave Fayetteville.

In that year too, after continued study, wide reading, and soul searching, which his increased responsibilities as a family man accelerated rather than impeded, Chesnutt decided that he would like most of all to write fiction. He had been struck by the popularity of Albion W. Tourgée's *A Fool's Errand* (1879) and Harriet Beecher Stowe's *Uncle Tom's Cabin* (1852). Moreover, he was increasingly concerned about the worsening plight of Afro-Americans–himself included. Writing in a journal now at Fisk University, he formulated, on 8 May 1880, his "high and holy purpose":

> The object of my writing would not be so much the elevation of the colored people as the elevation of the whites–for I consider the unjust spirit of caste which is so insidious as to pervade a whole nation, and so powerful as to subject a whole race and all connected with it to scorn and social ostracism–I consider this a barrier to the moral progress of the American people; and I would be one of the first to head a determined, organized crusade against it. Not a fierce indiscriminate onset, not an appeal to force, for this is something that force can but slightly affect, but a moral revolution which must be brought about in a different manner.
>
> The work is of a two-fold character. The Negro's part is to prepare himself for recognition and equality, and it is the province of literature to open the way for him to get it–to accustom the public mind to the idea; to lead people on, imperceptibly, unconsciously, step by step, to the desired state of feeling. If I can do anything to further this work, and can see any likelihood of obtaining success in it, I would gladly devote my life to it.

In 1883, when Chesnutt could write shorthand at a rate of two hundred words per minute, he resigned from the normal school, worked briefly in New York City, and then moved on to Cleveland, where he secured a clerkship and later a position as legal stenographer with the

and the security of the Colored Normal School principalship in Fayetteville.

That position he had attained through precocity and perseverance. Forced to go to work at fourteen to help support the family, Charles spent a year as a pupil-teacher at the normal school, and then became in turn peddler, teacher, and administrator in Fayetteville, Charlotte, and adjacent rural communities. Independent study and private tutoring–when he could afford it–enabled him to acquire the requisite skills and certification to teach. He also learned much not only about the folkways and mores of the North Carolinians with whom he came in contact but also about periods and peoples of Western civilization that he encountered only between the covers of books.

Teaching in a rural community and without friends who shared his interests, the adolescent Charles began in 1874 to keep journals which chronicle his passion for reading and–inspired by writers such as Charles Dickens–his growing inclination to become an author (a serialized story by

Chesnutt in 1874, the year in which he began his teaching career (Cleveland Public Library)

Nickel Plate Railroad Company. In less than a year his family, by then including two little girls and a baby boy, joined him in the city which became their permanent home. Chesnutt then began to write in earnest and to study law. His first adult story, "Uncle Peter's House," appeared in the *Cleveland News and Herald* in December 1885; others followed, published through a newspaper syndicate and in periodicals such as *Family Fiction* and *Tid-Bits*.

By 1887 Chesnutt's industry had begun to have tangible results. He stood at the head of the examinees admitted to the Ohio bar that year; he also became the first Afro-American to be published in the *Atlantic Monthly,* the most prestigious contemporary literary magazine. "The Goophered Grapevine," a folktale set in postbellum North Carolina, was chosen solely on its merit (Chesnutt made no mention of his race when he submitted it); and its appearance in the August 1887 issue of the *Atlantic* marked the formal beginning of his short-lived literary career. Chesnutt's fiction soon came to the attention of

Tourgée and George Washington Cable, both of whom shared Chesnutt's interest in improving race relations. Cable subsequently advised and encouraged Chesnutt in his literary endeavors.

In 1899 Houghton, Mifflin Company published Chesnutt's two volumes of short stories: *The Conjure Woman,* a collection of folk tales similar to "The Goophered Grapevine," and another group of related stories, *The Wife of His Youth and Other Stories of the Color Line,* whose title story (*Atlantic Monthly,* July 1898) treats middle-class blacks living in "Groveland" (Cleveland) after the Civil War. Also in 1899 Small, Maynard published a short biography of Frederick Douglass, which the firm had commissioned Chesnutt to write.

The future looked bright. His books were selling, and Chesnutt was being invited to lecture and read his stories so frequently that he decided that year to retire from court reporting and devote himself exclusively to literary endeavors. In what proved to be his most popular novel, *The House Behind the Cedars,* he further developed some of the themes introduced in *The Wife of His Youth.* The novel appeared in October 1900 and was in its fourth printing by April 1901. His second novel, *The Marrow of Tradition,* based on the Wilmington (North Carolina) Riot of 1898, was published in October 1901 and was not well received. Perhaps because race relations had continued to deteriorate during this period and because Chesnutt's more-overt criticism of race prejudice in his second novel was distasteful to his largely white reading audience, Chesnutt found it necessary in early 1902 to reopen and expand his court-reporting business in order to support his family properly. His last published novel, *The Colonel's Dream,* declined by Houghton, Mifflin because of previous losses, was brought out by Doubleday, Page in 1905. It too was a financial failure. Chesnutt published no more books after this point, although he continued to write novels until some time in the 1920s and to publish short fiction occasionally. He also continued to produce articles, essays, and speeches.

Thwarted in accomplishing his "high and holy purpose" through writing fiction, Chesnutt nevertheless persisted in trying to eradicate race and color prejudice in other ways. A highly respected businessman increasingly appreciated in cultural circles, he consistently promoted equal treatment for Afro-Americans on local, state, and national levels. He was among the 150 people invited to celebrate Mark Twain's seventieth birth-

Ethel, Edwin, and Helen Chesnutt in 1888 (Cleveland Public Library). Helen Chesnutt's 1952 biography of her father prompted a revival of interest in Chesnutt's writing.

day at Delmonico's in New York City in 1905. In 1910 he was elected to membership in the previously all-white Cleveland Rowfant Club, a literary group composed of a limited number of men who occasionally published privately printed books for its members. He received an honorary LL.D. from Wilberforce University in 1913, and in 1928 he was awarded the Spingarn Medal by the National Association for the Advancement of Colored People. Chesnutt was cited for his "pioneer work as a literary artist depicting the life and struggle of Americans of Negro descent, and for his long and useful career as scholar, worker, and freeman of one of America's greatest cities." Upon accepting the award Chesnutt declared, "My books were written, from one point of view, a generation too soon. There was no such demand then as there is now for books by and about colored people. I was writing against the trend of public opinion on the race question. And I had to sell my books chiefly to white readers." By that time all of Chesnutt's books were out of print. But in 1929, perhaps because of the upsurge of interest in Negro literature engendered by the Harlem Renaissance, Houghton Mifflin published a new edition of *The Conjure Woman.*

After Chesnutt's death in 1932, W. E. B. Du Bois eulogized him in "Postscript: Chesnutt" (*Cri-*

sis, January 1933): "Chesnutt was of that group of white folk who because of a more or less remote Negro ancestor identified himself voluntarily with the darker group, studied them, expressed them, defended them, and yet never forgot the absurdity of this artificial position and always refused to admit its logic or its ethical sanction. He was not a Negro; he was a man. But this fact never drove him to the opposite extreme. He did not repudiate persons of Negro blood as social equals and close friends. If his white friends (and he had legions) could not tolerate colored friends, they need not come to Mr. Chesnutt's home. If colored friends demanded racial segregation and hatred, he had no patience with them. Merit and friendship in his broad and tolerant mind knew no lines of color or race, and all men, good, bad, and indifferent, were simply men."

Despite the brevity of his career as an imaginative writer, Chesnutt is now considered one of the best American authors of short fiction at the turn of the century. Combining Euro-American, Afro-American, and African forms and techniques, he made phenomenal use of the seemingly simple folktale as a vehicle of social protest. Moreover, he enriched American literature with an unprecedented array of realistically portrayed Afro-American characters. As a literary artist, Chesnutt made a cogent commentary on American culture; and both in his treatment of character and in his choice of themes he anticipated many later writers.

In accord with his avowed purpose for writing–securing equal treatment of all Americans–Chesnutt took as his main themes the humanity of Afro-Americans and the inhumanity of man to man. Chesnutt treated both in the contexts of relations within and between races as they were defined by contemporary conditions and issues. Most of his Afro-American characters–especially the slaves–display much more sensibility and intelligence than in prior writings about them. Also, reacting to the worsening conditions for American blacks, especially in the South after 1877 and well into the twentieth century, Chesnutt focused on interpersonal issues such as miscegenation, intermarriage, and color prejudice among Afro-Americans and social issues such as racial discrimination in voting, the criminal justice system, employment, and education.

The Conjure Woman includes seven frame tales of antebellum times, superficially resembling the Uncle Remus tales retold by Joel Chan-

Mars Jeems's Nightmare 97

how er nuther I doan lak yo' looks sence
I come back dis time, en I'd much
ruther you would n' stay roun' heah.
Fac', I 's feared ef I 'd meet you alone in
de woods sometime, I mought wanter
ha'm you. But layin' dat aside, I be'n
lookin' ober dese yer books er yo'n w'at
you kep' w'iles I wuz 'way, en fer a yeah
er so back, en dere 's some figgers w'at
ain' des cl'ar ter me. I ain' got no time
fer ter talk 'bout 'em now, but I 'spec'
befo' I settles wid you fer dis las' mont',
you better come up heah ter-morrer,
atter I 's look' de books en 'counts ober
some mo', en den we straighten ou'
business all up.'

"Mars Jeems 'lowed atterwa'ds dat
he wuz des shootin' in de da'k w'en he
said dat 'bout de books, but howsom-
eber, Mars Nick Johnson lef' dat naber-
hood 'twix' de nex' two suns, en nobody
'roun' dere nebber seed hide ner hair
un 'im sence. En all de dahkies t'ank

98 *The Conjure Woman*

de Lawd, en 'lowed it wuz a good rid-
dance er bad rubbage.

"But all dem things I done tol' you
ain' nuffin 'side'n de change w'at come
ober Mars Jeems fum dat time on.
Aun' Peggy's goopher had made a noo
man un 'im enti'ely. De nex' day atter
he come back he tol' de han's dey neen-
ter wuk on'y fum sun ter sun, en he cut
dey tasks down so dey did n' nobody hab
ter stan' ober 'em wid a rawhide er a
hick'ry. En he 'lowed ef de niggers
want ter hab a dance in de big ba'n any
Sad'day night, dey mought hab it. En
bimeby, w'en Solomon seed how good
Mars Jeems wuz, he ax' 'im ef he would
n' please sen' down ter de yuther plantation fer his junesey. Mars Jeems say
sut'n'ly, en gun Solomon a pass en a
note ter de oberseah on de yuther plantation, en sont Solomon down ter Robe-
son County wid a hoss 'n' buggy fer ter
fetch his junesey back. W'en de nig-

Mars Jeems's Nightmare 99

gers see how fine Mars Jeems gwine
treat 'em, dey all tuk ter sweethea'tin'
en juneseyin' en singin' en dancin', en
eight er ten couples got married en
bimeby ev'ybody 'mence' ter say Mars
Jeems McLean got a finer plantation,
en slicker lookin' niggers, en dat he 'uz
makin' mo' cotton en co'n dan any
yuther gent'eman in de county. En
Mars Jeems's own junesey, Miss Libbie,
heared 'bout de noo gwines-on on Mars
Jeems's plantation, en she change' her
min' 'bout Mars Jeems en tuk 'im back
ag'in, en 'fo' long dey had a fine weddin',
en all de dahkies had a big feas', en dey
wuz fiddlin' en dancin' en funnin' en
frolic'in' fum sundown 'tel mawnin'."

"And they all lived happy ever after,"
I said, as the old man reached a full
stop.

"Yas, suh," he said, interpreting my
remarks as a question, "dey did. Solomon useter say," he added, "dat Aun'

100 *The Conjure Woman*

Peggy's goopher had turn't Mars Jeems
ter a nigger, en dat dat noo han' wuz
Mars Jeems hisse'f. But co'se Solomon
did n' das' ter let on 'bout w'at he
'spected, en ole Aun' Peggy would 'a'
'nied ef she had be'n ax', fer she 'd a got
in trouble sho' ef it 'uz knowed she 'd
be'n cunj'in' de w'ite folks.

"Dis yer tale goes ter show," concluded Julius sententiously, as the man
came up and announced that the spring
was ready for us to get water, "dat
w'ite folks w'at is so ha'd en stric' en
doan make no 'lowance fer po' ign'ant
niggers w'at ain' had no chanst ter l'arn,
is li'ble ter hab bad dreams, ter say de
leas', en dat dem w'at is kin' en good
ter po' people is sho' ter prosper en git
'long in de worl'."

"That is a very strange story, Uncle
Julius," observed my wife, smiling, "and
Solomon's explanation is quite improb-
able."

Mars Jeems's Nightmare 101

"Yes, Julius," said I, "that was
powerful goopher. I am glad too, that
you told us the moral of the story; it
might have escaped us otherwise. By
the way, did you make that up all by
yourself?"

The old man's face assumed an injured look, expressive more of sorrow
than of anger, and shaking his head he
replied : —

"No, suh, I heared dat tale befo' you
er Miss Annie dere wuz bawn, suh.
My mammy tol' me dat tale w'en I
wa'n't mo'd'n knee-high ter a hopper-
grass."

I drove to town next morning, on
some business, and did not return until
noon ; and after dinner I had to visit a
neighbor, and did not get back until
supper-time. I was smoking a cigar on
the back piazza in the early evening,
when I saw a familiar figure carrying a
bucket of water to the barn. I called
my wife.

102 *The Conjure Woman*

"My dear," I said severely, "what is
that rascal doing here? I thought I discharged him yesterday for good and
all."

"Oh, yes," she answered, "I forgot
to tell you. He was hanging round the
place all the morning, and looking so
down in the mouth, that I told him that
if he would try to do better, we would
give him one more chance. He seems
so grateful, and so really in earnest in
his promises of amendment, that I 'm
sure you 'll not regret taking him back."

I was seriously enough annoyed to let
my cigar go out. I did not share my
wife's rose-colored hopes in regard to
Tom ; but as I did not wish the servants
to think there was any conflict of authority in the household, I let the boy
stay.

Corrected proofs for pages in the first edition of The Conjure Woman *(Cleveland Public Library)*

v'iles her bref wuz gwine she call'
out : —

"'O Dan! O my husban'! come en
he'p me! come en sabe me fum dis wolf
w'at's killin' me!'

"W'en po' Dan sta'ted to'ds her, ez
any man nach'ly would, it des made her
holler wuss en wuss; fer she did n'
knowed dis yer wolf wuz her Dan. En
Dan des had ter hide in de weeds en
grit his teef en hol' hisse'f in 'tel she
passed out'n her mis'ry, callin' fer Dan
ter de las', en wond'rin' w'y he did n'
come en he'p her. En Dan 'lowed ter
hisse'f he'd ruther 'a' be'n killt a dozen
times'n ter 'a' done w'at he had ter
Mahaly.

"Dan wuz mighty nigh 'stracted, but
w'en Mahaly wuz dead en he got his
min' straighten' out a little, it did n'
take 'im mo' d'n a minute er so fer ter
see th'oo all de cunjuh man's lies, en
how de cunjuh man had fooled 'im en

made 'im kill Mahaly, fer ter git eben
wid 'im fer killin' er his son. He kep'
gittin' madder en madder, en Mahaly
had n' much mo' d'n drawed her' las bref
befo' he sta'ted back ter de cunjuh
man's cabin ha'd ez he could run.

"W'en he got dere de do' wuz standin'
open; a lighterd-knot wuz flick'rin' on
de h'a'th, en de ole cunjuh man wuz
settin' dere noddin' in de corner. Dan
le'p' in de do' en jump' fer dis man's
th'oat, en got de same grip on 'im w'at
de cunjuh man had tol' 'im 'bout half a'
hour befo'. It wuz ha'd wuk dis time,
fer de ole man's neck wuz monst'us
tough en stringy, but Dan hilt on long
ernuff ter be sho' his job wuz done
right. En eben den he did n' hol' on
long ernuff; fer w'en he tu'nt de cunjuh man loose en he fell ober on de flo',
de cunjuh man rollt his eyes at Dan, en
sezee: —

"'I 's eben wid you, Brer Dan, en

you er eben wid me; you killt my son
en I killt yo' 'oman. En ez I doan
want no mo' d'n w'at 's fair 'bout dis
thing, ef you 'll retch up wid yo' paw en
take down dat go'd hangin' on dat peg
ober de chimbly, en take a sip er dat
mixtry, it 'll tu'n you back ter a nigger
ag'in, en I kin die mo' sad'sfied'n ef I
lef' you lak you is.'

"Dan nebber 'lowed fer a minute dat
a man would lie wid his' las' bref, en
co'se he seed de sense er gittin' tu'nt
back befo' de cunjuh man died; so he
clumb on a chair en retch' fer de go'd en
tuk a sip er de mixtry. En ez soon ez he
done dat de cunjuh lafft his las' laf, en
gapsed out wid 'is las' gaps: —

"'Uh huh! I reckon I 's square wid
you now fer killin' me too; fer dat
goopher on you is done fix' en sot now
fer good, en all de cunj'in' in de worl'
won' nebber take it off.

'Wolf you is en wolf you stays,
All de rest er yo' bawn days.'

"Co'se Brer Dan could n' do nuffin.
He knowed it wa'n't no use, but he
clumb up on de chimbly en got down
de go'ds en bottles en yuther cunjuh
fixin's, en tried 'em all on hiss'f, but dey
did n' do no good. Den he run down
ter ole Aun' Peggy, but she did n' know
de wolf langwidge, en could n't 'a' tuk
off his yuther goopher nohow, eben ef
she 'd 'a' unnerstood w'at Dan wuz sayin'.
So po' Dan wuz bleedzd ter be a wolf all
de rest er his bawn days.

"Dey foun' Mahaly down by her own
cabin nex' mawnin', en eve'ybody made
a great 'miration 'bout how she 'd be'n
killt. De niggers 'lowed a wolf had bit
her. De w'ite fo'ks say no, dey ain' be'n
no wolves 'roun' dere for ten yeahs er
mo'; en dey did n' know w'at ter make
out'n it. En w'en dey could n' fin' Dan
nowhar, dey 'lowed he'd quo'lled wid
Mahaly en killt her en run erway; en
dey did n' know w'at ter make er dat.

fer Dan en Mahaly wuz de mos' lovin'
couple on de plantation. Dey put de
dawgs on Dan's scent, en track' 'im
down ter ole Unk' Jube's cabin, en
foun' de ole man dead; en dey did n'
know w'at ter make er dat; en den
Dan's scent gun out — en dey did n'
know w'at ter make er dat. Mars
Dugal' tuk on a heap 'bout losin' two er
his bes' han's in one day, en ole missis
'lowed it wuz a jedgment on 'im fer
sump'n he 'd done. But dat fall de
craps wuz monst'us big, so Mars Dugal'
say de Lawd had temper' de win' ter de
sho'n ram, en make up ter 'im fer w'at
he had los'.

"Dey buried Mahaly down in dat
piece er low groun' you er talkin' 'bout
cl'arin' up. Ez fer po' Dan, he did n'
hab nowhar e'se ter go, so he des stayed
'roun' Mahaly's grabe, w'en he wa'n't out
in de yuther woods gittin' sump'n ter
eat. En sometimes, w'en night would

come, de niggers useter heah him
howlin' en howlin' down dere, des fittin'
ter break his hea't. En den some mo'
un 'em said dey seed Mahaly's ha'nt
dere 'bun'ance er times, colloguin' wid
dis gray wolf. En eben now fifty yeahs
sence, long atter ole Dan has died en
dried up in de woods, his ha'nt en Mahaly's hangs roun' dat piece er low
groun', en eve'body w'at goes 'bout dere
has some bad luck er 'nuther; fer ha'nts
doan lak ter be 'sturb' on dey own
stompin' groun'.'"

The air had darkened while the old
man related this harrowing tale. The
rising wind whistled around the eaves,
slammed the loose window-shutters, and,
still increasing, drove the rain in fiercer
gusts into the piazza. As Julius finished
his story and we rose to seek shelter
within doors, the blast caught the angle
of some chimney or gable in the rear of
the house, and bore to our ears a long

dler Harris. They are the recollections of Uncle Julius, an emancipated slave who speaks in a North Carolina Negro dialect. The tales are introduced and commented upon in standard English by Julius's new employer, John, who has recently brought his wife, Annie, from northern Ohio to central North Carolina for health reasons and decided to engage in grape culture there. Annie as well as John is present while Julius spins his yarns, which usually contain some fantasy. The inner and outer narratives are always organically related–though the links are not equally apparent. Uncle Julius relates, in a seemingly uncritical manner, humane and sometimes inhumane reactions of slaves he has known to treatment they have received, primarily from owners but occasionally from free conjurers. The oppressive conditions include denial of recreation, insufficient food, conjuration, frequent selling or trading that sometimes results in separation of families, overwork, flogging, and murder. As John soon realizes, Uncle Julius seems to have an ulterior motive for telling each story.

In "The Goophered Grapevine," which Uncle Julius relates to the couple during their first encounter, he tries openly to dissuade John from buying a deserted plantation with a vineyard that is still somewhat productive, as is apparent because Uncle Julius is eating scuppernongs from the vineyard at the time. He describes the dire effects upon a slave newcomer, Henry, who inadvertently eats grapes which Mars' Dugal' has paid Aun' Peggy, who was born free, to "goopher" in order to stop the slaves from eating them and thus reducing his profits. Because Henry transgressed unknowingly, Aun' Peggy can ameliorate but cannot completely neutralize the power of the goopher, which would otherwise have caused his death within the year. Uncle Julius relates in detail how Henry was affected and how Mars' Dugal' capitalized on the situation– finally to his own detriment–to reinforce his advising John not to buy the plantation. The conjure is still effective, Uncle Julius avers, but he knows which vines were not goophered and can therefore eat the grapes with impunity. John, unbelieving, buys the plantation but hires Uncle Julius as the family coachman to compensate him for the revenue he would otherwise have derived from selling the grapes as he has in past years. Thus Julius is in the position to encounter, with John and Annie, circumstances which give rise to the other six tales in this collection.

The second tale Uncle Julius tells in *The Conjure Woman*, "Po' Sandy" (*Atlantic Monthly*, May 1888), grows out of Annie's desire to have a kitchen apart from the couple's new home on the old plantation and John's plan to use some of the lumber from a deserted schoolhouse on the premises in building the additional room. The whirring of a saw eating through a huge log at the sawmill, where Uncle Julius had driven the couple to purchase additional lumber, jogs his memory. He then relates the tragic events which took place when Sandy, a model slave whose first wife had been sold away from him, seeks to avoid being sent away from his equally devoted new wife, Tenie, a "cunjuh 'oman," by letting her change him back and forth into a tree. One of the outcomes of Uncle Julius's telling this tale is his securing for his church group the use of the old schoolhouse originally scheduled to be torn down.

Transformations which similarly influence plot development take place in several other tales. In "Mars' Jeems's Nightmare" (previously unpublished) a cruel master behaves differently after being changed temporarily into a slave. In "The Conjurer's Revenge" (*Overland Monthly*, June 1889) a headstrong, light-fingered slave, Primus, is turned into a mule and almost back again. In "Sis Becky's Pickaninny" (previously unpublished) Becky's little baby is transformed into a bird for a day at a time to keep his slave mother from dying of grief while they are separated. Finally, in "The Gray Wolf's Ha'nt" (previously unpublished) a loving slave couple, Mahaly and Dan, are changed permanently into a black cat and a gray wolf, who perish, at the will of a free conjurer, who also dies in the course of avenging his son's death.

In the inner narrative of "Hot-Foot Hannibal" (*Atlantic Monthly*, January 1899) Aun' Peggy conjures Hannibal, a favored house slave, at the request of Chloe, another house slave, and a field hand, Jeff, so that Hannibal will be unable to perform his duties well during the winter and thus fail to be rewarded with Chloe (who prefers Jeff) as a wife by their master as promised. The plan backfires, with disastrous results. There is also a love triangle among whites in the outer narrative, the happy resolution of which seems to be influenced greatly by the tragic fate of the slaves.

In each of the inner narratives in *The Conjure Woman* Chesnutt realistically portrays slaves striving to establish their identities as human beings. He reveals how they attempt to establish and maintain the same social relationships which goophers, now seems to acknowledge their power.

Contemporary reception of *The Conjure Woman* was generally good. In Cleveland interest was high. A special large-paper edition of 150 numbered copies requested by a member of the Rowfant Club was distributed to subscribers there before the trade edition appeared in March 1899. The volume was also the best-seller in Cleveland for April of that year.

As the author of what an anonymous southern reviewer called "the best book of short stories of the year" (*Raleigh News and Observer*, 30 April 1899), Chesnutt was compared favorably with Joel Chandler Harris, Ruth McEnery Stuart, Thomas Nelson Page, and Paul Laurence Dunbar. Other reviewers labeled Chesnutt a northerner and found him lacking in understanding of Southern mores and folkways. Critics commented more on the humor of the tales than the tragedy, and the dialect got mixed reactions. Little was said about John and Annie's reactions to Uncle Julius's tales, while commentary about Uncle Julius was both extensive and controversial. One reviewer found Julius's selfish motives distasteful; another said that his character was perfectly drawn and enriching to the stories as a whole. In one of the most perceptive, balanced, and detailed reviews (*Bookman*, June 1899) Florence A. H. Morgan declared, "these stories are so perfectly consistent with human nature, that, aside from the supernatural element, which is palpably a vehicle for the deeper thought underlying, the stories prove themselves."

Striking an informal note in his review of *The Conjure Woman* (*Conservator*, November 1902) Horace Traubel called "Sis' Becky's Pickaninny" "the poem of the book," advising readers "to go to the negro with soul. Soul will take you to the negro and give him to you. Nothing else will. And Chesnutt is soul. That one drop or two of negro blood has placed Chesnutt just right with justice." (Chesnutt evidently liked Traubel's reviews. In an undated note attached to a copy of *The Colonel's Dream* that is among the Traubel Papers in the Library of Congress, Chesnutt told Traubel, "I love to have you read my books, because you read them with my eyes—and with my heart.")

Although Chesnutt had been identified as a Negro in print early in 1891 and had so described himself in a 8 September 1891 letter to Houghton, Mifflin, the general reading public was largely unaware that he was an Afro-

Front cover for the collection of stories in which Chesnutt employed the Afro-American folktale as a vehicle of social protest

characterize all human societies, while these natural inclinations are usually disregarded by masters who, possessing absolute power over their human chattel, are often cavalier in their use of it. Moreover, residual attitudes of racial superiority and inferiority are reflected consciously or unconsciously in the postbellum interactions of John, Annie, and Uncle Julius.

Chesnutt also wrote seven other Uncle Julius tales, which were first collected in *The Short Fiction of Charles W. Chesnutt* (1974). In one of these stories, "The Marked Tree" (*Crisis*, December 1924 and January 1925), Uncle Julius traces through several generations of the Spencer family the fatal effects of a powerful goopher put on them by a slave conjure woman whose son died as a result of the family's having sold him. Significantly, John, who has previously scoffed at

American until after *The Conjure Woman* appeared. Reaction to the disclosure was mixed. An extreme position, not atypical for the times, was rejection of that truth because, according to one unidentified reader, a Negro was incapable of such creativity. Chesnutt himself considered his ethnic identity "a personal matter." As he declared years later in "Post-Bellum–Pre-Harlem" (*Colophon,* part 5, 1931) "It never occurred to me to claim any merit because of it, and I have always resented the denial of anything on account of it."

Chesnutt's second book, *The Wife of His Youth,* introduced subject matter more contemporary but less familiar to his readers than the Uncle Julius tales. For the first time in American fiction Chesnutt, an insider, explored the lives of those Americans whose African ancestry was so slight as to be hardly–if at all–evident in their appearance. Called "Blue Veins" in the vernacular– because, along with other physical attributes generally characterized as Caucasian, they had such fair skin that their wrist veins were easily discernible–they lived in many sections of the country, including Ohio, North Carolina, and Kentucky–the major settings for the ten stories in the volume.

The lead story, "The Wife of His Youth," had attracted critical attention upon its appearance in the July 1898 *Atlantic Monthly,* and in a review of both Chesnutt's collections Hamilton Wright Mabie found the story worthy to "take its place among the best short stories in American literature" (*Outlook,* 24 February 1900). Mr. Ryder is "dean of the Blue Veins" and president of Groveland's "Blue Vein Society," whose "purpose was to establish and maintain correct social standards among a people" eager to rise in the typical American manner. Ryder, having fled from the South before the Civil War to escape illegal enslavement, has for years cultivated a literary and musical bent while advancing himself through assiduous industry to a white-collar position, which has enabled him to buy a comfortable home and accumulate some savings. He is now about to propose to a young widow, Mrs. Molly Dixon, a former schoolteacher "even whiter and better educated" than himself, in whose honor he is giving a ball that evening. Relaxing on his front porch, Ryder is involved in reverie of recollection and anticipation when he is interrupted by the approach of a "very black," toothless, little old woman. She shows him a daguerreotype of her "husband," a "merlatter . . . Sam Taylor," who, to avoid being sold down the river illegally more

Charles Waddell Chesnutt (Western Reserve Historical Society, Cleveland)

than twenty-five years ago, had run away from the plantation where he was then apprenticed. She explains that she has been searching for him, and, though she obviously does not recognize Ryder as the young man in the daguerreotype, Ryder does. Though the "marriage" was not legally binding, he is faced with the moral dilemma of choosing between the faithful but uncultivated former slave and the more socially desirable Mrs. Dixon. His choice of the old woman climaxes the story.

Chesnutt demonstrates his ability to provide a striking variation on the theme of color prejudice among Afro-Americans in a companion piece, "A Matter of Principle" (previously unpublished), as satirical as "The Wife of His Youth" is serious. The prominent Cicero "Brotherhood" Clayton, "the richest colored man in Groveland," and his wife are faced with a dilemma; their "nearly white" daughter Alice receives a letter from the Honorable Hamilton M. Brown, a member of Congress. Having met Alice at the recent 1870s colored "inaugural" ball in Washington, D.C., he is asking permission to call on her during a trip to Groveland. The plot revolves around Alice's inability to recall Mr. Brown's complexion, and the overweening importance of his color in the Claytons' deciding whether or not to receive him.

Chesnutt presents admixture of blood from an altogether different angle in "The Sheriff's Children" (*Independent*, 7 November 1889). Set in Troy, North Carolina, in the 1870s, it discloses the far-reaching effects of racial mixing upon the law-abiding white Sheriff Campbell and a young mulatto accused of murder, Tom, whom the officer is protecting from a mob. While the sheriff is busy hastening the withdrawal of the would-be lynchers with rifle fire, Tom grabs a loaded pistol and threatens to kill Campbell unless he releases him from the jail. During a tense verbal exchange the younger man reveals that the sheriff is his father and former owner, who had sold Tom and his mother years before to a speculator. Only the timely arrival of the officer's daughter, who wounds her half-brother, prevents the sheriff's murder; but even more decisive action takes place before the story concludes the following morning.

In "The Web of Circumstance" (previously unpublished), social conditions determine the fate of enterprising Ben Davis, a former slave who, through industry and thrift, is prospering as a blacksmith and investing his money in real estate, including a home for his "good-looking yellow wife" and two children. His openly expressed desire to have a whip like the handsome fifteen-dollar one owned by Colonel Thornton and a probable affair between Ben's wife and his mulatto assistant pave the way for his downfall. Ben's misfortunes after he has been arrested for theft of the whip, which was apparently planted in his shop, are clearly attributable to race prejudice powerful enough to unbalance the scales of justice. The story thus becomes a searing indictment of a society greatly warped by its racial bias. The overt protest in this collection anticipates Chesnutt's more explicit social criticism in his last two novels, *The Marrow of Tradition* and *The Colonel's Dream*. Similarly, attitudes toward racial mixing in the stories are developed more fully in *The House Behind The Cedars*.

With the publication of *The Wife of His Youth* Chesnutt gained stature as a literary artist. Through it he demonstrated conclusively that he was capable not only of adding significantly innovative aspects to an already established and easily recognizable American literary form, but also that he could successfully treat in fiction a particular group of Americans in a "middle world" insofar as race was concerned and who, in their efforts to cope, became involved in situations seldom faced by other Americans. Hamilton Wright Mabie credited Chesnutt with "distinct gift and insight." In "Mr. Charles W. Chesnutt's Stories" (*Atlantic Monthly*, May 1900) William Dean Howells asserted that both Chesnutt's collections of short fiction were "remarkable above many, above most short stories by people entirely white, and would be worthy of unusual notice if they were not the work of a man not entirely white." Howells pointed out some flaws—mostly in *The Conjure Woman*—but emphasized Chesnutt's faithful portrayal of character. Overall he ranked Chesnutt with Guy de Maupassant, Ivan Turgenev, Henry James, Sarah Orne Jewett, and Mary E. Wilkins Freeman, as "one who sees his people very clearly, very justly, and he shows them as he sees them, leaving the reader to divine the depth of his feeling for them." Howells labeled "The Wife of His Youth" "altogether a remarkable piece of work [with] uncommon traits," citing "the novelty of the material . . . the author's thorough mastery of it . . . his unerring knowledge of the life he had chosen in its peculiar racial characteristics . . . the passionless handling of a phase of our common life which is tense with potential tragedy [and] the quiet self-restraint of the performance." Howells praised particularly Chesnutt's characterization of the "paler shades" (as Howells termed them), about whom Chesnutt wrote with unprecedented candor as an insider and whom—despite their sometimes startling resemblance to whites—were kept as far removed from whites as "the blackest negro."

Howell's positive, literary treatment of Chesnutt's efforts was less common than that of Nancy Huston Banks, who reviewed *The Wife of His Youth* in "Novel Notes" (*Bookman*, February 1900). While not entirely negative, she approved wholeheartedly only of the title story, which prompted her statement that Chesnutt "may perhaps be given the credit of the first publication of a subtle psychological study of the negro's spiritual nature, the first actual revelation of those secret depths of the dusky soul which no white writer might hope to approach through his own intuition." Yet, for her, romantic relations between blacks and whites were "all but unapproachable ground," and she criticized Chesnutt for "touching this and still more dangerous and darker race problems" which were not treated (in fact largely ignored) "by more experienced writers." Banks readily conceded that "The Sheriff's Children" contains a "too probable truth" and is "legitimate literary material," but in her opinion its verisimilitude made the story unsuitable for publication.

Commendatory reviews of *The Wife of His Youth* were quoted in probably the longest of the early articles about Chesnutt in an Afro-American publication, the short-lived *Colored American Magazine*. In "Charles W. Chesnutt. One of the Leading Novelists of the Race" (December 1901), John Livingston Wright discussed from an Afro-American point of view the grave problems of the " 'light-black' or the 'black-light' [individuals] whose mixture of blood makes them almost outcasts" as well as those of darker-skinned Negroes. Crediting Chesnutt with "practically pioneering in his especial vocation," Wright also commented about the author's "modest and charming manner" before "excellent audiences" during his recent reading tour of several eastern cities.

One of Chesnutt's stories that appeared after the publication of *The Wife of His Youth*, "Baxter's Procrustes" (*Atlantic Monthly*, June 1904), is an example of a facet of Chesnutt's work that has received almost no critical attention: fiction with only white characters. "Baxter's Procrustes" has been repeatedly cited for its literary excellence ever since *Atlantic* editor Bliss Perry found it "an ingenious and amusing story extremely well told" prior to its initial appearance in print.

This story is a satire of an all-male club devoted to books and book collecting–remarkably like the Cleveland Rowfant Club, which had denied Chesnutt membership in 1902. Suggesting that club members are too concerned with books as financial investments rather than with their contents, the story pointedly brings some of the group's values into question. It does not accuse them of racism, nor is it vengeful in tone, although Robert Hemenway finds social protest beneath the surface of what others have read as a "bagatelle." The Rowfanters enjoyed the story even though they realized that they were the ob-

jects of Chesnutt's raillery and elected him to membership in 1910. In 1966 the club published a special limited edition of "Baxter's Procrustes" accompanied by a biographical essay on Chesnutt by John B. Nicholson, Jr., a member.

After the publication of *The Colonel's Dream* in 1905 general interest in Chesnutt's work declined sharply. All of Chesnutt's books went out of print and, except for a financially successful new edition of *The Conjure Woman* in 1929, they were not republished until the late 1960s.

In 1974 *The Short Fiction of Charles W. Chesnutt* collected most of Chesnutt's short stories. Dating from 1885 to 1930, the previously uncollected stories range from anecdotes to long, rambling narratives. Except for the seven Uncle Julius tales mentioned earlier, they are about black and white life in the South and North as Chesnutt observed it. More often than not, even in seemingly frivolous short pieces such as "A Roman Antique" (*Puck*, 17 July 1889), Chesnutt's concern about race relations is manifested. In this little farce the narrator recounts his being asked for a handout by an old white-haired Negro who claimed to have been Julius Caesar's "fav'rite body-sarven' " and to have been wounded severely in Gaul while trying to protect his master. In turn Caesar had expressed his appreciation by giving him a quarter when he recovered and had left instructions in his will that the slave be emancipated by the time he became one hundred years old. In "The Doll" (*Crisis*, April 1912) Tom Taylor, the Negro proprietor of a barbershop in a high-class northern white hotel, finds himself weighing carefully the consequences of the various actions he may take when he is suddenly given the long-hoped-for opportunity to avenge the murder of his father by a white Southern colonel during Reconstruction. "Tom's Warm Welcome" (*Family Fiction*, 27 November 1886), about lower-class and middle-class whites near Fayetteville, North Carolina, some time after the Civil War, makes the distinction between "pore shote" Tom McDonald and more prosperous people such as grist-miller Dunkin Campbell and his daughter Jinnie. "White Weeds" (previously unpublished) focuses on the attitudes of cultivated northern white academicians.

Between 1906 and 1952, when Helen M. Chesnutt published her biography of her father and donated his papers to Fisk University, Chesnutt received only passing attention from the literati and none from the general white readership. Unlike Paul Laurence Dunbar, Chesnutt was little known among blacks as well. Nonetheless, during most of this period, a few scholars recognized Chesnutt's eminence as a black creator of short fiction. In 1931 Vernon Loggins stated that *The Conjure Woman* signaled the coming-of-age of Negro literature. Moreover, many other scholars of black literature in the 1930s and 1940s (themselves mostly Afro-Americans) were of the opinion that Chesnutt's short stories and novels equalled those of any other writer of his time. They also concurred with John Chamberlain's assertion in "The Negro as Writer" (*Bookman*, February 1930) that Chesnutt "pressed on to more tragic materials and handled them as no white novelist could have succeeded at the time in doing. And before he lapsed into silence all the materials of the Negro novel and short story as a vehicle for dramatizing racial problems had made their appearance, either explicitly or through adumbration, in his work."

In 1953, obviously moved by the Chesnutt biography, Russell Ames decried the neglect of Chesnutt by the literary establishment while comparing him favorably with other American writers such as Ernest Hemingway, John Dos Passos, William Faulkner, and John Steinbeck. Since then, interest in Chesnutt has been steadily increasing.

Chesnutt was recognized as a southern writer as early as 1900, and many times thereafter he was claimed as a North Carolina author, but until the 1960s Chesnutt was seldom represented in regional anthologies and critical literature on the South. The inclusion of his "The Conjurer's Revenge" in *The Local Colorists: American Short Stories 1857-1900* (1960), edited by Claude M. Simpson, was exceptional. In 1967 Julian Mason protested the exclusion which he considered "a disservice to Chesnutt, to his fiction and its concerns, to the South, and to the integrity and accuracy of histories of Southern literature." During the 1960s, however, a significant number of studies on regional aspects of Chesnutt's works appeared, including Sylvia Lyons Render's examinations of history, geography, character, ethnicity, beliefs, and customs in Chesnutt's stories and Charles W. Foster's article on nineteenth-century Negro dialect of the Fayetteville area as it is represented in Chesnutt's stories. Chesnutt's ambivalent feelings about the South have also been explored. Wayne Mixon has called him "A Southern writer in the best sense of the term because he wrote *about* the South, not *for* the South. . . . He refused to defend the region's short-

Susan Perry Chesnutt after her husband's death (Cleveland Public Library)

comings, hoping instead to excise them by facing them openly and presenting them realistically in his fiction."

Merrill Maguire Skaggs, in *The Folk of Southern Fiction* (1972), has found in Chesnutt's writings characters who fit into the "plain folk" (as opposed to the plantation) literary tradition and whom he calls "the core of the social structure [in the Old South], a massive body of plain [white] folk who were neither rich nor very poor". . . [whose] worth was not directly related to their income but [based] rather on good character . . . determined by the possession of four major traits—pride, courage, common sense, and a willingness to work." Ladell Payne has also determined that like other black and white southern writers, Chesnutt drew on the folk culture and story-telling traditions of his area. For some of the Uncle Julius tales Chesnutt was inspired by stories told him during his childhood by old Afro-American tale-spinners, and, according to Gloria C. Oden and Chikwenye Ogunyemi, the Uncle Julius tales are linked to African folklore by their literary methodology as well as by the beliefs and practices they portray. According to Sterling Stuckey the stories reflect "an ethos . . . a life style and set of values . . . an amalgam of Africanisms and New World elements," which gave the transported Africans a better chance of surviving under conditions of abject servitude. Hence "the tradition of subterfuge, indirection, and subtle manipulation of whites" in the Uncle Julius tales, which Jules Chametzky has labeled "the first fictional form given to the black ethos in America." (Joel Taxel has shown how black characters in other Chesnutt stories employ similar strategies.)

Recognition of Chesnutt's literary adaptation of this ethos is just one of many post-1970 indications that Chesnutt was being considered as an accomplished literary artist. Another was provided by Richard A. Baldwin in his cogent essay "The Art of *The Conjure Woman*," in which he shows how Chesnutt's Uncle Julius stories were "a perfect vehicle for his artistic needs." Chesnutt's effectiveness in creating structure and characterization in the tales prompted Melvin Dixon to label Chesnutt as well as Uncle Julius a trickster and a teller. Expanding on this theme, David D. Britt calls *The Conjure Woman* "primarily a study in duplicity that masks or reveals its meaning according to the predisposition of the reader." Britt points out that Chesnutt's use of the frame-tale device "gives the first and final word to the white man, implying that the latter is the 'official' interpreter of Julius's yarn" and thereby creating "a surface level of meaning that leaves the Southern caste system undisturbed." Thus, by minimizing the possibility of his readers' feeling threatened, Chesnutt maximized the chances of educating them. Yet it is important to recognize that because Uncle Julius is seen only through John's eyes, the portrait of the old storyteller is flawed by John's rationalism, materialism, racial bias, and ignorance of Southern folkways—as well as his apparent lack of awareness of these limitations. Julius is a product of a system under which a black was more likely to survive if, when expedient, he said one thing but meant another. Sometimes called "signifying," this ironic use of language was and still is characteristic of Afro-

American verbal communication. John frequently misses the underlying significance of Julius's words and is thus an unreliable narrator. The stories' ironic treatment of black-white interactions, as well as Uncle Julius's many recollections of the harshness of slavery, so unlike its nearly idyllic depiction by popular writers of the time, has prompted Robert Bone to classify *The Conjure Woman* as "antipastoral" and to praise Chesnutt for his skill in adapting the pastoral folk tale for his own ends, which David Britt has defined as "laying bare the nature of the slave experience, exploding myths about masters and slaves, and showing the limitations of the white man's moral and imaginative faculties."

Chesnutt's white characters also mask their true feelings and motives. According to P. Jay Delmar, the stories in *The Wife of His Youth* "show how both whites and Blacks are constrained to hide their true racial identities from themselves and each other" for better and for worse. Chesnutt's talent for characterization has also been recognized, as critics such as Delmar and Eugene Terry find many of Chesnutt's characters tragic according to classical standards rather than pathetic.

Still others, having read Chesnutt's works with the "new sensibility" which Terry propounded, have made sound metaphorical and allegorical interpretations. Pointing out "parallels in Ovid's *Metamorphoses* and *The Conjure Woman*, including similarities in Ovid's account of the fall of man and 'The Goophered Grapevine,'" Karen Magee Myers interprets Chesnutt's tale as "the old myth . . . skillfully molded by Chesnutt to represent the fall of the South, and the death of the utopian concept of the American Dream." Along the same lines Theodore Hovet calls the story "a parable which explains the consequence of an unbounded faith in economic progress and the way such a belief serves to conceal the cost in human dignity . . . a microcosm of the mental attitudes, economic methods and consequences of American imperialism." In another allegorical interpretation Harmut K. Selke calls Sheriff Campbell in "The Sheriff's Children" a representative of the "Founding Fathers," who have failed to recognize their Afro-American sons. Gerald Haslam has called this work "a parable for this nation's contemporary racial crisis and continuing moral atrophy," while Ronald Walcott has noted similarities between the biblical parable of Cain and Abel, and he believes that Chesnutt "may be suggesting, now, that the South, so long as it is unwilling to perceive the implications of the mulatto's life, may yet have to suffer the consequences of his death."

Such serious consideration of Chesnutt's short fiction suggests that more and more readers are agreeing with Robert Bone's assessment of him as "a literary artist of the first rank" who deserves to be placed, with Henry James, Mark Twain, and Stephen Crane, among the major American short-story writers of the late-nineteenth and early-twentieth centuries.

Bibliography:

Curtis W. Ellison and E. W. Metcalf, Jr., *Charles W. Chesnutt: A Reference Guide* (Boston: G. K. Hall, 1977).

Biographies:

Helen M. Chesnutt, *Charles Waddell Chesnutt: Pioneer of the Color Line* (Chapel Hill: University of North Carolina Press, 1952);

Frances Richardson Keller, *An American Crusade: The Life of Charles Waddell Chesnutt* (Provo, Utah: Brigham Young University Press, 1978).

References:

Russell Ames, "Social Realism in Charles W. Chesnutt," *Phylon*, 14 (Second Quarter 1953): 199-206;

William L. Andrews, *The Literary Career of Charles W. Chesnutt* (Baton Rouge: Louisiana State University, 1980);

Richard A. Baldwin, "The Art of *The Conjure Woman*," *American Literature*, 43 (November 1971): 385-398;

Robert A. Bone, *Down Home: A History of Afro-American Short Fiction From Its Beginnings to the End of the Harlem Renaissance* (New York: Putnam's, 1975);

William Stanley Braithwaite, "The Negro in American Literature," in *The New Negro*, edited by Alain Locke (New York: A. & C. Boni, 1925);

Benjamin Brawley, *The Negro in Literature and Art in the United States* (New York: Dodd, Mead, 1934);

David D. Britt, "Chesnutt's Conjure Tales: What You See Is What You Get," *College Language Association Journal*, 15 (March 1972): 269-283;

Jules Chametzky, "Regional Literature and Ethnic Realities," *Antioch Review*, 31 (Fall 1971): 385-396;

P. Jay Delmar, "Elements of Tragedy in Charles W. Chesnutt's *The Conjure Woman*," *College Language Association Journal*, 23 (June 1980): 451-459;

Delmar, "The Mask as Theme and Structure: Charles W. Chesnutt's 'The Sheriff's Children' and 'The Passing of Grandison,'" *American Literature*, 51 (November 1979): 364-375;

Melvin Dixon, "The Teller as Folk Trickster in Chesnutt's *The Conjure Woman*," *College Language Association Journal*, 18 (December 1974): 186-197;

Charles W. Foster, "The Representation of Negro Dialect in Charles W. Chesnutt's *The Conjure Woman*," Ph.D. dissertation, University of Alabama, 1968;

Hugh M. Gloster, *Negro Voices in American Fiction* (Chapel Hill: University of North Carolina Press, 1948);

Gerald Haslam, " 'The Sheriff's Children': Chesnutt's Tragic Racial Parable," *Negro American Literature Forum*, 2 (Summer 1968): 21-25;

Robert Hemenway, " 'Baxter's Procrustes': Irony and Protest," *College Language Association Journal*, 18 (December 1974): 172-185;

Hemenway, "The Functions of Folklore in Charles Chesnutt's *The Conjure Woman*," *Journal of the Folklore Institute*, 13, no. 3 (1976): 283-309;

Hemenway, "Gothic Sociology: Charles Chesnutt and the Gothic Mode," *Studies in the Literary Imagination*, 9 (Spring 1974): 101-119;

Theodore Hovet, "Chesnutt's 'The Goophered Grapevine' as Social Criticism," *Negro American Literature Forum*, 7 (Fall 1973): 86-88;

Vernon Loggins, *The Negro Author: His Development in America to 1900* (New York: Columbia University Press, 1931);

Julian D. Mason, Jr., "Charles W. Chesnutt as Southern Author," *Mississippi Quarterly*, 20 (Spring 1967): 77-89;

Wayne Mixon, "The Unfulfilled Dream: Charles W. Chesnutt and the New South Movement," *Southern Humanities Review*, Bicentennial Issue (1976): 23-33;

Karen Magee Myers, "Mythic Patterns in Charles W. Chesnutt's *The Conjure Woman* and Ovid's *Metamorphoses*," *Black American Literature Forum*, 13 (Spring 1979): 13-17;

Gloria C. Oden, "Chesnutt's Conjure as African Survival," *Melus*, 5 (Spring 1978): 38-48;

Chikwenye O. Ogunyemi, "The Africanness of *The Conjure Woman* and *Feather Woman of the Jungle*," *Ariel: A Review of International Literature*, 8 (April 1977): 17-30;

J. Saunders Redding, *To Make a Poet Black* (Chapel Hill: University of North Carolina Press, 1939);

Sylvia Lyons Render, *Charles W. Chesnutt* (Boston: Twayne, 1980);

Render, "Eagle with Clipped Wings: Form and Feeling in the Fiction of Charles W. Chesnutt," Ph.D. dissertation, George Peabody College for Teachers, 1962;

Render, Introduction to *The Short Fiction of Charles W. Chesnutt*, edited by Render (Washington, D.C.: Howard University Press, 1974; revised, 1981), pp. 3-56;

Render, "North Carolina Dialect: Chesnutt Style," *North Carolina Folklore*, 15 (November 1967): 69-70;

Render, "Tar Heelia in Chesnutt," *College Language Association Journal*, 9 (September 1965): 39-50;

H. K. Selke, "Charles W. Chesnutt's 'The Sheriff's Children,'" in *The Black American Short Story in the Twentieth Century*, edited by Peter Bruck (Atlantic Highlands, N.J.: Humanities Press, 1977), pp. 21-38;

Merrill Maguire Skaggs, *The Folk of Southern Fiction* (Athens: University of Georgia Press, 1972);

Sterling Stuckey, "Through the Prism of Folklore: The Black Ethos in Slavery," *Massachusetts Review*, 9 (Summer 1968): 417-437;

Joel Taxel, "Charles W. Chesnutt's Sambo: Myth and Reality," *Negro American Literature Forum*, 9 (Winter 1975): 105-108;

Eugene Terry, "Charles W. Chesnutt: Victim of the Color Line," *Contributions to Black Studies* (Amherst), 1 (1977): 13-44;

Ronald Walcott, "Chesnutt's 'The Sheriff's Children' as Parable," *Negro American Literature Forum*, 7 (Fall 1973): 83-85.

Papers:

The largest collection of Chesnutt manuscripts, including unpublished novels and journals, is at Fisk University. Other manuscripts and letters are at the Western Reserve Historical Society Library in Cleveland.

George Randolph Chester

(1869-26 February 1924)

Martha G. Bower
University of New Hampshire

BOOKS: *Get-Rich-Quick Wallingford. A Cheerful Account of the Rise and Fall of an American Business Buccaneer* (Indianapolis: Bobbs-Merrill, 1908);

The Cash Intrigue, A Fantastic Melodrama of Modern Finance (Indianapolis: Bobbs-Merrill, 1909);

The Making of Bobby Burnit (Indianapolis: Bobbs-Merrill, 1909);

Young Wallingford (Indianapolis: Bobbs-Merrill, 1910);

The Art of Short Story Writing (Cincinnati: Publishers Syndicate, 1910); republished as *The Art of Writing* (Cincinnati: Publishers Syndicate, 1910);

The Early Bird: A Businessman's Love Story (Indianapolis: Bobbs-Merrill, 1910);

The Jingo (Indianapolis: Bobbs-Merrill, 1912);

Five Thousand an Hour: How Johnny Gamble Won the Heiress (New York: Publishers Syndicate, 1912);

Wallingford and Blackie Daw (Indianapolis: Bobbs-Merrill, 1913);

Wallingford in His Prime (Indianapolis: Bobbs-Merrill, 1913);

A Tale of Red Roses (Indianapolis: Bobbs-Merrill, 1914);

The Ball of Fire, by Chester and Lillian Chester (New York: Hearst's International Library Co., 1914);

Blue Pete's Escape (New York: Winthrop Press, 1914);

Cordelia Blossom (New York: Hearst's International Library Co., 1914);

The Enemy, by Chester and Lillian Chester (New York: Hearst's International Library Co., 1915);

Runaway Jane, by Chester and Lillian Chester (New York: Hearst's International Library Co., 1915);

The Son of Wallingford, by Chester and Lillian Chester (Boston: Small, Maynard, 1921);

The Wonderful Adventures of Little Prince Toofat (New York: McCann, 1922);

George Randolph Chester

On the Lot and Off, by Chester and Lillian Chester (New York & London: Harper, 1924).

PLAY PRODUCTION: *Cordelia Blossom*, by Chester and Lillian Chester, New York, Gaiety Theatre, 31 August 1914.

MOTION PICTURES: *Black Beauty*, adaptation by Chester and Lillian Chester, Vitagraph, 1921;

The Son of Wallingford, story and scenario by Chester and Lillian Chester, Vitagraph, 1921;

The Top o' the Morning, scenario by Chester and Wallace Clifton, Universal, 1922;

The Lavender Bath Lady, adaptation and scenario by Chester, Universal, 1922;

The Altar Stairs, scenario by Chester, George Hively, and Doris Schroeder, Universal, 1922;

The Flaming Hour, scenario by Chester, Universal, 1922;

The Scarlet Car, scenario by Chester, Universal, 1923;

The First Degree, scenario by Chester, Universal, 1923;

The Bolted Door, scenario by Chester, Universal, 1923;

Soft Cushions, story by Chester, Paramount Famous Lasky, 1927.

OTHER: "Bargain Day at Tytt House," in *The Best American Humorous Short Stories*, edited by Alexander Jessup (New York: Boni & Liveright, 1920);

"The Triple Cross," in *Representative American Short Stories*, edited by Jessup (Boston & New York: Allyn & Bacon, 1923).

PERIODICAL PUBLICATIONS: "Skeezicks," *McClure's Magazine*, 25 (August 1905): 364-365;

"Strikebreaker," *McClure's Magazine*, 25 (September 1905): 451-468;

"Woman at Home," *American Magazine*, 61 (March 1906): 540-548;

"Edge of the Boom," *Collier's, The National Weekly*, 55 (8 May 1915): 5-7;

"Scropper Patcher," *Everybody's Magazine*, 35 (October 1916): 422-423;

"Heavenly Spat," *Everybody's Magazine*, 36 (January 1917): 86-97;

"Pouff," *Everybody's Magazine*, 42 (March 1920): 64-67;

"Boy Wonder," *Saturday Evening Post*, 195 (26 May 1923): 8-10;

"Dixie Day, Herself," *Saturday Evening Post*, 196 (28 July 1923): 9-10;

"All for the Ladies," *Saturday Evening Post*, 196 (11 August 1923): 16-17;

"Fish Eat Fish," *Saturday Evening Post*, 196 (13 October 1923): 8-10;

"Angel Child," *Saturday Evening Post*, 196 (3 November 1923): 12-14;

"Slump," *Saturday Evening Post*, 196 (18 March 1924): 16-18;

"Yesman Said No," *Saturday Evening Post*, 196 (19 April 1924): 9-11.

George Randolph Chester was both an interpreter and a paradigm of the times in which he lived. He was a writer who rose to the top of his genre by creating potboilers about humorous, devious swindlers and well-mannered confidence men. Chester's fame burgeoned when his stories were serialized in such magazines as *Collier's*, *Cosmopolitan*, and the *Saturday Evening Post*, but his "Get-Rich-Quick Wallingford" stories were primarily responsible for his great popular and financial success. The main character of the series, J. Rufus Wallingford, was an appealing villain who charmed women and made easy money by conning greedy, gullible investors.

A devotee of cigarettes, beer, and sauerkraut, Chester lived hard and worked hard, often producing several stories a week for the many magazines that published his work. Like his materialistic heroes, he spent his paychecks as fast as he earned them. In addition to his best-selling collection of stories, *Get-Rich-Quick Wallingford* (1908), much of his work was compiled in book form. Among his most popular books were *The Cash Intrigue, A Fantastic Melodrama of Modern Finance* (1909), *Young Wallingford* (1910), *Wallingford and Blackie Daw* (1913), and *The Son of Wallingford* (1921).

Chester was born in 1869, though the exact date is unknown; moreover, there has been some conjecture over the place of his birth. According to an article by Herbert Corey in Cosmopolitan (May 1911), Chester claimed he was born in Richmond, Indiana, but he also shrugged off his place of birth with the remark, "I really don't care. Do you prefer any particular city?" Most obituaries, including the one in the paper he once worked for–the *Cincinnati Enquirer*–record his birthplace as Hamilton County, Ohio. Chester's reluctance to recall where he was born reflected an undercurrent of bitterness that informed his childhood and adolescent memories. Chester was forced to leave home as a very small boy to earn his living. Before he became a reporter in his twenties, he tried his hand at an interesting mixture of trades. He was an engineer in a planing mill, a pen-and-ink artist, a cook, a plumber, a paperhanger, a ribbon salesman, a chaindragger for a civil engineer, and a worker in a chair factory producing furniture patterns.

Chester's first writing job was as a reporter for the *Detroit News* just prior to the turn of the cen-

"'No!' roared Uncle Billy. 'No, there wasn't, by gum!'"

BARGAIN DAY AT TUTT HOUSE
BY
GEORGE RANDOLPH CHESTER
ILLUSTRATED BY JAMES H. GARDNER-SOPER

I

JUST as the stage rumbled over the rickety old bridge creaking and groaning, the sun came from behind the clouds that had frowned all the way, and the passengers cheered up a bit. The two richly-dressed matrons, who had been so utterly and un- necessarily oblivious to the presence of each other, now suspended hostilities for the moment by mutual and unspoken consent, and viewed with relief the little, golden-tinted valley and the tree-clad road just beyond. The respective husbands of these two ladies exchanged a mere glance, no more, of comfort. They, too, were relieved, though more by the momentary truce than by anything else. They regretted very much to be compelled to hate each other, for each had

First page of Chester's story that appeared in the June 1905 McClure's Magazine

tury. But he was not destined to be merely an objective observer of human events. Instead, his facts were lost in the dramatic embellishments of the scenes of crime and tragedy he witnessed.

After leaving Detroit he was employed in 1901 by the *Cincinnati Enquirer* at a salary of twelve dollars a week. Six months later he was promoted to Sunday editor. Chester's career as a fiction writer began with the above position, for which he was required to produce from five to eighteen columns a week of original copy. The result of this proliferation was the eventual syndication of Chester's stories in twenty-five newspapers. After his first story, "Strikebreaker," was published in *McClure's Magazine* (September 1905), Chester gained immediate recognition. At that point he left the newspaper business to work full-time as a short-fiction writer.

The character of J. R. Wallingford was described in the first episode of the "Get-Rich-Quick" series mentioned above as being "a large gentleman, a suave gentleman, a gentleman whose clothes not merely fit him but distinguished him, a gentleman of rare good living, even though one of the sort whose faces turn red when they eat; the dignity of his worldly prosperousness surrounded him like a blessed aura." Chester was at his best when recounting the startling adventures of this slippery character. Wallingford's appeal lay in his engaging personality and his unflappable confidence. He would arrive in a strange town without a dime, sign the hotel register with a flourish, secure the most expensive suite, and have all the well-heeled businessmen in town hooked into his latest scam while they sipped champagne and smoked imported cigars.

The Author of "Wallingford"

By Herbert Corey

AN interviewer once called on George Randolph Chester. "In what city were you born?" he asked the author of the Wallingford stories. "Well," said Mr. Chester amiably, "I really don't care. Do you prefer any particular city?"

The record shows that, on this occasion at least, he selected Richmond, Indiana. But whether it was Richmond or another town, he left his birthplace so early in life that he has no sentiment to spare for "the dear old home." He is singularly free from flapdoodle, anyhow. It does not occur to him that there was anything romantic in the fact that a small boy had to go to work when other small boys were still running to their mothers to have their ears washed. Nor does he regard himself as having been a victim of hard luck. In fact, he had a fairly good time as a youngster, and for the next twenty years

or so he kept moving on. In that period he did about everything that can be done except to run a bank. A chronic case of "butter-fingers" kept him from handling money successfully. A dollar never seemed to him the foundation-stone of a fortune that should ultimately bulge. He recognized it only as available for the first payment on something he very greatly desired at the moment—subsequent payments to be made weekly over a period of ninety-nine years. In these early days he was always balanced between appetite and income.

He hasn't changed greatly since. Therefore his best friends can forgive his success. He still spends too much money, he keeps preposterous hours, he regards out-of-doors merely as a reason for the taximeter, he rolls his own cigarettes very badly, and he smacks his lips at the thought of

Photograph of Chester that appeared in the June 1912 Bookman

Chester traced Wallingford's devious career across the country from his first swindle involving a fictitious company that manufactured covered carpet tacks to his final coup—that of raising a million dollars in capital for a sham "traction system." His demise occurs when he is duped by a clever victim of one of his early stings. One of Chester's most valuable skills was his ability to engage the reader with his thorough and realistic characterizations, not only of Wallingford and the people he was swindling, but of such secondary characters as Wallingford's wife and his sidekick, Blackie Daw. The Wallingford stories were clearly a satire on the excesses of the nouveau

riche at the turn of the century. In describing Wallingford's first venture, Blackie Daw comments that "Wallingford himself might be a spendthrift and a nere-do-well," but his victims' "faith in the tack that was to make them all rich was supreme."

Chester's satiric style was flamboyant and melodramatic. In a scene in which Blackie Daw and Wallingford flip a coin to decide whether or not to try their luck in the strange town of Battlesburg, they stop in front of the local Baptist church: "Mr. Daw flipped the coin in the air over Mrs. Wallingford's lap. Upon the green broadcloth the bright silver piece came down

Publicity photograph for Black Beauty, *which Chester and his second wife, Lillian, adapted for the screen*
(Kevin Brownlow Collection)

with a spat, and the Goddess of Liberty faced upward to the sky." Chester's prose proved unwieldy at times when he tried his hand at metaphor: "Mr. Daw . . . stalked violently about the room like a huge pair of tongs." But Chester aspired to the satiric genius of Mark Twain in passages such as this one: "Mr. Daw stepped down upon the gravel, tall and slender, clad in glove-fitting 'Prince Albert,' his black mustache curled tightly, his black eyes glittering. Descended the beautiful, brown-haired Mrs. Wallingford, brave in dark green broadcloth. Descended the golden-haired Mrs. Daw, stunning in violet from hat to silken hose. Perfectly satisfactory, all of them; perfectly adapted to fill the ideal of what a quartette of genuine nabobs should look like!"

Chester, who artfully built suspense between capers by ending each story with an unresolved tension, closed the "Get-Rich-Quick Wallingford" series by resigning Wallingford to a fate that satisfied the moral sensibilities of his reading public: Wallingford is sent to prison before he can escape with his victims' money. However, to leave open the possibility that the adventures may be perpetuated at a later date, he is sprung from jail by a benefactor who has reaped the prof-

its of Wallingford's traction line scheme. Chester leaves his readers with the parting thought that expresses a motif that informs most of his writing. Wallingford is not to blame. He is "only the logical development of the American tendency to get there no matter how. It is the national weakness, the national menace," and Wallingford is "only an exaggerated molecule of it." Later in 1910 George M. Cohan wrote and produced a Broadway musical based on the Wallingford series. Chester himself wrote and produced a film version in Hollywood in 1921.

In 1909, one year after the publication of the Wallingford stories, Chester, a resident of New York City, wrote another series, "The Cash Intrigue." At the center of these episodes, serialized in *Cosmopolitan*, was another product of the American way, Philip Kelvin. In these stories, subtitled "A Ring of Complete Short Romances of Finance," Chester played on the typical American rags-to-riches plot. Kelvin, more of an authentic villain than the engaging Wallingford, amasses a fortune through gaining control of the railroad industry and is crowned emperor of the United States. A money-crazed madman, he keeps the general populace in check by means of force. In the last of the six episodes Chester pits the emperor Kelvin against the richest man in the world, who has gathered a huge cash treasury at his estate outside Washington, D.C. Kelvin plots to overtake this miser, aptly named Breed, and hence gain control of the world's largest store of cash.

In this saga America has been thrown into a chaos reminiscent of the French Revolution, complete with riots, strikes, and scenes of abject poverty. Chester's setting is reminiscent of Charles Dickens's *A Tale of Two Cities* (1859): "In a thousand gory spots the beasts of hate were loosed at once, and the places in which they chose to glut their rage were the cities; where vice had congregated, where crime had sought and found its fellows, where poverty had festered, where a deadly miasmic blight had settled upon all life, all thought, all social intercourse." The great bastion of Breed's cash store is invaded by the "Liberty, Equality, Fraternity" faction as well as by Kelvin's forces. But it is a third faction, armed with rifles and bayonets and led by a veteran of the Civil War, that wins the contest.

Chester depicted women in these stories as traitors to their sex. The street people are led by the dark-haired, ruby-gowned wife of Breed, who casts away her jewels for the cause. He describes her as "the incarnation of hell-apprenticed beauty. The incarnation of all the evil things that are red." Her female followers are "hideous travesties of their sex in all their grim frowsiness and defeminizing excitement." It is Lillian Breed, however, who boldly stabs the emperor.

Pandering to a patriotic reading public, Chester closed the tale with the new leader's oath of loyalty to the republic as he takes from his coat a tattered American flag "that had gone through the war between the North and the South." Chester's unpredictability and humor are in evidence as Kelvin's former adviser sums up the situation: "He was a wonderful study, and the nearest approach to absolute monarchy of any resident of this globe. In the meantime, gentlemen, America has had her orgasm, and her nerves will be quieter now." Chester ends this romance with the crowd singing "The Star-Spangled Banner"—an obvious touch of satire.

In 1910, shortly after the publication of the Wallingford series, Chester authored a writer's handbook, *The Art of Short Story Writing*, in which he cited the "business story" as the most popular genre of his times. Chester wrote: "The romance of millions and how they were made or stolen

... are the things which interest the live public of today." The chapter entitled "Democracy" advised aspiring authors to write not only of bank presidents but ditchdiggers, because "there is but very little difference in any of us as to the merest externals."

When Chester was at the height of his productivity and fame, he was divorced from his first wife, Elizabeth Bethermel, who was awarded the custody of their two sons, George Randolph, Jr., and Robert Fey. In 1911 he married Lillian De Rimo in Paris. The *New York Times* obituary (27 February 1924) stressed the particulars of the divorce, stating that Chester married Miss De Rimo "in ignorance of the need to wait for the final decree." The newspaper also named Chester's second wife as the correspondent in the case.

After their return from Paris the Chesters continued to live in New York City, where husband and wife became collaborators. There are no details available on the extent of Lillian Chester's participation, but her name is coupled with his as the author of several stories and plays. Her influence is apparent in stories such as "Edge of the Boom" (*Collier's*, 8 May 1915) and "The Son of Wallingford" (*Collier's*, 9 April 1921). In the former story the hero, Sam Arnold, is a real estate tycoon and town father. Arnold's wife has progressed from the obedient and superficial person that characterized Mrs. Wallingford to a sophisticated, educated, philanthropic club woman. Sam's deals are made legitimate by her charitable causes, and she plays an important role in the story. The exaggerated portraits of Chester's earlier writings become the understated characters which are presented to the reader in the story largely through dialogue. Expressions such as "Great Scott," "Holy Mackerel," and "ye gods and little fishes" are among Sam Arnold's most profound utterances. This new version of the American con man is educated and genteel, a sportsman who smokes a pipe and attends his college homecoming weekend, but he is also a conformist who lacks the originality of J. Rufus Wallingford.

The Wallingford capers were resurrected by the Chesters in 1921 under the title of *The Son of Wallingford*. This series of tales finds Wallingford superseded by his son, Jimmy, his junior partner in crime. But the younger Wallingford learns via the dire results of an oil well scam to mend his ways. The final episode takes the aging Wallingford, his wife, his son, and his son's fiancée to the brink of death. The Wallingfords' bravery is tested as they row across the lake through a screen of flames set off by a burst oil tank into the jaws of a hungry lynch mob. By the end of the adventure, however, Jimmy has saved the family name by proving that the oil scheme was not fake. The son of Wallingford assumes his position as the heir to the wit, charm, and canny business sense of his father. The difference between them is succinctly expressed in the following observation of Mrs. Wallingford: "he is so like his father; so like; but honest!"

Lillian Chester's influence surfaced again with an increase in the romantic interest and the civilizing influence of Jimmy's fiancée, Mary. The "Get-Rich-Quick" character so popular in the early 1900s has given way by the end of the series to the next generation of college-educated, honest businessmen. And Chester's racy, colorful style has lost some of its luster.

In the early 1920s George and Lillian Chester left New York and the world of popular fiction for the promise of Hollywood. The Chesters wrote and directed several screenplays. They were successful with only two, both produced in 1921: *Black Beauty* and *The Son of Wallingford*, based on their own series. The couple remained in Hollywood for two years, then returned to New York in 1923 to resume writing popular fiction. Inspired by his Hollywood experience, Chester began a new series, "The Adventures of Izzy Iskovitch," stories about a shyster film producer and the underside of Hollywood.

These Hollywood stories, the last series Chester would write, demonstrated a marked shift in his approach. The final episode, "Below Lay Hollywood," was published posthumously in the *Saturday Evening Post* (May 1924). The story is all but devoid of Chester's rich, flamboyant style of the early Wallingford stories, and his characters are flat and less sharply drawn. His account of how the Hollywood film magnate, Izzy, manipulates, swindles, and abuses lesser men for his own gain reads more like a movie script than a short story.

Cluttered with characters and framed within the filming of a movie, this story seems to defer to the taste of a public that has been acclimated to the silent-screen adventure. Imagery and metaphor are replaced by dialogue, and

what exposition remains is weakened by an overabundance of verbs modified by adverbs, such as "He packed fiercely their travelling bags" and they "thirsted unanimously." The character of Izzy runs true to form. He is a self-made millionaire who learned to fight his way out of poverty to achieve material success. In this late work, however, what Chester loses in style he gains in his authentic depiction of the golden age of silent film—the glamour, opulence, tragedy, and crime of the 1920s. But this story, written just prior to his death, is revelatory of a once vibrant writer who expended volumes of words to entertain his large popular audience, now at the end of his productive store. Chester died of a heart attack at his apartment in New York City with his wife at his side on 26 February 1924. He had been working on another installment for the *Saturday Evening Post* of the adventures of Izzy Iskovitch.

Chester, like many of his contemporaries, began as a journalist, but his propensities toward humor, satire, and the psychology of human behavior—especially of the American businessman—led him away from reporting and into the short-story genre. The appeal of his early and most popular work was founded in his lively and humorous character studies and his ability to sustain his readers through several episodes by his intriguing and extraordinary situations and sense of drama. Chester was able to make his scoundrels and confidence men sympathetic and human. At the same time, through his humorous satire, he remained critical of the often immoral pursuit of the American dream. His later work focused more on the action than the reaction of his characters and reflected his wife Lillian's collaboration when women played a more prominent and essential role in the stories.

Chester's last works were influenced by his Hollywood experience as a screenwriter, with more dialogue and short action scenes and less emphasis on character development. The importance and popularity of Chester's short fiction is that it serves as a chronicle both of the American businessman and the economic history of the times. Considered one of the most successful and the most widely read writers of the period, he provided in his stories a continuing reflection of and escape for the large reading public of middle-class America.

Kate Chopin
(8 February 1850-22 August 1904)

Tonette Bond Inge

See also the Chopin entry in *DLB 12: American Realists and Naturalists.*

BOOKS: *At Fault* (St. Louis: Privately printed, 1890);
Bayou Folk (Boston & New York: Houghton, Mifflin, 1894);
A Night in Acadie (Chicago: Way & Williams, 1897);
The Awakening (Chicago & New York: Herbert S. Stone, 1899);
The Complete Works of Kate Chopin, 2 volumes, edited by Per Seyersted (Baton Rouge: Louisiana State University Press, 1969);
A Kate Chopin Miscellany, edited by Seyersted and Emily Toth (Natchitoches, La.: Northwestern State University Press, 1979).

Kate O'Flaherty was born into one of St. Louis's most prominent families. Although Kate O'Flaherty Chopin later said she was born in 1851, Emily Toth discovered during her research for her forthcoming biography of Chopin that the future writer's baptismal certificate lists her birthdate as 8 February 1850. Her Irish immigrant father, Thomas O'Flaherty, was a successful St. Louis merchant; her mother, Eliza Faris O'Flaherty, a beautiful and gracious daughter of one of the city's oldest and most aristocratic Creole families. Kate received her formal education at the Academy of the Sacred Heart in St. Louis, where she was exposed to Catholic teachings and a French educational emphasis upon intellectual discipline. Her main interests were music, reading, and writing, though her commonplace book and the fable "Emancipation" are her only surviving writings from this early period. Between graduation in 1868 and marriage two years later Kate read ravenously, principally among the major classic and contemporary European writers. Fluent in French and German, she read in the original languages whenever possible. Though on the surface she appeared to be a conventional society belle, her commonplace book indicates that she gave a great deal of thought to the subject of the

Kate Chopin, 1894

independent woman, especially in response to her reading of Madame de Staël, one of her favorite authors. On 9 June 1870 she married Oscar Chopin, a member of a French-Creole family from Natchitoches Parish in northwestern Louisiana. On the way to New York, from which the couple would depart for a three-month honeymoon tour of Germany, Switzerland, and France, Kate Chopin met Victoria Claflin, later Victoria Woodhull, the radical-feminist publisher, stockbroker, spiritualist, and future nominee for president, who according to Chopin's diary advised her "not to fall into the useless degrading life of most married ladies. . . ." After their honeymoon the couple returned to New Orleans, where Oscar Chopin became a prosperous cotton factor. During the twelve and a half years of her married life—nine in New Orleans; three in Cloutierville, Natchitoches Parish—Chopin gave birth to six children: Jean (1871), Oscar (1873), George (1874), Frederick (1876), Felix (1878), and Lelia (1879). Devoting herself to her family and household, she still managed to reconcile the needs of her own being with the expectations of her conventional milieu. She dressed unconventionally and smoked cigarettes long before smoking was an approved practice among women in her class. In New Orleans she took long walks and streetcar rides through the city, absorbing all she could of its life and its people; in Cloutierville she walked and rode horseback and involved herself in the lives of both the Creole upper classes and the sharecropper tenants. Her charm, intelligence, and grace endeared her to all who knew her.

When Oscar Chopin died of swamp fever in December 1882, Kate Chopin stayed on in Cloutierville for more than a year to run the family plantation; but in 1884, at the age of thirty-four, she returned with her six children to her native St. Louis. Not long after her return her mother died, leaving her feeling alone and bereft. With the encouragement of her family doctor, Frederick Kolbenheyer, a man of broad learning and radical ideas, she began a course of reading in biology and anthropology, including works by Charles Darwin, Thomas Henry Huxley, and Herbert Spencer. Kolbenheyer also encouraged her to write fiction, for he appreciated the literary qualities of the letters she had written to him from Louisiana. Chopin made a return visit to Natchitoches Parish in 1887 and began writing fiction in late 1888.

Her first two published stories appeared in the summer of 1889. Over the next fifteen years, until her death in 1904, she published two novels and wrote almost a hundred stories and sketches, two-thirds of them set in Louisiana and peopled with characters drawn from the rich cultural mixture of the region.

Chopin found the inspiration for her themes and techniques among French writers, principally Guy de Maupassant, whom she seems to have discovered in 1888 or 1889, and—during her apprenticeship—the fiction of Sarah Orne Jewett and Mary E. Wilkins Freeman. In her realistic and outspoken treatment of human, especially female, sexuality, she was a pioneer among American fiction writers.

Though Chopin became a central figure in the literary and cultural activities of St. Louis, she had no direct contact with or influence upon

Chopin's parents, Thomas and Eliza O'Flaherty, in 1855

the major literary figures of the 1890s. Outside her honeymoon journey, she made only one trip to New York, in 1893, to try to interest the New York publishers in her second novel (later destroyed) and in a collection of her stories. The critics of her day classed her among the Louisiana dialect writers and gave particular praise to the sensitivity of her character portrayals and the artistry of her style. Her stories were published in such periodicals as *Harper's, Century, Atlantic, Vogue, Saturday Evening Post*, and magazines and newspapers of St. Louis and New Orleans. When in 1899 her novel *The Awakening* was published, she was censured both locally and nationally for its poisonous and "positively unseemly" theme. The St. Louis literary establishment refused to review the novel, the local library removed it from circulation, and its author was refused membership in the St. Louis Fine Arts Club.

Discouraged by the critical reception of *The Awakening*, Chopin published only five stories after its failure, two of them intentionally written for children's publications. When she died of a cerebral hemorrhage in August 1904, after a day at the St. Louis World's Fair, she passed from the literary scene almost entirely unappreciated for her pioneering contributions to American fiction.

Kate Chopin's earliest surviving story, written when she was nineteen and titled "Emancipation. A Life Fable" (first published in the Missouri Historical Society *Bulletin*, January 1963; collected in *The Complete Works of Kate Chopin*, 1969), announces the major theme of her later fiction. An allegory of the soul's movement from bondage to freedom, the fable describes an animal's bold flight from the confines of his cage, whose door was accidentally opened. Though the price of his freedom is pain, hunger, and thirst, "So does he live, seeking, finding, and joying and suffering. The door which accident had opened is open still, but the cage remains forever empty!" Much of Kate Chopin's best short fiction focuses on characters to whom spiritual emancipation becomes an issue, though each one responds differently to the challenge. Nor does Chopin avoid showing the sacrifices and suffering associated with the journey to self-realization.

"Wiser than a God" (*Musical Journal*, December 1889; collected in *The Complete Works*), the next story she wrote and the second one she published, treats the theme of emancipation in relationship to love and marriage, Chopin's most characteristic context for presenting her major thematic concerns. In this story Paula Von Stoltz chooses self-fulfillment through a career as a concert pianist over marriage to the man she loves, George Brainard. George marries a conventional woman whom he does not love; Paula seems destined for marriage with Max Kuntzler, a middle-aged composer-teacher who follows Paula to Leipsic and whose persistence and patience, the narrator says, are likely to win in the end. If Paula does marry Max Kuntzler, she will trade conventional marriage with the man she loves for a marriage of companionship with a man capable of appreciating her talent and accomplishments and of fostering her developing career. Whether this exchange is beneficial to Paula, the narrator does not say; but the story does show that even a young woman as independent as Paula is unlikely to resist altogether the marital expectations of her society, embodied by the middle-aged Prof. Max Kuntzler. In "A Point at Issue" (*St. Louis Post Dispatch*, 27 October 1889; collected in *The Complete Works*), Chopin's first published story, the opening line announces the marriage of Eleanor Gail to Charles Faraday. The couple has decided "to be governed by no precedential methods. Marriage was to be a form, that while fixing legally

Kate O'Flaherty in the mid 1860s

their relation to each other, was in no wise to touch the individuality of either. . . ." Yet sexual jealousy enters to drive both of them into a conventional relationship, with Faraday revealing at story's end his inability to view Eleanor as his equal. Chopin seems to suggest that human nature itself works against enlightened redefinitions of love and marriage.

Though in the second half of 1889 Chopin wrote four stories, she spent most of her creative energies on her first novel, *At Fault*. Her first story after the novel's publication at her expense in September 1890 was "Mrs. Mobry's Reason" (*New Orleans Times-Democrat*, 23 April 1893; collected in *The Complete Works*), a story which Chopin earlier had given a succession of revealing titles—"A Common Crime," "A Taint in the Blood," "The Evil that Men Do," "Under the Apple Tree." In the story's opening scene Editha Payne, "at a moment when inward forces were at

Kate O'Flaherty in the late 1860s

work with her to weaken and undo the determination of a lifetime," finally accepts John Mobry's marriage proposal. The action then shifts twenty-five years into the future, and the reader learns at the end of the story the reason for Editha's earlier refusals to marry: her family's hereditary insanity has been passed on to her daughter and in all likelihood to her son's children. As Chopin's image of the blossoming apple tree makes clear, the forces of biology weakened Editha's resolve not to marry and so the curse of tainted blood has been passed on. These early stories show Chopin's naturalistic interest in the operation of both internal and external forces in the determination of individual behavior and destiny, themes which Chopin treats with consummate artistry in her masterpiece, *The Awakening*.

The stories collected in *Bayou Folk* (1894) and *A Night in Acadie* (1897) continue the psychological explorations announced in Chopin's earliest stories. Chopin demonstrates the naturalist's concern with the influence of heredity and biology on her characters' thoughts and actions, particularly with the social and biological forces shaping individual female behavior. She investigates the potential for individual happiness to be found in love and marriage; she shows the dangers of the illusion-based life at the same time that she reveals an understanding of its psychological origins. In the joys and sufferings encountered by her protagonists along the journey to self-knowledge and spiritual awakening, a journey not always completed, Chopin found her most powerful and characteristic theme. Her thematic concern with the inner life led her to seek the artistic means for portraying its conflicts. The best stories in the two collections show Chopin using geography and landscape to establish a psychological terrain for her characters; the settings, though rich in local detail and indigenous characters, are used to objectify the states of mind of her protagonists, whose conflicts are universal to humankind. Technically, she develops toward an authorial detachment, generally resisting moral commentary upon her characters' situations; she moves toward an unobtrusive use of symbolism; she artfully weaves local characters, situations, and settings into stories of universal significance and striking thematic realism.

Bayou Folk contains twenty-three tales and sketches, all set in Louisiana and all written during the two-and-a-half-year period from mid 1891 to the end of 1893. The original printing of the book ran to 1,250 copies; it was reprinted in 1895 (500 copies), 1906 (150 copies), and 1911 (150 copies). The collection, receiving more than one hundred press notices, was widely and enthusiastically reviewed and established Chopin as a new and important writer, though the reviewers saw her almost exclusively as a Louisiana local colorist.

"A No-Account Creole" (*Century*, January 1894) tells the story of Wallace Offdean, a young New Orleans businessman who seeks a life with greater intellectual and spiritual content than the one led by most urban Americans. He vows to "keep clear of the maelstroms of sordid work and senseless pleasure in which the average American business man may be said alternately to exist, and which reduce him, naturally, to a rather ragged condition of soul." He therefore seizes upon a business assignment to inspect and salvage a derelict plantation as a chance to "retire and take counsel with his inner and better self." At the plan-

Oscar and Kate Chopin in the year of their marriage

tation he falls in love with Euphrasie, the fiancée of Placide Santien, the youngest member of the Creole family who originally owned the plantation. A central theme of the story is the redemptive power of love and the landscape, for Offdean finds the hope of spiritual rebirth in an agrarian life shared with Euphrasie. Another is the sacrificial quality of true love, for when Placide, a man of the fieriest passions, learns of Euphrasie's love for Offdean, he surrenders his claim to her. Yet Chopin refuses to let such a romanticized notion of love go unexamined. A complementary theme is the cultural pride behind Placide's refusal to allow himself, a Creole, to be lectured to by Offdean on how to love a woman. "The way to love a woman," counsels Offdean to the enraged Placide, who is threatening to shoot him, "is to think first of her happiness. If you love Euphrasie, you must go to her clean." These words give Placide something to think about, and he does not shoot Offdean; rather, he is challenged into a demonstration of the superiority of his love for Euphrasie by giving her up. This story is one of Chopin's longest and shows her making use of setting and landscape to objectify states of mind, a device perfected in her later fiction. The decaying plantation suggests the lack of spiritual order in the lives of Euphrasie, who is engaged to a man she respects but does not love,

and of Offdean, who arrives at the plantation in a state of spiritual unrest engendered by the emptiness of city life. In the process of giving order to the plantation, he discovers that love can order the wilderness of his emotional life. The restoration of the plantation, though not completed in the course of the story's action, is implicit in the clearing of the obstacles to Offdean's union with Euphrasie, for he has an inheritance large enough to permit him to buy the estate. Here marriage to the right person promises the spiritual liberation of the characters, a possibility that Kate Chopin was careful never categorically to dismiss. For Placide, however, the clearer understanding of love comes at the moment love is lost. His self-restraint and denial have earned him the reader's respect, making the story's title, "A No-Account Creole," ironic.

"Beyond the Bayou" (*Youth's Companion*, 15 June 1893) also deals with the liberating and ennobling power of love, not sexual love this time, but maternal love. La Folle, a middle-aged black woman whose childhood experience of the Civil War has made her morbidly afraid of crossing the bayou, musters the courage to cross that boundary in order to save the plantation owner's son, whom she loves as her own. Her foray into the unknown during the crisis gives her the courage the next morning to cross the bayou again on a mythic journey to self-discovery, where she encounters the memories of an earlier self. In the early dawn she experiences a rebirth of her senses in the rich fragrances and deep colors of high summer: "A look of wonder and deep content crept into her face as she watched for the first time the sun rise upon the new, the beautiful world beyond the bayou." Before La Folle's journey, animal imagery is employed to suggest her emotions and her actions: she is not unlike the cattle which are sent in dry periods to graze by the river and with which she feels a community. After her ordeal, however, she prepares for her courageous encounter with herself and with life by donning her new blue cottonade and white apron, emblems of her feminine role in the human community. The mythic suggestiveness of Chopin's theme is carried in the imagery of the setting and locale, as the following passage makes clear: "When La Folle had slowly and cautiously mounted the many steps that led up to the veranda, she turned to look back at the perilous ascent she had made. Then she caught sight of the river, bending like a silver bow at the foot of Bellissime. Exultation possessed her soul." Long before Eudora Welty's "A Worn Path," Kate Chopin gave female heroism a mythic context in the American short story.

If maternal instincts are a liberating force in La Folle's life, they lead the young half-breed Indian girl in "Loka" (*Youth's Companion*, 22 December 1892) to choose the restrictions of civilization over the freedom of the wild. Loka bears the same relationship to the agricultural and domestic order of the Padue farm that the farm bears to the wilderness that surrounds it. One day while all members of the family except the infant Bibine are off on an excursion, Loka feels the irresistible pull of the wild: stripping off her shoes, she starts for the woods, but she then remembers her responsibilities to Bibine. Grabbing him up, she disappears into the wild, only to return at day's end. Baptiste Padue recognizes his kinship with the animal wildness of the girl: "That girl, she done tole us how she was temp' today to turn *canaille*—like we all temp' sometimes." Because of her environmental heritage, Loka is not as practiced in repressing the animal side of her nature as are the Padues: "We got to rememba she ent like you an' me, po' thing; she's one Injun, her." In fact, it can be said that Loka's affection for the infant Bibine saves her from a life of brutality and exploitation, for the old Indian woman who kept Loka beat her for refusing

to steal. At least Baptiste views the situation this way: he says to Tontine, "W'at was it save her? That li'le chile w'at you hole in yo' arm." Chopin's treatment of her theme does not stop here. Baptiste chooses this moment, when his wife is emotionally exhausted by her anxiety over the disappearance of Loka and Bibine, to assert his masculine authority: " 'I want to say who's masta in this house—it's me,' he went on. Tontine did not protest; only clasped the baby a little closer, which encouraged him to proceed." Chopin suggests that Loka's maternal instincts bring her under the patriarchal power that characterizes the order of civilized society. Her immediate world on Bayou Choctaw offered her a greater range of experiences than the biologically determined choices imposed upon women in the world of the Acadians. Dominated by "old Marot, the squaw who drank whisky and plaited baskets and beat her," she was nevertheless free on Bayou Choctaw "to walk with moccasined feet over the spring turf, under the trees! What fun to trap the squirrels, to skin the otter; to take those swift flights on the pony that Choctaw Joe had stolen from the Texans!" Loka's choice of returning to the Padue farm with Bibine, then, represents the taking on of social responsibility that accompanies the entrance into sexual maturity. In the world of nineteenth-century America, doing so meant accepting the role limitations placed upon women by a patriarchal society.

"Ma'ame Pélagie" (*New Orleans Times-Democrat*, 24 December 1893) is the best of Chopin's early stories on the psychological dangers of a fantasy-ridden life. Though unmarried, the elder daughter of Philippe Valmêt is referred to as Madame Pélagie, for she has married herself to a moribund dream of restoring the family mansion to its antebellum splendor. Every penny not spent on necessities is saved for the fulfilling of this dream. She has succeeded in drawing her much younger and weaker sister Pauline into her dream; but La Petite, their brother's beautiful and vivacious daughter, who has come to live with them, refuses to participate further in the privations of their dream world because to do so, in her words, "is a sin against myself." Madame Pélagie has inherited the dreams and delusions of her past, and they have infected her soul to the point that she is unable to participate fully in the joys of the present, even after she renounces her dreams of recovering a lost past. The narrator summarizes the conclusion readers are to draw: "While the outward pressure of a young

Chopin with her first four children—Frederick, George, Jean, and Oscar—circa 1877

and joyous existence had forced her footsteps into the light, her soul had stayed in the shadow of the ruin." The psychological determinism inherent in the story's theme is made clear when Madame Pélagie's motive for renouncing her dream is considered. The part of the past most vivid to her involves the years just before the beginning of the Civil War when she was a young belle in the bloom of life and Pauline was a toddler. The story makes no direct mention of the children's mother, but it is clear that Pélagie has assumed that role in regard to Pauline. Her anxiety for the safety and well-being of the child has been formulated into a maxim governing her conscious and unconscious minds: "Il ne faut pas faire mal à Pauline." Had Pélagie followed her own impulses unimpeded, she would have died in the invaders' fire that destroyed the mansion—"to show them how a daughter of Louisiana can perish before her conquerors"—but it was necessary to save little Pauline, screaming in terror at her knees. Thus, when Pauline sinks into a depression from the despair of losing the redemptive presence of La Petite from their household, Pélagie surrenders her dream and uses their accumulated wealth to build a comfortable home for all of them upon the bricks of the ruined mansion. In a dream sequence intended to depict Pélagie's state of mind and the origins of the conflict she feels, Chopin injects a symbol for the morbid psychological effects of Pélagie's fantasies: "Ha! how low that bat has circled. It has struck Ma'ame Pélagie full on the breast. She does not know it." Chopin would later learn how to distance the narrative voice and to use images less obtrusively, but this story is important for its revelation of Chopin's interest in psychological motivation and her development of characterization consistent with those motives. Madame Pélagie demonstrates the clarity and the totality with which Chopin imagined her characters and her growing skill in realizing them as credible psychological entities. Pélagie's conflict is clearly between the maternal love she bears for Pauline and her own selfish commitment to an ideal. That she is able both to place her maternal responsibilities above her selfish dream and to suffer a spiritually disfiguring decline as a result are totally consistent with her nature, a nature which she is powerless to change.

In "Désirée's Baby" (*Vogue*, 14 January 1893), her most widely anthologized story and one which has consistently drawn favorable critical commentary over the years, Chopin treats the issues of race and heredity within the thematic context of love and marriage. Désirée was a foundling reared in an atmosphere of love by the Valmondés, a childless couple who view the girl as the gift of "a beneficent Providence." When grown, Désirée becomes the object of the headstrong, passionate love of Armand Aubigny. Chopin's imagery indicates that this passion is violent, even brutal, and destructive in its unrestraint: "The passion that awoke in him that day, when he saw her at the gate, swept along like an avalanche, or like a prairie fire, or like anything that drives headlong over all obstacles." Armand's French mother, who died in Paris when the boy was eight, "loved her own land too well ever to leave it." The narrator assigns an air of sad, even moribund, neglect of the plantation house to this fact, which serves to foreshadow the events at story's end. Armand's marriage to Désirée soon produces an heir; when her child begins to show signs of a racially mixed heritage, however, Armand feels unjustly betrayed by God. He avenges himself through inhumane treatment of Désirée, whom he stops loving "because of the unconscious injury she had brought upon his home and his name." Cast out from his home, Désirée disappears with her child into the dim marshes of the bayou. After her disappearance Armand has a huge bonfire built, and he feeds into it the household remains of Désirée and her baby. In a drawer from which he is removing Désirée's billets doux, he finds a love letter his mother had written to his father disclosing the information that she "belongs to the race that is cursed with the brand of slavery." In this story the artistic emphasis is on plot, and the portraits lack psychological depth. The characters become mere stick figures in the universal struggle between the enfranchised and the disenfranchised. Armand fits the stereotype of the cruel slave-beating plantation owner down to the last detail of possessing an octoroon mistress. The emotional impact of the story is supplied by the perfect skill with which Chopin employs irony and with her highly effective use of symbolism. In the imagery of the story Armand's pride of sexual and racial superiority aligns him with Satan; also like Satan, Armand seeks to avenge himself against what he perceives as God's injustice. In stark contrast Désirée is viewed as the instrument of "a beneficent Providence," for she has brought maternal joy to the barren Madame Valmondé and a male heir to her plantation-owning husband. Désirée is portrayed as the passively suffering victim of Armand's racial pride and a social system in which her sexual function is her only source of identity and value. The narrative presents only two scenes of direct confrontation between Armand and Désirée. In the second he tells her to leave him; in the first, in which Chopin makes strikingly subtle and restrained use of dialogue, he cruelly puts her in the same category as La Blanche, his ironically named octoroon mistress. In her ongoing examination of the institution of marriage and of woman's place in society, Chopin in "Désirée's Baby" courageously and artfully combines localized setting, situation, and characters to link female bondage with chattel slavery.

"Madame Célestin's Divorce" (written in May 1893 and first published in *Bayou Folk*), one of Chopin's best stories, treats the theme of the independent woman with remarkable honesty, lightness of touch, and conscious artistry. Madame Célestin, the mother of two toddlers and wife of a no-account drunk, who probably beats her and who abandons her for months on end, begins a flirtation with the lawyer Paxton. Paxton encourages her to seek redress in divorce court, an idea which Madame Célestin pursues both with her family and with the Church. The reader and Paxton are convinced Madame Célestin has the determination and independence of mind to carry out a divorce, for she remains undaunted by the arguments against it offered by her family, her confessor, and the bishop: "The Pope himse'f can't make me stan' that any longer, if you say I got the right in the law to sen' Célestin sailing." The independence of her character is shown by her industriousness in finding alternate ways of supporting herself and her children: she takes in sewing and gives music lessons. Every time the reader sees her, she has a broom in her hand and wields it with efficient determination. If she chose to do so, she could sweep Célestin out of her life. It is she who orchestrates her encounters with Paxton, using her broom to punctuate her remarks. There is also a sensuous side to Madame Célestin's nature, suggested by the pink ribbon that she wears at her neck. One morning "Her face seemed to the lawyer to be unusually rosy"– Célestin had returned the night before. She tells Paxton to "neva mine about that divo'ce," clearly preferring Célestin, as the color imagery suggests, because of the sexual attraction he holds for her. Célestin's promise to "turn ova a new leaf" surely rings as false to Madame Célestin as it does to the lawyer; but, the story implies, such matters ultimately have little bearing when a woman loves.

A theme treated with a comic touch in "Madame Célestin's Divorce" comes in for tragic display in "A Lady of Bayou St. John" (*Vogue*, 21 September 1893). Madame Delisle too is lonely and discontented with marriage as circumstances have created it for her. Her husband, Gustave, is away in Virginia with Gen. P. T. Beauregard's troops. She, too, finds sympathy in the eyes of a man not her husband. Sépincourt, a neighboring Frenchman, regards the war only as a disruption to his comforts, while Madame Delisle is a child-woman whose seeming preoccupation with her own beauty and youth is really the manifestation of strange emotional stirrings which she cannot understand. She and Sépincourt quickly exhaust each other intellectually: "a time came–it came very quickly–when they seemed to have nothing more to say to one another." Her husband recedes into the dim mists of memory, but she indulges herself in sentimental kisses upon his portrait. Addicted to imaginative escape through the stories told by her black nurse, she finds a new kind of stimulation for her imagination in Sépincourt's suggestion that they escape her wartorn country by going to Paris together. With this new escape fantasy to occupy her imagination, she can discharge Manna-Loulou from her nightly story-telling duties. In her fantasies, "She had suddenly become a woman capable of love or sacrifice." In the real world, however, she is frightened by the passion she arouses in Sépincourt: "in the quiver of his sensitive lip and the quick beating of a swollen vein in his brown throat ... she withdrew from him, frightened...." In her mind she can become the central figure in a sentimental romantic drama, but the curtain falls on this short-lived fantasy when news of Gustave's death arrives. Returning in the early spring to press his suit upon the young widow, Sépincourt finds that she has made an altar of Gustave's portrait, scarf, and sword and that a world of dead memories is more real to her than the promises of love and life with him in Paris. Her imaginative longings now have some-

thing sustaining upon which to nourish themselves: "My husband has never been so living to me as he is now.... We walk once more together beneath the magnolias...." Like Sépincourt, the reader is left "trying to comprehend that psychological enigma, a woman's heart." Though the reader does not comprehend fully Madame Delisle's heart, she is a credible personality whose motives are buried deep in her particular psychology, most likely in a morbid fear of her own sexuality.

As its frame establishes, "La Belle Zoraïde" (*Vogue*, 4 January 1894) is one of the stories Manna-Loulou tells Madame Delisle to help her fall asleep. All Manna-Loulou's stories are true, "for Madame would hear none but those which were true." Zoraïde, the lady-in-waiting of one of the most fashionable ladies of la rue Royale, is a light-skinned beauty who has been trained by her mistress, Madame Delarivière, to be a valuable commodity on the marriage market. "Remember, Zoraïde," counsels Madame Delarivière, "when you are ready to marry, it must be in a way to do honor to your bringing up. It will be at the Cathedral." Madame chooses for Zoraïde M'sieur Ambroise, the mulatto body servant of Madame's friend Doctor Langlé. Zoraïde, however, has only contempt for M'sieur Ambroise and insists upon marrying her heart's choice, Mésor. To prevent the marriage Madame has Doctor Langlé sell Mésor away to a distant state. By this time, however, Zoraïde is pregnant. In a last effort to control Zoraïde's destiny–"to have her young waiting-maid again at her side, free, happy, and beautiful as of old"–Madame removes Zoraïde's child from her at its birth and tells her falsely that it died. When Zoraïde slips into a physical and mental decline that culminates in her taking a bundle of rags to her breast as her lost infant, Madame attempts to restore Zoraïde's living child to her: "Reaching out a hand she thrust the little one mistrustfully away from her. With the other hand she clasped the rag bundle fiercely to her breast; for she suspected a plot to deprive her of it." Zoraïde, who becomes known as Zoraïde la folle, lives to be an old woman; her child is returned to the plantation, where "she was never to know the love of mother or father." Madame Delisle's expressed sympathies are with "the poor little one"; "better had she died!" is her conclusion. Chopin's ending establishes a strong social theme for the story: the violations of individual freedom and happiness created by a caste system form a poisonous legacy from one generation to the next. Under the grip of this system Madame Delarivière never questions her right to violate the fundamental humanity of someone she professes to love, for under such a system love itself cannot escape corruption.

The most recent story in *Bayou Folk*, "In Sabine" (written in November 1893 and previously unpublished), is about a young Acadian woman who, with the aid of the sympathetic young Creole gallant Grégoire Santien, succeeds in breaking away from her abusive husband, Bud Aiken. Grégoire earlier figured in Chopin's first novel, *At Fault*, and the Santien brothers are recurring characters in Chopin's Louisiana stories. 'Tite Reine is a prisoner in her husband's cabin, for in spite of her spunk and because of her illiteracy–itself a comment upon female education–she cannot even write a letter to her family. The story's humor resides in the ease with which Grégoire and 'Tite Reine dupe Aiken. But what keeps this story from being just a scintillating piece of local-color writing is its complex psychological base. For one thing, Chopin seems to be using the device of the alter ego to add psychological complexity. Bud Aiken recognizes in Grégoire "a spirit not altogether uncongenial to his own," for Grégoire's essential nature is violent too. When 'Tite Reine tells him of Aiken's drunken beatings of her, Grégoire wonders "if it would really be a criminal act to go then and there and shoot the top of Bud Aiken's head off." Though the "inward revolt" of 'Tite Reine is Chopin's primary interest, the peculiarities of male psychology also interest her. For example, the narrative establishes an identity between Aiken and Buckeye, "an unkempt, vicious-looking little Texas pony" that is Aiken's prized possession. Buckeye is also associated with Aiken's pride of masculine supremacy: when 'Tite Reine complained to Aiken of the monotony of her life, he suggested that she ride Buckeye "knowing that the little brute wouldn't carry a woman; . . . it had amused him to witness her distress and terror when she was thrown to the ground." Thus, when Aiken hears that with Grégoire's help his wife has left him and that Grégoire was riding Buckeye, Aiken's humiliation is compounded. The outwitting of Aiken does not stop there, however, for the person who has the pleasure of delivering this news to Aiken is Mortimer, a black farmer with whom Aiken shares the crop and who, undaunted by Aiken's violent nature, acted as 'Tite Reine's protector until Grégoire arrived. When Mortimer arms himself with an ax before delivering the news, the sym-

bolic emasculation of Aiken is complete, for he is blocked from venting his rage upon a member of a race he considers inferior.

A Night in Acadie, published in November 1897, contains twenty stories and sketches. The stories make use of the same Louisiana settings and employ some of the same characters that figure in *Bayou Folk*. Published by the little-known firm of Way and Williams in Chicago, *A Night in Acadie* received fewer reviews than *Bayou Folk*. Though the notices were quite favorable, they were somewhat less enthusiastic than those for the earlier collection. The largest proportion of the stories collected in *A Night in Acadie* were written in 1895, though stories composed as early as December 1891 and as late as the spring of 1896 were included as well. In this second collection the psychological themes become bolder, for the internal conflicts portrayed are rooted in the passions, which can be a source sometimes of destruction, at other times of liberation.

"A Respectable Woman" (*Vogue*, 15 February 1894) leaves its heroine on the verge of adultery. The boldness of Chopin's handling of the theme is remarkable, for Mrs. Baroda is not even unhappy in her marriage. The reader is told that after a winter in New Orleans, "She was looking forward to a period of . . . undisturbed tête-à-tête with her husband. . . . " Her husband "was also her friend," which may to some extent suggest that a certain note of sexual boredom has entered their marriage. Her husband, Gaston, has invited an old college friend, the journalist Gouvernail, to visit their plantation for a week or two. Though Mrs. Baroda has heard a great deal about Gouvernail, she has never met him. When she does, she feels a strong and immediate sexual attraction to him that throws her into a state of mental confusion. She decides to leave for New Orleans, but before she does, Chopin gives the reader a direct look at the feelings of a woman aroused by the presence of a man to whom she feels sexually attracted: "Her mind only vaguely grasped what he was saying. Her physical being was for the moment predominant. She was not thinking of his words, only drinking in the tones of his voice. She wanted to reach out her hand in the darkness and touch him with the sensitive tips of her fingers upon the face or the lips. She wanted to draw close to him and whisper against his cheek–she did not care what–. . . ." She then fights an internal battle over what to do about these feelings. Resolute at first, she refuses to allow Gouvernail to be invited back during the summer. "However, before the year ended, she proposed, wholly from herself, to have Gouvernail visit them again." Her husband expresses his surprise and pleasure upon learning that she has overcome her dislike of Gouvernail, to which she replies, "I have overcome everything! You will see. This time I shall be very nice to him." Chopin's ironic use of color symbolism prepares for her heroine's implied capitulation at story's end. One night Mrs. Baroda has seated herself upon an outdoor bench. Her husband has Gouvernail bring her "a filmy, white scarf with which she sometimes enveloped her head and shoulders" to protect her against the dangers of the night air. "She accepted the scarf from him with a murmur of thanks, and let it lie in her lap." By declining to wrap herself in the white scarf that symbolizes her wedding vows, she symbolically asserts her independence of them.

"Regret" (*Century*, May 1895) tells the story of Mamzelle Aurélie, a physically strong, self-sufficient, determined woman of fifty who efficiently manages a farm and wears a man's hat, an old blue army overcoat, and topboots when the ·weather calls for it. At twenty she turned down the only marriage proposal she received and "had not yet lived to regret it." When circumstances conspire to place "a small band of very small children" in her care for two weeks, she learns, however, that she would have lived a much happier, more fulfilled life if she had a family. Ironically, this self-knowledge comes too late. This summary does not do justice to the artistry of Chopin's handling of her materials. The lightness of touch, the narrative detachment that nevertheless regards its protagonist with sympathy and understanding, the economy of dialogue, and the sure handling of the local-color elements in the service of characterization show that Chopin has mastered her form.

"A Sentimental Soul" (*New Orleans Times-Democrat*, 22 December 1895) tells the story of Mamzelle Fleurette, whose desire to cherish the memory of the dead Lacodie, another woman's husband whom she has loved from afar, leads her to rebel against the established order: "There was a great, a terrible upheaval taking place in Mamzelle Fleurette's soul. She was preparing for the first time in her life to take her conscience into her own keeping." She finds a new confessor at a church in another section of town so that she can tend the grave and preserve Lacodie's memory as she chooses. There is much light humor at Mamzelle's expense–something of the mock he-

roic in Chopin's handling of Mamzelle's growing independence of mind–but the reader never loses interest in or sympathy for the moral dilemma of this being tortured by the conflict between body and soul. Chopin's target for her sharpest satire seems to be the view espoused by Mamzelle's church that the human psyche is irreconcilably divided into the eternally warring factions of body and soul; she gives her protagonist the courage to arrive at a resolution of her conflict that reconciles the two into a kind of whole, one in which soul does not bruise body, as William Butler Yeats would say.

'Polyte, the responsible young store manager on Mr. Mathurin's plantation in "Azélie" (*Century*, December 1894), learns about the destructive power of love. So strong is his passionate longing for Azélie that he resigns his job to follow her back to Little River, a place 'Polyte associates with the grave: "To me it's like a person mus' die, one way or otha, w'en they go on Li'le river." Long before 'Polyte discovers what has destroyed his peace of mind and led him to choose a kind of moral death, the imagistic qualities associated with the moon foreshadow his fate: "The edge of the moon crept up–a keen, curved blade of light above the dark line of the cotton-field." 'Polyte's feelings for Azélie are purely sexual; in fact, they do not assert themselves with any urgency until after he has caught her trying to steal goods from the store: "The very action which should have revolted him had seemed, on the contrary, to inflame him with love. He felt that love to be a degradation. . . ; and he knew that he was hopelessly unable to stifle it." Azélie embodies the amoral, rebellious, instinctual forces in 'Polyte's nature: his obsessive longing for sexual union with her is actually a manifestation of the longing for freedom and expression of the repressed side of his own personality. In "Azélie" Chopin provides a specifically sexual context within which to treat a broader theme–the mysterious influence of the unconscious mind on human behavior.

In "Caline" (*Vogue*, 20 May 1893) the young heroine's sexual awakening leads her to disillusionment; in "Athénaïse" (*Atlantic Monthly*, August and September 1896) the protagonist wakes to a sense of identity and fulfillment. A story of some thirteen thousand words, "Athénaïse" shows Chopin at the very height of her artistic powers. The story is remarkable for the economy and precision with which the psychology of the main characters is etched. After her marriage to Cazeau, a well-

Letter to Chicago publisher Stone and Kimball regarding a collection of stories and sketches that may have been an early version of A Vocation and a Voice *(Kate Chopin Collection [#9442-a], Clifton Waller Barrett Library, Special Collections Department, University of Virginia Library)* established and respected Cane River widower, Athénaïse discovers that she has "a constitutional disinclination for marriage." The narrative description and the imagery indicate that the sources of her disinclination are to some extent in Athénaïse's sexual immaturity; but, more significantly, they lie in her sense that marriage, especially the sexual side of it, is an invasion of her sense of self, though it is through indirection that we learn the true nature of her objections: "I can't stan' to live with a man; to have him always there; his coats an' pantaloons hanging in my room; his ugly bare feet–washing them in my tub, befo' my very eyes, ugh!" She longs for "a blessed life in the convent," where she would be absolved from such violations of her being. With the help of her brother Montéclin, who aids her out of a grudge against Cazeau and his own romantic sense of youthful adventure and revolt, Athénaïse secrets herself in New Orleans. Her first action is to order two new dresses, one of sprigged muslin and another "pure white" to announce to the world the inviolate state of her being now that she has slipped her matrimonial yoke. She chooses the sprigged muslin to wear on a lake outing with Gouvernail, the same journalist who so attracts Mrs. Baroda in "A Respectable Woman," suggesting the eternal tension within the soul between retraction into self and extension toward the other. Gouvernail already knows what during the course of the story Cazeau has to learn through a painful encounter with the past: that unless a marriage is based on mutual love and free, mature choice, it is no marriage at all: "He [Gouvernail] hoped some day to hold her with a lover's arms. That she was married made no particle of difference to Gouvernail . . . when the time came that she wanted him, . . . he felt he would have a right to her. So long as she did not want him, he had no right to her,–no more than her husband had." Cazeau confronts this fundamental human truth for the first time through a discomfiting recollection he has while bringing Athénaïse back home after the first time she has run away to her parents' home: he realizes the parallel between his bringing Athénaïse home and his father's bringing in a runaway slave and finds the whole impression "hideous." Cazeau comes to recognize that the conventions of marriage can violate individual freedom as monstrously as can chattel slavery. Chopin's portrait of Cazeau is one of the most-fully realized in her canon, making it possible for the reader to sympathize with both him and Athénaïse as each

makes a symbolic journey into fuller knowledge. Cazeau expresses his hard-won insights in a letter to Athénaïse: "he disclaimed any further intention of forcing his commands upon her. He did not desire her presence ever again in his home unless she came of her free will, uninfluenced by family or friends. . . ." As for Athénaïse, when she learns that she is pregnant, "Her whole being was steeped in a wave of ecstasy. . . . Cazeau must know. As she thought of him, the first purely sensuous tremor of her life swept over her. . . . Her whole passionate nature was aroused as if by a miracle." More fortunate than Ma'ame Pélagie or Mamzelle Aurélie, Athénaïse finds sexual awakening and the promise of fulfillment and self-knowledge. Her spiritual reconciliation is indicated by her new concern for others. She makes little gifts of her belongings to the servant Pousette; she buys "little presents for nearly everybody she knew." Moreover, for the first time she begins to think of herself as Cazeau's wife, as evidenced by the confidence with which she draws money from her husband's account merchant. In this beautifully crafted story Chopin shows that marriage, if conceived in justice, has the potential to be a liberating, maturing force.

On 20 January 1897 one of the editors at Houghton, Mifflin returned Chopin's third collection of stories, *A Vocation and a Voice*, with a note suggesting that Chopin might have greater success publishing a novel. Later the same year she began writing *The Awakening*, but she continued to seek a publisher for her collection. In March 1898 Way and Williams accepted both *The Awakening* and a second version of *A Vocation and a Voice*. Not long afterward, however, they went out of business and transferred the rights to Herbert S. Stone and Company of Chicago, which published *The Awakening* on 22 April 1899, but in February 1900 the publisher returned *A Vocation and a Voice* without explanation. The list of stories to be collected under this title went through several versions, for Chopin continued to seek a publisher for the collection almost until the time of her death. In his 1932 biography of Chopin, Daniel Rankin listed the stories and sketches projected for the second version of the collection, which is growing in critical recognition as Chopin's best work next to *The Awakening*: "A Vocation and a Voice," "Elizabeth Stock's One Story," "Two Portraits," "An Idle Fellow," "A Mental Suggestion," "An Egyptian Cigarette," "The White Eagle," "The Story of an Hour," "Two Summers and Two Souls," "Night," "Juanita," "The Unexpected," "Her Letters," "The Kiss," "Suzette," "Fedora," "The Recovery," "The Blind Man," "A Morning's Walk," "Lilacs," "Ti Démon," and "The Godmother."

The composition dates of the stories in *A Vocation and a Voice* (collected for the first time in *The Complete Works of Kate Chopin*, 1969) fall within a six-year period extending from spring 1894 to spring 1900. The best stories in this collection, in their universality of theme and in the honesty with which they explore human passions and the complicated relationship between the self and society, establish Chopin as a writer of major importance in the early development of the modern short story.

In "The Story of an Hour" (*Vogue*, 6 December 1894) the death of Mrs. Mallard's husband brings upon the young widow a confrontation with her essential self. She learns that it is not love but the "possession of self-assertion" that is "The strongest impulse of her being." She welcomes the freedom and independence of the years before her in which "she would live for herself." With the death of her husband, Mrs. Mallard awakes to a new consciousness of self, just as nature has moved into spring, the period of nature's cycle awakening. In fact, Mrs. Mallard is sensitively attuned to nature, for it is the sounds and fragrances and signs of spring that inspire her inner explorations. In the story's surprise ending Brently Mallard, who has not died in the train crash as thought, walks unharmed through the door, and the shock brings a fatal heart attack upon his wife. Only the reader knows of the anarchic thoughts that Mrs. Mallard entertained in her last hour. Ironically, the doctors, representing the male-dominated establishment, think she died of the "joy that kills." As in *The Awakening*, Chopin seems unable to conceive of a fully enlightened woman's finding a place in society as it was then constituted: after their enlightenment, the two most self-conscious characters in her fiction–Mrs. Mallard and Edna Pontellier–find in death the release from the frustrations of living at odds with a society that forces repression and role confinement upon its female population.

In May 1894, a month after writing "The Story of an Hour," Chopin was still exploring the psychology of the independent-minded woman in conflict with herself and her society. "Lilacs" (*New Orleans Times-Democrat*, 20 December 1896) follows a neat circular structure composed of three scenes. In the first, Madame Adrienne Farival, a young widow living in Paris, returns for the fourth consecutive year to spend a fortnight among the sisters at the convent school she attended as a girl. She luxuriates in the sensuous pleasures of the rural spring and delights in the wholesome and robust playfulness she shares with the nuns in their recreational hours. In returning to the simplicities of an all-female world, she symbolically returns to the preadolescent state of innocence and security. But the restraints upon her independence and her individuality which sent her as an adolescent up a tree "to see if she could get a glimpse of Paris" also keep her in Paris fifty weeks out of the fifty-two. The next scene shows Adrienne in Paris, where she is called Mademoiselle, not Madame, indicating that her widowhood might be a fabrication. The reader also learns that Adrienne is a successful performer, probably a singer in light opera, and that she has a lover; that, in short, she is a woman of the world with perhaps extravagantly sensual habits. The settings are aptly chosen to represent the two contrary states of mind which define the protagonist's character. In Paris Adrienne's apartment is furnished luxuriously. It is characterized by a "picturesque disorder. Musical scores were scattered upon the open piano. Thrown carelessly over the backs of chairs were puzzling and astonishing-looking garments." Adrienne herself is shown pelting her exasperated maid in the face with hothouse roses and then shaking her "till the white cap wobbled on her head." The third scene depicts Adrienne's return to the convent the next spring, when the urgent call to innocence and simplicity, signaled by the lilacs coming into bloom, sweeps Adrienne away from her new lover and from "a breakfast of a hundred francs" ordered for the next morning. This time, however, she is denied entrance at the door, her expensive gifts to the convent of previous years are returned, and she is handed a letter that "banished her forever from this haven of peace, where her soul was wont to come and refresh itself."

Like William Blake, Chopin was interested in the two contrary states of the human soul, innocence and experience; and, like Blake, she recognized that the instinctual longings for both states must find expression in a mode of being that reconciles them rather than keeping them divided from each other. Those who remain cloistered from the world and its taints are just as psychologically fractured as the Adriennes of the world, as Chopin makes clear in her characterization of Sister Agathe, who weeps bitter tears when her contact with the world through Adrienne is severed. In spite of the inconsistency of tone in the handling of the three scenes–the middle scene employs some of the antics of a music hall variety show–the story offers an interesting treatment of the theme of the divided self that so preoccupied the greatest writers of the nineteenth century and which was of especial concern to Chopin in the stories she collected in *A Vocation and a Voice.*

In "Her Letters" (*Vogue*, 11 and 18 April 1895) Chopin treats female sexuality with the frankness that characterizes her treatment of the theme in *The Awakening* and an 1898 story, "The Storm." The characters in "Her Letters" are a middle-aged, apparently childless wife and her husband, both of whom remain nameless throughout the story. Four years before, the wife's passionate love affair with an unnamed lover ended. Seriously ill from some wasting disease, the wife attempts to destroy her letters, but she realizes that to do so would deprive her of the spiritual sustenance necessary to life. Though generally perceived as cold and passionless by her husband and her friends, the wife has become in fact fully acquainted with her capacity for passion: her lover "had changed the water in her veins to wine, whose taste had brought delirium to both of them." Chopin draws a powerfully graphic scene to show the woman's hunger for the life and love slipping from her: "With her sharp white teeth she tore the far corner from the letter, where the name was written; she bit the torn scrap and tasted it between her lips and upon her tongue like some god-given morsel." Unable to destroy the letters, but fearful of hurting her husband should he read them after her death, she settles upon a plan to appeal to his sense of honor. She leaves the letters in an unsealed bundle with a note reading "I leave this package to the care of my husband. With perfect faith in his loyalty and love, I ask him to destroy it unopened." The remainder of the story is devoted to the psychological analysis of a husband whose "man-instinct of possession" has been aroused by doubt of his wife's fidelity. He casts the package unopened into the river, but the knowledge that his wife had a life unknown to him destroys his sense of identity and purpose and leaves him marooned alone in a "black, boundless universe"; he finds his only solace in suicide.

"A Vocation and a Voice" (*St. Louis Mirror*, 27 March 1902) is one of Chopin's longest–some eleven thousand words–and most finely woven stories. Written much earlier–in November

1896–it brings together her major themes and treats them within the mythic context of the journey to self-knowledge. Brother Ludovic does a better job of psychic integration than Adrienne Farival in "Lilacs" or Edna Pontellier in *The Awakening.* And unlike the first-person narrator in "An Egyptian Cigarette" (*Vogue*, 19 April 1900), written half a year later, he transcends his earlier fear of the dark mysteries hidden in his own psyche: rather than continue a life of repression and denial, he takes to the road again on an arduous journey toward psychic wholeness, toward integration of the instinctual and the social in his own nature.

The story's initially unnamed protagonist, a young boy who has been sent on an errand into the outskirts of the city by his foster mother, confuses the directions given to him and finds himself marooned at the entrance to Woodland Park without money for a return trip. Discovering a harmony and a reality in nature that he has never known in the city, he recognizes that he "belonged under God's sky in the free and open air." Because he has no real roots in the city, he is free to take up with a pair of "movers"–Gutro, a hawker of herbal medicines, and Suzima, an "Egyptian" fortune-teller. Suzima is really Susan, a twenty-year-old girl who befriends the boy and defends him against the drunken Gutro, whom Susan calls the Beast and whose only care is for his two mules. On their long journey south for the winter, the boy develops a mystical awareness of nature: "he felt as if he were alone and holding communion with something mysterious, greater than himself, that reached out from the far distance to touch him. . . ." Because he is unable to give expression to his feelings himself, the song Susan sings in her moments of joy and harmony while walking beside the wagon becomes in the boy's mind the symbol of life lived in the freedom and harmony of nature. The biological changes associated with puberty soon bring him in touch with another aspect of nature. The sight of Susan naked arouses in him the complex emotions of sexual desire which, when consummated, bring him into even closer sympathy with the whole living universe. But these changes in him also bring about a crisis that forces him to confront the destructive power of his passions and instincts. In a fit of jealous, protective rage, he almost kills Gutro: "He had never dreamed of a devil lurking unknown to him, in his blood, that would someday blind him, disable his will and direct his hands to deeds of violence." Up to this point in the story Chopin's interest has been in the impact of biology and instinct upon the boy's psychological development. When the boy becomes conscious of the conflict between the elements in his makeup, he withdraws in fear to the safety of a monastery and there seeks to imprison all that he fears within himself behind a massive wall that he builds around the cloister with his own hands. In choosing his vocation, however, he has denied the voice whose song rises from his unconscious in haunting dreams. One day while laboring at his wall, Brother Ludovic, as he is now called, hears Susan's voice: "The trowel fell from Brother Ludovic's hand and he leaned upon the wall and listened; not now like a frightened animal at the approach of danger." Chopin has brought her character to the brink of psychological maturity, for in conquering his fear of the dark elements within him, which are also the sources of creativity and psychic energy, he can now set out on the journey that can lead to spiritual wholeness: "Brother Ludovic bounded down from the wall and followed the voice of the woman." Though there is no guarantee that Brother Ludovic will reconcile vocation and voice–the call of society with the call of the self–Chopin seems to want her readers to think that the possibility is there.

The story has a few failures; for example, Chopin's attempts at a kind of mock-epic hyperbole do not have the desired comic effect but come off merely as stilted and overblown language. Yet in its symbolic handling of setting to reflect the psychology of her characters, in its thematic richness, and in its plot interest, "A Vocation and a Voice" is one of Chopin's best stories.

"Ti Démon" (written in November 1899 and first published in *The Complete Works*), one of the few good stories Chopin wrote after the critical failure of *The Awakening*, treats another universal theme: that of the fall brought about by hubris. Chopin's protagonist is a good man, better than the general run even, a man whose eyes "reflected a peaceful soul." As in Greek tragedy, Ti Démon's punishment seems far greater than his offense. With classic economy and inevitability Chopin traces the protagonist's move from a position of respect and love to that of social outcast. Using with consummate skill the elements of local color to ground her tale, she places the source of Ti Démon's fall fully within his own character: "Perhaps no other man in town could so have tempted and prevailed with Ti Démon. It

flattered his self-complacency to be seen walking down the street with Aristides whose distinction of manner was unquestionable, whose grace and amiability made him an object of envy with the men and a creature to be worshipped by susceptible women." Thus it is that Ti Démon wavers from his Saturday night routine and goes with Aristides Bonneau to a tavern. There the atmosphere, charged with drinking and gambling, clouds the rational, peace-loving side of Ti Démon's mind and frees the irrational elements in his makeup: he nearly kills Aristides with his bare hands when he finds him walking along the moonlit road with his fiancée. "That was Ti Démon's one and only demoniacal outburst during his life, but it affected the community in an inexplicable way," comments the narrator with all the ironic understatement of a Greek chorus.

Another late story projected for inclusion in the unpublished third collection is "The White Eagle" (*Vogue*, 12 July 1900), in which Chopin shows her mastery in the skillful and unobtrusive use of symbolism for ironic effect and in the use of symbolic settings for representing the psychology of her characters. Chopin also achieves a remarkable consistency in narrative voice, which is almost reportorial in its detachment. The bird of the title is a cast-iron eagle with outspread wings. The story presents the psychological history of the woman to whom the bird is a much-prized possession, for it becomes an emblem of her childhood dreams of the future. The statue comes into her private possession when the family estate is divided among the heirs. Through lack of financial expertise, the woman loses her small estate and becomes a seamstress to support herself; "No mate came to seek her out." She lives out her life in a single overstuffed room of a tenement building, where the eagle occupies a dark corner. After her death a relative places the statue at the head of the woman's grave.

Clearly a masculine image, the eagle embodies the woman's dreams for sexual fulfillment through marriage and family. In her old age these dreams turn into unconscious frustrations and disappointments that prey upon her: on her deathbed, she has a nightmare vision in which the eagle, leaving its dark corner, "perched upon her, pecking at her bosom." In the opening and closing sentences of the story, the narrator describes the eagle's expression as one "which in a human being would pass for wisdom." The eagle, then, also represents the whole sum of questionable social wisdom that would limit women's chances for self-fulfillment to those ordained by biology. In the course of a lifetime of diminishing opportunities, the woman has moved from the spacious lawn of her childhood homestead to a series of cramped rooms to finally a coffin placed in a grave that after her interment sinks "unkept to the level." In a final image that captures the irony inherent in the statue's symbolism, the reader is told, "With the sinking grave the white eagle has dipped forward as if about to take his flight." Chopin's ironic ending carries clear social implications–implications not far removed from those of *The Awakening*: women's chances for spiritual fulfillment are sadly limited in a society that sees their primary value in their biological functions as wives and mothers.

Several of Chopin's most important stories were not collected during her lifetime. After their publication in Per Seyersted's edition of *The Complete Works of Kate Chopin* in 1969, these stories have increasingly attracted critical praise and reader interest, as evidenced by their recurring appearance in anthologies. In the best of these stories, composed over a four-and-a-half-year period from late 1895 to April 1900, Chopin produced psychological portraits striking in their artistic integrity and stunning in the frankness of their subject matter.

In "A Pair of Silk Stockings" (*Vogue*, 16 September 1897) the protagonist, Mrs. Sommers, receives an unexpected boon of fifteen dollars. Intending to buy much-needed clothing for her brood of children, she instead buys new silk stockings and well-fitting leather shoes and gloves for herself and treats herself to expensive magazines, an exquisite lunch at a fashionable restaurant, and a matinee at the theater. In this crisply drawn psychological portrait with its touches of irony, Chopin makes no direct judgment of her protagonist, whose actions and thoughts reveal a character with a fully realized psychology. In marrying, Mrs. Sommers left a life much easier and more comfortable than her present one. Her reduced circumstances have forced her to be a bargain hunter: "she had learned to clutch a piece of goods and hold it and stick to it with persistence and determination till her turn came to be served, no matter when it came." She is sometimes appalled by a vision of the future as "some dim, gaunt monster," but the absorbing needs of the present have taught her to live with a reckless disregard for the future, for "luckily tomorrow never comes." As Chopin uses it, this cliché is rich in ambiguity, for it provides insights into

Mrs. Sommers's character that prepare the reader for the hedonism of her subsequent actions. Mrs. Sommers's possession of the fifteen dollars "gave her a feeling of importance such as she had not enjoyed for years." During her shopping expedition she stops to rest at the hosiery counter. She at first only caresses the stockings. Then with both hands she holds "them up to see them glisten, and to feel them glide serpent-like through her fingers." The imagery evokes the story of Eve, also a sensuous woman, who succumbed to the snake's entreaties because she was promised a new sense of place and respect in the hierarchy of existence. Mrs. Sommers's purchases are tastefully chosen to present her in a better light to the world and to herself. After her spree Mrs. Sommers is left with the poignant wish' that the cable car taking her home would never stop.

Two other stories that Chopin never included in a collection are of current interest to scholars and readers: "Elizabeth Stock's One Story" (written in March 1898 and first published in the Missouri Historical Society *Bulletin*, January 1963) and "Vagabonds" (written in December 1895 and first published in Rankin's 1932 biography). Each makes use of a first-person narrator; but "Elizabeth Stock's One Story" is a story unusually contrived, saccharine, and moralistic for Chopin, while "Vagabonds," skillfully employing the device of the alter ego, is one of Chopin's artistic explorations into human psychology. The narrator is a woman of substantial family and social position who seems to have a plantation to run. The vagabond is Valcour, a distant relation of the narrator, who has asked to see her. Though the narrator does not understand fully why he wants to see her, the reader understands that Valcour has sensed a spiritual kinship with her, which is apparent in the ease with which they slip into unrestrained banter on subjects and in an idiom the woman would never use with members of her own class. Valcour is associated in the narrator's mind with the earth and with nature: "His clothes, his battered hat, his skin, his straggling beard which he never shaved, were all of one color–the color of clay." She quizzes him about his life as a wanderer; he tells her how he lives off the land, content to take what nature puts in his way: "I called him names; but all the same I could not help thinking that it must be good to prowl sometimes; to get close to the black night and lose oneself in its silence and mystery." By keeping her rendezvous with Valcour, she can enter the world of the vagabond for a short time

First page of the manuscript for a story written in July 1898 and posthumously published in the 1969 collection of Chopin's works (Missouri Historical Society, St. Louis) and satisfy an unrealized side of her own nature, so that the story is aptly titled "Vagabonds," plural.

"A Family Affair" (*Saturday Evening Post*, 9 September 1899) tells the story of a greedy, grasping, miserly old woman, grossly fat and confined to a wheelchair, who is outmaneuvered by her young niece, whom she brought in to keep house for her. In general Chopin uses local-color devices to achieve her effects, but the honesty of its conclusion gives it a place among Chopin's realistic works. After the niece has left to marry the young doctor whom she has called in to treat her aunt, the unregenerated old woman, outraged at the niece's management of her affairs, gets up from her wheelchair and is last seen tyrannically reversing all the improvements instituted by the niece and calling for a lawyer.

"The Storm," written on 19 July 1898 but not published until 1969 in *The Complete Works*, has won general critical acceptance as Chopin's finest short story. Through the perfect subordination of setting, atmosphere, and character to theme, Chopin reached the peak of her artistic development. The story is subtitled "A Sequel to 'The 'Cadian Ball' '" and treats the chance encounter of Calixta and Alcée five or six years after their flirtation at the Acadian ball was interrupted by Clarisse's claiming Alcée for herself. "At the 'Cadian Ball" (*Two Tales*, 22 October 1892; collected in *Bayou Folk*) is one of Chopin's best pieces of local-color writing, but it lacks the thematic richness and psychological realism of her best stories. Only around two thousand words in length, "The Storm" proceeds through five divisions constituting three dramatic scenes followed by two divisions using nondramatic means to reveal the relationship between Alcée and Clarisse. In the first scene Calixta's husband, Bobinôt, and their son, Bibi, are shown waiting out a violent summer storm at Friedheimer's store. In the next scene Alcée takes refuge against the same storm at Bobinôt's house, where Calixta is home alone. Chopin makes masterly use of dialogue to suggest the growing sexual tension between them: "If this keeps up, *Dieu sait* if the levees goin' to stan' it," exclaims Calixta. Sexually aroused by Alcée's passionate desire for her, Calixta releases the "generous abundance of her passion," which is like "a white flame which penetrated and found response in depths of his own sensuous nature that had never yet been reached." In their lovemaking both tap the rich resources of their own and the other's sexual pas-

Kate Chopin, 1899 (Missouri Historical Society, St. Louis)

sion and in so doing renew themselves in the life-giving sources of nature. In statement and imagery stunningly frank for the time, Chopin describes Calixta's sexual awakening in positive terms that link sexual fulfillment with the life-sustaining forces of nature: "Her firm, elastic flesh that was knowing for the first time its birthright, was like a creamy lily that the sun invites to contribute its breath and perfume to the undying life of the world."

The next scene describes Bobinôt's rather anxious homecoming, for Calixta has become "an over-scrupulous housewife." Both Bobinôt and Bibi are delighted to find Calixta in an unusually good humor, and the evening ends in much happiness and merrymaking for the little family. Alcée writes Clarisse "a loving letter, full of tender solicitude," telling her not to hurry back. Clarisse feels relieved to have her release from their "intimate conjugal life" extended for a while longer. The fundamental nature of neither marriage is disturbed by the encounter. Chopin never tried to publish "The Storm," for the unfavorable critical reception of *The Awakening* taught her that the literary establishment would not accept such bold treatments of human sexuality.

Less important is "Charlie" (written in April 1900 and first published in *The Complete Works*), a lengthy and loosely structured story that treats a young tomboy's awakening to her own femininity. Through much of the story the author's major interest is in Charlie as an eccentric, at times to the point of patronizing her. Until the last part of the story, there is little emphasis on the inner workings of the characters' minds and a great deal on their social behavior. After the maiming of Charlie's father and Charlie's return from finishing school in New Orleans to run the plantation, however, Chopin treats the relationship between Charlie and her father with the psychological truth and artistic subtlety of her best works.

Kate Chopin exerted no influence upon the realist writers of her day or upon those who followed her: there is no evidence that she was read by Willa Cather or Ellen Glasgow, women writers of whom she is an important forerunner. Categorized by literary historians as a Louisiana local colorist to be included with George Washington Cable, Lafcadio Hearn, Grace King, and Ruth McEnery Stuart, Chopin has had to wait until the third quarter of the twentieth century for an accurate assessment of her literary significance. Earlier there were a few isolated voices speaking with sensitivity to Chopin's accomplishment: for example, Leonidas Rutledge Whipple, in his entry on Chopin in the *Library of Southern Literature* (1907), acknowledged the "delicate sensuous realism" of her stories; and in 1939 Shields McIlwaine recognized that Kate Chopin had "joined the movement away from local color and propaganda toward a purer art" and that her primary concern was with "emotional reality."

Two European scholars have led the way toward the general recognition of Chopin as a pioneering American realist. In 1952 Cyrille Arnavon published a French translation of *The Awakening* with an introduction that discusses the novel as an important work in early American literary realism. His essay has been republished in *A Kate Chopin Miscellany* (1979). Per Seyersted's 1963 reconsideration of Chopin, which was included with six Chopin stories (four previously unpublished) in the Missouri Historical Society *Bulletin*, labeled Chopin a "forgotten early realist." In 1969 Seyersted published his critical biography of Chopin and *The Complete Works*, launching the major reassessment of Chopin in the 1970s. Seyersted shows that in applying a "unique pessimistic realism" to woman's unchanging condition, Chopin "broke new ground in American literature"; she is allied more closely with Theodore Dreiser than with any other American writer of her day.

In the first half of the twentieth century critics treated the stories and generally ignored *The Awakening;* beginning in the late 1950s, however, critics tended to view the stories as marred by local colorism and to praise the thematic realism and artistry of *The Awakening.* Larzer Ziff's comments are representative: he finds the situations in the stories "conventionalized" and even exploited for quaintness; the novel "was the most important piece of fiction about the sexual life of a woman written to date in America. . . ." In the 1970s, however, critics devoted more attention to the individual stories and gave greater place to Chopin's short story in their assessments of her literary achievement. In the wake of this new expression of interest a flurry of editions of selected stories by Chopin came out, many with laudatory prefaces. Helen Taylor's edition of twenty-nine stories from Chopin's three collections, *Portraits* (1979), includes an introduction that classifies Chopin among the nineteenth-century female local colorists who were the literary ancestors of such twentieth-century women writers as Willa Cather, Eudora Welty, Carson McCullers, and Flannery O'Connor.

Bibliographies:

Marlene Springer, *Edith Wharton and Kate Chopin: A Reference Guide* (Boston: G. K. Hall, 1976);

Jerry T. Williams, *Southern Literature, 1968-1975: A Checklist of Scholarship* (Boston: G. K. Hall, 1978), pp. 55-57;

Tonette Bond Inge, "Kate Chopin," in *American Women Writers: Bibliographical Essays*, edited by Maurice Duke, Jackson R. Bryer, and M. Thomas Inge (Westport, Conn.: Greenwood Press, 1983), pp. 47-69.

Biographies:

Daniel Rankin, *Kate Chopin and Her Creole Stories* (Philadelphia: University of Pennsylvania Press, 1932);

Per Seyersted, *Kate Chopin: A Critical Biography* (Baton Rouge: Louisiana State University Press, 1969);

Emily Toth, *Kate Chopin* (New York: Atheneum, forthcoming 1989).

References:

George Arms, "Kate Chopin's *The Awakening* in the Perspective of Her Literary Career," in *Essays in American Literature in Honor of Jay B. Hubbell*, edited by Clarence Gohdes (Durham, N.C.: Duke University Press, 1967), pp. 215-228;

Robert D. Arner, "Kate Chopin," *Louisiana Studies*, 14 (Spring 1975): 11-139;

Arner, "Pride and Prejudice: Kate Chopin's 'Désirée's Baby,'" *Mississippi Quarterly*, 25 (Spring 1972): 131-140;

Bert Bender, "Kate Chopin's Lyric Short Stories," *Studies in Short Fiction*, 11 (Summer 1974): 257-266;

Thomas Bonner, Jr., "Kate Chopin's European Consciousness," *American Literary Realism*, 8 (Summer 1975): 281-284;

Margaret Culley, ed., *Kate Chopin, The Awakening: An Authoritative Text, Contexts, Criticism* (New York: Norton, 1976);

Barbara Ewell, *Kate Chopin* (New York: Unger, 1986);

Clarence Gohdes, "Exploitation of the Provinces," in *The Literature of the American People: An Historical and Critical Survey*, edited by Arthur Hobson Quinn (New York: Appleton-Century-Crofts, 1951), pp. 639-660;

Kate Chopin Newsletter (Spring 1975-Winter 1976-1977); titled *Regionalism and the Female Imagination* (Spring 1977-Winter 1979);

Patricia Hopkins Lattin, "Kate Chopin's Repeating Characters," *Mississippi Quarterly*, 33 (Winter 1979-1980): 19-37;

Shields McIlwaine, *The Southern Poor-White from Lubberland to Tobacco Road* (Norman: University of Oklahoma Press, 1939);

Joseph J. Reilly, "Something About Kate Chopin," in his *Of Books and Men* (New York: Julian Messner, 1942), pp. 130-136;

James E. Rocks, "Kate Chopin's Ironic Vision," *Revue de Louisiane/Louisiana Review*, 2 (Winter 1972): 110-120;

Per Seyersted, "Kate Chopin: An Important St. Louis Writer Reconsidered," Missouri Historical Society *Bulletin*, 19 (January 1963): 89-114;

Seyersted and Emily Toth, eds., *A Kate Chopin Miscellany* (Natchitoches, La.: Northwestern State University Press, 1979);

Merrill M. Skaggs, *The Folk of Southern Fiction* (Athens: University of Georgia Press, 1972);

Peggy Skaggs, "The Boy's Quest in Kate Chopin's 'A Vocation and a Voice,'" *American Literature*, 51 (May 1979): 270-276;

Cynthia G. Wolff, "Kate Chopin and the Fiction of Limits: 'Désirée's Baby,'" *Southern Literary Journal*, 10 (Spring 1978): 123-133;

Larzer Ziff, *The American 1890s: Life and Times of a Lost Generation* (New York: Viking, 1966), pp. 296-305.

Papers:

The primary repository of the Kate Chopin materials is the Missouri Historical Society. This collection includes all but one and a part of another of the extant manuscripts: some twenty stories and forty poems by Chopin; clippings of magazine versions of her stories; translations from Maupassant; diaries and notebooks; an assortment of photographs and letters from friends.

James B. Connolly

(28 October 1868-20 January 1957)

Albert J. Miles
Pennsylvania State University—Ogontz Campus

BOOKS: *Jeb Hutton: The Story of a Georgia Boy* (New York: Scribners, 1902);

Out of Gloucester (New York: Scribners, 1902; London: Hodder & Stoughton, 1906);

The Seiners (New York: Scribners, 1904; London: Hodder & Stoughton, 1904);

The Deep Sea's Toll (New York: Scribners, 1905; London: Bickers, 1906);

On Tybee Knoll: A Story of the Georgia Coast (New York: Barnes, 1905);

The Crested Seas (New York: Scribners, 1907; London: Duckworth, 1907);

An Olympic Victor: A Story of the Modern Games (New York: Scribners, 1908);

Open Water (New York: Scribners, 1910; London: Nelson, 1920);

Wide Courses (New York: Scribners, 1912; London: Duckworth, 1912);

Sonnie-Boy's People (New York: Scribners, 1913);

The Trawler (New York: Scribners, 1914);

Head Winds (New York: Scribners, 1916; London: Nelson, 1920);

Running Free (New York: Scribners, 1917; London: Nelson, 1921);

The U-Boat Hunters (New York: Scribners, 1918);

Hiker Joy (New York: Scribners, 1920);

Tide Rips (New York: Scribners, 1922);

Steel Decks (New York: Scribners, 1925; London: Hodder & Stoughton, 1926);

Coaster Captain: A Tale of the Boston Waterfront (New York: Macy-Masius, 1927);

The Book of the Gloucester Fishermen (New York: John Day, 1927); republished as *Fishermen of the Banks* (London: Faber & Gwyer, 1930); revised and enlarged as *The Book of the Gloucester Fishermen* (New York: John Day, 1930);

Gloucestermen, Stories of the Fishing Fleet (New York: Scribners, 1930);

Navy Men (New York: John Day, 1939);

American Fishermen, photographs from the collection of Albert Cook Church with text by Connolly (New York: Norton, 1940; London: Hale, 1947);

James B. Connolly, circa 1904

The Port of Gloucester (New York: Doubleday, Doran, 1940);

Canton Captain: The Story of Captain Robert Bennet Forbes (Garden City, N.Y.: Doubleday, Doran, 1942);

Master Mariner: The Life and Voyages of Amasa Delano (Garden City, N.Y.: Doubleday, Doran, 1943);

Sea-Borne: Thirty Years Avoyaging (Garden City, N.Y.: Doubleday, Doran, 1944).

OTHER: Roman J. Miller, *Around the World with the Battleships*, introductory essay by Connolly (Chicago: McClurg, 1909);

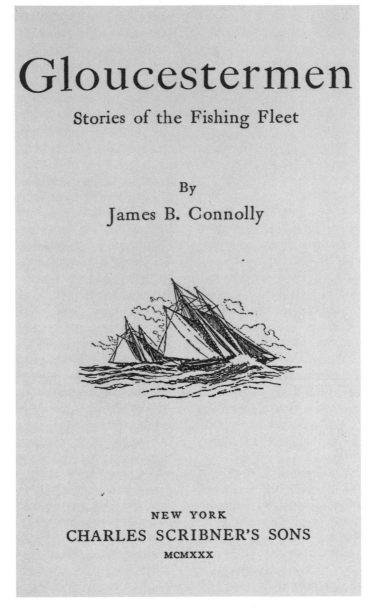

Gloucestermen

Stories of the Fishing Fleet

By

James B. Connolly

NEW YORK

CHARLES SCRIBNER'S SONS

MCMXXX

Title page for Connolly's selection of the best stories from his earlier collections

"Cooper and Stories of the Sea," in *Fiction by Its Makers,* edited by Francis X. Talbot (New York: America Press, 1928), pp. 171-178;

"How I Write Sea Stories," in *How to Write for a Living,* edited by Trentwell Mason White (New York: Reynal & Hitchcock, 1937), pp. 284-291.

James Brendan Connolly, the man Joseph Conrad once called the best sea-story writer in America, has been justly celebrated as a realistic chronicler of the Gloucester fishermen and their lonely, heroic struggles with the implacable sea. Others have written of the sailor's life;

Connolly lived it–and then wrote about it. He was born on 28 October 1868 to John and Ann O'Donnell Connolly, descendants of a long line of Aran Islands seafaring folk who had left the islands off the west coast of Ireland when quite young to settle in South Boston (Little Ireland). In addition to instilling James with "a strong body and love of old-fashioned virtues–courage, justice, honesty, reliability," virtues which would later manifest themselves in his depiction of character, his family brought him into close contact with the sea. His father sailed with the Boston fishing fleet; his mother's brother Jim, who lived with the family, sailed with the Gloucester fleet and was later a skipper and owner of a ship in the Boston fleet. These stalwart men recounted their sea stories casually, minimizing the danger in their experiences, while providing young Jim with the germs for many of his future short stories and helping to establish the restraint and understatement which would infuse the best of them. As early as his seventh year, Connolly sailed with his uncle to the fishing banks during summer vacation and was washed out of his cabin bunk during a great storm, the first of many encounters with the sea, encounters which would also help furnish the material for his vivid renderings of sea life. Having received little formal schooling (though later he completed high school by correspondence) and being dissuaded by his mother from fishing as a way of living, Connolly took a job as a clerk in an insurance company and then became a clerk and later inspector with the U.S. Engineers Corps in Savannah, where he did his first writing for money—a sports column—and captained the Savannah football team. He entered Harvard in 1895 to study engineering, but because Harvard refused to give him a leave of absence, he quit the university to attend the first modern revival of the Olympic Games being held in Athens in April 1896. He became the first Olympic champion since 369 A.D., winning the hop-step-and-jump contest with a distance of forty-five feet. Later he based his novel *An Olympic Victor* (1908) on this experience.

An expanded short story, *An Olympic Victor* was called "soul stirring" by E. K. T. (Mrs. J. H. Temple, Jr.) in 1920; yet it now seems a formula-ridden, somewhat stilted boys' book about a Greek peasant boy, Loues, who beat his rival for the affection of a local girl by winning the Olympic marathon. In it, however, is revealed Connolly's keen observation of detail (particularly in his description of the athletes' entrance to the stadium), his ability to demonstrate character through dialogue, his celebration of virtues such as courage, endurance, and modesty, and his Whitmanesque love of the common man. Above all, the novel illustrates Connolly's penchant for transmuting his experiences to fiction. Clearly, however, this material worked against his writing in his own individualistic, authentic voice.

After the Olympics Connolly found himself back in Boston writing for Boston newspapers and dabbling in athletics. In 1898 he fought with the Ninth Massachusetts Infantry, United States Volunteers, against the Spanish at San Juan Hill.

During the year of this expedition one-seventh of his regiment died, most from yellow fever, malaria, and dysentery. Connolly survived a long bout with typhoid malaria, after which he took a sailing trip on a cattle boat to Liverpool before his important stay at Gloucester.

His time in Gloucester proved to be the most seminal period of his life. Offered a position as the physical director at the Gloucester Athletic Club, Connolly accepted it because it enabled him to coach the football team. His duties were not onerous and left him much time to loaf on the docks and converse with the Gloucester fishermen, "the greatest sailormen who ever lived," who augmented his supply of fascinating anecdotes. By spring 1900 he had tired of the inside work in the gymnasium, and he sailed steerage to Paris to enter the Olympics, where he finished second in his old event. After returning home he wrote two boys' stories for money, feeling it would be easy to get fifty dollars for "something a fellow could write between breakfast and lunch of a morning." A few months later, after some fishing trips with the Gloucester fleet and some urging by a friend who suggested he should write down some of the tales he told, Connolly wrote—on one end of the kitchen table while his mother rolled pie crust on the other—the short stories "A Chase Overnight" (*Scribner's Magazine,* April 1901) and "From Reykjavik to Gloucester" (*Scribner's Magazine,* August 1901). First collected in *Out of Gloucester* (1902), both stories were later included in Connolly's selection of his best stories, *Gloucestermen* (1930). At last, Connolly had found his métier.

The stories in *Gloucestermen* are representative of this modern mariner's work. Told in a spare, forceful vernacular, they move swiftly and with apparent artlessness. Usually ordered chronologically, Connolly's stories evince little concern for experimental technique; yet his realistic narratives are well crafted, impressive for their ability to sustain interest in these humble fishermen, their sacrifice and endurance. In depicting the elemental passions of these men, the stories move from the merely provincial to the universal, touching the wellsprings of human nature. "Dory-Mates" (*Scribner's Magazine,* May 1905; collected in *The Deep Sea's Toll,* 1905), which rivals Jack London's "To Build a Fire" (1902) in its evocation of cold and ice, depicts the almost incredible loyalty and friendship of Martin Carr, who freezes his hands to fit the oars so he can help to save the life of his dory mate and later delays his

James B. Connolly, Montrose J. Moses, Edwin Lefevre, Margaret Sutton Briscoe Hopkins, Irving Bacheller, Ellen Douglas Deland, and John D. Barry at a party celebrating the seventieth birthday of Henry Mills Alden, managing editor of Harper's Weekly *(photograph from* Harper's Weekly, *15 December 1906)*

own recovery by first making sure his friend is buried properly. In "His Three Fair Wishes" (first published in *Tide Rips*, 1922), based on a true story, seaman Danny Bergin, to protect the woman he loves, serves fourteen years in jail for a crime he did not commit. Connolly asks, "should we not honor even more highly that man who does a great deed but who from the humility of his soul knows not that it is a great deed? Such men, by making little or nothing of their great deed, do impress on men's minds that here is something for all men to attempt on all days, thereby advancing not the mere glory of a single man, but raising the standard of an entire community, or even of a whole race; and, yes, of all men for all time it may be."

Typically the stories are narrated by some participant in the tale; often Connolly employs the frame-story device. In "A Chase Overnight" two fishermen looking for their own ship overhear a conversation which recounts the race home in which Billy Sims in the *Parker* beat Tom O'Donnell aboard the *Lucy Foster*. In "From Reykjavik to Gloucester" old Peter, the garrulous lookout of the crow's nest who appears in several stories as raconteur, tells of the race home of

Wesley Marrs aboard the *Lucy Foster* as it beats the English ship *Bouncing Billow* by three days. The same technique is employed in stories such as "On the Echo o' the Morn." (*Scribner's Magazine*, June 1901; collected in *Out of Gloucester*), "The Truth of Oliver Cromwell" (*Scribner's Magazine*, January 1905; collected in *The Deep Sea's Toll*, 1905), "The Trawler" (*American Magazine*, March 1909; separately published in 1914), "The Drawn Shutters" (*Scribner's Magazine*, October 1906; collected in *The Crested Seas*, 1907), "Loose Oilskins," and "A Man Dies."

In "Clancy," another story from *Out of Gloucester*, Connolly introduces a character who seems to have come out of the western tall-tale tradition. Tommy Clancy–a devil-may-care fellow who drinks, gambles, and womanizes–manages to outwit a customs official and save a case of wine. In Connolly's Gloucester stories the legendary exploits of the captains, their finely honed navigational skills, their courage in sailing with full sail into the fiercest storm while attempting to race to market with their catch, along with the amazing seaworthiness of their vessels and the courage of their men, are made credible and given immediacy by the verisimilitude of the setting and the au-

Toiling he is out there on the wide ocean.

The Book of the
GLOUCESTER FISHERMEN
by
JAMES B. CONNOLLY
Illustrated by
HENRY O'CONNOR

New York
THE JOHN DAY COMPANY
1927

Frontispiece and title page for Connolly's nonfiction book about the all-sail fishing fleet that inspired his popular sea stories

thenticity of the dialogue. Drawing on oral tradition, Connolly offers little authorial comment and is content to let the story tell itself with economy and directness. In his refusal to romanticize and sentimentalize these men, Connolly did much to aid the cause of realism and reject the limitations of the O. Henry "surprise ending" convention popular when many of these stories were written. Instead he honestly depicts the joys and rigors of fishing life as he experienced it. In doing so, Connolly renders concretely a now-vanished era of American life.

Connolly married Elizabeth Frances Hurley of South Boston on 28 September 1904; they later had a daughter, Brenda. In 1905 he returned to Harvard for the first time, not as a student but as a guest speaker before the Harvard Union. In the same year he collected eight more of his sea stories in *The Deep Sea's Toll*. The thirteen tales in *The Crested Seas* present many of his old characters in new roles, including sea captain

Wesley Marrs and the comic character Tommy Clancy.

Open Water (1910) contains more sea tales, but it also includes stories such as "The Emigrants," "Gree Gree Bush" (*Hampton's Magazine*, July 1910), and "The Christmas Handicap" (*Scribner's Magazine*, December 1908), which show Connolly's ability to write about life on shore. *Wide Courses* (1912), like earlier collections, contains some humorous stories and some that–in Connolly's words–dramatize "man in his indomitable courage doing battle with storm and wave, with the hardships of life that have hardened him."

"The Trawler," which appeared in the 31 December 1914 issue of *Collier's* and in book form that same year (it was later published in *Head Winds,* 1916), is a long, powerful story of a man who sacrifices his life for another. Notable for its restrained pathos, it is told with simplicity, and it includes some of Connolly's best descriptions of the stormy sea. The heroic stature of Hugh Glynn, who freezes to death after giving his sweater and shirt to his dory mate Simon, is superbly realized through his dialogue and actions as "the man who thought that 'twas better for one to live than for two to die, and that one not to be himself." In 1914 "The Trawler" won first prize in *Collier's* twenty-five-hundred-dollar short-story contest. Theodore Roosevelt, one of the judges and later a friend, felt it deserved the award because of its "elevation of sentiment, rugged knowledge of rugged men, strength and finish of writing." Later, Roosevelt was to call Connolly "the author of the best sea stories ever written" and to say, "If I were to pick one man for my sons to pattern their life after, I would choose Jim Connolly." Another judge, Mark Sullivan, liked "The Trawler" because of Connolly's "length of reach into the depths of human nature, a sort of second sight about the springs of human emotion and human action."

By 1922 Connolly had sailed aboard every sort of navy ship but a repair ship and a garbage scow, having crossed the Atlantic Ocean twenty-five times. He had served in the navy in 1907 and 1908, and, as a naval correspondent for *Collier's*, he arrived in Mexican waters aboard the battleship *New York* toward the end of the April 1914 battle of Vera Cruz. He covered the European naval war for *Collier's* in 1917 and was aboard an American destroyer when it was attacked by torpedoes.

During this period Connolly was refining his conception of style, which is probably best explained in his 1920 novel, *Hiker Joy*: "the first thing in telling a story is to tell it, not to stop to preach a sermon." The novel also advises storytellers to "lay off too much talky-talky and don't try to make yuhself out too wise a guy in tellin' your

story." The short-story collection *Tide Rips* was followed by the novels *Steel Decks* (1925) and *Coaster Captain* (1927). In the same year Connolly offered a factual account of the gallant Gloucestermen in *The Book of the Gloucester Fishermen*, which shows clearly the base for many of his fictional accounts. By 1930 Connolly was widely acclaimed as the best modern writer of the sea, and *Gloucestermen* was well received. Some of the true stories Connolly tells are as thrilling as his fictional versions. No matter what genre he employed, he seems to have been incapable of telling a bad story.

Although he continued to write well into his seventies, Connolly never surpassed his stories of the Gloucestermen. Little known today, Connolly achieved in the narrow compass of these tales a wholesome, robust prose distinguished by simplicity, clarity, and vividness. As Temple put it, "The sublimity, the pathos, the charm, the power of human character are brought out in every tale." What other local colorists did to immortalize their regions, James Brendan Connolly–with his passion for the sea–did for Gloucester.

References:

Ernest Cummings Marriner, *Jim Connolly and the Fishermen of Gloucester: An Appreciation of James Brendan Connolly at Eighty* (Waterville, Maine: Colby College Press, 1949);

E. K. T. (Mrs. J. H. Temple, Jr.), "James Brendan Connolly," in *Our Short Story Writers*, by Blanche Colton Williams (New York: Moffat, Yard, 1920), pp. 85-104.

Papers:
Colby College in Maine has an extensive collection of Connolly's papers, as well as autographed and inscribed first editions of his books.

Stephen Crane

(1 November 1871-5 June 1900)

Glen M. Johnson
Catholic University of America

See also the Crane entries in *DLB 12: American Realists and Naturalists* and *DLB 54: American Poets, 1880-1945*.

SELECTED BOOKS: *Maggie: A Girl of the Streets*, as Johnston Smith (New York: Privately printed, 1893); revised edition, as Stephen Crane (New York: Appleton, 1896; London: Heinemann, 1896);

The Black Riders and Other Lines (Boston: Copeland & Day, 1895; London: Heinemann, 1895);

The Red Badge of Courage: An Episode of the American Civil War (New York: Appleton, 1895; London: Heinemann, 1896);

George's Mother (New York & London: Edward Arnold, 1896);

The Little Regiment and Other Episodes of the American Civil War (New York: Appleton, 1896; London: Heinemann, 1897);

The Third Violet (New York: Appleton, 1897; London: Heinemann, 1897);

The Open Boat and Other Stories [17 stories] (London: Heinemann, 1898); republished, in part, as *The Open Boat and Other Tales of Adventure* [8 stories] (New York: Doubleday & McClure, 1898);

War is Kind (New York: Stokes, 1899);

Active Service (New York: Stokes, 1899; London: Heinemann, 1899);

The Monster and Other Stories (New York & London: Harper, 1899; enlarged edition, London & New York: Harper, 1901);

Whilomville Stories (New York & London: Harper, 1900);

Wounds in the Rain: A Collection of Stories Relating to the Spanish-American War of 1898 (New York: Stokes, 1900; London: Methuen, 1900);

Great Battles of the World (Philadelphia: Lippincott, 1901; London: Chapman & Hall, 1901);

Last Words (London: Digby, Long, 1902);

Stephen Crane, 1899 (Public Library, Newark, New Jersey)

The O'Ruddy: A Romance, by Crane and Robert Barr (New York: Stokes, 1903; London: Methuen, 1904);

The Sullivan County Sketches of Stephen Crane, edited by Melvin Schoberlin (Syracuse: Syracuse University Press, 1949);

Stephen Crane: Uncollected Writings, edited by O. W. Fryckstedt (Uppsala: Studia Anglistica Upsaliensia, 1963);

The War Dispatches of Stephen Crane, edited by

R. W. Stallman and E. R. Hagemann (New York: New York University Press, 1966);

The New York City Sketches of Stephen Crane, edited by Stallman and Hagemann (New York: New York University Press, 1964);

Sullivan County Tales and Sketches, edited by Stallman (Ames: Iowa State University Press, 1968);

The Notebook of Stephen Crane, edited by Donald and Ellen Greiner (Charlottesville, Va.: A John Cook Wylie Memorial Publication, 1969);

Stephen Crane in the West and Mexico, edited by Joseph Katz (Kent, Ohio: Kent State University Press, 1970);

The Red Badge of Courage: A Facsimile Edition of the Manuscript, 2 volumes, edited by Fredson Bowers (Washington, D.C.: Bruccoli Clark/ NCR Microcard Edition, 1973).

Collections: *The Work of Stephen Crane*, 12 volumes, edited by Wilson Follett (New York: Knopf, 1925-1926);

The Collected Poems of Stephen Crane, edited by Follett (New York & London: Knopf, 1930);

The Poems of Stephen Crane, edited by Katz (New York: Cooper Square, 1966);

The Works of Stephen Crane, 10 volumes, edited by Bowers (Charlottesville, Va.: University Press of Virginia, 1969-1976).

Stephen Crane lived fast and aggressively, and although he died at age twenty-eight, he managed to exceed a normal lifetime's experience in travel and exposure to extremes of human condition and endeavor. Out of his experience came a body of work equal in extent and quality to that of many longer-lived contemporaries. Crane produced one novel and a handful of short stories which are securely in place among the masterworks of fiction in English. Perhaps due to the unique character of his genius, the relationship between his hectic life and his best art is even more problematical than is usually the case with writers. He produced the greatest of American war novels before he ever saw combat, but perhaps his best short story came directly out of his experience in an endangered lifeboat. Another of his masterpieces seems to have developed from a single visual impression, caught at a railroad junction on the Nebraska plains—a hotel painted incongruously blue. Crane the man is enigmatic, but the artist survives in his work and is approachable when the man, lost in the past and in legend, is not.

Crane was born on 1 November 1871, a close contemporary of W. E. B. Du Bois, Edwin Arlington Robinson, Theodore Dreiser, Robert Frost, Frank Norris, and Jack London. He was descended on both sides from clergymen, and through his father from a Revolutionary patriot, Stephen Crane, president of the Colonial Assemblies. The former circumstance helps to explain his religious symbolism and the anguish of his agnosticism; the latter illuminates his paradoxical combination of aristocratic attitudes with empathy for the lapsed, those who fail to live up to received standards or a more heroic past. Crane's father, the Reverend Dr. Jonathan Townley Crane, was Presiding Elder of Methodist churches in and around Newark; his mother, Mary Peck Crane, was an active public speaker on religious and reform issues. A man of liberal inclinations and charity, Jonathan Crane was a beloved presence in his small world; his death early in 1880 put the family of nine surviving children (five others had died in early childhood) in straitened circumstances and left Stephen, his youngest son, with an unstable personal identity. Crane's short life was a series of experiments with various personas: athlete, bohemian, muckraking urban journalist, western adventurer, war correspondent, English country gentleman. The only identity he settled on, however, was that of artist.

After Rev. Crane's death, the family lived in Port Jervis and in Asbury Park, New Jersey. Crane developed conventional attitudes of adolescent rebelliousness: he smoked, drank, and gambled, though without getting himself irrevocably into trouble, even in straitlaced Asbury Park. His brother Townley was a newspaperman working for the *New York Tribune*, and Crane began at about sixteen to help Townley with his column. He went to two preparatory schools and to Lafayette College and Syracuse University; he did not graduate from any of these institutions, and his main distinction seems to have been as a baseball player. After leaving Syracuse in mid 1891, he lived a bohemian life for two-and-a-half years, mainly in New York City. He published newspaper reports and features, many about low life in the city, but he never quite established himself as a professional journalist. Early in 1893 Crane had *Maggie: A Girl of the Streets* privately printed and published under a pseudonym.

The Red Badge of Courage, his best-known work, was syndicated in abridged form late in 1894 and published as a book late in 1895. It

Crane (bottom right) and friends at Syracuse University, 1891 (Clifton Waller Barrett Library, University of Virginia Library)

made Crane lastingly famous, gave him leverage with publishers, and loaded him with the burden of equaling a youthful masterpiece. He parlayed initial reaction to the novel into support by a newspaper syndicate for a trip into the American West and Mexico early in 1895; that experience eventually produced some of his most distinguished short stories.

During 1895-1897, Crane published *The*

Black Riders and Other Lines, a collection of poems; a revised version of *Maggie*; a new "Bowery" novel, *George's Mother*; *The Little Regiment*, consisting of war stories; and *The Third Violet*, a novel based on his life among artists in New York. By late 1896 his journalistic interest in police corruption and his testimony in support of a prostitute in a harassment case made New York uncomfortable for him, and he went south to cover the

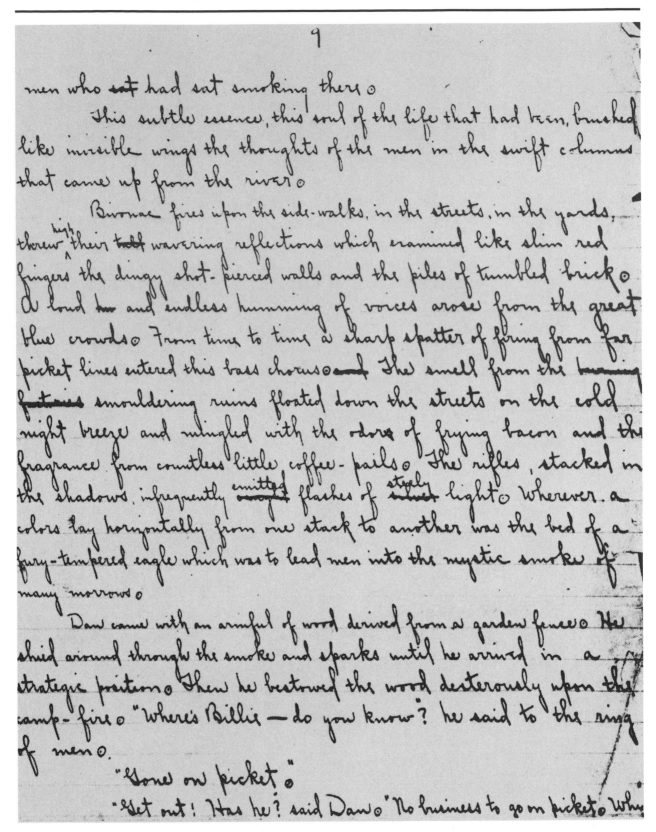

9

men who ~~sat~~ had sat smoking there.

This subtle essence, this soul of the life that had been, brushed like invisible wings the thoughts of the men in the swift columns that came up from the river.

Bivouac fires upon the side-walks, in the streets, in the yards, threw their ~~tall~~ wavering reflections which examined like slim red fingers the dingy shot-pierced walls and the piles of tumbled brick. A loud ~~hu~~ and endless humming of voices arose from the great blue crowds. From time to time a sharp spatter of firing from far picket lines entered this bass chorus. ~~and~~ The smell from the ~~burning~~ ~~fires~~ smouldering ruins floated down the streets on the cold night breeze and mingled with the ~~odors~~ of frying bacon and the fragrance from countless little coffee-pails. The rifles, stacked in the shadows, infrequently ~~emitted~~ flashes of ~~steely~~ light. Wherever a colors lay horizontally from one stack to another was the bed of a fury-tempered eagle which was to lead men into the mystic smoke of many morrows.

Dan came with an armful of wood derived from a garden fence. He shied around through the smoke and sparks until he arrived in a strategic position. Then he bestowed the wood dexterously upon the camp-fire. "Where's Billie — do you know? he said to the ring of men.

"Gone on picket."

"Get out! Has he? said Dan. "No business to go on picket. Why

Cuban insurrection. Headed out of Jacksonville on the gun-running *Commodore*, Crane spent over twenty-seven hours in a dinghy after the ship sank on 2 January 1897. From that experience developed "The Open Boat" (*Scribner's Magazine*, June 1897; collected in *The Open Boat and Other Stories*, 1898). In April he was in Europe to cover the brief Greco-Turkish War, accompanied by Cora Taylor, formerly proprietor of a sporting house in Jacksonville. By mid 1897 Crane and Cora were settled in England as husband and wife, though they never legally married. That year and the next brought Crane's greatest productivity in the short story, the pieces collected in *The Open Boat* and *The Monster and Other Stories* (1899).

In 1898 Crane headed back across the Atlantic to cover the Spanish-American War. Reckless and ill with tuberculosis and malaria, he was evacuated to the United States in July; soon, however, he was back on the scene, living for a time in Havana while it was still under Spanish control. In January 1899 he returned to England, where he and Cora lived in high style at Brede Manor in Sussex. Joseph Conrad was a good friend, Henry James a visitor. That year Crane published a collection of poems, *War is Kind*, and another novel, *Active Service*. Beset by debts, he worked feverishly despite progressive evidence of tuberculosis. By March 1900 he was desperately ill, and on a recuperative journey he died in Germany on 5 June. He was buried in Hillside, New Jersey. He left behind an unfinished novel, *The O'Ruddy*, completed by Robert Barr and published in 1903. *Whilomville Stories* (1900), *Wounds in the Rain*, a collection of stories (1900), and *Last Words*, a miscellany (1902), were published posthumously.

Restlessness and experimentation were central forces in Crane's life, and as concepts they help to illuminate his art as well. Just as he tried out personal identities of various sorts, he explored a number of literary genres and styles. He produced news reports and features, historical sketches, novels, poetry, and short stories; he was, variously, realist, naturalist, symbolist, impressionist, and expressionist. In all of these writings restlessness is an essential theme. Crane's characters live out dissatisfaction, often inchoate for them but attributed by the stories to a world of circumscribed possibilities, social and spiritual. They seem compelled to seek what is denied by, or simply not available in, their normal environments. One kind of compensation is in action:

Crane's characters wander in search of adventures, and usually they find them. Another compensation is in thought: they seek ways to order experience meaningfully, often with the help of what they have read in fiction. These alternate visions of order reflect widely varying degrees of confusion or clear thinking, but all express a yearning born in discontent. Crane's deepest ironies come out of the conflict–inevitable and, he thought, finally irresolvable–between yearning and reality, between desires and the way things happen, between what an individual seeks and what his experience can reasonably be expected to offer. In a letter, Crane wrote that an artist's responsibility came down to "his quality of personal honesty," and for him that meant both rejecting the kinds of assurance that ordered the world of his father and acknowledging the anguish of the loss and the impulse to seek compensations. Elsewhere Crane denied that his literature tried to uphold any specific "moral or lesson"–"preaching is fatal to art"–but he went on to hope that an honest literature might provide assurance of some sort, which a reader could "find . . . for himself."

Crane's earliest writings include a group of pieces now known as the Sullivan County tales. Most appeared in the *New York Tribune* during 1892, and Crane reprinted none of them during his lifetime. They are apprentice work, but they show thematic preoccupations and technical approaches that characterize many later stories. The plots are often repetitious: "Four Men in a Cave" (3 July 1892), "The Octopush" (10 July 1892), "A Ghoul's Accountant" (17 July 1892), and "The Black Dog" (24 July 1892); each recounts an encounter between comically pompous campers in the woods and someone or something spooky. The campers are terrified, but eventually they receive knowledge that clarifies what appeared inexplicable and thus deflates their horror. Crane's irony is directed at the campers, who through a combination of unfamiliar surroundings, unclear perception, and constitutional pomposity mislead themselves. They thus anticipate the typical Crane protagonist, for whom terror is an ironically self-imposed punishment for muddleheadedness born in self-importance.

In setting and in characterization the Sullivan County tales have the simplicity of allegory. Though named after a specific locale, they convey little sense of a particular place: the settings are stylized mountains, forests, caves, and lakes. Similarly, the characters, such as "the little man" and "the fat, pudgy man," act in the generalized,

An 1896 letter from Crane to William Dean Howells (Clifton Waller Barrett Library, University of Virginia Library)

Stephen Crane in his study at Brede Manor, in Sussex, England, September 1899

broadly exaggerated ways of fable. ("The Octopush," indeed, begins "Once upon a time.") What contrasts with the simplifications of plot, setting, and character is a style vigorous with movement and color, disorienting the world of the fiction with its sense of an immanently violent environment: "In the cave-atmosphere the torches became studies in red blaze and black smoke. . . . Things that hung, seemed to be upon the wet, uneven ceiling, ready to drop upon the men's bare necks. Under their hands the clammy floor seemed alive and writhing. When the little man endeavored to stand erect, the ceiling forced him down. Knobs and points came out and punched him . . . " ("Four Men in a Cave").

The sense of threat immanent in the landscape is here clearly psychological, as suggested by the repetition of "seem." But the prose *reproduces* the little man's disorientation. Crane's stylistic mark is that he does not distance the disorientation: the narrative tends to adopt the hysterical, and ultimately false, point of view of the character. This technique anticipates expressionism, and like expressionist playwrights and filmmakers of the early twentieth century, Crane uses it to do more than just trick readers and elicit easy

chills. "A Ghoul's Accountant," for example, begins with a landscape where "a campfire lay dying in a fit of temper. . . . A mass of angry, red coals glowered and hated the world. Some hemlocks sighed and sung. . . ." At this point all the characters are asleep–"four imperturbable bundles . . . near the agonized campfire." Perhaps the outer world's agony reflects the dreams of the sleepers–but "imperturbable" suggests otherwise. To some extent, undetermined and perhaps indeterminable, ominousness and agony inhere in the world apart from psychology or viewpoint. Unstable perceptions meet unstable "reality." Even in his earliest work, then, Crane's disorienting, vibrant but ominous fictional world is a product of style, and his technical resources were equal to it. Only later did he begin self-consciously to explore the interaction of psychology, perception, and external order that is his fiction's chief preoccupation. But he was at twenty-one already preoccupied.

Between 1893 and 1895 Crane's most serious efforts went into novels and poems. His short works tended to come out of his newspaper career in New York–occasional pieces and, more often, what would now be called features. Their main value for him, apart from the financial, was in allowing him further to develop his craft in pieces short and highly focused. He was apparently pleased by the results, since he chose a group of the short works from this period to appear, grouped as "Midnight Sketches," in the 1898 British edition of *The Open Boat*.

The Midnight Sketches reveal important developments in Crane's art since the Sullivan County tales. Urban in locale and in action, they are more realistically detailed in physical and social settings. Crane's tendency toward generalization is thus restrained or directed toward social statements, as "An Ominous Baby" (*Arena*, May 1894) and "The Men in the Storm" (*Arena*, October 1894) illustrate. The "ominous baby" is a slum child who wanders into a fashionable neighborhood and tries to play with a "pretty child" there. Rejected as "all dirty," he steals a toy and vanishes like a "barbarian" or a "vandal . . . down a dark side street as into a swallowing cavern." The plot here is as fablelike as before, and the characters are still nameless and representative rather than individualized. The setting, however, is far more specifically realized: carriages, "a man with a chrysanthemum . . . going up steps," trucks in the street, nursemaids with perambulators, buildings whose cornices and windows reflect light, "heaps of rugs and cushions" on which pampered children play. In the second sketch, "the men in the storm" are similarly generalized, treated as a "tossing crowd" or even a "mob," and compared to "ogres," among other things. They are representative, however, less of some general conception about human nature than of a specific social situation, the aftermath of the panic of 1893. Crane realizes their situation by making the mob part of an environment whose metaphorical power lies in its particularization: "The whirling snows acted as drivers, as men with whips, and at half-past three, the walk before the closed doors of the house was covered with wanderers of the street, waiting. For some distance on either side of the place they could be seen lurking in doorways and behind projecting parts of buildings, gathering in close bunches in an effort to get warm. A covered wagon drawn up near the curb sheltered a dozen of them. Under the stairs that led to the elevated railway station, there were six to eight, their hands stuffed deep in their pockets, their shoulders stooped, jiggling their feet. Others always could be seen coming, a strange procession. . . ."

"An Experiment in Misery" (*New York Press*, 22 April 1894), among the best of the Midnight Sketches, re-creates the world of saloons, flophouses, and cheap hash restaurants, using observed details to construct a "fantastic nightmare" in which these seedy places have the "strange effect of a graveyard." But the most significant technical quality of "An Experiment in Misery" is the center of consciousness, "the youth." The plot recounts Crane's own experiences when he decided to dress and live as "an outcast" on the city's streets. The idea is gimmicky, but the story is not, largely because Crane focuses intently on the youth's psychology and presents the reality of slum experience as it is discovered *within* a man living it. The result is thus not a sentimental identification with the downtrodden, but an ironic discovery of how easy it is to *be* downtrodden. As the final sentence has it: "He confessed himself an outcast, and his eyes from under the lowered rim of his hat began to glance guiltily, wearing the criminal expression that comes with certain convictions."

The "convictions" mentioned here are complex. The youth feels outcast because the fine world, "frieze-like," ignores him; but he is more fundamentally outcast because he has discovered within himself an "infinite distance from all that he valued." In a letter of November 1896 Crane spoke about the "cowardice" of the poor, and this story defines that word as an interaction of indifferent environment and weak character. Even amid scenes of degradation, however, Crane discovers a strange human resiliency—the "unholy atmosphere" of a flophouse, for example, is easily forgotten under the influence of coffee and a roll. And this resiliency is connected to an irrepressible egotism that is both ironic and heroic. As the youth and his ragged companion assure each other that they are "respecter'ble gentlem'n" and "souls of intelligence and virtue," they are being simultaneously ridiculous and human. Perhaps survival itself, with any sort of contentment in an indifferent world, requires being a coxcomb.

It is important that these insights develop in a story where Crane identified closely with the protagonist. His interest in the outcast, in the loser, probably originated in his own problems of identity; his sense of irony was most fundamentally directed at himself. But in his earlier works, the characters are too one-dimensional and the irony seems nothing more than facile adolescent cynicism. By 1894 he had learned to dramatize his sen-

The Five White Mice
By Stephen Crane.

Freddie was mixing a cock-tail. His hand with the long spoon was whirling and the ice in the glass hummed and rattled like a cheap watch. Over by the window, a gambler, a millionaire, a railway conductor and the agent of a vast American syndicate were playing seven-up. Freddie surveyed them with the ironical glance of a man who is mixing a cocktail. From time to time a swarthy Mexican waiter came with his tray from the rooms at the rear and called his orders across the bar. The sounds of the indolent stir of the city, awakening from its siesta, floated over the screens which barred the sun and the inquisitive eye. From the faraway kitchen could be heard the roar of the old French chef, driving, herding and abusing his Mexican helpers.

A string of men came suddenly in from the street. They stormed up to the bar. There were impatient shouts. "Come now, Freddie dont stand there like a portrait of yourself. Wiggle!" Drinks of many kinds and colors, amber, green, mahogany, strong and mild began to swarm upon the bar with all the attendants of lemon, sugar, mint and ice. Freddie with Mexican support worked like a sailor in the provision of them, sometimes talking with that scorn for drink and admiration for those who drink which is the attribute of a good bar-keeper.

At last a man was afflicted with a stroke of dice-shaking. A herculean discussion was waging and he was deeply engaged in it but at the same time he lazily flirted the dice. Occasionally he made great combinations. "Look at that, would you? he cried proudly. The others paid little heed. Then suddenly the craving took them. It went along the line like an epidemic and involved them all. In a moment they had arranged a carnival of dice-shaking with money penalties and liquid prizes. They clamorously made it a point of honour with Freddie that he too should play and take his chance of sometimes providing this large group with free refreshment. With bended heads like foot-ball players they surged over the tinkling dice, jostling, cheering and bitterly arguing. One of the quiet company playing seven-up at the corner table said profanely that now reminded him of a bowling contest at a picnic.

Page from the manuscript for "The Five White Mice" (Henry E. Huntington Library, San Marino, Cal.)

sibility by localizing human irony within characters sharing his own complicated, honest if slightly confused, awareness.

Two additional stories from 1893-1895 reflect the crucial influence on Crane of the realism movement in American fiction. In a letter of 1894 Crane described William Dean Howells as one of his "literary fathers": "I developed all alone a little creed of art. . . . Later I discovered that my creed was identical with the one of Howells." Crane's ironic view of human egotism and pomposity undoubtedly found reinforcement in the ethical stance of Howells and other realists, their disbelief in "romantic" self-assertions or extravagant expectations about life in the real world. Crane may have gotten from Howells the idea that "unrealistic" notions are nurtured by bad literature. Crane's "Why Did the Young Clerk Swear?" (*Truth*, March 1893; collected in *Last Words*) presents a haberdashery clerk who reads, between interruptions by customers, "a French novel with a picture on the cover." Crane's story provides long quotations from this novel; the joke is that the clerk skips parts dealing with "money transactions," "life in the coalpits," and other real-life matters, concentrating instead on titillating passages where characters "blushed," "felt faint with rapture," were "enchanted," and "burst into tears" with little provocation. Eventually the promised seduction fails, and the clerk reacts with "a wild scream of disappointment." The novel-within-a-story anticipates Crane's later tales that withhold promised climaxes. More important, the clerk is the earliest exemplar of Crane's ironic insight, learned probably from realism that humans perversely seek out literature that sensationalizes existence and reinforces "romantic" predilections.

Realism's attack on sensationalizing was accompanied by a positive ethical stance, reflected in "The Pace of Youth" (*Dayton Daily Journal* and *Kansas City Star*, 17 and 18 January 1895; collected in the British edition of *The Open Boat*), perhaps Crane's first mature story. This piece begins as a comic romance between Lizzie Stimson, the ticket taker, and Frank, the keeper of brass rings, on a Coney Island merry-go-round. The courtship, conducted through long-distance glances and awkward meetings on the beach, is delicately handled by Crane in a tone both mocking and respectful. The key figure in the story, however, is the girl's father, the owner of the carousel. He has forbidden the courtship and, at the story's climax, pursues the eloping couple's carriage. They

outrun him and, in the end, he experiences the kind of recognition central to realist ethics: "That other vehicle, that was youth, with youth's pace, it was swift-flying with the hope of dreams. He began to comprehend those two children ahead of him, and he knew a sudden and strange awe, because he understood the power of their young blood, the power to fly strongly into the future and feel and hope again." There is sentiment here, but it is subordinated to and validated by a realist's ethical position. Stimson is not gushing about young love; he is not even happy. But he is willing to accept what he cannot change and, more than that, perhaps to choose to be optimistic. That stance is as far as Crane's stories ever go: at best, his protagonists acquiesce in the world as they find it and hope, though with no extravagant expectations, for the best.

"The Pace of Youth" is longer and better developed than Crane's earlier stories, a fact that perhaps reflects the impact on his career of *The Red Badge of Courage*. The celebrity following from that novel had two immediate effects. First, Crane found a ready market for stories that could be more developmental, less journalistic in format or occasion. The pieces in his first published collection, *The Little Regiment*, are free from the sketchlike constraints of his earlier short works. Second, Crane was able to spend three months traveling through the West and Mexico. The first products of the trip were newspaper features; but after a significant gestation period there appeared several stories that rank among Crane's best.

The Little Regiment stories, all relating to the Civil War (and one, "The Veteran," which was first published in the August 1896 *McClure's Magazine*, featuring Henry Fleming in later life), were obvious attempts to exploit *The Red Badge of Courage*. But they are notable works in their own right, and they develop some of Crane's themes. Most important is the consistent contrast in these stories between veterans and the uninitiated. In quiet moments the veteran soldiers gripe and posture, but in battle they are thoroughly dependable, professional, and admirable. Those qualities come out of a psychological balance born of experience and of what is called in *The Red Badge of Courage* "forgotten vanities"—with, as always for Crane, a considerable dose of cynicism about the world. In "The Little Regiment" (*Chapman's Magazine*, June 1896) the veterans do not "grow nervous" in the "jumble" of battle: "They had learned to accept such puzzling situations as a consequence of their position in the ranks." Larger questions they meet with "the veteran's singular cynicism": "Their duty was to grab sleep and food when occasion permitted, and cheerfully fight wherever their feet were planted. . . . This was a task sufficiently absorbing." As for the individual's ultimate importance: "The terrible voices from the hills told him that in this wide conflict his life was an insignificant fact. . . . The solemnity, the sadness of it came near enough to make him wonder why he was neither solemn nor sad."

For Crane, war is the chief metaphor for human existence. ("The sense of a city is battle," he wrote in "Mr. Binks' Day Off," *New York Press*, 8 July 1894.) So there is general relevance in the veteran's "neither solemn nor sad" ethics–a development of the clearheadedness forwarded by realism, accepting life's "jumble" but learning to function usefully and perhaps safely within it. A contrast is provided in "Three Miraculous Soldiers" (*Omaha Daily Bee* and *Omaha Evening Bee*, 14 March 1896), whose protagonist, a naive Southern girl, reacts to a dangerous wartime situation in terms of "carefully constructed ideals" compounded from "all the stories she had read" and from "years of dreaming." Predictably, her romantic notions prove in reality useless if not dangerous; she wants to be a "heroine," but she ends up just being in the way.

Crane's stories satirize "romantic" expectations and the extravagant gestures they lead to. But Crane does not deny the possibility of heroism; one concern of *The Little Regiment* is to define the concept. In "The Veteran" Henry Fleming retells his adventures of *The Red Badge of Courage*, freely admitting that he panicked and ran at Chancellorsville, before "I got kind of used to it. A man does." Later Fleming goes into a flaming barn to save two colts: "I must try. . . . The poor little things," is his only reason. The story makes clear that the veteran's honest self-knowledge and his ability to act unselfishly when need arises are related. A longer story, "A Mystery of Heroism" (*Philadelphia Press*, 1 and 2 August 1895), further probes the issue. In it, Fred Collins risks death to fetch water during a skirmish. Collins's motives are mixed, and hardly heroic: he's thirsty, and when his comrades mock his bragging about making a dash to the well, his pride leads him to try. If heroes are people without fear or shame, Collins reflects during his trip, he is a "disappointment," "an intruder in

the land of fine deeds." That irony cuts both ways: conventional heroic notions are false to experience, but people still *act* heroically, if only for foolish reasons. And yet on his return from the well Collins stops under fire to comfort a dying officer on the field, and this is genuine heroism of the sort also illustrated by old Fleming in "The Veteran." Then a final twist: Collins's water is spilled by two lieutenants before anyone gets a drink. Crane's irony here is characteristic: it twists, it deflates, it denies ultimates. But it leaves Collins's action, his personal gesture toward the dying officer, untouched.

After 1896 Crane wrote no more Civil War stories; in settings and situations his best short works derive more directly from specific experiences. The most fertile of these experiences was the western journey of 1895, on which Crane drew in nine stories published as late as 1900, the year of his death. On the simplest level, these stories parody the shoot-'em-up westerns that were staples of the dime novel industry. Crane's basic tactic is to set up a conventional violent climax and then withhold it: the last sentence of "The Five White Mice" is "Nothing had happened" (*New York World*, 10 April 1898; collected in the British edition of *The Open Boat*). This technique for exposing the artificialities of literary conventions was anticipated in Crane's aptly titled Midnight Sketch, "The Duel that Was Not Fought" (*New York Press*, 9 December 1894). In the stories published beginning in 1896, however, Crane uses his skill in manipulating point of view to carry the works beyond parody, developing further insights about the relationship among romantic expectation, perception, and event in the human world.

"Horses–One Dash" (*Buffalo Commercial* and *Kansas City Star*, 3 and 4 January 1896; collected in *The Open Boat*) sets the pattern. Apparently based on one of Crane's actual experiences, it tells of an American dude who is menaced by bandits at a Mexican cantina. After a night of terror the American, Richardson, slips away and, after a dash across the plain with the bandits pursuing, is saved by cavalry. In the end nothing happens. But Crane adds to the parodic sellout of expectations an emphasis on Richardson's psychology and on how it both creates his terror and hinders the clear thinking that might give him a measure of control in the situation. Crane's irony develops through manipulation of perspectives. At times the narrative adopts Richardson's point of view

Crane at Brede Place in August 1899 (Clifton Waller Barrett Library, University of Virginia Library)

and presents a world of "threatening gloom," in which even bedsheets are "grim" and a blanket a "horrible emblem." The story makes clear that this hysterical perspective is psychological, the product of "tumultuous emotions" that result not just from the situation but from a combination of Richardson's exhaustion, unfamiliar surroundings, and—significantly—his recollection of "all the tales of such races." The opposite of Richardson's "tingling and twitching" perception is what the narrator calls "careful process of thought," and this is exemplified in the story by a detached, ironic perspective that alternates with Rich-

ardson's. If Richardson sees the bandit chief as a "serpent," the ironic perspective describes him as "a fat, round-faced Mexican" who poses "in the manner of a grandee" and who is probably as "disconcerted" by Richardson as the dude is by him.

The irony of "Horses—One Dash" rests on a simple contrast of involved and detached points of view, where the involved individual is satirized for exaggerated, unrealistic emotional interpretations of events, interpretations at least partly owing to his readings in romantic fiction. But the narrative perspective, undoubtedly realistic in its detachment, is also smug: the situation is, after

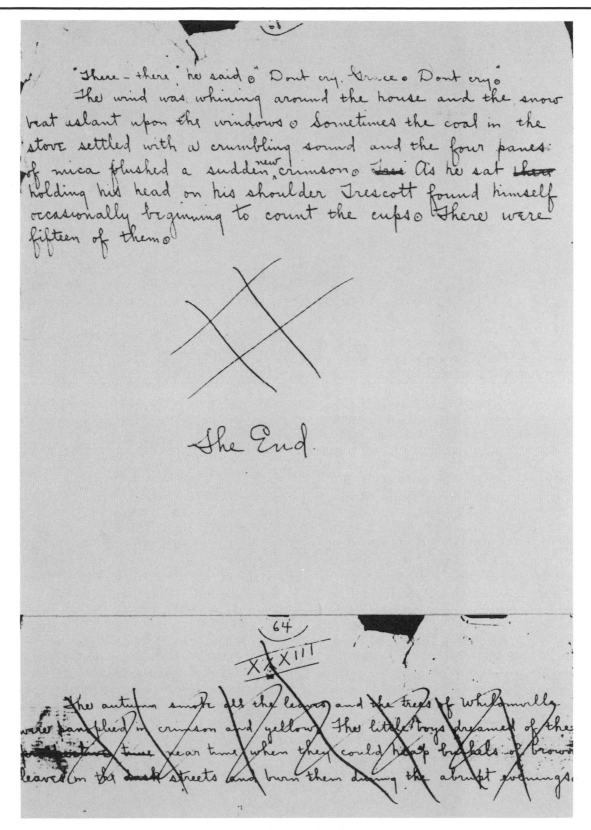

Verso (top) and recto of the only extant leaf of the manuscript for "The Monster" (Columbia University Libraries)

Cora and Stephen Crane, 23 August 1899, at a benefit held in the rectory gardens of the Brede village church (Syracuse University Library)

all, dangerous, and ironic detachment is hardly a reasonable expectation of one caught in a potentially lethal confrontation. In later western stories Crane tried to find a synthesis of involvement and detachment, essentially a more active and responsible version of the veteran soldier's ability to function under fire. The solution, synthesizing perspectives by allowing an involved character to earn an ironic insight about himself, is illustrated by "The Five White Mice." Here another dude, the "New York Kid," and two drunken companions have a confrontation with threatening natives on a street in Mexico City. At first the story adopts the involved perspective of the Kid in a long, vivid presentation of fears "perfectly stereopticon, flashing in and away . . . with an inconceivable rapidity [in] one quick dismal impression." Then comes the deflating switch in perspectives, only now it is the Kid, not a detached narrator, who achieves irony. The Mexicans suddenly show fear, and the Kid realizes that he has been "seduced" by his romanticizing of their grand postures. "He had never dreamed that he did not have a complete monopoly of all possible trepidations. . . . The Kid was able to understand swiftly that they were all human beings. They were unanimous in not wishing for too bloody combat. There was a sudden expression of the equality." This is a saving insight. It is compounded of two things: a recognition of common humanity—an equal susceptibility to fear or pomposity among people apparently different; and a realization that the tendency to superhumanize or otherwise romanticize what one does not understand is itself a chief cause of conflict and terror. For Crane, as for other realists, the essential value is understanding, defined in humanistic terms. Still, for Crane more than for older realists, understanding cannot *guarantee* safety in a world that is not always understandable; characteristically, "The Five White Mice" ends with an ironic twist, referring to a throw of the dice which the Kid loses. He has lost one game and won another more lethal; his ironic insight into human nature helped this time, but whether it would in the next cast of the dice is open to question.

These western stories are part of Crane's period of greatest productivity in the short form, 1896-1898. His most famous stories are products of these years; of them, "The Bride Comes to Yellow Sky" (*Chapman's Magazine*, February 1898; collected in *The Open Boat*) and "The Blue Hotel"(*Collier's Weekly*, 26 November and 3 December 1898; collected in *The Monster*) are westerns. "The Bride Comes to Yellow Sky" parodies the western duel, concluding as marshal and desperado face each other in a deserted street. Only now the marshal is unarmed and has his wife along, while the desperado is an aging drunk dressed in a maroon shirt from New York and in red-topped boots "of the kind beloved in winter by little sledding boys on the hillsides of New England." Throughout, Crane self-consciously plays with western conventions. Marshal Potter, for example, feels "heinous" for marrying; the stock literary sheriff is, of course, the strong, single type. Matrimony has a deeper significance as well. The arrival of domestic values—"the environment of the new estate"—signals historical change: Yellow Sky is no longer frontier, wild or not. Scratchy Wilson, "a simple child of the earlier plains," no longer belongs, and the "funnel-shaped tracks" he makes as he walks away symbolize the passing of the old order. However much Crane mocks Potter's uneasiness in new clothes or his bride's lack of romantic qualities (she "was not pretty, nor was she very young. . . . It was quite apparent that she had cooked, and that she expected to cook"), the story wastes no nostalgia on the frontier days. And it is significant in Crane's realist ethics that even Scratchy Wilson can eventually adapt: he turns up in "Moonlight on the Snow" (*Frank Leslie's Popular Monthly*, April 1900; added to the 1901 edition of *The Monster*) as Potter's deputy.

Crane's use of multiple perspectives is again evident in "The Bride Comes to Yellow Sky." Part 2 of the story is told from the point of view of a traveling salesman sitting in the Weary Gentleman Saloon as Scratchy advances. Like holders of similar perspectives in other Crane stories, the drummer is unfamiliar with his surroundings and the situation and thus reacts with "increasing anxiety and bewilderment." Through the drummer Crane sets up a tense, foreboding atmosphere that is humorously sold out when Scratchy finally appears in his maroon shirt and red-topped boots. The reader, moving from part 2 to the objective narration of parts 3 and 4, finds again that a real situation is usually less horrific and more manageable than an involved and muddled perception has suggested.

In "The Blue Hotel" a character not unlike the drummer becomes the center of attention. Like Yellow Sky, Fort Romper, Nebraska, is a town passing beyond its frontier days: it already has four churches and plans a line of streetcars next spring. But a "badly frightened" Swede arrives full of notions he got "reading dime-novels," convinced "he's right out in the middle of it–the shootin' and stabbin' and all." Sure that he will be murdered, the Swede behaves more and more erratically, drinking heavily, repulsing reassurances, and interpreting as hostile the most innocuous actions of others. Eventually he becomes "demoniac" and gets himself stabbed by a gambler who is a "trusted and admired" citizen of the town. The Swede falls beside a cash register on which is the legend: "This registers the amount of your purchase." Thus Crane conveys an insight he shared with other realists: life can imitate bad art when people act out confused notions derived from romantic literature.

But Crane does not stop with the simple irony of having unrealistic perceptions backfire on their holders. Again there is an alternate perspective, provided in the story's final section by the Easterner, heretofore a mostly silent observer. An initial step in the Swede's hysterical progress toward death was his charge that Johnnie, son of the hotel's proprietor, cheated at cards. Now the Easterner reveals that the charge was true, and that by their silence the others present contributed to the circumstances causing a man's death: "Johnnie was cheating. I saw him. I know it. I saw him. And I refused to stand up and be a man.... We are all in it! ... Every sin is the result of a collaboration. We, five of us, have collaborated in the murder of this Swede."

This doctrine of complicity is a development of Crane's notion of responsibility, anticipated by the emphasis on solidarity and teamwork that marks the stories of soldiers. In Crane's increasingly complex vision of how the world operates, the individual's "quality of personal honesty" now involves social responsibilities as well as clarity of perception.

"The Blue Hotel" is perhaps Crane's most highly symbolic short story, and it provides a good example of his evocative imagery. A consistent pattern of religious imagery in the story is characteristic of many of Crane's works. Thus Scully, the proprietor of the blue hotel, is compared to an "old priest" and refers to his guests' "sacred privileges." The center of the hotel is a stove, "humming with god-like violence" in a parlor which is its "temple." The Swede has "flame-lit eyes," is volatile "like a fire-wheel," and is compared to a martyr. The association of religion and fire imagery suggests that Crane's point of reference is a Calvinistic belief in which hell looms larger than heaven, and indeed, as the Easterner says, the Swede "thinks he's right in the middle of hell." But the imagery has an additional dimension. The religious and fire imagery is associated with an inside world, human habitations and the human mind. Outside is a chaos of wind and snow that is less Calvinistic than nihilistic. Near the story's conclusion, as the Swede makes his way from the hotel to the saloon where he will die, Crane comments explicitly:

It was hard to imagine a peopled earth. One viewed the existence of man then as a marvel, and conceded a glamour of wonder to these lice which were caused to cling to a whirling, fire-smote, ice-locked, disease-stricken, space-lost bulb. The conceit of man was explained by this storm to be the very engine of life. One was a coxcomb not to die in it.

Man's "conceit" is associated through imagery with the world of religion. The fire within is paradoxically both hellish and the engine of life–Crane's ambiguous symbolic evocation of the soul. The soul belongs to a coxcomb, and seems bent on vexing itself; but it also provides whatever "glamour" or "wonder" is available to human life.

Central to "The Open Boat," the third great story of Crane's most productive years, is a thematic statement similar to the one in "The Blue Hotel":

When it occurs to a man that nature does not regard him as important, and that she feels she would not maim the universe by disposing of him, he at first wishes to throw bricks at the temple, and he hates deeply the fact that there are no bricks and no temples....

He feels, perhaps, the desire to confront a personification and indulge in pleas, bowed to one knee, and with hands supplicant, saying, "Yes, but I love myself."

A high cold star on a winter's night is the word he feels that she says to him. Thereafter he knows the pathos of his situation.

What Crane saw in his earliest stories as strutting pomposity and in "The Blue Hotel" as coxcombry has become, in this most mature of his works, a sad assertion of self-worth within a "cold," unresponsive universe. Subtitled "A Tale Intended to Be After the Fact," "The Open Boat" derived from Crane's own experience after the sinking of the *Commodore*. Hours in a fragile dinghy provided Crane with his best metaphor for human existence in a universe that is "flatly indifferent" and capable of "disposing" of any individual at any time. Against this universal oblivion is asserted love of self, exemplified by the desperate attempt to survive and even to understand that marks the four men in the open boat. Crane's word "pathos" is carefully chosen; he will not claim tragedy. Nevertheless, this story offers a wisdom about existence that makes human vulnerability potentially tragic: the last line—"they felt that they could then be interpreters"—suggests that experience does offer, finally, some meaning.

The meaning is of two sorts, both actively achieved rather than received, and both extensions of themes in earlier stories by Crane. First is "the subtle brotherhood of men," a development of the social responsibility and solidarity upheld in his previous works. The men in the dinghy comfort each other: they share gripes, talk about pies, huddle for warmth, and smoke cigars together. They cooperate for mutual survival: each does his appointed task in navigating, rowing, or bailing. It is significant to Crane's cooperative ethics that the only casualty among the four is the strongest, who at the crisis depends on his own unaided strength; he drowns while the others, weaker but working together, survive.

The second value in "The Open Boat" is self-knowledge, honesty tinctured, as always in Crane's works, with self-irony. The representative here is the correspondent, the obviously auto-

biographical center of consciousness. The correspondent presents a successful collation of the involved and detached perspectives which are distinct in most stories by Crane. The story begins by rejecting an abstracting sort of detachment: "Viewed from a balcony," the experience of the men "would doubtlessly have been weirdly picturesque," but for the correspondent the exigencies of survival forbid such "leisure." Deeply and desperately involved, he agonizes and rails at fate. But at the same time he achieves a distanced perspective, an irony, that Crane previously managed only in superimposed viewpoints. In the open boat it is possible to achieve *through* involvement "a profound and perfectly impersonal comprehension." The interpretation that the correspondent becomes capable of is that life is "an actuality—stern, mournful, and fine" all at once. "Stern" and "mournful" comprise Crane's assessment of universal indifference; "fine" suggests that solidarity and awareness can give life value, perhaps even zest, beyond a merely "realistic" assessment of fate.

"The Open Boat" offers a more subtle integration of imagery and point of view than "The Blue Hotel." From the first sentence—"None of them knew the color of the sky"—the presentation develops out of the limited but lucid perception of the characters. Such elements as "canton-flannel gulls," "uncanny and sinister in their unblinking scrutiny," and a shark seen only as "a gleaming trail of phosphorescence, like blue flame," are effective both as parts of the setting and as symbols of nature. Objects on shore—an omnibus, people waving, a tower that seems like "a giant, standing with its back to the plight of the ants"—become full of uncanny significance when described from the point of view of men so near but so far removed from "the average experience, which is never at sea in a dinghy." In "The Open Boat" Crane achieved a nearly ideal integration of style and substance and wrote what is generally considered one of the best stories in the English language.

Crane never again equaled the subtle solemnity of "The Open Boat," the delicacy of "The Bride Comes to Yellow Sky," or the vividness of "The Blue Hotel." The stories of his last two years were written increasingly in haste, under financial pressure, and in ill health; despite frequent felicities, they show the effects. Besides westerns, which continued to appear, the late stories are of two general sorts: tales of war and nostalgic social comedies. The war stories developed mainly out of Crane's experiences in Cuba and were collected as *Wounds in the Rain*. Some deal with soldiers, others with correspondents. Themes are much the same as in earlier war stories: the professionalism and unselfish bravery of the veteran, the confusion of the novice (here often a reporter). There is occasionally vivid expressionistic writing such as the disoriented atmosphere evoked in "The Sergeant's Private Mad-House" (*Saturday Evening Post*, 30 September 1899). But the essential value of these short works lies in the observed circumstantial detail. Though thematically like the Civil War stories, the best Cuban pieces, particularly "The Price of the Harness" (*Cosmopolitan*, December 1898; *Blackwood's Edinburgh Magazine*, December 1898) and "The Clan of No-Name" (*Black and White*, Christmas Number, 1899), have a solidity of specification that comes from Crane's direct observations of men under fire. To an extent, however, this virtue is also a weakness. The stories are often too journalistic, insufficiently rethought as fictions and close to the dispatches from which many of them derive.

The best of the later war stories is the first written, "Death and the Child" (*Black and White*, 5 and 12 March 1898; collected in *The Open Boat*), a product of Crane's experience covering the brief Greco-Turkish War. The story focuses on two characters: Peza, a correspondent who combines Henry Fleming's patriotic braggadocio with the self-consciousness of the correspondent in "The Open Boat"; and the child, abandoned by his peasant parents and playing at battle as the real thing rages around him. Peza, full of patriotic fervor, plans to fight, until the sight of real death ("the clutch of a corpse about his neck") causes him to flee. As he runs he meets the child, "fearless [and] cherubic," who asks, " 'Are you a man?' " The confrontation is evocative. But its irony is rather facile, more like Crane's earliest sketches than "The Open Boat." Peza is left a spectacle of deflated ego: "Peza gasped in the manner of a fish. . . . He knew that the definition of his misery could be written on a wee grass-blade." He is not allowed, like the correspondent of "The Open Boat," to become "an interpreter." The story is striking in its symbolic pairing of two victims of the life of war—one asks, for example, if Peza is "Death" or just another "Child"—but by 1898 Crane's insights could take him beyond this point.

Crane, had, perhaps, exhausted war as a metaphorical setting for his fiction. During the last

two years of his life, he began to explore a new vein, bourgeois comedy of the sort central to the work of Howells and other realists. Crane's Whilomville, based on Port Jervis, became the setting for fifteen stories, the best of which is the first and least typical, "The Monster" (*Harper's Magazine*, August 1898; collected in *The Monster*). The monster is Henry Johnson, a black servant maimed and maddened while rescuing from a house fire his young pal, Jimmie Trescott. Jimmie's father, Dr. Trescott, tries to do right by Henry, but gradually the town turns against him for saving and then sheltering this horrific creature. In the last scene, ostracism is poignantly symbolized by the fifteen untouched teacups left in Mrs. Trescott's drawing-room after no one has called on her receiving day.

"The Monster" is a rich story which suggests what Crane might have accomplished had he lived long enough to explore a new direction. There are finely realized scenes, ranging from the grotesque when Henry breaks up a child's party to the comic in depictions of the barbershop and kitchen gossip. The social scope is wide, including poor blacks, loafers, gossipy housewives, and the gentry. But the real distinction of "The Monster" is its moral outlook. Though Dr. Trescott's sense of responsibility is a given, Crane provides in Judge Hagenthorpe a "realistic" commentator who suggests that in preserving Henry when "Nature has very evidently given him up," Trescott has in a sense created the monster. To impose on Whilomville something its complacent social world cannot accommodate is, says the doctor, a "blunder of virtue." The town's complacency is clearly exposed, but again Crane refuses to rest in easy moralism. Mr. Winter insults Dr. Trescott, but only after Winter's daughter has been terrified by the escaped Henry. Jimmie and his friends act cruelly toward Henry, but Crane suggests that they are less uncaring than simply unable to deal with what they cannot integrate into their world. Throughout the story, Crane's flatly objective tone works: his refusal to condemn, the justification allowed even to the callous, adds to the reader's awareness of a pathetic, irresolvable dilemma that is, in effect, a social equivalent of the world of the open boat.

No other Crane work equals "The Monster" in complexity of social setting and outlook. The later Whilomville stories concentrate almost exclusively on the town's children; the adult world enters mostly as pranks by Jimmie and his chums disrupt it or as childish behavior parodies adult foibles. These late stories belong to a recognizable genre, the "boy's book," epitomized by Mark Twain's *The Adventures of Tom Sawyer* (1876). Crane's boys engage in the same activities as Twain's: they play pirates or cowboys, fight with new kids, fall in love with cute little girls, mope and write love letters, and "show off " in ways that irk adults–though never too seriously. The boy book's psychology, which Crane adopts, is simple. Principal motives are pride and romantic fantasy: in "Lynx-Hunting" (*Harper's Magazine*, September 1899; collected in *Whilomville Stories*) Jimmie recklessly shoots at a cow because he fears the derision of his companions; in "The Lover and the Tell-tale" (*Harper's Magazine*, October 1899; collected in *Whilomville Stories*), he pens an extravagant love letter and then fights with equal extravagance the children who mock it. The problem in Crane's version of the boy book is inconsistency of tone. Whereas *The Adventures of Tom Sawyer* treats youthful folly with a mixture of nostalgia and indulgence ("to pleasantly remind adults of what they once were"), the tales collected in *Whilomville Stories* have a sardonic undercurrent that pulls awkwardly against their general lightheartedness. In "Lynx-Hunting," for example, a boy shoots at a bird, "and blew this poor thing into a mere rag of wet feathers. Of which he was proud." That harsh note jars against the story's general tone of bemused toleration. It suggests that Crane was unable fully to manage two divergent reactions to his material: the indulgence arising from nostalgia and the irony arising from yet another enactment of human vanity and recklessness.

In their fablelike simplicity and their sardonic view of human nature, the *Whilomville Stories* are reminiscent of Crane's earliest work in the Sullivan County tales. The similarity suggests less that he had come full circle than that, under the pressures of his last months and in trying out a new kind of setting, he reverted to his most fundamental preoccupations. He was never able to follow up on the complexities of vision or sophisticated technical manipulations of the "The Open Boat," "The Bride Comes to Yellow Sky," "The Blue Hotel," and "The Monster." What he might have done had he lived is a tantalizing but useless question. What he *did* do is more than promising work by a developing writer: his stories are a chief accomplishment of America's literature.

Nine decades after his death Crane's critical and popular reputation seems secure. His best works have never been out of print and the flow of scholarship and criticism has been steady always and at times a flood. The great events of the past thirty years have been the straightening out of Crane's biography, previously full of confusions and romanticizations, and the editorial work leading to identification and republication of his journalism and more obscure short works. These materials provide the basis for a more comprehensive study of Crane's rapid but traceable development as an artist. Fuller understanding of this enigmatic man and sophisticated artist can only highlight his remarkable achievement.

Letters:

Stephen Crane: Letters, edited by R. W. Stallman and Lillian Gilkes (New York: New York University Press, 1960).

Bibliography:

R. W. Stallman, *Stephen Crane: A Critical Bibliography* (Ames: Iowa State University Press, 1972).

Biography:

R. W. Stallman, *Stephen Crane: A Biography* (New York: Braziller, 1968).

References:

Thomas Beer, *Stephen Crane: A Study in American Letters* (New York: Knopf, 1923);

Frank Bergon, *Stephen Crane's Artistry* (New York: Columbia University Press, 1975);

John Berryman, *Stephen Crane* (New York: Sloane, 1950);

Edwin H. Cady, *Stephen Crane*, revised edition (Boston: Twayne, 1980);

James B. Colvert, *Stephen Crane* (San Diego, New York & London: Harcourt Brace Jovanovich, 1984);

Donald B. Gibson, *The Fiction of Stephen Crane* (Carbondale: Southern Illinois University Press, 1968);

Thomas A. Gullason, ed., *Stephen Crane's Career: Perspectives and Evaluations* (New York: New York University Press, 1972);

Daniel Hoffman, *The Poetry of Stephen Crane* (New York: Columbia University Press, 1956);

Milne Holton, *Cylinder of Vision: The Fiction and Journalistic Writing of Stephen Crane* (Baton Rouge: Louisiana State University Press, 1972);

Joseph Katz, ed., *Stephen Crane in Transition: Cente-*

nary Essays (De Kalb: Northern Illinois University Press, 1972);

Marston LaFrance, *A Reading of Stephen Crane* (Oxford: Clarendon Press, 1971);

James Nagel, *Stephen Crane and Literary Impressionism* (University Park: Pennsylvania State University Press, 1980);

Donald Pizer, "Stephen Crane," in *Fifteen American Authors Before 1900: Bibliographic Essays on Research and Criticism*, edited by Robert A. Rees and Earl N. Harbert (Madison: University of Wisconsin Press, 1971), pp. 97-137;

Eric Solomon, *Stephen Crane: From Parody to Realism* (Cambridge: Harvard University Press, 1966).

Papers:

The principal holdings of Crane's manuscripts and other papers are at the Clifton Waller Barrett Library at the University of Virginia, and at the Columbia University Libraries.

Richard Harding Davis

(18 April 1864-11 April 1916)

James F. Smith, Jr.
Pennsylvania State University–Ogontz Campus

See also the Davis entries in *DLB 12: American Realists and Naturalists* and *DLB 23: American Newspaper Journalists, 1873-1900*.

BOOKS: *The Adventures of My Freshman* (Bethlehem, Pa.: Privately printed, 1884);

Gallegher and Other Stories (New York: Scribners, 1891; London: Osgood, McIlvaine, 1891);

Stories for Boys (New York: Scribners, 1891; London: Osgood, McIlvaine, 1891);

Van Bibber and Others (New York: Harper, 1892; London: Osgood, McIlvaine, 1892);

The West from a Car-Window (New York: Harper, 1892);

The Rulers of the Mediterranean (New York: Harper, 1894; London: Gay & Bird, 1894);

Our English Cousins (New York: Harper, 1894; London: Low, Marston, 1894);

The Exiles and Other Stories (New York: Harper, 1894; London: Osgood, McIlvaine, 1894);

The Princess Aline (New York: Harper, 1895; London: Macmillan, 1895);

About Paris (New York: Harper, 1895; London: Gay & Bird, 1896);

Three Gringos in Venezuela and Central America (New York: Harper, 1896; London: Gay & Bird, 1896);

Cinderella and Other Stories (New York: Scribners, 1896);

Dr. Jameson's Raiders vs. the Johannesburg Reformers (New York: Russell, 1897);

Cuba in War Time (New York: Russell, 1897; London: Heinemann, 1897);

Soldiers of Fortune (New York: Scribners, 1897; London: Heinemann, 1897);

A Year from a Reporter's Notebook (New York & London: Harper, 1897); republished as *A Year from a Correspondent's Notebook* (London & New York: Harper, 1898);

The King's Jackal (New York: Scribners, 1898; London: Heinemann, 1898);

The Cuban and Porto Rican Campaigns (New York: Scribners, 1898; London: Heinemann, 1899);

The Lion and the Unicorn (New York: Scribners, 1899; London: Heinemann, 1899);

With Both Armies in South Africa (New York: Scribners, 1900);

In the Fog (New York: Russell, 1901);

Ranson's Folly (New York: Scribners, 1902; London: Heinemann, 1903);

Captain Macklin: His Memoirs (New York: Scribners, 1902; London: Heinemann, 1902);

"Miss Civilization": A Comedy in One Act (New York: Scribners, 1905);

Richard Harding Davis [signature]

Farces: The Dictator, The Galloper, "Miss Civilization" (New York: Scribners, 1906; London: Bird, 1906);

Real Soldiers of Fortune (New York: Scribners, 1906; London: Heinemann, 1907);

The Scarlet Car (New York: Scribners, 1907);

The Congo and Coasts of Africa (New York: Scribners, 1907; London: Unwin, 1908);

Vera, the Medium (New York: Scribners, 1908);

The White Mice (New York: Scribners, 1909);

Once upon a Time (New York: Scribners, 1910; London: Duckworth, 1911);

Notes of a War Correspondent (New York: Scribners, 1910);

The Consul (New York: Scribners, 1911);

The Man Who Could Not Lose (New York: Scribners, 1911; London: Duckworth, 1912);

The Red Cross Girl (New York: Scribners, 1912; London: Duckworth, 1913);

The Lost Road (New York: Scribners, 1913; London: Duckworth, 1914);

Who's Who: A Farce in Three Acts (London: Bickers, 1913);

Peace Manoeuvres: A Play in One Act (New York & London: French, 1914);

The Zone Police: A Play in One Act (New York & London: French, 1914);

The Boy Scout (New York: Scribners, 1914);

With the Allies (New York: Scribners, 1914; London: Duckworth, 1914);

"Somewhere in France" (New York: Scribners, 1915; London: Duckworth, 1916);

The New Sing Sing (New York: National Committee on Prisons and Prison Labor, 1915);

With the French in France and Salonika (New York: Scribners, 1916; London: Duckworth, 1916);

The Boy Scout and Other Stories for Boys (New York: Scribners, 1917);

The Deserter (New York: Scribners, 1917);

Adventures and Letters of Richard Harding Davis, edited by Charles Belmont Davis (New York: Scribners, 1917).

Collection: *The Novels and Stories of Richard Harding Davis*, Crossroads Edition, 12 volumes (New York: Scribners, 1916).

PLAY PRODUCTIONS: *The Other Woman*, New York, Theatre of Arts and Letters, 1893;

The Disreputable Mr. Raegen, Philadelphia, Broad Street Theatre, 4 March 1895;

The Taming of Helen, Toronto, Princess Theatre, 5 January 1903; New York, Savoy Theatre, 30 March 1903;

Ranson's Folly, Providence, Rhode Island, Providence Opera House, 11 January 1904; New York, Hudson Theatre, 18 January 1904;

The Dictator, New York, Criterion Theatre, 4 April 1904;

The Galloper, Baltimore, Ford's Theatre, 18 December 1905; New York, Garden Theatre, 22 January 1906;

"Miss Civilization," New York, Broadway Theatre, 26 January 1906;

The Yankee Tourist, book by Davis, lyrics by Wallace Irwin, and music by Alfred G. Robyn, New York, Astor Theatre, 12 August 1907;

Vera, the Medium, Albany, New York, Bleecker Hall, 2 November 1908; revised as *The Seventh Daughter*, Cleveland, Colonial Theatre, 10 November 1910;

Blackmail, New York, Union Square Theatre, 17 March 1913;

Who's Who, New Haven, Connecticut, Hyperion Theatre, 28 August 1913; New York, Criterion Theatre, 11 September 1913;

Davis (second from right, standing) and his younger brother, Charles (second from left, standing), with the Lehigh University football team, circa 1884

The Trap, by Davis and Jules Eckert Goodman, Boston, Majestic Theatre, September 1914; New York, Booth Theatre, 19 February 1915;

The Zone Police, Tunkhannock, Pa., Piatt's Opera House, 11 August 1916;

Peace Manoeuvres, Bernardsville, New Jersey, Somerset Hills Dramatic Association, 13 September 1917.

Richard Harding Davis once said that "There is no training for a novelist as thorough as that received in the local room of a daily newspaper." Davis served just such an apprenticeship at newspapers in Philadelphia and New York and remained a journalist throughout his writing career, believing that as such he made his most significant contributions to his age. Nevertheless, Davis produced an enormously popular body of fiction—both short stories and novels—which captured the spirit of the "Strenuous Age" and which earned for him the designation of an "American Kipling." Because his impressionistic journalism and fiction so closely mirror its era of Rough Riders and Victorian sentimentality, it was at odds with the naturalistic visions of Stephen Crane, Frank Norris, and other contemporaries. Davis's critical fortunes suffered further as Americans turned their attention to realists such as Theodore Dreiser, Sherwood Anderson, F. Scott Fitzgerald, and Ernest Hemingway. Yet, if only by his own success—by the end of his career American magazines were paying him their highest fees for short fiction—Richard Harding Davis provided the inspiration for even those later writers who repudiated the chivalrous and genteel world he idealized. Although his stories have been criticized as shallow, they effectively capture the style and the popular ideals of America of the 1890s and early-twentieth century and present them to readers in vivid and memorable fiction.

Richard Harding Davis, the first child of Lemuel Clarke Davis and his wife, Rebecca Blaine Harding Davis, was born in Philadelphia on 18 April 1864. His father was an editorial writer for the *Philadelphia Inquirer* and later the editor of the *Public Ledger*. His mother had established a reputation as a notable writer, with her "Life in the Iron Mills," a novella describing the plight of Wheeling, West Virginia, mill workers, in the April 1861 issue of *Atlantic Monthly*. Davis, and his younger siblings, Charles and Nora, en-

W. W. Mills, Charles Clapp, and Richard Harding Davis, 1884. Davis was the editor of the Lehigh Burr; *Mills and Clapp were associate editors.*

joyed a genteel and cultured home life with their parents. Family friends included well-known literary and theatrical people. Davis was anything but a dedicated scholar. After five years at Philadelphia's Episcopal Academy, he left without a diploma and went to live with his uncle, Hugh Wilson Harding, a professor at Lehigh University in Bethlehem, Pennsylvania, who tutored Davis in Latin and mathematics. After attending preparatory schools in Swarthmore and Bethlehem, Davis was admitted to Lehigh as a conditional student in the Latin-scientific curriculum, having failed the mathematics entrance exam.

At Lehigh Davis won recognition outside the classroom, writing for the school literary magazine and the yearbook, playing football, and involving himself in theatrical productions. Unfortunately, his scholarship suffered, and Davis was expelled at the end of his third year. At his expulsion Davis is said to have told the professors assembled, "You don't think that I am worthy to remain in this school. But in a few years you will find that I have gone farther than you will ever go." Having decided on a writing career, Davis en-

rolled in Johns Hopkins to study political economy, but after a year of struggling academically while enjoying himself socially, he left academe for journalism.

One of Davis's later short stories, "The Grand Cross of the Crescent" (*Saturday Evening Post*, 20 January 1912; collected in *The Red Cross Girl*, 1912) may be seen as its author's appraisal of higher education. Peter Hallowell, a student at Stillwater College and son of the school's major benefactor, Cyrus Hallowell, has been routinely passed in all examinations because of a kind of unspoken conspiracy among professors to prevent Stillwater's fall from favor. In his last semester at Stillwater Peter–who has distinguished himself at football, theatricals, and other extracurricular activities–takes a history course with Dr. Henry Gillman, author of *The Rise and Fall of the Turkish Empire*. For some reason Gillman, a thirty-year veteran of Stillwater, is not part of the conspiracy to pass Peter, and instead of the "gentleman's" score of fifty, Gillman awards Peter a five on his final examination. This failure cancels Peter's graduation, but he refuses to join friends in ridiculing

Davis (center) with other journalists in Johnstown, Pennsylvania, after the devastating flood of 1889

the professor and shows good sportsmanship: "Old Man Gillman fought fair. He gave me just what was coming to me. I think a darn-sight more of him than I do of that bunch of bootlickers that had the colossal nerve to pretend that I scored fifty." That summer while he is in Constantinople Peter arranges for Gillman to receive the Grand Cross of the Crescent, a high distinction, bestowed by the sultan on particularly worthy individuals. After Gillman is given this decoration–which, unlike lesser ones, cannot be bought through bribes–Peter returns to Stillwater for his reexamination, and again Gillman cannot pass him. When he gently chides Peter for not studying during his summer in Turkey, Peter cheerfully replies: "To tell you the truth, Professor, . . . you're right. I got working for something worthwhile–and I forgot about the degree."

With his father's help Davis obtained a reporting job at the *Philadelphia Record* in 1886. Because of the weight of his cub-reporting assignments and the merciless cutting of his prose to fit traditional journalistic style, Davis disliked the city editor, who–in turn–did not approve of

Davis's dandified bearing. After only three months Davis was fired from the *Record* and was hired by the *Philadelphia Press* where he remained until 1889. Always egotistical, he never lost his taste for genteel society and always fastidiously maintained his cultivated dress and demeanor, but he was sobered by his firing and used his time at the *Press* to develop into a good reporter. During these years Davis continued to submit fiction to magazines, as he had done since his college days. *St. Nicholas* magazine published "Richard Carr's Baby," a football story, in 1886, and in 1889 that magazine paid him fifty dollars, the sum his mother had earned for "Life in the Iron Mills," for "Midsummer Pirates" (August 1889). Both stories were later collected in *Stories for Boys* (1891).

When "Gallegher: A Newspaper Story" (collected in *Gallegher and Other Stories*, 1891) appeared in the August 1890 issue of *Scribner's Magazine*, Richard Harding Davis gained the attention of a national audience. The model for the subject of Davis's story was a ten-year-old copyboy at the *Press*, whose personality, wit, and penchant for crime detection had earned him the right to be called by his real name, "Gallagher," instead of "Boy" in the newsroom. Drawing heavily from the real-life Gallagher, whose name he changed only slightly, Davis made his fictional copyboy bright and audacious. Himself fascinated by crime stories, Davis, who occasionally disguised himself as a disreputable street character to do undercover reporting, has Gallegher solve a crime that is national front-page news. A streetwise boy adept at recognizing wanted men, Gallegher deduces that Stephen S. Hade, wanted for the murder of his employer, Richard F. Burrbank, would be dressed like a gentleman so that he can look natural wearing gloves to conceal a missing index finger. Sure enough, Gallegher encounters the well-dressed Hade at a Philadelphia train station. He trails Hade to the Eagle Inn, which is to be the scene of an illegal prizefight. After Gallegher learns that Hade will attend, he and Michael Dwyer, the sporting editor at the *Press*, arrange for Hefflefinger, a New York police detective, to arrest Hade in return for the promise that it be done discreetly so that the *Press* can have an exclusive on the capture of the notorious criminal. The plan works admirably until the fight is raided by the local police. In the confusion Hefflefinger manages to arrest Hade and leave for New York, but Dwyer is arrested with others at the fight. He passes the story he has written to Gallegher who uses all his street wisdom and a borrowed hansom cab to rush the story to the *Press*. Gallegher succeeds in the fashion of Alger's heroes, earning the admiration of his coworkers and his editor as well as the cash reward for Hade's capture.

From the publication of "Gallegher" until the turn of the century Davis was one of America's most popular authors. During the same time, having been hired by Arthur Brisbane in December 1889 as a reporter for the *New York Evening Sun*, he became one of New York's star journalists. He thrived on this recognition and on New York itself. His good looks, his taste for fashion, his attention to genteel courtesy and decorum made him a darling of New York society, a favorite among the ladies, and the model for his friend Charles Dana Gibson's pen-and-ink drawings of the male counterpart of the "Gibson Girl." New York afforded him the opportunity to indulge his interest in the theater, fine dining, and events inside the well-to-do social circles to which he was more and more frequently admitted. The only drawback to his new position was

Charles Dana Gibson and Richard Harding Davis on E. C. Benedict's yacht, Oneida, *1893*

that the *Sun* reporters had short weekends: only Sunday was free unless the reporter could produce additional copy which would release him after work on Friday. This restriction made it virtually impossible for Davis to make weekend trips to visit his family in Philadelphia.

Acting on a suggestion from Brisbane, Davis solved this problem by developing a series of weekly feature stories centering on Cortlandt Van Bibber, wealthy man-about-town, through whose eyes *Sun* readers could observe New York and Newport society in the 1890s. The first of these stories, "The Master and the Man," appeared in the 1 March 1890 issue of the *Evening Sun*. In August 1890 *Harper's* published "A Walk Up the Avenue," a story Davis claims to have written in one sitting and the one which briefly introduced Van Bibber to readers outside New York. An incidental character who appears only at the very end of the story, Van Bibber sees the unnamed protagonist embracing his fiancée in Central Park and comments later to a friend at his club that it was "very bad form" even if the couple is engaged.

Stories featuring Van Bibber appear in *Gallegher and Other Stories*, *Van Bibber and Others* (1892), and *Cinderella and Other Stories* (1896), and their popular hero became a kind of social barometer and spokesman for polite society. Characterized by a "genial purposelessness" (he has no profession) and an unflinching loyalty to social proprieties (he descends from Dutch aristocracy in "old" New York), Van Bibber represents the sentimental ideals of all American Victorians. In "Van Bibber's Man-servant" (first published in the 14 June 1890 issue of the *New York Evening Sun* as "Mr. Walters's Temptation"; collected in *Van Bibber and Others*) Walters, his English valet, steps beyond his place by eating a dinner he has ordered for his master, and when he is found out, he is so embarrassed that he leaves Van Bibber's service after paying the cost of the meal. Van Bibber teaches social propriety to a beggar in "The Hungry Man Was Fed" (*New York Evening Sun*, 2 June 1890; collected in *Van Bibber and Others*). Claiming not to have eaten for more than a day, a ragged man cadges several donations, including three from Van Bibber, without buying any food. Van Bibber hustles him off to a cheap eating house, stuffs him with a hearty breakfast, and forces him to pay for it with the money he has begged. "Van Bibber and the Swan-Boats" (*New York Evening Sun*, 7 June 1890; collected in *Gallegher and Other Stories*) takes the aristocrat to Central Park, where he muses on the silliness of the swan boats for hire on the lake. When he encounters three "little ladies from Hester Street" who wish to ride but have no money, however, he escorts them on a ride. Embarrassed when he is observed by "A Girl He Knew and Her Brother," Van Bibber is comforted when the young lady praises him for his gallantry and buys the tenement girls a week's worth of tickets. In "Van Bibber as Best Man" (*New York Evening Sun*, 26 July 1890; collected in *Gallegher and Other Stories*) he is "down from Newport" to meet with his attorney on a summer Saturday. While lunching at a French restaurant he encounters a young couple in the process of eloping. He recognizes young Ted Standish from a proper Boston family, and when the couple is frightened by the appearance of Standish's elder brother in pursuit, Van Bibber resolves not only to send the brother on a wild-goose chase, but to see young Standish and Miss Cambridge married "properly." He gathers whatever friends he can find in town to be "guests" at the wedding and acts as best man. When the ceremony and celebration are over,

Van Bibber resolves to send an account of the day to the paper, and "when it is printed tomorrow it will read like one of the most orthodox and one of the smartest weddings of the season." In a later Van Bibber story, "Cinderella" (*Scribner's Magazine*, April 1896; collected in *Cinderella and Other Stories*), Van Bibber and his friend Travers attend a servants' ball at the Hotel Salisbury along with several theater people. An extraordinary girl on the dance floor captures the attention of all the society-page visitors, and Van Bibber and Travers conspire to cultivate the girl as a professional dancer. But when the two patrons return to the hotel to tell Annie Crehan, the chambermaid "La Cinderella" of their plan, they meet her elevator-boy fiancé on their way to the seventh floor. He tells them of his love for Annie and begs them not to change her, for he fears that he will lose her when she becomes famous. Van Bibber is touched by the boy's plea and with a look "partly of respect and partly of pity," he tells the boy to return them to the lobby, where they will leave her to her faithful but lowly prince.

Van Bibber and his world of Delmonico's, clubs, and "the several hundred" became closely identified with Davis himself in the 1890s, earning for him the reputation of a society dilettante and poseur and the title "prose laureate of snobocracy." Davis left the *Sun* in February 1891 to become managing editor of *Harper's Weekly*. In "The Editor's Story" (*Harper's New Monthly*, August 1894; collected in *Cinderella and Other Stories*) he fictionalizes an incident from his own life. An unnamed editor is sent a plagiarized poem signed "Edward Aram," who gives no return address. After the editor receives three additional plagiarized submissions, each signed by Aram, he and his reporter friend Bronson seek out the "author," who is found to be the son of a city commissioner. He finally admits copying others' work and begs to be forgiven, claiming not to have done it viciously or with intent to defraud (he has asked for no money for his contributions) but only to impress his wife, a reader of the editor's publication. Just as the editor and Bronson resolve to expose Aram in the next day's newspaper to make an example of him, his wife makes an unexpected appearance. Her apparent vulnerability and good breeding melt the heart of the editor and change his mind.

Although Davis was part of polite society, he maintained an interest in the lower strata of urban life, and he occasionally treated these char-

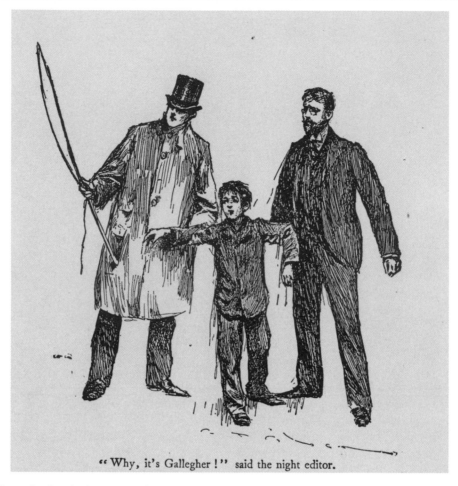

" Why, it's Gallegher ! " said the night editor.

Illustration by Charles Dana Gibson included in a later edition of Gallegher and Other Stories,
Davis's first collection of short stories

acters and their humble surroundings, revealing their quiet dignity. In "My Disreputable Friend, Mr. Raegen" (*Scribner's Magazine,* December 1890; collected in *Gallegher and Other Stories*) Davis writes of an ice-cart man from the tenements, "Rags" Raegen, who is being chased by the police because he has struck "Pike" McGonegal, a member of a rival gang. Fearing that because of his previous record the law will not believe that he acted in self-defense, he takes refuge in a deserted apartment, where he hides under some blankets on the floor as the police make a cursory search of the premises. As he waits for an opportunity to escape, he hears the police mention that the apartment is empty because the man and woman who live there have been sent to jail after a domestic dispute, and he later discovers their young daughter abandoned in the apartment, forgotten by her drunken parents, and overlooked by the authorities. Rags tries to care for the toddler for two days, but the

summer heat and lack of proper food finally force him to take the child to the twenty-first precinct house and turn himself in, even though he has learned from the cries of a newsboy that he is now wanted for murder because McGonegal has died. Three months later, a reformed Raegen is back at work; the police were impressed by his turning himself in to save the child, and one has testified in his behalf saying that he acted in self-defense. Virtue is rewarded, even in the tenements.

A similar character is "Hefty" Burke, "a young man of honest countenance who had been born by some mischance in the Fourth Ward" and who frequently finds himself in scrapes with the police. In "A Leander of the East River" (first published in the 22 August 1890 issue of the *New York Evening Sun* as "How Hefty Left the Island"; collected in *Van Bibber and Others*) he is imprisoned for thirty days after an altercation with McClure, a policeman who beat Hefty for celebrat-

Humorist Finley Peter Dunne, Richard Harding Davis, and novelist John Fox, Jr.

ing his new job and forthcoming engagement a little too noisily. Burke escapes his prison by jumping into the river. Although the current at Hell's Gate proves to be stronger than he expected, he is rescued by a sympathetic canal-boat captain and appears for his date with his beloved Mary Casey in time to thwart another suitor. "How Hefty Burke Got Even" (*New York Evening Sun,* 3 January 1891; collected in *Van Bibber and Others*) continues the story as Burke borrows a suit of armor and wins prizes at a masquerade ball that he and Mary Casey attend at his social club. Though he finds the suit heavy and complains that he looks "like a locomotive," he finds it handy when McClure appears to harass him and the other revelers. He thrashes McClure in a fight and makes a clean getaway, but he cannot claim his prizes lest anyone find out the identity of the armored man. In "The Romance in the Life of Hefty Burke" (*Harper's New Monthly,* January 1893; collected in *The Exiles and Other Stories,* 1894) the young man is confronted by exotic temptations. While sailing in the harbor he saves the life of a young woman who has fallen while try-

ing to board a freighter at anchor. He learns that she and her father, Juan Alvarez, are returning to Colombia, where political oppression has robbed them of their fortune and social position, and her grateful father is impressed enough by Burke to offer him a captaincy in the revolutionary army and the good favor of the young woman. He turns down the offer in deference to his obligations to Mary Casey, but as he is leaving, he accidentally discovers that the freighter is loaded with contraband arms. Unfortunately, he is not the only one to see the contraband: "Big" Marks, an acquaintance of Burke's, is intent on reporting the contraband to collect a reward, but Hefty distracts him with force long enough for the freighter to depart. Burke, like Raegen, has an innate sense of what is right and "proper," even if it does not always agree with the mores of polite society or with the law.

Always eager to travel and to broaden his horizons, Davis insisted on covering stories firsthand. He traveled in the western United States in 1892, and in 1893 he spent several months in Europe and North Africa. When he returned, he was made an advisory associate editor at *Harper's New Monthly Magazine*. Severing himself from even this less-demanding tie by the mid 1890s, Davis became a roving journalist, earning good sums for his pieces and traveling widely in Latin America, Europe, Africa, and Asia. Davis's articles on life in other countries were criticized as sensationalized and ill-informed, and he took this criticism into account when revising them for collections. He found that his experiences abroad helped broaden his understanding of human nature; and this deeper insight coupled with his first-hand knowledge of exotic settings inspired several of his best short stories.

"The Exiles" (*Harper's New Monthly*, May 1894; collected in *The Exiles and Other Stories*) begins: "The greatest number of people in the world prefer the most highly civilized places of the world, because they know what sort of things are going to happen there, and because they also know by experience that those are the sort of things they like." Young Holcombe, the son of Judge Henry Howard Holcombe, is such a person, a man of high ideals, stiff ethics, and deep self-righteousness: "It was measures, not men, to Holcombe, and law and order were his twin goddesses, and 'no compromise' his watchword." After a particularly intense period of reform work and difficult prosecutions, Holcombe is sent to Tangier for his health. He finds there a new civilization where the only whites, except for some officials, are people of dubious background, including some escaping the law. At first Holcombe is appalled, but as the prejudices of his civilization break down he comes to understand and even befriend those he would have shunned in other circumstances. He finds that he knows three members of this exiled society already: former Police Commissioner Meakem, who recently jumped bail to avoid prosecution; Lloyd Carroll, the correspondent in a divorce action Holcombe handled for Mr. Thatcher; and Mrs. Carroll (formerly Mrs. Thatcher). Into this world comes Winthrop Allen, an embezzler who has stolen a quarter-million dollars, including sixty thousand dollars from Martha Field, an elderly teacher known and admired by Holcombe. Since the thief is beyond the reach of New York justice, the young prosecuting attorney takes the law into his own hands, holds Allen at gunpoint, and forces him to hand over Martha Field's sixty thousand dollars. As he leaves Tangier for New York, where he will return the teacher's money, Holcombe observes, "All my life I have been fight-

Davis at the front during World War I

ing causes . . . and principles. I have been working with laws against law breakers. . . . Now . . . I have been thrown with men and women on equal terms. . . . I have been brought face to face . . . with my fellow man."

"A Question of Latitude," published sixteen years later (*Scribner's Magazine*, August 1910; collected in *Once upon a Time*, 1910), presents a much darker picture of exotic locations. Everett, a young man of wealth and good breeding, gains a reputation as a muckraking journalist for *Lowell's Weekly*. Always scrupulous in his personal conduct, he is sent by *Lowell's* to investigate conditions in the Congo, where he finds a world very different from his Boston upbringing, Harvard education, and New York social life—though he finds the appointed officials similar to New York

City politicians. Africa to him seems unexpectedly barbaric, and he begins to find his own "heart of darkness." He makes a sporting wager on the outcome of a feud between an Italian doctor and the local chief of police, and he is only slightly concerned when "his" man is murdered beneath his hotel window. Although he is shocked by tales of white brutality against natives, he beats a black boy for questioning his measurement of cloth. While on a cruise up the Congo Everett draws a pistol on a ship's officer for unbecoming manners at table. Later, he becomes infatuated with Mrs. Ducret, wife of a wealthy ivory trader and a former supper girl at Maxim's in Paris. He propositions her in daringly frank prose; but, because Mrs. Ducret is more used to receiving such advances than Everett is to making them, she effectively blunts his attack long enough to make an early morning getaway with her husband, leaving Everett only a good-bye note for comfort. At the story's ironic conclusion Everett realizes just how much he has changed from his former self: "To Everett, the roar of the great river, and the echoes from the land he had set out to reform, carried the sound of gigantic, hideous laughter."

From the mid 1890s through the turn of the century, Davis found himself covering battles around the world, and earned a reputation as war correspondent during the Greco-Turkish War, the Spanish-American War, and the Boer War. On 4 May 1899 he married Cecil Clark, whom he had known for several years. A fancier of show dogs, she introduced her husband to a new facet of society, which provided for him stories such as "The Bar Sinister" (*Scribner's Magazine*, March 1902; collected in *Ranson's Folly*, 1902), a fictional version of a true story about a street-fighting bull terrier who becomes a champion show dog. His sire was a pure white champion of noble lineage, but his mother was only a "black and tan" mongrel. Yet he beats his father in show competition, for as a dog-companion advises him, "Blood will out, Kid, blood will out."

In 1902 Davis settled down at Crossroads Farm, his home in Mount Kisco, New York, to write. When his novel *Captain Macklin* (1902) was harshly treated by critics, Davis began to devote more and more of his energy to writing and producing plays, activities which occupied him for the next several years, interrupted by an assignment to cover the Russo-Japanese War in 1904 and a trip to the Congo in 1907. Although he won a great deal of recognition for his plays, fic-

Davis with his daughter, Hope Harding Davis

tion writing was too profitable to ignore. In 1910 he separated from his first wife, and after an amicable divorce, Davis married, on 8 July 1912, Elizabeth Genevieve McEvoy, an actress whose stage name was Bessie McCoy.

Davis's later short stories echo earlier works and in some cases emphasize romantic over realistic themes. For example, in "The Man Who Could Not Lose" (*Collier's*, 20 and 27 August 1910; separately published in 1911) a struggling young writer, Champneys Carter, and Dolly Ingram marry against the wishes of Dolly's mother, who cuts off her daughter from her considerable family fortune. The couple's financial problems are solved, however, when Carter begins to dream the winners of horse races and to win money by betting on them. He earns a fortune and the reputation as "the man who could not lose," but Dolly Ingram Carter is not really satisfied. Hiring a publicity man to promote Carter's first novel, which has not sold well, she uses several thousand dollars to buy up the first edition, advertising that it had "sold out in one day," and to subsidize the printing of a second edition. Thanks to Carter's newfound reputation for picking horses–and the somewhat ambiguous title of the novel, *The Dead Heat* (it is actually a mystery)–Dolly's investment is safe. By the end of the story Carter has a fifteen thousand dollar advance for his next book to supplement the fortune they have in the bank. The story reads as a struggling writer's dream come true, with love conquering all.

Similarly, "The Red Cross Girl" (*Saturday Evening Post*, 2 March 1912; collected in *The Red Cross Girl*), which he dedicated to his second wife, tells the story of a star reporter who finds true love. Sam Ward is sent by the New York *Republic* to cover the dedication of The Flagg Home for Convalescents, named after its millionaire benefactor. Ward is not really interested in the facts and figures, and he focuses his story on a beautiful girl in a Red Cross uniform whom he believes to be Sister Anne, a sweet, innocent, and self-sacrificing nurse at the home, taking a photograph of her and even going so far as to arrange a date in the city with her for the following Saturday. Sister Anne is actually Anita Flagg, the millionaire's daughter, playing a role on opening day, and Ward is stung when his story of Sister Anne is printed intact, but she is correctly identified in the caption under her photo as Anita Flagg. Believing that he has been deliberately fooled, he will not answer Anita's phone calls, and, when she telegraphs him as Sister Anne, he replies, "Sister Anne is dead." Nevertheless, he carries out the plan for the date he was to have with the girl of his dreams, though he dines and goes to the theater alone. At the final stop, a musical comedy, he meets Anita, who has come with some friends. She joins him at intermission, and they make up. Coincidentally, each is traveling to London for the winter, and the future looks romantic indeed as they sail together.

In October 1913 Davis worked on the production of the motion-picture version of his 1897 book *Soldiers of Fortune*, and although he had virtually retired from being a war correspondent, he traveled to Vera Cruz in April 1914 to report on strife between the United States and Mexico. Later that same year he journeyed to England, Belgium, and France to report on World War I, collecting his accounts in *With the Allies* (1914). On 4 January 1915 Bessie Davis gave birth to Hope Harding Davis, their only child. That summer, Davis spent a month in a military-training camp, an experience that was hard on him physically even though he had always tried to stay fit; and before the year was out, he was back in Europe, covering World War I. By this time he had come to believe that there was really a question of good versus evil rather than simply imperialistic competition. When he returned to Mount Kisco in February 1916, it was clear that his health was failing. Nevertheless, he continued to work and was busy with the proofs of *With the French in France and Salonika* (1916) when he died suddenly on 11 April.

Any appraisal of Richard Harding Davis's short stories must be made in terms of the period during which he lived. By the time of his death the tastes of the literary world had changed dramatically from the 1890s, and by the 1920s Davis's fiction was regarded as nostalgic trivia. Yet like F. Scott Fitzgerald, Davis both admired and recognized the limitations of the society whose ways he recorded. While he was identified with and embraced the values of his character Cortlandt Van Bibber, he also gently satirized Van Bibber's shallowness. Like Fitzgerald a generation later, Davis was "within and without" at the same time, attracted to high society but mindful of its shortcomings.

Richard Harding Davis chronicled and celebrated the sentimentality, the genteel traditions, and the chauvinistic imperialism of America just as they were about to break down in the crucible of twentieth-century change. His writing, whether nonfiction or fiction, is a valuable social record.

Bibliographies:
Henry Cole Quinby, *Richard Harding Davis: A Bibliography* (New York: Dutton, 1924);

Fannie Mae Elliott, Lucy Clark, and Marjorie D. Carver, *The Barrett Library: Richard Harding Davis, A Checklist of Printed and Manuscript Works of Richard Harding Davis in the Library of the University of Virginia* (Charlottesville: University Press of Virginia, 1963);

John M. Solensten, *Richard Harding Davis (1864-1916)* (Arlington: University of Texas Press, 1970);

Clayton L. Eichelberger and Ann McDonald, *Richard Harding Davis (1864-1916): A Checklist of Secondary Comment* (Arlington: University of Texas Press, 1971).

Biographies:
Fairfax Downey, *Richard Harding Davis: His Day*

(New York & London: Scribners, 1933);

Gerald Langford, *The Richard Harding Davis Years: A Biography of Mother and Son* (New York: Holt, Rinehart & Winston, 1961).

References:

"Notes on Richard Harding Davis," *Bookman*, 43 (June 1916): 353-363;

Scott C. Osborn and Robert L. Phillips, Jr., *Richard Harding Davis* (Boston: Twayne, 1978);

John M. Solensten, "The Gibson Boy: A Reassessment," *American Literary Realism*, 4 (Fall 1971): 303-312.

Papers:

There are three major collections of Davis manuscripts and letters: in the Richard Harding Davis Collection, in the Clifton Waller Barrett Library at the Alderman Library, University of Virginia; letters in the files of Charles Scribner's Sons at Princeton University; and letters in the library of Lehigh University.

Margaret Deland

(23 February 1857-13 January 1945)

B. A. St. Andrews
State University of New York, Health Science Center

BOOKS: *The Old Garden and Other Verses* (Boston & New York: Houghton, Mifflin, 1886; London: Longmans, Green, 1888);

John Ward, Preacher (Boston & New York: Houghton, Mifflin, 1888; London: Longmans, Green, 1888);

A Summer Day (Boston: Prang, 1889);

Florida Days (Boston: Little, Brown, 1889; London: Longmans, Green, 1889);

Sidney (Boston & New York: Houghton, Mifflin, 1890; London: Longmans, Green, 1890);

The Story of a Child (Boston & New York: Houghton, Mifflin, 1892; London: Longmans, Green, 1892);

Mr. Tommy Dove and Other Stories (Boston & New York: Houghton, Mifflin, 1893; London: Longmans, Green, 1893);

Philip and His Wife (Boston & New York: Houghton, Mifflin, 1894; London: Longmans, Green, 1894);

The Wisdom of Fools (Boston & New York: Houghton, Mifflin, 1897; London: Longmans, Green, 1897);

Old Chester Tales (New York & London: Harper, 1899);

Dr. Lavendar's People (New York & London: Harper, 1903);

The Common Way (New York & London: Harper, 1904);

The Awakening of Helena Ritchie (New York & London: Harper, 1906);

An Encore (New York & London: Harper, 1907);

RJ's Mother and Some Other People (New York & London: Harper, 1908);

Where the Laborers Are Few (New York & London: Harper, 1909);

The Way to Peace (New York & London: Harper, 1910);

The Iron Woman (New York & London: Harper, 1911);

The Voice (New York & London: Harper, 1912);

Partners (New York & London: Harper, 1913);

The Hands of Esau (New York & London: Harper, 1914);

Around Old Chester (New York & London: Harper, 1915);

The Rising Tide (New York & London: Harper, 1916);

Small Things (New York: Appleton, 1919);

Margaret Deland (photograph from the Critic, *February 1904)*

The Promises of Alice: The Romance of a New England Parsonage (New York & London: Harper, 1919);

An Old Chester Secret (New York & London: Harper, 1920);

The Vehement Flame (New York & London: Harper, 1922);

New Friends in Old Chester (New York & London: Harper, 1924);

The Kays (New York & London: Harper, 1926);

Captain Archer's Daughter (New York & London: Harper, 1932; London: Cape, 1932);

If This Be I, As I Suppose It Be (New York & London: Appleton-Century, 1935);

Old Chester Days (New York & London: Harper, 1937);

Golden Yesterdays (New York & London: Harper, 1941).

PERIODICAL PUBLICATIONS:
NONFICTION
"A Menace to Literature," *North American Review*, 250 (February 1894): 157-163;

"The Ethics of the Novel," *Independent*, 51 (13 April 1899): 1007-1009;

"Individualism and Social Responsibility," *Independent*, 53 (23 May 1901): 1172-1174;

"The Change in the Feminine Ideal," *Atlantic Monthly*, 105 (March 1910): 289-302;

"Woman in the Market Place," *Independent*, 86 (22 May 1916): 286-288;

"The Light Which is Darkness," *Harper's Monthly*, 139 (June 1919): 34-35.

POETRY
"The Night Mist," *Harper's Monthly*, 74 (May 1887): 927;

"Whence These Tears?," *Century*, 34 (June 1887): 320;

"The Peony," *Century*, 39 (November 1889): 131;

"Deaf," *Harper's Monthly*, 110 (February 1905): 430.

So firmly established were Margaret Deland's achievements in the minds of her generation that in 1936 *Encyclopedia of American Biography* could correctly cite her "international reputation" as precluding any need for extensive introduction. Extolled as a writer who could make her considerable audience not only read but think, she was among the first women elected to the National Institute of Arts and Letters (1926), and she was awarded honorary degrees by Rutgers University (1917), Tufts University (1920), Bates College (1920), and Bowdoin College (1921). Margaretta Wade Campbell Deland now needs not only introduction but reconsideration, for historical and artistic reasons.

Her life covered years of monumental change in American society and was filled with honors and opportunities, despite its difficult beginnings. Born near Allegheny, Pennsylvania, she was named Margaretta Wade Campbell after her mother, who had died in giving birth to her. Her father, Sample Campbell, died when she was about four, and Margaretta, who—when she was somewhat older—shortened her name to Margaret, was raised by her maternal aunt, Lois Wade Campbell, who like her sister had married a man named Campbell, though the two men were not related. Margaretta Wade Campbell grew up in a privileged household on the estate of Louis and Benjamin Bakewell Campbell in Manchester, on the Ohio River near Allegheny. She was educated in Pittsburgh and at Pelham Priory in New Rochelle, New York. Then, in a characteristically independent act, she moved alone in 1875 to New York City, where she studied art and design

Front cover for the first collection of Deland's stories set in a town resembling Manchester, Pennsylvania, where Deland spent her childhood

at Cooper Union. The following year she became an assistant instructor of drawing and design at the Normal College of the City of New York (now Hunter College) and remained there until her marriage on 12 May 1880, to Lorin Fuller Deland, the junior partner of. the Boston printing house Deland and Son, whom she had met during a summer 1878 vacation in Vermont. Childless, the Delands created a fruitful union based upon mutuality and a shared moral vision. For four years early in their marriage they shocked some segments of the public by bringing some sixty unmarried mothers into their home, helping them to understand, to accept, and to overcome the censure of society. To help support this household Deland first painted china and then turned to writing greeting-card verses. A friend sent some of Deland's poems to *Harper's New Monthly Magazine*, which published "The Succory" in its March 1885 issue; more poems appeared in magazines, and in 1886 Houghton,

Mifflin published her first book, *The Old Garden and Other Verses*, whose first printing of one thousand copies sold within a week. The book was reprinted for the fifteenth time in 1899, by which time Deland had also made a name for herself as a fiction writer. After the success of Deland's first novel, *John Ward, Preacher* (1888), the Delands bought a summer house in Kennebunkport, Maine, where Deland spent part of each year for the rest of her life. Lorin Deland's success in advertising as well as the income from his wife's books gave the couple financial security, and they became leaders of Boston society.

In her fiction Deland was interested in preserving the lost places and mores of the past while analyzing the customs and values of the present. She examined the tensions between old orthodoxies and new ideas, between urban and rural sensibilities, between individual goals and those of the community. The characters in the stories dealing with the community of "Old Chester"– many of them collected in *Old Chester Tales* (1899), *Dr. Lavendar's People* (1903), *Around Old Chester* (1915), and *New Friends in Old Chester* (1924)–are poised precariously on the edge of a new age; yet they are emotionally rooted in agricultural America.

Deland's first published short story, "Mr. Tommy Dove" (*Atlantic Monthly*, January 1889; collected in *Mr. Tommy Dove and Other Stories*, 1893), is set in Old Chester, but most of the stories she wrote before 1898 are set elsewhere. From this date until *Old Chester Days*, a selection of previously collected Old Chester stories, appeared in 1937, the first families of Old Chester–the Kays, the Wrights, the Dales, the Jay girls, the Ferris women, the Barkleys, the Doves–and the village's presiding moral consciousness, Dr. Lavendar, became increasingly familiar to American readers of Deland's short stories, novels, and novelettes. These villagers, their doings and undoings, provided a microcosm for the study of human character. In fact, in fiction set in Old Chester and elsewhere Deland often set up characters and stories as mirror images; that is, she presented two approaches to similar problems in order to show the complexity of moral decisions. In "Where Ignorance is Bliss, 'Tis Folly to be Wise," in *The Wisdom of Fools* (1897), for example, she studies the effects of complete honesty between two lovers: Amy Townsend breaks faith with William West after his confessing an act of youthful forgery. "Good for the Soul" (*Harper's New Monthly*, May 1898; collected in *Old Chester Tales*) indicates, con-

WENT PLODDING OUT TO SEE HIS PEOPLE WHO WERE SICK

Dr. Lavendar making his rounds, an illustration by Howard Pyle for Old Chester Days

versely, that keeping one's own counsel may prove equally destructive.

William West also appears in "The House of Rimmon" (first published in the April 1897 issue of *Harper's New Monthly* as "The Wisdom of Fools"; collected in *The Wisdom of Fools*), where he saves the good and dutiful Lydia Blair from a life of struggle and loneliness. This repetition of certain characters underscores Deland's understanding of the nineteenth century's interest in communal history as well as her affection for the people she created. In his influential book *A History of American Literature Since 1870* (1917) Fred Lewis Pattee praised Deland's stylistic blend of feminine tenderness and masculine analysis, stating that Deland's purposes were "to expose the human soul to its own view, to show it its limitations and dangers, that the soul may be purged through fear of what may be–the aim indeed of the Greek drama." Thus, Deland's Old Chester is not a fairyland place but a microcosm where the classic problems of class, change, knowledge, and responsibility exist and demand solution.

Deland's Old Chester–based upon the Manchester of her childhood–parallels Kate Chopin's Grand Isle and bayou country or William Faulkner's fabled Yoknapatawpha County. Other regionalists have created literary places populated with beleaguered, universal characters, while preserving a region's peculiarities. At times the response of these long-suffering characters to struggle seems less a form of virtue than of resignation. As Alexander Cowie notes in *The Rise of the American Novel* (1948), local colorists, including Deland, express a nostalgia for the past, offering characters who are "as authentic as the soil that supports them," while calling for change, exposing a community that "subtly discourages initiative." Deland's insistence on probing unpopular, sometimes "unspeakable" problems brought both approbation and opprobrium. Dedicated to ideas of religious freedom and individual conscience, she forswore the ossifying influences of Calvinism. An anecdote in her autobiographical volume *Golden Yesterdays* (1941) seems to reveal the wellspring of her position: At the funeral of a young cousin the minister chastised the child's father for not attending church regularly, linking the father's absence and the child's death. Though she was raised in a strict, Calvinist household, Deland rejected this pitiless side of orthodoxy, becoming an Episcopalian after her marriage and later rejecting some of the articles of that faith.

Her questioning of religious orthodoxy contributed to her first novel, *John Ward, Preacher*, for which she was both lauded and condemned. At a time when Darwinian thought was challenging religious dogma, many readers wanted an affirmation of old ways and old beliefs. Deland chose instead to face the problem directly. In *Golden Yesterdays* she ponders but cannot explain why her *John Ward, Preacher* appeared at roughly the

Riverbank Court, Cambridge, Mass.
February 8, 1929.

My dear Miss Piercy:-

I am sorry to have been so very long answering your
letter asking me if you might print the letter I wrote you, in the
textbook which you are going to bring out.   I have been not very
well, and *have been* very busy -- and the combination of these two things has
interfered with letter writing.

You are quite welcome to publish the letter I wrote you
about "Helena Richie", with the one or two slight changes which I
have made ✓ *see inclosure.* As I did not write that letter for publication, I did
not make as clear as I should the statement about Helena's mental
processes.

So far as I am concerned, you may print one of the Old
Chester stories, but I think you could make a better choice than "The
Promises of Dorothea"? Wouldn't "The Note" be more interesting to
most readers? Or possibly "An Encore", which has more humor in it? *Howev*
I leave the choice to you --
The Harpers are my publishers, and I suppose that it is to them that you
should apply for permission to reprint any of my stuff.

Again with apologies for not writing to you before,

I am,

Sincerely yours,

Margaret Deland

*I think that the Elliots Katy - in New Friends
in Old Chester, is more interesting than the
Promises ———— but perhaps it is too long —*

Letter to Josephine Ketcham Piercy, editor of the 1930 English-composition textbook Modern Writers at Work, *for which she asked writers to send a paragraph or chapter of "What you consider your best writing with an explanatory or supplementary letter as to your methods, habits of writing, revisions, etc." Deland had sent part of chapter 24 from her 1906 novel,* The Awakening of Helena Ritchie, *with a letter explaining that it "indicates how hard I have to work to acquire lucidity and precision. . . ." This letter grants Piercy permission to publish the previous letter, and suggests other possible inclusions, none of which appeared in the book (Lilly Library, Indiana University).*

same time as two other books, Olive Schreiner's *The Story of An African Farm* (1883; first American edition, 1888) and Mrs. Humphry Ward's *Robert Elsmere* (1888), wondering if there were "a 'Plan' which caused three women who had never heard of each other, on three different continents, Africa, Europe, and America, to write–at almost the same time, books attacking religious beliefs?" Deland's wondering if a Divine directive might have inspired these literary attacks on religion indicates her ability to hold what appear to be contradictory beliefs firmly in mind.

As in her later fiction, the characters in *John Ward, Preacher* are drawn with such balance and dignity that the readers' sympathies are divided between the unyielding Calvinism of John Ward and the loving piety of his Episcopalian wife, who resolutely refuses to accept the essential Calvinist belief in the existence of hell. Such stylistic ability is largely responsible for Deland's enormous success: she was able to cloak controversial ideas in beautiful descriptions and present them through well-drawn, sympathetic, honorable characters.

Yet to present Margaret Deland as a pioneer for new ideas and new morals is but a half-truth. She held many traditional, conservative social ideas, including the primacy of motherhood, the sanctity of marriage, and the concept of self-sacrifice. More Kantian than Calvinist, she believed that no one should engage in activities which, if engaged in by all, would destroy the fabric of society. Thus, she called for moderation. Her definition of individual freedom precluded revolutionary action even in the name of just causes. She examined divorce in *The Iron Woman* (1911), feminism in *The Rising Tide* (1916), pacifism in *The Kays* (1926), adultery in *The Vehement Flame* (1922), rejecting any fashionable dogma which might condemn her characters or simplify their dilemmas.

Deland opposed universal female suffrage; her essay "The Change in the Feminine Ideal," which appeared in *Atlantic Monthly* (March 1910), advocates selective suffrage, an elitist notion based upon class, education, and economic conditions. Frederica Payton, the protagonist in Deland's *The Rising Tide*, for example, participates in suffrage rallies and experiences modest success in her own real-estate firm. Yet Freddy must learn the settling benefits of mature love and modify her feminist fervor. A review in *Nation* (October 1916) summarized the popular attitude to-

ward Deland's character and message: "If her story shows the folly of current militant and aggressive methods, it does not deny the existence of a goal." In her own life, however, from the time she emancipated herself from her adoptive parents to attend art school in New York, Deland insisted on feminist prerogatives and a modicum of individual freedom. Deland's charitable works also provided her a forum in which to examine the complexity of moral issues. In *Old Chester Tales* Mary Dean of "The Child's Mother" (*Harper's New Monthly*, August 1898) represents moral regeneration, while in an earlier story, "The Law or the Gospel" (first published in the February 1896 issue of *Cosmopolitan* as "One Woman's Story: A Study"; collected in *The Wisdom of Fools*), the efforts of Sarah Wharton to uplift Nellie Sherman are wasteful, destructive, and futile because Nellie does not want to be reformed. *The Awakening of Helena Ritchie* (1906) extends the study of how a woman who has violated the established moral order can find regeneration through the love of a child.

In this novel, as in many short stories, Dr. Lavendar is the kindly and insightful moral leader of Old Chester. Rector of St. Michael's Church, Dr. Lavendar preaches (and embodies) a religion of duty. His wise directives help citizens of Old Chester to regain the path of moral rectitude. Through this character, who is just, yet tolerant, Deland invited her readers to contemplate a range of tangled, ethical issues.

In December 1917–following her husband's death the previous May–Deland went to France to engage in war-relief work. *Small Things* (1919) collects Deland's articles about her trip to war-torn France, recording the reactions of civilians, soldiers, and relief workers to their experiences. For her work in France Deland was awarded the Legion of Honor. Born before the Civil War and dying near the end of World War II, Deland lived during a period of monumental change. Her autobiographical volumes, *If This Be I, As I Suppose It Be* (1935) and *Golden Yesterdays*, provide important insights into the course of American history during the nearly ninety years of her life.

Many of Deland's best-known stories–"Many Waters" (*Collier's*, 13 May 1905; collected in *RJ's Mother and Some Other People*, 1908); "Justice and the Judge" (*Harper's New Monthly*, September 1898; collected in *Old Chester Tales*,); "An Old Chester Secret" (separately published in 1920; collected in *New Friends in Old Chester*); "The Grass-

Margaret Deland (photograph © Brown Brothers)

hopper and the Ant" (*Harper's Monthly*, October 1903; collected in *Dr. Lavendar's People*); and "Good for the Soul" (*Harper's Monthly*, May 1898; collected in *Old Chester Tales*)–examine characters and issues which transcend the historical moment. Whether her writings are reactionary or progressive, sentimental or hardheaded is still under debate. Perhaps what the *Boston Transcript* prophesied about Deland's works in 1924 may still prove true: "They have a vitality in them that has endured and that will endure when the literary fads and eccentricities of the first quarter of the twentieth century have disappeared and are forgotten." The reader will find in Deland's short stories meticulously wrought characters who, whatever their political or religious views, aspire to courage, honorable conduct, and love for humanity.

References:

Mary W. Ford, "Some Representative Story Tellers," *Bookman*, 25 (July 1907): 511-519;
Marjorie Gould, "Of Margaret Deland and Old 'Chester,' " *Colby Library Quarterly*, series two, 10 (May 1949): 167-171;
James Humphry III, "The Works of Margaret Deland," *Colby Library Quarterly*, series two, 8 (November 1948): 134-140;
David J. Nordloh, *The Popular Novel 1865-1920* (Boston: Twayne, 1980), pp. 156-162;
Grant Overton, *The Women Who Make Our Novels* (New York: Dodd, Mead, 1928), pp. 105-106;
Fred Lewis Pattee, *A History of American Literature Since 1870* (New York: Century, 1917), pp. 394-397;
Diana C. Reep, *Margaret Deland* (Boston: Twayne, 1985);
Blanche Colton Williams, *Our Short Story Writers* (New York: Moffat, Yard, 1926), pp. 129-145.

Papers:

A substantial collection of letters, work sheets, and corrected typescripts is housed in the Miller Library at Colby College.

Paul Laurence Dunbar

(27 June 1872-9 February 1906)

James R. Giles
Northern Illinois University

See also the Dunbar entries in *DLB 50: Afro-American Writers Before the Harlem Renaissance* and *DLB 54: American Poets, 1880-1945.*

SELECTED BOOKS: *Oak and Ivy* (Dayton, Ohio: Press of United Brethren Publishing House, 1893 [i.e., 1892]);

Majors and Minors: Poems (Toledo, Ohio: Hadley & Hadley, 1895);

Lyrics of Lowly Life (New York: Dodd, Mead, 1896; London: Chapman & Hall, 1897);

Folks from Dixie (New York: Dodd, Mead, 1898; London: Bowden, 1898);

The Uncalled: A Novel (New York: Dodd, Mead, 1898; London: Service & Paton, 1899);

Lyrics of the Hearthside (New York: Dodd, Mead, 1899);

The Strength of Gideon and Other Stories (New York: Dodd, Mead, 1900);

The Love of Landry (New York: Dodd, Mead, 1900);

The Fanatics (New York: Dodd, Mead, 1901);

The Sport of the Gods (New York: Dodd, Mead, 1902); republished as *The Jest of Fate: A Story of Negro Life* (London: Jarrold, 1902);

Lyrics of Love and Laughter (New York: Dodd, Mead, 1903);

In Old Plantation Days (New York: Dodd, Mead, 1903);

The Heart of Happy Hollow (New York: Dodd, Mead, 1904);

Lyrics of Sunshine and Shadow (New York: Dodd, Mead, 1905);

The Life and Works of Paul Laurence Dunbar, edited by Lida Keck Wiggins (Naperville, Ill. & Memphis, Tenn.: J. L. Nichols, 1907);

The Complete Poems (New York: Dodd, Mead, 1913);

The Best Stories of Paul Laurence Dunbar, edited by Benjamin Brawley (New York: Dodd, Mead, 1938);

The Paul Laurence Dunbar Reader, edited by Jay Martin and Gossie H. Hudson (New York: Dodd, Mead, 1975).

Paul Laurence Dunbar (Ohio Historical Society)

OTHER: "Representative American Negroes," in *The Negro Problem: A Series of Articles by Representative Negroes* (New York: James Pott, 1903), pp. 189-209;

"The Tuskegee Song," in *Selected Songs Sung by Students of Tuskegee Normal and Industrial Institute* (Tuskegee, Ala.: Tuskegee Institute, 1904), p. 3.

Paul Laurence Dunbar was born in Dayton, Ohio, to Joshua and Matilda Murphy Dunbar, both former slaves, on 27 June 1872. He was educated in public schools, graduating from Central High School in 1891. Dunbar composed the class song, and several of his poems appeared in local

Dayton newspapers. His first book, a collection of poems, *Oak and Ivy*, was privately printed and appeared just before Christmas, 1892. His second collection, *Majors and Minors* (1895), caught the attention of William Dean Howells, who published a lengthy laudatory review in the 27 June 1896 *Harper's Weekly*. On 6 March 1898 Dunbar married Alice Ruth Moore, a writer and teacher who would achieve a measure of fame in her own right. The marriage, however, was plagued with tensions, both artistic and personal, and the couple divorced in 1904, two years before Dunbar's death from tuberculosis.

During his brief career Dunbar produced a considerable body of poetry, four novels, and four collections of short stories. With the active encouragement and support of Howells, Dunbar became one of the first black American writers to benefit from a large public following. His predominately comic black-dialect poetry and southern plantation stories were widely admired by turn-of-the-century American readers. The rapidly changing literary tastes and values of the twentieth century have not, however, treated Dunbar's reputation kindly. Both the dialect poems and the plantation stories increasingly have been under attack for their dependence upon degrading stereotypes of black people. Several modern critics have made the telling point that, while Dunbar achieved popularity through romanticizing the Old South, his personal experience was largely limited to the post-Civil War North.

While it is impossible to refute totally the view of Dunbar as an apologist for a racist southern society, one can say that the complexity of his overall achievement demands a close examination. In fact, he published considerably more lyric poetry written in standard English than dialect verse and is increasingly remembered for his powerful coded protest poem, "We Wear the Mask." Similarly, his four collections of short stories are not made up exclusively of southern plantation tales. The majority of his stories can be divided into four categories: the plantation tall tale; didactic stories warning his readers against certain vices; fiction decrying overt and brutal southern social repression; and protest fiction aimed at more covert northern racism. The didactic fiction is the least interesting; it is dominated by a suffocating puritanism and is technically weak. The protest stories set in the North are the most memorable. With the exception of an unprofitable 1897 lecture tour of England, Dunbar spent most of his adult life in Washington, D.C.,

Photograph of Dunbar used as the frontispiece for Majors and Minors *(1895), the collection of poems that established his reputation*

(where he worked as a reading-room assistant at the Library of Congress), Chicago, and Dayton, and outrage arising from his experience gives these tales a legitimate power.

Dunbar's first collection of stories, *Folks from Dixie*, appeared in 1898. It is dominated by plantation tall tales depicting southern blacks who are fiercely loyal servants as well as intensely, if comically, religious. Dunbar editorializes in one story about "that characteristic reverence for religion which is common to all their race, and not lacking even in the most hardened sinner among them. . . ." The motif of slaves freely choosing loyalty to their masters over loyalty to themselves runs throughout the volume. The didactic Dunbar is present in this volume as well. For instance, "The Ordeal at Mt. Hope" comes closer to being a lecture on the necessity of black spiritual "uplift" than a story. "Jimsella" is reminiscent of Dunbar's most successful novel, *The Sport of the Gods* (1902), in its warning against the moral destruction awaiting blacks in the North. The volume's three most important stories are "Nelse Hatton's Vengeance," "At Shaft 11," and "The Colonel's Awakening." In the first, Nelse Hatton, a former slave living comfortably in Ohio, welcomes a white beggar into his house only to discover that the man is his former sadistic master. Briefly tempted to take revenge, Nelse remembers instead the teachings of the New Testament and feeds the man. Dunbar's concern with spiritual "uplift" is clearly evident in this story; but, in contrast to "The Ordeal at Mt. Hope," it is developed dramatically. "At Shaft 11" is an intriguing and somewhat disturbing story dominated by Dunbar's unique kind of conservatism. The setting is a West Virginia mine at which the once happy workers have been led astray by union organizers. Dunbar seems to imply that labor trouble can be solved without unionization, if only the best and strongest white workers will cooperate with the best and strongest blacks. "The Colonel's Awakening," the least typical story in the volume, is essentially a portrait of an old Virginia aristocrat unable to adjust to post-Civil War reality and the loss of his two sons. It is one of Dunbar's most effectively crafted, moving achievements.

The Strength of Gideon and Other Stories (1900) is generally considered Dunbar's most ambitious and most successful collection. Still, it does have its share of both overly sentimental stories focusing on loyal servants and didactic tales warning against the evils of dissipation and vice, especially as found in the North. For instance, the title story, first published in October 1899 in *Lippincott's Monthly Magazine*, is an approving account of how Gideon, when emancipation is finally achieved, turns his back on freedom and his fiancée out of loyalty to the white family which had owned him. "The Trustfulness of Polly" describes the moral destruction of Polly Jackson's husband Sam as he falls prey to the "policy game" in New York City's "tenderloin" district. Much more effectively written is "An Old-Time Christmas," in which 'Liza Ann Lewis carefully saves her money so that she can give her thirteen-year-old son Jimmy a "down-home" Christmas, only to have her plans shattered when Jimmy is arrested for shooting dice.

Perhaps no story so emphatically reveals Dunbar's confusing and even contradictory stance regarding both black loyalty and the evil lure of the North as "Viney's Free Papers." In it patient, hardworking Ben Raymond struggles desperately to buy freedom for himself and for Viney, first his girl and then his wife. Ultimately he is able to secure freedom for Viney, but not for himself. The woman immediately becomes arrogant with other blacks who are still slaves and offends virtually every friend she and Ben have. Even worse, she betrays her husband and plans to desert him in order to go north. In a last-minute conversion she realizes her love for Ben and burns the papers which document her freedom. The story conveys the horror of a system which separated loved ones; nevertheless, one feels that Dunbar is much more concerned with warning blacks against the vice of pride and the dangers of the sinful North. In contrast, "The Ingrate" (*New England Magazine*, August 1899) and "The Tragedy at Three Forks" represent unqualified protest against southern racism. Dunbar's father had escaped to Canada on the Underground Railroad before the Civil War and later served in the Union Army; and, according to Darwin T. Turner in his introduction to the 1969 Arno Press edition of *The Strength of Gideon*, "The Ingrate" is a fictionalized account of his experience. The story ends on an effective note of irony when the master learns that his former slave is now a sergeant in the Union Army and lapses into a self-pitying tirade. One of Dunbar's two lynching stories, "The Tragedy at Three Forks" is saved from triteness by its penetrating insights into the sexual hysteria of the white girl who initiates the "tragedy."

By far the most intriguing stories in Dunbar's second collection, however, are those which investigate the black love-hate relationship with the post-Civil War Republican party. "Mr. Cornelius Johnson, Office-Seeker" (*Cosmopolitan*, February 1899) vividly depicts the disintegration of the title character after the party has promised him a government position, then stalled him interminably before disappointing him entirely. Elaborately plotted, "A Council of State" recounts the party's successful plot to reduce an Afro-American convention to a meaningless formality. In sharp contrast to these two stories is "A Mess of Pottage" (*Saturday Evening Post*, 16 December 1899), which painfully conveys the outrage of Deacon Swift, a fanatically loyal Republican, when his own son sells his vote to an ambitious Democratic candidate. Judging from these stories, Dunbar seems to have felt that, while the Republican party offered black people their only hope, they should expect disappointment and even occasional betrayal from it. Perhaps the most bitter story Dunbar ever wrote, "One Man's Failure" touches on the black man's relationship to the political party of Lincoln and emancipation. "One Man's Failure" is, however, broader in focus–its

Dunbar in his study, which he called "Loafin' Holt" (Ohio Historical Society)

real concern is with the ever-present, inescapable northern hypocrisy toward the black American.

For the most part, *In Old Plantation Days* (1903) is an artistic lapse after *The Strength of Gideon*. As its title indicates, its twenty-five stories are dominated by plantation tall tales heavily dependent upon the stereotypes of the loyal servant and the comically religious black. While occasional sadistic overseers appear in these stories and are clearly condemned, the pervasive emphasis is upon the need for black slaves to learn responsibility through loyalty and obedience to their white masters. Moreover, a majority of these works are not true stories, but character sketches or nostalgic vignettes of plantation life. While "Ash-Cake Hannah and Her Ben" (*Saturday Evening Post*, 8 December 1900) describes the pain of husband and wife separated by the slavery system, it is not developed into a truly well-rounded story. In contrast, "The Conjuring Contest" (*Saturday Evening Post*, 8 July 1899) contains comic ambiguity and a clearly developed resolution, but its tone implies nostalgic approval of the slavery system. *In Old Plantation Days* does contain a few stories which are exceptions to its overall mediocrity. Reminiscent of "The Colonel's Awakening," "The Stanton Coachman" presents a white aristocratic family completely unable to

face reality after the loss of their fortune. "The Easter Wedding" is the volume's best story, emphasizing the vulnerability of the black slave to his master's weaknesses. A decent, but impractical, plantation owner loses his land to a cruel overseer and then has to perform a wedding ceremony for two of his slaves. Throughout the ceremony everyone knows that the couple will almost certainly be sold separately by their new owner as a fate symbolically foreshadowed by an owl's ominous hooting.

The Heart of Happy Hollow (1904) contains Dunbar's best short story, "The Scapegoat," a deliciously ironic account of the revenge which Mr. Robinson Asbury, a black party boss, takes upon the political establishment after it has temporarily purged him in the name of reform. Asbury is the most memorable character in all of Dunbar's stories—not quite honest, but a masterful manipulator. The sheer anger at the political system which dominates such a story as "Mr. Cornelius Johnson, Office-Seeker" is here refined to a restrained, but savagely effective, satire.

Irony and satire appear in other stories in Dunbar's last volume. "The Mission of Mr. Scatters" is highly reminiscent of Mark Twain's "The Man That Corrupted Hadleyburg" (1899) in its characterization of an elegant, but deceitful,

Dunbar's bedroom in the house in Dayton, Ohio, where he lived from 1903 until his death in 1906. The bicycle was a gift from Orville Wright, Dunbar's high-school friend.

"stranger" who tricks a complacent community. Dunbar does descend to his worst stereotypical impulses in such an anecdote as "The Race Question"; one is, nevertheless, pleased to find "Old Abe's Conversion," which at least grants the possibility of a rational, socially concerned black religion. Still, apart from the obvious brilliance of "The Scapegoat," *The Heart of Happy Hollow* can generally be said to demonstrate the same aesthetic inconsistency and occasional authorial confusion that typified Dunbar's first two collections. "The Triumph of Ol' Mis' Pease" is a memorable portrait of a once-decent woman embittered by unrelenting bad luck and severe blows to her pride. "The Lynching of Jube Benson" presents inherently emotional and dramatic subject matter in a trite, cliché-ridden manner; the story contains none of the psychological insight found in "The Tragedy at Three Forks." Like "Viney's Free Papers," "The Wisdom of Silence" is marred by confusing authorial intent. While the story does give a graphic picture of the horrendous odds against which the newly freed slave had to struggle, its message seems to be that the freedman should guard against the sin of pride in his new socioeconomic position.

Paul Laurence Dunbar is not a major figure in the history of the short story. Technically, he perfected nothing original and even had trouble in plotting the most traditional kind of stories. There is, in fact, considerable evidence that he viewed fiction as a literary form inherently inferior to poetry. Still, Dunbar should be remembered as the author of a few excellent stories distinguished by powerful characterization and as one of the most popular American writers of his time. The contradictions often implicit in his authorial stance are in themselves interesting for what they reveal about the unique pressures felt by a black writer addressing a predominately white audience at the turn of the century.

Bibliography:
E. W. Metcalf, Jr., *Paul Laurence Dunbar: A Bibliography* (Metuchen, N.J.: Scarecrow Press, 1975).

Biographies:
Virginia Cunningham, *Paul Laurence Dunbar and His Song* (New York: Dodd, Mead, 1947);
Addison Gayle, Jr., *Oak and Ivy: A Biography of Paul Laurence Dunbar* (Garden City, N.Y.: Doubleday, 1971).

References:

Benjamin Brawley, *Paul Laurence Dunbar: Poet of His People* (Chapel Hill: University of North Carolina Press, 1936);

Darwin T. Turner, Introduction to *The Strength of Gideon and Other Stories* (New York: Arno Press, 1969);

Turner, "Paul Laurence Dunbar: The Rejected Symbol," *Journal of Negro History*, 52 (1967): 1-13.

Papers:

The Ohio Historical Society, Columbus, holds the major collection of Dunbar manuscripts, letters, related documents, and correspondence. The Dunbar home at 219 North Summit Street in Dayton, which is maintained by the society as a state memorial, has Dunbar's personal library. The Schomburg Center for Research in Black Culture, New York Public Library, has an important collection of Dunbar letters and related correspondence.

Mary E. Wilkins Freeman
(31 October 1852-15 March 1930)

Perry D. Westbrook
State University of New York at Albany

See also the Freeman entry in *DLB 12: American Realists and Naturalists*.

BOOKS: *Decorative Plaques: Designs by George F. Barnes, Poems by Mary E. Wilkins* (Boston: Lothrop, 1883);

Goody Two-Shoes and Other Famous Nursery Tales, by Clara Doty Bates and Mary E. Wilkins (Boston: Lothrop, 1883);

The Cow with Golden Horns and Other Stories (Boston: Lothrop, 1884?);

The Adventures of Ann: Stories of Colonial Times (Boston: Lothrop, 1886);

A Humble Romance and Other Stories (New York: Harper, 1887); republished in two volumes as *A Humble Romance and Other Stories* and *A Far-Away Melody and Other Stories* (Edinburgh: Douglas, 1890);

A New England Nun and Other Stories (New York: Harper, 1891; London: Osgood, McIlvaine, 1891);

The Pot of Gold and Other Stories (Boston: Lothrop, 1892; London: Ward, Lock, Bowden, 1892);

Young Lucretia and Other Stories (New York: Harper, 1892; London: Osgood, McIlvaine, 1892);

Jane Field: A Novel (London: Osgood, McIlvaine, 1892; New York: Harper, 1893);

Giles Corey, Yeoman: A Play (New York: Harper, 1893);

Pembroke: A Novel (New York: Harper, 1894; London: Osgood, McIlvaine, 1894);

Comfort Pease and Her Gold Ring (New York, Chicago & Toronto: Revell, 1895);

Madelon: A Novel (New York: Harper, 1896; London: Osgood, 1896);

Once Upon a Time and Other Child Verses (Boston: Lothrop, 1897; London: Harper, 1898);

Jerome, A Poor Man: A Novel (New York & London: Harper, 1897);

Silence and Other Stories (New York & London: Harper, 1898);

The People of Our Neighborhood (Philadelphia: Curtis/New York: Doubleday, McClure, 1898); republished as *Some of Our Neighbours* (London: Dent, 1898);

The Love of Parson Lord and Other Stories (New York & London: Harper, 1900);

The Hearts Highway: A Romance of Virginia in the Seventeenth Century (New York: Doubleday, Page, 1900; London: Murray, 1900);

Understudies (New York & London: Harper, 1901);

Mary E. Wilkins Freeman

The Portion of Labor (New York & London: Harper, 1901);

Six Trees (New York & London: Harper, 1903);

The Wind in the Rose-Bush and Other Stories of the Supernatural (New York: Doubleday, Page, 1903; London: Murray, 1903);

The Givers (New York & London: Harper, 1904);

The Debtor: A Novel (New York & London: Harper, 1905);

"Doc." Gordon (New York & London: Authors & Newspapers Association, 1906);

By the Light of the Soul: A Novel (New York & London: Harper, 1907);

The Fair Lavinia and Others (New York & London: Harper, 1907);

The Shoulders of Atlas: A Novel (New York & London: Harper, 1908);

The Winning Lady and Others (New York & London: Harper, 1909);

The Green Door (New York: Moffat, Yard, 1910; London: Gay & Hancock, 1912);

The Butterfly House (New York: Dodd, Mead, 1912);

The Yates Pride: A Romance (New York & London: Harper, 1912);

The Copy-Cat & Other Stories (New York & London: Harper, 1914);

An Alabaster Box, by Freeman and Florence Morse Kingsley (New York & London: Appleton, 1917);

Edgewater People (New York & London: Harper, 1918).

PLAY PRODUCTIONS: *Giles Corey, Yeoman*, Boston, Theatre of Arts and Letters, 27 March 1893; New York, Palmer's Theatre, 17 April 1893.

OTHER: "The Long Arm," by Freeman and J. Edgar Chamberlin, in *The Long Arm, by Mary E. Wilkins, and Other Detective Stories, by George Ira Brett, Professor Brander Matthews, and Roy Tellet* (London: Chapman & Hall, 1895), pp. 1-66;

"Emily Brontë and Wuthering Heights," in *The Booklovers Reading Club Handbook to Accompany the Reading Course Entitled the World's Great Woman Novelists* (Philadelphia: Booklovers Library, 1901), pp. 85-93;

"The Old-Maid Aunt," in *The Whole Family: A Novel by Twelve Authors* (New York & London: Harper, 1908), pp. 30-59;

"The Girl Who Wants to Write," *Harper's Bazar*, 47 (June 1913): 472.

Mary E. Wilkins Freeman ranks among the foremost interpreters of New England village and rural life. Though she may correctly be described as a local colorist, she is much more, for in her short stories and novels she deals perceptively with the 250-year-old Puritan heritage of her region so convincingly, with such objectivity, that she takes an honored place in the development of realism in American literature, a place that the "high priest of realism," William Dean Howells, readily assigned her. Her local color–her presentation of the social and physical aspects of the New England countryside–is unexceptionable; but she either avoids or greatly modifies some of the conventions of local-color writing. Thus she does not dwell on "quaintness," whether of character or folkways, merely for the sake of quaintness. Nor does she record regional dialect with the relentless phonetic accuracy that has rendered much nineteenth-century local-color writing repugnant to present-day readers. In her dialogue she attempts, usually success-

A HUMBLE ROMANCE

AND OTHER STORIES

BY

MARY E. WILKINS

NEW YORK
HARPER & BROTHERS, FRANKLIN SQUARE
LONDON: 30 FLEET STREET
1887

A NEW ENGLAND NUN

AND OTHER STORIES

BY

MARY E. WILKINS
AUTHOR OF "A HUMBLE ROMANCE" ETC.

NEW YORK
HARPER & BROTHERS, FRANKLIN SQUARE
1891

Title pages for the collections of short stories that established Freeman's reputation as a local-color writer

fully, to catch the rhythms of regional speech and to give the flavor, rather than an exact transcription, of pronunciation. Most important, unlike most local colorists, in her best writing she is preoccupied with the psychology, especially as it is derived from cultural roots, underlying her characters' attitudes and actions. For example, she was fascinated by what may be called the anatomy of the New England will—that legacy from early Puritanism—which she found in a hypertrophied, or warped, condition in the remote villages and on the isolated farms of the area. At the beginning of her career, she earned recognition for her insights into the impulses and motives that ruled the lives of the fiercely independent, stubborn, often pathetic, and at times hateful rural characters that people her stories.

Yet her insights were not solely in the realm of psychology. She was also keenly aware of the social and economic conditions with which her country folk had to contend. Seriously depopulated of its men by the Civil War and by migration to the West and to the industrial cities, the countryside of which she wrote was one of run-down or abandoned farms. Her villages, where the churches,

the schools, and the town-meeting governments had lost their original vigor or seemed hardly to function, were communities where women, disenfranchised politically and barred from the ministry, far outnumbered the men and where the men who remained were more often than not moral and intellectual weaklings. Thus Freeman wrote of a woman's world, and since her women, many of them strong characters but others weak and neurotic, somehow cope, she has attracted the attention of feminist literary critics—a development which, after a period of neglect, has contributed to her rehabilitation as an important American author. But mostly the renewal of her reputation is ascribable to the fact that in her skill at evoking atmosphere and mood and in her psychological perceptions she anticipates such authors as Katherine Anne Porter and Katherine Mansfield. And as a depicter of rural New Englanders she must be considered in the company of Sarah Orne Jewett, Edwin Arlington Robinson, and Robert Frost.

Freeman wrote about conditions, places, and people that she had known at firsthand all her life. She was born Mary Ella Wilkins in Ran-

Portrait of Freeman used as the frontispiece for The Love of Parson Lord and Other Stories *(1900)*

dolph, Massachusetts, in 1852. (Her middle name was later changed to Eleanor.) Both her father, Warren E. Wilkins, who was a carpenter, and her mother, Eleanor Lothrop Wilkins, were descended from seventeenth-century settlers in the Colony of Massachusetts Bay. Randolph, though only fourteen miles from Boston, was an agricultural community with a considerable amount of shoe manufacturing, much of it carried on in individual homes. Orthodox Congregationalism held sway in the town, and the Wilkins family strictly observed the Sabbath with its Sunday school, morning and afternoon services, and evening prayer meeting. Later in life Mary Wilkins took a somewhat relaxed view of the Calvinism in which she had been brought up, but she remained a member of the Congregational Church. When she was fifteen years old, she moved with her family to Brattleboro, a town of some cultural pretensions in southern Vermont, where her father went into the retail dry-goods business. Graduating from Brattleboro High School in 1870, she entered the strictly religiously oriented Mt. Holyoke Female Seminary but dropped out because of ill health after a year. Returning home, she took courses at Glenwood Seminary in West Brattleboro during 1871-1872. A series of misfortunes then beset the Wilkins family. Between the years 1873 and 1880

Warren Wilkins's business failed, forcing him to return to carpentry; Mary's only sister, Anna, died in 1876 at the age of seventeen; and Mary's mother died in 1880 at the age of fifty-three. In 1882 Warren Wilkins, in poor health, moved to Florida, where he continued his trade as a builder until his death a year later. Soon after, Mary returned to Randolph, continuing to live there until her marriage to Dr. Charles Manning Freeman on 1 January 1902 and her consequent removal to his home in Metuchen, New Jersey, where she died of a heart attack in 1930. During her seventeen years in Brattleboro she had gained an intimate knowledge of rural New England life, especially as it was lived in the nearby hill towns.

Before her return to Randolph, Freeman had tried her hand at writing and had placed juvenile poetry and fiction in such reputable magazines for children as *Wide Awake* and *St. Nicholas*. She had also won a prize for an adult story, "The Shadow Family," published in the 1 January 1882 *Boston Sunday Budget*, had placed several others in *Harper's Bazar*, and as a final triumph had had her story "A Humble Romance" (collected in *A Humble Romance and Other Stories*, 1887) accepted by the prestigious *Harper's New Monthly Magazine*, where it appeared in the June 1884 issue. Mary Booth, the editor of *Harper's Bazar*, was especially fond of Freeman's fiction, and, though Booth died in 1889, the magazine continued to publish Freeman's work for many years. A stickler for grammar, Mary Booth forbade Freeman to end sentences in prepositions.

Thus launched, Freeman continued to turn out a steady flow of stories and poems for both children and adults. Her first collection of adult short fiction, *A Humble Romance and Other Stories*, was published in 1887 by Harper and Brothers. This volume is one of her most distinguished and is thoroughly representative of her best work both stylistically and thematically. In the preface to an 1890 Edinburgh edition Freeman carefully defined her purpose and the scope of her subject matter. She was writing, she stated, about "the descendants of the Massachusetts Bay Colonists, in whom can *still* be seen traces of will and conscience, so strong as to be almost exaggerations and deformities, which characterized their ancestors." Her hope was "to present in literature . . . this old and disappearing type of New England character." In this purpose she was highly successful. William Dean Howells, though he found a few of the stories in *A Humble Romance* too sentimental for his taste, praised the stories in the aggregate for "their directness and simplicity" and their distinctively American flavor and compared her work favorably with that of Sarah Orne Jewett, Ivan Turgenev, and Henry James for its avoidance of the superficiality of much of the fiction of the day. To Howells, Freeman was an outstanding practitioner of the realism that he was sponsoring in the criticism he was writing for his "Editor's Study" column in *Harper's New Monthly* and exemplifying in his own fiction. Hamlin Garland was even more impressed. He considered Freeman's work to be in close accord with his theory of literary "veritism" (essentially realism). Visiting her in Randolph in 1886 or 1887, he thought "her home might have been used as a typical illustration for her [characters' homes]"–a confirmation that she was a countrywoman whose writing reflected her own life and experience. Eventually Freeman's work also received acclaim as social commentary; for example, Rollin Lynde Hartt, in an article for the April and May 1899 issues of the *Atlantic Monthly*, cited her accuracy in describing life in areas of New England which were suffering from severe economic and spiritual decline.

Indeed, conditions in the New England countryside and in the villages were deplorable. Although Freeman did not write about the most severe social and economic deterioration as it existed in the more remote regions, the villages and farms in her fiction–modeled as they were on localities she had known in the upper Connecticut River Valley and in eastern Massachusetts– were in a state of chronic and deepening depression. Farming the rocky soil was unprofitable in the face of western competition made possible by the railroads. Small-scale village industries–once prolific in number and variety–were succumbing to the city manufacturers, who were also aided by the railroads in their marketing. Whole families of rural people, in some cases whole communities, had migrated in search of a livelihood, leaving the abandoned countryside slowly to revert to forest and the villages to languish in semidesertion and a grinding poverty that kept the poorhouses, those most dismal and inhumane of New England institutions, fully inhabited. As already stated, of those who did not emigrate, the majority were women. Many of the men who had gone in search of better things undoubtedly intended to return, and some did, to rejoin their families or to marry a hometown girl. But many never returned, and the women, in disproportionate numbers, were left to guard what

Photograph of Freeman that appeared in the March 1903 issue of Cosmopolitan

was left of the old culture and to make do as best they could–which often was quite well. Of course, some farmers and shopkeepers remained, but the farmers were victims of the stultifying and dehumanizing labor required to wrest even the barest subsistence from the sterile land, and the shopkeepers in their efforts to wring a profit from their impoverished customers earned the reputation–often deserved–of being heartless skinflints ever on the alert to cheat widows and orphans of their last pennies.

Such was the environment of many of Freeman's stories. In evoking the sounds and sights and the atmosphere of one of these backcountry villages or upland farms she was supreme. A dusty, dreamy village street lined with picket fences and houses from which the white paint had cracked and flaked away; a grassy country road with a thunderstorm rumbling on the horizon; a single woman's kitchen on a frosty autumn evening; the bleak common room of a poorhouse set among stubble cornfields across which slants a November rain–these and other such scenes form the backdrop of her tales. The reader is struck by the number of stories in which the first or second paragraph skillfully

(FACSIMILE PAGE OF MANUSCRIPT FROM DOC. GORDON)

Doc. Gordon

Chapter I

It was very early in the morning, it was scarcely dawn when the young man started upon a walk of twenty-five miles in order to reach Alton where he was to be assistant to the one physician in the place: Doctor Thomas Gordon, or Doc Gordon as he was familiarly called.

Mary E. Wilkins Freeman.

Facsimile in Freeman's 1906 novel, "Doc." Gordon

and economically creates a setting and establishes a mood: "The house was an infinitesimal affair, containing only two rooms besides the tiny lean-to which served as a wood-shed. It stood far enough back from the road for a pretentious mansion, and there was one curious feature about it—not a door nor window was there in front, only a blank unbroken wall"—thus begins "An Honest Soul" (*Harper's New Monthly*, July 1884; collected in *A Humble Romance*), the story of Martha Patch, an unmarried, impoverished seamstress. Another tale, "A Conflict Ended" (*Harper's New Monthly*, February 1886; collected in *A Humble Romance*), the theme of which is a man's pathologically developed volition, begins: "In Acton there were two churches, a Congregational and a Baptist. They stood on opposite sides of the road, and the Baptist edifice was a little farther down than the other. One Sunday morning both bells were ringing. The Baptist bell was much larger, and followed quickly on the soft peal of the Congregational with a heavy bronze clang, which vibrated a good deal."

But Freeman is most interested in the people who inhabit her vividly, sometimes starkly, etched settings. In a preface to *Pembroke* (1894), a fine novel of village life, she wrote that her book "was originally intended as a study of the human will in several New England characters, in different phases of disease and abnormal development and to prove . . . the truth of a theory that its cure depended entirely upon the capacity of the individual for a love which could rise above all considerations of self. . . ." These remarks apply as well to her short fiction. She explains that by "abnormal" she does not mean "unusual." She insists that in the remote areas of New England eccentricity of character in the form of a stiff-necked stubbornness, or a refusal to yield on even the most trivial matters, or a pathologically developed conscience is the norm. She traces these characteristics back to the Calvinism of the original colonists, in whom an indomitable will was indispensable for survival in a strange and hostile land. In the nineteenth century the old strengths, warped and exaggerated, often become obstacles to personal happiness and community harmony. Yet in meek, seemingly weak-willed persons these same strengths would sometimes suddenly awake from dormancy with startling intensity and release their possessors from their own incapacities or from the domination of others.

A Humble Romance and Other Stories, then, like most of Freeman's best writing, is to a great ex-tent a study of residual Puritanism as it existed in the rural New England of her day or a generation earlier. The gallery of character portraits that she presents in this first volume of her serious fiction is varied and fascinating, and each one typifies a different but more-or-less prevalent form of eccentricity or aberration. Martha Patch, in "An Honest Soul," is the victim of a morbidly overrefined conscience. Living precariously near starvation in her tiny cottage, she exists by sewing for her neighbors. Commissioned by two customers to make patchwork quilts from bags of rags that they leave with her, she finds, on finishing the quilts, that she has sewn into one a scrap belonging to the other customer. A person of normal conscience would let the matter go. A person of a rather finicky conscience would inform her customers of the error on the assumption that they would be unconcerned. A person with a post-Puritan conscience pathologically developed would do what Martha Patch does—tear the two quilts apart and resew them, not once but twice, since she makes a similar mistake the second time. Meanwhile Martha has made no money and hence has not eaten for days. She faints from malnutrition and is found lying on the floor by a neighbor, who revives her. The title of the story is in part, at least, ironic, for in conclusion Freeman poses the question whether "there were any real merit in such finely strained honesty, or whether it were really a case of morbid conscientiousness." The question, of course, is rhetorical. Martha's scruples—which she has learned from her father, and he from his father, and so on back through the generations—have been "so intensified by age and childlessness that they have become a little off the bias of reason."

The reference to "age and childlessness" adds another dimension to the story. After the death of her parents, Martha had lived entirely alone. Her solitary state was common in New England villages of the time. Without implying that marriage is a cure-all for the problems of either men or women, one can assume, as Freeman did, that Martha would have worried less about two misplaced scraps of cloth had she had a family to occupy her thoughts. In addition to her loneliness, Martha is wretchedly poor, as her family has been. So poverty-stricken was her father, in fact, that in building the little house Martha occupies, he could not afford to put a window on the end facing the street, and thus its inhabitants have had no outside view except from the back—a fitting symbol of the narrow horizons of these vil-

Portrait of Freeman by W. D. Stevens

lagers' lives. At the end of the story neighbors take pity on Martha and pay to have a window cut in the front of the cottage. Presumably her life and outlook broaden accordingly. At least she can look onto the street and, watching her fellow villagers, enjoy some sense of rapport with them. "An Honest Soul" touches on a number of Freeman's major themes–the overdeveloped will; the post-Puritan conscience, which in this story motivates the will; the economic distress endemic in the New England countryside; and the loneliness that was the lot of many villagers, especially women. In the breadth of its thematic concerns the story deserves close attention.

There is variety in the eccentricities of Freeman's New Englanders. While Martha Patch's will is coupled with a grotesquely overdeveloped conscience, will alone, without the proddings of conscience, is the theme of other stories in *A Humble Romance*. In "On the Walpole Road" (*Harper's Bazar,* 9 February 1884), for example, a

couple, having decided to marry, go through with the ceremony even though both know that the woman has fallen in love with another man since the engagement, as she openly states to the minister officiating at the wedding. Both the man and the woman are so determined to do what they have set out to do that the prospect of a loveless marriage is no deterrent. The story is told by one woman to another as the two ride in a buggy along a country road. Freeman here, as in other stories, has adopted one of the oldest forms of narration, that of gossip. The suitability of this device to her subject is obvious. The account of this married couple is clearly a topic for gossip, whether in a kitchen or during a buggy ride on a summer afternoon.

Another story in this collection, "Gentian" (*Harper's Bazar,* 23 January 1886), records a different manifestation of overdeveloped volition. A woman married to a domineering man, who has become seriously ill and who hates doctors and medicines, doses his food, unbeknownst to him, with gentian. The clandestine medication works, but the wife, afflicted with a conscience comparable to Martha Patch's, decides to tell her spouse what she has done. Thenceforth, the husband, determined to know exactly what he is eating, purchases and cooks his own food, refusing any that she has prepared. "I'm just a-goin' to make sure I hev some tea, an' somethin' to eat without any gentian in it," he snarls. No longer permitted to perform the wifely function of cooking for her husband, the woman suggests that it might be better if she went to live with her sister. In one of Freeman's masterstrokes of dialogue, the man laconically says, "It might be just as well." Later the couple is reunited—a somewhat sentimental ending suited to the Victorian tastes of the predominantly feminine readership of *Harper's Bazar*.

In stories such as "Gentian" and "An Honest Soul" the hypertrophied will exerts a negative influence. It is volition become "cussedness," "setness," "meanness." Yet other stories in the same collection demonstrate that such wills may be directed to constructive ends, as in Freeman's "A Taste of Honey" (*Harper's Bazar*, 6 September 1884), in which a young girl, Louisa, through years of grinding labor pays off the mortgage on her and her widowed mother's farm. Her determination costs her a chance to marry; her lover, tired of waiting, marries another girl on the day Louisa makes the last payment on the mortgage. But at least she accomplishes something of value, and she has perhaps learned that marriage is not the only worthwhile goal a woman may choose to pursue.

At times in these stories the action of a strongly developed will leads to an unexpected and even violent revolt. In "A Tardy Thanksgiving" (*Harper's Bazar*, 15 December 1883) the Widow Muzzy refuses to observe Thanksgiving, that most hallowed of New England holidays, because she has lost her husband and has nothing for which to thank God. In the religious context of her village and her upbringing, her decision constitutes the most serious of all rebellions—a revolt against God by a refusal to accept his ordering of things. Despite pleas by her niece, she insists on spending the day doing "pig work," that is, cutting up and curing the meat of her recently butchered hog. She is deterred from her purpose only when she scalds her foot with boiling water—an event that she takes as a divinely directed punishment for her revolt. Another story of rebel-

lion is "A Moral Exigency" (*Harper's Bazar*, 26 July 1884), in which a rather plain but passionate woman, a minister's daughter, defies her father's wish that she marry a widower with four children. Instead she steals another girl's lover, but relinquishes him when that girl is about to die. In this story, as in "A Tardy Thanksgiving," the rebellious woman is eventually brought back into line; but the fact that either woman had even dared to defy authority that was unquestioned in that time and place—in the one case the divine Father and in the other an earthly father—required extraordinary force of character and willpower.

Yet the seemingly unswervable post-Puritan will can be softened in various ways. In "A Tardy Thanksgiving" the protagonist's determination is broken by what she considers an intervention by God. In "A Conquest of Humility" (*Harper's Bazar*, 29 January 1887) a change of the will's direction is brought about by an act of confession and an abnegation of self. This is a strong story—though not one generally singled out for discussion among feminist critics—for it draws on the old Puritan practice of public confession to break an iron will. At the hour of her wedding, a girl named Delia and the assembled guests are informed by the groom's father that his son, who has become infatuated with another woman, will not appear. Delia's handling of her rage and humiliation is to repress both by an almost superhuman effort. She resumes her former life as if nothing has happened. This indifference, of course, is a front that she presents to the townspeople; but it is also her way of showing her contempt for her former fiancé. Later he is jilted in turn and learns a lesson deeply rooted in Calvinist practice and theology: that of humility, repentance, and public admission of guilt. Before a gathering of the same people who had been present at the cancellation of the wedding, he confesses his wrong, asks Delia to forgive him, and offers to marry her. Her refusal is immediate and triumphant. The man, knowing the strength of the girl's will, prepares to leave. Delia, who has recognized the sincerity of the confession, notices a look of contempt on the face of one of the guests. Foreseeing the ordeal or ridicule facing her repentant lover, she exclaims to the sneering guest, "You needn't look at him that way. I am going to marry him." There has indeed been a conquest of humility. A story like this might easily have been engulfed in sentimentality, but Freeman's handling of the situation is far from sentimental. The sequence of repentance, humil-

Photograph of Freeman that accompanied an article titled "Beauty and The Woman of Fifty" in the March 1904 issue of Ladies' Home Journal

ity, confession, and its results are psychologically convincing and, in the light of New England theology, reflect a traditional process of breaking an emotional and moral deadlock. Freeman's setting of the story against a village background where gossip, ridicule, and contempt for those who fail or deviate from the accepted moral norm adds a dimension of realism that successfully neutralizes any traces of sentimentality inherent in such a plot.

Village opinion is a governing force in many of Freeman's stories. Yet in New England villages eccentricity or extreme independence in one's manner of living would not necessarily invite censure or ridicule. Indeed, an oddity, so long as no moral or religious rule is broken, might be a subject of tolerant interest or good-natured amusement in a community. Most villages had their "characters" to whom their neighbors often pointed with the same kind of pride as to an outstanding geographical or architectural feature. In later stories (such as some of those in *Six Trees*, 1903) Freeman sometimes

writes of harmless, even likable eccentrics; but in cases where normal people commit unacceptable or injurious acts–like the breaking of a betrothal on one's wedding day–public opinion is merciless against the offender.

Most sensitive, perhaps, to village opinion were the poor. According to Calvinism prosperity in one's earthly life might be taken as a sign, though not a proof, of one's favorable standing with God. The righteous, the elect, would more likely than not be blessed with material possessions. The poor–though again the evidence would be considered far from conclusive–would be suspected to be among those whom God had destined for damnation. Thus the poor would be at great pains to conceal their condition, especially if they had once known better times. For example, in "Old Lady Pingree" (*Harper's Bazar*, 2 May 1885) an eighty-year-old gentlewoman who is permitted to continue living in her foreclosed mansion and to take in impoverished boarders accepts charity but not openly. Donations from her neighbors must be left behind a door, and her pride makes her balk at the thought of being buried at the town's expense. She also insists on helping those of her boarders who are as poor as she, paying the funeral costs for one with money saved for her own burial. By such actions she is able to keep her self-respect, and ultimately, by several lucky chances, she comes into possession of funds sufficient to save her from a pauper's burial. In another story, "A Mistaken Charity" (*Harper's Bazar*, 26 May 1883), two elderly women of lowlier social status than Old Lady Pingree survive only by the charity of the townspeople. In deadly fear of the poorhouse, commitment to which was the ultimate disgrace in New England one hundred years ago, the two accept, but find fault with, the handouts by which they survive, thus, they think, proving that they are not paupers.

Though the overdeveloped will and its aberrations are the subjects of the majority of the stories in *A Humble Romance*, several selections deal with a total immobilization of the will. In one of these, "A Symphony in Lavender" (*Harper's Bazar*, 25 August 1883), the protagonist has drifted into a completely passive way of life. A woman allows a dream to prevent her from marrying a man who courts her and whom she loves. Having chosen not to marry him, she is agonizingly uncertain for the remainder of her life as to whether she has made the right decision. Poor Martha Patch, resewing her quilts, experiences no such uncertainty. Others among Freeman's characters, such as the husband in "Gentian," may realize the wrongness of their course and change it, but once having made a choice they do not question its rightness.

A Humble Romance and Other Stories deserves close and detailed attention because it contains material that was to characterize the best of Freeman's later work. Her second volume of short fiction, *A New England Nun and Other Stories* (1891), also focuses on village and rural settings and characters and elaborates on themes found in her earlier collection. It contains, moreover, several of her best-known and most skillfully narrated tales, among them "A Village Singer" (*Harper's Bazar*, 6 July 1889), "Louisa" (*Harper's Bazar*, 13 September 1890), "Sister Liddy" (*Harper's Bazar*, 2 March 1889), "A Village Lear" (*Harper's Bazar*, 10 November 1888), "The Revolt of Mother" (*Harper's New Monthly*, September 1890), and the title piece, "A New England Nun" (*Harper's Bazar*, 7 May 1887). The volume also includes stories far below these in quality—in fact,

below the average of those in *A Humble Romance*. Freeman, a fast and prolific writer, was already giving indications of an inability to hold to a consistently high level of literary excellence.

Two of the selections in *A New England Nun*, the title story and "Sister Liddy," deal with the theme of passivity. In "A New England Nun" Louisa Ellis has been engaged for fifteen years to a man who has gone to Australia to seek his fortune. During his absence Louisa has fallen contentedly into a way of life that centers about—and is symbolized by—her caged canary and her dog, Caesar, which, because as a puppy he playfully nipped someone, has been chained all his life. (Freeman had known of a dog confined in this way, and, as a lover of animals, she pitied it.) Moreover, Louisa has shunned any participation in the life of her sleepy little village. When her fiancé returns, flushed with success, it becomes apparent to both that they are no longer suited to one another. In fact, they are no longer in love. Louisa, like certain of Henry James's characters, has, over the years, let herself become unfit for marriage or any other active role in life. Yet, conscientious New Englanders that they are, the two proceed to plan their wedding. A betrothal is not lightly to be broken. At length Louisa learns that her fiancé has fallen in love with a younger and more-vivacious woman, but the betrothed still persist in their plans of marriage—another loveless union like that described in "On the Walpole Road." Louisa, however, does finally make a decision of sorts, though it is prompted mostly by her reluctance to abandon the peaceful, inert existence to which she has become so pleasantly accustomed. She releases her fiancé, and "all alone by herself that night, wept a little, she hardly knew why; but the next morning, on waking, she felt like a queen, who after fearing lest her domain be wrested away from her, sees it fully insured in her possession. . . . If Louisa Ellis had sold her birthright she did not know it, the taste of the potage was so delicious, and had been her sole satisfaction for so long. Serenity and placid narrowness had become to her as the birthright itself." Unlike the young woman in "A Taste of Honey," who forgoes marriage for the sake of saving the family farm, Louisa retreats into self-indulgence as an escape from involvement in the responsibilities and hazards of a shared life.

"Sister Liddy," a plotless sketch evoking the grim atmosphere of a New England poorhouse, records the dreary existence of a group of paupers and psychopaths. (The poorhouses often

Ridgely Torrence, Elizabeth Jordan, Rossiter Johnson, F. T. Leigh, Edward Penfield, Mary E. Wilkins Freeman, Will N. Harben, and Mrs. William Dana Orcutt at a party celebrating the seventieth birthday of Henry Mills Alden, managing editor of Harper's Weekly *(photograph from* Harper's Weekly, *15 December 1906)*

served as asylums for the mentally ill as well.) These unfortunates are utterly in the clutch of circumstance; if they have ever possessed any willpower, they have long since lost it. Presented to the reader are a tall, demented old woman who predicts the end of the world; a stupid, fat old woman who amuses herself with vicious gossip and the needling of a pretty old woman whose only comfort is in her memories of her past beauty; Polly Moss, homely and pathetic, who regales the others with stories about a lovely and glamorous sister named Liddy (on her deathbed Polly admits that Liddy never existed); an insane old woman named Sally whose pastime is tearing apart her bed; and a sickly and depressed young woman, whose lover has abandoned her. Not in the starkest tales of the naturalistic writers has so desolate a group been assembled.

In two other stories in this collection, "A Village Singer" and "The Revolt of Mother," women who for years had lived in passive submission revolt with a suddenness and a violence utterly unexpected by their friends or family. In "A Village Singer" Candace Whitcomb erupts with fury when she is supplanted by a younger woman as soprano in her church choir. Candace

manages to break up a Sabbath service, and she defies her minister when he attempts to mollify her. Her rage is likened to a forest fire whose glow may be seen from her window. Though she softens somewhat on her deathbed, Candace's revolt has been total and fiercer than that described in "A Tardy Thanksgiving" or "A Moral Exigency" in Freeman's previous volume.

"A Village Singer" is one of Freeman's most dramatic stories. More popular, but less convincing psychologically, is the frequently anthologized story "The Revolt of Mother," in which a farm wife, in defiance of her husband, moves with her children from their shabby dwelling into the much more commodious new barn that the farmer has constructed for his animals. Her act reduces the man to tears, and he bestirs himself to provide the better living arrangements that for years he has promised his wife. This story has often been taken as feminist in its implications. For example, Theodore Roosevelt interpreted it as such in a speech he made before a group of women while he was governor of New York. Yet Freeman herself considered the story flawed by a lack of realism. No New England farm woman, she declared, would place her and her children's comfort before the welfare of the animals that were the family's livelihood.

The fact is that Freeman did not take a strong stand on woman's rights, though the chief appeal of her stories was to women. *Harper's Bazar*, which published so much of her early fiction (though "The Revolt of Mother" appeared in *Harper's Monthly*), was a woman's magazine addressing a great variety of subjects from New York fashions to employment opportunities for women. Mary Booth, its able editor, had been quick in appreciating the suitability of Freeman's fiction for the magazine, and indeed she provided an outlet for other New England writing women, including Rose Terry Cooke and Harriet Prescott Spofford. Always, however, Booth insisted on literary merit. For some months during the mid 1880s Freeman's stories appeared side by side with installments of Thomas Hardy's *The Woodlanders*.

Among the stories in *A New England Nun* are several in which revolt is combined with a masochistic self-punishment, not an expiation of guilt at having rebelled but an added dimension of defiance and an assertion of independence. In "A Poetess" (*Harper's New Monthly*, July 1890) an elderly single woman has won recognition in her village as a writer of sentimental verse. When she hears that her pastor, who has himself actually published some poetry, regards her compositions as trash, she burns all her poems and apostrophizes God, "I'd like to know if you think it's fair. Had I ought to have been born with the wantin' to write poetry if I couldn't write it—had I? Had I ought to have been let to write all my life, an' not know before there wa'n't any use in it?" Henceforth she writes no more, goes into a decline, and before her death makes her minister promise to have the ashes of her poems buried with her and requests that he, a published poet, write a poem about her. In another story, "A Solitary" (*Harper's Bazar*, 8 November 1890), the main character, Nicholas Gunn, has suffered a series of misfortunes, including the death of his wife. His recourse is to avoid all human associations, to refuse to heat his house in winter, to eat only food that he dislikes, and to keep reminding himself of his sorrows. By spiting himself, he reasons, he will not suffer any more disappointments. Nicholas, unlike the poetess, who dies embittered, eventually forsakes his misanthropic and masochistic way of life when he takes in an ill neighbor and cares for him, thus finding a focus other than himself and his grievances.

As does *A Humble Romance*, *A New England Nun* contains stories in which a determined but healthy will is directed toward worthwhile accomplishments. One such is "Louisa," the story of a country girl who, refusing marriage to a wealthy but surly suitor, struggles successfully to support herself and her mother on a single acre of tillable land. A story in a lighter vein, "A Church Mouse" (*Harper's Bazar*, 28 December 1889), tells of a woman who, becoming sexton of her church, sets up housekeeping in the meeting house. Despite the efforts of the congregation and head selectman to evict her, she remains harmlessly and usefully in the church.

Critics are generally agreed that most of Freeman's best short fiction is included in *A Humble Romance* and *A New England Nun*. For example, F. O. Matthiessen wrote in 1931 that in these two collections Freeman "told all she knew about life." In them, Matthiessen thought, she revealed a profound insight into the tragic aspects of life, "though she never achieved a complete expression of it in any of her stories.... The struggle of the heart to live by its own strength alone is her constant theme, and the sudden revolt of a spirit that will endure no more from circumstance provides her most stirring dramas."

During the decade after 1891 Freeman wrote seven novels, several of which possess much literary merit. The best is *Pembroke* (1894), which resembles her collections of short stories in its analyses of various mutations of the Puritan will as it persisted in nineteenth-century New England. As a gallery of rural characters and a record of life in a New England village, this novel is unsurpassed, if not unequaled. *Jane Field* (1892) is also an effective novel of New England village life, centering on a struggle between a strong-minded woman's will and her conscience. *Madelon* (1896), a somewhat romantic novel built around an attempted murder of passion, illustrates Freeman's theory that in every New England town some dark secret lies hidden. *Jerome, A Poor Man* (1897), more realistic in its social background than *Madelon*, describes the plight of a country town when its chief industry, that of shoemaking, succumbs to competition by urban manufacturers. *The Portion of Labor* (1901) deals with the strife and hardship occasioned by a textile strike in a large factory town. Like her short stories, these novels, as well as other lesser ones written during the same decade, draw heavily on Freeman's own experiences and observations in eastern Massachusetts and the area around Brattleboro.

During this period Freeman also published five books for children (four volumes of fiction and one of verse); a play, *Giles Corey, Yeoman* (1893), set in Salem at the time of the witch trials; and enough adult short fiction to fill four other volumes–*Silence and Other Stories* (1898), *The People of Our Neighborhood* (1898), *The Love of Parson Lord and Other Stories* (1900), and *Understudies* (1901). None of these collections equals her first two in sustained literary merit. Yet in them are several stories that rank with all but the best of her earlier ones. In *Silence*, in which with one exception the tales deal with the historic past, "A New England Prophet" (*Harper's New Monthly*, September 1894) imaginatively evokes the atmosphere and emotions aroused by the apocalyptic prophecies of the Millerites in the 1840s. In "The Cat" (*Harper's New Monthly*, May 1900) in *Understudies*–a collection of stories on various animals and plants in relation to, or symbolic of, human types–Freeman convincingly presents her favorite animal in what amounts to a partnership for survival with a man during a long winter of confinement in a remote cabin. Yet in most of her short fiction in the decade following 1891 there is unmistakable evidence of either a loss of talent or an exhaustion of subject matter. Freeman, it is clear, was straining for new topics and effects.

Nor did her writings improve after 1901, though her prolificacy, if anything, increased. (In the course of her life she wrote about two hundred short stories.) In 1902, at the age of forty-nine, she married Dr. Charles Manning Freeman, a nonpracticing physician engaged at that time in a coal business in Metuchen, New Jersey, where she had met him during visits to the Metuchen home of Henry Alden, editor of *Harper's New Monthly*. Thus Freeman's contact with the New England scene, about which she had done her best writing, was attenuated. The six volumes of short fiction and the seven novels that she wrote on a wide variety of themes after her marriage reveal a continuing deterioration of her abilities. Part of her problem may have been her husband's insistence that she produce in an unreasonable quantity, for he was impressed by the money that her writings brought in. Indeed, it is reported that he supplied her with two typewriters so that she might work on two pieces simultaneously. Another cause for Freeman's decline in talent may have been the breakdown of the

marriage itself. Dr. Freeman, an alcoholic, spent time in the New Jersey State Hospital for the Insane, and eventually Mary Freeman obtained a legal separation.

So far had Freeman's writing ability slipped that many of her late stories were never collected, nor did they deserve to be. *Six Trees* parallels *Understudies* in that it uses six different arboreal species as symbols of human types. In the same year she tried her hand, with only mild success, at writing about the occult in *The Wind in The Rose-Bush and Other Stories of the Supernatural* (1903). *The Givers* (1904) is for the most part a gathering of sentimental Christmas stories. *The Fair Lavinia and Others* (1907) is devoted to feeble, if not mawkish, accounts of the insignificant doings of village gentlefolk who are startlingly in contrast to the farm men and women and artisans of her earlier tales. One is amazed that those stories had originally been published in *Harper's New Monthly*. *The Winning Lady and Others* (1909), though generally undistinguished, contains one striking story, "Old Woman Magoun" (*Harper's Monthly*, October 1905), an account of rural degeneracy, in which an old woman stands by while her granddaughter, born out of wedlock to the old woman's daughter, eats a lethal dose of poison berries. The old woman would rather have the child die than have her possessed by her depraved father. In this grim tale is a glimmering of the author who wrote "Sister Liddy" and "A Village Singer." *The Copy-Cat & Other Stories* (1914) includes several selections–notably two stories of revolt, "Dear Annie" (*Harper's Monthly*, October and November 1910) and "The Balking of Christopher" (*Harper's Monthly*, September 1912)–which mark a partial revival of their author's powers. *Edgewater People* (1918), the last of Freeman's volumes of short fiction, contains no noteworthy stories.

During the final decade of Freeman's life, none of her writings appeared in book form, though she still occasionally had stories published in magazines. Yet on the strength of her earlier work she deserved to be awarded the William Dean Howells Gold Medal for Fiction in 1926 and to be elected, in the same year, to the National Institute of Arts and Letters. During her life and after, other critics have concurred with Howells and Matthiessen in singling out for praise her realism, her insight into the New England mind, the economy of her prose, and the direct simplicity of her plot structure. Fred Lewis Pattee emphasizes Freeman's awareness of the cultural roots of her characters' motives and way of life as well as her depiction of the social and economic straits of the New England of her day. Van Wyck Brooks agrees with Pattee, and in comparing Freeman with Sarah Orne Jewett finds that Freeman possesses a deeper psychological insight into her characters' attitudes and actions. Carlos Baker also considers Freeman superior to Jewett as an analyst of rural New England character, a view adopted and elaborated on by Austen Warren.

Letters:

The Infant Sphinx: Collected Letters of Mary E. Wilkins Freeman, edited by Brent L. Kendrick (Metuchen, N.J.: Scarecrow Press, 1985).

Biography:

Edward Foster, *Mary E. Wilkins Freeman* (New York: Hendricks House, 1956).

References:

Van Wyck Brooks, *New England: Indian Summer* (New York: Dutton, 1940), pp. 464-473;

F. O. Matthiessen, "New England Stories," in *American Writers on American Literature,* edited by John Macy (New York: Liveright, 1931), pp. 339-413;

Fred Lewis Pattee, "On the Terminal Moraine of New England Puritanism," in his *Side-Lights on American Literature* (New York: Century, 1922), pp. 175-209;

Charles M. Thompson, "Miss Wilkins: An Idealist in Masquerade," *Atlantic Monthly,* 83 (May 1899): 665-675;

Susan A. Toth, "A Defiant Light: A Positive View of Mary Wilkins Freeman," *New England Quarterly,* 46 (March 1973): 82-93;

Toth, "Mary Wilkins Freeman's Parable of Wasted Life," *American Literature,* 42 (January 1971): 564-567;

Austin Warren, *The New England Conscience* (Ann Arbor: University of Michigan Press, 1967), pp. 157-169;

Perry D. Westbrook, *Acres of Flint: Sarah Orne Jewett and Her Contemporaries* (Metuchen, N.J.: Scarecrow Press, 1981), pp. 86-104;

Westbrook, "Mary E. Wilkins Freeman (1852-1930)," *American Literary Realism, 1870-1910,* 2 (Summer 1969): 139-142;

Westbrook, *Mary Wilkins Freeman,* revised edition (Boston: Twayne, 1988);

Blanche C. Williams, *Our Short Story Writers* (New York: Moffat, Yard, 1920), pp. 160-181.

Papers:

Sizable collections of Mary E. Wilkins Freeman's papers may be found in the Library of the American Academy of Arts and Letters, in the New York Public Library, and in the libraries of Columbia University, Princeton University, the University of Virginia, and the University of Southern California.

Zona Gale

(26 August 1874-27 December 1938)

John F. Moe
Ohio State University

See also the Gale entry in *DLB 9: American Novelists, 1910-1945*.

BOOKS: *Romance Island* (Indianapolis: Bobbs-Merrill, 1906);

The Loves of Pelleas and Etarre (New York & London: Macmillan, 1907);

Friendship Village (New York: Macmillan, 1908);

Friendship Village Love Stories (New York: Macmillan, 1909);

Mothers to Men (New York: Macmillan, 1911);

Christmas (New York: Macmillan, 1912);

When I Was a Little Girl (New York: Macmillan, 1913);

Civic Improvement in the Little Towns (Washington, D.C.: American Civic Association, 1913);

Neighborhood Stories (New York: Macmillan, 1914);

Heart's Kindred (New York: Macmillan, 1915);

A Daughter of the Morning (Indianapolis: Bobbs-Merrill, 1917);

Birth (New York: Macmillan, 1918);

Peace in Friendship Village (New York: Macmillan, 1919);

The Neighbours (New York: Huebsch, 1920);

Miss Lulu Bett [novel] (New York & London: Appleton, 1920);

Miss Lulu Bett: An American Comedy of Manners [play] (New York: Appleton, 1921);

The Secret Way (New York: Macmillan, 1921);

Uncle Jimmy (Boston: Baker, 1922);

What Women Won in Wisconsin (Washington, D.C.: National Woman's Party, 1922);

Why I Shall Vote for Senator Robert M. La Follette (Madison, Wis., 1922);

Faint Perfume [novel] (New York: Appleton, 1923);

Mr. Pitt (New York & London: Appleton, 1925);

Preface to a Life (New York & London: Appleton, 1926);

Yellow Gentians and Blue (New York & London: Appleton, 1927);

Portage, Wisconsin and Other Essays (New York: Knopf, 1928);

Borgia (New York: Knopf, 1929);

Zona Gale

Bridal Pond (New York: Knopf, 1930);

Evening Clothes (Boston: Baker, 1932);

Papa La Fleur (New York & London: Appleton, 1933);

Old Fashioned Tales (New York & London: Appleton-Century, 1933);

Faint Perfume, A Play with a Prologue, and Three Acts (New York & Los Angeles: French, 1934);

The Clouds (New York: French, 1936);

Light Woman (New York & London: Appleton-Century, 1937);

Frank Miller of Mission Inn (New York & London: Appleton-Century, 1938);

Magna (New York & London: Appleton-Century, 1939).

OTHER: "The Novel of Tomorrow," in *The Novel of Tomorrow and the Scope of Fiction, by Twelve American Novelists* (Indianapolis: Bobbs-Merrill, 1922), pp. 65-72.

Zona Gale belongs to the relatively large group of American midwestern regionalist authors that includes Sinclair Lewis, Edgar Lee Masters, Willa Cather, Floyd Dell, Sherwood Anderson, Susan Glaspell, Theodore Dreiser, and Ruth Suckow. Like other midwestern writers of the years between 1890 and 1930, Gale addressed the problems of a rural society that was becoming increasingly urban. Her short stories present a panorama of small-town life in Wisconsin at the beginning of the twentieth century.

Zona Gale was born in Portage, Wisconsin, on 26 August 1874, the only child of Charles Franklin Gale (1842-1929), a railroad engineer, and Eliza Beers Gale (1846-1923), a teacher. Zona Gale noted later in her life that "I inherited predominant elements of character from both parents. From my mother imagination and initiative, from my father reflective and meditative tendencies; from both, power of concentration, and whatever of kindness and a socialized nature I have carried on." Her parents, who served as models for some of her fictional characters, strongly influenced her attitudes and actions, and, as August Derleth noted in his biography of Gale, "Zona was devoted to both of them; she loved them with a fierce, passionate intensity; she did everything in her power to convey to them her great affection for them." In many ways Gale's parents were a source of strength for her during her formative years and into her middle years. She did not marry until several years after her mother died, devoting most of her adult life to literary and political activities.

Gale attended the University of Wisconsin, earning a B.L. in 1895 and an M.L. in 1899. After working in Milwaukee from 1895 until 1901, first for the *Milwaukee Evening Wisconsin* and later for the *Milwaukee Journal*, she went to New York, where she became a reporter for the *New York Evening World*. In New York Gale became deeply involved in the literary scene, resigning her job with the *Evening World* after eighteen months to devote full time to free-lance writing. Her career as a published short-story writer had begun in 1899 with the appearance of one of her

Zona Gale, circa 1900 (photograph by Histed)

stories in the *Evening Wisconsin*, and in 1903 she had a story published in a national magazine, *Success*. During this time she became romantically involved with poet Ridgely Torrence, but the relationship ended, and in 1904 Gale returned to Portage, where she lived for the rest of her life. The highlight of her writing career came in 1921 when she was awarded a Pulitzer Prize for her play *Miss Lulu Bett*. In October 1928 she married William Llewellyn Breese, a banker. They adopted a child, Leslyn.

Strongly committed to social reform, Gale was a pacifist, and she supported the LaFollette progressive movement in Wisconsin as well as woman suffrage. She also maintained a close connection with her alma mater. First appointed to the University of Wisconsin's Board of Regents in 1923, she was instrumental in the selection of Glenn Frank as president of the university in 1925. In 1936 and part of 1937 she became involved in the controversy over Frank's dismissal. A statement she gave to the press in December 1936 may be read as a concise summary of her political philosophy: "I have been a progressive since progressivism was born as a social movement in Wisconsin. I was never more convinced than now of the state's need of the idealism, the democracy, and the social devotion of the progressive movement." This strong social commitment pervades her regionalist fiction.

Like many other midwestern writers between 1890 and 1930, Gale found herself making portraits of her own hometown, focusing on what she knew best: midwestern life and family values. These writers focused on the virtues and vices of the midwestern town, aware that encroaching urbanization would soon alter the relative homogeneity of small-town life. While some writers mourned the passing of small-town values and traditions, others were critical of these communities' restrictive mores, and many writers were ambivalent about their roots. Portage, Wisconsin, was for Zona Gale what Clyde, Ohio, was for Sherwood Anderson in *Winesburg, Ohio* (1919). Floyd Dell, Susan Glaspell, and Ruth Suckow drew their material from Iowa towns, while Sinclair Lewis drew on his life in Minnesota. Edgar Lee Masters, Willa Cather, and Hamlin Garland also wrote of midwestern town life. The same era was the heyday of midwestern regionalist painters such as Grant Wood, John Steuart Curry, and Thomas Hart Benton. In the foreword to her last collection of short stories, *Old Fashioned Tales* (1933), Gale remarked, "One writes a story because one sees, in some sharper light, an aspect of event or of character or of relationship, and one is 'obsessed' to record it. Without troubling to admit it, one believes oneself momentarily to have divined a little *more*—more man, more woman, more event—than meets the daily eye." Gale added, "If a story . . . lets one briefly look within people or moments, then it *is* a story."

Gale's first collection of stories, *The Loves of Pelleas and Etarre* (1907), contains seventeen loosely connected stories with titles such as "The Elopement," "The Dance," "The Honeymoon," "The Baby," "The Wedding," and "Christmas Roses." Gale explores the eternal problems of and attitudes toward love and fidelity, expressing herself in typically Victorian language, as in these lines from "The Baby": "To see Enid with her baby in her arms was considerably like watching a wild rose rock a butterfly, and no one can fancy how tenderly we two observed her. I think that few sweet surprises of experience or even of wisdom have so confirmed our joy in life as the sight of our grandniece Enid with her baby."

The Loves of Pelleas and Etarre is reminiscent of much late-nineteenth-century American fiction. Within a few years, however, the quality and tone of her fiction changed. In 1908, one year after the publication of *The Loves of Pelleas and Etarre*, she published her first collection of stories about the imaginary hamlet of Friendship Village, Wisconsin. *Friendship Village* begins with "The Side Door," in which Gale describes the landscape and people of the town.

In this town, Gale says in her introduction to the volume, "Calliope characterized us when she said: 'This town is more like a back door than a front—or, givin' it full credit, *anyhow*, it's no more'n a side door. . . .'" Gale goes on to explain, "we are a kind of middle door to experience, minus the fuss of official arriving and, too, without the old odours of the kitchen savoury beds; but having, instead, a serene side-door existence, partaking of both electric bells and of neighbours with shawls pinned over their heads."

During the next twelve years Gale collected more Friendship Village stories in *Friendship Village Love Stories* (1909), *When I Was a Little Girl* (1913), *Neighborhood Stories* (1914), and *Peace in Friendship Village* (1919). The community is also the setting for Gale's novel *Mothers to Men* (1911), her novelette *Christmas* (1912), and her one-act play *The Neighbours* (1920). Later in her career Gale published two collections of short stories not set in Friendship Village: *Yellow Gentians and Blue* (1927), which contains some of Gale's best writing, and *Old Fashioned Tales*, which collects stories that return to the familiar community themes of the Friendship Village stories.

In her Friendship Village stories Zona Gale examined how communities work, how its members interact, and how its life benefits its individual citizens. Literary critics tend to identify Friendship Village with Portage, Wisconsin. While there are strong similarities between them, the imaginary town and the real town are not necessarily the same place. She begins her introduction to Friendship Village with a disclaimer—"Friendship Village is not known to me, nor are any of its people, save in the comradeship which I offer here." Yet, she adds later, addressing readers familiar with small-town life, "Our improvements, like our entertainments, our funerals, our holidays, and our very lives, are but Friendship Village exponents of the modern spirit." Like many of her contemporaries, she created a microcosm of the midwestern hamlet, and whatever the village's faults, she concludes in *Neighborhood Stories*, "any

Zona Gale, with her mother, Eliza Beers Gale (seated), and her father, Charles Franklin Gale

one who takes seriously our faint feuds or even our narrow judgements does not know and love the Middle Western villages, nor understand that seeds and buds are not the norm of bloom."

In each of the collections of Friendship Village stories, Gale reiterates that they "are told in the words" of Calliope Marsh and that the theme running through the stories is Calliope's message to the reader. As Gale writes in the introduction to *Peace in Friendship Village*, "always I hear most clearly as her conclusion: 'Life is something other than that which we believe it to be.' " In *Friendship Village* Gale paints a bucolic picture of the town, but by *Peace in Friendship Village*, the last volume of Friendship Village stories, Gale was attempting to address the deeper social issues of the day.

Even earlier, in the preface to her 1914 collection, *Neighborhood Stories*, she contends that the vitality of the midwestern "home town" lies in the mixture of old and new. Citing the traditional midwestern county fair, where the old and the new have always coexisted, Gale notes, "From design in our County Fair fancy work to our attitude toward the home, new things are come upon us." She recognizes the value of the old and the need to preserve it, but she concludes that adaptation and change stand "for a special and precious form of vitality, in little towns." This theme is especially apparent in some of the stories in the last collection of Friendship Village stories. In "The Feast of Nations" Gale addresses the question of the mixture of old and new immigrants. One of her primary characters, Mis' Postmaster Sykes (many of the women in the village are identified by their husbands' jobs), says, "I can*not* help feeling pride that I've lived in Friendship Village for three generations of us, unbroken." Yet later in the story she dresses as "Columbia" for a pageant celebrating the new immigrants. In the same

Zona Gale, Eleanor Roosevelt, Robert Dessureau, Mary Waterstreet, and William Llywelyn Breese at an October 1938 peace conference in Green Bay, Wisconsin

book Gale writes about Jewish immigration in "The Story of Jeffro" (first published in *Everybody's Magazine*, March 1915), one of her most powerful stories, and about an Afro-American who has moved into the community in "Dream" (first published in the *Bookman*, July 1901).

Throughout her shorter fiction Zona Gale exhibits a clear message of midwestern self-assurance, a sense that the "folks" who reside in Friendship Village can resolve the tensions of modern society on their own terms. In these poignant vignettes, Gale's "home town" people face worldly questions and make decisions about them without having their relatively stable society tumble down. Yet her Friendship Village represents only part of midwestern society during the first two decades of the twentieth century. The problems of the people in Friendship Village do not give the reader that wider sense of the issues related to America's quickly growing urban society that Theodore Dreiser's *Sister Carrie* (1900)

provides, but the tensions the Friendship Villagers face were real social and political dilemmas that needed to be worked out within the developing midwestern culture. Though uneven in quality, Gale's short stories were popular with her contemporaries, and the best of them compare favorably with fiction by the other midwestern writers of her period.

References:

August Derleth, *Still Small Voice: The Biography of Zona Gale* (New York: Appleton-Century, 1940);

Harold P. Simonson, *Zona Gale* (New York: Twayne, 1962).

Papers:

The principal collection of Zona Gale papers is at the State Historical Society of Wisconsin in Madison. An important collection of letters is included in the Ridgely Torrence Collection in the Princeton University Library.

Hamlin Garland
(14 September 1860-5 March 1940)

Joseph B. McCullough
University of Nevada at Las Vegas

See also the Garland entry in *DLB 12: American Realists and Naturalists* and *DLB 71: American Literary Critics and Scholars, 1850-1880.*

BOOKS: *Under the Wheel: A Modern Play in Six Scenes* (Boston: Barta, 1890);

Main-Travelled Roads: Six Mississippi Valley Stories (Boston: Arena, 1891; London: Unwin, 1892; enlarged edition, New York & London: Macmillan, 1899; enlarged again, New York & London: Harper, 1922; enlarged again, New York & London: Harper, 1930);

A New Declaration of Rights (N.p., 1891?)

Jason Edwards, an Average Man (Boston: Arena, 1892);

A Member of the Third House (Chicago: Schulte, 1892);

A Little Norsk; or Ol' Pap's Flaxen (New York: Appleton, 1892; London: Unwin, 1892);

A Spoil of Office: A Story of the Modern West (Boston: Arena, 1892; revised edition, New York: Appleton, 1897);

Prairie Songs: Being Chants Rhymed and Unrhymed of the Level Lands of the Great West (Cambridge, Mass. & Chicago: Stone & Kimball, 1893);

Prairie Folks (Chicago: Schulte, 1893; London: Sampson Low, 1893; enlarged edition, New York & London: Macmillan, 1899);

Crumbling Idols: Twelve Essays on Art Dealing Chiefly with Literature, Painting, and the Drama (Chicago & Cambridge, Mass.: Stone & Kimball, 1894);

Impressions on Impressionism: Being a Discussion of the American Art Exhibition at the Art Institute, Chicago, by A Critical Triumvirate, by Garland, Charles Francis Browne, and Lorado Taft (Chicago: Central Art Association, 1894);

Five Hoosier Painters: Being a Discussion of the Holiday Exhibit of the Indianapolis Group, in Chicago, by The Critical Triumvirate, by Garland, Browne, and Taft (Chicago: Central Art Association, 1894);

Hamlin Garland, 1883

Rose of Dutcher's Coolly (Chicago: Stone & Kimball, 1895; London: Beeman, 1896; revised edition, New York & London: Macmillan, 1899);

Wayside Courtships (New York: Appleton, 1897; London: Beeman, 1898);

Ulysses S. Grant: His Life and Character (New York: Doubleday & McClure, 1898);

The Spirit of Sweetwater (Philadelphia: Curtis/New York: Doubleday & McClure, 1898; London: Service & Paton, 1898); revised and enlarged as *Witch's Gold* (New York: Doubleday, Page, 1906);

Boy Life on the Prairie (New York & London: Macmillan, 1899; revised edition, New York: Macmillan, 1908);

The Trail of the Goldseekers: A Record of Travel in Prose and Verse (New York & London: Macmillan, 1899);

The Eagle's Heart (New York: Appleton, 1900; London: Heinemann, 1900);

Her Mountain Lover (New York: Century, 1901; London: Dollar Library, 1901);

The Captain of the Gray-Horse Troop (New York & London: Harper, 1902; London: Grant Richards, 1902);

Hesper (New York & London: Harper, 1903);

The Light of the Star (New York & London: Harper, 1904);

The Tyranny of the Dark (New York & London: Harper, 1905);

The Long Trail: A Story of the Northwest Wilderness (New York & London: Macmillan, 1907);

Money Magic (New York & London: Harper, 1907);

The Shadow World (New York & London: Harper, 1908);

The Moccasin Ranch (New York & London: Harper, 1909);

Cavanagh, Forest Ranger (New York & London: Harper, 1910);

Other Main-Travelled Roads (New York & London: Harper, 1910);

Victor Ollnee's Discipline (New York & London: Harper, 1911);

The Forester's Daughter (New York & London: Harper, 1914);

They of the High Trails (New York & London: Harper, 1916);

A Son of the Middle Border (New York: Macmillan, 1917; London: John Lane, 1921);

A Daughter of the Middle Border (New York: Macmillan, 1921);

The Book of the American Indian (New York & London: Harper, 1923);

Trail-Makers of the Middle Border (New York: Macmillan, 1926; London: John Lane, 1926);

Prairie Song and Western Story (Boston & New York: Allyn & Bacon, 1928);

Back-Trailers from the Middle Border (New York: Macmillan, 1928);

Roadside Meetings (New York: Macmillan, 1930; London: John Lane, 1931);

Companions on the Trail (New York: Macmillan, 1931);

My Friendly Contemporaries: A Literary Log (New York: Macmillan, 1932);

Afternoon Neighbors (New York: Macmillan, 1934);

Forty Years of Psychic Research (New York: Macmillan, 1936);

The Mystery of the Buried Crosses: A Narrative of Psychic Exploration (New York: Dutton, 1939);

Hamlin Garland's Diaries, edited by Donald Pizer (San Marino, Cal.: Huntington Library, 1968);

Hamlin Garland's Observations on the American Indian, 1895-1905, edited by Lonnie E. Underhill and Daniel F. Littlefield (Tucson: University of Arizona Press, 1976).

During a productive and varied literary career Hamlin Garland published almost fifty volumes. But his reputation rests principally on his short fiction written before 1895, and particularly on his volume of short stories *Main-Travelled Roads* (1891) and on his autobiographies, *A Son of the Middle Border* (1917) and *A Daughter of the Middle Border* (1921). In these volumes Garland demonstrated that it had at last become possible to deal realistically with the American farmer in literature instead of seeing him simply through the veil of literary convention. By creating new types of characters, Garland hoped not only to inform readers about the realities of western farm life but to touch the deeper feelings of the nation.

One of America's foremost local colorists, Garland graphically depicted the countryside of his native Middle West in verse, fiction, and powerful autobiographical narratives in which he memorably portrays the futility of farm life. His writings include realistic and propagandistic novels and short stories, a biography of President Ulysses S. Grant, and several books on spiritualism. He also wrote about the struggle for woman's rights in the 1890s and the American Indian. He made significant contributions to the development of realism and naturalism in American literature and was a leading advocate of impressionism at the turn of the century.

Garland was born in West Salem, Wisconsin, on 14 September 1860 to Richard and Isabelle McClintock Garland. After his early formative years growing up on family farms in Wisconsin, Iowa, and the Dakota Territory, Garland made the most crucial decision in both his personal life

Garland, age twenty-one

and his artistic career in the fall of 1884 when he journeyed to Boston, then the intellectual and literary center of the country. By the time he arrived, he was already familiar with the work of Hippolyte Taine and Robert Ingersoll. While in Boston he eagerly read Walt Whitman's poetry, absorbing the poet's view of the spiritual brotherhood of workers as well as much of his nationalistic feeling. He also studied Charles Darwin, Herbert Spencer, and others in an effort to understand not only how evolutionary and biological processes in nature led from simple to complex forms, but also how these processes could be applied to society. His reading of Henry George's *Progress and Poverty* (1879) in early 1884 confirmed his own experiences of farm life and quickly converted him into an advocate of the single tax, which sought to correct the injustice of the unearned increment (profits made from the increased value of land) that favored property own-

ers at the expense of the laboring farmer. Involved with the intellectual and philosophical currents of the time, Garland desired to participate in them; but he had not the vaguest idea about where such involvement would take him. It was not until his meeting with William Dean Howells in 1887, after which a long and fruitful friendship evolved, and a trip back to the West that same year that Garland began to consider an artistic career. After having spent three years in the East, the barrenness of farm life made a deeper impression on him than ever before. He remarked that "Something deep and resonant vibrated within my brain as I looked out upon this monotonous commonplace landscape. I realized for the first time that the east had surfeited me with picturesqueness. It appeared that I had been living for six years amid painted, neatly arranged pasteboard scenery. Now I dropped to the level of nature unadorned down to the ugly unkempt lanes I knew so well, back to the pungent realities of the streamless plain." And his associations with Richard Watson Gilder, editor of the prestigious *Century*, and B. O. Flower, editor of the radical *Arena*, gave impetus to his publishing career. However, it soon became evident that the contrasting positions of literary art espoused by Gilder and Flower provided a tension within Garland, one which he never fully reconciled. Garland not only wanted to tell the truth about life on the middle border, and hopefully change conditions through his art, as Flower urged, but he also desired the recognition and the success as an artist that the praise and respect by Gilder would give him. Flower was his social and ethical conscience; Gilder was his artistic conscience. Fundamentally, Garland's was a struggle to identify his artistic mission which troubled him in one form or another for the rest of his life.

A consideration of Garland's development of his literary theory is important, for it both sheds light on his own fictional practices and reflects turn-of-the-century debates concerning the function of American literature. *Crumbling Idols* (1894) was Garland's only major contribution to literary theory; but it marked the culmination in the evolution of his ideas which had occupied his attention from the time he had entered Boston nearly a decade earlier. Through his reading and his professional associations he was extensively involved in the critical debates over realism and the nature of American literature. Though the sources of Garland's ideas are relatively complicated ones, and his applications of the ideas are occasionally simplistic, he vigorously clung to the belief that local color should be the dominant form in American literature.

Garland identified with the local colorists, who, he felt, sought to present life more truthfully by presenting the facts of the immediate present. They attempted to reproduce the texture and background of life which they had personally experienced, and they observed American life in order to produce a national literature through national character.

By the time he wrote *Crumbling Idols*, Garland had accepted most of Howells's convictions set forth in his *Criticism and Fiction* (1891). However, Garland's reading and lectures during the period also indicate that he was influenced by many other critics, artists, philosophers, and scientists, including Ralph Waldo Emerson, Whitman, Taine, Darwin, Spencer, and Eugene Véron. Garland accepted Taine's deterministic formula expressed in *The History of English Literature* (1865), according to which literature or art, like natural phenomena, is the by-product of time, place, and race and which, therefore, ought to tell the truth about a nation at a particular moment in its history. Important, too, were Spencer's revolutionary terms and ideas which he explained in detail in his *First Principles* (1860-1862), and his two principal ideas that influenced Garland's thought were a belief in progress and the need for individual liberty.

In 1885 Garland began work on a large project entitled "The Evolution of American Thought." In it he intended to treat American literature according to the formulas prescribed by Taine and Spencer. But he also believed that literature itself must depend on varying physical and social conditions. And, because literature should reflect progress, to ask writers to conform to past standards would be retrogressive. Since he was convinced of both the increased heterogeneity in modern American life and the need for a national literature, he felt that American literature should reflect contemporary American life in all its diversity and complexity. It had to deal, therefore, with the primary characteristics of the present, the common experiences of the people.

Besides Whitman's works, which seemed to Garland to epitomize the foremost in contemporary literary development because of Whitman's treatment of contemporary life, the common man, and his democratic individualism, Garland felt that the local-color movement was the only existing one capable of responding to the dictates es-

tablished by Spencer. To Garland, local color, which he defined simply as that which "*has such a quality of texture and background that it could not have been written in any other place or by anyone else than a native*," would become the dominant literary form because it was the only one capable of depicting the diversity and complexity of American life. Using the leading local colorists of the day as examples of this trend, notably Joel Chandler Harris, George Washington Cable, Joseph Kirkland, Sarah Orne Jewett, Mary E. Wilkins, and Bret Harte, Garland further believed that the local-color movement was a form of literary nationalism, for it not only indicated the truth of life of a particular region but also minimized foreign influence.

During 1886 and 1887, while Garland was insisting on the importance of the local-color novel, he came upon Véron's *Aesthetics* (1879), which Garland cited as the major source of ideas for *Crumbling Idols*. Like Garland, Véron, also influenced by evolutionary thought, insisted that the artist must free himself from the past and deal with the present. To enable artists to do so, Véron advocated a theory of literary impressionism; he maintained that "there are but three ways open to art: the imitation of previous forms of art; the realistic imitation of actual things; the manifestation of individual expression." Of these three, the last was the essential constituent of art, for the value of impressionistic art is derived from the character and personality of the artist, corrected by observed fact: "TRUTH AND PERSONALITY: these are the alpha and omega of art formulas: *truth* as to facts, and the *personality* of the artist."

Crumbling Idols deals with a variety of critical issues, but particular themes run throughout. Garland emphasizes the necessity for originality and individuality in authorship, freedom from past models for modern literature, Americanism and nationalism, and a proclamation of western literary independence.

While Garland basically advocated a form of literary realism, after the manner of Howells, he was concerned with the terminology of realism. In order to avoid confusion between Howells's view of realism—which aimed at a truthful representation of American life but avoided the extremes by attempting to depict the commonplace—and the exponents of a "harsher realism," after the manner of Emile Zola, Garland propounded a form of literary impressionism called "veritism."

By arguing that, at bottom, "realism," "veritism," and "Americanism" meant "practically the same thing," and by distinguishing between his form of realism and that practiced by the followers of Zola, Garland resolved the problem of defending traditional morality within the limits imposed by accurate observation and realistic detail. Like Henry James, Howells, and the early Mark Twain, Garland's realism was infused with a strain of ethical idealism which implied moral responsibility and an abiding faith in man's moral nature. Garland's veritism differs from Howells's realism in its emphasis on impressionism, an insistence on the centrality of the artist's individual vision. Though Garland's depiction of farm life in *Main-Travelled Roads* is harsher than Howells's suggestion that literature should deal with "the more smiling aspects of life," Garland's ethical idealism and his romantic individualism precluded his accepting the view of life and the treatment of material practiced by American literary naturalists.

While Garland made several unsuccessful attempts at writing fiction during his stay in Boston before 1887, he was primarily involved as a teacher, critic, and lecturer. He did, however, manage to publish one story during this period which made incidental use of western material. In "Ten Years Dead" (*Every Other Saturday*, 28 March 1885), which, as Garland later recalled, was influenced by Nathaniel Hawthorne, the narrator meets a man named Gregory, who had previously suffered an attack from brain fever, had remained in a coma for ten years, and on awakening had retained no recollection of what had happened during the period of his illness. While Garland placed the action of the story in the West, however, he had not yet learned to develop themes and characters from western life.

His next two stories, though, written after a return to the Dakota Territory in 1887 had filled him with moral outrage against the economic injustices which brought about tragedy and despair for the farmer, foreshadow in theme, tone, and subject matter the direction of his fiction for the next several years. In both "A Common Case" (*Belford's Monthly*, July 1888; revised as "Before the Low Green Door," *Wayside Courtships*, 1897) and "John Boyle's Conclusion" (written in 1888, unpublished) Garland depicts the barrenness and futility of western farm life.

"A Common Case" deals with Matilda Bent, a defeated farm wife. Through Garland's surrogate spokesman, Rance Knapp, the author dis-

Garland in his Cheyenne tepee, 1899

cusses the dying mother who "has lived in that miserable little hovel for a quarter of a century. She has heard nothing, seen nothing of the grandeur and glory of this great age we boast about, . . . the American farmer living in semi-solitude, his wife a slave, both denied things that make life worth living. Fifty per cent of these farms mortgaged, in spite of the labors of every member of the family and the most frugal living." In the second half of the story Garland depicts Matilda's painful death: resentful of her husband, the farm, and the world, she desires only peace and rest. Also, since Garland was rapidly moving to become a propagandist for the single tax, the story implicitly discusses the tragedy of farm life which Garland felt was the direct result of unfair economic and social conditions. Even at this early stage in his career Garland was already becoming the literary spokesman for the discontented farmers of the middle border.

"John Boyle's Conclusion" is similar in tone, theme, and framework to "A Common Case"; it is also one of the most bitter stories Garland was ever to write. The story deals with the effects of farm life on John and Sairy Boyle, an elderly farm couple, and on Porter and Ida Alling, a young couple. By contrasting two reactions to a devastating hailstorm, Garland effectively dramatizes the effect of the continuous defeats on the Boyles. They have previously lost several farms because of war and financial problems created by a prairie fire and cinch bugs. In July they are again on the verge of losing their farm because of a drought. Their hopes are momentarily raised when they think a coming storm will bring the necessary rain; however, a devastating hailstorm occurs that ruins not only the crops for the last time but breaks John Boyle's spirit.

In the second part of the story the point of view shifts to the Allings, who are also ruined by the storm. But, because they are still young and resilient, they are able to absorb the defeat, deciding to leave farm life for good. They function not so much to suggest that escape is possible (although Garland himself escaped the hardships of farm life early in his own life) but to comment on the social, economic, and natural conditions that bring about the tragedy. After the storm the Allings go to the Boyle farm only to find that the farm is ruined, Sairy Boyle has gone mad, and John has committed suicide by drowning.

While the dialogue is somewhat crude in the story, and while Garland gets too melodramatic in some scenes and propagandizes too much in others, "John Boyle's Conclusion" provokes a sympathetic response to the plight of the farmers. And both the subject matter and techniques make it clear that Garland had become committed to the local-color story and the "new realism," and that his locale was to be the middle border.

Garland's best stories are those found in *Main-Travelled Roads*, which he wrote and collected at the suggestion of B. O. Flower. While some of the six individual stories which comprise the original edition are flawed, the book as a whole is a powerful and evocative treatment of western farm life. Its poignant portrayal of man's struggles against overwhelming forces in nature and social injustices led Howells to observe in his "Editor's Study" (*Harper's Monthly*, August 1891):

> If any one is still at a loss to account for that uprising of farmers in the West which is the translation of the Peasant's War into modern and republican terms, let him read *Main-Travelled Roads*, and he will begin to understand, unless, indeed, Mr. Garland is painting the exceptional rather than the average. The stories are full of those gaunt, grim, sordid, pathetic, ferocious figures, whom our satirists find so easy to caricature as Hayseeds, and whose blind groping for fairer conditions is so grotesque to the newspapers and so menacing to the politicians. They feel that something is wrong, and they know that the wrong is not theirs. The type caught in Mr. Garland's book is not pretty; it is ugly and often ridiculous; but it is heart-breaking in its rude despair.

Garland uses the metaphor of the western road as the symbolic and structural center for *Main-Travelled Roads*, and he also employs an epigraph before each story in the first edition to achieve unity. A prefatory statement to the volume sets the dominant tone and contains a hint of what is to follow:

> The main-travelled road in the West (as everywhere) is hot and dusty in the summer, and desolate and drear with mud in fall and spring, and in winter the winds sweep the snow across it; but it does sometimes cross a rich meadow where the songs of the larks and the bobolinks and blackbirds are tangled. Follow it far enough, it may lead past a bend in the river where the water laughs eternally over its shallows.
>   Mainly it is long and wearyful and has a dull little town at one end, and a home of toil at the other. Like the main-travelled road of life, it is traversed by many classes of people, but the poor and the weary predominate.

Throughout the volume Garland emphasizes that, while farm life was sometimes tragic and generally desolate, it also contained exhilarating moments. But, unlike many local-color stories of the time that sentimentally expressed the charm of quaint country villages and that characterized American rural life as a pastoral idyll, the stories here express outrage at the social injustices suffered by the farmer. Garland's tendency to dispel past myths is clearly present in all of the stories, as they depict the ugliness, monotony, and hopelessness of the average American farmer. But it is also possible to overemphasize Garland's disillusionment, for, despite the pervasive deterministic forces at work, a persistent strain of romantic optimism is evident. Moreover, Garland reflects an ethical idealism which sets him apart from the naturalists who believed that, since man was determined, he necessarily had less moral responsibility. Throughout, Garland stresses the strength of individual will. While it is true that Garland's realistic portrayal of hardship did much to shatter any romanticism about the American pastoral idyll, and that the submission of many of his characters to the inevitable demands of the world suggests the futility of farm life, his characters also continue to strive because of their will. Since several of the stories have a hopeful ending, they also indicate Garland's compassionate view of human nature and his love for the land. This moral stance contradicts the diffused pessimism of the stories. However, such an ambiguity, far from being an impediment, gives his work its vitality.

The ambivalence of isolation and companionship, optimism and pessimism, is illustrated in "The Return of the Private" (first published in the December 1890 *Arena*), a moving story of post-Civil War disillusionment. Here is found a richness of detail, and the characters and their actions are presented credibly and authentically as Garland develops the three main scenes: Private Smith's return with his fellow soldiers to La-Crosse, Wisconsin; the terrible loneliness of his wife, relieved by the companionship and affection afforded to her and her children at Sunday dinner with the kind "Widder" Gray; and finally the reunion itself of the soldier and his family. Private Smith's return is filled with high expectations, and his first views of the land justify those hopes. But, despite the beauty of the landscape, his harmony with nature, and the hospitality of the neighbors, the return of the exhausted, aged veteran is shattering because he finds his farm in shambles. The story, however, does not end on this despondent note, for he resumes with courage "his daily running fight with nature and against the injustice of his fellow-man."

In "A Branch Road" (previously unpublished), this ambivalence is clearly expressed. Here, Will Hannan, who has left the farm to make his way in the world, returns seven years later only to discover the pitiable condition of his former sweetheart, who has since married and reared her family on a farm. In the first half of the story the rustic idyll seems to be confirmed by a lyrical and poetic ecstasy for nature; and the observer is Hannan, a romantic young man who seems uncommonly sensitive to divine beauty in nature. As the dawn unfolds, nature is depicted as both beautiful and bountiful; and the farmer, to Will, seems bound in a mystical relationship with nature in the ritual of the harvest. But as he sees the scene at close range, his angle of vision changes, and Will, like Garland himself who returned to the West after several years in Boston and found his mother in a desolate state, finds his former sweetheart married to an insensitive brute, living in squalor, her beauty gone, her health failing, beaten by her life of toil.

Again, however, the story does not end on a despondent note, for Will persuades Agnes to flee with him into a completely new life despite the fact that she is still married to Grant, and the story closes with the sun shining "on the dazzling, rustling wheat, the fathomless sky blue, as a sea, bent above them." Howells, in his September 1891 *Harper's Monthly* "Editor's Study," judged the ending to be "morally wrong," but Garland intended to oppose the sacred right of individuals to conventional morals.

A spirit of guilt permeates several stories in the collection, a theme that unquestionably resulted from Garland's personal guilt over the plight of his family, and especially of his mother. In "Up the Coulé" (previously unpublished), the most powerful and in a sense the most autobiographical story in the volume, Garland depicts the return of Howard McLane, a successful actor, to Wisconsin from the East to visit his mother and his brother Grant. Garland uses several contrasts to present his theme, while at the same time creating a vivid sense of the emptiness and hopelessness of farm life. Two of these contrasts are most important: the beauty of the countryside as against that of the barrenness in the lives of the farmers, and the life of Howard as against that of Grant. But the most striking tension is contained in the conflict between success and failure. After first being awed by the beauty of nature upon his return, Howard is overwhelmed by the irrelevancy of this beauty in the lives of his family. When he confronts his brother Grant and his family, he finds them living in poverty on a small, unproductive farm, for the family property has been sold to pay a mortgage. Grant makes it plain that he blames Howard for the loss of the farm, for he is convinced that if Howard had shared his wealth, the farm could have been saved and his mother spared much of her misery. And Howard's gifts of fine silk from Paris, a parasol for Grant's wife, and a copy, ironically, of General Grant's autobiography for Grant additionally enrage his brother. But Garland implies here, as later, that Grant's destruction is not primarily a result of Howard's neglect; it is really caused by the overpowering evils of contemporary farm conditions. Societal pressures and injustices have inevitably led to Grant's final somber view of a life in which he feels hopelessly trapped: "A man like me is helpless.... Just like a fly in a pan of molasses. There ain't

Garland at the South Dakota homestead where he wrote the first of the six short stories for the 1891 edition of
Main-Travelled Roads

any escape for him. The more he tears around the more liable he is to rip his legs off."

While "Up the Coulé" suggests inequities in the economic system, "Under the Lion's Paw" (*Harper's Weekly*, 7 September 1889), the best-known story in the collection, is the only one which makes explicit use of the single-tax doctrine. Written as an illustration of Henry George's thesis of the harmful social effects of the unearned increment, Garland habitually used the text when he was campaigning for Populist candidates. In the story the Haskins family, forced to settle in Kansas because of the high price of land in the East, is plagued by grasshoppers and forced to move again. Aided by a hospitable family, they rent a farm in Iowa from Jim Butler, a villainous land speculator. After three years of hard labor Haskins is ready to buy, but Butler doubles the price because of the improvements Haskins himself has made upon the land. Enraged, Haskins determines to murder Butler, refraining only at the last moment when he sees his child. Though cursed under the economic system, he resolves to renew his struggle for her sake.

Generally Garland's treatment of farm life is anti-idyllic; and, because of the harsh demands of that life, his treatment of the possibilities of romantic love is no less so. The emotional center of many of his stories is the demoralizing condition of the farm wife. Cut off from human community, she is destined to live a depressing, lonely life, with no fulfillment. Some, like Agnes in "A Branch Road," Julia in "Among the Corn Rows" (*Harper's Weekly*, 28 June 1890), or Nellie Sanford in "A 'Good Fellow's' Wife" (*Century*, April 1898; added to the 1922 edition of *Main-Travelled Roads*), are fortunate enough to escape before they are utterly ruined. Others, like Delia Markham in "A Day's Pleasure" (added to the 1899 edition of *Main-Travelled Roads*) or Grandma Ripley in "Mrs. Ripley's Trip" (*Harper's Weekly*, 24 November 1888), are afforded temporary release from their monotonous routine. But the point is always the same: the loneliness and hardships for which a prairie wife is destined serve as an ironic comment on the beauty of the landscape and finally defeat the reader's expectations of romantic love.

"Mrs. Ripley's Trip," the final story in the volume, is a tender, moving tale about the relationship of an old couple who are settled into the burdens of daily life and who have nothing to look forward to. Frustrated with her life, Mrs. Ripley desires to make a last trip to the East where she was born, but she feels guilty about leaving her husband, even for a short time. However, she finally accomplishes her dream and then returns to the farm to resume her misery. "Her trip was a fact now; no chance could rob her of it. She had looked forward twenty-three years toward it, and now she could look back at it accomplished. She took up her burden again, never more thinking to lay it down."

Garland's later additions to *Main-Travelled Roads*, though dealing with the same subject matter, disturb the tight unity of the first edition. These later stories tend to be milder, to lack the possibility of tragedy and the sense of outrage at farm conditions that characterize the original text. Though the stories contain Garland's best writing and create some memorable characters, with the exception of the moving "A Day's Pleasure," the subtle tensions and stark contrasts which give the original collection its vitality are lacking. In "A Day's Pleasure" Markham takes his wife and child from the farm to the city for a day. Mrs. Markham's misery is temporarily relieved by a sympathetic acquaintance. However, since the relief is only temporary, the return to the grim conditions of the farm seems even more depressing once she has been given a taste of human companionship.

Frequently the stories added to subsequent editions, like much of Garland's later fiction, are closer to being anecdotal expressions and lack the deeper emotions of his earlier writings. But, taken as a whole, and particularly considering the original text, *Main-Travelled Roads* is Garland's best work. It is not only a significant social and historical document but, despite its flaws, illustrates Garland's capacity to transform artistically personal feelings, attitudes, and experiences into compelling themes for his fiction.

Although *Prairie Folks* (1893) appeared two years later than *Main-Travelled Roads*, its stories were written contemporaneously. In fact, Garland thought of it as a "companion volume" to the earlier collection. The 1893 edition of *Prairie Folks* initially contained nine stories, but, like *Main-Travelled Roads*, Garland made several additions in the 1899 edition. While *Prairie Folks* is never given the prominence of *Main-Travelled Roads*, the two volumes are closely related, as Garland intended. In both volumes the presiding subject matter is farm life; many of the same characters appear in both volumes; and Garland precedes each story with a poem which sets the tone for the story which follows.

There are, however, two important differences between the two. In *Prairie Folks* there is an insistence on the life of the community; in *Main-Travelled Roads* the emphasis is on the individual. And the movement in *Prairie Folks* is more toward the romantic. With the exception of "Sim Burns's Wife" (first published as "A Prairie Heroine," *Arena*, July 1891), the stories are similar in tone to the later additions to *Main-Travelled*

Roads. Several stories in the volume belong to Garland's "lighter" or "milder" fiction, reflecting his attraction, at this time, to Gilder rather than Flower.

"William Bacon's Hired Man" (first published as "A Spring Romance," *Century*, June 1891) specifically belongs to these milder stories which do not portray the hardships and toil of farm life. Here, Lyman Gilman, working for William Bacon, decides to marry Bacon's daughter, Marietta. Bacon, however, whose wife and only son are dead, is enraged, feeling that he has a claim on Marietta. Although Lyman is told to leave the farm, he returns at night and convinces Marietta to elope with him. They leave together but return after they are married to live with Bacon, who finally accepts the marriage. Garland uses the escape-return motif here as he did frequently in *Main-Travelled Roads* and also suggests the difficulty of freedom for women; but, unlike his other stories, he does not hint at the drudgery of farm life awaiting the couple (especially Marietta) when they resume their place on the farm. Rather, the story focuses on a romantic interlude in the spring which, when isolated from the total picture of farm life, suggests the possibilities of romantic love. Since there is no complication in nature and since youth and love triumph, these circumstances contrast with Garland's more frequent treatment of the irrelevance of romantic love and the beauty of nature.

Both "The Test of Elder Pill" (*Arena*, March 1891) and "A Day of Grace" (first published as "Grace . . . A Reminiscence," *Philadelphia Press*, 17 October 1895, added to the 1899 edition of *Prairie Folks*) depict the religious flavor of the times. The philosophy of both episodes is a plea for simple humanitarianism; if heaven exists, people must know how to find it on this earth. Donald Pizer has suggested that "The Test of Elder Pill" dramatizes a Spencerian distrust of the "barbarism" of evangelism and calls for an earnest "morality" to replace "antiquated terrorism" as Elder (Andrew) Pill comes to town to preach. Through an ambitious evangelism, he throws terror into the hearts of his listeners. However, in the middle of one of his sermons, William Bacon interrupts him; cynic Radbourne follows him; and Pill is defeated. After seeking advice from Radbourne, Pill meditates on his "old morality" and realizes that, although he has no religion left, he still has morality. He leaves and eventually returns to preaching, but the changed man has replaced terrorism with humanitarianism.

Garland with John Burroughs, the popular American naturalist (Special Collections Department, Doheny Memorial Library, University of Southern California)

Drawing upon a similar theme, "A Day of Grace" deals with the antiquated terrorism of the revival meeting and with the emotional excesses of rural religion. Although Ben Griswold saves Grace Cole from "falling" under the influence of the preacher at the meeting, Ben changes as a result of his experience at the meeting and his growing closeness to "Grace."

The most powerful story in the volume is "Sim Burns's Wife." There is little in this story, which fully treats the despair of the farm wife, that lightens its pessimism. Lucretia Burns is initially described in a realistic, unromantic way: "It was a pitifully warm, almost tragic face—long, thin, sallow, hollow-eyed. The mouth had long since lost the power to shape itself into a kiss, and had a droop at the corners which seemed to announce a breaking-down at any moment into a

despairing wail. The collarless neck and sharp shoulders showed painfully. And even Sim Burns had long since ceased to kiss his wife or even speak kindly to her. There was no longer any sanctity to life or love." The story dramatizes the sympathetic feeling Garland had for farm wives. For Lucretia there is no escape from her monotonous, unromantic life. She contemplates suicide but finally resolves to go on. The tone tends toward despair, but the characters have an abiding endurance and cannot be defeated. Again Garland places blame on economic conditions which produce the misery. Through the appearance in the story of Radbourne, the young radical, Garland explicitly voices his view of the economic system, insisting that the downfall of the farmer can be attributed specifically to his economic situation.

In a lighter vein, "Some Village Cronies" (first published as "An Evening at the Corner Grocery: A Western Character Sketch," *Arena*, September 1891) deals with the baiting of Colonel Peavy about his bald head by Squire Gordon during a checker game at the town grocery one winter evening. A humorous story, Garland presents in it well-drawn local types and focuses on the local, colorful scene. This story was not a product of Garland's reactions against western conditions, but of his nostalgic memories of his boyhood.

"Daddy Deering" (*Belford's Magazine*, April 1892) also belongs to Garland's "milder fiction." It is a simple, uncomplicated tale of a vibrant, fun-loving man who simply grows old and dies. There is not much dramatic tension in the story, except at the end when, for a brief moment, the reader suspects that Daddy Deering has committed suicide. But it is soon apparent that Daddy, knowing he was going to die, went out into the snow to "defiantly meet his death." The story does not depict the tragedy and toil of farm life; Daddy is vibrant as long as he can work. It is only when he can no longer function, when old age comes and the past becomes a nostalgic memory, that the character is pitiable. However, he never succumbs to despair.

"Drifting Crane" (*Harper's Weekly*, 31 May 1890) illustrates Garland's early interest in the Indian problem and announces a long series of stories to come. Here, Chief Drifting Crane tries to convince Henry Wilson, a solitary pioneer, to leave his ranch, which borders an Indian reservation. But Wilson refuses and tries to explain to Drifting Crane that the Indian's fate is doomed, that the white settlers will eventually come. Garland briefly indicates the injustices of the whites in their treatment of the Indian and his land. At the same time, he attempts to evoke the tragedy of a dying race.

Prairie Folks, like *Main-Travelled Roads*, deals with material which Garland knew well. The pleasant scenes Garland depicts were as much a part of his personal experiences of growing up in the West as were the pitiable pictures found in *Main-Travelled Roads*. Yet, though the stories in *Prairie Folks* depict a wide range of western material, though the picturesque renderings of the local scenes are memorable, and though the volume has an attractive lyrical quality that is reinforced by the poems which run throughout, the collection ultimately suffers from the distinct lack of sufficient plot and character development. It fails to touch the "deeper life" of the people which *Main-Travelled Roads* accomplishes so well. It fails primarily because here Garland withheld the possibility of tragedy. The lighter aspects of life painted in *Prairie Folks* were unquestionably a part of the farmers' experiences, but their lives contained much more. And such a failure to capture their total lives, to produce the tensions and ironies as he had done earlier, ultimately harms the volume, despite the charm of the individual pieces.

In February 1897 Garland signed a contract with D. Appleton and Company for a new volume of collected short stories to be entitled *Wayside Courtships*. For this volume Garland collected eleven diverse stories, most of which had previously appeared in journals between 1887 and 1897. The stories, while including a variety of themes, deal with the relations of men and women and serve, in many ways, as companion pieces to those in *Main-Travelled Roads* and *Prairie Folks*. Although the title of the volume suggests a collection of romances, several stories deal with the harsher side of love, giving his treatment of the theme of love more complexity and, on the whole, more strength.

The main stories are contained between an opening vignette, "At the Beginning" (first published as "Before the Overture," *Ladies' Home Journal*, May 1893), which briefly depicts two young lovers full of youthful romance moved emotionally by the sight and presence of each other at an opera, and a concluding piece, "The End of Love is Love" (first published as "Forgetting," *Ladies' Home Journal*, December 1892), which portrays an old married couple resting on a beach after life has driven the romance from their marriage. The elderly man wants to forget that he is old and timid and that youthful romanticism and love are gone and urges his wife to forget and help him forget the intervening years.

Unlike the characters in *Main-Travelled Roads* and *Prairie Folks*, the main characters of *Wayside Courtships* are not found on the farm; generally college-bred, they are usually encountered by the reader on a train either going to or passing through a small town. The first tale, "A Preacher's Love Story" (first published as "An Evangel in Cyene," *Harper's Monthly*, August 1895), portrays Wallace Stacey, who is just out of college and on his way by train to Illinois to look for a position as a preacher and teacher. He finds a position in Cyene through a man he meets on the train, Herman Allen, a cynical, worldly college dropout who intends to make his fortune on the Wheat Exchange in Chicago. Stacey, a Baptist, intends to stay with Allen; but after he meets Allen's sister Mattie, their father, a confirmed Methodist, learns of Stacey's religion and asks him to leave the house. Stacey finds the church run-down; and, because of the religious divisions, he is offered no help by either the Methodists or Baptists to rebuild it. However, after a series of inspirational sermons, he brings everyone together. When Stacey becomes ill, the town rebuilds the church; he falls in love with Mattie; and the story ends with their anticipated marriage. A romantic story, it suggests the unity of all people and the power of love. But the story has poor dramatization, is overly sentimental, and is weak in depicting local color.

Like "A Preacher's Love Story," romance penetrates "A Meeting in the Foothills" (first published as "A Girl from Washington," *Philadelphia Press*, 16-18 January 1896). After searching in vain Arthur Ramsey finally accepts a position as a common hand with wealthy Major Thayer. Eventually Ramsey is able to win the major's niece Edith and to convince everyone that he is more than a commoner, and the story ends again with the promise of marriage. But here again the story lacks sufficient tension, dramatization, and character development to carry the theme.

"A Stop-over at Tyre" (first published as "A Girl of Modern Tyre," *Century*, January 1897) is more successful and also has closer ties with the best stories in Garland's first two volumes of stories. Torn between his love for Maud and his desire to finish school, Albert Lohr finally decides to marry. The story effectively depicts the tensions involved in Lohr's loss of ambition and aspiration because of his marriage, but it also discloses a greater skepticism concerning the possibilities of romantic love than the previous two stories.

Not everything in marriage is similarly delightful. In "An Alien in the Pines" (first published as "Only a Lumberjack," *Harper's Weekly*, 8 December 1894) the reader is confronted by a man who calls himself Williams who was formerly a talented violinist but who works as a woodcutter in the pine forests of Wisconsin. Destroyed by drink, he left his family; but he sends part of his check each month for their welfare. However, at the end of the story a burst of shame overcomes him, and he decides to return to his wife and try to make their marriage successful.

In "The Owner of the Mill Farm" (first published as "A Graceless Husband," *Northwestern Miller*, Extra Christmas Number, December

1893) Garland focuses on brutality and jealousy which have disastrous consequences. Remedies to cure the problems are only temporary, and the tone of the story remains somber throughout.

In "Of Those Who Seek" (1897) the same young man appears in four separate vignettes. In one he notices a young Indian girl who is deaf, dumb, and blind. He perceives that, having "the prisoned soul," her life must remain a cruel fragment, imprisoned in darkness. In another, while running for public office, he envies the sheltered life of a rich, well-protected girl who longs to be released from her humdrum existence and to join him in his struggle. Each idealizes the other's way of life and is dissatisfied with his or her own.

Another unnamed young man appears in "A Fair Exile" (first published as "A Short-Term Exile," *Literary Northwest*, July 1893) on his way to Boomtown. He overhears a story by a young woman who had gone through a difficult childhood with a coarse father and who is now in the midst of a divorce from a drunken, dissolute man. Now she is alone, with only sympathetic listeners. But in "The Passing Stranger" (first published in *Wayside Courtships*), Garland suggests that redemption is always possible for lost souls. The young man passes an infamous bar in New York where he sees a young woman. When she sees him, she feels herself compelled to leave the bar and return to her village. This piece is much more mystical than any of the others in the volume.

In "Before the Low Green Door" (a revision of "A Common Case") Garland depicts a broken farm wife, Matilda Bent, who is dying from cancer. The tone is utterly antiromantic and is a contrast with the dominant positive tone of the volume. Garland then ends the volume with a more idyllic story, "Upon Impulse" (*Bookman*, January 1897), in which Mr. Jenkins Ware, a lawyer, becomes infatuated at a social gathering with Miss Powell, a teacher. Reminded of a schoolteacher he once idolized, Ware acts on an impulse and asks her to marry him. After hesitating, she finally accepts, deciding to follow her own impulses and feelings and not to rationalize them.

Garland's next collection of stories was not published until 1916, under the title *They of the High Trails*, although all of the pieces had seen prior publication. By this time Garland had shifted his locale to the mountains of the West. In retitling all of the stories, he attempted to delineate the various western types to be found: "The Grub-Staker," "The Cow-boss," "The Remittance

*Garland in Chicago at the 1933-1934 Century of
Progress Exposition*

Man," "The Lonesome Man," "The Trail
Tramp," "The Prospector," "The Outlaw," "The
Leaser," "The Ranger," and "The Tourist." The
stories often capture the idiosyncrasies of his picturesque mountain people, and the scenes are
often compelling; however, the characters seldom
emerge from their type. What was lacking was
the emotional identification with his subject matter that Garland had in *Main-Travelled Roads*. In
the western mountains, Garland remained a sympathetic observer, but an outsider nevertheless.
Another weakness, one which characterized
much of Garland's longer fiction after 1895, was
the lack of significant tension to carry the stories'
themes. Such weaknesses were not apparent, however, in his treatment of the American Indian.

Before his marriage in 1899 to Zulime Taft,
Garland traveled extensively and spent a considerable amount of time living with and observing various Indian tribes. Consequently, he reacted
strongly against those writers who treated the Indians as nothing more than savages. As he told
Major Stouch, the Indian agent at Darlington,
Oklahoma, "We have had plenty of the 'wily red-
skin' kind of thing. . . . I am going to tell of the

red man as you and [John Homer] Seger have
known him, as a man of the polished stone age trying to adapt himself to steam and electricity." Garland became indignant over the unjust treatment
of the Indian. He was not concerned with the
forces which subjugated the Indian as much as
he was with the conflicts which arose when the Indian attempted to come to terms with an alien culture. He had little patience with white programs
which attempted to rehabilitate a defeated race
but which had little understanding of the Indian's way of life. However, he also appreciated the
inherent tragedy and futility in the attempt of
many Indians to retain their way of life in modern society. But Garland ultimately makes it clear
that the Indian must change. His primary concern, as James K. Folsom has observed, is the nature of the process of conversion.

In Garland's stories collected in *The Book of
the American Indian* (1923), which also contains
"The Silent Eaters"—a previously unpublished fictionalized biography of Sitting Bull—he manifests
an engaging and genuine sympathy for the American Indian. In his best stories his treatment has
an authenticity unmatched in his other writings
during this period. The theme of the necessity of
conversion to modern life, which is apparent
throughout the collection, is most effectively
treated in "Wahiah—A Spartan Mother" (first published as "Spartan Mother," *Ladies' Home Journal*,
February 1905). Here John Seger, the Indian
agent among the Cheyennes and Arapahoes,
tries to convince the Indians to send their children to school. Most comply, but Tomacham and
his wife, Wahiah, resist sending their son,
Atokan, since it would mean that he would be
forced to change his dress and to follow the
white man's road. They eventually agree, recognizing that "we are on the road—we cannot turn
back." When Seger resolves to whip the offend-
ers, because of flagrant truancy, many parents
are unhappy; they feel that "It was pivotal, this
question of punishment—it marked their final subjugation to the white man." When Atokan is truant, Seger whips him in front of his parents and
others until the boy's spirit is broken. Seger justi-
fies his actions to Atokan's parents by telling
them that the children must learn to plow and
reap as the white man does or they will die. The
parents surrender; and, in a symbolic gesture,
Wahiah breaks her son's "symbols of freedom,"
his bows and arrows, and orders him henceforth
to obey the agent. The story is central to the collection, for it effectively dramatizes the painful real-

ization by Wahiah of the necessity to reject old ways.

This theme is also treated in "Nistina" (*Harper's Weekly*, 4 April 1903) and "The New Medicine House" (*Harper's Weekly*, 6 December 1902), but it is handled more directly in "Rising Wolf, Ghost Dancer" (*McClure's*, January 1899). Rising Wolf recounts how in his young life he became a medicine man. After the Indian defeat, Rising Wolf and his people are placed on reservations where his powers are no longer needed. However, their hopes are raised when a stranger teaches them the Ghost Dance, which promises to bring back their lost past. If they arrange to dance for four days, the white man would presumably disappear on the fourth day, the buffalo would return, and the Indians would be reunited with their dead on earth. The dance is performed but is unsuccessful. Convinced that the Ghost Dance and the Indian medicine have both been in error, Rising Wolf renounces them and resolves to take up white ways.

To be sure, not all Indians are converted. In "Big Moggasen" (*Independent*, November 1900) the chief of a Navajo band, living high in the mountains, refuses to have anything to do with the white man and rejects any help for his desolate tribe. Finally, persuaded to visit Little Father, he is offered aid in return for sending his children away to be schooled by whites. He refuses and leaves, for he has resolved to resist.

Generally, Garland's heroes are either Indian agents or schoolteachers who show a tolerance and sympathetic understanding toward the Indian. The villains tend to be missionaries who attempt to convert the Indian not by teaching him new ways but by eradicating all of his customs. In one of his most poignant stories, "The Iron Kiva" (first published as "Iron Khiva," *Harper's Weekly*, 29 August 1903), Garland tells of two children who escape and kill themselves rather than be taken away to school in the East by a missionary. The Indians' attitude toward the missionaries is directly stated: "They came to love one of those who taught them—a white woman with a gentle face—but the man in the black coat who told the children that the religion of their father's was wicked and foolish—him they hated and bitterly despised." Garland thus indicated that, to convert the Indian, it was not necessary to destroy his customs entirely but to teach him the skills necessary to endure in a dominant white society.

Not all of the stories treat the theme of conversion, for some deal with Indian customs. In "The Remorse of Waumdisapa" (previously unpublished) Garland concentrates on dissension in the camp of Waumdisapa, chief of the Tetons. Matawan, his cousin, jealous of the chief's great fame, conspires to degrade and destroy him. At a council meeting Waumdisapa announces that he will step aside if his doing so is the will of the members. But when each speaks in his defense and Matawan accuses the group of cowardice, Waumdisapa, losing control, leaps up and stabs him to death. Full of remorse for the murder, he removes himself as chief and takes his place outside the council circle—self-accused and self-deposed.

In "The Decree of Council" (previously unpublished) Garland indicates that the white man's road cannot nor should not always be followed. Here, Big Nose, an inveterate gambler, foolishly loses both his wives and his belongings. After consideration the council decree is to give him back one of his wives—the older one who was difficult to manage. Unhappy with the decision, he nevertheless endures for several years, gives up gambling, works hard, and becomes one of the most progressive men in the camp. However, no longer able to endure his wife, and wanting to take a new one, he approaches Seger, the superintendent of the school, to get advice, feeling that since he is conforming he does not care what the other Indians have to say. But Seger, recognizing the cultural differences, accepts the judgment of White Shield that, from the decree of the council, there is no appeal.

The most powerful story in the collection, "The Story of Howling Wolf" (previously unpublished), is also the most somber because it seriously questions the positive view expressed elsewhere of the potential for conversion by following the white man's road. Seven years after Howling Wolf's brother was shot by two white cattlemen, Howling Wolf vows to kill those responsible. Captain Cook, the Indian agent, attempts to gain his trust; but to Howling Wolf, "It was hard to trust the white man even when he smiled, for his tongue had ever been forked like a rattlesnake and his hand exceedingly cunning.... They brought plows that tore the sod, machines that swept away the grass. They all said, 'Dam Injun,' and in those words displayed their hearts."

But Howling Wolf finally decides to trust Cook, with whom he makes friends, renounces his vengeance, resolves to win the respect of whites, and writes his resolution on a piece of paper. He gets a job hauling hides, but the whites continue to taunt him. When a cowboy picks a fight with him and fires a wild shot, wounding another white man in the knee, Howling Wolf is blamed. He is jailed, and the Indian agent's efforts to get him released are futile. One day he is taken from the jail by the sheriff, who wants to attend a baseball game but is afraid to leave Howling Wolf unattended. Howling Wolf, however, thinks that he is being taken to his execution and tries to escape. He is pursued by a mob and caught after being abandoned by the sheriff, and the mob "With the light of hell on their faces ... shot down the defenseless man and then alighted, and, with remorseless hate, crushed his face beneath their feet as if he were a rattlesnake.... They fought for a chance to kick him. They lost all resemblance to men. Wolves fighting over the flesh of their own kind could not have been more heartlessly malevolent— more appalling in their ferocity." Although the Indian miraculously recovers, he is so misshapen and battered that even his wife cannot recognize him.

Howling Wolf's attempt to walk the white man's road ends tragically. As Folsom observes, Howling Wolf's story, like others in the volume, is a treatment of education, but what he learns stands in direct opposition to the lesson learned elsewhere; for, except for the actions of the agent, his education teaches the cruelty, savagery, and selfishness of the whites. Their evil is not a product of different social values, which could be corrected through social action, but an expression of the bestiality in man. The lesson here is that while change may be inevitable, it does not necessarily represent progress.

Through his fiction, Garland became a principal spokesman for nineteenth-century agrarian society. Faithful to his innate instinct for telling the truth, he used particular settings in the Midwest to bring to his readers the problems which men and women in crude surroundings had to face and solve in order to survive. He succeeded in reflecting the severe restrictions of prairie life, with its loneliness and drudgery, and suggested the waste of finer values exacted by life on the farm.

Most readers acknowledge that Garland's finest work, *Main-Travelled Roads*, is an important historical document, for it portrays more vividly than any other work of its time the conditions which led to the Populist revolt. But it is also important for its artistic success. In praising the book William Dean Howells observed that "these stories are full of the bitter and burning dust, the foul and trampled slush, of the common avenues of life, the life of the men who hopelessly and cheerlessly make the wealth that enriches the alien and the idler, and impoverishes the producer."

In addition to Garland's historical importance, he is significant for another reason: while not an original thinker, Garland reflected in his works the most vital intellectual, social, and aesthetic ideas of his time, responding as a zealous reformer to such issues as the rise of Populism, the single tax, Indian rights, the struggle for woman's rights, and evolution; and to such creative concepts as local color and impressionism. Whenever Garland was able to integrate his social and literary theories with the materials he gathered from personal experience and observation, and whenever he was able to maintain a tension between his radical individualism and the oppressive social and economic forces threatening individual freedom, his work retained a compelling vitality. Garland died 5 March 1940.

Biographies:

Eldon C. Hill, "A Biographical Study of Hamlin Garland from 1860 to 1895," Ph.D. dissertation, Ohio State University, 1940;

Jean Holloway, *Hamlin Garland: A Biography* (Austin: University of Texas Press, 1956);

Robert Mane, *Hamlin Garland: L'homme et l'oeuvre (1860-1940)* (Paris: Didier, 1968).

References:

Lars Ahnebrink, *The Beginnings of Naturalism in American Fiction* (Cambridge, Mass.: Harvard University Press, 1950), pp. 63-89;

Thomas Becknell, "Hamlin Garland's Response to Whitman," *The Old Northwest: A Journal of Regional Life and Letters*, 7 (Fall 1981): 217-235;

Thomas Bledsoe, Introduction to *Main-Travelled Roads* (New York: Rinehart, 1954), pp. ix-xliii;

Michael Clark, "Herbert Spencer, Hamlin Garland, and *Rose of Dutcher's Coolly*," *American Literary Realism*, 17 (Autumn 1984): 203-208;

Bernard I. Duffy, "Hamlin Garland's 'Decline' from Realism," *American Literature*, 25 (March 1953): 69-74;

M. H. Dunlop, "Unfinished Business: Hamlin Garland and Edward MacDowell," *The Old North-*

west: *A Journal of Regional Life and Letters*, 10 (Summer 1984): 175-185;

James K. Folsom, *The American Western Novel* (New Haven, Conn.: College and University Press, 1966), pp. 149-155, 180-184;

Clyde E. Henson, "Joseph Kirkland's Influence on Hamlin Garland," *American Literature*, 23 (January 1952): 458-463;

Walter Herrscher, "The Natural Environment in Hamlin Garland's *Main-Travelled Roads*," *The Old Northwest: A Journal of Regional Life and Letters*, 11 (Spring-Summer 1985): 35-50;

Marcia Jacobson, "The Flood of Remembrance and the Stream of Time: Hamlin Garland's *Boy Life on the Prairie*," *Western American Literature*, 17 (November 1982): 227-242;

Frances W. Kaye, "Hamlin Garland's Feminism," in *Women and Western American Literature*, edited by Helen Winter and Susan J. Rosowski (Troy, N.Y.: Whitston, 1982), pp. 135-161;

Albert Keiser, *The Indian in American Literature* (New York: Oxford University Press, 1933), pp. 279-292ff;

James D. Keorner, "Comment on 'Hamlin Garland's "Decline" from Realism,'" *American Literature*, 26 (November 1954): 427-432;

Joseph B. McCullough, *Hamlin Garland* (Boston: Twayne, 1978);

McCullough, "Hamlin Garland's Letters to James Whitcomb Riley," *American Literary Realism*, 9 (Summer 1976): 249-260;

McCullough, "Hamlin Garland's Quarrel with *The Dial*," *American Literary Realism*, 9 (Winter 1976): 77-80;

Warren Motley, "Hamlin Garland's *Under the Wheel*: Regionalism Unmasking America," *Modern Drama*, 26 (December 1983): 477-485;

James Nagel, ed., *Critical Essays on Hamlin Garland* (Boston: G. K. Hall, 1982);

Donald Pizer, *Hamlin Garland's Early Work and Career* (Berkeley: University of California Press, 1960);

Pizer, "Herbert Spencer and the Genesis of Hamlin Garland's Critical System," *Tulane Studies in English*, 7 (1957): 153-168;

Pizer, Introduction to *Main-Travelled Roads* (Columbus, Ohio: Merrill, 1970), pp. v-xviii;

Pizer, "'John Boyle's Conclusion': An Unpublished Middle Border Story by Hamlin Garland," *American Literature*, 31 (March 1959): 59-75;

Pizer, "Romantic Individualism in Garland, Norris and Crane," *American Quarterly*, 10 (Winter 1958): 463-475;

Lewis O. Saum, "Hamlin Garland and Reform," *South Dakota Review*, 10 (Winter 1972): 36-62;

Charles L. P. Silet, Robert E. Welch, and Richard Boudreau, eds., *The Critical Reception of Hamlin Garland* (Troy, N.Y.: Whitston, 1985);

Claude Simpson, "Hamlin Garland's Decline," *Southwest Review*, 26 (Winter 1941): 223-234;

James B. Stronks, "A Realist Experiments with Impressionism: Hamlin Garland's 'Chicago Studies,'" *American Literature*, 36 (March 1964): 38-52;

Walter F. Taylor, *The Economic Novel in America* (Chapel Hill: University of North Carolina Press, 1942), pp. 148-183;

Robert Thacker, "Twisting toward Insanity: Landscape and Female Entrapment in Plains Fiction," *North Dakota Quarterly*, 52 (Summer 1984): 181-194;

Charles C. Walcutt, *American Literary Naturalism, A Divided Stream* (Minneapolis: University of Minnesota Press, 1956), pp. 53-63.

Papers:
The chief collection of Garland's papers is in the Doheny Library of the University of Southern California; the Garland-Gilder Correspondence is in the New York Public Library; Garland's diaries are at the Huntington Library in San Marino, California.

Katharine Fullerton Gerould

(6 February 1879-27 July 1944)

Kenneth A. Robb

Bowling Green State University

BOOKS: *Vain Oblations* (New York: Scribners, 1914; London: Sidgwick & Jackson, 1914);

The Great Tradition and Other Stories (New York: Scribners, 1915; London: Methuen, 1916);

Hawaii: Scenes and Impressions (New York: Scribners, 1916);

A Change of Air (New York: Scribners, 1917);

Modes and Morals (New York: Scribners, 1920);

Lost Valley, A Novel (New York & London: Harper, 1922);

Valiant Dust (New York: Scribners, 1922);

Conquistador (New York: Scribners, 1923; London: Harrap, 1924);

The Aristocratic West (New York & London: Harper, 1925);

The Light That Never Was (New York: Scribners, 1931);

Ringside Seats (New York: Dodd, Mead, 1937).

In *The Best Short Stories of 1917* Edward J. O'Brien stated that Katharine Gerould's stories sustained "her claim to rank as one of the three most distinguished contemporary writers of the American short story," and he also included stories by her in the collections for 1920, 1921, 1922, and 1925, while including her name on the "roll of honor" in other volumes of this series. Yet today her stories are seldom read.

Katharine Elizabeth Fullerton, born in Brockton, Massachusetts, was adopted by her uncle, the Reverend Bradford Morton Fullerton, and his wife, Julia Maria Bell Fullerton. After attending Miss Folsom's School, Katharine Fullerton entered Radcliffe College, where she earned an A.B. (1900) and an A.M. (1901). She then served ten years as a reader in English at Bryn Mawr. About 1903, she learned that she had been adopted and that the older "brother" for whom she had always felt an extraordinary affection, William Morton Fullerton, was really her cousin. When he returned from Europe to America briefly in 1907, they became engaged, but soon he and Edith Wharton entered into an affair in Paris. On leave in Paris, 1908 to 1909, Kath-

arine Fullerton attempted to write a novel and to gain certainty about the engagement, but upon her return to the United States, Morton Fullerton became unresponsive to her letters. The engagement was broken off in early 1910. On 9 June 1910 she married a prominent medieval scholar at Princeton University, Gordon Hall Gerould, and resided at Princeton the rest of her life. The Geroulds had two children, Christopher and Sylvia.

In 1900 Gerould's "The Poppies in the Wheat" won the *Century Magazine* prize for the best short story by an undergraduate and was published in the January 1902 issue, but she was displeased with the story and did not finish another until "Vain Oblations" in 1908. Edith Wharton helped her to have her work published by Charles Scribner's Sons. From 1911 until the early 1930s, about fifty stories by Gerould appeared in periodicals such as *Century, Scribner's Magazine, Harper's Monthly,* and the *Atlantic Monthly.* Later in life, Gerould focused her efforts on lecturing and on writing novels, book reviews, and essays. She died of lung cancer at the age of sixty-five.

Speaking of her essays, Fred Millett described Gerould as "the least ingratiating of the Brahmins." In her stories Gerould frequently analyzes "the New Englander," but they do not display so blatantly the regional and class prejudices apparent in her essays. Many of Gerould's characters are people of independent means. Some have religious vocations, while others are artists, writers, or academicians. Gerould's style is reminiscent of Henry James's or Edith Wharton's, and her use of narrators and of exotic settings reminds one of Joseph Conrad. One of her many male narrators, Hoyting, who appears in several stories, is similar to Conrad's Marlowe. A main theme in many of her stories is the preservation of the self, or of one's image of one's self, in extreme circumstances.

Writing in 1930, Fred Lewis Pattee called Gerould's "Vain Oblations" (*Scribner's Magazine,*

March 1911; collected in *Vain Oblations*, 1914) a "sinister tale" that "placed her at a bound near the head of the new school of short-story writers." Mary Bradford has been kidnapped by marauding natives in an African village as she helped her missionary father. She was once "the finest flower of New England," but when her fiancé, Saxe, finds a woman who is said to be Mary, the woman who stands before him has been so disfigured and has painted herself so gaudily that he cannot identify her with certainty, and he can evoke no sign of recognition from her. Nevertheless, he buys her from the chief, but before they are to leave, the woman commits suicide. After making his way to the coastal mission, Saxe dies, believing he has not found Mary. Several weeks later, "incontrovertible proof" is received that the woman was indeed she. The masculine narrator speculates that Mary committed suicide—against all her former beliefs—to save Saxe from the woman she had become, but it is also suggested that her soul saves herself by destroying her disfigured body. The power of Mary's character can be inferred from her ability to survive her capture, to abase herself before her captor in her fiancé's presence, to refuse to recognize him, and finally, to commit suicide. Pattee seems justified in commenting that the story can be classed "with those few tales that burn themselves into one's memory like scorpion bites and will not be erased."

Two other, lesser, stories collected in *Vain Oblations* are set in a Conradian Africa: "The Tortoise" (*Scribner's Magazine*, January 1914), an interesting variation of "Vain Oblations," and "The Case of Paramore" (*Scribner's Magazine*, October 1913), in which the title character, like Conrad's Lord Jim, seeks to atone for an early failure of duty.

When summarized, many of Gerould's story plots sound quite melodramatic, and her frequent use of coincidence is exposed, but in the stories themselves these weaknesses are frequently masked by a slightly elevated, dignified style, by effective characterization and deployment of narrators, and by convincing psychological motivation of the characters. Among such stories are her ghost tales. "On the Staircase" (*Scribner's Magazine*, December 1913; collected in *Vain Oblations*) may suggest the author's belief in Fate lurking behind the seeming randomness of life, for ghosts haunt a new house, and gradually the narrator comes to realize that they are ghosts foretelling the futures of those who see them,

rather than spectres from the past. The ghosts of "Blue Bonnet" (*Century*, February 1915; collected in *Valiant Dust*, 1922), on the other hand, turn out to be the psychopathological delusions of a neglected wife. Similarly, the apparently supernatural occurrences of "Belshazzar's Letter" (*Metropolitan*, June 1922; collected in *Valiant Dust*) turn out to originate in a human mind.

Gerould's stories of marital and parent-child relationships are often impressive. Hatred between husband and wife is portrayed in "The Wine of Violence" (*Scribner's Magazine*, July 1911; collected in *Vain Oblations*), in which an actress allows her actor-husband to be executed for her supposed murder. She does not come forward to clear him because they had become so inimical to each other that "to walk the same earth was too oppressive, too intimate a tie." "Pearls" (*Harper's Monthly*, July 1914; collected in *The Great Tradition*, 1915) treats not only marital discord but two other Gerould themes: egotism and a parent's self-sacrifice for a child. The wife of a struggling artist reveals their mutual hatred to the narrator after her husband has collected a fifteen-thousand-dollar reward for finding a pearl necklace, sent her a thousand dollars of it, and decamped to the South Seas with the rest. Considering herself "dead and done for," Mrs. Parmenter decides to take their daughter to Europe on the little money remaining and to devote her life to bringing out the beauty she is convinced her daughter possesses.

The effect of egocentrism in marriage is also portrayed in Dr. Dorrien of "The Divided Kingdom" (*Century*, June 1912; collected in *Vain Oblations*). Reminiscent of Dr. Lydgate in George Eliot's *Middlemarch* (1871-1872), Dorrien longs to solve the problem of leprosy while ministering to the lepers of Molokai, but—like Lydgate's wife, Rosamond—Dorrien's delicate, vain wife defeats his aspirations. After a few years of "normal" practice, sporadic research, and community service, he accidentally infects himself with tuberculosis and then commits suicide. Similarly, in "The Weaker Vessel" (*Century*, December 1913; collected in *The Great Tradition*), Basil Targett's plan to undertake an extended archaeological expedition is frustrated by his wife's insistence that such a separation violates her religious beliefs—even though she has come to his study to tell him she is going abroad to get over her love for another man. Targett finds that "an egotist intrenched in a sacred right is the one antagonist you cannot afford to meet," and he yields, despairingly, to her demands.

Sadie Chadwick, the wife in "Wesendonck" (*Harper's Monthly*, April 1913; collected in *The Great Tradition*) is portrayed somewhat more sympathetically. When a great German chemist comes to visit the college where her husband works as a chemistry professor, Sadie's husband expects her to give a dinner party for the visitor, but finding it impossible to mask their shabbiness, Sadie flees home to her mother with the baby. Returning some weeks later, she finds that, ironically, her flight has cost her husband a promotion that would have made the family more comfortable. Gerould portrays effectively a wife's misery and frustration in trying to "make do" on her husband's small salary in a context that requires refined appearances, but she betrays some superciliousness in describing Sadie's education and her midwestern hometown.

Parental self-sacrifice is the main theme of "The Great Tradition" (*Century*, July 1914; collected in *The Great Tradition*); Mrs. Boyce is the central intelligence, and since her husband never appears, the horrors of marriage to him are conveyed only through her thoughts and actions as she prepares to run away to her lover in England, Ambrose Hale. Just as her stratagems are about to succeed, however, she receives a letter from her nineteen-year-old daughter, Monica, announcing that she has run away to Europe with a married man. Although Monica's actions alone would be viewed tragic so long as Mrs. Boyce herself remained "impeccable," Mrs. Boyce realizes that the conjunction of two such scandals in the same family could be seen only as a "nasty farce." Therefore, she gives up her plans, facing a desolate future yoked to her detestable husband. Mrs. Boyce seems pretentious but also curiously sympathetic, and, while modern readers might consider her too concerned with her reputation, she sees herself, after all, as part of a "great tradition" in which "it hurt to be good."

Harmonious marriages are portrayed in "The Bird in the Bush" (*Scribner's Magazine*, August 1913; collected in *The Great Tradition*) and "The Miracle" (*Harper's Monthly*, November 1914; collected in *The Great Tradition*), in both of which Gerould uncharacteristically verges on the saccharine. "Leda and the Swan" (*Scribner's Magazine*, February 1915; collected in *The Great Tradition*), however, portrays most effectively the deep bond between husband and wife. As Leo Farrant—a respected artist who lost his right arm

in an accident five years earlier—lies dying, Marie, his wife and model for Leda in his greatest painting, knows they have little money left and doubts her ability to resist Mannheimer's offer to purchase the great painting, the symbol of their perfect union. Fearing its desecration, the careworn Marie destroys the masterpiece. The contrasts between Marie of the past and Marie of the present, between Marie talking with Leo and Marie reflecting in solitude, create a powerful characterization.

In one of her most intriguing stories, Gerould sets up a cliché situation in "The Penalties of Artemis" (*Harper's Monthly*, December 1915; collected in *Valiant Dust*) with brittle, sardonic humor. When the *Owara* sinks in the South Seas, lovely young Persis Lambert, engaged to a lawyer back home, is rescued by "tall and dark" Angier. Marooned with him on a desert island for six weeks, Persis early establishes what their relationship is to be, and Angier agrees: he will be the epitome of chivalry. Indeed, both suppress any sexual impulses. On the island they do not talk about their pasts or their futures; it is "an existence that is limited to itself" as they focus on "the little details" of life, with Persis "clinging desperately . . . to some privacy of the mind." They are rescued; they separate; and Persis makes her way home. Yet once there, she goes into seclusion and then breaks her engagement, explaining that, although she disliked Angier, "I feel as if I had been married to him, and I'm quite incapable of marrying again. . . . Every nerve in me has been violated." In establishing the grounds of "saving herself" for her fiancé, Persis created a relationship of dreadful intimacy which can never be dismissed, excused, rationalized, or forgotten.

No substantial studies of Katharine Fullerton Gerould and her work exist, though she is referred to in footnotes and discussed briefly in reference works. Austin Wright calls her one of the "old tradition" writers who flourished before and into the 1920s, contrasting them to the "new tradition" of Sherwood Anderson, F. Scott Fitzgerald, Ernest Hemingway, William Faulkner, and Katherine Anne Porter. By way of contrast he suggests that moral issues are far more clear-cut in Gerould's "The Great Tradition" than in Hemingway's "The End of Something," which was published just eleven years later.

Gerould's stories are notable for their style. Occasionally, one of her narrators comments at too great a length at the end of a story, but most often Gerould shows expertise in her sense of form, in her use of language, and in the psychological motivation of her characters.

References:
R. W. B. Lewis, *Edith Wharton: A Biography* (New York: Harper & Row, 1975);
Fred Lewis Pattee, *The New American Literature, 1890-1930* (New York: Century, 1930);

Stuart P. Sherman, *The Genius of America* (New York: Scribners, 1923);
Austin McGiffert Wright, *The American Short Story in the Twenties* (Chicago: University of Chicago Press, 1961).

Papers:
There are collections of Gerould's letters at Princeton University and Yale University.

Susan Glaspell

(1 July 1876-27 July 1948)

Arthur Waterman
Georgia State University

See also the Glaspell entries in *DLB 7: Twentieth-Century American Dramatists* and *DLB 9: American Novelists, 1910-1945*.

BOOKS: *The Glory of the Conquered: The Story of a Great Love* (New York: Stokes, 1909; London: Pitman, 1909);
The Visioning: A Novel (New York: Stokes, 1911; London: Murray, 1912);
Lifted Masks: Stories (New York: Stokes, 1912);
Fidelity: A Novel (Boston: Small, Maynard, 1915; London: Jarrolds, 1924);
Suppressed Desires, by Glaspell and George Cram Cook (New York: Shay, 1917);
Trifles (New York: Shay/The Washington Square Players, 1917);
The People, and Close the Book: Two One Act Plays (New York: Shay, 1918);
Plays (Boston: Small, Maynard, 1920);
Inheritors: A Play in Three Acts (Boston: Small, Maynard, 1921; London: Benn, 1924);
The Verge: A Play in Three Acts (Boston: Small, Maynard, 1922; London: Benn, 1924);
Bernice, a Play in Three Acts (London: Benn, 1924);
Tickless Time: A Comedy in One Act, by Glaspell and Cook (Boston: Baker, 1925);
Trifles and Six Other Short Plays (London: Benn, 1926);
The Road to the Temple (London: Benn, 1926; New York: Stokes, 1927);

The Comic Artist, a Play in Three Acts, by Glaspell and Norman Matson (New York: Stokes, 1927; London: Benn, 1927);
A Jury of Her Peers (London: Benn, 1927);
Brook Evans (New York: Stokes, 1928; London: Gollancz, 1928);
Fugitive's Return (New York: Stokes, 1929; London: Gollancz, 1929);
Alison's House: A Play in Three Acts (New York & London: French, 1930);
Ambrose Holt and Family (New York: Stokes, 1931; London: Gollancz, 1931);
Cherished and Shared of Old (New York: Messner, 1940);
The Morning Is Near Us: A Novel (New York: Stokes, 1940; London: Gollancz, 1940);
Norma Ashe: A Novel (Philadelphia: Lippincott, 1942; London: Gollancz, 1943);
Judd Rankin's Daughter (Philadelphia: Lippincott, 1945).

PLAY PRODUCTIONS: *Suppressed Desires*, by Glaspell and George Cram Cook, Provincetown, Mass., Wharf Theatre, 1 August 1915;
Trifles, Provincetown, Mass., Wharf Theatre, 8 August 1916;
The People, New York, Provincetown Playhouse, 9 March 1917;
Close the Book, New York, Provincetown Playhouse, 2 November 1917;

Susan Glaspell (Berg Collection, Astor, Lenox and Tilden Foundation, New York Public Library)

The Outsider, New York, Provincetown Playhouse, 28 December 1917;

Woman's Honor, New York, Provincetown Playhouse, 26 April 1918;

Tickless Time, by Glaspell and Cook, New York, Provincetown Playhouse, 20 December 1918;

Bernice, New York, Provincetown Playhouse, 21 March 1919;

Inheritors, New York, Provincetown Playhouse, 21 March 1921;

The Verge, New York, Provincetown Playhouse, 14 November 1921;

Chains of Dew, New York, Provincetown Playhouse, 27 April 1922;

The Comic Artist, by Glaspell and Norman Matson, London, Strand Theatre, 24 June 1928;

Alison's House, New York, Civic Repertory Theatre, 1 December 1930.

PERIODICAL PUBLICATIONS: "Finality in Freeport," *Pictorial Review*, 17 (July 1916): 14-15, 32;

"The Hearing Ear," *Harper's Magazine*, 134 (January 1917): 234-241;

"Jury of Her Peers," *Everyweek*, 5 March 1917;

"Government Goat," *Pictorial Review* (April 1918): 147-166;

"The Busy Duck," *Harper's Magazine*, 137 (November 1918): 828-836;

"Pollen," *Harper's Magazine*, 138 (March 1919): 446-451;

"The Escape," *Harper's Magazine*, 140 (December 1919): 29-38.

Susan Glaspell's literary reputation derives chiefly from the fourteen plays she wrote between 1915 and 1930, most of them for the Provincetown Players. Along with Eugene O'Neill she was the most important playwright for that influential little theater. In addition to her plays, she wrote nine novels, forty-three short stories, a children's tale, plus a few essays and a biography of her husband, George Cram Cook. Like almost everything she wrote, her short stories reveal her midwestern background in both setting and attitude. Her beginnings as a writer closely parallel the development of the so-called local colorists, whose work, especially in short fiction, dominated magazine writing at the turn of the century. As she matured as a writer she developed techniques and themes that helped her avoid the excessive triteness and formula plots of much local-color writing, so that her later tales retain the romantic appeal of the earlier tradition while adding the sharpness of detail and objective treatment of material brought in by the new school of realism.

Glaspell was born in Davenport, Iowa, to Elmer S. and Alice Keating Glaspell on 1 July 1876. Her father's family was among the first settlers of that region, and from him she learned to cherish the independence, integrity, idealism, and practicality of her pioneer heritage. Glaspell was educated in Davenport's public schools and graduated from Drake University in Des Moines in 1899. She then worked for two years as a court and legislative reporter for the *Des Moines Daily News*. Glaspell accepted and conveyed the values of her region as easily as she used herself, with her feminine point of view, as the narrator in the stories she began to write while still in college. When she turned to full-time writing in 1901, she chose the themes, attitudes, and techniques that would appeal to readers of the ladies' magazines of the period, such as *Good Housekeeping* and *Woman's Home Companion;* so she wrote fiction that was sentimental, escapist, romantic, and idealistic. Twenty-six of her stories are set in Freeport, her fictional name for Davenport, and they all follow the convention of local-color writing. After an opening scene that establishes the main character and her problem, a flashback fills in background detail and information, then the plot develops, and the tale ends with an unexpected, sometimes comic, twist. This is a formula fairly close to the French well-made play tradition so popular in the nineteenth-century theater, which is ironic because as a playwright Glaspell was in conscious revolt against the French school.

In addition to their similarities in structure, many of these stories center on a romantic problem where, after several obstacles, love triumphs. All end happily, even when a state senator votes against the will of his constituents to pardon a young murderer, thereby committing political suicide; and most of these stories convey a heavy sentimental tone, as when a hardened city editor breaks down and cries as he listens to an appeal from a condemned man's wife. Glaspell sometimes saves a story from too much sentiment by a clever ending. In "Everything You Want to Plant" a country schoolteacher is attracted to a seed salesman. He tells her that a year ago he lost a woman he loved, so to share his grief she invents a lost lover too. The difficulty is that he respects her grief so much he will not even kiss her and

Glaspell, age eighteen

eventually leaves her. When he returns, she confesses that her lost lover was a fat man who chased her and that she hated him. He confesses that he never had a former love and only invented one to gain her sympathy; and the story ends with their marriage.

In 1912 Glaspell published a collection of thirteen stories, entitled *Lifted Masks*. The reviewer for the *Boston Evening Transcript* (19 October 1912) indicates the basic appeal of these stories: "Rarely do we meet with a writer who lifts the masks of life, who shows us the naked souls of men, their dreams, their sufferings, their hopes. Here is a book that holds one's breathless attention, a series of short stories, each revealing the innermost promptings of the heart." And, while suggesting that some of the stories were mere sketches, the reviewer for the *New York Times* (29 September 1912) praised the volume as "finely human pictures of human people, full of human tenderness and human laughter, and some of them are among the best stories of the sort that have appeared for a long time." These favorable comments indicate how well Glaspell had mastered the techniques and material of local-color writing, how skillfully she could reach her readers by giving them emotional satisfaction and idealistic reassurance balanced by a realistic setting and credible characters. In her later tales she would strengthen this balance by adding an ironic tone, a more ambiguous attitude toward the Midwest, and much sharper dialogue, stemming obviously from her experience as a playwright.

Sometime in 1907 Susan Glaspell met George Cram Cook, whom she married in 1913. Cook was also a native of Davenport, but, unlike Glaspell, he set out to shock the more conservative elements in the town. He came from a well-known and well-to-do family, so his outrageous behavior was all the more upsetting. With Floyd Dell, a fellow rebel, he founded the Monist Society, which was open to "freethinkers," and the two men, on at least one occasion, caused a furor at a meeting of the Contemporary Club—the leading intellectual club in town—by mocking its seriousness. Although Cook and Dell admired Glaspell's literary ability and envied her success (she won a five-hundred-dollar short-story award), they thought she needed to change. In his autobiography, *Homecoming* (1933), Dell writes that "Susan was a slight, gentle, sweet, whimsically humorous girl, a little ethereal in appearance, but evidently a person of great energy, and brimful of talent; but, we agreed, too medieval-romantic in her views of life." Under their tutelage she began to see her region in other than "medieval-romantic" terms, and to discover a literary tradition concerned with an immediate, realistic sense of the contemporary, often with political overtones. Their effect on her thinking and writing can be seen in her second novel, *The Visioning* (1911), which overflows with socialist ideas, antimilitary notions, and a vision for a better world. Indeed, Cook strengthened Glaspell's idealism with his own vision of a classical revival in America, where, especially in the theater, all the arts would unite in a creative totality. For a few years Cook realized this dream as director of the Provincetown Players. Influenced by Cook's vision, Glaspell's later stories would shift away from the local-color tradition, with its emphasis on escapism and sentimentality, to a more realistic art which treated more contemporary themes. Cook also helped her to see the Midwest in more complex and less simplistic terms. When they met, Glaspell had spent a year in France, and another year studying in Chicago, so she was already distancing herself from the easy acceptance of midwestern attitudes revealed in her early stories. Her years as a court and legislative reporter not only trained her in journalistic realism, but also made her aware of the often wide discrepancy between the real world of brutal crime and hypocritical politics and the ideal world that existed in slogans and schoolbooks. Like other midwestern children, Glaspell, Cook, and Dell found that, as they matured, their pioneer heritage was being adulterated by small-town morality, commercial greed, and political hypocrisy; and they fled their homeplace, going first to Chicago then to New York to experiment with new life-styles and new art. So, when Glaspell married Cook in Weehawken, New Jersey, on 14 April 1913, she was ready to establish a new life in the East and begin a new career as a playwright.

During her years with Cook and the Provincetown Players (1913-1922) Glaspell wrote one novel, seven one-act and four full-length plays, and twenty short stories. These stories were written to earn the money needed to keep the Cooks solvent while they lived in Greenwich Village and were involved with the theater. Consequently, these stories are designed to appeal to the same readers of the same magazines as were her earlier stories. None of them reflects the Bohemian life she encountered in the Village. She did write a few stories about the Portuguese fishermen who lived on Cape Cod, but her treatment of them is in the local-color tradition; all that has changed is the locale. What she did find in the Village were people who affirmed her belief that the individual should seek out his or her meaning of life regardless of convention or societal restrictions. These modern "pioneers" were creating for themselves new frontiers of feeling, thinking, and living, often at considerable psychological and financial cost. One of Glaspell's most persistent themes is the painful, albeit necessary, journey of someone to pursue her (they are all women, except for Ambrose Holt) life's meaning, in spite of love, money, acceptance—anything that stands in the way of personal fulfillment. The best example of a character seeking this goal is Ambrose Holt in *Ambrose Holt and Family* (1931), and the most extreme example is Claire in Glaspell's most shocking play, *The Verge*, first produced at the Provincetown Playhouse in 1921 and published in 1922.

In "The Escape" (*Harper's Magazine*, December 1919) Glaspell depicts one of these exceptional people. Because she insists on trying to discover the meaning of life, Margaret Powers is

Ida Rauh and Susan Glaspell in the Provincetown Players' production of Glaspell's play Bernice *(Fales Library, Elmer Holmes Bobst Library, New York University)*

considered "different" by the townspeople of Freeport. She invites a horse into her house because she wants to know what, if anything, horses think about houses. She comforts animals as if they were human. But what is most upsetting to her neighbors is that Margaret cares little about the war then raging in Europe and refuses to share their jingoistic fervor. When a young soldier returns home with one leg missing and rebuffs any expression of sympathy or aid, Margaret realizes that, like herself, he wears a mask of indifference to hide his deeper feelings. She shows him that he is not alone, that others, who are different as he is, can live happy lives in spite of, or because of, those differences. The tale is saved from its obviously trite theme and sentimental characters by Glaspell's skillful dramatizing of Margaret's character. She is shown in action, onstage as it were, and the reader is at first puzzled by her actions; only as the story unfolds through her actions and witty reactions to situations does the reader understand and, finally, sympathize with her. By emphasizing Margaret's refusal to get excited about the recent war and by emphasizing its terrible effect on the young soldier, Glaspell was echoing the pacifism so prevalent in the Village during the war years. This story illustrates the beneficial influence of her play writing and also demonstrates that her work was concerned with contemporary themes.

Glaspell's first plays were one-acts that satirized current Village fads. One, *Suppressed Desires* (produced in 1915; published in 1917), written in collaboration with Cook, has become a little theater classic and is still performed today. Encouraged by her success at satire, Glaspell soon began to write short stories that were also satires, except that her stories made fun of midwestern pretensions and shortcomings. The best of these is "Finality in Freeport" (*Pictorial Review*, July 1916), which was based on an actual event that happened in Davenport. In the story a member of the town's literary club discovers that the public library has refused to stock a supposedly heretical book, *The Finality of Christ*. Outraged at this censorship, she begins a campaign to force the library to buy and lend the book. The affair becomes a cause célèbre; sides are taken, letters to the editor are written, and a literary war is initiated. An enterprising bookseller stocks the book and sells copies as quickly as he can keep them available. The literary club invites the author to address them, hoping he will champion their cause on behalf of his book. A timid man, the author is terrified by the furor he has caused and lectures on Greek culture. His disappointing appearance convinces the town that the tempest has been silly; the book is available whether the library buys it or not, and its author and contents are too slight to fuss over. The author, however, is asked to write another book because his first has sold so well, thanks to the citizens of Freeport. With great skill, Glaspell wittily spoofs both the naive pursuit of culture that newer towns in the Midwest were insisting on, as well as the "Bible-belt" mentality that saw heresy in every new idea. The sometimes serious conflict between morality and freedom is treated in this story with comic detachment and delightful insight. The story succeeds because Glaspell knows her town and its people well, and because she keeps an objective view, letting the satire emerge from the situation in good dramatic fashion.

The story that shows the influence of her play writing on her stories most directly is "Jury of Her Peers" (*Everyweek*, 5 March 1917; published separately in 1927), a fictional retelling of her one-act play *Trifles* (produced in 1916; published in 1917). Based on a case Glaspell had covered in Des Moines, the story is about Minnie Wright, who is in jail, accused of killing her husband. Minnie does not appear in either the play or the story, but is presented through indirection. The sheriff, the county attorney, and a neighbor have come to the Wright farm to seek out evidence that will prove Minnie killed her husband. The men are accompanied by Mrs. Peters, the sheriff's wife, and Mrs. Hale, the neighbor's wife. While the men search the house, the women gather things Minnie will need while in jail. The women uncover the evidence the men seek: in a piece of irregular stitching they read Minnie's emotional tension; in a dead canary (killed by the husband) they find the motive for the killing. As they move through the house, the women gossip about Minnie's unhappy marriage and the abuse she suffered under her brutal husband, and gradually, each woman reveals her own reasons for sympathizing with Minnie's final act of desperation. They argue over whether they should inform the men about their discovery of the clues that will convict Minnie, but they decide not to say anything; they are a jury of Minnie's peers, women who know what a woman can suffer and what she must do, if necessary, to escape from male tyranny.

"Jury of Her Peers" is Glaspell's best story, and it has become a classic of its genre. It com-

Glaspell and her husband, novelist and playwright George Cram Cook, in Greece, 1924

bines an exact sense of place and a strong emotional appeal, especially to women, with the suspense and objectivity of a play. Compared to her other stories, "Jury of Her Peers" has an extraordinary amount of dialogue, which helps keep the sentiment from becoming mawkish and builds the suspense: first about the uncovering of the domestic details that show Minnie is guilty, then whether the women should tell the men about what they have discovered. "Jury of Her Peers" transcends the limits of most local-color writing to evoke from the reader a universal response. The true conflict in the story is a sexual one, where the men insist on logic and masculine superiority, while the women judge Minnie from love and sympathy. The bleak Iowa homestead becomes a courtroom where women band together in common protest against arrogant, brutal, and stupid men.

When Glaspell stopped writing short stories in 1922, she had written several stories that exemplify the best in local-color writing. She had learned to convey the shallowness and hypocrisy of her region along with its strength and goodness. In these stories style suits content. Her tone, often ironical, protects and reinforces her sentiment, and her characters represent more than the midwesterner speaking in his quaint drawl; they are unique in their quest for "otherness," for that elusive something that makes life worthwhile.

Local-color writing grew from the desire of writers to preserve, through their art, the special qualities of a region that made it different. Midwestern and Southern writers in particular held to the agrarian dream of the native son or daughter renewed and strengthened by his association with the land. In their zeal to convey the values and benefits they felt derived from this bond between man and nature, they tended to romanticize their locale and its people. The better local colorists, like Glaspell and Zona Gale, soon grew away from this ideal (and false) portrayal; they showed the limitations as well as the uniqueness of their region, and they warned, as Glaspell does in her last novel, *Judd Rankin's Daughter* (1945), of the dangers of clinging to the past and ignoring the present.

Glaspell's career as an experimental playwright ended at about the same time as her career as a short-story writer. After Cook's death in Greece in 1924 (the couple had moved there in 1922), she married Norman Matson and returned to Provincetown, where she lived until her death in 1948. Aside from two plays, she also

returned to fiction, writing between 1928 and 1945 six novels, all of which are regional works with a midwestern emphasis. An overview of her career, therefore, should see that the short stories she wrote between 1903 and 1922 were the early steps of a literary journey that would radically alter her life and her art, without ever changing her lifelong commitment to and dependence on her midwestern roots.

Bibliographies:

Arthur E. Waterman, "Susan Glaspell," *American Literary Realism*, 4 (Spring 1971): 183-191;

Marcia Noe, "A Susan Glaspell Checklist," *Books at Iowa*, no. 27 (November 1977): 14-20.

References:

Clarence Andrews, "Parnassus on the Prairie," in his *A Literary History of Iowa* (Iowa City: University of Iowa Press, 1972), pp. 65-185;

Gerhard Bach, *Susan Glaspell und die Provincetown Players* (Frankfurt: Lang, 1979);

Marcia Noe, "A Critical Biography of Susan Glaspell," Ph.D. dissertation, University of Iowa, 1976;

Noe, "Susan Glaspell's Analysis of the Midwestern Character," *Books at Iowa*, no. 27 (November 1977): 3-14;

Arthur E. Waterman, *Susan Glaspell* (New York: Twayne, 1966).

Papers:

Most of Glaspell's papers are in the Henry and Albert Berg Collection, New York Public Library. Some clippings, photographs, and correspondence can be found in the Billy Rose Theatre Collection of the Library and Museum of the Performing Arts at Lincoln Center. The Library at St. Ambrose College in Davenport, Iowa, has a Susan Glaspell collection, including a copy of "Chains of Dew," an unpublished Glaspell play.

Joel Chandler Harris

(9 December 1848-3 July 1908)

Doty Hale
California State University, Los Angeles

See also the Harris entries in *DLB 11: American Humorists, 1800-1950; DLB 23: American Newspaper Journalists, 1873-1900;* and *DLB 42: American Writers for Children Before 1900.*

BOOKS: *Uncle Remus: His Songs and His Sayings* (New York: Appleton, 1881 [i.e., 1880]); republished in part as *Uncle Remus and His Legends of the Old Plantation* (London: Bogue, 1881); first edition republished as *Uncle Remus, or Mr. Fox, Mr. Rabbit, and Mr. Terrapin* (London & New York: Routledge, 1881); revised as *Uncle Remus: His Songs and His Sayings* (New York: Appleton, 1895; London: Osgood, 1895);

Nights with Uncle Remus: Myths and Legends of the Old Plantation (Boston: Osgood, 1883; London: Routledge, 1884);

Mingo and Other Sketches in Black and White (Boston: Osgood, 1884; Edinburgh: Douglas/ London: Hamilton Adams, 1884);

Free Joe and Other Georgian Sketches (New York: Scribners, 1887; London: Routledge, 1888);

Daddy Jake the Runaway and Short Stories Told After Dark (New York: Century, 1889; London: Unwin, 1889);

Balaam and His Master and Other Sketches and Stories (Boston & New York: Houghton, Mifflin, 1891; London: Osgood, McIlvaine, 1891);

A Plantation Printer: The Adventures of a Georgia Boy During the War (London: Osgood, McIlvaine, 1892); enlarged as *On the Plantation: A Story of a Georgia Boy's Adventures During the War* (New York: Appleton, 1892);

Uncle Remus and His Friends: Old Plantation Stories, Songs, and Ballads with Sketches of Negro Character (Boston & New York: Houghton, Mifflin, 1892; London: Osgood, McIlvaine, 1893);

Little Mr. Thimblefinger and His Queer Country: What the Children Saw and Heard There (Boston & New York: Houghton, Mifflin, 1894; London: Osgood, McIlvaine, 1894);

Joel Chandler Harris, age thirty-four

Mr. Rabbit at Home: A Sequel to Little Mr. Thimblefinger and His Queer Country (Boston & New York: Houghton, Mifflin, 1895; London: Osgood, 1895);

The Story of Aaron (So Named) The Son of Ben Ali (Boston & New York: Houghton, Mifflin, 1896; London: Osgood, 1896);

Stories of Georgia (New York, Cincinnati & Chicago: American Book Company, 1896);

Sister Jane: Her Friends and Acquaintances (Boston & New York: Houghton, Mifflin, 1896; London: Constable, 1897);

Aaron in the Wildwoods (Boston & New York: Houghton, Mifflin, 1897; London: Harper, 1897);

Tales of the Home Folks in Peace and War (Boston & New York: Houghton, Mifflin, 1898; London: Unwin, 1898);

Plantation Pageants (Boston & New York: Houghton, Mifflin, 1899; London: Constable, 1899);

The Chronicles of Aunt Minervy Ann (New York: Scribners, 1899; London: Dent, 1899);

On the Wing of Occasions (New York: Doubleday, Page, 1900; London: Murray, 1900);

The Making of a Statesman and Other Stories (New York: McClure, Phillips, 1902; London: Isbister, 1902);

Gabriel Tolliver: A Story of Reconstruction (New York: McClure, Phillips, 1902);

Wally Wanderoon and His Story-Telling Machine (New York: McClure, Phillips, 1903; London: Richards, 1904);

A Little Union Scout (New York: McClure, Phillips, 1904; London: Duckworth, 1905);

The Tar-Baby and Other Rhymes of Uncle Remus (New York: Appleton, 1904);

Told by Uncle Remus: New Stories of the Old Plantation (New York: McClure, Phillips, 1905; London: Hodder & Stoughton, 1906);

Uncle Remus and Brer Rabbit (New York: Stokes, 1907);

The Bishop and the Boogerman (New York: Doubleday, Page, 1909); republished as *The Bishop and the Bogie-Man* (London: Murray, 1909);

The Shadow Between His Shoulder-Blades (Boston: Small, Maynard, 1909);

Uncle Remus and the Little Boy (Boston: Small, Maynard, 1910; London: Richards, 1912);

Uncle Remus Returns (Boston & New York: Houghton Mifflin, 1918);

The Witch Wolf: An Uncle Remus Story (Cambridge, Mass.: Bacon & Brown, 1921);

Joel Chandler Harris: Editor and Essayist, edited by Julia Collier Harris (Chapel Hill: University of North Carolina Press, 1931);

Qua: A Romance of the Revolution, edited by Thomas H. English (Atlanta: The Library, Emory University, 1946);

Seven Tales of Uncle Remus, edited by English (Atlanta: The Library, Emory University, 1948);

The Complete Tales of Uncle Remus, compiled by Richard Chase (Boston: Houghton Mifflin, 1955).

OTHER: "Uncle Remus' Little Red Speckle Steer," in *St. Jacobs Oil Family Calendar 1883-4 and Book of Health and Humor for the Million* (Baltimore: Vogeler, 1883?), pp. 29-30; republished in *Emory University Quarterly*, 10 (December 1954): 266-270;

"Biographical Sketch of Henry W. Grady," in *Joel Chandler Harris' Life of Henry W. Grady*, compiled by Grady's coworkers and edited by Harris (New York: Cassell, 1890), pp. 9-68;

Evening Tales; Done into English from the French of Frédéric Ortoli, translated by Harris (New York: Scribners, 1893; London: Low, 1894);

" 'Uncle Remus' Has a Word to Say of Putnam As It Was and Is," in *A Guide to Immigration: Putnam County, Georgia and Its Resources*, edited by D. T. Singleton (Atlanta: Methodist Book & Publishing Company, 1895), pp. 90-92; republished in *Emory University Quarterly*, 4 (December 1948): 229-231.

PERIODICAL PUBLICATIONS:
FICTION
"A Georgia Fox Hunt," *Atlanta Constitution*, 16 December 1877; republished in *Uncle Remus's Magazine*, 30 (October 1911): 24-25;

"*The Romance of Rockville*," *Atlanta Weekly Constitution*, 16 April-24 September 1878; republished in *The Life of Joel Chandler Harris: From Obscurity in Boyhood to Fame in Early Manhood*, by Robert Lemuel Wiggins (Nashville, Dallas & Richmond: Methodist Episcopal Church, South, 1918);

"Uncle Remus's 'Ha'nt," *Youth's Companion*, 58 (17 December 1885): 544;

"Miss Irene," *Scribner's Magazine*, 27 (February 1900): 216-229;

"Rosalie," *Century*, 62 (October 1901): 916-922;

"Cousin Annie Crafton," *Ainslee's*, 11 (April 1903): 50-61;

"Billy Boring and His Drum," *Saturday Evening Post*, 178 (7 October 1905): 5-7;

"Miss Little Sally," *Uncle Remus's Magazine*, 1 (December 1907): 18-20, 27, 35, 41;

"King Philpo," *Uncle Remus's Magazine*, 31 (May 1912): 7, 18;

"A Romantic Tragedy," *Uncle Remus's Magazine*, 32 (November 1912): 8-9;

"Mr. Billy Sanders, Detective," *Emory University Quarterly*, 4 (December 1948): 194-216.

NONFICTION
"An Accidental Author," *Lippincott's*, 37 (April 1886): 417-420;

Frontispiece by J. H. Moser for Uncle Remus: His Songs and His Sayings *(1881)*

"The Poor Man's Chance," *Saturday Evening Post*, 173 (7 July 1900): 12;

"Events in Middle Georgia," *Harper's Weekly*, 47 (10 October 1903): 1621;

"The Negro of To-Day: His Prospects and His Discouragements," *Saturday Evening Post*, 176 (30 January 1904): 2-5;

"The Negro Problem: Can the South Solve It—And How?," *Saturday Evening Post*, 176 (27 February 1904): 6-7.

Joel Chandler Harris is remembered by many readers as a collector of black folklore in the Uncle Remus stories, an amanuensis for slaves whose forced illiteracy prevented them from writing down their own stories. Often, however, Harris is also seen as a white Southern apologist, with the happy Uncle Remus perpetuating the plantation myth, which is at the same time undermined by the tales' poetic irony—an irony that, according to some critics, Harris probably did not recognize.

Both views are partly correct; several critics, primarily Thomas H. English, have pointed out that there are two fictional characters called Uncle Remus—one living in Atlanta and the other in rural Putnam County. The Atlanta Uncle Remus is often a minstrel figure, puzzled by such things as the phonograph, opposed to education for blacks, and sometimes the butt of jokes for more-sophisticated whites. At other times, however, he uses biting humor to counterattack. The rural Uncle Remus is a far more interesting literary figure–a complex, dignified, clever, controlling, occasionally dishonest, hardworking character whose most important role is to be the chief explicator of a world ruled sometimes by joy, justice, and liberty but more often by cleverness, ruthlessness, self-interest, and greed. Moreover, Harris was aware of the ironic mood of Remus's tales; in the introduction to *Uncle Remus: His Songs and His Sayings* (1881) Harris claimed that his publishers were presenting the book as humor, but "however humorous it may be in effect, its intention is perfectly serious; and, even if it were otherwise, it seems to me that a volume written wholly in dialect must have its solemn, not to say melancholy features." Nor were the Uncle Remus tales Harris's sole preoccupation: from the time he was thirteen until he died at fifty-nine, Harris earned his living by printing and writing, producing many newspaper columns (now largely of historical interest), at least six novels, a biography, a history of Georgia, a translation of French folktales, six volumes of stories for children, and seven volumes of non-Remus short stories for adults. Some of the characters in the non-Remus stories are not successful; too many of the blacks in them do tend to perpetuate the "happy darky" stereotype, and his attempts at portraying the white southern gentry are almost all failures. Other characters are more memorable, particularly society's perpetual underdogs–black women, freed slaves, runaway slaves, and poor southern whites.

Harris's identification with the downtrodden stems from his early life. Born on 9 December 1848 in or near Eatonton in middle Georgia to Mary Harris, an unmarried woman, and an unidentified man, who may have been an Irish day laborer, the small, red-haired, freckled-faced Harris was almost pathologically shy and stuttering in front of strangers, but he was known among his young friends as the leader of their gang of pranksters–"borrowing" dogs for rabbit hunting, stealing melons and peaches, and playing practical jokes. A childhood friend told Harris's biographer and daughter-in-law, Julia Collier Harris, that "Joe" Harris was often truant from school, but it "was a strange thing to all of us that Joe, although he did not seem to study much, was always well prepared when it came to reciting his lessons, and got along as well as any of us."

Joel Chandler Harris, 1873

Much of his success then and as an adult was due to his mother. Formerly of an educated, middle-class Georgia family, Mary Harris had been abandoned by her family as well as her lover. She gave her child her last name and set about rearing him, supporting him by weaving and sewing and fostering his intellect by talking to him about affairs of the day and reading to him from the classics. Harris later remembered Oliver Goldsmith as one of his childhood favorites. Several of the citizens of Eatonton helped Mary Harris and her son; an Andrew Reid in particular gave her a small house to live in and paid her son's tuition at school. Thus Harris and his mother were spared many of the hardships that might have resulted from her social ostracism. Yet Harris's childhood was difficult. Later in life he rarely spoke of his early years in Eatonton, even to his wife. He referred to "the humblest sort of circumstances" in which he had been reared, and another time he said that his early history was "a peculiarly sad and unfortunate one."

When Harris was thirteen, he was hired as a printer's devil for the *Countryman*, a weekly newspaper published at a nearby plantation, Turnwold. According to Harris, "it was on this and neighboring plantations that I became familiar with the curious myths and animal stories that form the basis of the volumes accredited to 'Uncle Remus.' " The owner of the plantation, Joseph Addison Turner, also lent the young Harris books from his extensive library. Soon Harris was writing short pieces for the newspaper, but more important than these early attempts at writing was the knowledge that he was absorbing, both from the almost exclusively white literary world of the owner's library and from the stories, songs, and myths he heard from the black slaves, some of whom became prototypes for his fictional characters.

The end of the Civil War forced the end of the *Countryman*, and it also marked the end of the most important part of Harris's life; all his successful writings are based on his years at Eatonton and Turnwold. For the next decade he had jobs on the *Macon Telegraph* (spring-fall 1866), the *Crescent Monthly* in New Orleans (late 1866-May 1867), the *Monroe Advertiser* in Forsyth, Georgia (summer 1867-fall 1870), and the *Savannah Morning News* (fall 1870-September 1876). In Savannah he lived in the same boardinghouse as Esther LaRose, the attractive, vivacious, intelligent daughter of a French-Canadian sea captain. They married on 20 April 1873, and for thirty-five years she provided a calm, stable center to his life, bearing nine children, three of whom died in childhood.

Harris's responsibilities as a writer increased as he went from newspaper to newspaper; he contributed editorials and other features but became best known for his ability to write short humorous anecdotes, or "paragraphs," many of which were picked up and reprinted in other newspapers. One clipping in the Harris family scrapbook says "Harris, the inimitable paragraphist and wag of the Savannah News has a peculiar knack at turning every thing into the ludicrous." Some of the "paragraphs" seem overtly racist; the one most often quoted in this context is: "A Lumpkin negro seriously injured his pocketknife recently by undertaking to stab a colored brother in the head." However, that anecdote is like many others by Harris's contemporaries, an example of the crude humor of the day. Harris's columns contain similarly demeaning jokes that make no reference to color: "When a banana skin pulls a Macon man to the pavement, he invariably gets up and looks around to see if he has bro-

ken any of the bricks. This is a singular trait, and is probably owing to the climate."

Harris's real achievements as a writer began when he took his family to live in Atlanta in September 1876 to avoid a yellow fever epidemic in Savannah. He was first hired by the *Atlanta Constitution* as an editorial paragrapher and telegraph editor and rose to associate editor. The subjects of his editorials ranged from local and national politics to farming methods, but one of his major themes (and the one most relevant to his fiction) was to urge understanding and reconciliation in the postwar South. Locally as well as nationally in publications such as the *Saturday Evening Post*, he would try to explain the South to itself and to counter what he felt were mistakenly negative views from the North. His ideas, especially about southern blacks, were enlightened for his time. He enjoyed the blacks' clever wit and humor and, according to Julia Collier Harris, hated the "debased and burlesqued" depictions presented in vaudeville and minstrel shows. He called black deportation to Africa–seriously proposed at the time–"folly." He consistently denied accusations that blacks were idle or unthrifty, insisting that each person had to be judged as an individual and that individual blacks held these traits in no greater proportion than any other people. He saw black education as essential: "If education of the negro is not the chief solution of the problem that confronts the white people of the South then there is no other conceivable solution." He did, however, hold the opinion that slavery had been beneficial to Afro-Americans because it "grew into a university in which millions of savages served an apprenticeship to religion and civilization, and out of which they graduated into American citizens. We cannot perceive in these momentous results anything less powerful than the hand of the Almighty."

While Joel Chandler Harris the journalist was encouraging efforts to bring the blacks into white culture, educational system, and religion, Joel Chandler Harris the creative writer, especially in the Uncle Remus animal fables, was educating his largely white readers about the different world of the blacks. Brer Rabbit and the other creatures live in a land that is usually comic and exuberant, but simultaneously savage and even cruel, with self-preservation its primary goal. Harris recognized the dual, almost contradictory nature of his writing. In an 1898 letter to his daughters he said that he himself wrote his newspaper editorials but that some "other fellow" wrote the stories: "when night comes, I take up my pen, surrendering unconditionally to my 'other fellow,' and out comes the story, and if it is a good story I am as much surprised as the people who read it."

The tale-teller began as part of Harris's editorial job. The *Atlanta Constitution* had a black-dialect feature in which an "Old Si" commented on topics of the day. Old Si was a stock black-minstrel figure, and his "dialect" was all too often a mishmash of misspelled English, but the feature was popular. When its creator, Sam W. Small, left the *Constitution*, Harris was asked to take over. "Markham's Ball," his first dialect piece for the newspaper (he had experimented with writing dialect as early as his teenage years at Turnwold), was largely an imitation of Small's work, but Harris quickly hit his own stride. In the same issue (26 October 1876) appeared "Jeems Roberson's Last Illness," in which an unnamed "Jonesboro negro," when asked about a mutual acquaintance, replies using story-telling elements that were later to be used by Uncle Remus: Although two people are speaking in this sketch, one just asks questions, and thus the story itself is essentially a dramatic monologue like the Uncle Remus stories; the dialect is middle Georgia black; the story, though quasi-comic, is told solemnly; indirection is a key device (the narrator, when asked if Roberson is sick, insists that he is not and goes on to tell a cliff-hanging story about Roberson and a difficult mule); he forces his listeners to ask for more of the tale; he insists that "I done tole you all I knew" and then relents with the comic, ironic, deadly ending: the mule "sorter hump herself," and Roberson fell off and died "sorter accidental-like. Hit's des like I tell you: de nigger wuzn't sick a minnit."

This narrator evolved into the Atlanta Uncle Remus. The first animal fable, "The Story of Mr. Rabbit and Mr. Fox as Told by Uncle Remus," did not appear until almost three years after this sketch, in the 20 July 1879 issue of the *Constitution*. In the meantime Harris published *Constitution* articles about country life, plantation songs, Atlanta Uncle Remus sketches, and a wandering, episodic, serialized novel, *The Romance of Rockville* (*Atlanta Weekly Constitution*, 16 April-24 September 1878), that even Harris considered an artistic failure. The immediate popularity of the Remus animal fables after they began to appear led D. Appleton and Company to publish, in November 1880, Harris's first book, *Uncle Remus: His Songs and His Sayings*, with the date 1881 on

Esther LaRose Harris in 1873

its title page. Despite the subtitle, the songs, sayings (slightly revised versions of the Atlanta Uncle Remus sketches), "Plantation Proverbs" (short, pithy lines of practical advice), and an isolated short story–"A Story of the War" (a revision of "Uncle Remus as a Rebel," which had appeared in the *Constitution*), in which the plantation Remus, here in a faithful old retainer role, shoots a Yankee sniper aiming at his master–take up only 83 pages at the end of the 231-page first edition. These have chiefly sociological interest today. Richard Chase's definitive modern edition, *The Complete Tales of Uncle Remus* (1955), omits them entirely. The bulk of *Uncle Remus: His Songs and His Sayings* is devoted to the animal fables told by the rural Putnam County Uncle Remus that have proved to be both the most popular and the most controversial of Harris's works.

Harris insisted that the tales had been told to him by blacks and that he had not "cooked" (altered) any of them, but some filtration must have taken place. For one thing, after his personal memories were largely used up in the early Uncle Remus books, he openly solicited plot outlines and bits of stories from other people. Still, he would not publish any tale he could not authenticate as being in the black tradition. Recent studies of black oral stories have discovered some ribald tales; the nineteenth-century Harris omitted all of these–although "Miss Meadows" and the "gals" are conveniently around when flirtatious animals wish to dress up and "cum a callin'."

Nevertheless, most critics today agree that the fables themselves accurately reflect black oral tradition and that for an amateur linguist, Harris rendered black dialect quite well. The character of Uncle Remus and the narrative framework in which he tells the stories to the little boy, however, are far more controversial. Harris insisted that the tales were more important than their frames, but his friend Mark Twain disagreed, writing to Harris on 10 August 1881: "You can argue *yourself* into the delusion that the principle of life is in the stories themselves & not in their setting," but "Uncle Remus is most deftly drawn, & is a lovable & delightful creation; he, & the little boy, & their relations with each other, are bright fine literature, & worthy to live, for their own sakes." The fables are "only alligator pears–one merely eats them for the sake of the salad-dressing."

Most modern critics reverse Twain's assessment–Robert Bone, for example, claims that Uncle Remus himself furthers the white "plantation myth. . . . it is the author's avowed purpose to create a sympathetic, nostalgic, and untroubled portrait of plantation life before the war. The point of view, he tells us frankly, will be that of an old Negro 'who has nothing but pleasant memories of the discipline of slavery–and who has all the prejudices of caste and pride of family that were the natural results of the system. . . .' " In the source from which Bone is quoting, Harris's sentence goes on to say: "if the reader can imagine all this, he will find little difficulty in appreciating and sympathizing with the air of affectionate superiority which Uncle Remus assumes as he proceeds to unfold the mysteries of plantation lore to a little child who is the product of that practical reconstruction which has been going on to some extent since the war in spite of the politicians."

Thus, although Uncle Remus has "pleasant memories" of slavery, his position in regard to his auditor is "affectionate superiority." The stories demonstrate this superiority. If, for example, in trying to push a story along, the little boy asks "premature questions," he is told "hol' on dar!

Wait! Gimme room!" Nor does Remus hesitate to usurp white parental authority. In "A Plantation Witch" the boy tells Remus, "Papa says there aren't any witches." Remus replies, "Mars John ain't live long ez I is," and proceeds to tell a story so frightening that the boy is afraid to go home alone.

Usually the interaction between the boy and Uncle Remus is very short, but Remus as controller and educator is present throughout the stories. A prime example of Remus's role is in the "The Tar Baby" story. Usually the reader thinks of the story as beginning with Brer Fox's building a tar baby; then after the angry Brer Rabbit hits the mute black baby and gets stuck, he turns to trickery and emerges triumphant and free, shouting "Bred en bawn in a brier-patch, Brer Fox– bred en bawn in a brier-patch!" But both in the original version, which appeared in the 16 November 1879 issue of the *Constitution*, and in the version published in *Uncle Remus: His Songs and His Sayings*, the story is broken into two tales. The first one stops as Brer Rabbit is held fast by the tar, and Brer Fox is planning to have him for dinner. The little boy asks, "Did the Fox eat the Rabbit?"; but Remus is adamant, "Dat's all de fur de tale goes. . . . You better run 'long." The little boy persists, and one evening later (in the book, two stories later) he again asks the question, and Uncle Remus relents, not grinning broadly but "chuckling slyly" and claiming that "I 'clar ter gracious I ought er tole you dat." Only then does he conclude the story.

Several tricks are being played in this story of cleverness and guile, with the creatures reflecting Uncle Remus's attitudes. Harris saw the connection; his introduction to this volume says, "it needs no scientific investigation to show why he [the black] selects as his hero the weakest and most harmless of all animals, and brings him out victorious in contests with the bear, the wolf and the fox." As Bernard Wolfe and other critics have pointed out, however, the rabbit is often more malevolent than mischievous; in one tale, for example, he persuades Mrs. Fox to boil her husband's head for dinner. Despite its humor, the world of the creatures is often a melancholy, dark, and savage one, and Remus clearly thinks the boy needs to know about it. The first fable published in the *Constitution* is also the first fable in this collection, but it has been significantly retitled from "The Story of Mr. Rabbit and Mr. Fox as Told by Uncle Remus" to "Uncle Remus Initiates the Little Boy." As he "beamed so kindly" upon the

Henry W. Grady, managing editor of the Atlanta Constitution; *Joel Chandler Harris; John H. Estill, managing editor of the* Savannah Morning News; *and an unidentified man at Lookout Mountain, Tennessee, circa 1880*

boy, Remus initiated him into a world where Brer Fox invites Brer Rabbit to a dinner in which the rabbit is to be the main course. The clever rabbit catches on, and with the pretense of seeking calamus root for seasoning, "Brer Rabbit gallop off home."

Usually the tales speak for themselves, but occasionally in this volume Uncle Remus openly declares that the tales represent the real world. When the boy complains that the terrapin has cheated by placing his relatives as decoys along the race track, Uncle Remus replies, "Co'se honey. De creeturs 'gun ter cheat, en den folks tuck it up, en hit keep on spreadin'. Hit mighty ketchin', en you min' yo' eye, honey, dat somebody don't cheat you 'fo' yo' ha'r git gray ez de ole nigger's."

The book did well, selling out several printings during its first months of publication. Its early proceeds allowed Harris to move his growing family to a larger house on the outskirts of Atlanta, and as late as 1904 a letter from Appleton to Harris notes, "certainly, for a book twenty-

four years old, a regular sale of four thousand copies yearly is most gratifying and unusual."

Since Harris was a working journalist with a large family, the warm reception given the first collection of Uncle Remus tales prompted him to write more stories and to try a new publishing strategy. Upon Mark Twain's suggestion he secured a book agent and reduced the frequency of Uncle Remus's appearances. He also found himself caught up in an exploration of folktales in general and black folktales in particular. His next volume, *Nights with Uncle Remus: Myths and Legends of the Old Plantation* (1883), contains a long introduction exploring the genesis of various tales and commenting on the wide correspondence generated by the first volume: "Much of this correspondence was very valuable, for it embodied legends that had escaped the author's memory." Harris also discovered tales that had been told by coastal blacks as well as middle Georgia blacks, and consequently *Nights with Uncle Remus* has several narrators. Uncle Remus tells the bulk of the tales but he is joined by Aunt Tempy, a woman of "large authority on the place" and a covert rival of Uncle Remus; 'Tildy, a young house girl; and Daddy Jack, who—because he was born in Africa and was sold to a Sea Island family—speaks in Gullah dialect. The setting has been moved back to before the Civil War, but the little boy is still the auditor, and the stories take place in Uncle Remus's cabin. The storytellers vie among themselves over tale-telling ability and the best versions of the stories, but otherwise these fables are similar in form and content to those of the first book— dramatic monologues in which the rabbit and other weaker creatures usually triumph by guile and quickness. Uncle Remus as a slave does seem to have the pleasant attitude that Harris noted in the earlier volume. For example, when his mistress sends 'Tildy with his dinner on a rainy day he makes a "great demonstration," saying, "Ef she ain't one blessid white 'oman," but he defers to none other than her and continues to undermine white Christian values, even at one point suggesting that they are hypocritically professed: "w'en you sorter grow up so you kin knock 'roun', 'twon't be long 'fo' some un'll take en take you off 'roun' de cornder en tell you dat 'tain't make no diffunce whar de money come fum so de man got it. Dey won't tell you dat in de meeting-house, but dey'll come mighty nigh it."

Nights with Uncle Remus has more overall structure than the earlier book, some of it believable (the story swapping, the culminating Christmas party); some of it not (the flirtation and engagement between young 'Tildy and eighty-year-old Daddy Jack).

Harris's next two collections of short stories, *Mingo and Other Sketches in Black and White* (1884) and *Free Joe and Other Georgian Sketches* (1887), were not animal fables but local-color stories centering on the lower strata of Southern society. Most of the blacks are, unlike Uncle Remus, stereotypical "happy darkies." The title character of "Free Joe and the Rest of the World" (*Century*, November 1884) is a notable exception. Freed by a master who then committed suicide, Free Joe is a pathetic, lost creature in a society that has no place for him. Harris blames white paranoia: "he was the embodiment of that vague and mysterious danger that seemed to be forever lurking on the outskirts of slavery, ready to sound a shrill and ghostly signal in the impenetrable swamps, and steal forth under the midnight stars to murder, rapine, and pillage,—a danger always threatening, and yet never assuming shape; intangible, and yet real; impossible, and yet not improbable. Across the serene and smiling front of safety, the pale outlines of the awful shadow of insurrection sometimes fell." Joe himself is a danger to none; his greatest ambition is to see his wife, still a slave. He is tolerated but not befriended by a poor white family, the Staleys. In this story, more than any other except Uncle Remus's, Harris ignores romantic idealization to give a believable picture of the relationships between blacks and whites. Harris's revision of the original manuscript (now in the collection at the Henry E. Huntington Library) shows in part how he accomplished such realism. For example, in the original Harris has a white woman say, " 'Well, I reckon he's like lots of folks,' said Miss Becky, smiling a little grimly." The revised version far better depicts the ambivalent relationship between these two underdogs of society: " 'Niggers is niggers,' said Miss Becky, smiling grimly, 'an' you can't rub it out; yit I lay I've seed a heap of white people lots meaner'n Free Joe.' "

Because of Harris's financial background, it is not surprising that, except for Free Joe, poor whites are the strongest characters in these local-color collections. Harris places many of these characters in the moonshining area of the north Georgia mountains—as in "Trouble on Lost Mountain" (*Century*, January 1886; collected in *Free Joe and Other Georgian Sketches*) and "At Teague Poteet's: A Sketch of the Hog Mountain Range" (*Century*, May and June 1883; collected in *Mingo and Other*

Photograph of Harris, age forty-three, used as the frontispiece for On the Plantation: A Story of a Georgia Boy's Adventures During the War, *1892 (Baldwin Library, University of Florida Libraries)*

Sketches in Black and White)—but others, such as Mrs. Feratia Bivins of "Mingo: A Sketch of Life in Middle Georgia" (*Harper's Christmas Pictures & Papers* for 1882), are tough survivors of the hardscrabble white life in middle Georgia. Reconciliation—a constant theme in the stories—occurs somewhat uneasily between black and white unless the black humbly submits, but it takes place on a more equal footing between a Union and a Confederate soldier ("Little Compton," *Century*, April 1887; collected in *Free Joe and Other Georgian Sketches*) or between a tax revenue man and a moonshiner's beautiful daughter ("At Teague Poteet's"). Also shown is the fierce independence of the mountain people.

Daddy Jake the Runaway and Short Stories Told After Dark (1889) contains Uncle Remus tales and a long local-color story about runaway slaves. The title character of "Daddy Jake, the Runaway" is another subservient "darky," who happily returns home when he finds that his master is not angry at him for striking an incompetent overseer. But his fellow runaways hiding in a canebrake more realistically depict the tragic aspects of slavery. Especially pathetic is Crazy Sue, who fell asleep nursing her twins and was punished by being assigned to field work: "whiles I wuz hoein' I kin year dem babies cryin'. . . . Dey des fade away, an' bimeby dey died." The son of Jake's master offers his father's help, but there are no easy solutions for Crazy Sue: "yo' pa is a mighty good man, an' a mighty good doctor, but he ain't got no medicine w'at could 'a' kyored me an' my marster." The rabbit and the terrapin can survive by trickery and guile, Daddy Jake can return to a decent master, and even Free Joe can die in peace, but Crazy Sue must hide in the canebrake, remembering the cries of her babies who died.

In "Daddy Jake, the Runaway" Crazy Sue tells a story in which Mr. Rabbit tricks the frogs and they "fuss," trying their best to drive him out of the swamp–a parallel to the whites' pursuit of the runaway slaves hiding in the same swamp. Uncle Remus's "after dark" stories in the same book are partly animal fables, but they also involve human characters including male and female witches. One of Remus's tales, "How the Birds Talk," tries to explain his relationship with his mistress, Miss Sally, whom he still regards as a child. He takes a "dictatorial, overbearing and quarrelsome" attitude toward her; and yet he is also respectful and affectionate. Harris admits that their relationship is "peculiar" and difficult to describe to "those not familiar with some of the developments of slavery in the South."

Balaam and His Master and Other Sketches and Stories (1891) is another collection of local-color stories about blacks and poor whites. Again the blacks are simultaneously subservient to and protective of the whites, and the north Georgia white mountaineers are fiercely independent, as in "A Conscript's Christmas" (*Century*, December 1890), which shows their resistance to conscription in the Confederate army. The plots in this volume tend to be more melodramatic and the characters less memorable than Free Joe, Crazy Sue, and Mrs. Bivins. The title character of "Mom Bi," however, is the most outspoken black in all of Harris's stories. She openly quarrels with whites and even jeers at Confederate soldiers as they evacuate Charleston: "Hi! Wey you gwine? Whaffer you no stop fer tell folks good-by? Nummine! Dem Yankee buckra, dee gwine shaky you by de han'. Dee mek you hot fer true. Wey you no stop fer see de nigger come free?" Still, as a slave, she is dependent on her master and is more devoted to their son than to her own daughter. Freedom is not much better; poverty and smallpox kill her daughter and granddaughter, and she again becomes dependent on her master, a mild-mannered stick figure. She dies at his house, defiant to the last: "I done bin come back. I bin come back fer stay; but I free, dough!"

Harris's best sustained piece of long fiction, the autobiographical novel *On the Plantation: A Story of a Georgia Boy's Adventures During the War* (1892) is the last good book of Harris's earlier years; *Uncle Remus and His Friends: Old Plantation Stories, Songs, and Ballads with Sketches of Negro Character*, published in the same year, shows Harris's flagging interest. He said it would be the last of the Uncle Remus stories, and the "old man will bother the public no more with his whimsical stories." The stories are mostly not based on Harris's own memories but obtained from others, and the book returns to the uneven format of the first Uncle Remus–tales supplemented with sketches, songs, and ballads. The sketches are an unfortunate return to the obsequious Atlanta Uncle Remus, and the songs and ballads are again mainly of sociological interest.

For more than a decade (1892-1905) Harris kept his word, publishing a few Uncle Remus tales but turning most of his attention to an immense quantity of other work: four volumes of local-color short stories (*Tales of the Home Folks in Peace and War*, 1898; *The Chronicles of Aunt Minervy Ann*, 1899; *On the Wing of Occasions*, 1900; and *The Making of a Statesman and Other Stories*, 1902), three completed novels (*Sister Jane*, 1896; *Gabriel Tolliver: A Story of Reconstruction*, 1902; and *A Little Union Scout*, 1904), an unfinished novel (*Qua: A Romance of the Revolution*, published from the manuscript in 1946), several uncollected stories, one volume of verse (*The Tar-Baby and Other Rhymes of Uncle Remus*, 1904), a translation (*Evening Tales; Done into English from the French of Frédéric Ortoli*, 1893), a history for high-school students (*Stories of Georgia*, 1896), and six volumes of children's stories (*Little Mr. Thimblefinger*, 1894; *Mr. Rabbit at Home*, 1895; *The Story of Aaron*, 1896; *Aaron in the Wildwoods*, 1897; *Plantation Pageants*, 1899; and *Wally Wanderoon and His Story-Telling Machine*, 1903).

Always an extremely shy man, seldom leaving his Gordon Street home except to pick up his editorial assignments, Harris even left his job at the *Constitution* in 1902 to devote himself to his

"Brer Rabbit ain't see no peace w'atsumever."

"Ef you don't lemme loose I'll knock you agin!"

Frontispiece and illustration by Arthur B. Frost for the revised edition of Uncle Remus: His Songs and His Sayings *(1895)*

"other fellow." Unfortunately, most of his literary work from these years is distinguished more by its quantity than its quality. Harris could not really handle the novel form; as Julia Collier Harris noted, he had "a deep-seated conviction that the handling of a sustained plot would be beset with difficulties." She felt that "for more than thirty years [he] had been a victim to the routine of newspaper work, and . . . deprived of the leisure of unbroken hours, he had had scant opportunity for the cultivation of the technique of his craft." Both the human characters and the writing style of the children's stories condescend in a way that Uncle Remus would never permit; the history is slanted in a way that the mountaineers of Teague Poteet's and "A Conscript's Christmas" would have denied.

Even Harris's volumes of adult local-color short stories are inferior to his earlier ones. The folks at peace in *Tales of the Home Folks in Peace and War* are largely romanticized southern gentry, although "The Late Mr. Watkins of Georgia" (*Lippincott's*, April 1894) is fun because it jeers at the pretensions of folklore specialists, including Harris's own: "When I say, therefore, that the introduction [to *Nights with Uncle Remus*] is wonderfully learned, I mean that I do not understand it." The more-interesting folks at war are mountaineers introduced from earlier volumes, but even they lose vigor when transplanted to the flatland battlefields of the Civil War.

The title character of *The Chronicles of Aunt Minervy Ann* (stories first published in the February, May, June, July, September, and October 1899 issues of *Scribner's Magazine*) has been praised for her liveliness, but her energy is alternately directed to correcting uppity reconstruction blacks and to serving whites. Darwin T.

Turner is right when he dismisses her as a "colorful mammy."

In *On the Wing of Occasions*, a series of Confederate spy stories, the first story, "Why the Confederacy Failed" (*Saturday Evening Post*, 23 December 1899), indicates one of the problems Harris had in creating suspense. The reason for the South's loss–"Providence has a hand in the matter"–further removes any chance of realism or even excitement. Only the earthy middle Georgia humor of Billy Sanders, for example, redeems an otherwise implausible account of "The Kidnapping of President Lincoln" (*Saturday Evening Post*, 2-23 June 1900). Three of the four narratives in *The Making of a Statesman and Other Stories* are ruined by sentimentality, as is most of the fourth, the title story (*Saturday Evening Post*, 25 January and 1 February 1902). The first third, however, is a convincing portrait of a "statesman" being created by image makers working behind the scenes.

Harris's best book to come out of this period was not a new volume but a new edition of his first book, *Uncle Remus: His Songs and His Sayings*, with illustrations by Arthur B. Frost (1895). In the preface to the new edition Harris noted the popularity that this volume of Uncle Remus stories had enjoyed for fifteen years but suggested "it would be no mystery at all if this new edition were to be more popular than the old one. Do you know why? Because you have taken it under your hand and made it yours. . . . The book was mine, but now you have made it yours, both sap and pith." The tribute is deserved. The modern reader's vision of Brer Rabbit and his fellow creatures is nearly as influenced by Frost's drawings as Harris's tales. Subsequent collections of the Uncle Remus stories have preferred Frost's illustrations over the originals. A comment in a letter to Harris from Rudyard Kipling perhaps best sums up the appeal of these drawings: "They fit, as Tenniel's did to Alice in Wonderland." So "natural is their unnaturalness," Kipling felt, that "the beasts just naturally *had* to wear clothes."

Despite his farewell to Uncle Remus in 1892, Harris published some eight Remus tales in 1904-1905, and in 1905 he collected these and others into the best book of his last years, *Told by Uncle Remus: New Stories of the Old Plantation*. Darwin Turner has said that in *Nights with Uncle Remus* (1883), "particularly in those [stories] in which he and the boy are the only human characters, Remus is merely a stereotyped old-time

Andrew Carnegie and Joel Chandler Harris at Snap Bean Farm, Harris's home in the West End section of Atlanta, in 1906 (photograph by William F. Nelson)

Negro. . . . In his relationships with other Negroes, however, Remus appears as an individual subject to human frailties. He is superstitious, petulant, hypocritical, vain, and jealous." Yet, Turner adds, in "later stories, Harris, with increasing frequency, projected his own ideas through Uncle Remus." Thus the later Uncle Remus often "transcends the stereotype of the 'old-time darky.'" Uncle Remus probably has more control, both covert (through the tales) and overt (sometimes openly defying the authority of white parental and religious tradition), in the earlier stories than Turner grants, but he is right about the later tales. In *Told by Uncle Remus* the old man takes complete control of blacks and whites alike. The framework is familiar–Uncle Remus tells black tales to a white boy–but the boy is the son of the former little boy and far more in need of Remus's education: "Small as the lad was, he was old-fashioned. He thought and spoke like a grown person; and this the old Negro knew was not according to nature. The trouble with the

Joel Chandler and Esther Harris with two of their grandchildren, 1907

boy was that he had had no childhood; he had been subdued and weakened by the abnormal training he had received." Miss Sally of the earlier tales, the boy's grandmother, also sees the problem but is powerless to interfere: "A grandmother doesn't count for much these days," she complains and sends the child to Remus's cabin. In the first story, "The Reason Why," Remus initiates this new little boy into nonverbal language (a message Miss Sally "writ wid de dishes" she sent along with the boy) and into the ambiguity and humor of the spoken language (an elaborate pun on "cuff").

In the second tale the little boy is imprisoned in the parlor for wiping his mouth on his sleeve, and Uncle Remus must act alone: "He knew that in a case of this kind, Miss Sally could not help him. She had set herself to win over the young wife of her son, and she knew that she would cease to be the child's grandmother and become the mother-in-law the moment her views clashed with those of the lad's mother." Speaking loudly so that the mother can hear, Remus tells the little boy that jailing in the parlor will irresistibly lead to jail in "Atlanty" for nothing, and that

he'll be glad for real jail after the dampness of the parlor gives him croup and pneumonia.

The mother relents, releases the little boy, and cries, but the boy races to Uncle Remus to hear a tale. Here and in the rest of the book the stories work to undermine what Harris calls the "modern spirit of scientific doubt." Remus also forces the reticent boy to question in order to get tales and to break up his "prematurely grave face" with laughter. Again, the stories are from and about the imaginative world of the blacks: "I don't like ter tell no tale ter grown folks, speshually ef dey er white folks." Weak creatures such as the rabbit and the cricket continue to triumph, and the strong continue to contribute to their own downfalls. When the little boy complains that the creatures lie and are cruel, Remus replies, "de creeturs ain't much ahead er folks, an' yit folks is got preachers fer ter tell um when dey er gwine wrong. Mo' dan dat, dey got de Bible; an' yit when you git a little older, you'll wake up some fine day an' say ter yo'se'f dat de creeturs is got de 'vantage er folks, spite er de fac' dat dey ain't know de diffunce 'twix' right an' wrong. Dey got ter live 'cordin' ter der natur', kaze dey ain't know no better." The boy is also uneasy with some of the more-violent stories but soon gets hardened; despite Remus's fears the boy does not quail when he hears "How Old Craney-Crow Lost His Head" (*Collier's*, 28 May 1904)–the wolf bites it off.

Eventually the tales succeed, and the little boy loses his repressions. In fact, they succeed so well that the boy becomes "wilful and obstinate," and Remus must now teach him other black virtues, flexibility and patience. In "The Hard-Headed Woman" (*Metropolitan*, August 1905) a quarrelsome woman is killed by an enchanted pot. At the end Remus tells the little boy, "An' when you wanter be hard-headed, an' have yo' own way, you better b'ar in min' de 'oman an' de dinner-pot."

In 1906 Harris's son Julian and a group of Atlanta businessmen raised enough money to start *Uncle Remus's Magazine*. Feeling somewhat "bedeviled," Harris came out of retirement to edit the magazine and also contributed lead articles, book reviews (signed "Anne Macfarland"), poems, stories, and a serialized novel. Six new Uncle Remus stories appeared in the next two years as well as a reprint of "Free Joe and the Rest of the World," but most of Harris's contributions were nonfiction. In 1907 a small volume of six tales and five poems, *Uncle Remus and Brer Rabbit*, came out. The younger little boy is still the auditor for the tales, and he is less repressed than before, but the narrative framework is minimal. The fables are similar to earlier ones and break no new ground.

Harris's health began to decline in the spring of 1908, and after being baptized in the Roman Catholic church by his wife's pastor, he died of acute nephritis and chronic cirrhosis of the liver on 3 July. Reticent to the end, he warned his son that if anyone tried "to start any monument business, don't let them do it."

Several collections of short stories were published posthumously, all of them involving Uncle Remus. *Uncle Remus and the Little Boy* (1910) contains the six fables from *Uncle Remus's Magazine*; *Uncle Remus Returns* (1918) includes six plantation stories and five Atlanta Remus stories that Julia Collier Harris found in old newspaper and magazine files; *The Witch Wolf: An Uncle Remus Story* (1921) is a story from *Daddy Jake*; and in 1948 Thomas English edited *Seven Tales of Uncle Remus* (five rewritten in standard English). Like the 1907 *Uncle Remus and Brer Rabbit*, however, the posthumously published tales are enjoyable, but add little new to the canon.

Harris's chief contributions to American literature are his short stories. His first book of Uncle Remus tales has remained as popular as it was during his lifetime. It has never been out of print and has been translated into many languages. R. Bruce Bickley, Jr., is right when he says, "Harris's fame would be secure today had he written no other volumes." Critics of Harris's time almost unanimously praised the subsequent Uncle Remus stories, but modern critics are more divided. Most give Harris credit for being the first to recognize the literary value of the black oral tradition and appreciate his role in preserving the tales and the dialect in which they were told. Some, however, question the value of Remus's character and of the narrative framework.

Harris's local-color stories have received much less attention, and indeed most of them do not have the compact complexity of the black fables. But Harris could write memorably and poignantly in these stories as well, especially when creating characters such as Free Joe, Becky Staley, Mom Bi, and Crazy Sue. At his best Harris transcended the prejudices of his time, place, and race in order to initiate his readers into the harsh, even brutal world inhabited by society's underdogs.

Bibliographies:
William Bradley Strickland, "A Check List of the Periodical Contributions of Joel Chandler Harris (1848-1908)," *American Literary Realism*, 9 (Summer 1976): 207-229;
R. Bruce Bickley, Jr., and Strickland, "A Checklist of the Periodical Contributions of Joel Chandler Harris: Part 2," *American Literary Realism*, 11 (Spring 1978): 139-140;
Bickley, *Joel Chandler Harris: A Reference Guide* (Boston: G. K. Hall, 1978).

Biographies:
Julia Collier Harris, *The Life and Letters of Joel Chandler Harris* (Boston & New York: Houghton Mifflin, 1918);
Robert Lemuel Wiggins, *The Life of Joel Chandler Harris: From Obscurity in Boyhood to Fame in Early Manhood* (Nashville, Dallas & Richmond: Methodist Episcopal Church, South, 1918);
Paul M. Cousins, *Joel Chandler Harris: A Biography* (Baton Rouge: Louisiana State University Press, 1968).

References:

Florence E. Baer, *Sources and Analogues of the Uncle Remus Tales* (Helsinki: Suomalainen Tiedeakatemia, Acadmia Scientiarum Fennica, 1980);

R. Bruce Bickley, Jr., *Joel Chandler Harris* (Boston: Twayne, 1978);

Robert Bone, "The Oral Tradition," in his *Down Home: A History of Afro-American Short Fiction from Its Beginnings to the End of the Harlem Renaissance* (New York: Putnam's, 1975), pp. 19-41;

Stella Brewer Brookes, *Joel Chandler Harris—Folklorist* (Athens: University of Georgia Press, 1950);

Louise Dauner, "Myth and Humor in the Uncle Remus Fables," *American Literature*, 20 (May 1948): 129-143;

Thomas H. English, "In Memory of Uncle Remus," *Southern Literary Messenger*, 2 (February 1940): 77-83;

English, "The Other Uncle Remus," *Georgia Review*, 21 (Summer 1967): 210-217;

Lyle Glazier, "The Uncle Remus Stories: Two Portraits of American Negroes," *Journal of General Education*, 22 (April 1970): 71-79;

Daniel G. Hoffman, *Form and Fable in American Fiction* (New York: Oxford University Press, 1961), p. 341;

Thomas Nelson Page, "Immortal Uncle Remus," *Book Buyer*, 12 (December 1895): 642-645;

Louis D. Rubin, Jr., "Southern Local Color and The Black Man," *Southern Review*, new series 6 (October 1970): 1014-1015, 1016-1022;

Rubin, "Uncle Remus and the Ubiquitous Rabbit," *Southern Review*, new series 10 (October 1974): 784-804;

Darwin T. Turner, "Daddy Joel Harris and His Old-Time Darkies," *Southern Literary Journal*, 1 (December 1968): 20-41;

Bernard Wolfe, "Uncle Remus and the Malevolent Rabbit," *Commentary*, 8 (July 1949): 31-41.

Papers:

Most of Harris's manuscripts and letters are in the Harris Memorial Collection at Emory University. The Henry E. Huntington Library in San Marino, California, has a few manuscripts and letters, as do the Berg Collection at the New York Public Library, the Harry Ransom Humanities Research Center at the University of Texas, and the Alderman Library at the University of Virginia.

Lafcadio Hearn

(27 June 1850-26 September 1904)

Yoshinobu Hakutani
Kent State University

See also the Hearn entry in *DLB 12: American Realists and Naturalists*.

SELECTED BOOKS: *Stray Leaves from Strange Literature: Stories Reconstructed from the Anvarisoheïli, Baitál, Pachísí, Mahabharanta, Pantchatantra, Gulistan, Talmud, Kalewala, Etc.* (Boston: Osgood, 1884; London: Paul, Trench, Trübner, 1889);

Some Chinese Ghosts (Boston: Roberts, 1887);

Chita: A Memory of Last Island (New York: Harper, 1889);

Two Years in the French West Indies (New York: Harper, 1890);

Youma: The Story of a West-Indian Slave (New York: Harper, 1890);

Glimpses of Unfamiliar Japan, 2 volumes (Boston & New York: Houghton, Mifflin, 1894; London: Osgood, McIlvaine, 1894);

"Out of the East": Reveries and Studies in New Japan (Boston & New York: Houghton, Mifflin, 1895; London: Osgood, McIlvaine, 1895);

Kokoro: Hints and Echoes of Japanese Inner Life (Boston & New York: Houghton, Mifflin, 1896; London: Osgood, McIlvaine, 1896);

Gleanings in Buddha-Fields: Studies of Hand and Soul in the Far East (Boston & New York: Houghton, Mifflin, 1897; London: Harper, 1897);

Exotics and Retrospectives (Boston: Little, Brown, 1898; London: Low, 1899);

In Ghostly Japan (Boston: Little, Brown, 1899; London: Low, 1899);

Shadowings (Boston: Little, Brown, 1900; London: Low, 1900);

A Japanese Miscellany (Boston: Little, Brown, 1901; London: Low, 1901);

Kottō: Being Japanese Curios, with Sundry Cobwebs (New York & London: Macmillan, 1902);

Kwaidan: Stories and Studies of Strange Things (Boston & New York: Houghton, Mifflin, 1904; London: Kegan Paul, 1904);

Japan. An Attempt at Interpretation (New York & London: Macmillan, 1904);

Lafcadio Hearn, 1889 (photograph by Gutekunst)

The Romance of the Milky Way and Other Studies & Stories (Boston & New York: Houghton, Mifflin, 1905; London: Constable, 1905);

Leaves from the Diary of an Impressionist: Early Writings (Boston & New York: Houghton Mifflin, 1911);

Fantastics and Other Fancies, edited by Charles Woodward Hutson (Boston & New York: Houghton Mifflin, 1914);

Karma, edited by Albert Mordell (New York: Boni & Liveright, 1918; London: Harrap, 1921);

Essays in European and Oriental Literature, edited by Mordell (New York: Dodd, Mead, 1923; London: Heinemann, 1923);

Hearn, circa 1873

Creole Sketches, edited by Hutson (Boston & New York: Houghton Mifflin, 1924);

An American Miscellany: Articles and Stories, 2 volumes, edited by Mordell (New York: Dodd, Mead, 1924); republished as *Miscellanies: Articles and Stories* (London: Heinemann, 1924);

Occidental Gleanings: Sketches and Essays, 2 volumes, edited by Mordell (New York: Dodd, Mead, 1925; London: Heinemann, 1925);

Editorials, edited by Hutson (Boston & New York: Houghton Mifflin, 1926);

Essays on American Literature, edited by Sanki Ichikawa (Tokyo: Hokuseido Press, 1929);

Barbarous Barbers and Other Stories, edited by Ichiro Nishizaki (Tokyo: Hokuseido Press, 1939);

Buying Christmas Toys and Other Essays, edited by Nishizaki (Tokyo: Hokuseido Press, 1939);

Literary Essays, edited by Nishizaki (Tokyo: Hokuseido Press, 1939);

The New Radiance and Other Scientific Sketches, edited by Nishizaki (Tokyo: Hokuseido Press, 1939);

Oriental Articles, edited by Nishizaki (Tokyo: Hokuseido Press, 1939);

The Buddhist Writings of Lafcadio Hearn, edited by Kenneth Rexroth (Santa Barbara: Ross-Erikson, 1977).

Collection: *The Writings of Lafcadio Hearn*, 16 volumes (Boston & New York: Houghton Mifflin, 1922).

OTHER: Théophile Gautier, *One of Cleopatra's Nights and Other Fantastic Romances*, translated by Hearn (New York: Worthington, 1882);

La Cuisine Creole. A Collection of Culinary Recipes from Leading Chefs and Noted Creole Housewives, Who Have Made New Orleans Famous for Its Cuisine, compiled by Hearn (New York: Coleman, 1885);

"Gombo Zhèbes." Little Dictionary of Créole Proverbs, Selected from Six Créole Dialects, compiled and translated by Hearn (New York: Coleman, 1885);

Anatole France, *The Crime of Sylvestre Bonnard*, translated by Hearn (New York: Harper, 1890).

Born on the Ionian island of Lafcadio to Rosa Cassimati, a young woman of Greek descent, and Charles Bush Hearn, an Irish military surgeon in the service of the British army, Lafcadio Hearn's life was a procession of restless wandering and exotic travels. When he was two years old his father was transferred to the West Indies, but Hearn, his younger brother James, and his mother were dispatched to Dublin to live with paternal relatives. Hearn's mother, shy and unaccustomed to Irish life, soon suffered a physical and emotional breakdown, and in 1854 she left her children and returned to Greece. His father later married an English woman, an event for which Hearn never forgave him. Charles Hearn was eventually stationed in India, where he died from fever, and his two children were raised separately by relatives. Lafcadio became the ward of his great-aunt, Sarah Brenane, a devout Catholic who attempted to educate the young Hearn for the priesthood. At thirteen he was sent to a Catholic school in Paris, and while he became fluent in French, as indicated by his superb translations of works by Théophile Gautier, Alphonse Daudet, and Pierre Loti, he detested not only the Catholic temperament but Christianity in general; he was secretly determined not to become a priest. Hearn was then enrolled in St. Cuthbert's school

Hearn and his wife, Setsu Koizumi

in England and there suffered an accident that would shape his entire life. While playing a game in the schoolyard he injured his left eye, which subsequently atrophied and caused his right eye to become abnormally enlarged. Hearn was extremely sensitive about his deformity, and as an adult he seemed to think of himself as a freak and an outcast.

At age nineteen he learned that the Hearn estate was bankrupt and that he was, therefore, no longer entitled to financial support. To find his fortune he sailed to America in 1869. He first went to Cincinnati and eventually found employment as a journalist on the *Enquirer* and the *Commercial*. "His Greek temperament and French culture," says Yone Noguchi, "became frost-bitten as a flower in the North." So Hearn sought and found a milder climate in the South. In 1877 he traveled down the Mississippi River and settled in New Orleans. By the time he arrived there he had become a printer by trade, and a newspaper reporter and editor as well, but he seldom wrote about such experiences. He first secured a responsible position on the *New Orleans Item* and a few

years later on the *New Orleans Times-Democrat*. In 1882 he translated Gautier's *One of Cleopatra's Nights and Other Fantastic Romances*; he later tried his hand at the Gothic tale, completing *Stray Leaves from Strange Literature* (1884), his first book of legends and stories. In 1885 he made a trip to Florida; two years later his second book of fiction, *Some Chinese Ghosts*, appeared. He also traveled to Martinique, French West Indies; from this experience came his first novel, *Chita* (1889), which brought him instant recognition.

In 1890 *Harper's Magazine* sent him to Japan. Although he was to return to the United States a year later, when his writing assignment was complete, he remained there for the fourteen remaining years of his life. He married Setsu Koizumi, the daughter of an ancient samurai family, raised four children, became a naturalized citizen, and changed his name to Koizumi Yakumo. Despite his busy schedule, including an editorial stint with the *Kobe Chronicle*, he took time out teaching English at the middle school in Matsue, a provincial city, during 1890-1891 and at the higher middle school in Kumamoto on the island of Kyushu from 1891 to 1894. Soon after, he went to Tokyo to hold a chair of English literature at the Imperial University from 1896 to 1903. At the wave of antiforeign sentiments that swept the political circles, he was forced to resign and took a lectureship at Waseda University. He was invited to lecture at Cornell and London Universities, but these offers were withdrawn or declined for various reasons. Within a year he died of heart failure at age fifty-four. His last words were spoken in Japanese, as remembered by his son Kazuo: "Ah, byoki no tame" (Ah, because of illness). While in Japan, Hearn wrote and published several books of fiction, and since 1904 over a dozen books of various genres have been posthumously collected in the United States and Japan.

Hearn's earliest effort to write fiction in New Orleans was in the form of sketches rather than short stories, collected and published posthumously under the title of *Fantastics and Other Fancies* (1914). Such pieces as "The Vision of the Dead Creole," "All in White," and "The Ghostly Kiss" are tinged by a decadent vision of lust and death. More refined tales in the Gothic tradition appear in *Stray Leaves from Strange Literature*, a collection of twenty-seven legends and fables based on the English and French sources. "The Fountain Maiden" focuses on a Polynesian's adoration of the legendary maiden; "The Bird Wife" deals

Hearn's funeral procession in Okubo, Japan

with an Eskimo's love of a bird woman. As fantasies, both the fountain and the bird must return to their respective worlds, leaving their husbands behind. "The Cedar Closet" (*Enquirer*, 2 March 1874), on the other hand, represents a more ambitious attempt at the ghost story, though it lacks the type of psychic intensity that characterizes the best work in the genre. However, Hearn's penchant for the Gothic tale is explained in a letter written at that time: "But I think a man must devote himself to one thing in order to succeed: so I have pledged me to the worships of the Odd, the Queer, the Strange, the Exotic, the Monstrous. It quite suits my temperament."

His predilection for the exotic is evident in another early book, *Some Chinese Ghosts* (1887). His purpose, stated in the preface, is to seek "especially for *weird* beauty" and reconstruct it in his own words. "The Soul of the Great Bell," the opening story, is derived from a well-known Chinese legend about filial obedience and sacrifice. The casting of the perfect bell is made possible only by fusing its metals with the very flesh of the craftsman's daughter. "The Legend of Tchi-Niu" (*Harper's Bazaar*, 31 October 1885) treats a similar theme, whereas "The Return of Yen-Tchin King" dramatizes the immortality of the soul in Oriental philosophy. In "The Tale of the Porcelain-God," with the help of a whisper he hears from God, a potter ultimately triumphs in creating a vase with the perfect tint of living flesh without sacrificing himself. In these stories Hearn's emphasis is on the intensity of the weird passion rather than the moral of the story.

Hearn's sojourn in the South and the West Indies in the late 1880s resulted in a number of fragmentary travelogues and tales, some of which show the ideas and style of his later fiction. *Leaves from the Diary of an Impressionist* (1911) is a posthumous collection of lesser sketches and travelogues. "A Midsummer Trip to the Tropics" (first published as "A Midsummer Trip to the West Indies," *Harper's Monthly Magazine*, July, August, September 1888) and "Martinique Sketches" (*National Geographic*, June 1902) are also assemblages of fragmentary and impressionistic writing. His best work in this period is a group of four exotic tales later collected under the title *Karma* (1918): "Karma" (*Lippincott's*, May 1890); "A Ghost" (*Harper's Magazine*, December 1889); "Bilâl" (*New Orleans Times-Democrat*, 1884); and "China and the Western World" (*Atlantic Monthly*, April 1896). "Karma" depicts the suffering of a man whose love refuses to forgive him because of an old sin. The ideal love portrayed in this story, according to Albert Mordell, the editor, was based on Hearn's own experience.

Hearn's first books written in Japan are decidedly less accomplished than the later ones. *"Out of the East"* (1895) is a hurried collection of stories, travelogues, and folktales. "The Red Bridal" (*Atlantic Monthly*, July 1894), for instance, is an awkward attempt to build a bridge between the ancient Urashima folktale and contemporary Japanese scenes. *Kokoro* (1896), which in Japanese means "heart," contains several stories but consists primarily of essays on Japanese "inner life." However, *Gleanings in Buddha-Fields* (1897), the last collection in Hearn's early Japanese period, is more fictional than philosophical. Among the eleven pieces included, the best conceived and executed are "A Living God" (*Atlantic Monthly*, December 1896), which describes the moments of panic preceding a man's setting fire to his ricestacks, and "Ningyō-no-Haka" (A Doll's Grave), in which a child narrator tells a series of superstitious episodes surrounding her family.

Some of Hearn's best work appeared in the late 1890s and the early 1900s, his final period. *In Ghostly Japan* (1899) and *Shadowings* (1900) collect horror stories reminiscent of the work of Edgar Allan Poe. "Ingwa-Banashi" (Tales of Fate), collected in *In Ghostly Japan*, presents an unexpected terror in the midst of a death scene where the ghost of the dead wife possesses the body of the new bride, much like Poe's "Ligeia" (1838). With obvious differences in theme and character, both Hearn's "The Reconciliation," collected in *Shadowings*, and Poe's "The Fall of the House of Usher" (1839) feature long passages describing a decayed house that foreshadow the doom of the stories' endings.

A Japanese Miscellany (1901) is derived mainly from various legends and folktales. "Of a Promise Kept," the first story, is a translation of a tale in the eighteenth-century work *Ugetsu Monogatari* (Tales of Rain and Moon) by Ueda Akinari, but Hearn quickly changes the theme of homosexual love into that of the supernatural will to return. Translated also from another tale in *Ugetsu Monogatari* is "The Story of Kōgi the Priest." In the original the priest becomes a fish, but in Hearn's version he remains a human victim; Hearn nevertheless manages to sustain a sense of horror as poignantly as in the original. "The Story of Kwashin Koji," like many of the stories in Hearn's later period, abounds in irony and humor: an enterprising collector misled into purchasing a copy of a famous painting instead of the original; a murderer deluded into taking an empty wine gourd instead of the victim's head; a thief deceived into stealing a lump of filth instead of gold.

Hearn's greatest single achievement in Japan came in 1904 with the publication of *Kwaidan* (Weird Tales), a volume of seventeen short stories transformed from medieval Japanese folktales and legends. As recognized by most critics, *Kwaidan* exhibits more of Hearn's creative originality than any other collection published in this period. Because the moral of each story is legend, he concentrates on the effects of character and action. In "The Story of Mimi-Nashi-Hōichi" (The Story of Hōichi the Ear-less), first published in August 1903 *Atlantic Monthly*, the grotesque action yields an extraordinary sense of pathos and a powerful denouement. In "Diplomacy" the horrific presence of a ghost is juxtaposed with a samurai's outwitting of the apparition; in "The Dream of Akinosuké" (*Atlantic Monthly*, March 1904) the dream world is counterbalanced by the real. In such stories Hearn's realism is intricately woven into the traditional Buddhist thoughts; to the weirdness inherent in the story he adds his sense of irony and reflection.

In the light of the legend behind it, as well as the story itself, "The Story of Mimi-Nashi-Hōichi" skillfully reveals Hearn's artistic goals and sensibility. It is a tale of a blind lute player who resides at a Buddhist temple. Hōichi is so good at reciting the songs for the perished warriors of the Heike clan that even the goblins weep. The spirits of the departed warriors return nightly to hear his music. To chase the spirits away, the priest at the temple writes the text of the holy Sutra all over Hōichi's body, except for his ears. When the spirits of the ghosts visit him again, he can hear their talks but cannot utter a word because his mouth is covered by the holy texts. The angry ghosts then tear off Hōichi's ears and leave him in writhing pain. Ironically the vengeance the ghosts take on Hōichi immortalizes him. As do many of Hearn's exotic tales, this story offers a parable on the relation of life and art. Indicative of the artist's extreme position in life, Hōichi's craftsmanship is scarcely appreciated by the measure of this world.

In his own life Hearn looked for extraordinary experience and sought to make art out of his troubled life. Despite the wide vision and profound philosophy he had acquired in Japan, in many ways Hearn remained a lonely skeptic, as indicated by the haiku he chose as the epigraph for one of his last travel essays, "Fuji-no-yama" (*The Writings of Lafcadio Hearn*, volume 9, 1922): "Kité miréba/Sahodo madé nashi/Fuji no yama!" ("Seen on close approach, the mountain of Fuji does not come up to expectation"). To Hearn, disillusionment was the catalyst in an unusual search.

Letters:

Letters from the Raven, Being the Correspondence of Lafcadio Hearn with Henry Watkin, edited by

Milton Bronner (New York: Brentano's, 1907; London: Constable, 1908);

The Japanese Letters of Lafcadio Hearn, edited by Elizabeth Bisland (Boston & New York: Houghton Mifflin, 1910; London: Constable, 1911);

Some New Letters and Writings of Lafcadio Hearn, edited by Sanki Ichikawa (Tokyo: Kenkyusha, 1925).

Biographies:

Elizabeth Bisland, *The Life and Letters of Lafcadio Hearn*, 2 volumes (Boston & New York: Houghton, Mifflin, 1906);

Edward Larocque Tinker, *Lafcadio Hearn's American Days* (New York: Dodd, Mead, 1924).

References:

George M. Gould, *Concerning Lafcadio Hearn* (Philadelphia: Jacobs, 1908);

Yoshinobu Hakutani, "Lafcadio Hearn," *American Literary Realism*, 8 (Summer 1975): 271-274;

Arthur E. Kunst, *Lafcadio Hearn* (New York: Twayne, 1969);

Yone Noguchi, "Lafcadio Hearn: A Dreamer," *Current Literature*, 38 (June 1905): 521-523;

Elizabeth Stevenson, *Lafcadio Hearn* (New York: Macmillan, 1961);

Beongcheon Yu, *An Ape of Gods: The Art and Thought of Lafcadio Hearn* (Detroit: Wayne State University Press, 1964).

Papers:

The major collections of Hearn's manuscripts and letters are located at the Houghton Library, Harvard University; the Henry W. and Albert A. Berg Collection of English and American Literature, New York Public Library; and the Humanities Research Center, University of Texas, Austin.

Robert Herrick

(26 April 1868-23 December 1938)

Richard J. Thompson
Canisius College

See also the Herrick entries in *DLB 9: American Novelists, 1910-1945* and *DLB 12: American Realists and Naturalists.*

BOOKS: *The Man Who Wins: A Novel* (New York: Scribners, 1897);

Literary Love-Letters, and Other Stories (New York: Scribners, 1897);

The Gospel of Freedom (New York & London: Macmillan, 1898);

Love's Dilemmas (Chicago: Stone, 1898);

Composition and Rhetoric for Schools, by Herrick and Lindsay Todd Damon (Chicago: Scott, Foresman, 1899);

Methods of Teaching Rhetoric (Chicago: Scott, Foresman, 1899);

The Web of Life (New York & London: Macmillan, 1900; London: Mills & Boon, 1900);

The Real World (New York & London: Macmillan, 1901);

Their Child (New York & London: Macmillan, 1903);

The Common Lot (New York & London: Macmillan, 1904);

The Memoirs of an American Citizen (New York & London: Macmillan, 1905);

The Master of the Inn (New York: Scribners, 1908);

Together (New York & London: Macmillan, 1908);

A Life for a Life (New York: Macmillan, 1910);

The Healer (New York: Macmillan, 1911);

One Woman's Life (New York: Macmillan, 1913; London: Mills & Boon, 1913);

His Great Adventure (New York: Macmillan, 1913; London: Mills & Boon, 1914);

Clark's Field (Boston & New York: Houghton Mifflin, 1914);

The World Decision (Boston & New York: Houghton Mifflin, 1916);

The Conscript Mother (New York: Scribners, 1916; London: Bickers, 1916);

Homely Lilla (New York: Harcourt, Brace, 1923);

Waste (New York: Harcourt, Brace, 1924);

Wanderings (New York: Harcourt, Brace, 1925; London: Cape, 1926);

Robert Herrick

Chimes (New York: Macmillan, 1926);

Little Black Dog (Chicago: Rockwell, 1931);

The End of Desire (New York: Farrar & Rinehart, 1932);

Sometime (New York: Farrar & Rinehart, 1933).

PERIODICAL PUBLICATIONS: "The Emigration of the Calkins," syndicated by the Century Association in 1895;

"A Bull Market," *Saturday Evening Post*, 172 (27 January 1900): 655-657, 678-679;

"Mother Sims," *Saturday Evening Post*, 173 (17 November 1900): 10-11, 19;

"The Professor's Chance," *Atlantic Monthly*, 87 (May 1901): 723-732;

"The Polity of Nature," *Lippincott's Magazine*, 68 (October 1901): 458-471;

"Common Honesty," *Saturday Evening Post*, 176 (19 September 1903): 2-5, 28-30;

"The End of Desire," *Atlantic Monthly*, 92 (October 1903): 462-469;

"Avalanche," *Scribner's Magazine*, 41 (June 1907): 705-714;

"Papa's Stratagem," *Collier's*, 40 (19 October 1907): 21-23;

"In the Doctor's Office," *Scribner's Magazine*, 43 (January 1908): 105-115;

"The General Manager," *Scribner's Magazine*, 43 (March 1908): 270-282;

"The Temple of Juno," *Atlantic Monthly*, 101 (March 1908): 353-360;

"Found Out," *Saturday Evening Post*, 183 (25 March 1911): 16-17, 57-58;

"The Miracle," *Harper's Monthly*, 124 (December 1911): 138-147;

"His Leetle Trees," *Everybody's Magazine*, 27 (July 1912): 35-44;

"The Rainbow Chasers," *Canadian Magazine*, 44 (December 1914): 175-186.

Herrick's three collections of short stories written over a thirty-year period from 1895 to 1925 do not alter the reputation established for him by his seventeen novels and five novellas. He is considered a brilliant, minor realist who fused Theodore Dreiser's power of social observation and Henry James's talent for character psychology in a way that approached but never achieved an epic synthesis. While his short stories reflect debts to both branches of the American writer's "divided stream," they are for the most part too limited in scope and theme to allow the sweeping social vision of his longer work to come through.

Robert Welch Herrick was born in Cambridge, Massachusetts, the fourth child of William Augustus Herrick, a lawyer, and Harriet Peabody Emery Herrick, daughter of a Congregational minister. His family's Brahmin roots went back to the earliest settlers of New England. Educated at Harvard, where he served as editor of the *Monthly*, he earned an A.B. in 1890 and then went to teach composition at M.I.T. In 1893 he and his lifelong friend Robert Morss Lovett were hired by William Rainey Harper to install a program based on the Harvard method of teaching composition and rhetoric at the new University of Chicago. The following year, on 9 June 1894, he married his first cousin Harriet Peabody Emery, with whom he had one child, Philip Abbot. The marriage gradually soured as did Herrick's regard for his occupation of teaching.

His early stories, first published in *Scribner's Magazine* and the *Atlantic Monthly* and collected in *Literary Love-Letters, and Other Stories* (1897) and *Love's Dilemmas* (1898), won him the toehold he sought in the literary world, while his much-reprinted textbook on composition helped to assure his rise in academe. Herrick's major creative period as a novelist was launched by *The Man Who Wins* (1897) and extended to *Clark's Field* (1914). Its high point was the superbly structured novel *The Memoirs of an American Citizen* (1905). In their variety and depth of social observation his novels surpass those of Frank Norris and Winston Churchill and deserve comparison with those of Dreiser and William Dean Howells, both of whom admired Herrick's work.

World War I incited disenchantment in Herrick. The most pronounced contradiction of his literary work in general–the conflict between his respect for traditional decency and for the exhilarating pragmatic urgencies of the modern world–emerged to engage him in a constantly shifting response to the war that proved finally enervating. He ignored fiction in favor of polemics, arguing first for isolationism, but after he went to Europe in 1915 as a correspondent for the *Chicago Tribune* he began to call for "national chivalry" and for the destruction of Teutonic materialism. The frustration and spite that had been generated by his unhappy marriage and teaching career and by his failure to bring his writing ability to full fruition are reflected in bitter war essays. The Herricks had separated in 1913, and their divorce was finalized in January 1916. In December 1923 Herrick resigned his academic position in order to travel and to write polemical novels, of which *Waste* (1924) and *Chimes* (1926) are the best. In general his work of the 1920s and 1930s seems dated when compared to the postwar realism of Ernest Hemingway and John Dos Passos or to the technical freshness of F. Scott Fitzgerald and William Faulkner. In Herrick's last, utopian works the old social scrutinizer takes long views in favor of fuzzy escapism. In 1934 his familiarity with life in the Caribbean brought him to the attention of Harold Ickes, secretary of the interior, who in January 1935 appointed Herrick (reluctantly, Ickes's diary later showed) to be government secretary of the Virgin Islands. He died there on 23 December 1938.

It is customary and just to say that Herrick's novels have been regrettably undervalued. His manifest talents–for depicting the vitality of frontier Chicago, for dealing with basic human compli-

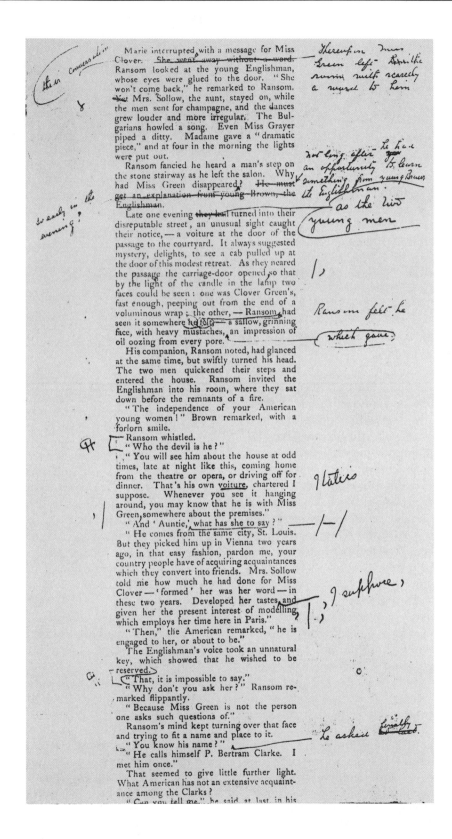

Marie interrupted, with a message for Miss Clover. ~~She went away without a word.~~ Ransom looked at the young Englishman, whose eyes were glued to the door. "She won't come back," he remarked to Ransom. ~~Yet~~ Mrs. Sollow, the aunt, stayed on, while the men sent for champagne, and the dances grew louder and more irregular. The Bulgarians howled a song. Even Miss Grayer piped a ditty. Madame gave a "dramatic piece," and at four in the morning the lights were put out.

Ransom fancied he heard a man's step on the stone stairway as he left the salon. Why had Miss Green disappeared? ~~He must get an explanation from young Brown, the~~ Englishman.

Late one evening ~~they had~~ turned into their disreputable street, an unusual sight caught their notice,—a voiture at the door of the passage to the courtyard. It always suggested mystery, delights, to see a cab pulled up at the door of this modest retreat. As they neared the passage the carriage-door opened, so that by the light of the candle in the lamp two faces could be seen : one was Clover Green's, fast enough, peeping out from the end of a voluminous wrap ; the other, — Ransom had seen it somewhere he felt — a sallow, grinning face, with heavy mustaches, an impression of oil oozing from every pore.

His companion, Ransom noted, had glanced at the same time, but swiftly turned his head. The two men quickened their steps and entered the house. Ransom invited the Englishman into his room, where they sat down before the remnants of a fire.

"The independence of your American young women !" Brown remarked, with a forlorn smile.

Ransom whistled.

"Who the devil is he ?"

"You will see him about the house at odd times, late at night like this, coming home from the theatre or opera, or driving off for dinner. That's his own voiture, chartered I suppose. Whenever you see it hanging around, you may know that he is with Miss Green, somewhere about the premises."

"And 'Auntie,' what has she to say ?"

"He comes from the same city, St. Louis. But they picked him up in Vienna two years ago, in that easy fashion, pardon me, your country people have of acquiring acquaintances which they convert into friends. Mrs. Sollow told me how much he had done for Miss Clover — 'formed' her was her word — in these two years. Developed her tastes, and given her the present interest of modelling, which employs her time here in Paris."

"Then," the American remarked, "he is engaged to her, or about to be."

The Englishman's voice took an unnatural key, which showed that he wished to be reserved.

"That, it is impossible to say."

"Why don't you ask her ?" Ransom remarked flippantly.

"Because Miss Green is not the person one asks such questions of."

Ransom's mind kept turning over that face and trying to fit a name and place to it.

"You know his name ?"

"He calls himself P. Bertram Clarke. I met him once."

That seemed to give little further light. What American has not an extensive acquaintance among the Clarks ?

"Can you tell me," he said, at last, in his

A portion of the corrected galley proofs for "A Pension Love Story" in Herrick's 1898 short-story collection,
Love's Dilemmas (The Newberry Library, Chicago)

cations with moral authority (that is, the "Anglo-Saxon" and the "Continental" spheres of his art)–sometimes compete with and defeat one another. Likewise Herrick's short stories are often full of many-sided promise but devoid of a coherent, realized focus. They come across to a present-day reader as appetizers for the novels that expand their themes. In broad outline his short stories fall into three groupings: apprentice work of the 1890s, stories that widen out into the mode of the big-circulation periodicals in the first years of the new century, and short fiction that trails off into noninvolvement and utopianism in the 1920s.

Literary Love-Letters, and Other Stories, containing seven stories of roughly thirty-five pages each, opens with the first story that Herrick composed upon reaching Chicago in the fall of 1893, "Literary Love-Letters: A Modern Account" (*Atlantic Monthly*, December 1894). The entire exchange of letters between a rich, somewhat naive middle-aged man and an arch, outspoken middle-aged woman exudes pseudosophistication. Herrick's youthful effort to appear old, wise, full of ennui, the story contains headings such as "Number X. The Limitation of Life" and parenthetical author's headnotes such as "Miss Armstrong vindicates herself by scorning" before each letter. While mocking the male protagonist's moral earnestness, the story unintentionally indicts Herrick's own wish to demonstrate his eastern, in fact European, elegance. Affected worldliness also taints the volume's second story, "A Question in Art" (*Scribner's Magazine*, April 1895), in which the painter Clayton's lordly unconcern for the frumpish landlady who has supported him while his talent slowly ripened again produces an aversion within the reader that Herrick did not intend.

This first volume is full of questions-in-art; it emphasizes those philosophical enigmas that dominated the Aesthetic Movement: What is the social role of beauty? Is art superior to life? The most typical story in the book is the third, "Mare Morto," in which the allegory is undisguised. When the enchanting Miss Barton takes the American Lawrance to her elfin grotto on the *laguna morto* in Venice, she takes him to both a larger world than he could ever find for himself and to a land where Life must be sacrificed for Love. In Herrick's judgment, Lawrance in this story and Clayton in "A Question in Art" wisely choose the ideal over the mundane. Persistently Herrick keeps the questions theoretical, the settings ex-

Robert Herrick, circa 1914

otic, the characters older and full of Jamesian social polish. The high price of experiencing beauty might well be called the theme of "The Price of Romance" (*Scribner's Magazine*, July 1895), "A Rejected Titian" (*Scribner's Magazine*, July 1897), and "Payment in Full." The volume concludes with an experimental piece, "A Prothalamion," in which the discourse of "He" and "She," discussing activities in the afterlife, is sophomoric. In sum, *Literary Love-Letters* seems to have been written to impress by a writer whose experience of the world is rather limited.

Love's Dilemmas, a collection of six stories written between 1895 and 1897, constitutes an improvement after the tepid opening piece, "Mute." "A Temporary Infidelity" offers a daring early illustration of lesbian attraction winning out over heterogeneity. The longest story in the book, "Miss Atherton's Mission," breaks even newer ground, for Judge Jerome Hale is the first evocation of Herrick's strongman, amalgamated from his reading of Friedrich Nietzsche and Horatio Alger and set down in the American melting pot. Hale's view of life looks forward to characters in novels from *The Gospel of Freedom* (1898) to *The Memoirs of an American Citizen* (1905): "The only way is to kick it; then it respects you. A strong man is strong by himself. He carries the gospel of force and discipline into the realms of the mean and uprighteous." Yet strength is not enough by itself; Alice Atherton Hale must humanize her husband's powerful character by teaching him "the habit of mercy" at the story's up-lifting close.

The best effort in *Love's Dilemma* is "A Pension Love Story" (*Scribner's Magazine*, December 1897), for in it is one of Herrick's most interesting and believable women, Clover Green, who resembles Henry James's Daisy Miller. She subtly dismisses the suitor Ransom while ostensibly analyzing for him a picture by Frans Hals as they stand before it in the Louvre. There are in Clover also fleeting reminders of Henry Adams's wife, whose nickname was Clover. The device by which Ransom rids Clover of the cad, P. Bertram Clarke—parading Clarke and an acquiescent woman past her on a street near the Madeleine—is dramatically effective, though Clover's reasons for rejecting Ransom remain cloudy. The story and the two that follow it, "A Marriage by Proxy" and "The Psychological Moment," successfully adumbrate a major Herrick theme, the extremely risky nature of marriage.

Herrick's fifteen short stories published between his first two collected volumes and his final collected volume of 1925 appeared, predominantly, during the period from the turn of the century to the outbreak of World War I in Europe, in *Scribner's Magazine* and the *Atlantic Monthly*, but also in mass-circulation periodicals (which Herrick referred to as "huge advertising billboards") such as *Collier's*, *Everybody's Magazine*, and *Lippincott's Magazine;* four of them appeared in the *Saturday Evening Post*. Their quality is uneven. Herrick appears to have had no general, controlling conception of what the short story should be. He depended purely on his sharp eye for isolating moral and philosophical cruxes in characters' lives, but he only rarely resolved them. Thus in "The Professor's Chance" (*Atlantic Monthly*, 1901), the choice that Professor Drake is asked to make between remaining at his overworked and underpaid teaching post and moving to a remunerative administrative job in Washington, D.C., is left undecided. Drake's own inertia seems a reflection of

Robert Herrick and his dog, Mickey

Herrick's in leaving the story open ended. The ending of "The Avalanche" (*Scribner's Magazine*, June 1907) arrives at the same sort of inconclusiveness: will Mrs. Archer and Greenhow, who have just confessed their mutual affection on a mountain pass in the Alps after Mr. Archer's snowy demise, ever make it back to civilization? Herrick is diverted by a penchant for maundering on the lovers' parts ("At last heart may speak to heart. . . .") and for turgid allegory ("It seems as if we [have] come a long way up the hill of life. . . ."). Most adventitious and sentimentalized of all is the ending of "In the Doctor's Office" (*Scribner's Magazine*, January 1908). The story attenuates the great medical man's needless examination of the heroine, who is estranged from her husband and wasting away for want of love, love which is then conveniently provided by her husband, who suddenly materializes out of the waiting room.

Increasingly Herrick's theme becomes that of failure—of isolation, acedia, angst, marriages and careers in bittersweet disarray—and, at the very end, of flight. Stearns, the journalist-turned-novelist in "The General Manager" (*Scribner's Magazine*, March 1908), loses his beloved, Mrs.

Bracefield, to the vulgar lawyer Puvis when he goes off to Asia. He gains a profounder sense of life while she rises in society, but they lose their real goal of having one another. No better off are the Marshalls in "The Temple of Juno" (*Atlantic Monthly*, March 1908), separated for ten years though not divorced and accidentally reunited on the island of Stromboli. Their temporarily renewed passion is inadequate to incite any genuine reinvolvement, and in the end they again drift apart. Worst off of all is the ruined financier Langdon in "The Miracle" (*Harper's Monthly*, December 1911). He falls into a reservoir that is under construction near his estate and considers ending it all before his overcoincidental rescue and bathetic conversion to the belief that "the world out there is big and beautiful." In the main Herrick's middle stories are gray and bleak. They reflect indecision, confusion, and a lapsed faith in life.

Wanderings (1925) contains four long stories that resort to various utopian alternatives to counter the disordered state in which Herrick considered the postwar world to be. In "Magic" the sacred mountain Tshikimo, where "the shroud that life had woven was lifted," is the place held out. Here on the Black Mesa, near the Rio Grande, Eleanor Lamont is transfigured into Shimana, the Flower Girl, and achieves perfect spiritual union with the rancher Ezra Groves. Yet later she comes back down to earth and deserts both Groves and her son in favor of a fresher illusion, Russian communism. The quest for visionary perfection in "Magic" sets the tone for the volume as a whole.

The quest led ultimately to the islands of the Caribbean, where both "The Stations of the Cross" and "The Adventures of Ti Chatte" are set. In "The Stations of the Cross" the lovers are transcendentally moved by watching the priest and his congregation go along the ancient volcanic route of the "Calvaire"; at the same time, the cockfights exert a competing black-magical hold on the couple. The reader is reminded of D. H. Lawrence and Malcolm Lowry only momentarily, however, for the conclusion of the story is pat and the narrative flow glacial. In "The Adventures of Ti Chatte" the anthropologist Charlotte Day prefigures Serena Massey in *The End of Desire* (1932), who is herself a fictionalization of Margaret Mead. The woman takes over in Herrick's last works, and the feminist Charlotte gradually accepts the docile Lapin as mate. The cat of the title is self-sufficient and free of human foible, as is the dog (Trotsky) in the concluding story of *Wanderings*, "The Passions of Trotsky." Animals finally are the only dependable and caring creatures in Herrick's nostalgic last stories.

Herrick's short stories are today largely neglected by readers. The two main published critical studies of his life and work concentrate on his novels. His stories have not been republished in anthologies or textbooks in the last sixty-five years; his three short-story collections are difficult to locate, although the Books For Libraries Press reprinted *Love's Dilemmas* in 1970. With the exception of the half-dozen stories that act as portents for Herrick's major novels, his stories have only historical interest, and the neglect is probably justified.

References:

Louis J. Budd, *Robert Herrick* (New York: Twayne, 1971);

Blake Nevius, *Robert Herrick, The Development of a Novelist* (Berkeley & Los Angeles: University of California Press, 1962).

Papers:

The Robert Herrick Papers are in the Division of Archives and Manuscripts of the University of Chicago Library.

Grace King

(29 November 1852-12 January 1932)

David Kirby
Florida State University

See also the King entry in *DLB 12: American Realists and Naturalists.*

BOOKS: *Monsieur Motte* (New York: Armstrong, 1888; London: Routledge, 1888);

Tales of a Time and Place (New York: Harper, 1892);

Jean Baptiste le Moyne, Sieur de Bienville (New York: Dodd, Mead, 1892);

Balcony Stories (New York: Century, 1893; London: Warne, 1893);

A History of Louisiana, by King and John R. Ficklen (New Orleans: Graham, 1893; revised, 1905);

New Orleans: The Place and the People (New York & London: Macmillan, 1895);

De Soto and His Men in the Land of Florida (New York & London: Macmillan, 1898);

The Pleasant Ways of St. Médard (New York: Holt, 1916; London: Constable, 1917);

Creole Families of New Orleans (New York: Macmillan, 1921);

La Dame de Sainte Hermine (New York: Macmillan, 1924);

Mount Vernon on the Potomac: History of the Mount Vernon Ladies' Association of the Union (New York: Macmillan, 1929);

Memories of a Southern Woman of Letters (New York: Macmillan, 1932);

Grace King of New Orleans: A Selection of Her Writings, edited by Robert Bush (Baton Rouge: Louisiana State University Press, 1973).

Grace King

A realist in the manner of William Dean Howells, Edith Wharton, and such French authors as Guy de Maupassant, Grace King never attained the stature of these literary giants. But it is often the special gift of a minor author to reveal the particular and the peculiar in a way that a major author cannot, and at this King was unparalleled. She spoke with artistry and feeling for a class of people who were all but voiceless, the disenfranchised and penniless women, black and white, who lived in the South after the Civil War.

Ignored for decades, King is now benefiting from the recent upsurge of interest in folklore, regional literature, and women's studies. As traditional literary hierarchies are challenged by new critical approaches, King, like other minor writers, is being examined anew, and her contribution is at last receiving its true valuation.

King's subject is one of which she had firsthand knowledge. The third child and eldest daughter of a prosperous New Orleans lawyer, William Woodson King, and his wife, the former Sarah Ann Miller, Grace Elizabeth King recalled in later years a comfortable family life and the pleasant rigors of convent schooling, but the Civil

War changed all that. With her parents and siblings the nine-year-old fled the city in the spring of 1862 and sat out the conflict in the comparative safety of the family plantation. The period following the war was hard, and when the King family returned to New Orleans, it was to a small house in a poor neighborhood; years passed before the once-proud family was able to extricate itself from the humbling confines of poverty. The young Grace King was determined to write and to travel, however, and she succeeded at both, profiting along the way by the many friendships that she made. Beginning in 1887 she spent several summers with the Charles Dudley Warner family in Connecticut, where she was introduced to many important literary people of the day, including Samuel Clemens, who became her close friend, and William Dean Howells. She traveled in Europe in 1891-1892. In England King was asked to speak to the young women of Newnham College, Cambridge, on the subject of Sidney Lanier and his work. In France, a country for which King had a lifelong affinity, she heard Ernest Renan lecture at the Sorbonne and saw Alexandre Dumas *fils* in the audience of the Théâtre d'Art. She met the most-noted *femmes de lettres* in Paris, including Madame Blanc and Baronne de Bury, and frequented their salons.

For all these connections, King remained a child of her past. In *The American Scene* (1907) Henry James noted that whereas the "ancient order" in the South was "masculine, fierce and mustachioed," the post-Civil War era was marked by a "strange feminization." The reason for the change is obvious: the "fierce and mustachioed" men had died on the battlefields, leaving their wives and daughters behind. Writers such as King elaborated the feminine Southern viewpoint in a way that James, with all his mastery, could not. The specific incident that propelled King into the world of letters was a conversation in 1885 with Richard Watson Gilder, editor of the *Century Illustrated Monthly Magazine*. Gilder had asked King for the reason behind the enmity of the people of New Orleans toward George Washington Cable and his works. King replied that Cable, a native son, had treated the Creoles unfairly in order to please his northern readers. Gilder replied, "If Cable is so false to you, why do not some of you write better?"

The result was King's first published story, "Monsieur Motte," which appeared in the January 1886 issue of the *New Princeton Review*. The story is set in a young ladies' boarding school in

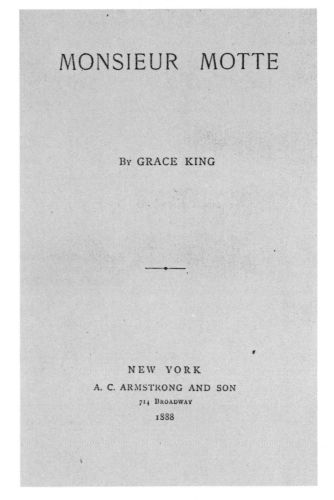

Title page for King's first book, an expanded version of the short story that she wrote in response to George Washington Cable's fictional treatment of New Orleans Creoles

New Orleans on the eve of the school's annual celebration. The heroine is Marie Modeste, whose parents are dead (her father, like many of King's fictional fathers, was killed in the war). An uncle provides for her, but Marie Modeste has not seen him since she was four. After he does not appear at the party, she learns that he too is long dead and that her benefactor has actually been the black Marcélite, a hairdresser. As in other King stories, men are fallible, and women must bond together if they are to survive in a harsh world. King wrote three more sketches involving the same characters and published the whole as *Monsieur Motte* (1888), a thoroughly padded "novel" in which Marie Modeste marries someone much like herself, a young man who has lost his parents and has been raised largely by a faithful black female.

Of the five stories in King's first collection, *Tales of a Time and Place* (1892), "Bayou L'Ombre:

An Incident of the War" (*Harper's New Monthly*, July 1887) is one of King's most accomplished. Though the story's details are invented, its genesis is autobiographical. It concerns three young girls who are removed to their family's plantation when it becomes apparent that their city will be taken by Federal troops. The girls have an idealized notion of war; they are intensely patriotic, and their every thought is of "soldiers, flags, music, generals on horseback brandishing swords, knights in armor escalating walls, cannons booming through clouds of smoke." In the tragicomedy of errors which follows, the girls "free" some Confederate soldiers who are actually Yankee troops in disguise. Warfare is revealed as farcical, even if the girls themselves are noble and courageous.

One reviewer of *Tales of a Time and Place* noted of King that "in narrating a slight episode, as in sketching a simple character, her touch is at once strong and delicate, but her power of invention fails to sustain a complicated plot. She dashes spasmodically from incident to incident, and though she always has her end in view, arrives at it through much incoherence" (*Nation*, 14 July 1892). Yet the reviewer for *Harper's New Monthly* (June 1892)–calling *Monsieur Motte* "as perfect a representation of creole [*sic*] conditions and social life as Hawthorne ever made of New England"–proclaimed that *Tales of a Time and Place* "increases this writer's reputation as an original force in American literature." The reviewer found "Bayou L'Ombre" especially praiseworthy, noting that a scene depicting the march of some rebellious slave women "has a dramatic quality and a raciness of humanity that our critics have been accustomed to find only in the French masters of fiction."

King's second collection of short fiction, *Balcony Stories* (1893), consists of an introductory sketch, "The Balcony"(*Century*, December 1892), and thirteen stories, all of which are relatively short. The average story in *Tales of a Time and Place* is nearly four times as long as the average story in this collection. The characters here are largely widows, spinsters, and orphans, and each story deals implicitly or explicitly with one or more of King's major themes: male fallibility, female strength in the face of despair, the need for solidarity among women. "The Balcony" creates an ambience that pervades the stories proper. A balcony is a gathering place where, on summer nights, women may sit in hearing distance of their sleeping children and tell stories: "experi-

ences, reminiscences, episodes, picked up as only women know how to pick them up from other women's lives,–or other women's destinies, as they prefer to call them,–and told as only women know how to relate them." If one of the children should wake, "through the half-open shutters the still quiet eyes" might "look across the dim forms on the balcony to the star-spangled or the moon-brightened heavens beyond; while memory makes stores for the future, and germs are sown, out of which the slow, clambering vine of thought issues, one day, to decorate or hide, as it may be, the structures or ruins of life." In *Memories of a Southern Woman of Letters* (1932) King said that she got the idea for *Balcony Stories* after listening to her mother tell stories about the family, and in "The Balcony" she seems to be writing about herself when she treats the eavesdropping child as nascent artist. In terms of fiction and its origins King is writing about a process of subtle collusion between women and children, art and anecdote–a process from which men and male activities are conspicuously absent.

Balcony Stories was for the most part favorably received by King's contemporaries. H. E. Scudder, the reviewer for the *Atlantic Monthly* (April 1894), noted that "Miss King ... moves among her people and scenes as one who has drawn from like sources of life, and simply has this apart from her characters, that she is gifted with the power of giving them independent existence. With a careless ease born of familiarity with her material, she seems to take this or that bit of stuff and ... turn what would have been a disregarded scrap into a revelation of beauty." Another reviewer observed in the *New Orleans Daily Picayune* (22 October 1893) that the stories "are among the best things that have appeared ... of late; sweet, tender pictures, mostly of Louisiana life and manners that the accomplished author has grown up in the midst of, and knows thoroughly well." These reviewers, and others, were describing one particular method of the local-color writer, who, according to Jay Martin, either romantically reconstructs the myth of the past or realistically destroys it or embodies both tendencies in his work because of the need to "reconstruct a glorious past, along with a simultaneous recognition that such a paradise never existed." In the course of her career King ran the gamut of all three possibilities when writing about her native region. Yet the sentimentally reminiscent approach that characterizes most *Balcony Stories* puts that book squarely in the romantic mythmaking

Grace King (photograph by Moses & Son)

school of local-color writing. Evidently it was one of the things King did best. *Balcony Stories* was republished in 1914 and again in 1925; it is interesting to note that, thirty-three years after the stories' first appearance, the reviewer for the *Boston Transcript* (11 November 1925) found them "all well worth the re-reading." *Balcony Stories* is King's most artistically accomplished work, both in the achievement of the individual stories and the unity of the volume as a whole.

If King is somewhat difficult to classify as a writer, perhaps that is because her American realism has a distinctly French aspect due to the New Orleans settings of her fictions as well as her French convent-school training (like Marie Modeste's in "Monsieur Motte") and her travels in France. In *A History of American Literature Since 1870* (1922) Fred Lewis Pattee called "Monsieur Motte" in the *New Princeton Review* "another step in the development of the short story. It was as distinctively French in its atmosphere and its art as if it had been a translation from Maupassant, yet it was as originally and peculiarly American as even [Cable's] *Madame Delphine*, which in so many ways it resembles." And in *The Development of the American Short Story* (1923) Pattee noted that "no

other native American short-story writer has been so thoroughly French. Her tales are like well-made translations from the school of Flaubert and Daudet. Like Norris and Garland, she affected veritism: it was in the air of the times; she had learned of Zola to tell the Truth, but not after the manner of Zola." Commenting on the lifelong feud between King and George Washington Cable that sparked the writing of "Monsieur Motte," Pattee wrote that King thought Cable "had romanticized New Orleans beyond toleration and misrepresented it: she would present the charming side of her people, their pride, their uniqueness, their distinction, their lovable unselfishness. If romance came into her tales it would be only because romance in New Orleans was the Truth." As King herself said, "I am a realist *á la mode de la Nouvelle-Orleans*. I have never written a line that was not realistic, but our life, our circumstances, the heroism of the men and women that surrounded my early horizon—all that was romantic."

Like many writers, King worked in a variety of genres. As a historian, she wrote solid and readable works which still commend themselves today, even though professional historians would no doubt take issue with her purely narrative method. As a novelist, she achieved great passages of lyric beauty, even if she might have profited from a sterner editorial hand to curb her prolixity and her occasionally deficient organizational sense. As a writer of short stories, she left tightly constructed, insightful tales of life during the Civil War and Reconstruction periods. It is for these that she will be remembered.

References:

Robert Bush, *Grace King: A Southern Destiny* (Baton Rouge: Louisiana State University Press, 1983);

Bush, "Grace King: The Emergence of a Southern Intellectual Woman," *Southern Review*, new series 13 (Spring 1977): 272-288;

Bush, "Grace King (1852-1932)," *American Literary Realism*, 8 (Winter 1975): 43-49;

Bush, "Grace King and Mark Twain," *American Literature*, 44 (March 1972): 31-51;

Bush, Introduction to *Grace King of New Orleans: A Selection of Her Writings*, edited by Bush (Baton Rouge: Louisiana State University Press, 1973);

David Kirby, *Grace King* (Boston: Twayne, 1980);

Fred Lewis Pattee, *The Development of the American Short Story* (New York & London: Harper, 1923);

Pattee, *A History of American Literature Since 1870* (New York: Century, 1922);

Bess Vaughan, "A Bio-Bibliography of Grace Elizabeth King," *Louisiana Historical Quarterly*, 17 (October 1934): 752-770.

Papers:

The Grace King Papers are in the Louisiana State University Library Department of Archives, Baton Rouge, Louisiana.

Peter B. Kyne

(12 October 1880-25 November 1957)

James F. Smith, Jr.
Pennsylvania State University–Ogontz Campus

BOOKS: *The Three Godfathers* (New York: Doran, 1913; London: Hodder & Stoughton, 1914);

The Long Chance (New York: H. K. Fly, 1914; London: Hodder & Stoughton, 1919);

Cappy Ricks; or, The Subjugation of Matt Peasley (New York: H. K. Fly, 1916; London: Hodder & Stoughton, 1919);

Ireland über Alles; A Tale of the Sea (London: Nash, 1917); republished as *The Stolen Ship* (London: Hodder & Stoughton, 1919);

Webster–Man's Man (Garden City, N.Y.: Doubleday, Page, 1917; London: Hodder & Stoughton, 1919);

The Valley of the Giants (Garden City, N.Y.: Doubleday, Page, 1918; London: Hodder & Stoughton, 1919);

The Green Pea Pirates (Garden City, N.Y.: Doubleday, Page, 1919; London: Hodder & Stoughton, 1920); republished as *Captain Scraggs; or, The Green-Pea Pirates* (New York: Grosset & Dunlap, 1921);

Peter B. Kyne: An Autobiography, by Request (New York: International Magazine Company, 1919);

Kindred of the Dust (New York: Cosmopolitan Book Corporation, 1920; London: Hodder & Stoughton, 1920);

The Go-Getter: A Story That Tells You How to Be One (New York: Cosmopolitan Book Corporation, 1921; London: Hodder & Stoughton, 1921);

Peter B. Kyne

The Pride of Palomar (New York: Cosmopolitan Book Corporation, 1921; London: Hodder & Stoughton, 1921);

Cappy Ricks Retires (New York: Cosmopolitan Book Corporation, 1922; London: Hodder & Stoughton, 1922);

Never the Twain Shall Meet (New York: Cosmopolitan Book Corporation, 1923; London: Hodder & Stoughton, 1923);

The Enchanted Hill (New York: Cosmopolitan Book Corporation, 1924; London: Hodder & Stoughton, 1924);

The Understanding Heart (New York: Cosmopolitan Book Corporation, 1926; London: Hodder & Stoughton, 1926);

They Also Serve (New York: Cosmopolitan Book Corporation, 1927);

Made of Money (London: Hodder & Stoughton, 1927);

Money to Burn (New York: Grosset & Dunlap, 1928);

The Silent Comrade (London: Hodder & Stoughton, 1928);

The Tide of Empire (New York: Cosmopolitan Book Corporation, 1928; London: Hodder & Stoughton, 1928);

Jim the Conqueror (New York: Cosmopolitan Book Corporation, 1929; London: Hodder & Stoughton, 1929);

The Parson of Panamint and Other Stories (New York: Cosmopolitan Book Corporation, 1929; London: Hodder & Stoughton, 1929);

The Thunder God, A Romantic Story of Love, Hatred and Adventure (New York: Grosset & Dunlap, 1930);

Outlaws of Eden (New York: Cosmopolitan Book Corporation, 1930; London: Hodder & Stoughton, 1931);

Golden Dawn (New York: Cosmopolitan Book Corporation, 1930; London: Hodder & Stoughton, 1930);

The Gringo Privateer and Island of Desire (New York: Cosmopolitan Book Corporation, 1931);

The Gringo Privateer (London: Hodder & Stoughton, 1932);

Island of Desire (London: Hodder & Stoughton, 1932);

Two Make a World (New York: H. C. Kinsey, 1932; London: Hodder & Stoughton, 1933);

Lord of Lonely Valley (New York: H. C. Kinsey, 1932; London: Hodder & Stoughton, 1932);

Comrades of the Storm (New York: H. C. Kinsey, 1933; London: Hodder & Stoughton, 1933);

Cappy Ricks Comes Back (New York: H. C. Kinsey, 1934; London: Hodder & Stoughton, 1934);

The Golden West: Three Novels by Peter B. Kyne (New York: Farrar & Rinehart, 1935)–comprises *Kindred of the Dust*, *Never the Twain Shall Meet*, and *The Pride of Palomar*;

The Cappy Ricks Special (New York: H. C. Kinsey, 1935; London: Hodder & Stoughton, 1936);

Soldiers, Sailors and Dogs (New York: H. C. Kinsey, 1936);

Lloyds of London (New York: Twentieth Century-Fox, 1936);

Dude Woman (New York: H. C. Kinsey, 1940; London: Hodder & Stoughton, 1940);

The Book I Never Wrote (San Francisco: Privately printed by Taylor & Taylor, 1942).

MOTION PICTURES: *The Beautiful Gambler*, story by Kyne, Universal, 1921;

The Innocent Cheat, story by Kyne, Ben Wilson Productions, 1921;

Brothers Under the Skin, titles by Kyne, Goldwyn, 1922;

Homeward Bound, story by Kyne, Famous Players-Lasky, 1923;

Never the Twain Shall Meet, titles by Kyne, Cosmopolitan, 1925;

The Shamrock Handicap, story by Kyne, Fox, 1926;

War Paint, story by Kyne, M-G-M, 1926;

California, story by Kyne, M-G-M, 1927;

Foreign Devils, story by Kyne, M-G-M, 1927;

The Rawhide Kid, story by Kyne, Universal, 1928;

Freedom of the Press, story by Kyne, Universal, 1928;

Stampede, story by Kyne, Columbia, 1936;

Headline Crasher, story by Kyne, Independent, 1937;

Ride, Kelly, Ride, story by Kyne, 20th Century-Fox, 1940;

Belle Le Grand, screenplay by Kyne, Republic, 1951;

Bronco Buster, story by Kyne, Universal, 1952.

OTHER: "Point," in *My Story That I Like Best, by Edna Ferber, Irving [sic] S. Cobb, Peter B. Kyne, James Oliver Curwood, Meredith Nicholson, H. C. Witwer* (New York: International Book Company, 1924).

PERIODICAL PUBLICATIONS:
FICTION
"A Little Matter of Salvage," *Saturday Evening*

Post, 182 (25 September 1909): 17-18, 43-44;

"The Ten-Dollar Raise," *Saturday Evening Post*, 182 (4 December 1909): 18-20, 48-50;

"A Little Flyer in Junk," *Saturday Evening Post*, 182 (19 March 1910): 8, 46-48;

"The Buzz Saw of Chance," *Saturday Evening Post*, 182 (7 May 1910): 49-50;

"The Great Mono Miracle, An Echo of Mark Twain," *Sunset: The Pacific Monthly* (July 1912): 37-49;

"Mr. Burdock's Insurance," *Collier's*, 53 (23 April 1914): 5-7, 25, 26-30;

"The Last Survivor," *Collier's*, 56 (11 March 1916): 5-7, 26, 28-29;

"The Halcyon Comes Back," *Collier's*, 57 (2 September 1916): 5-7, 20-23;

"Reynard of the Seas," *Collier's*, 58 (7 October 1916): 9-11, 24-26;

"Salvage," *Collier's*, 58 (9 December 1916): 17-18, 34-35, 37-41;

"Over and Back," *Collier's*, 58 (10 March 1917): 16-18, 28-29, 32-34;

"Private Cappy Ricks," *Cosmopolitan*, 67 (August 1919): 31-35, 128-134;

"Cappy Ricks Comes Back," *Cosmopolitan*, 69 (August 1920): 39-43, 104-111;

"Back to Yellow Jacket," *Cosmopolitan*, 69 (September 1920): 26-31, 123-130;

"The Go-Getter," *Cosmopolitan*, 71 (November 1921): 19-24, 108;

"The Sea Anchor," *Cosmopolitan*, 72 (June 1922): 51-57, 122-124;

"Point! A Story of Man's Best Friend," *Cosmopolitan*, 73 (July 1922): 36-42, 137;

"The Curious Tribe of McFee," *Cosmopolitan*, 73 (September 1922): 95-98, 118;

"Semper Fidelis: A New Dog Story," *Cosmopolitan*, 74 (March 1923): 40-45, 153-156;

"Discipline," *Cosmopolitan*, 74 (April 1923): 32-37, 184-188;

"The Bluebird," *Cosmopolitan*, 78 (February 1925): 16-21, 145;

"Cappy Ricks and the Mystic Isles," *Cosmopolitan*, 78 (March 1925): 36-39, 166;

"Cappy Bells the Cat," *Cosmopolitan*, 79 (October 1925): 30-33, 122-128;

"The Beloved Leader," *Cosmopolitan*, 79 (December 1925): 36-39, 161-164;

"Rustling for Cupid," *Cosmopolitan*, 80 (February 1926): 68-71, 100-108;

"For His Money," *Cosmopolitan*, 82 (January 1927): 74-77, 126-133;

"Round-the-World," *Cosmopolitan*, 82 (February 1927): 38-41, 174-183;

"Soldier's Sleep," *Collier's*, 80 (1 October 1927): 5-7, 40-42;

"The Golden Heart," *Collier's*, 81 (7 January 1928): 5-7, 32, 34, 36;

"Chivalry," *Collier's*, 82 (1 September 1928): 5-6, 39-41;

"Good Dog," *Cosmopolitan*, 85 (September 1928): 100-103, 117;

"Getaway Day," *Cosmopolitan*, 85 (November 1928): 60-63, 178;

"The Mud-Lark," *Cosmopolitan*, 85 (December 1928): 90-93, 157;

"A Ringer," *Cosmopolitan*, 86 (January 1929): 70-71, 126-130;

"Old Man Tooker's Investment," *Cosmopolitan*, 86 (January 1929): 48-49, 234-242;

"Lionized," *American Magazine*, 108 (July 1929): 26-29, 137-138;

"Old-Fashioned Pete," *Collier's*, 84 (27 July 1929): 5-7, 58, 60, 61;

"Let Freedom Ring," *Collier's*, 84 (12 October 1929): 7-9, 57-58;

"An Officer, Not a Gentleman," *Cosmopolitan*, 88 (January 1930): 28-31, 119-124;

"O'Bannion Rules the Roost," *Cosmopolitan*, 88 (March 1930): 82-85, 137-140;

"S-t-u-t-t-e-r-i-n-g Cowboy," *Cosmopolitan*, 91 (August 1931): 76-79, 138-143;

"The Perfect Secretary," *Collier's*, 89 (25 June 1932): 7-8, 29-30, 32;

"Some Heroes Are Like Men," *Cosmopolitan*, 93 (October 1932): 52-55, 96-101;

"Old Man of the Sea," *Cosmopolitan*, 95 (August 1933): 62-65, 130-133;

"Call a Cop," *Collier's*, 94 (25 August 1934): 7-9, 46;

"The Playboy Champion," *Collier's*, 94 (17 November 1934): 7-9, 53-56;

"Sky Pilot," *Collier's*, 97 (28 March 1936): 12-13, 71-72, 74-75;

"Home Is the Sailor," *Collier's*, 97 (9 May 1936): 7-8, 102-104, 106, 108;

"Troubled Sea," *Collier's*, 106 (16 November 1940): 18-19;

"Rich Girl, Poor Man," *Collier's*, 121 (29 May 1948): 18-19;

"Memory Test," *Collier's*, 123 (11 June 1949): 20-21.

NONFICTION

"Double and Redouble," *Collier's*, 83 (23 March 1929): 44;

The Go-Getter

A Story That Tells You How to be One

—By—

Peter B. Kyne

Who is One Himself

He is also the author of
CAPPY RICKS
KINDRED OF THE DUST
THE PRIDE OF PALOMAR
. . . etc. . . .

The Real Secret of Success—Told in the Best of All the Cappy Ricks Stories

Dust jacket illustration for one of Kyne's most-popular stories, in which Cappy Ricks proves his superiority over his son-in-law, a member of "the choicest aggregation of mental duds since Ajax defied the lightning"

"Ahoy, Australia Ahoy New Zealand," *Saturday Evening Post*, 204 (24 November 1931): 69-74;

"Dogs," *Cosmopolitan*, 91 (December 1931): 36-37, 118-120;

"I Used to Be a Business Man," *American Magazine*, 115 (June 1935): 58-59, 105-106;

"Turning Point," *American Magazine*, 146 (December 1948): 126-128.

Peter B. Kyne, self-proclaimed businessman-turned-author, displayed no pretension to liter-ary greatness when he referred to his "alleged lit-erary output" in the dedication to his novel *Never the Twain Shall Meet* (1923). He also stated that "with the years I developed into a journeyman suf-ficiently skilled to make my cockeyed profession pay well." Author of twenty-five novels and some one thousand short stories and articles during his long writing career, Kyne was certainly prolific, if not profound. Though he observed that "the world lost a good salesman when I became a writer," one may safely say that Kyne found the formula for commercial literary success and sold

VOLUME 57 NUMBER 25   SEPTEMBER 2 1916

Collier's
THE NATIONAL WEEKLY

Entered at the New York Post
Office as Second-Class Matter   MARK SULLIVAN, EDITOR   Entered as Second-Class Matter at the
                                                                     Post Office Department, Ottawa, Canada

THE HALCYON COMES BACK
BY PETER B. KYNE

San Francisco probably possesses more picturesque traditions and unwritten romances than any other of our ports. This is the first of a series of San Francisco shipping tales which Mr. Kyne is writing for Collier's

ILLUSTRATED BY PERCY E. COWEN

THE story really begins back in the hard, old days when the Department of Commerce had nothing to do with deciding on the merits of a sailor for a job as mate or the fitness of a mate for a skipper's berth. It will be recalled that Christopher Columbus did not have a certificate as master, in a neat oak frame, screwed into the cabin wall of the *Santa Maria*, and neither did young Andy Royce at the time he gave old man Bates an opportunity to take his dunnage out of the forecastle and come aft. That was an era when a man came aboard, as the saying was, "through the hawsepipes," fought his way aft, learned navigation, and in the fullness of time persuaded an owner to intrust him with a ship. At the time old man Bates made his first voyage in the *Halcyon* a knowledge of navigation was considered an asset in a mate, although lack of it was not regarded as a disability. Seamanship, brute courage, and brute strength, coupled with a certain sense of responsibility and a pride in his vocation, were the prime requisites in future skipper material.

Old man Bates was probably the last person in the world the average skipper would have selected for a mate, even before his jet-black hair turned snowy white and brought him the cognomen of "Pop" Bates. Forty years ago masters disliked being bothered with details, so they hired mates who could handle men—both ways. Pop Bates could only hope to handle men one way, and that was by moral persuasion. Of course he was a seaman, but in an age of seamanship that was taken for granted and considered nothing remarkable; while he had courage, it was the quiet, unobtrusive kind that nobody ever suspected any more than they did the fact that as far back as ten years before Captain Andrew Royce crooked his finger at him and said: "You're the mate of the *Halcyon*," Pop Bates had commenced a nodding acquaintance with Bowditch. However, he had never gone to school very long, so the logarithms bothered him. Added to his retarded ambition to become a master, Pop Bates was also the proprietor of a sense of responsibility. He always put away a little money at the end of every voyage, and he never got drunk. He would buy a round or two of drinks and stow away a modest allowance of grog, just to prove he wasn't holding himself better than his shipmates, but he had never been known to acquire such a cargo of rum that he got out of trim. However, this peculiarity was known only to his intimates of the forecastle, while, as to his vast pride in

his calling, that was known only to himself. He was a thin, spare little man, with an alert, smiling, kindly, wistful face and a retiring disposition; in all his movements he was alert and precise; he was a model of neatness, even in his dungarees, and he could play the concertina better than most Italians. Whenever a shipmate died aboard a vessel in which Pop Bates happened to be shipped, the little man would invariably be called upon to play "Nearer, My God, to Thee" and "Lead, Kindly Light," at the brief burial service, and unless you saw him swinging the concertina you would have been willing to wager a month's pay that somebody was playing a church organ.

There are millions of capable but repressed men such as Pop Bates was when young Andy Royce decided, out of the generosity of his youth, to give the old man a chance, and, like all of his kind, all the little man needed was the opportunity; thereafter his ability manifested itself as inevitably as water runs downhill.

Andy Royce was the youngest representative of the tribe of Royce, which had been engaged in building, sailing, and owning ships on the western ocean for a century. They had a scarlet house flag, with a blue R on a white diamond, and time was when that proud emblem was no stranger in the ports of the seven seas. It was a family custom, hallowed by much precedent, that a male Royce had to be a master mariner before he could be a managing owner, so when young Andy got out of college his Yankee father took him down to a dock in Boston and pointed to a clipper ship, from whose main truck floated the family house flag.

"My son," he said, "that is my ship. Some day she will be yours. Learn to sail her. You will start in at the forecastle and work aft, and when the master of the *Southern Cross* says you can be trusted with a ship I'll build you the finest steel clipper that ever flew the American flag."

YOUNG ANDY performed his part of the contract, so the old man kept his word. He built for his boy the full-rigged steel ship *Halcyon*, twenty-

"*Get your duds and come aboard. You're first mate of the Halcyon*"

seven hundred and eighty-four tons net register, and loaded her with coal. She was Andy's first command, and he was very proud of her (and prouder of himself) when he sailed her from Delaware Breakwater around Cape Horn and up the Pacific to San Francisco in a smashing voyage that brought a smile to the grim face of old Royce and fame and fortune to the *Halcyon's* designer.

In San Francisco, after discharging her coal, the *Halcyon* was chartered for

First page for one of Kyne's short stories about sea captain "Pop" Bates

his publishers and his public exactly what they wanted.

Peter Bernard Kyne was born in San Francisco, California, to John and Mary Cresham Kyne. He had his only formal education in a one-room public school, from which, in his words, he "did not graduate at the age of 15." After leaving school he worked for his father's cattle business and attended six months of classes at a local business college. At sixteen he left the family farm for a town seven miles away and took a job as clerk in a general merchandise store, where he worked from six in the morning until nine at night for room, board, and twenty dollars per month.

Though he found that he "loved to sell things," he left the store after only nine months to join the army, lying about his age and bribing a corporal with five dollars to pass him on the eyesight test. An infantryman, Kyne saw action during a year of service in the Philippines in 1898-1899 and used this experience as the foundation for his first literary output. For seven years after leaving the army Kyne worked at several enterprises, much of the time for a wholesale-lumber and shipping firm. During that period Kyne became acquainted with San Francisco waterfront life, which was to provide him with still more characters and incidents for his fiction. His self-avowed talent for salesmanship was tested when he became the proprietor of his own haberdasher's shop in San Francisco and a lumber broker. Later in life he was given to investing heavily in gold mines, inventions, and manufacturing schemes, and he bought a farm, where he successfully raised purebred cattle and swine.

When he was fourteen, Kyne had read a story that he had written for a weekly assignment to the county superintendent of schools, who was visiting his class. The man was moved by Kyne's story about destroying an infirm horse and declared, "My boy, whatever you attempt in after life in the way of commercial pursuits will be a monumental failure, because God made you for a writer." During the year before his marriage to Helene Catherine Johnston on 2 February 1910, he decided to take the superintendent's advice to heart, and by 25 September 1909, when his short story "A Little Matter of Salvage" appeared in the *Saturday Evening Post*, he was a published writer. His first novel, *The Three Godfathers*, appeared in 1913. *Cappy Ricks* (1916), Kyne's third novel, introduced his best-known character, patterned after Capt. Robert Dollar, a bewhiskered

shipping tycoon who also owned extensive lumber interests. The subject of two novels and more than fifty short stories—as well as an unsuccessful play adapted to the stage by Edward E. Rose in 1919—this lively, skinny little tyrant, who is always portrayed sympathetically, is prone to overreaching himself and making mistakes and takes delight in beating his son-in-law, Matt Peasley, in business deals.

For example, in "The Go-Getter" (*Cosmopolitan*, November 1921; separately published in the same year) Ricks demonstrates his superior reading of a man's character to the skeptical Peasley. Cappy has supposedly retired from active involvement in his businesses, leaving Peasley in charge of the Blue Star steamship company and Mr. Skinner in charge of the lumber business. He cannot resist "interfering," however, especially when the younger men have trouble with an employee who has run off with thirty thousand dollars of company funds. Peasley defends his having appointed the embezzler to a position of trust by noting that the man had moved up in the company through hard and diligent work, but Cappy points out: "Henderson *was* a good man—a crackerjack man—when he had a better man over him." Further, when Skinner consoles them with the fact that Henderson was bonded, Cappy breaks in: "Not a peep out of you, Skinner. . . . Permit me to remind you that I'm the little genius who placed that insurance unknown to you and Matt." The story centers on Cappy's shrewd and seasoned judgment in giving employment to a young, aggressive war veteran, Bill Peck, when Skinner and Peasley are unwilling to try him. Cappy's decision proves sound, and Peck is triumphantly successful. The reader likes the irascible, but softhearted, Cappy Ricks whether he wins or loses, and he is regarded as Kyne's most fully drawn character, perhaps the only one who has any individual importance.

Kyne's "go-getter" businessman was only one among a gallery of character types he created: seamen, cowboys, lumbermen, miners, soldiers. There is little doubt that Kyne was catering to the tastes of the largest possible audience, for he wrote, "When an editor buys a story from me for a good price, he expects it to help his circulation. If I sell him a product which is not a good story or a serial with not as much pull as I can give it, I'm not an honest business man." Kyne's product is often a stereotyped character, a hero who is always daring, courageous, clever, and courteous—one who always wins in the end—in short, tuned to popular taste. Nevertheless, Kyne's heroes and heroines are not too obvious, and many remain appealing.

One of Cappy Ricks's clones is the sea captain "Pop" Bates, who is nicknamed "Reynard of the Seas" in the story of the same name, which appeared in the 7 October 1916 issue of *Collier's*. Bates displays down-to-earth American ingenuity, resourcefulness, daring, and, above all, honor. The setting is wartime on the high seas. Bates has bought a ship which he discovers to be on the British blacklist of enemy vessels. Consequently, even though the *Montara* now has an American skipper and American registry, British warships are likely to capture and impound the ship, depriving Bates of his investment as well as the cargo entrusted to him. His first ploy is to change the name of the ship and use counterfeit papers. During a journey from California to New York via the Straits of Magellan the ruse works in his first meeting with a British ship, but the disguise is dropped later in the voyage, and the *Montara* is intercepted by the same British vessel as it is steaming through the Straits of Magellan. In a daring bluff Bates and his crew capture the boarding party, and, as a thick fog rolls in to shroud the treacherous straits, the *Montara* comes about and the foxy Bates makes a break to the open Pacific. The getaway is successful, but a distress call from the British ship, which has run aground in pursuit, turns Pop Bates around. Obeying the mandates of a sailor's honor, he returns to his pursuer, frees the vessel from the reef, and tows it to safe harbor and the waiting British navy. He expects to surrender his vessel and cargo, but in recognition of Bates's honor and chivalry, the British navy removes the *Montara* from its blacklist.

It has been argued that Kyne uses racial stereotyping in many of his novels and stories to assert that Aryan and other "pure" races are superior to mixed races. Using a varied array of characters, frequently in ordinary, innocent, or superficial situations, Kyne often depicted, complete with dialect, national and racial stereotypes that were commonly accepted by the majority of his contemporaries. At a time when dialect stories were a staple of public speakers' jokes, Kyne's stereotyping did not arouse resentment among his readers, though readers today may be offended.

"The Thunder God" is one of Kyne's most obvious uses of "Mendel's Law" of racial and national supremacy. Old Man Hickman, owner of a

Front cover for the 1934 book about Kyne's best-known character, based on shipping and lumber tycoon Capt. Robert Dollar

steamship line, takes a liking to one of his seamen, Valdemar Sigurdson, "the damndest, finest, white man [he'd] ever seen." Sigurdson, a huge man of Viking descent, is taken under the old man's wing and educated as a ship's master, becoming Hickman's right-hand man. Years later, as Sigurdson is about to take Hickman's newest and finest ship on her maiden voyage, its turbines are sabotaged by a member of the crew. The villain turns out to be a Frenchman, a card-carrying member of the International Workers of the World. Sigurdson's rage at this "enemy of the world" is righteous, and he is prevented from killing the saboteur only at the intervention of Hickman, his son, and five other men. "Score one for Capitalism," exults Old Man Hickman, as the Viking and his ship are both saved.

Kyne's first collection of short fiction was *The Parson of Panamint and Other Stories* (1929), which reflects Kyne's fascination with the West, primarily the mining towns of California and Nevada. Chuckawalla Bill Redfield, an old-timer straight from the Western-genre tradition, provides Kyne's first-person narrator with the title story. Panamint, now a ghost of a town marked only by rusty tin cans, lives in the heart of Chuckawalla Bill, who reminds the narrator, "I was mayor o' that city oncet." To make the town respectable he arranged for a school to be established, and, although he is not a particularly religious man himself, he pushed for the establishment of a Protestant church. His search for a parson leads him to San Francisco, where he finds the Reverend Philip Pharo, a man as good in a fight as he is in front of a congregation. Bill takes an immediate liking to this somewhat unorthodox preacher and agrees to hire him as parson, providing he is not a Baptist: "I shore ain't no bigot ... but we got to haul our water in bar'ls twelve mile to camp." Pharo proves to be a most fortunate choice. Gamblers, drinkers, and women of easy virtue find a champion in the parson, who prefers people with their "souls turned inside out" rather than hypocrites who wear "their best side outside when they meet up with the minister."

In an effort to attract even more lost sheep, Pharo enters a gambling den and chastises Chappie Ellerton, the roulette dealer, for taking the Lord's name in vain. Good-natured banter turns into a friendly wager, with the parson agreeing to take a chance on the wheel if Chappie takes a chance by coming to church the following Sunday. Against the laws of probability, the "sky pilot" breaks the bank in an improbable series of no-limit bets, which the parson tries to lose, and Pharo becomes the covert owner of the gambling hall. Many men of the mining camp become regulars at Pharo's church, but word of the parson's gambling spreads among conservative members of the congregation, who demand Pharo's resignation. Finally, several members of the church vestry attempt to block the funeral services for a gambler in the church. The funeral entourage, including gamblers and prostitutes, enters the church after Chuckawalla shoots padlocks off the door, but the parson is brought to task for his unbecoming behavior. A new pastor is brought in to run the church; but Pharo continues with an outlaw ministry until he succumbs to "mining-camp pneumonia." Chappie Ellerton, not the new preacher, officiates at Pharo's funeral. The story ends with Chuckawalla Bill showing the narrator the parson's epitaph: "On July 20, 1884, he saved two men and a woman from everlasting

fire, receiving burns from which he never recovered."

Similar tales of unorthodox virtue are found in *Soldiers, Sailors and Dogs* (1936), a collection that demonstrates Kyne's continuing interest in sea stories, hunting tales, and military life. Drawing from his experiences during World War I as a captain in the 144th Field Artillery, Kyne had a special affection for soldiers. In "The Bluebird" (*Cosmopolitan*, February 1925) Kyne offers the story of a "repeater"—a soldier who reenlists without acknowledging his previous military record. "Old Peep Sight," the battery commander at a field-artillery training post, quickly recognizes that his new recruit, Private Callahan, has had previous military experience, but he tells him, "This is a new war, Callahan, and you're starting from scratch." Peep Sight learns that Callahan is Gene Paddock, a veteran of several campaigns with a distinguished service record until he served three years in an army prison and was dishonorably discharged for drinking and sleeping on sentry duty. Not able to return home, "because [he] had the kind of a mother [he] couldn't face with a dishonorable discharge," Paddock has allowed his mother to believe he had been killed in action at Luzon. Now he hopes to vindicate himself through honorable service.

Promoted to sergeant by the sympathetic battery commander, Callahan performs up to expectations and risks his life to save an old woman who has accidentally wandered into range of a practice barrage. The salvo also has damaged the old lady's shanty and beehives in a deserted area near the training camp. Calling her "Mother," Callahan vows to do all he can to repair the damage and help the old lady. Only later does he discover that the woman is actually his mother, whom he has not seen in twenty years. Callahan feels that he cannot reveal his identity, but just before he is to leave for action in the war, he tells her that he has "adopted" her as his mother, allotting his pay to her, leaving her his will, and signing over his army insurance to her. Callahan goes "down the path of glory—to the grave." After the war, when his former top sergeant visits Mrs. Paddock's home, now abandoned, he finds a gold star on Callahan's service flag and realizes that "the Bluebird at last got his honorable discharge from the service."

Kyne's most productive period was during the 1920s when many of his short stories were published in leading popular magazines. In addition to war and sea stories, he wrote business romances and hunting stories. He was part owner of a duck hunting club in northern California, and stories in *Soldiers, Sailors and Dogs*, such as "Point!" (*Cosmopolitan*, July 1922) and "Semper Fidelis" (*Cosmopolitan*, March 1923), reflect his interest in hunting dogs and their trainers. Also, for a number of years Kyne owned race horses and served a term as president of the California Jockey Club.

During the 1930s Kyne's health failed, and the reading public seemed to lose interest in the old-time heroics and typed characters in Kyne's stories. In 1939 a thirty-thousand-dollar judgment was rendered against him for failure to pay income taxes. When his last published novel, *Dude Woman*, appeared in 1940, it did not sell well. Two novels written in the 1940s were never published. An occasional short story or magazine article appeared in the late 1940s, and Kyne was involved in negotiations for sales of old stories to radio, movies, and television. While he traveled as widely as his health allowed, he continued to maintain his home in San Francisco. Kyne's wife died in 1956, and he died on 25 November 1957.

Peter Kyne's short stories and novels will never be listed among the most notable works of American fiction from the first half of the twenti-

eth century. Yet the honest, forthright courage of Pop Bates, the irascible common sense of Cappy Ricks, the aggressive confidence of Bill Peck, and the homespun Christianity of Philip Pharo are traits that his readers could admire and emulate. By writing heartwarming tales that reinforced traditional American virtues and reflected the popular culture of their times, Kyne became one of the most popular and prolific authors of twentieth-century fiction.

References:

Charles C. Baldwin, "Peter B. Kyne," in his *The Men Who Make Our Novels*, revised edition (New York: Dodd, Mead, 1924), pp. 317-320;

Carl Bode, "Cappy Ricks and The Monk in the Garden," *PMLA*, 64 (March 1949): 59-69;

Two San Francisco Writers: Inventory of the Papers of Dean S. Jennings and Inventory of the Papers of Peter B. Kyne, University of Oregon Library Occasional Paper Number 6 (Eugene, Oreg., August 1974).

Papers:

A collection of Kyne's papers, including more than 130 manuscripts and 3,400 letters dating from 1917 to 1957, may be found at the University of Oregon Library.

Jack London

(12 January 1876-22 November 1916)

Earle Labor
Centenary College of Louisiana

See also the London entries in *DLB 8: Twentieth-Century American Science-Fiction Writers* and *DLB 12: American Realists and Naturalists*.

BOOKS: *The Son of the Wolf: Tales of the Far North* (Boston & New York: Houghton, Mifflin, 1900; London: Isbister, 1902);

The God of His Fathers & Other Stories (New York: McClure, Phillips, 1901; London: Isbister, 1902);

Children of the Frost (New York: Macmillan, 1902; London: Macmillan, 1902);

The Cruise of the Dazzler (New York: Century, 1902; London: Hodder & Stoughton, 1906);

A Daughter of the Snows (Philadelphia: Lippincott, 1902; London: Isbister, 1904);

The Kempton-Wace Letters, anonymous, by London and Anna Strunsky (New York: Macmillan, 1903; London: Isbister, 1903);

The Call of the Wild (New York: Macmillan, 1903; London: Heinemann, 1903);

The People of the Abyss (New York: Macmillan, 1903; London: Isbister, 1903);

The Faith of Men and Other Stories (New York: Macmillan, 1904; London: Heinemann, 1904);

The Sea-Wolf (New York: Macmillan, 1904; London: Heinemann, 1904);

War of the Classes (New York: Macmillan, 1905; London: Heinemann, 1905);

The Game (New York: Macmillan, 1905; London: Heinemann, 1905);

Tales of the Fish Patrol (New York: Macmillan, 1905; London: Heinemann, 1906);

Moon-Face and Other Stories (New York: Macmillan, 1906; London: Heinemann, 1906);

White Fang (New York: Macmillan, 1906; London: Methuen, 1907);

Scorn of Women (New York: Macmillan, 1906; London: Macmillan, 1907);

Before Adam (New York: Macmillan, 1907; London: Werner Laurie, 1908);

Love of Life and Other Stories (New York: Macmillan, 1907; London: Everett, 1908);

Jack London

The Road (New York: Macmillan, 1907; London: Mills & Boon, 1914);

The Iron Heel (New York: Macmillan, 1908; London: Everett, 1908);

Martin Eden (New York: Macmillan, 1909; London: Heinemann, 1910);

Lost Face (New York: Macmillan, 1910; London: Mills & Boon, 1915);

Revolution and Other Essays (New York: Macmillan, 1910; London: Mills & Boon, 1920);

Burning Daylight (New York: Macmillan, 1910; London: Heinemann, 1911);

Theft: A Play in Four Acts (New York: Macmillan, 1910);

When God Laughs and Other Stories (New York: Macmillan, 1911; London: Mills & Boon, 1912);

Adventure (London: Nelson, 1911; New York: Macmillan, 1911);

The Cruise of the Snark (New York: Macmillan, 1911; London: Mills & Boon, 1913);

South Sea Tales (New York: Macmillan, 1911; London: Mills & Boon, 1912);

The House of Pride and Other Tales of Hawaii (New York: Macmillan, 1912; London: Mills & Boon, 1914);

A Son of the Sun (Garden City, N.Y.: Doubleday, Page, 1912; London: Mills & Boon, 1913);

Smoke Bellew (New York: Century, 1912; London: Mills & Boon, 1913);

The Night-Born (New York: Century, 1913; London: Mills & Boon, 1916);

The Abysmal Brute (New York: Century, 1913; London: Newnes, 1914);

John Barleycorn (New York: Century, 1913; London: Mills & Boon, 1914);

The Valley of the Moon (New York: Macmillan, 1913; London: Mills & Boon, 1913);

The Strength of the Strong (New York: Macmillan, 1914; London: Mills & Boon, 1917);

The Mutiny of the Elsinore (New York: Macmillan, 1914; London: Mills & Boon, 1915);

The Scarlet Plague (New York: Macmillan, 1915; London: Mills & Boon, 1915);

The Jacket (London: Mills & Boon, 1915); republished as *The Star Rover* (New York: Macmillan, 1915);

The Acorn-Planter: A California Forest Play (New York: Macmillan, 1916; London: Mills & Boon, 1916);

The Little Lady of the Big House (New York: Macmillan, 1916; London: Mills & Boon, 1916);

The Turtles of Tasman (New York: Macmillan, 1916; London: Mills & Boon, 1917);

The Human Drift (New York: Macmillan, 1917; London: Mills & Boon, 1919);

Jerry of the Islands (New York: Macmillan, 1917; London: Mills & Boon, 1917);

Michael Brother of Jerry (New York: Macmillan, 1917; London: Mills & Boon, 1917);

The Red One (New York: Macmillan, 1918; London: Mills & Boon, 1919);

Hearts of Three (London: Mills & Boon, 1918; New York: Macmillan, 1920);

On the Makaloa Mat (New York: Macmillan, 1919); republished as *Island Tales* (London: Mills & Boon, 1920);

Dutch Courage and Other Stories (New York: Macmillan, 1922; London: Mills & Boon, 1923);

The Assassination Bureau, Ltd. (New York: McGraw-Hill, 1963; London: Deutsch, 1964);

Jack London Reports: War Correspondence, Sports Articles, and Miscellaneous Writings, edited by King Hendricks and Irving Shepard (Garden City, N.Y.: Doubleday, 1970);

Curious Fragments: Jack London's Tales of Fantasy Fiction, edited by Dale L. Walker (Port Washington, N.Y.: Kennikat, 1975);

No Mentor But Myself: A Collection of Articles, Essays, Reviews and Letters, by Jack London, on Writing and Writers, edited by Walker (Port Washington, N.Y.: Kennikat, 1979);

A Klondike Trilogy: Three Uncollected Stories, edited by Earle Labor (Santa Barbara, Cal.: Neville, 1983);

With a Heart Full of Love: Jack London's Presentation Inscriptions to the Women in His Life, edited by Sal Noto (Berkeley: Twowindows Press, 1986).

OTHER: H. D. Umbstaetter, *The Red Hot Dollar and Other Stories from THE BLACK CAT,* introduction by London (Boston: Page, 1911);

The Cry for Justice: An Anthology of the Literature of Social Protest, edited by Upton Sinclair, introduction by London (Philadelphia: John C. Winston, 1915);

Francis A. Cox, *What Do You Know About a Horse?,* foreword by London (London: G. Bell & Sons, 1915);

Osias L. Schwarz, *General Types of Superior Men: A Philosophical-Psychological Study of Genius, Talent, and Philistinism in Their Bearings upon Human Society and Its Struggle for a Better Social Order,* preface by London (Boston: R. G. Badger, 1916).

"No literary historian but sooner or later must reckon with Jack London," Fred Lewis Pattee asserts in *The Development of the American Short Story* (1923), for "he represented more than an individual: he was the product of a literary condition in America. To understand the opening years of the new century one must study Jack Londonism."

London and his first wife, Bessie Maddern

Since the publishing of Pattee's pioneering study two generations ago, Jack London has become universally acclaimed as one of the most dynamic figures in American literature. Sailor, hobo, Klondike argonaut, social crusader, war correspondent, scientific farmer, self-made millionaire, global traveler, and adventurer: London captured the popular imagination worldwide as much through his personal exploits as through his literary efforts. But it is the quality of his writings, more than his personal legend, that has won him a permanent place in world literature and distinguished him as our most widely translated author. The Danish critic Georg Brandes considered him the best of our new twentieth-century writers: "He is absolutely original," wrote Brandes, "and his style is singularly forcible and free from all affectation." Anatole France remarked that "London had that particular genius which perceives what is hidden from the common herd, and possessed a special knowledge enabling him to anticipate the future." More recently, the Russian scholar Vil Bykov, comparing London favorably with Tolstoy and Chekhov, has observed that it is the "life-asserting force" in London's writings and particularly the portrayal of "the man of noble spirit" which have "helped London to find his way to the heart of the Soviet reader." Among a number of contemporary European critics he is considered "possibly the most powerful of all American writers."

London was, in fact, a writer of extraordinary vitality. He pioneered in the literature of social protest and apocalypse as well as in the fiction of escape and adventure. He excelled in the "plain style": the terse, imagistic prose so well suited to the depiction of physical violence and to the stringent demands of the modern short story. The publication of "An Odyssey of the North" in the January 1900 *Atlantic Monthly* and of *The Son of the Wolf: Tales of the Far North* a few months later was like a draught of bracing Arctic air: "Except for the similar sensation caused by the appearance of Mark Twain's mining-camp humor in the midst of Victorian America, nothing more disturbing to the forces of gentility had ever happened to our literature," remarks Kenneth Lynn, "and it decisively changed the course of American fiction." London was a major force in establishing for the American short story a respectable middle ground between the saloon and the salon, and he trailblazed the way for the later generations of Ernest Hemingway, Ring Lardner, and Norman Mailer. During the first fifteen years of this century, the golden era both of the American magazine and of the American short story,

London dominated the literary marketplace as perhaps no author has done before or since: scarcely a month passed without the appearance of his name in the newspapers and of his stories in popular magazines such as *Cosmopolitan* and the *Saturday Evening Post*. In less than two decades he produced two hundred short stories and four hundred nonfiction pieces, fifty books on such varied subjects as agronomy, architecture, astral projection, economics, gold-hunting, penal reform, political corruption, prizefighting, seafaring, and socialism. His vitality seemed inexhaustible; yet he died before reaching his forty-first birthday, his body finally rebelling against the incredible pace he had forced it to maintain through sheer effort of will. In spirit his brief career was a dramatic epitome of America's "strenuous age"; in mythic terms, his spectacular rise from rags to riches was paradigmatic of the American dream of success.

In *The American Adam* (1955) R. W. B. Lewis has defined this central figure in New World mythology as "a radically new personality, the hero of the new adventure; an individual emancipated from history, happily bereft of ancestry, untouched and undefiled by the usual inheritances of family and race; an individual standing alone, self-reliant and self-propelling, ready to confront whatever awaited him with the aid of his own unique and inherent resources." This definition might have been personally tailored to suit London, who was born a "natural" child, literally if not happily "bereft of ancestry"; for his paternity has never been conclusively established. The biographical consensus is that his father was William Henry Chaney, a "Professor of Astrology" with whom his mother, Flora Wellman, was living as a fellow spiritualist and common-law wife in 1875. She named the child "John Griffith Chaney," even though Chaney had deserted her in a rage of denial when he learned of her pregnancy. On 7 September 1876 she married John London, a Civil War veteran and widower who had been forced to place his two youngest daughters, Eliza and Ida, in an orphanage while he worked as a carpenter. Evidently it was a marriage of convenience rather than of love, providing a father for the infant boy and a home for the two girls.

While the literal truth of London's paternity may never be definitely known, the psychological truth is evident: in his case particularly, the child was clearly the father of the man. Out of the circumstances of his childhood were shaped the essential attitudes of his adulthood, and throughout his mature years he compensated, both creatively and self-destructively, for what he considered to have been a deprived childhood. "My body and soul were starved when I was a child," he wrote; and he never fully outgrew his deep-seated resentment of his boyhood poverty and of his mother's detachment. Flora Wellman London was an unhappy, restless woman whose body had been dwarfed by a girlhood attack of typhoid fever and whose dreams of the genteel life had been aborted by the birth of an unwanted child. Too frail to nourish the infant herself, she had been forced to find a wet nurse, a black woman named Mrs. Virginia Prentiss, whose own baby had been lost in childbirth. What little maternal affection London received as a youngster, he got from his "Aunt Jennie" and from his older stepsister Eliza, not from Flora. Psychologically, one of the most significant factors in London's development was his conscious rejection of the occult, the supernatural, the mystical—all of which he associated with his mother's cold spiritualism.

His childhood loneliness led London at a very early age to seek companionship in the world of books. "I always could read and write," he claimed, "and have no recollection antedating such a condition. Folks say I simply insisted upon being taught." Washington Irving's exotically romantic *The Alhambra* (1832; revised, 1851) and Ouida's *Signa* (1875), the story of a peasant girl's illegitimate son who rises to fame as a great Italian composer, were among his early favorites—as were *The Voyages of Captain James Cook* (1842) and Horatio Alger's success stories. One of the great discoveries of his life occurred in 1885 when his family moved back to the city after several farming ventures and he found that he could check out books from the Oakland Public Library as fast as he could read them. "It was this world of books, now accessible, that practically gave me the basis of my education," he later wrote.

Other, coarser worlds also played notable roles in his education: the worlds of the gutter, the slum, the factory, the saloon, the sea. Although John London was a conscientious provider, his vitality had been sapped by war injuries and poor health, and his efforts to succeed in various storekeeping and farming enterprises were repeatedly thwarted by Flora's get-rich-quick schemes. Consequently, even as a grade-schooler, the boy "Johnny," as he was called, had been forced to help support the family, later attesting that "from my ninth year, with the exception

London with his husky, Brown Wolf, 1905

of hours spent at school (and I earned them by hard labor), my life has been one of toil." At first the work was part-time: delivering newspapers, setting pins in a bowling alley, sweeping saloon floors, and doing whatever odd jobs would bring a few extra pennies into the family budget. When he finished grade school, he went to work full-time in a West Oakland cannery, spending as many as eighteen hours a day at ten cents an hour stuffing pickles into jars. It was a traumatic ordeal, impressing upon him a lifelong loathing of physical labor. Years later that trauma was translated into art in one of London's most powerful stories, "The Apostate" (*Woman's Home Companion*, September 1906; collected in *When God Laughs and Other Stories*, 1911). Describing the plight of his protagonist–a teenaged factory slave significantly named "Johnny"–London wrote: "There was no joyousness in life for him. The procession of days he never saw. The nights he slept away in twitching unconsciousness. . . . He had no mental life whatever; yet deep down in the crypts of his mind, unknown to him, were being weighed and sifted every hour of his toil, every movement of his hands, every twitch of his muscles, and preparations were making for a future course of action that would amaze him and all his little world." That "course of action" was escape: just as London himself had done, the hero

of "The Apostate" suddenly deserts the tattered army of "work beasts," hopping a freight train to parts unknown.

The pattern of London's life, reflected in much of his fiction, might be viewed as a series of escapes–first from the drudgery of poverty, later from the monotony of work: a constant alternation between commitment and escape, routine and recreation, work and adventure. At the age of fifteen, after borrowing three hundred dollars from Aunt Jennie to buy a sloop from one of the hoodlums who made their living by raiding the commercial oyster beds in the Bay Area, "Jack" (by now he had disavowed his childhood name of "Johnny") achieved notoriety as "Prince of the Oyster Pirates." He followed this dangerous career for a year, until, apprehensive that like a number of his comrades he would wind up dead or in prison, he switched sides to become a member of the California Fish Patrol. Many of his escapades during these two years were later fictionalized as juvenilia in *The Cruise of the Dazzler* (1902) and *Tales of the Fish Patrol* (1905).

London's maritime adventures continued into the next year when, a few days after his seventeenth birthday, he shipped as an able-bodied seaman aboard the *Sophia Sutherland*, a sealing-schooner bound for hunting grounds in the northwest Pacific. This seven-month voyage provided the raw materials not only for his later novel *The Sea-Wolf* (1904) but also, more immediately, for his first successful literary effort: "Story of a Typhoon off the Coast of Japan," a prize-winning sketch published in the *San Francisco Morning Call* on 12 November 1893.

Subsequent experiences as "a work beast" in a jute mill and a power plant intensified his wanderlust: "The thought of work was repulsive," he recollected in his autobiographical treatise *John Barleycorn* (1913). "It was a whole lot better to royster and frolic over the world in the way I had previously done. So I headed out on the adventure-path again, starting to tramp East by beating my way on the railroads." At first he rode with the west coast contingent of Coxey's Army, a group of jobless men who marched on Washington, D.C., in 1894; after deserting the army at Hannibal, Missouri, he hoboed northeast on his own. Arrested for vagrancy in Niagara, New York, in late June 1894, he served thirty days in the Erie County Penitentiary, then headed back home, determined to raise himself out of "the submerged tenth" of American society.

London's tramping experiences, later recounted in a series of sketches entitled *The Road* (1907), were profoundly influential in the shaping of his career. First, they helped develop his natural talents as a raconteur: "I have often thought that to this training of my tramp days is due much of my success as a storywriter," he said. "In order to get the food whereby I lived, I was compelled to tell tales that rang true. At the back door, out of inexorable necessity, is developed the convincingness and sincerity laid down by all authorities on the art of the short-story." Second, they transformed him from what he termed a "blond-beastly" bourgeois adventurer into a socialist: "It is quite fair to say that I became a Socialist in a fashion somewhat similar to the way in which the Teutonic pagans became Christians," he recollected, "it was hammered into me." Finally, they convinced him that to raise himself from "the shambles at the bottom of the Social Pit," he must resume his formal education: consequently, he wrote, "I ran back to California and opened the books."

By 1895 London was reading Charles Darwin's *Origin of Species* (1859), Herbert Spencer's *First Principles* (1860-1862), and Karl Marx's *Communist Manifesto* (1848). At the first of the year he enrolled in Oakland High School and began contributing essays and sketches regularly

London in 1906

to the student literary journal, the *High School Aegis*. The following spring he joined the Socialist Labor Party, and his activism won him notoriety as Oakland's "Boy Socialist." In the late summer of 1896, after feverish cramming, he was admitted to the University of California at Berkeley. Forced to withdraw after one semester for financial reasons, he launched his writing career in earnest: "Heavens, how I wrote!" he recalled in *John Barleycorn*. "I wrote everything–ponderous essays, scientific and sociological, short stories, humorous verse, verse of all sorts from triolets and sonnets to blank verse tragedy and elephantine epics in Spenserian stanzas. On occasion I composed steadily, day after day, for fifteen hours a day. At times I forgot to eat, or refused to tear myself away from my passionate outpouring in order to eat." But all his efforts earned him nothing but rejection slips, and he was forced to return again to manual labor, this time in the laundry at the Belmont Academy, where Frank Norris had been a student a few years before. Escape came once again in July 1897 when he left for the Klondike gold rush with his brother-in-law, Capt. J. H. Shepard, who had mortgaged his home for their grubstake.

The Klondike was the turning point of London's career, acting as a catalyst for his creative vitality. "It was in the Klondike that I found myself," he confessed. "There you get your perspective. I got mine." Forced by an attack of scurvy to return home the next spring, he brought back no gold, but a wealth of experiences—not only his own but also those of the argonauts and sourdoughs with whom he had spent the richest winter of his life, experiences which the artistic genius could then transmute into marketable stories.

The fall of 1898 was a time of furiously intense work—an incredible outpouring of creative energy subsequently documented in his autobiographical novel *Martin Eden* (1909) as well as in *John Barleycorn*. This period, unlike the spring of 1897, was one of concentrated effort. London had found his métier; and having discovered that, he now found a market for his work. By January of 1899 he had broken into print in the *Overland Monthly;* within a year his fiction was appearing in the most prestigious magazine in the country, the *Atlantic Monthly;* and in April of 1900 his first book was released by the highly respected Boston publishing firm, Houghton, Mifflin. His rise to fame was truly meteoric. He was hailed by American critics as the "Kipling of the Klondike," and by the time his "instant classic" *The Call of the Wild* had appeared in 1903 he had become an international celebrity.

A reading public that had dieted on propriety and pap for more than a generation and whose appetite for strenuous action had been whetted by the colorful melodramas of Kipling and by the melodramatics of Theodore Roosevelt was hungry for the meaty fare of London's Northland. The opening sentence of "An Odyssey of the North" is the harbinger of a new kind of American fiction: "The sleds were singing their eternal lament to the creaking of the harnesses and the tinkling bells of the leaders; but the men and dogs were tired and made no sound." Others had already used the Klondike materials for profit, but their writings lacked the vividness and poetic cadence of London's style, which fused the vigorous and the picturesque. Furthermore, his was a fresh breed of fictional heroes—not the maudlin gentlemen of sentimental romances, but a "lean and wiry type, with trail-hardened muscles, and sun-browned faces, and untroubled souls which gazed frankly forth, clear-eyed and steady." Kip-

ling had introduced a kindred type the decade before, and London was quick to acknowledge his debt to the master of the "plain tale."

But the Klondike argonauts were not merely copies of those leathery cockneys and Irishmen in the Queen's Army whose individualism was subverted to the uses of British imperialism and whose sporting ethic was at times gratuitously cruel. London's Northland heroes were, by contrast, a ruggedly independent yet a remarkably compassionate breed who not only paid allegiance to the inexorable laws of nature and to the authority of conscience, but who also possessed a capacity for selflessness and comradeship very much like the agape of primitive Christianity. Theirs was a situational ethic, predicated on integrity, charity, and pragmatism. They had invaded a hostile land where the ruling law was "survival of the fittest" and where the key to survival was adaptability, but this did not simply mean physical fitness or brute strength: "The man who turns his back upon the comforts of an elder civilization, to face the savage youth, the primordial simplicity of the North, may estimate success at an inverse ratio to the quantity and quality of his hopelessly fixed habits," explains the narrator in his prologue to the story "In a Far Country" (*Overland Monthly,* June 1899; collected in *The Son of the Wolf*). "The exchange of such things as a dainty menu for rough fare, of the stiff leather shoe for the soft, shapeless moccasin, of the feather bed for a couch in the snow, is after all a very easy matter. But his pinch will come in learning properly to shape his mind's attitude toward all things, and especially toward his fellow man. For the courtesies of ordinary life, he must substitute unselfishness, forbearance, and tolerance. Thus, and thus only, can he gain that pearl of great price,—true comradeship. He must not say 'Thank you'; he must mean it without opening his mouth, and prove it by responding in kind. In short, he must substitute the deed for the word, the spirit for the letter."

This Code of the Northland, with the mystique of comradeship at its heart, is dramatized in "To the Man on Trail," the first of London's Klondike stories published by the *Overland Monthly* (January 1899). This Yuletide story is trimmed with the rich assortment of symbols, pagan as well as Christian, appropriate to the occasion. The setting is Christmas Eve in the cabin of the Malemute Kid, who dominates *The Son of the Wolf* collection as high priest of the Code. Gathered together are representatives from a dozen

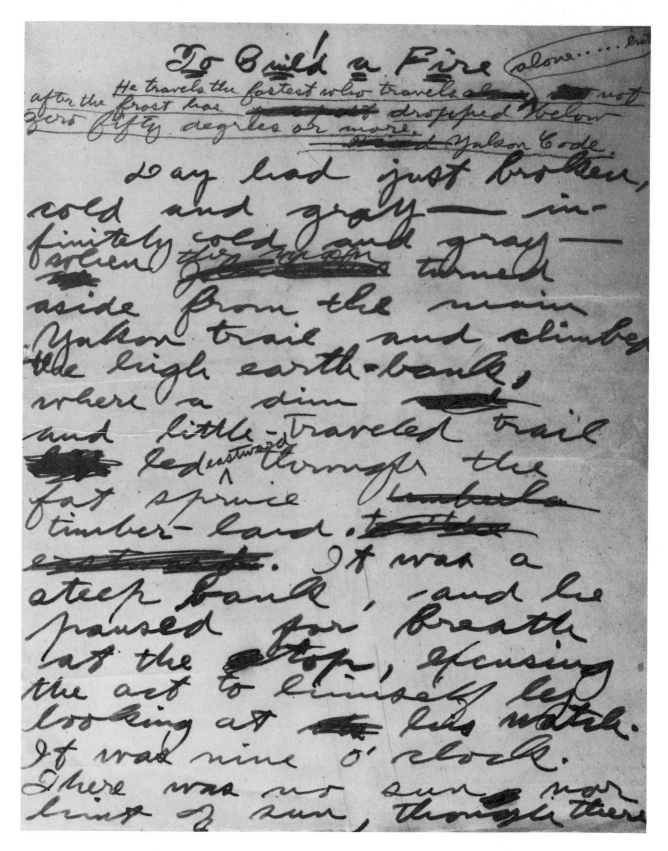

Pages from the manuscript for one of London's best-known stories (Henry E. Huntington Library and Art Gallery)

2.

was not a cloud in the sky.
It was a clear day, and
yet there seemed an
intangible pall over the
face of things, a subtle
gloom that made the
day dark, and that
was due to the absence
of sun. This fact did
not worry ~~the man~~.
He was ~~used~~ to the lack
of sun. It had been
days since he had
seen the sun, and
he knew that a few
more days ~~must the~~ ^cheerful orb,
pass ere that ~~cheerful orb~~
~~permit it but~~ due
south, would just peep
above the sky-line and
dip ^immediately from ~~sight~~ view.
~~The this~~ ^The man flung a look
back along the ~~way~~ he

different lands who are swapping yarns, reminiscing about home, and sharing the heady Christmas punch concocted by the Kid. At midnight the convivialities are suddenly interrupted by the jingling of bells, "the familiar music of the dogwhip, the whining howl of the Malemutes, and the crunch of a sled"; then comes "the expected knock, sharp and confident" and the entrance of "the stranger": "a striking personage, and a most picturesque one, in his Arctic dress of wool and fur. Standing six foot two or three, with proportionate breadth of shoulders and depth of chest, . . . his long lashes and eyebrows white with ice, . . . he seemed, of a verity, the Frost King, just stepped in out of the night. . . . An awkward silence had fallen, but his hearty 'What cheer, my lads?' put them quickly at ease, and the next instant Malemute Kid and he had gripped hands. Though they had never met, each had heard of the other, and the recognition was mutual."

The apparition suggests Saint Nicholas himself—but in a peculiar Klondike guise. He has been on the frozen trail for twelve hours running, and he is burdened not with the traditional sack of gifts but, instead, with "two large Colt's revolvers and a hunting knife . . . the inevitable dogwhip, a smokeless rifle of the largest bore and latest pattern." Jack Westondale, the stranger, explains that he is pursuing a gang of dog thieves. While the guest is eating the Christmas snack hospitably prepared for him, the Kid studies his face and finds him worthy: "Nor was he long in deciding that it was fair, honest, and open, and that he liked it. Still youthful, the lines had been firmly traced by toil and hardship. Though genial in conversation, and mild when at rest, the blue eyes gave promise of the hard steel-glitter which comes when called into action, especially against odds. The heavy jaw and square-cut chin demonstrated rugged pertinacity and indomitability. Nor, though the attributes of the lion were there, was there wanting the certain softness, the hint of womanliness, which bespoke the emotional nature."

Westondale apparently embodies all the vital traits of the Code Hero (including the notable feminine quality); and, while he is taking a quick nap before again taking to the trail, his authenticity is confirmed by the Kid: "Been in going on three years, with nothing but the name of working like a horse, and any amount of bad luck to his credit. . . . The trouble with him is clean grit and stubbornness." A short three

hours later the Kid rouses the young giant and—maguslike—sends him on his way with fresh provisions and wise counsel. Fifteen minutes later the festivities are stopped a second time—by a nearly exhausted stranger who wears the red coat, not of St. Nick, but of the Royal Canadian Mounted Police. He demands fresh dogs and information about Westondale, who is running—he discloses—not for, but *from*, the law after having robbed a Dawson gambling casino of forty thousand dollars.

Though the revelers have kept silent according to the Kid's example, they furiously demand an explanation after the Mountie has gone: Why has the Kid given sanctuary and aid to a man who has doubly violated the Code by robbery and by deception?

> "It's a cold night, boys—a bitter cold night," was the irrelevant commencement of his defense. "You've all traveled trail, and know what that stands for. Don't jump a dog when he's down. You've only heard one side. A whiter man than Jack Westondale never ate from the same pot nor stretched blanket with you or me. Last fall he gave his whole clean-up, forty thousand, to Joe Castrell, to buy in on Dominion. To-day he'd be a millionaire. But while he stayed behind at Circle City, taking care of his partner with the scurvy, what does Castrell do? Goes into McFarland's, jumps the limit, and drops the whole sack. Found him dead in the snow the next day. And poor Jack laying his plans to go out this winter to his wife and the boy he's never seen. You'll notice he took exactly what his partner lost,—forty thousand. Well, he's gone out; and what are you going to do about it?"
>
> The Kid glanced around the circle of his judges, noted the softening of their faces, then raised his mug aloft. "So a health to the man on trail this night; may his grub hold out; may his dogs keep their legs; may his matches never miss fire. God prosper him; good luck go with him; and"—
>
> "Confusion to the Mounted Police!" [they] cried, to the crash of empty cups.

Without belaboring his symbolism, London has provided a fitting epiphany as the conclusion of his Christmas carol; moreover, the situational ethic which informs the story was sure to appeal to a reading public less than one generation removed from frontier justice.

The mystique of comradeship is obversely dramatized in the fourth story in *The Son of the Wolf* collection, "In a Far Country." In this tale about "two Incapables" named Carter Weatherbee and Percy Cuthfert, who elect to spend the long Arctic winter snugly marooned in a deserted cabin rather than suffer the hardships of breaking trail with their comrades for the thousand remaining miles to Dawson, London reiterates the idea that survival is not primarily a matter of physical fitness.

Both Incapables are healthy, husky men, whereas Merritt Sloper, the wiry little argonaut who functions as a moral norm in this and in several other Klondike episodes, weighs less than a hundred pounds and is still yellow from the fever he had picked up in South America: "The fresh young muscles of either Weatherbee or Cuthfert were equal to ten times the endeavor of his; yet he could walk them into the earth in a day's journey.... He was the incarnation of the unrest of his race, and the old Teutonic stubbornness, dashed with the quick grasp and action of the Yankee, held the flesh in the bondage of the spirit." Sloper predicts the Incapables' fate as he and the remaining members of the party pull out from the cabin: "[Ever] hear of the Kilkenny cats?" he asks Jacques Baptiste, the party's halfbreed guide. "Well, my friend and good comrade, the Kilkenny cats fought till neither hide, nor hair, nor yowl, was left.... Now, these two men don't like work. They won't work. We know that. They'll be all alone in that cabin all winter, —a mighty long, dark winter."

At first, Sloper's prophecy appears to be wrong, for the Incapables seem determined to prove their compatibility; in addition, they are plentifully stocked with food and fuel. But, representatives of a degenerate society, they are fatally undersupplied in the moral staples needed for subsistence in the Northland. Weatherbee, formerly a clerk, is an unimaginative, materialistic fool who has joined the gold rush to make his fortune; Cuthfert, opposite as well as apposite, is an overripe cultural dilettante afflicted with "an abnormal development of sentimentality [which he mistakes] for the true spirit of romance and adventure." Moreover, the two men lack that "protean faculty of adaptability"–the capacity to slough off the callus of "self" along with the specious comforts of civilization–which is the most vital insurance against the dangers of the wilderness.

After an overeager show of industrious cooperation, they abandon the austere discipline of the Code. Their spiritual degeneration, as they succumb to each of the Seven Deadly Sins, is initially dramatized in their social relationship.

First, Pride is manifest in a foolish arrogance which precludes the mutual trust requisite to survival in the wilderness: "Save existence, they had nothing in common,–came in touch on no single point. Weatherbee was a clerk who had known naught but clerking all his life; Cuthfert was a master of arts, a dabbler in oils, and had written not a little. The one was a lower-class man who considered himself a gentleman, and the other was a gentleman who knew himself to be such. From this it may be remarked that a man can be a gentleman without possessing the first instinct of true comradeship.... He deemed the clerk a filthy, uncultured brute whose place was in the muck with the swine, and told him so; and he was reciprocally informed that he was a milk-and-water sissy and a cad."

Next appears Lust, as they consume with sensual promiscuity their supply of sugar, mixing it with hot water and then dissipating "the rich, white syrup" over their flapjacks and breadcrusts. This is followed by Sloth, as they sink into a lethargy which makes them "rebel at the performance of the smallest chore," including washing and personal cleanliness, "and for that matter, common decency." Accelerated by Gluttony, their moral deterioration now begins to externalize itself in their physical appearance: "As the sugarpile and other little luxuries dwindled, they began to be afraid they were not getting their proper shares, and in order that they might not be robbed, they fell to gorging themselves. The luxuries suffered in this gluttonous contest, as did also the men. In the absence of fresh vegetables and exercise, their blood became impoverished, and a loathsome, purplish rash crept over their bodies.... Next, their muscles and joints began to swell, the flesh turning black, while their mouths, gums, and lips took on the color of rich cream. Instead of being drawn together by their misery, each gloated over the other's symptoms as the scurvy took its course." Covetousness and Envy appear when they divide their sugar supply and hide their shares from each other, obsessed with the fear of losing the precious stuff.

The last of the cardinal sins, Anger, is delayed awhile by another trouble: "the Fear of the North.... the joint child of the Great Cold and the Great Silence," which preoccupies each man according to his nature. For the dilettantish Cuthfert, Fear manifests itself quietly and inwardly: "He dwelt upon the unseen and unknown till the burden of eternity appeared to be crushing him. Everything in the Northland had that crushing effect,–the absence of life and motion; the darkness; the infinite peace of the brooding land; the ghastly silence, which made the echo of each heart-beat a sacrilege; the solemn forest which seemed to guard an awful, inexpressible something, which neither word nor thought could compass." The coarser sensibilities of the clerk are more sensationally aroused in necrophilic nightmares: "Weatherbee fell prey to the grosser superstitions, and did his best to resurrect the spirits which slept in the forgotten graves. It was a fascinating thing, and in his dreams they came to him from out of the cold, and snuggled into his blankets. . . . He shrank from their clammy contact as they drew closer and twined their frozen limbs about him, the cabin rang with his frightened shrieks."

The symbolism grows richer as the drama moves toward its ghastly climax. Though London had not yet read the works of Sigmund Freud, his metaphors reveal an instinctive grasp of dream symbolism, particularly of the unconscious associations of sexual impotency and death. Cuthfert is obsessed with the absolute stillness of the phallic, arrow-shaped weathervane atop the cabin: "Standing beneath the wind-vane, his eyes fixed on the polar skies, he could not bring himself to realize that the Southland really existed, that at that very moment it was a-roar with life and action. There was no Southland, no men being born of women, no giving and taking in marriage. . . . He lived with Death among the dead, emasculated by the sense of his own insignificance. . . ." The metaphors of potency-life versus emasculation-death coalesce in the story's vivid climax, as Anger completes the allegoric procession of the deadly sins. Thinking that his companion has pilfered his last tiny cache of the symbol-laden sugar, Weatherbee attacks Cuthfert in the cold fury of insanity and severs his spine with an axe, thereby fulfilling the premonition of symbolic emasculation; he then falls heavily upon his victim as Cutherfert shoots him in the face.

The closing tableau–a grotesque inversion of the primal scene–dramatically reveals London's pre-Freudian intuitions: "The sharp bite of the axe had caused Cuthfert to drop the pistol, and as his lungs panted for release, he fumbled aimlessly for it among the blankets. Then he remembered. He slid a hand up the clerk's belt to the sheath-knife; and they drew very close to each other in that last clinch." Passages like this one apparently substantiate Maxwell Geismar's observation that London seemed to be more at home in the "world of dream and fantasy and desolate, abnormal emotion . . . than the world of people and society" and that "his best work was often a transcript of solitary nightmares." But such an assessment, notwithstanding the brilliance of Geismar's Freudian interpretation of London's life and work, is too limited. Though a considerable amount of his fiction does fit into this category, London's best is something more than "a transcript of solitary nightmares": it is the artistic modulation of universal dreams, of myths and archetypes.

Beyond the dramatization of such major themes as primitivism, atavism, Anglo-Saxonism, environmental determinism, stoicism, fair play, and compassionate humanism, what is perhaps most distinctive about London's Northland saga is the curious intermingling of naturalism and supernaturalism–of the materialistic and the mythic. "His gallery of supermen and superwomen has about it the myth atmosphere of the older world," says Fred Lewis Pattee. "It is not the actual North: it is an epic dream of the North, colored by an imagination adolescent in its love of the marvelous, of fighting and action, and of headlong movement."

Born into an age when the larger religious structures of Western civilization were tottering, reared in a home without any formal religious orientation, and negatively conditioned by his mother's weird spiritualism, London gravitated logically toward the secular doctrines of Marx, Ernst Haeckel, Darwin, and Spencer, describing himself as a revolutionary socialist and materialistic monist. But while he remained reasonably true to these convictions in theory, he betrayed himself time and again in fictional practice as an individualist and a philosophic dualist. And notwithstanding his assertions to the contrary, the best of his creative writing is informed by an instinctive mysticism, what C. G. Jung has called the "visionary mode." The following paragraph from "The White Silence" (*Overland Monthly*, February 1899), the first story in *The Son of the Wolf,* is exemplary: "The afternoon wore on, and with the awe, born of the White Silence, the voiceless travelers bent to their work. Nature has many tricks wherewith she convinces man of his finity,–the ceaseless flow of the tides, the fury of the storm, the shock of the earthquake, the long roll of heaven's artillery,–but the most tremendous, the most stupefying of all, is the passive phase of the White Silence. All movement ceases, the sky clears, the heavens are as brass; the slightest whisper seems

London with his daughters Bess and Joan, circa 1905

sacrilege, and man becomes timid, affrighted at the sound of his own voice. Sole speck of life journeying across the ghostly wastes of a dead world, he trembles at his audacity, realizes that his is a maggot's life, nothing more. Strange thoughts arise unsummoned, and the mystery of all things strives for utterance. And the fear of death, of God, of the universe, comes over him,—the hope of the Resurrection and the Life, the yearning for immortality, the vain striving of the imprisoned essence,—it is then, if ever, man walks alone with God."

London's Northland deity, like the "inscrutable tides of God" in Herman Melville's *Moby-Dick* (1851), is the polar opposite of the philanthropic God-in-Nature celebrated by such sentimental "exoticists" as Jean-Jacques Rousseau and Vicomte François René de Chateaubriand. Furthermore, in conveying the awesome ruthlessness of this deity, London drew his metaphors from the same mythic stockpile that Melville had used a half-century before him. Melville had fashioned his own unique metaphor, or "autotype," by combining two archetypes: the *fish*, an ancient life-symbol of divine creative force and wisdom, and *whiteness*, the emblematic all-color of universal mys-

tery and the metonymy for an impersonal, incomprehensible deity of infinite paradoxes and incommunicable truth. For London, as for Melville, whiteness becomes "the most meaning symbol of spiritual things, . . . the intensifying agent in things the most appalling to mankind."

But where Melville had combined whiteness with the fish, an archetype of creation and the life-force, London fused it with images of space, silence, and cold—and he thereby created an autotype more subtly terrifying than the warm-blooded whale. Thus conceived, London's "White Silence" is not merely a convenient setting for adventurous plots; it emerges as a dramatic antagonist charged with the special potency of universal dream symbolism—that is, of myth.

This potency is displayed nowhere to better advantage than in "To Build a Fire" (*Century*, August 1908; collected in *Lost Face*, 1910), a masterpiece of short fiction which has become one of the most widely anthologized works ever produced by an American author. The central motif is simple enough, as London himself suggested: "Man after man in the Klondike has died alone after getting his feet wet, through failure to build a fire." Plot and characterization are equally uncomplicated: a nameless *chechaquo* (newcomer to the Northland), accompanied by a large husky, is taking a day's hike across the frozen wilderness to join his partners at their mining claim. Although he has been warned by the old-timers against traveling alone in the White Silence, he is a strong, practical man, confident of his ability to cope with the forces of nature. Yet the reader senses from the outset that the *chechaquo* is doomed, as the narrator begins to weave his dark spell: "Day had broken cold and gray, exceedingly cold and gray, when the man turned aside from the main Yukon trail and climbed the high earth-bank, where a dim and little-traveled trail led eastward through the fat spruce timberland."

The key to the story's impact is not plot, but—as in much of London's best work—mood and atmosphere, which is conveyed through repetitive imagery of cold and gloom and whiteness: "There was no sun nor hint of sun, though there was not a cloud in the sky. It was a clear day, and yet there seemed an intangible pall over the face of things, a subtle gloom that made the day dark, and that was due to the absence of sun.... The man flung a look back along the way he had come. The Yukon lay a mile wide and hidden under three feet of ice. On top of this ice were as many feet of snow. It was all pure white.... North and south, as far as his eye could see, it was unbroken white, save for a dark hair-line [trail]."

London's story manifests in its stark eloquence many of those same elements that Aristotle indicated in his *Poetics* as requisite to tragedy. It is a representation of an action that is serious, whole, complete, and of a certain magnitude. The action is rigorously unified, taking place between daybreak and nightfall. The protagonist, neither an especially good man nor an especially bad man, falls into misfortune because of a tragic flaw, notably hubris—an overweening confidence in the efficacy of his own rational faculties and a corresponding blindness to the dark, nonrational powers of nature, chance, and fate: "But all of this—the mysterious, far-reaching hair-line trail, the absence of sun from the sky, the tremendous cold, and the strangeness and weirdness of it all—made no impression on the man.... He was quick and alert in the things of life, but only in the things, and not in the significances. Fifty degrees below zero meant eighty-odd degrees of frost. Such fact impressed him as being cold and uncomfortable, and that was all. It did not lead him to meditate upon his frailty as a creature of

temperature, and upon man's frailty in general, able only to live within certain narrow limits of heat and cold; and from there on it did not lead him to the conjectural field of immortality and man's place in the universe."

Here, as throughout the story, the narrator functions as the chorus, who mediates between the action and the reader and who provides moral commentary upon the action. The setting, a mask of the scornful gods, functions as antagonist. Aside from these, the only other character is the dog, who acts as foil or "reflector" by displaying the humility and natural wisdom which the man fatally lacks: "Its instinct told it a truer tale than was told to the man by the man's judgment. In reality, it was not merely colder than fifty below zero; it was colder than sixty below, than seventy below. It was seventy-five below zero.... The dog did not know anything about thermometers.... But the brute had instinct. It experienced a vague but menacing apprehension that subdued it and made it slink along at the man's heels, and that made it question eagerly every unwonted movement of the man as if expecting him to go into camp or to seek shelter somewhere and build a fire."

Also in keeping with the tragic mode is the sense of inevitability in the catastrophe which must befall the hero. Even when he builds his first fire for lunch, it is clear that the reprieve is temporary: "For the moment the cold of space was outwitted." There is no slackening of suspense, only a dreadful waiting for disaster. "And then it happened": the curt announcement is almost a relief. Still, knowing the cruel irony of the gods, the reader senses that although the man must surely die, he will first be mocked in his delusion of security. The man himself does not know this, of course, but he does know the gravity of his situation. Having broken through the snow crust over a hidden spring and wet his legs halfway to the knees, he realizes he must immediately build a fire: "He knew there must be no failure. When it is seventy-five below zero, a man must not fail in his first attempt to build a fire—that is, if his feet are wet. If his feet are dry, and he fails, he can run along the trail for half a mile and restore his circulation. But the circulation of wet and freezing feet cannot be restored by running when it is seventy-five below. No matter how fast he runs, the feet will freeze the harder."

The man is fully cognizant of these facts, for they have been told him by the sourdoughs, yet he remains obtuse to their significance. "The

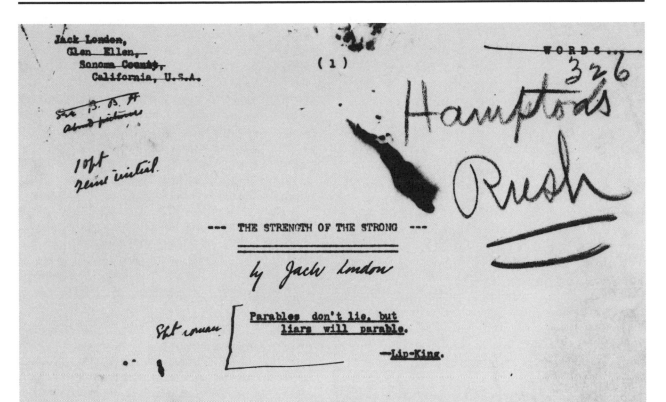

Jack London,
Glen Ellen,
Sonoma County,
California, U.S.A.

(1)

WORDS
326

Hampton's
Rush

--- THE STRENGTH OF THE STRONG ---

by Jack London

Parables don't lie, but
liars will parable.

—Lip-King.

Old Long Beard paused in his narrative, licked his greasy fingers, and wiped them
on his naked sides where his one piece of ragged bearskin failed to cover him. Crouched around
him, on their hams, were three young men, his grandsons, Deer-Runner, Yellow-Head, and Afraid-
of-the-Dark. In appearance they were much the same. Skins of wild animals partially covered
them. They were lean and meager of build, narrow-hipped and crooked-legged, and at the same
time deep-chested, with heavy arms and enormous hands. There was much hair on their chests
and shoulders, and on the outsides of their arms and legs. Their heads were matted with uncut
hair, long locks of which often strayed before their eyes, beady and black and glittering like
the eyes of birds. They were narrow between the eyes and broad between the cheeks, while their
lower-jaws were projecting and massive.

It was a night of clear starlight, and below them, stretching away remotely, lay range
on range of forest-covered hills. In the distance the heavens were red from the glow of a vol-
cano. At their backs yawned the black mouth of a cave, out of which, from time to time,
blew draughty gusts of wind. Immediately in front of them blazed a fire. At one side, partly
devoured, lay the carcass of a bear, with about it, at a respectable distance, several large
dogs, shaggy and wolf-like. Beside each man lay his bow and arrows and a huge club. In the
cave-mouth a number of rude spears leaned against the rock.

Setting copy for London's story that appeared in the March 1911 issue of Hampton's Magazine *(Jack London Collection
[#6240-l], Clifton Waller Barrett Library, Special Collections Department, University of Virginia Library)*

cold of space smote the unprotected tip, received the full force of the blow. The blood of his body recoiled before it. The blood was alive, like the dog, and like the dog it wanted to hide away and cover itself up from the fearful cold." But the man, working rationally and carefully, manages to build his fire and believes himself safe: "He remembered the advice of the old-timer on Sulphur Creek and smiled. The old-timer had been very serious in laying down the law that no man must travel alone in the Klondike after fifty below. Well, here he was; he had had the accident; he was alone; and he had saved himself. Those old-timers were rather womanish, some of them, he thought. All a man had to do was to keep his head, and he was all right." The irony is dramatic as well as tragic.

"Tragedy," according to Aristotle, "is a representation of an action that is not only complete but that consists of events inspiring fear and pity; and this effect is best produced when the events are at once unexpected and casually related." Moreover, the greatest tragedies are complex: the catastrophe is attended by a sudden reversal in the hero's situation to its opposite and by a discovery, or a change from ignorance to knowledge; and "of all discoveries the best is that which arises from the action itself, where the shock of surprise is the outcome of a plausible succession of events."

Being human and therefore fallible, London's protagonist makes a simple, human mistake: he builds his fire under a large, snow-laden spruce tree; and the heat precipitates a small avalanche that blots out the fresh blaze. Reversal and discovery are virtually simultaneous: "The man was shocked. It was as though he had just heard his own sentence of death. For a moment he sat and stared at the spot where the fire had been. Then he grew very calm. Perhaps the old-timer on Sulphur Creek was right. If he had only had a trail-mate he would have been in no danger now. The trail-mate could have built the fire."

From this dramatic climax, the story moves through a brilliant denouement toward its inescapable conclusion. Fighting off panic, the man tries vainly to build another fire; but his fingers are already dead from the cold. Next, he tries ineffectually to kill the dog, thinking he can warm his hands in its body. Then, panic-stricken, he tries running on his frozen feet until he falls exhausted into the snow. Finally, he grows calm and decides to meet death with dignity: "His idea

of it was that he had been making a fool of himself, running around like a chicken with its head cut off. . . . Well, he was bound to freeze anyway, and he might as well take it decently. . . . There were lots worse ways to die." In thus resigning himself to his fate, the man achieves a kind of heroic stature; and his tragic action inspires both pity and fear in leading his audience toward the cathartic relief prescribed by Aristotle.

> "You were right, old hoss; you were right," the man mumbled to the old-timer of Sulpher Creek.
>
> Then the man drowsed off into what seemed to him the most comfortable and satisfying sleep he had ever known. The dog sat facing him and waiting. The brief day drew to a close in a long, slow twilight. There were no signs of a fire to be made, and, besides, never in the dog's experience had it known a man to sit like that in the snow and make no fire. . . . A little longer it delayed, howling under the stars that leaped and danced and shone brightly in the cold sky. Then it turned and trotted up the trial in the direction of the camp it knew, where were the other food-providers and fire-providers.

With this concluding image the tone of the action has been transmuted from dramatic irony into cosmic irony. Gazing at the cold mockery of the heavens, one senses that one is not on the side of the gods and that the man's frailty is one's own. Such is the effect of London's artistry that few finish "To Build a Fire" without a subtle shiver of relief to be—at least for the moment—among the "food-providers and fire-providers."

"To Build a Fire" has established itself as a world classic, and while it is instructive to see how much of Aristotle's formula is dramatically reflected in this remarkable work of short fiction, the story's greatness does not depend on this formal coincidence; London himself was probably unaware of these nice parallels with Greek tragedy. The story is great because it derives its informing power from the common mystery that animates the plays of Sophocles and Aeschylus—and all great tragedians—and because it has articulated this mystery with such force that the reader becomes a mutual participant in the celebration of what Joseph Conrad called "the unavoidable solidarity" of human destiny. The ultimate source of tragedy is, as Herbert Muller points out, the simple fact that man must die; the great wonder is that, being the one animal who knows this fact, man is still capable of achieving dignity. So long as he possesses this heroic capability, "all is not vanity."

The modulating of naturalism into supernaturalism through the visionary mode is nowhere better illustrated than in *The Call of the Wild* (1903), composed during the winter of 1902-1903 when London had reached his full maturity as a prose craftsman. Read superficially, the familiar story of Buck's transformation from ranch pet to Ghost Dog of the Wilderness is entertaining escape literature, often relegated to the children's sections of libraries. However, mere tales of escape do not become world classics—and *The Call of the Wild* has become one of the great books in world literature, published in hundreds of editions in more than seventy languages. In the strictest sense, London's book (only thirty thousand words long) is scarcely a novel but, as Maxwell Geismar has classified it, "a beautiful prose poem, or *nouvelle*, of gold and death on the instinctual level." Its plot is animated by one of the most universal of thematic patterns: the Myth of the Hero. The call to adventure, departure, initiation through ordeal, the perilous journey to the "world navel" or mysterious life-center, transformation, and final apotheosis—these are the phases of the Myth, and all are evident in Buck's progress from the civilized world to the raw frontier of the Klondike gold rush, and then through the natural and beyond to the supernatural world. These rites of passage carry him not only through space but also through time and, ultimately, into the still center of a world that is timeless. London's style is modulated to conform to this transformation, becoming increasingly lyrical as Buck moves from the naturalistic world into that of myth; and the final chapter contains some of his most poetical writing: "The months came and went, and back and forth they twisted through the uncharted vastness, where no men were and yet where men had been if the Lost Cabin were true. They went across divides in summer blizzards, shivered under the midnight sun on naked mountains between the timber line and the eternal snows, dropped into summer valleys amid swarming gnats and flies, and in the shadows of glaciers picked strawberries and flowers as ripe and fair as any the Southland could boast. In the fall of the year they penetrated a weird lake country, sad and silent, where wild-fowl had been, but where then there was no life nor sign of life—only the blowing of chill winds, the forming of ice in sheltered places, and the melancholy rippling of waves on lonely beaches."

This weird land is appropriate to the "call to adventure" described by Joseph Campbell in *The Hero with a Thousand Faces* (1949), which "signifies that destiny has summoned the hero and transferred his spiritual center of gravity from within the pale of society to a zone unknown. This fateful region of both treasure and danger may be variously represented: as a distant land, a forest, . . . or profound dream state; but it is always a place of strangely fluid and polymorphous beings, unimaginable torments, superhuman deeds and impossible delight." This "fateful region" is a far cry from the pastoral California ranch where the story begins, and equally remote from the raw frontier of the Klondike gold rush. Buck's party discovers at last a fabulously rich placer-valley at the heart of this "zone unknown," where "Like giants they toiled, days flashing on the heels of days like dreams as they heaped the treasure up."

Buck's master John Thornton is killed along with the rest of the party, thereby releasing the hero to complete his transformation into the Ghost Dog of Northland legend—an incarnation of the eternal mystery of creation and the life-force: "When the long winter nights come on and the wolves follow their meat into the lower valleys . . . a great, gloriously coated wolf, like, and yet unlike, all other wolves . . . may be seen running at the head of the pack through the glimmering borealis, leaping gigantic above his fellows, his great throat a-bellow as he sings the song of a younger world, which is the song of the pack."

In Buck's escape from the bondage of civilization, one may see a psychological parallel with London's own yearnings; for during the composition of this story the author was evidently growing increasingly restive in his own domesticity.

As a younger man, London had experienced a number of affairs and one highly idealized romantic relationship with Mabel Applegarth, the frail aristocratic beauty later fictionalized as Ruth Morse in *Martin Eden*; none of these affairs, however, had satisfied his deep emotional need for female companionship. His rational solution to this problem was to marry a solid, sensible woman—not for romantic love, but for settling him down and rearing, as he hoped, "seven sturdy Saxon sons and seven beautiful daughters." With these objectives in mind, on 7 April 1900 he married Bessie Maddern, a good friend who had helped him pass the University of California entrance exams in 1896 by tutoring

Jack London (photograph by Arnold Genthe)

him in math. The marriage had seemed to make a good deal of sense at the time: London needed someone to tame his wildness, to give him a sense of roots and stability–in short, to domesticate the wolf in him. Maddern–a well-educated, maternally attractive young woman who had lost her fiancé in the Spanish-American War–needed someone to make a home for. They seemed well matched, even though, while good friends, neither had truly loved the other. Love apparently came to Bessie after the wedding–but not to Jack–and it became evident fairly early in the marriage that the personalities and the interests of the two were not really compatible. Moreover, the increasing attention London received as a new literary celebrity–and the presence of his

mother as a member of their household–put further strains on both himself and Bessie. A year or so after the marriage London fell in love with Anna Strunsky, a brilliant Stanford student he had met in 1899 and with whom he later collaborated on an epistolary dialogue about love published in 1903 as *The Kempton-Wace Letters*. Arguing behind the persona of a young economics professor named Herbert Wace, London–obviously trying to rationalize his own marriage–contended that romantic love was nothing more than "pre-nuptial madness." A wise union, he insisted, "is based upon reason and service and healthy sacrifice." But these fine qualities, as he painfully came later to realize, were not enough to sustain a marriage without love on both sides.

Writing to his friend Cloudesley Johns in the late summer of 1903, London remarked, "It's all right for a man sometimes to marry philosophically, but remember, it's damned hard on the woman."

Although Strunsky was implicated when Bessie filed suit for divorce in 1904, there is no real evidence that her affair with London was ever physically consummated; and she had apparently decided to end their romance when he left for England in the summer of 1902. They remained lifelong friends, but there is no passion in their correspondence after that summer, and Strunsky subsequently enjoyed a successful marriage to the wealthy socialist William S. Walling.

London had gone to England presumably en route to South Africa to report the aftermath of the Boer War for the American Press Association; that assignment was canceled, however, and he reported, instead, the aftermath of the Industrial Revolution that he had found in the London slums. After spending six weeks in the notorious East End (disguised as a stranded and broke American seaman), he produced *The People of the Abyss* (1903), "his masterpiece of nonfiction writing," according to sociologist Clarice Stasz: "[His style,] with its clipped, brisk rhythms, was radical for the time. . . . a style often erroneously credited to Hemingway, when in fact it took birth with journalists of the yellow presses—London, a leader among them."

London returned home from Europe in the fall of 1902, shortly after the birth of his second daughter, determined to make his marriage work; but despite his efforts, it was increasingly obvious that he and Bessie could not live happily together. In May of 1903 he took his family to Glen Ellen, California, a picturesque hamlet nestled in the heart of the Sonoma Valley (the "Valley of the Moon") fifty-five miles north of Oakland. There he rented a summer cottage from Ninetta and Roscoe Eames, the managing editor of the *Overland Monthly*; and that summer he fell in love with Mrs. Eames's niece Charmian Kittredge. Though she was four years older than he, and though she was not beautiful, Charmian was a comely, vivacious woman who not only knew how to make the most of her physical charms but also possessed an independent spirit that set her apart from the other young intellectuals, artists, and dilettantes who constituted "The Crowd" of London's acquaintances. The better he came to know her, the more it seemed to him that she was endowed with all the qualities he asso-

ciated with the ideal comrade and "mate-woman" he had long dreamed about. In late July, without revealing that he was in love with another woman, he announced to Bessie that he was leaving her. Shortly afterwards he moved his belongings from their Piedmont bungalow into an Oakland apartment rented for him by his boyhood friend Frank Atherton. So discreet were he and Charmian in their affair that it was more than a year before Bessie discovered the true identity of her husband's lover. In the meantime London was finishing his novel *The Sea-Wolf* (1904), using Charmian as the model for Maud Brewster, and putting his own romantic sentiments into the mouth of Humphrey Van Weyden.

In early January 1904, leaving the manuscript of *The Sea-Wolf* with Charmian and his poet-friend George Sterling to edit and proofread, he sailed on the SS *Siberia* for Yokohama, to report the Russo-Japanese War for the Hearst Syndicate. London managed to get closer to the front than any other reporter, but he was continually frustrated by the Japanese officials, who had imposed strict censorship on all military activities. "Personally, I entered upon this campaign with the most gorgeous conceptions of what a war correspondent's work in the world must be," London wrote. "I had read 'The Light that Failed.' I remembered Stephen Crane's descriptions of being under fire in Cuba. I had heard . . . of all sorts and conditions of correspondents in all sorts of battles and skirmishes, right in the thick of it, where life was keen and immortal moments were being lived. In brief, I came to war expecting to get thrills. My only thrills have been those of indignation and irritation." After six months of frustrated attempts to get into the action London returned home with a high opinion of the Japanese soldier's toughness but only disgust for the Japanese military bureaucrat's obtuseness.

The year following London's return from Japan was a crucially important one. In the spring of 1905, following his unsuccessful campaign for mayor of Oakland on the Socialist ticket, he took up permanent residence in the Valley of the Moon with Charmian and in June purchased the 130-acre Hill Ranch, which would ultimately grow into the 1,500-acre Jack London Ranch, or "Beauty Ranch," as he preferred to call it. During the same period he wrote some of his best tales, including "The Unexpected," (*McClure's Magazine*, August 1906; *Blackwood's*, August 1906; collected in *Love of Life and Other Stories*, 1907); "The Sun-Dog Trail" (*Harper's Monthly*

London sitting for a portrait by his friend Xavier Martinez

Magazine, December 1905; collected in *Love of Life*), and "All Gold Cañon" (*Century*, November 1905; collected in *Moon-Face and Other Stories*, 1906).

"All Gold Cañon" is one of London's most significant stories. Not only does it embody some of his best lyrical description and dramatic narrative; it also demonstrates his newly awakened ecological conscience. There had been little evidence of such concern in his Klondike stories; all his sympathies were with the brave souls who pit their heroic will against the awesome intractability of the White Silence. The gold itself is incidental, the moral fiber of the man himself being the important thing; but it is nonetheless a positive reward for those select few upon whom fate has endowed the rare combination of grit, determination, adaptability, good comradeship, and—most important—good luck. London's bonanza kings are almost invariably men of exceptional character who have also been blessed by special providence. Like their Puritan forebears they see in wildness not the preservation of the world, but profit for the individual who has strength of will to match force with force.

The main character in "All Gold Cañon," a pocket-miner simply called "Bill," is such a frontier type, possessing the best qualities of the North-

land heroes: courage, decency, industriousness, a sense of fair play, and humor. There is but one major shortcoming: he lacks the touch of feminine tenderness we find in such ideal protagonists as Jack Westondale of "To the Man on Trail," and, consequently, he regards nature as something to be exploited rather than nurtured. His materialistic spirit is clearly out of harmony with the spirit of the beneficent Southland wilderness, which London introduces in imagery that is both pastoral and feminine:

It was the green heart of the canyon, where the walls swerved back from the rigid plan and relieved their harshness of line by making a little sheltered nook and filling it to the brim with sweetness and roundness and softness. Here all things rested....

There was no dust in the canyon. The leaves and flowers were clean and virginal.... Sunshine and butterflies drifted in and out among the trees. The hum of the bees and the whisper of the stream were a drifting sound. And the drifting sound and drifting color seemed to weave together in the making of a delicate and intangible fabric which was the spirit of the place.

The quietness of this western "Sleepy Hollow" is a far cry from the terrifying silence of "the frozen-hearted Northland Wild," and its spirit is unmis-

London, his second wife, Charmian, and their dog, Possum, November 1916

takably Edenic (at one point London even refers to it as "the canyon-garden"): "It was a spirit of peace that was not of death, but of smooth-pulsing life, of quietude that was not silence, of movement that was not action, of repose that was quick with existence without being violent with struggle and travail. The spirit of the place was the spirit of the peace of the living, somnolent with the easement and content of prosperity, and undisturbed by rumors of far wars."

This spirit is abruptly ruptured by the pocket-miner, who bursts noisily upon the scene in a cloud of dust, the metal of his hobnailed boots clanging harshly against the rocks as he mechanically chants a hymn about "them sweet hills of grace." The man is immediately struck by the loveliness of the place, but his aesthestic sensibilities have been blunted by his hypermasculinity and by his materialistic motives, so that he can merely respond with cheap commercial clichés: "A pocket-hunter's delight an' a cayuse's paradise! Cool green for tired eyes! Pink pills for pale people ain't in it."

In London's new pastoral wilderness—so strikingly different from the Northland—the roles between Man and Nature are now reversed: it is Man who has become the savage destructive force, Nature the passive victim. Bill the gold hunter proceeds methodically to desecrate the virginal canyon, digging a series of scientifically calculated holes into the gently sloping hill until he has penetrated to the secret gold-pocket. But, while discovering his treasure, he has also brought death into the garden: the deep hole he has dug in gratifying his lust for gold almost becomes his own grave and does, indeed, become the grave of the dark stranger who attempts to ambush him after he has excavated his treasure. London's message is clear: modern man's heedless exploitation of nature is likely to produce fatal results.

Shortly after "All Gold Cañon" had been written, during the summer of 1905, Jack and Charmian read Joshua Slocum's *Sailing Alone Around the World* (1900)–and this book was the inspiration for what was to become the most highly publicized of all London's adventures: the cruise of the *Snark*. London, encouraged by his fiancée (they would be married that November, as soon as his divorce became final), decided that he would design his own boat for circumnavigating the globe. He had calculated that the boat would cost him about seven thousand dollars, but his careful planning had anticipated neither the San Francisco earthquake of April 1906 nor the subtler disasters of twentieth-century production standards. Consequently, the *Snark* cost five times the original estimate, was a half-year late in leaving Oakland, and was so badly botched in the building that extensive repairs were needed when the boat reached Hawaii in May of 1907. Moreover, the voyage, originally planned as a seven-year round-the-world cruise, lasted less than two years. By the fall of 1908, all seven members of the crew had been stricken with various tropical ailments–malaria, dysentery, Solomon Island sores–and, in addition to these, London himself suffered from a double fistula and a mysterious skin disease that caused his hands to swell and peel so badly that he could use them only with great pain. That December, on the advice of his physicians in Sydney, Australia, he called off the *Snark* voyage; and the following spring he and Charmian returned home, via Ecuador, Panama, New Orleans, and the Grand Canyon, arriving in Oakland on 21 July 1909.

While the *Snark* voyage had been disastrous from the standpoint of London's health and finances, it nevertheless provided vital new material for his stories. Hawaii, for example, had first struck him as a paradise of flower-swept valleys peopled by bronzed youths and golden maidens. "When Hawaii was named the Paradise of the Pacific, it was inadequately named," he wrote. "Hawaii and the Hawaiians are a land and a people loving and lovable. By their language may ye know them, and in what other land save this one is the commonest form of greeting, not 'Good day,' nor 'How d'ye do,' but 'Love'? That greeting is *Aloha*–love, I love you, my love to you. . . . It is a positive affirmation of the warmth of one's own heart-giving."

Further experience revealed, however, that Hawaii was, in truth, Paradise Lost: a lovely land whose economy had been commercialized, whose politics had been usurped, and whose inhabitants had been contaminated by the "civilized" haoles. "They came like lambs, speaking softly," remarks the title character in "Koolau the Leper" (*Pacific Monthly*, December 1909; collected in *The House of Pride and Other Tales of Hawaii*, 1912): "They were of two kinds. The one kind asked our permission, our gracious permission, to preach to us the word of God. The other kind asked our permission, our gracious permission, to trade with us. That was the beginning. Today all the islands are theirs, all the land, all the cattle–everything is theirs." Also theirs, insidiously shared with the Hawaiians, is the "rotting sickness" of civilization, the leprosy which has metamorphosed a beautiful people into hideous monsters with stumps for arms and gaping holes for faces: "The sickness is not ours," says Koolau. "We have not sinned. The men who preached the word of God and the word of Rum brought the sickness with the coolie slaves who work the stolen land."

But if Hawaii was Paradise Lost, the Solomon Islands, which the *Snark* reached in the summer of 1908, was the Inferno. "If I were a king, the worst punishment I could inflict on my enemies would be to banish them to the Solomons," London reminisced in *The Cruise of the Snark* (1911). "On second thought, king or no king, I don't think I'd have the heart to do it." He was drawing from first-hand experience when he wrote that in the Solomons "fever and dysentery are perpetually on the walk about, . . . loathsome skin diseases abound, . . . the air is saturated with a poison that bites into every pore, cut, or abrasion and plants malignant ulcers, [and] many strong men who escape dying there return as wrecks to their own countries." It was this region, rather than the Klondike, that inspired London's bitterest naturalistic writing. Here the wilderness-as-Eden symbolism is wholly inverted. Unlike the golden youths of Hawaii, the Solomon Islanders are ugly myrmidons of the Prince of Blackness himself–"a wild lot, with a hearty appetite for

Caricature of London drawn by James Montgomery Flagg for Charmian London's 1921 biography of her husband

human flesh and fad for collecting human heads." The moral effect of this rotting green hell, unlike the Northland, is to bring out the worst in those who survive. Among the natives the "highest instinct of sportsmanship is to catch a man with his back turned and to smite him a cunning blow with a tomahawk that severs the spinal column at the base of the brain. It is equally true that on some islands, such as Malaita, the profit and loss account of social intercourse is calculated in homicides." The white man is reduced to like savagery: "I've been in the tropics too long," confesses a character in *A Son of the Sun* (1912), London's series of David Grief stories. "I'm a sick man, a damn sick man. And the whiskey, and the sun, and the fever have made me sick in morals, too. Nothing's too mean and too low for me now, and I can understand why the niggers eat each other, and take heads, and such things. I could do it myself."

Occasionally, London's dark irony assumes the form of a grim poetic justice in his Melane-

sian tales, as in the story "Mauki" (*Hampton's Magazine*, December 1909; collected in *South Sea Tales*, 1911). The protagonist is an inversion of the stereotyped hero: "He weighed one hundred and ten pounds. His hair was kinky and negroid, and he was black. He was peculiarly black. He was neither blue-black nor purple-black, but plum-black. His name was Mauki, and he was the son of a chief." His appearance belies his sinister heroism: "There was no strength nor character in the jaws, forehead, and nose. In the eyes only could be caught any hint of the unknown quantities that were so large a part of his make-up and that other persons could not understand. These unknown quantities were pluck, pertinacity, fearlessness, imagination, and cunning; and when they found expression in some consistent and striking action, those about him were astounded."

Mauki's antagonist is Max Bunster, a hulking, psychopathic German whose principal delight is beating cripples, old men, and defenseless blacks. Bunster symbolizes the inevitable white man at his degenerate worst: "Semi-madness would be a charitable statement of his condition. He was a bully and a coward, and a thrice-bigger savage than any savage on the island. Being a coward, his brutality was of the cowardly order." "Mauki," a racial chiaroscuro, presents a dramatic tableau of the white man's sadistic cruelty juxtaposed against the black man's primitive capacities for endurance and revenge. Theirs is an unwholesome "marriage" like that of Cuthfert and Weatherbee in London's early Klondike story: "For better or worse, Bunster and he were tied together. Bunster weighed two hundred pounds. Mauki weighed one hundred and ten. Bunster was a degenerate brute. But Mauki was a primitive savage. While both had wills and ways of their own." Bunster finds many ways to torment the black–depriving him of his tobacco allowance, beating his head against the wall, knocking out his teeth, "vaccinating" him with the live end of a cigar, as examples; but his most ingenious method of torture is "caressing" his servant with a mitten made of ray-fish skin: "The skin of a shark is like sandpaper, but the skin of a ray fish is like a rasp. In the South Seas the natives use it as a wood file in smoothing down canoes and paddles. . . . The first time he tried it on Mauki, with one sweep of the hand it fetched the skin off his back from neck to armpit. Bunster was delighted."

Mauki endures this treatment for week after week, but his chance for retribution finally comes when Bunster is stricken with a severe case of black-water fever. After the worst of the illness has passed, leaving the white man enervated and bedridden, Mauki carefully provisions a boat for his escape and then returns to bid farewell to his tormentor:

> The house deserted, he entered the sleeping-room, where the trader lay in a doze. Mauki first removed the revolvers, then placed the ray fish mitten on his hand. Bunster's first warning was a stroke of the mitten that removed the skin the full length of his nose.
>
> "Good fella, eh?" Mauki grinned, between two strokes, one of which swept the forehead bare and the other of which cleaned off one side of his face. "Laugh, damn you, laugh." . . .
>
> When Mauki was done, he carried the boat compass and all the rifles and ammunition down to the cutter, which he proceeded to ballast with cases of tobacco. It was while engaged in this that a hideous, skinless thing came out of the house and ran screaming down the beach till it

fell in the sand and mowed and gibbered under the scorching sun. Mauki looked toward it and hesitated. Then he went over and removed the head, which he wrapped in a mat and stowed in the stern-locker of the cutter.

The irony is dark but clear: Bunster has paid for his moral callousness by having his thick hide removed entirely, and his sadistic head has become the trophy of its principal victim.

If the Solomons can be said to have had any salutary effect on London, it was perhaps to convince him that the Eden he sought was not halfway round the globe but in his own backyard. "I also have a panacea," he confessed after suffering through the hellish ailments inflicted on him and his crew by the tropics. "It is California. I defy any man to get a Solomon Island sore in California."

His ranch in the Valley of the Moon seemed, indeed, to be the panacea London needed after the *Snark* cruise; and for awhile after returning home he thrived as he devoted his time and energy to fulfilling his agrarian dream. "I believe the soil is our one indestructible asset," he said. "I am rebuilding worn-out hillside lands that were worked out and destroyed by our wasteful California farmers. . . . Everything I build is for the years to come." Between 1909 and 1916 he increased the size of "Beauty Ranch" to fourteen hundred acres, one of the largest in the Sonoma Valley; and during those seven years he came to be regarded by the agricultural experts as "one of California's leading farmers," whose ranch was "one of the best in the country." By combining modern agronomy with the wisdom of Oriental agriculture (such as terracing, drainage, and tillage), he succeeded in growing bumper crops of prunes, grapes, and alfalfa on land that had been abandoned by previous owners. He built the first concrete-block silo in California and constructed a "pig palace" which was a model of sanitation and efficiency. His livestock regularly took high honors in the county and state fairs and brought top breeding prices. One of the finest tributes he ever received was that by the famous horticulturist Luther Burbank in his autobiographical reminiscence *The Harvest of Years* (1927): "Jack London was a big healthy boy with a taste for serious things, but never cynical, never bitter, always good-humored and humorous, as I saw him, and with fingers and heart equally sensitive when he was in my gardens."

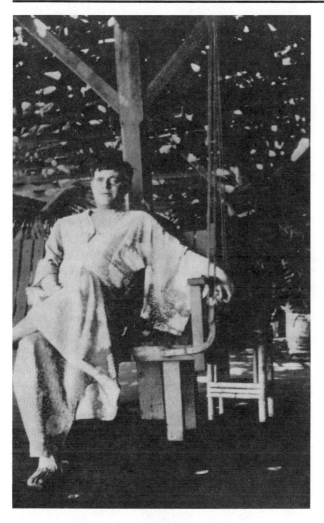

London in Honolulu, 1916

During the next six years following his return from the *Snark* voyage, London produced fewer short stories, devoting his energies to the building of Beauty Ranch and deriving his income mainly from novel-writing. He had working arrangements during this period with both *Cosmopolitan* and the *Saturday Evening Post* for the serialization of his longer works before their publication in book form. He seemed to be tireless, but the various ailments he had suffered in the tropics had evidently left his body–particularly his kidneys–permanently damaged. While he tried to maintain a vigorous public image, his health was clearly failing from 1913 onward: the symptoms of uremia–edema, swollen ankles, bloated body, kidney stones, ghouty rheumatism– were increasingly apparent. Yet he refused to heed the warnings of his physician that he must restrict his diet and get more rest. He cut his consumption of alcohol drastically, but he kept on

smoking heavily, more than two packs of cigarettes a day. He spent several months in Hawaii in 1915 and 1916, trying to recapture his lost health in that benevolent climate; but his body continued to deteriorate.

Paradoxically, even as his health failed, London's creative energies were once more renewed; and during the last half-year of his life he not only returned to short-story writing but brought to that craft a significant new element. While in Hawaii in the spring of 1916, he discovered the recently translated work of Jung and was immediately enthralled: "I tell you I am standing on the edge of a world so new, so terrible, so wonderful, that I am almost afraid to look over into it," he announced to Charmian. Suddenly, the Polynesian myths he had listened to with good-natured disbelief over the past several years came to life within the Jungian context of "racial memory" and "the archetypes of the collective unconscious." The literary results of this new discovery were a series of extraordinary stories written during the last six months of his life, published posthumously in *The Red One* (1918) and *On the Makaloa Mat* (1919), and signifying not only an advance in his own work but a new dimension in twentieth-century literature: London became the first American fictionist to make use of Jung's theories consciously as well as creatively. "The Water Baby" (*Cosmopolitan*, September 1918), for example, involves a dialogue between the world-weary narrator, John Lakana (the Hawaiian name for London), and Kohokumu, an ancient Hawaiian diver who claims the sea as his true mother. " 'But listen, O Young Wise One, to my elderly wisdom,' " the old man admonishes his skeptical listener:

"This I know: as I grow old I seek less for the truth from without me, and find more of the truth from within me. Why have I thought of my return to my mother and of my rebirth from my mother into the sun? You do not know. I do not know, save that, without whisper of man's voice or printed word, without prompting from otherwhere, this thought has arisen from within me, from the deeps of me that are as deep as the sea. . . . Is this thought that I have thought a dream?"

"Perhaps it is you that are a dream," I laughed. . . .

"There is much more in dreams that we know," he assured me with great solemnity. "Dreams go deep, all the way down, maybe to before the beginning. . . ."

London himself, the self-avowed materialistic monist, was evidently undergoing a sea-change during the last six months of his life, coming to terms at last with those nonrational psychic elements he had so rigorously rejected in his earlier years. He finished "The Water Baby" on 2 October 1916; seven weeks later, his meteoric career was ended by a fatal attack of a "gastrointestinal type of uraemia." In his copy of Jung, Charmian reports, he had underscored the following biblical quotation: "Think not carnally or thou art carnal, but think symbolically and then thou art spirit."

The nation mourned London's death as that of one of its heroes, the newspapers allotting more space to him than to Francis Joseph I, the Emperor of Austria, who had passed away on the preceding evening of 21 November. Yet, despite this enormous popularity, Joan Sherman remarks, "when he died his rating as an artist among pre-eminent men of letters was zero." William Dean Howells, who had encouraged such other young writers as Stephen Crane and Frank Norris, never so much as mentioned the name of Jack London in his hundreds of literary reviews and essays. "Jack London's reputation in America exemplifies the split between 'high' and 'low' culture," Sherman writes; and London was the victim of "critical standards established by the New England Sages and their New York heirs in 'The Age of Innocence,' 'The Age of Decorum,' 'The Genteel Decades,' 'The Purple Cow Period'–as the years from 1870 through the early 1900's were variously called." Those same critical standards were implicit in Arthur Hobson Quinn's attempt to write London's literary epitaph in 1936: "It is almost certain that his vogue is passing, for there is something impermanent in the very nature of the literature of violence." The New Critics of the succeeding generation–attuned to the verbal complexities of writers such as Henry James and William Faulkner–were equally willing to see London buried and forgotten. London's name was discreetly expunged from the college textbooks while such classics as *The Call of the Wild* and "To Build a Fire" were relegated to junior high school classes.

But a change in London's reputation began in the 1960s with the publication of three important books by reputable scholars: *Letters from Jack London* (1965), edited by King Hendricks and Irving Shepard; Hensley C. Woodbridge, John London, and George H. Tweney's comprehensive *Jack London: A Bibliography* (1966); and Franklin

Walker's *Jack London and the Klondike: The Genesis of an American Writer* (1966). At the same time the publication of the *Jack London Newsletter*, edited by Woodbridge, provided a forum for London scholars as well as buffs. The London "nascence" was readily apparent in the following decade with the publication of book-length critical studies by Earle Labor and James McClintock, along with additional bibliographies by Dale Walker, James Sisson, and Joan Sherman.

In 1976, the centennial of London's birth as well as the nation's bicentennial, three scholarly journals–*Modern Fiction Studies*, *Western American Literature*, and *The Pacific Historian*–confirmed his academic reputation by issuing special Jack London numbers. That reputation has been enhanced still further during the past ten years through the publication of major biographical studies by Russ Kingman and Andrew Sinclair, and of significant scholarly and critical books by David Mike Hamilton, Carolyn Johnston, and Charles N. Watson, Jr. And in January 1986 the United States Postal Service provided official national recognition by issuing a Jack London stamp in its Great Americans series.

Such recognition would have been as gratifying perhaps to Fred Lewis Pattee as to London himself; for it was Pattee who a half-century ago remarked that "To study Jack London is to be impressed first of all with his Americanism. He was as indigenous as Mark Twain." Truly, no other American writer, except possibly Twain, has so captivated the vital imagination of his countrymen. And none has made a greater contribution to the development of the American short story.

Letters:
Letters from Jack London, edited by King Hendricks and Irving Shepard (New York: Odyssey, 1965);
The Letters of Jack London, edited by Earle Labor, Robert C. Leitz III, and I. Milo Shepard, 3 volumes (Stanford: Stanford University Press, 1988).

Bibliographies:
Hensley C. Woodbridge, John London, and George H. Tweney, *Jack London: A Bibliography* (Georgetown, Cal.: Talisman, 1966; enlarged edition, Millwood, N.Y.: Kraus, 1973);
Dale L. Walker and James E. Sisson III, *The Fiction of Jack London: A Chronological Bibliogra-*

phy (El Paso: Texas Western University Press, 1972);

Joan Sherman, *Jack London: A Reference Guide* (Boston: G. K. Hall, 1977).

Biographies:

Charmian K. London, *The Book of Jack London*, 2 volumes (New York: Century, 1921);

Irving Stone, *Sailor on Horseback: The Biography of Jack London* (Boston: Houghton Mifflin, 1938);

Joan London, *Jack London and His Times: An Unconventional Biography* (New York: Doubleday, Doran, 1939);

Richard O'Connor, *Jack London: A Biography* (Boston: Little, Brown, 1964);

Andrew Sinclair, *Jack: A Biography of Jack London* (New York: Harper & Row, 1977);

Russ Kingman, *A Pictorial Life of Jack London* (New York: Crown, 1979).

References:

Gorman Beauchamp, *Jack London* (Mercer Island, Wash.: Starmont House, 1984);

Richard W. Etulain, *Jack London on the Road: The Tramp Diary and Other Hobo Writings* (Logan: Utah State University, 1979);

Philip Foner, ed., *Jack London: American Rebel* (New York: Critical Press, 1947);

Maxwell Geismar, "Jack London: The Short Cut," in *Rebels and Ancestors; the American Novel, 1890-1915* (Boston: Houghton Mifflin, 1953);

David Mike Hamilton, *"The Tools of My Trade": Annotated Books in Jack London's Library* (Seattle: University of Washington Press, 1987);

Joan D. Hedrick, *Solitary Comrade: Jack London and His Work* (Chapel Hill: University of North Carolina Press, 1982);

Carolyn Johnston, *Jack London—An American Radical?* (Westport, Conn.: Greenwood Press, 1984);

Earle Labor, *Jack London* (New York: Twayne, 1974);

James Lundquist, *Jack London: Adventures, Ideas, and Fiction* (New York: Ungar, 1987);

James I. McClintock, *White Logic: Jack London's Short Stories* (Grand Rapids, Mich.: Wolf House Books, 1975);

Ray Wilson Ownbey, ed., *Jack London: Essays in Criticism* (Santa Barbara, Cal.: Peregrine Smith, 1978);

Fred Lewis Pattee, *The Development of the American Short Story* (New York: Harper, 1923);

Jacqueline Tavernier-Courbin, ed., *Critical Essays on Jack London* (Boston: G. K. Hall, 1983);

Franklin Walker, *Jack London and the Klondike: The Genesis of an American Writer* (San Marino, Cal.: The Huntington Library, 1966);

Charles N. Watson, Jr., *The Novels of Jack London: A Reappraisal* (Madison: University of Wisconsin Press, 1983).

Papers:

The Henry E. Huntington Library in San Marino, California, houses the largest collection of Londoniana, comprising some sixty thousand items: the major portion of London's manuscripts and letters, as well as scrapbooks, most of London's personal library, and Charmian London's diaries. The Merrill Library at Utah State University in Logan, Utah, has the second largest collection of London materials, including many letters, some manuscripts and notes, along with a significant portion of Charmian London's correspondence. The New York Public Library houses London's correspondence with George P. Brett and the Macmillan Company, as well as some manuscripts. The Clifton Waller Barrett Library at the University of Virginia includes more than one hundred London letters (most of them to his agent Paul Revere Reynolds). The Jack London State Historical Park in Glen Ellen, California, houses the Holman Collection of London materials, including important letters to his friend Frederick Irons Bamford. Other smaller but noteworthy collections of London materials are on file at the following libraries: the Bancroft Library at the University of California, Berkeley; Stanford University; the Cresmer Collection at the University of Southern California; the Irving Stone Collection at the University of California, Los Angeles; and the Oakland Public Library.

Brander Matthews
(21 February 1852-31 March 1929)

Perry D. Westbrook
State University of New York at Albany

See also the Matthews entry in *DLB 71: American Literary Critics and Scholars, 1880-1900.*

BOOKS: *Edged Tools. A Play in Four Acts* (New York: French, 1873);

Too Much Smith; Or, Heredity, A Physiological and Psychological Absurdity in One Act, as Arthur Penn, adapted from *La Postérité d'arun Bourgmestre* by Mario Uchard (New York: Werner, 1879);

The Theaters of Paris (London: Low, Marston, Searle & Rivington, 1880; New York: Scribners, 1880);

French Dramatists of the 19th Century (New York: Scribners, 1881; London: Remington/New York: Scribners, 1882; revised and enlarged, New York: Scribners, 1891; revised and enlarged again, 1901);

The Home Library, as Arthur Penn (New York: Appleton, 1883);

In Partnership: Studies in Story-Telling, by Matthews and H. C. Bunner (New York: Scribners, 1884; Edinburgh: Douglas, 1885);

The Last Meeting: A Story (New York: Scribners, 1885; London: Unwin, 1885);

A Secret of the Sea (New York: Scribners, 1886; enlarged edition, London: Chatto & Windus, 1886);

Cheap Books and Good Books (New York: American Copyright League, 1888);

Check and Counter-Check, A Tale of Twenty-five Hours, by Matthews and George H. Jessop (Bristol: Arrowsmith, 1888; republished as *A Tale of Twenty-five Hours* (New York: Appleton, 1892);

Pen and Ink: Papers on Subjects of More or Less Importance (New York & London: Longmans, Green, 1888; revised and enlarged edition, New York: Scribners, 1902);

American Authors and British Pirates (New York: American Copyright League, 1889);

A Family Tree, and Other Stories (London & New York: Longmans, Green, 1889);

Brander Matthews

With My Friends: Tales Told in Partnership, by Matthews and others (New York: Longmans, Green, 1891);

Americanisms and Briticisms, with Other Essays on Other Isms (New York: Harper, 1892);

In the Vestibule Limited (New York: Harper, 1892);

Tom Paulding: The Story of a Search for Buried Treasure in the Streets of New York (New York: Century, 1892);

The Decision of the Court: A Comedy (New York: Harper, 1893);

The Story of a Story, and Other Stories (New York: Harper, 1893);

The Royal Marine: An Idyl of Narragansett Pier (New York: Harper, 1894);

Studies of the Stage (New York: Harper, 1894);

This Picture and That: A Comedy (New York: Harper, 1894);

Vignettes of Manhattan (New York: Harper, 1894; London: Harper, 1912);

Bookbindings Old and New: Notes of a Booklover, with an Account of the Grolier Club of New York (New York & London: Macmillan, 1895);

Books and Play-books: Essays on Literature and the Drama (London: Osgood, McIlvane, 1895);

His Father's Son: A Novel of New York (New York: Harper, 1895; London: Longmans, Green, 1895);

Aspects of Fiction and Other Ventures in Criticism (New York: Harper, 1896; New York & London: Harper, 1900; enlarged edition, New York: Scribners, 1902);

An Introduction to the Study of American Literature (New York & Cincinnati: American Book Co., 1896; enlarged, 1911);

Tales of Fantasy and Fact (New York: Harper, 1896);

Outlines in Local Color (New York & London: Harper, 1898);

The Action and the Word: A Novel of New York (New York & London: Harper, 1900);

A Confident Tomorrow: A Novel of New York (New York & London: Harper, 1900);

The Historical Novel, and Other Essays (New York: Scribners, 1901);

Notes on Speech-making (New York & London: Longmans, Green, 1901);

Parts of Speech: Essays on English (New York: Scribners, 1901);

The Philosophy of the Short Story (New York & London: Longmans, Green, 1901);

Cuttyback's Thunder; Or, Frank Wylde. A Comedy in One Act, adapted from *Serment d'Horace* by Henry Mürger (Boston: Baker, 1902);

The Development of the Drama (New York: Scribners, 1903);

Recreations of an Anthologist (New York: Dodd, Mead, 1904);

American Character (New York: Crowell, 1906);

The Spelling of Yesterday and the Spelling of Tomorrow, circular no. 4 (New York: Simplified Spelling Board, 1906);

Inquiries and Opinions (New York: Scribners, 1907);

A Gold Mine, A Play in Three Acts, by Matthews and Jessop (New York & London: French, 1908);

The Spelling of the Poets, circular no. 21 (New York: Simplified Spelling Board, 1908);

The American of the Future, and Other Essays (New York: Scribners, 1909);

Molière, His Life and His Works (New York: Scribners, 1910; London: Longmans, 1910);

A Study of the Drama (Boston & New York: Houghton Mifflin, 1910);

A Study of Versification (Boston & New York: Houghton Mifflin, 1911);

Fugitives from Justice (New York: Corlies, Macy, 1912);

Gateways to Literature, and Other Essays (New York: Scribners, 1912);

Vistas of New York (New York & London: Harper, 1912);

Shakspere As a Playwright (New York: Scribners, 1913; London: Longmans, Green, 1913);

On Acting (New York: Scribners, 1914);

A Book About the Theater (New York: Scribners, 1916);

These Many Years, Recollections of a New Yorker (New York: Scribners, 1917);

The Principles of Playmaking, and Other Discussions of the Drama (New York & London: Scribners, 1919);

The Englishing of French Words, published with *The Dialectal Words in Blunden's Poems* by Robert Bridges (Oxford: Clarendon, 1921);

Essays on English (New York: Scribners, 1921);

The Tocsin of Revolt, and Other Essays (New York & London: Scribners, 1922);

Playwrights on Playmaking, and Other Studies of the Stage (New York & London: Scribners, 1923);

The Clown: In History, Romance and Drama (Springfield, Ohio: Crowell, 1924);

Suggestions for Teachers of American Literature (New York: American Book Co., 1925);

Rip Van Winkle Goes to the Play, and Other Essays on Plays and Players (New York & London: Scribners, 1926);

Papers on Playmaking, edited, with a preface, by Henry W. Wells (New York: Hill & Wang, 1957);

Papers on Acting, edited, with a preface, by Wells (New York: Hill & Wang, 1958).

PLAY PRODUCTIONS: *Very Odd,* Indianapolis, Academy of Music, 13 October 1871;

Marjory's Lovers, London, Royal Court Theatre, 18 February 1884; New York, Madison Square Theatre, 11 January 1887;

A Gold Mine, by Matthews and George H. Jessop, Memphis, New Memphis Theatre, 1 April 1887;

This Picture and That, Denver, Lyceum Theatre, 15 April 1887;

On Probation, by Matthews and Jessop, Decatur, Illinois, 9 September 1889;

Decision of the Court, New York, Hermann's Theatre, 23 March 1893;

Frank Wylde, Denver, Lyceum Theatre, 30 December 1894;

Peter Stuyvesant, Governor of New Amsterdam, by Matthews and Bronson Howard, Providence, Rhode Island, 25 September 1899; New York, Wallack's, 2 October 1899.

OTHER: *Comedies for Amateur Acting*, edited, with a prefatory note, by Matthews (New York: Appleton, 1880);

Poems of American Patriotism, edited by Matthews (New York: Scribners, 1882; revised and enlarged, 1922);

Richard Sheridan, *Sheridan's Comedies: "The Rivals" and "The School for Scandal,"* edited, with an introduction, notes, and a biographical sketch, by Matthews (London: Osgood, 1885; New York: Crowell, 1904);

Actors and Actresses of Great Britain and the United States, from the Days of David Garrick to the Present Time, edited by Matthews and Laurence Hutton, 5 volumes: volume 1, *Garrick and His Contemporaries;* volume 2, *The Kembles and Their Contemporaries;* volume 3, *Kean and Booth and Their Contemporaries;* volume 4, *Macready and Forrest and Their Contemporaries;* volume 5, *The Present Time* (New York: Cassell, 1886); volume 5 revised and republished as *The Life and Art of Edwin Booth and His Contemporaries* (Boston: Page, 1900);

William Dunlap, *André; A Tragedy in Five Acts*, introduction by Matthews (New York: Dunlap Society, 1887);

John Daly Burk, *Bunker Hill; or, The Death of General Warren*, introduction by Matthews (New York: Dunlap Society, 1891);

Charles Lamb, *The Dramatic Essays of Charles Lamb*, edited, with an introduction and notes, by Matthews (New York: Dodd, Mead, 1891);

Washington Irving, *Washington Irving's Tales of a Traveller*, edited, with an introduction, by Matthews (New York & London: Longmans, Green, 1895);

Great Plays (French and German) by Corneille, Molière, Racine, Lessing, Schiller, and Hugo, edited, with an introduction and notes, by Matthews (New York: Appleton, 1901);

American Familiar Verse, Vers de Société, edited, with an introduction, by Matthews (New York & London: Longmans, Green, 1904);

The Short Story: Specimens Illustrating Its Development, edited, with an introduction and notes, by Matthews (New York: American Book Co., 1907);

The Oxford Book of American Essays, edited by Matthews (New York: Oxford University Press, 1914);

The Chief European Dramatists: Twenty-one Plays from the Drama of Greece, Rome, Spain, France, Italy, Germany, Denmark, and Norway, from 500 B.C. to 1879 A.D., edited, with notes, biographies, and bibliographies, by Matthews (Boston & New York: Houghton Mifflin, 1916);

H. C. Bunner, *The Poems of H. C. Bunner*, edited by Matthews (New York: Scribners, 1917);

The Chief British Dramatists, Excluding Shakespeare; Twenty-five Plays from the Middle of the Fifteenth Century to the End of the Nineteenth, edited, with notes, bibliographies, and biographies, by Matthews and Paul Robert Lieder (Boston & New York: Houghton Mifflin, 1924).

Brander Matthews has been described as "perhaps the last of the gentlemanly school of critics and essayists that distinguished American literature in the last half of the nineteenth century." The description is reasonably accurate, though to it should be added that he was also a writer of drama and fiction. Most assuredly he was a gentleman by birth. Born in New Orleans to Edward and Virginia Brander Matthews, on his father's side he was descended from William Brewster of Plymouth and on his mother's side from a first family of Virginia. The Matthews family did not remain long in New Orleans; but, as the father's business demanded, they resided in various cities in America, traveled abroad, and eventually settled in New York, where Matthews spent much of his boyhood. In 1868, after another sojourn in Europe, he entered Columbia College, graduated three years later, and was admitted to Columbia Law School, from which in 1873, at the age of twenty-one, he received his LL.B. degree. That same year he married the English actress Ada S. Smith (known on the stage as Ada Harland).

Matthews did little with his training in law. His main interest was literature and drama, and he aspired to be a playwright. However, his initial success was in literary and dramatic criticism.

Engraving of Matthews used as the frontispiece for Pen and Ink: Papers on Subjects of More or Less
Importance *(1888)*

Among the periodicals to which he contributed critical essays were *Galaxy, Nation, Scribner's Monthly, Saturday Review*, and *Century*. During the 1880s he published two books on drama, *The Theaters of Paris* (1880) and *French Dramatists of the 19th Century* (1881), and edited several others. At the same time he was making some headway as a playwright. His comedy *Marjory's Lovers* was performed in London in 1884 and later in America. Two one-act plays by him and two comedies that he wrote in collaboration with George H. Jessop were also successfully produced during this period. In addition, he had begun writing short fiction and novels. During these years also he was becoming a prominent figure in the literary and artistic circles of New York and London, counting among his friends Rudyard Kipling and Thomas Hardy. An extremely sociable man, he belonged to a number of clubs, several of which he was instrumental in founding.

On the basis of these credentials and proclivities, he was appointed to the faculty of Columbia University as a professor of literature. Eight years later his title was changed to professor of dramatic literature, the first such chair in the nation. For the remainder of his life he continued to publish voluminously, mainly on subjects connected with the theater but including a rather impressive quantity of fiction. Honors were heaped

upon him. France conferred upon him the decoration of the Legion of Honor, of which he later became an officer; he was elected president of the Modern Language Association of America in 1910; he was elected to the American Academy of Arts and Letters and later became its chancellor. In 1924 he resigned from the Columbia faculty, but for the remaining five years of his life he retained his position as an academic and literary luminary.

That a man who expended so much energy and time on the peripheries of creative literature—on clubs, on teaching, on scholarship—could yet write successful drama and produce an appreciable amount of fiction, especially short stories, of creditable quality is little less than phenomenal. Not only did he write a sufficiency of short fiction to fill six volumes and parts of two others, but he also formulated a theory of the short story based on his study of masters of the genre as well as on his own experience as a writer.

Reflecting his attachment to New York, Matthews's best fiction mirrors the city's life on all social levels. Indeed, at a time when local color was a vogue among American authors, he very consciously took on the role of New York's own local colorist, and his performance in this role was impressive. However, his first short fiction did not qualify as local color. In 1884, in a vol-

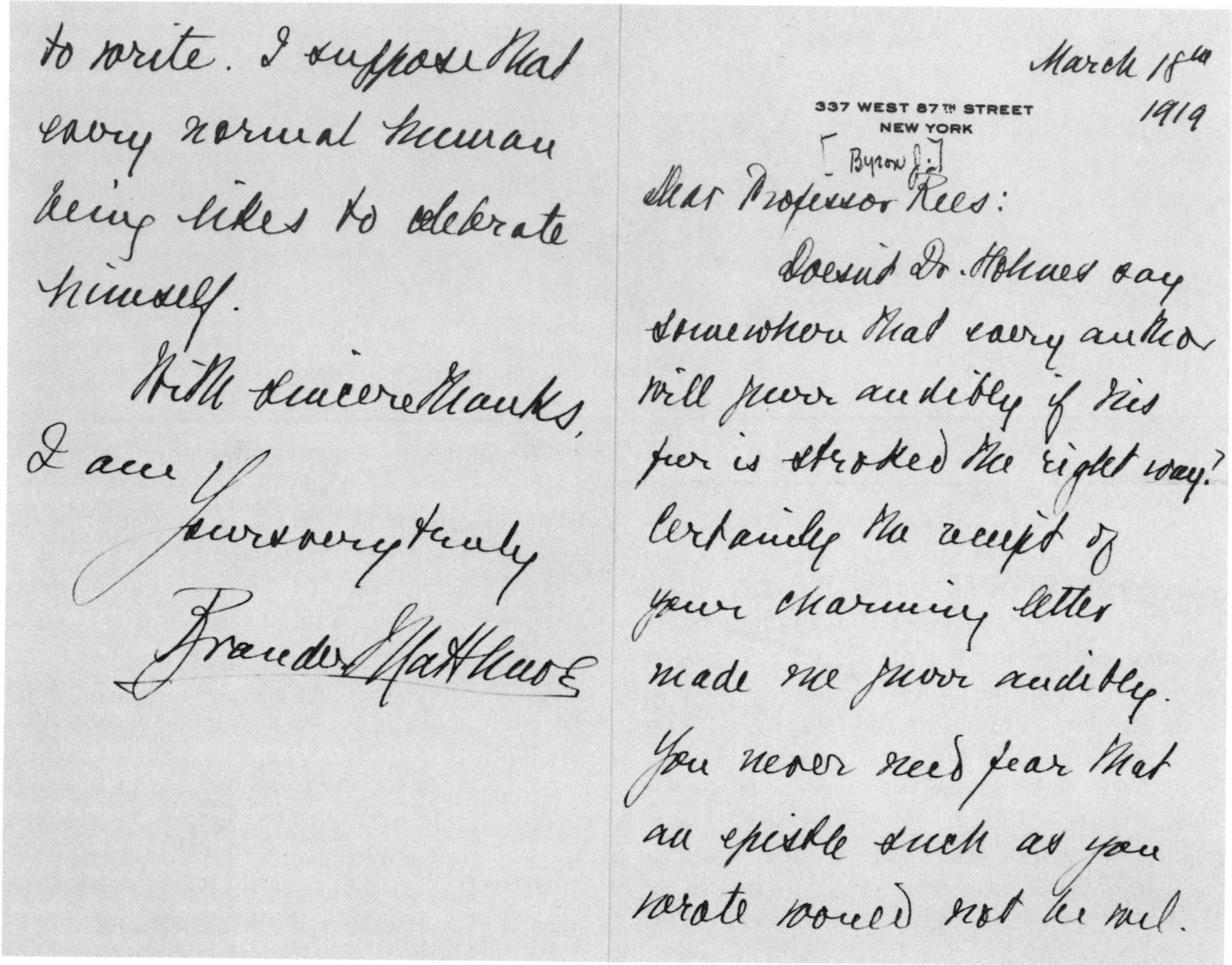

to write. I suppose that
every normal human
being likes to celebrate
himself.

    With sincere thanks,
I am
      Yours very truly

    Brander Matthews

337 WEST 87TH STREET
NEW YORK

March 18th
1919

[Byron J.]

Dear Professor Rees:

    Doesn't Dr. Holmes say
somewhere that every author
will purr audibly if his
fur is stroked the right way?
Certainly the receipt of
your charming letter
made me purr audibly.
You never need fear that
an epistle such as you
wrote would not be mel-

Letter from Matthews to Professor Byron J. Rees (James Brander Matthews Collection [#8006], Clifton Waller Barrett Library, Special Collections Department, University of Virginia Library)

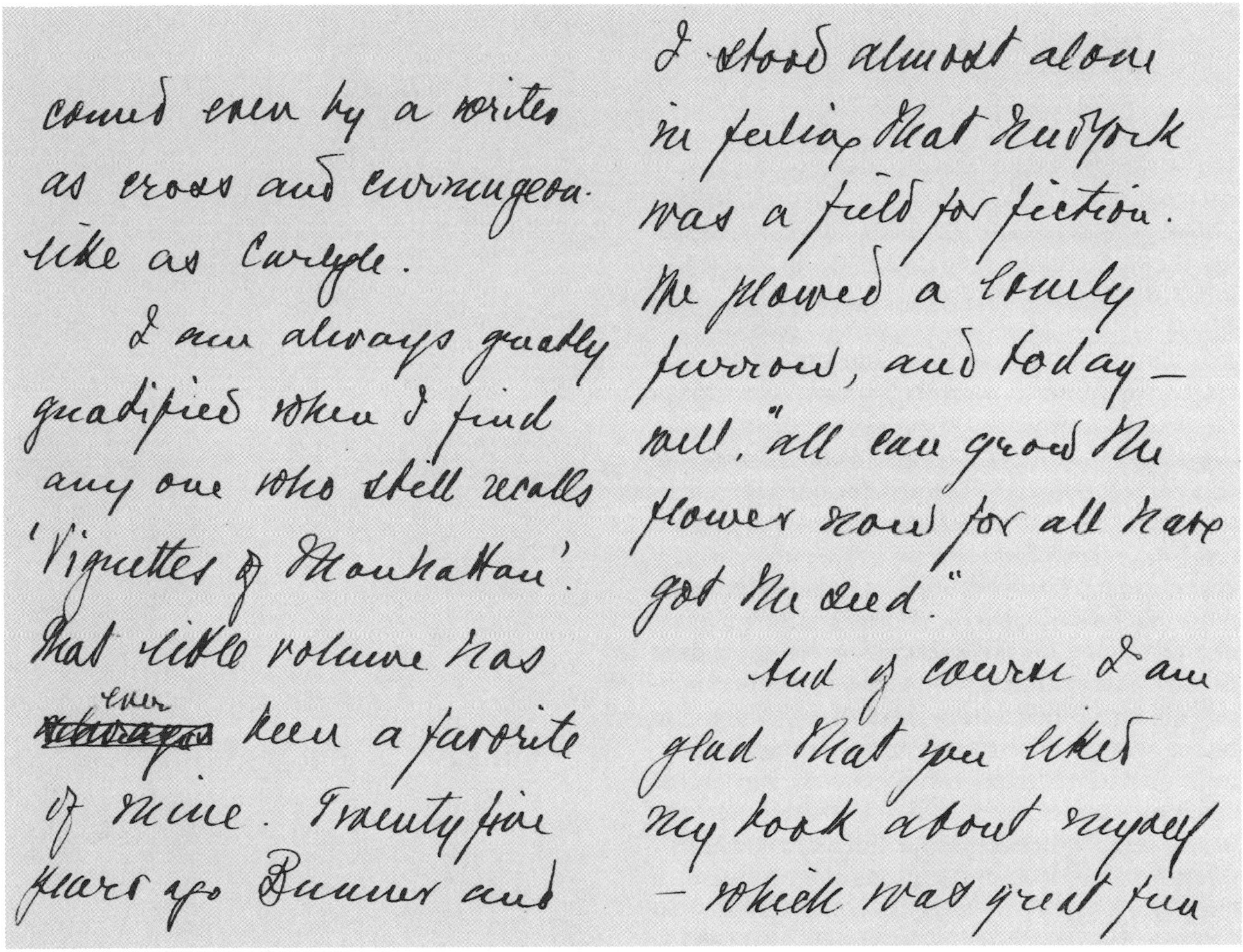

comed even by a writer
as cross and curmudgeon-
like as Carlyle.

I am always greatly
gratified when I find
any one who still recalls
'Vignettes of Manhattan'.
That little volume has
~~always~~ ever been a favorite
of mine. Twenty five
years ago Bunner and

I stood almost alone
in feeling that New York
was a field for fiction.
We plowed a lonely
furrow, and today —
well, "all can grow the
flower now for all have
got the seed."

And of course I am
glad that you liked
my book about myself
— which was great fun

ume entitled *In Partnership: Studies in Story-Telling*, he collaborated with H. C. Bunner on two stories and contributed three of his own. The efforts of both men seem to have been to devise original techniques and construct clever plots. In 1886 Matthews published *A Secret of the Sea*, a collection of his own stories, notable mainly for labored plotting and an urbane style. Three years later, in 1889, another gathering of his own work, *A Family Tree, and Other Stories*, in which he was still concentrating on originality and cleverness, was published. The title piece, first published in the February 1889 issue of *Scribner's Magazine*, is so freighted with coincidences as to be ludicrous. But one story, "In a Bobtail Car" (*Century Magazine*, September 1886), reprinted years later in *Vistas of New York* (1912), presages the skill that was to flourish in the next decades as Matthews recorded New York life in three volumes of sketches or, as he called them, snapshots.

In 1891 Matthews again contributed to a collaborative volume, *With My Friends: Tales Told in Partnership*, in which two stories were written with Bunner, two with Walter H. Pollock, and one each with Jessop and F. Amsty. Included was an introductory essay by Matthews, "The Art and Mystery of Collaboration," in which he convincingly argues that collaboration is a legitimate, time-honored literary activity. However, the contents of the volume do not substantiate his contention that collaboration has produced work of the highest quality. The stories, several of which appeared earlier in *In Partnership*, are competent entertainments, notable for cleverness, variety of techniques, and a sophisticated but rather flat prose style. These same qualities are illustrated in an exaggerated, almost grotesque, degree by a long story, *In the Vestibule Limited*, published in *Harper's Monthly Magazine* in March 1891 and as a book in 1892. The action takes place in a New York to Chicago limited train, which picks up a sleeping car from Boston at Albany. The scenes, or chapters, of the story shift from one car to another as the train speeds westward. During the journey it develops that a young man and a young woman, who would have been married on that day had not their engagement been broken off by a lover's quarrel, are both on the train. By a not very deft series of contrivances, the two are brought together and are married by a clergyman, conveniently on board, on the day originally planned.

In 1893 a full-length volume of Matthews's fiction, *The Story of a Story, and Other Stories*, was published. Here again the author depends heavily on gimmickry in his technique and plotting. For example, the title piece, "The Story of a Story" (*Century Magazine*, October 1891), follows the vicissitudes of a story from its dictation by a dying author to his wife, through the editorial office of a magazine, to a number of readers scattered across the country in such spots as an Indian reservation, a slum in Chicago, and a summer resort in New England. Matthews does not reveal the contents of the story beyond the fact that it includes a fight in which an exemplary and selfless hero kills a man for unspecified reasons. The chief interest is intended to lie in the story's effects on different readers. Its illustrators and printer are bored with it, the critics barely notice it, but to members of the public it brings joy and inspiration. To the son of a Chicago scrubwoman, for example, it is a stimulus that carries him to a distinguished law career. Years later he seeks out the author to thank him but learns that he had died two weeks after completing the story which constitutes his message to the world. The potential influence of literature, obviously, is the theme, but the artificiality of its presentation and its sentimentality go far to negate its effectiveness. Much the same could be said of the other stories in this collection, especially "Etelka Talmeyer: A Tale of Three Cities" (*Harper's New Monthly Magazine*, May 1893), the plot of which is built around an unlikely case of mistaken identity.

Matthews's best fiction–and the most likely to attract present-day readers–is contained in three collections of stories with settings exclusively in New York City: *Vignettes of Manhattan* (1894), *Outlines in Local Color* (1898), and *Vistas of New York* (1912). These, along with several novels also set in New York, qualify Matthews as an important literary reporter of life in his "strange and manysided city," a distinction which he shares with O. Henry, Thomas Wolfe, and John Dos Passos. In a prefatory note to *Vignettes of Manhattan* addressed to Theodore Roosevelt, Matthews wrote that his offerings were "not stories really, I am afraid–not sketches even, nor studies; they are, I think, just what I have called them–vignettes." And ever one for a gimmick, he added, "And there are a dozen of them, one for every month in the year, an urban calendar of times and seasons." *Outlines in Local Color* follows the same pattern, as does *Vistas of New York*, though less rigorously. The "calendar" idea actually works, giving a certain unity to each volume and providing the author with an opportunity to do one of the things he did best—portray the physical aspects of the city under ever-varying conditions.

The three volumes may be conveniently discussed together, for each has the same purpose of catching the strangeness and variety of the city's life through a series of brief but vivid glimpses of episodes, places, and persons. The reader of these collections will be rewarded with a sense of the almost organic life of the city as it was during the three decades before World War I. In his composite picture Matthews omits few segments of the city's population. He includes portraits of immigrants in the slums and members of high society on Fifth Avenue, as well as criminals, policemen, journalists, college professors, and students. He shows people at work and at play. He re-creates the city's odors; the roar of its traffic, the bells of its fire engines, and the steamboat whistles on the East and North Rivers; its massive buildings, its crowded streets, the smoke of the steam locomotives on the elevated railways; the shimmering heat of July and the keen winds of December. Above all, Matthews makes the reader aware of the constant motion on the streets and in other public places—the thronging pedestrians, the horse and the cable cars, the carriages and the drays, the spectators at a picture gallery, strollers in Central Park. As a playwright, Matthews knew the value of movement on stage to hold an audience's attention. In a sense, in these stories he has taken New York as a huge stage where constant motion holds the viewer's eye. Similarly, when he focuses on a particular scene, perhaps in a restaurant or private house, his placement of his characters and their movements are the work of a competent dramatist. Indeed, he describes his settings as he would in stage directions in a play. The use of these devices of the playwright's art gives the stories of this period a commanding power his earlier stories, for all their clever plotting and tricky techniques, lack.

In 1896, between the appearance of his first two volumes of New York stories, Matthews published a collection entitled *Tales of Fantasy and Fact*. Several of the pieces in it recount visions seen in dreams or states of self-hypnosis. They qualify as fantasy, surely, and some readers may find them enjoyable. The most entertaining story, written much earlier, is "The Rival Ghosts"

(*Harper's Magazine*, May 1884). Combining humor and suspense, the tale is a rare and highly successful experiment in fiction of the supernatural. The collection also includes a straight story of detection, "The Twinkling of an Eye," which won second prize in a competition conducted by the Bacheller Syndicate. (The first prize went to "The Long Arm," by Mary E. Wilkins Freeman and J. Edgar Chamberlain.)

Perhaps Matthews's major contribution to the short story was not in his fiction but in criticism, especially *The Philosophy of the Short Story* (1901), in which he made the claim that he "had no predecessor in asserting that the Short-story differs from the Novel essentially—and not merely in the matter of length," and that "the Short-story is in reality a *genre*." However, he does admit that Edgar Allan Poe came very close to making this distinction in his review of Nathaniel Hawthorne's *Twice Told Tales* (1842). Matthews's essay for many years was considered authoritative on its subject. Three years after its first appearance in *Lippincott's Magazine* in October 1885, it was reprinted in a volume of Matthews's nonfiction entitled *Pen and Ink: Papers on Subjects of More or Less Importance* (1888). In 1901 it was issued with revisions and an appendix as a separate book. Edward J. O'Brien, in the 1931 revised edition of *The Advance of the American Short Story*, praised it as the "finest critical contribution I know to the technique" of the genre.

Influenced undoubtedly by his study and admiration of classical French drama, Matthews in *The Philosophy of the Short Story* laid down rather strict rules for the genre. He agrees with Poe that a short story differs from a novel "in its essential unity of impression ... the effect of 'totality.'" Furthermore, the short story must have action. It differs from a sketch, for "while a Sketch may be a still-life, in a Short-story something always happens." Essential to the form are "ingenuity, originality, and compression," and, if possible, a "touch of fantasy." And it must have "form," though the choice of form should be left to the author's decision, so long as he achieves "symmetry of design." Matthews warns, however, against an "over-elaboration of ingenuity" in the matter of form—a flaw in much of his own early fiction. Finally, Matthews makes a case for the short story as a preeminently American genre. The British, with their predilection for long novels, were inept in the form, though such French writers as Guy de Maupassant and Prosper Mérimée ranked as masters of the short story.

Oddly, Matthews's stories about New York, which are the most deserving of attention, hardly follow his formula. Rather, they are sketches– "vignettes" or "vistas" as the title of two of the volumes describes them–suggestive of a scrapbook of photographs of the city a hundred years ago, nostalgic in their effect today though vitally contemporary when written. Since Matthews's death in 1929, critics have paid little attention to him as writer of fiction, whether short or long; however, during his lifetime he received favorable reviews. In 1920 Blanche Colton Williams, in her *Our Short Story Writers,* devoted a chapter to Matthews in which she singled out his New York stories for special praise, but O'Brien, who had good things to say about *The Philosophy of the Short Story,* had nothing to say about Matthews's short stories except to compare the New York sketches to "pressed flowers without fragrance or color," though he conceded that they possessed "formal technical correctness." The first part of this criticism seems unduly harsh.

References:

Edward J. O'Brien, *The Advance of the American Short Story,* revised edition (New York: Dodd, Mead, 1931);

Blanche Colton Williams, *Our Short Story Writers* (New York: Moffat, Yard, 1920).

Papers:

Matthews's books, manuscripts, letters, and papers are located at the Butler Library, Columbia University.

Thomas Nelson Page
(23 April 1853-1 November 1922)

Kathryn L. Seidel
University of Central Florida

See also the Page entry in *DLB 12: American Realists and Naturalists.*

SELECTED BOOKS: *In Ole Virginia: or Marse Chan and Other Stories* (New York: Scribners, 1887);

Befo' de War: Echoes in Negro Dialect, by Page and A. C. Gordon (New York: Scribners, 1888);

Two Little Confederates (New York: Scribners, 1888; London: Unwin, 1888);

On Newfound River (New York: Scribners, 1891; London: Osgood, 1891; enlarged edition, New York: Scribners, 1906);

Elsket and Other Stories (New York: Scribners, 1891; London: Osgood, 1892);

Among the Camps, or Young People's Stories of the War (New York: Scribners, 1891; London: Scott, 1892);

The Old South: Essays Social and Political (New York: Scribners, 1892);

Pastime Stories (New York: Harper, 1894);

The Burial of the Guns (New York: Scribners, 1894; London: Ward, Lock & Bowden, 1894);

The Old Gentleman of the Black Stock (New York: Scribners, 1897);

Two Prisoners (New York: Russell, 1897; revised, 1903);

Red Rock (New York: Scribners, 1898; London: Heinemann, 1899);

Santa Claus's Partner (New York: Scribners, 1899; London: Sands, 1900);

Gordon Keith (New York: Scribners, 1903; London: Heinemann, 1903);

Bred in the Bone (New York: Scribners, 1904);

The Negro: The Southerner's Problem (New York: Scribners, 1904);

The Coast of Bohemia (New York: Scribners, 1906);

Under the Coast (New York: Scribners, 1907);

The Old Dominion: Her Making and Her Manners (New York: Scribners, 1908);

Tommy Trot's Visit to Santa Claus (New York: Scribners, 1908);

Frontispiece for Roswell Page's 1923 biography of his brother, Thomas Nelson Page: A Memoir of a Virginia Gentleman

Robert E. Lee, The Southerner (New York: Scribners, 1908; London: Laurie, 1909);

John Marvel, Assistant (New York: Scribners, 1909; London: Laurie, 1910);

Robert E. Lee, Man and Soldier (New York: Scribners, 1911);

The Land of the Spirit (New York: Scribners, 1913; London: Laurie, 1913);

Italy and the World War (New York: Scribners, 1920; London: Chapman & Hall, 1921);

Dante and His Influence: Studies (New York: Scribners, 1922; London: Chapman & Hall, 1923);

Washington and Its Romance (New York: Doubleday, Page, 1923; London: Heinemann, 1923);

The Red Riders (New York: Scribners, 1924).

Collection: *The Novels, Stories, Sketches, and Poems of Thomas Nelson Page,* Plantation Edition, 18 volumes (New York: Scribners, 1906-1912).

Thomas Nelson Page's importance to southern literature results from his nostalgic short stories that articulate and popularize the myth of the South's Edenic origins, its prelapsarian heroes and heroines, and its fall. A self-proclaimed Homer, Page created panegyrics that look back upon a civilization which Page called in his history, *The Old South* (1892), "a civilization so pure,

so noble, that the world to-day holds nothing equal to it." Page's plantation settings and characters became the popular images of the antebellum South; of the southern belle, for example, he writes, "She was a creature of peach-blossom and snow; languid, delicate, saucy. . . . She was not versed in the ways of the world, but she had no need to be; she was better than that; she was well bred."

As a local colorist, Page gives his characters the dialect and customs of the region and paints settings of sparkling plantations and charming "servant cottages." But the perils of local color are its demand for accuracy and its requirement that an author imagine the thoughts of the rustic persons he presents. By selecting as his narrators and main characters for many stories the black southern rustic, Page inadvertently reveals the flaws of the Eden he so assiduously extols.

Page was born to John and Elizabeth Burwell Nelson Page at Oakland plantation, Hanover County, Virginia, in 1853, an ideal time for one whose mission would be to laud the glories of the Old South. Page's actual experiences of the Old South were those of a young boy who witnessed the end of his apparently carefree childhood as simultaneous with the debacle that ended the social order he had assumed would be perpetual. His aristocratic Virginia family lived at Oakland

"Marse Chan."
(A Tale of Old Virginia.)

One afternoon in the Autumn of 1872, I was riding leisurely down the sandy road that wind along the top of the watershed between two of the smaller rivers of Eastern Virginia, when I made a chance acquaintance with an "ole family nigger" as he proudly styled himself, who ... with the close union of the comical and the pathetic which is so striking a characteristic of his race.

His narrative, which I have endeavored to reproduce in his own language, ... illustrates strikingly the loving fidelity to his old master so inexplicable to the outside world, and so touching to those who alone know and appreciate the negro at his true worth.

The road I was travelling, following "the ridge" for miles had just struck me as most significant of the character of the race whose only avenue of communication with the outside world it had been. Their once splendid mansions now fast falling to decay appeared to view from time to time set back far from the road, in proud seclusion among groves

Manuscript pages for the best-known story in Page's first book (Thomas Nelson Page Collection [#8641], Clifton Waller Barrett Library, Special Collections Department, University of Virginia Library)

(2)

of oaks and hickories, now scarlet and gold with the early frost. Distance was nothing to this people; time was of no consequence to them. They desired but a level path in life, and that they had though the way was longer and the outer world strode by them as they dreamed.

~~Such were~~ from my reflections ~~when~~ I was aroused by hearing ~~someone~~ ahead of me calling, "Heah!—hiah,—whoo—oop, hiah!—" Turning the curve in the road, I saw just before me with a hoe and a watering pot in his hand a negro ~~standing~~ ~~a negro standing~~. He had evidently just gotten over the "worm-fence" into the road, out of the path which could be seen for a short distance ~~leading zigzag~~ across the "old field" until it was lost to sight in the dense ~~jungle~~ growth of sassafras. When I rode up he was looking anxiously back down this path for his dog. So engrossed was he, that he did not even hear my horse, and I reined in to wait until he should turn around, and ~~I could~~ satisfy my curiosity as to the handsome old place whose pillars and chimneys peeped out from the grove of scarlet oaks and yellow maples some half a mile off from the road.

with sixty slaves. Page saw his father ride off in glory to war and return, a poor and disillusioned man, to a ruined plantation. The poverty of the Reconstruction South influenced Page's youth; he entered Washington and Lee College in 1869 but left for a lack of funds. He tutored children; then, in the tradition of the southern gentleman, he studied law at the University of Virginia. After passing the bar in 1874 Page moved to Richmond and practiced law until 1893, when his success as a writer enabled him to leave his vocation to engage full time in his avocation. In 1886 he married Anne Seddon Bruce, who died only two years later; in 1893 he married Mrs. Florence Lathrop Field, widowed sister-in-law of department-store magnate Marshall Field, and moved to Washington, D.C., where he established himself as a man of letters and much sought-after lecturer and dinner guest. In 1912 Page was active in Woodrow Wilson's presidential campaign, and in 1913 he was appointed ambassador to Italy, where he served for six years. Page died on 1 November 1922, at Oakland.

Page's oeuvre contains short-story collections, novels, essay collections, children's stories, literary criticism, and poetry, but it is his stories that are his most significant contribution to American literature and to popular culture. Page's first published work, "Uncle Gabe's White Folks," a dialect poem that appeared in the April 1877 *Scribner's Monthly*, presents a black servant's eulogy to the way of life his master enjoyed before the Civil War; this motif continues in "Marse Chan: A Tale of Old Virginia" (*Century*, April 1884), "Unc' Edinburg's Drowndin': A Plantation Echo" (*Harper's New Monthly Magazine*, January 1886), "Meh Lady: A Story of the War" (*Century*, June 1886), and "Ole 'Stracted" (*Harper's New Monthly Magazine*, October 1886). These stories, with the addition of "No Haid Pawn" and "Polly," comprise *In Ole Virginia: or Marse Chan and Other Stories* (1887), Page's first, and most uniform, short-story collection.

Of these, "Marse Chan" has attracted the most critical attention. While narrated from the point of view of a northern visitor, the story within the story is that of Unc' Sam, the black slave, now a "servant" as Page calls him, who recounts to the northerner the story of the noble and heroic deeds of his former master, Mr. Channing, in the prelapsarian tranquillity of the plantation South. Sam says, "Dem was good ole times, marster–de bes' Sam ever see! Dey wuz, in fac'! Niggers didn't hed nothin' 't all to do–jes' hed to

'ten' to de feedin' an' cleanin' de hosses an' doin' what de marster tell 'em to do. . . . Dyar warn' no trouble nor nothin." But there was trouble, even in this purposeful eulogy to the past. Sam tells the story of the chivalrous, pure love of Tom Channing and Anne Chamberlain, and of Tom's courage. But his courage is necessitated by the undercurrents of abuse within the plantation society itself. In an incident whose symbolic content unintentionally speaks to a modern audience, Channing orders one of his slaves, Ham, into a burning barn to rescue horses, an incident that is a precursor to William Faulkner's "Barn Burning," as Lucinda MacKethan points out in her essay on Page in *The Dream of Arcady: Time and Place in Southern Literature* (1980). Channing saves him but is blinded in the process. The modern reader perceives an ironic parallel of the master's blindness to his capricious decisions which Ham had no choice but to obey with the blindness of an entire society with this power of life and death, and the inevitable self-destructiveness of this power. In another instance, when Channing chooses not to duel with the story's antagonist, Colonel Chamberlain, Channing proves his manly courage by overturning the chivalric ritual. These incidents suggest that Page could not, even when he desired, ignore the underlying tensions of the Old South's codes and the anxiety of those who try to defend it.

In "Unc' Edinburg's Drowndin': A Plantation Echo," Page attempts to record the antebellum world of order and stability. Another unconsummated love affair allows Page to show the idealism and courtliness of the true southern gentleman, his lady, and closeness of the black families, particularly the warmth of the mammy.

"Meh Lady: A Story of the War" is intended to convey the courage, strength, and purity of the southern women who "singlehandedly" ran the plantations while the men were at war. In fact, however, it is the former slave, Unc' Billy, the narrator of the story, who has held the plantation together. In this story Page proposes as a solution to the North/South schism: the marriage of a plantation owner's daughter, Miss Anne, to a northerner. This allegorical solution to the sectional rivalry typifies a good deal of the fiction of the postwar South, as can be seen in the works of John William De Forest, Sarah Josepha Hale, and Thomas Dixon, Jr., and Page would re-create the situation in his own novel, *Red Rock* (1898). The portrait of the southern belle is of a woman so virginal, courageous, and defenseless that she inspires courtesy even from the northern captain whom Miss Anne eventually marries. The quiet courage of the long-suffering and admirable Unc' Billy has in large part kept the plantation safe, and he is rewarded for his service with the honor of giving away "Meh Lady" on her wedding day.

In "Ole 'Stracted: The Derangement of Loyalty," Page writes a poignant tale of a slave who has been sold away from his wife and child. The breaking up of families which slavery fostered was often more horrifying to the Victorian reader than slavery per se. It is remarkable to see such a story, then, in a volume Page wrote as part of his avowed effort to establish southern ideals as the basis of a new "age of Pericles." When Ole 'Stracted loses his memory and has no recollection of his past, even his name, Page wanders into a chilling territory whose metamorphic significance to black identity foreshadows some of the major themes of contemporary black fiction. Page blames the Civil War and Reconstruction on Ole 'Stracted's fate–had the Old South persisted, all would be well. But Page forgets it was during the Edenic times that the master sold Ole 'Stracted.

While "No Haid Pawn" does not ostensibly focus on the southern past, its gothic qualities place it well within the southern tradition; in Page's story a boy recounts legends of a blood-drinking superhuman, a haunted house, and a ghost. The characters and themes are descendants of those of Edgar Allan Poe and ancestors of the grotesques of Carson McCullers, Flannery O'Connor, and Faulkner.

The last story in *In Ole Virginia* is "Polly." Here Page presents a child's world before the war, but the story is slight and the characters stereotyped. The child's point of view, however, was of continuing interest to Page, as it was also to his contemporaries Mark Twain and Joel Chandler Harris. The child's point of view, moreover, was an appropriate vantage point since Page was himself an eight-year-old boy at the war's opening. In the novella *Two Little Confederates* (1888), Page describes two boys who witness their father's heroic entry to war, his despair over the war's loss, their mother's courage, and their slaves' loyalty even after emancipation. The story is well controlled, not maudlin (Page's frequent problem), and effective. In other children's tales Page lapses into the sentimental mode his Victorian readers tolerated well but which modern readers find cloying. In "A Captured Santa Claus" (*Harper's Young People*, December 1888; collected in *Among the Camps*, 1891), a son helps his father

join his family and still do his duty to the Confederate Army; in "Kittykin and The Part She Played in the War" (*Harper's Young People*, 17 and 24 February 1891; collected in *Among the Camps*), the war stops for a time when both sides unite to rescue a cat from a tree; in "Nancy Pansy" (*Harper's Young People*, 3 and 10 December 1889; collected in *Among the Camps*), an innocent girl reconciles North and South; and in "Two Prisoners" (*Harper's Young People*, 10 and 17 May 1892; expanded and published separately in 1897), the courage of a war widow is revealed through the eyes of children.

Until 1898, when he published *Red Rock*, Page wrote stories concerned with the notion that a person's "breeding," his "noble blood," was his chief and most telling characteristic. This idea, grotesquely exaggerated by Dixon in *The Clansman: An Historical Romance of the Ku Klux Klan* (1905), was nonetheless the current and popular explanation of human behavior and accounted for the differences in race and sex. In "Elsket" (*Scribner's*, August 1891; collected in *Elsket and Other Stories*, 1891), which is set in Norway, Page emphasizes the loyalty and faithfulness of an Anglo-Saxon "belle" who is "the last of her race." The story is another dirge for a dying civilization, though this time not the South. In "Run to Seed" (*Scribner's*, August 1891; collected in *Elsket and Other Stories*), an impoverished young southern fellow, with an act of courage, proves his family's seed is good after all.

These stories are populated with eccentric characters whom Page nonetheless presents affectionately. "My Cousin Fanny" (*Century*, December 1892; collected in *The Burial of the Guns*, 1894), gives a reminiscence of a hypochondriacal "poor" relation. "The Gray Jacket of No. 4" (*Century*, May 1892; collected in *The Burial of the Guns*), is the story of a Civil War veteran who lost all in the war and who has become an alcoholic obsessed with the gray jacket that represents the bravery and honor he once possessed. Now he is adrift in the fallen South. There is a metaphorical undertone to many of Page's stories that adds depth to his otherwise stereotypical characters. The attitudes of his characters represent the South's attitudes toward itself; his characters are projections, personifications of those attitudes.

Pastime Stories, which appeared in 1894, is a collection of poorly done sketches and anecdotes. Even Page was embarrassed about what he admitted were the many "demerits" of these stories, but in keeping with his avowed purpose to make

Dr. H. C. McCook, C. F. Thwing, John Burroughs, Elizabeth B. Custer, Moncure D. Conway, Edwin Markham, and Thomas Nelson Page at a celebration honoring the seventieth birthday of Henry Mills Alden, the managing editor of Harper's Weekly

out of his work a "chronicle of Virginia life," they have historical value. They elaborate Page's notions of the behavior of blacks and also explore his experiences as a lawyer. Page portrays blacks in these sketches often as thieves, tricksters, and drunkards; they embody his notion of the basic inferiority of the race, on which he later writes in *The Negro: The Southerner's Problem* (1904), and represent Page's conclusion that for blacks, the loyalty and goodness of the Unc' Billys and Unc' Sams are exceptional. The pieces that concern lawyers, more sketches or caricatures than stories, are interesting because Page can be credited with beginning in earnest a tradition in southern literature: the southern gentleman as lawyer. Page imagines that the South "in the supreme moment of her existence.... found herself arraigned at the bar of the world without an advocate and without a defense." The image of the South as the defendant before the Judge recalls the Miltonic version of God's jurisprudence in the cases of Adam and Eve.

In 1894 Page wrote three stories that give full attention to his evaluation of the postwar disintegration of the South. "The Burial of the Guns" (*Scribner's*, April 1894; collected in *The Burial of the Guns*) is an intriguingly symbolic story because these Civil War guns are buried but not destroyed. These sources of strength and power are waiting for resurrection; they will, like the South, "rise again." The mythic pattern of the return of the fallen hero, from King Arthur to the legends of Sir Walter Scott, of whom Page was an ardent reader, was a particularly apt way of assuaging southerners' need for solace in the face of their defeat. Southerners, says the inevitable colonel in the story, "fought a good fight" and now must return home ever vigilant and proud, for although the South has lost the war, it has emerged more "noble" than ever. In "Little Darby" (*Scribner's*, September and October 1894; collected in volume 11 of the Plantation Edition, 1908), Page writes of a poor young white man who leaves his beloved to go to war; in this story Page is questioning whether it is possible not to be an aristocrat but still to possess courage and loyalty. But while Darby proves brave in war, he is weak in love; he deserts without a furlough to see Vashti. She accuses him of being a coward and deserter, and only a courageous death in battle redeems him. "The Old Gentleman of the Black Stock" (*Harper's New Monthly Magazine*, October 1894), one of

Page's most popular tales, concerns a young lawyer whose mentor tells him what to read and whom to marry. The lawyer needs not learning but love, needs the pastoral innocence of country life, not the corruption of the city. Hence, while not focusing exclusively on the South, Page's themes in this story are consistent with the pastoral and Edenic impulse of his earlier work.

Page's later fiction repeats most of his major themes, though he turned increasingly toward nonfiction works such as biography and literary criticism. Stories written after *Red Rock* repeat the motif of identifying the true southern aristocrat. "Bred in the Bone" (*Century*, October 1901; collected in *Bred in the Bone*, 1904), for example, deals with the pedigree, the "blood" of racehorses, an unsubtle parallel typical of Page's tendency to use obvious literary devices. "Mam Lyddy's Recognition" (*Collier's*, 16 April 1904) depicts a mammy whose behavior is the sort Page prizes; she refuses emancipation, which is what one must do to be in the company of Page's black aristocrats.

In the early 1900s Page wrote extensively in nonfiction about race, southern culture, and southern history. *The Negro: The Southerner's Problem* concluded, as did many works by southerners, that it was the crass, rapacious northerner who tempted the Negro from his normally placid and more noble condition of subservience. Negroes revert all too easily, says Page, to barbarism. During this time Page also wrote two biographies of Robert E. Lee. His short fiction of this period was limited mainly to moralistic, Dickensian Christmas stories.

Page's present critical reputation in no way matches the popular acclaim he met in his lifetime. Even before his stories appeared in collections, Page published most of them in the popular magazines of the day, such as *Scribner's Monthly*, *North American Review*, and *Atlantic Monthly*. His contemporaries prized the stories because they revitalized southern patriotism and provided an ordered, harmonious myth with which southerners could assuage their feelings of failure and defeat.

Current assessment of Page's work finds most of it wanting aesthetically–maudlin, repetitive plots, didactic imagery, and undeveloped characters are among Page's worst creative flaws. His first work was his best. The stories comprising *In Ole Virginia* are vital because their conflicts result from the tensions inherent in well-drawn characters and also because of their vivid use of dialect and local setting.

Page was the most successful articulator of the southerner's attitudes after the Civil War, and as such is largely responsible for the popular image of the Old South, with its code of chivalry, its ideal race relations, its honorable gentleman and pure ladies, its faithful black retainers, and all-loving mammies. Most crucial, Page tapped the American myth of the New World as Eden and transformed it into a peculiarly southern myth, with the gentleman as Adam, the belle as Eve, and the northerner and his black proxies as serpent.

Biography:
Roswell Page, *Thomas Nelson Page: A Memoir of a Virginia Gentleman* (New York: Scribners, 1923).

References:
Theodore L. Gross, *Thomas Nelson Page* (New York: Twayne, 1967);
Kimble King, Introduction to *In Ole Virginia* (Chapel Hill: University of North Carolina, 1969);
Lucinda MacKethan, "Thomas Nelson Page: The Plantation Arcady," in *The Dream of Arcady: Time and Place in Southern Literature* (Baton Rouge: Louisiana State University Press, 1980).

William Sydney Porter
(O. Henry)

(11 September 1862-5 June 1910)

Luther S. Luedtke and Keith Lawrence
University of Southern California

See also the Porter entry in *DLB 12: American Realists and Naturalists*.

BOOKS: *Cabbages and Kings* (New York: McClure, Phillips, 1904; London: Nash, 1904);

The Four Million (New York: McClure, Phillips, 1906; London: Nash, 1916);

The Trimmed Lamp (New York: McClure, Phillips, 1907; London: Hodder & Stoughton, 1916);

Heart of the West (New York: McClure, 1907; London: Nash, 1912);

The Voice of the City (New York: McClure, 1908; London: Nash, 1916);

The Gentle Grafter (New York: McClure, 1908; London: Nash, 1916);

Roads of Destiny (New York: Doubleday, Page, 1909; London: Nash, 1913);

Options (New York & London: Harper, 1909; London: Harper, 1910);

Strictly Business (New York: Doubleday, Page, 1910; London: Nash, 1916);

Whirligigs (New York: Doubleday, Page, 1910; London: Hodder & Stoughton, 1916);

Sixes and Sevens (Garden City, N.Y.: Doubleday, Page, 1911; London: Hodder & Stoughton, 1916);

Rolling Stones (Garden City, N.Y.: Doubleday, Page, 1912; London: Nash, 1916);

Waifs and Strays (Garden City, N.Y.: Doubleday, Page, 1917; London: Hodder & Stoughton, 1920);

O. Henryana (Garden City, N.Y.: Doubleday, Page, 1920);

Postscripts, edited by Florence Stratton (New York & London: Harper, 1923);

O. Henry Encore, edited by Mary S. Harrell (Dallas: Upshaw, 1936; New York: Doubleday, Doran, 1939; London: Hodder & Stoughton, 1939).

Collections: *The Complete Writings of O. Henry*, 14

William Sydney Porter

volumes (Garden City, N.Y.: Doubleday, Page, 1917);

The Biographical Edition, 18 volumes (Garden City, N.Y.: Doubleday, Doran, 1929);

The Complete Works of O. Henry, 2 volumes (Garden City, N.Y.: Doubleday, 1953).

PLAY PRODUCTION: *Lo!, A Musical Comedy*, book and lyrics by Porter and Franklin P. Adams, music by A. Baldwin Sloane, Aurora, Ill., 25 August 1909.

OTHER: J. W. Wilbarger, *Indian Depredations in Texas*, illustrated with woodcuts by Porter (Austin, Tex.: Hutchings Printing House, 1889).

Perhaps the reputation of no other American writer has undergone a more rapid and drastic reversal than that of William Sydney Porter. Writing under the pseudonym O. Henry during the first decade of the twentieth century, Porter commanded a readership in the millions. Critics spoke of "the Yankee Maupassant," discussed Porter in the same breath with Gustave Flaubert, Rudyard Kipling, and Robert Louis Stevenson, and regarded him as "the master of the American short story." C. Alphonso Smith declared in 1916 that "O. Henry's work remains the most solid fact to be reckoned with in the history of twentieth-century American literature." "The time is coming," Canadian critic Stephen Butler Leacock wrote in the same year, "when the whole English-speaking world will recognize in him one of the great masters of modern literature."

Soon after Porter's death in 1910, however, the serious litterateur was removing *The Four Million* (1906) and *The Trimmed Lamp* (1907) from his bookshelf to accommodate what he perceived as the more enduring titles of Stephen Crane, Frank Norris, and Theodore Dreiser. Critics of the 1920s satirized mercilessly the hundreds of would-be writers who emulated Porter's formulaic plot constructions. H. L. Mencken dismissed Porter as a cheap stage magician with a repertoire of four or five shopworn tricks. After crediting his humor, journalistic sense, "ingrained Americanism" in storytelling technique, and "verbal precision and wide range of vocabulary," Fred Lewis Pattee concluded that Porter "worked without truth, without moral consciousness, and without a philosophy of life." Pattee remonstrated, "He was a harlequin Poe with modern laughter in place of gloom." After Cleanth Brooks and Robert Penn Warren's relentless attack on Porter in 1943, the New Critics were indifferent, at best, to the sentimental characterizations, impostures, scene changing, and rhetorical constructs of Porter's tales. While he continues to attract biographers, critics have shown little interest in Porter's work for several decades.

In American popular culture, however, his renown persists. Collected editions of his works continue to sell. Stories such as "The Gift of the Magi" frequently are dramatized for television or the stage. Hardly an American student leaves high school without having read "The Ransom of Red Chief" or analyzing "A Municipal Report." For many, Porter captures the spirit and flavor of early-twentieth-century America as memorably as another "popular" artist, Norman Rockwell. The gap between public and critical opinion of Porter's work is tenuously, and ironically, bridged by one of America's most prestigious short-story awards, named in O. Henry's honor.

If by style and literary craftsmanship Porter has been relegated to the second rank of authors, his place in American literary history is assured by other considerations. He retains a solid base in the popular culture. He left an imposing volume of work and perhaps, after Edgar Allan Poe and Mark Twain, is the most widely read of any American short-story writer. He almost single-handedly proved—to the benefit of more-talented writers who succeeded him—that the short story was a credible and lucrative art form. He originated a number of character types that have been incorporated in the American mythos with effects on both society and literature. He shaped perceptions of America and Americans abroad, particularly in the Soviet Union, where he continues to be much read and admired. Finally, postmodern critics have begun to discover narrative and rhetorical triumphs in Porter's storytelling that lie outside the ken of traditional criticism.

William Sydney Porter was born on 11 September 1862 in Greensboro, North Carolina. His mother, Mary Jane Virginia Swain Porter, was a well-educated Southern belle who died when the boy was three. His father, Algernon Sydney, was an unlicensed medical doctor who devoted less time to his practice than to drinking and to building a perpetual-motion machine. William was largely raised by his paternal grandmother and by Miss Lina, his paternal aunt, who operated a small private school. When asked in later life to list his favorite authors, Porter claimed that he seldom read fiction because it was all tame compared with the romance of his own life. Nevertheless, even as a child he was an avid reader and by age nine or ten entertained himself with the tales of Charles Dickens and Sir Walter Scott as well as his own collection of dime novels. He left school at age fifteen to clerk in his uncle Clark Porter's pharmacy in Greensboro and was a licensed pharmacist at nineteen. Acquaintances remembered him as a "thin pale youth with dark hair and a cough."

Worried about the cough, James K. Hall, a Greensboro physician, and his wife invited Porter to accompany them to Denison, Texas, in 1882. He remained there on an extensive sheep ranch as a houseguest of their son Richard for the next two years. The impressionable youth was fasci-

*William Sydney Porter as a child in Greensboro,
North Carolina*

nated by the stories of Richard Hall's brother, Lee Hall, who had been a captain with the Texas Rangers, and later used him as the basis for several of his Western tales. Porter spent most of his time on the ranch reading books he borrowed from the Hall family and from a local library. He was partial to the British classics and to Webster's dictionary.

Early in 1885 Porter was hired as a bookkeeper in an Austin real-estate office at a salary of one hundred dollars per month. When Richard Hall was elected Texas land commissioner in 1887, Porter became an assistant draftsman in the state land office in Austin. He learned his new duties quickly and was popular among his co-workers, who later remarked that his personality was grounded in a "rather odd combination of wit and reserve." His four years at the land office became the happiest of his life.

The same year, Porter eloped with Athol Estes, the stepdaughter of prominent grocer P. G. Roach, on 1 July 1887. Although Athol's parents had opposed the marriage, they quickly forgave their daughter and new son-in-law. Within a few months the Porters had settled in a small home near Athol's parents. In later years the Roaches supported and encouraged Porter when he had few other friends. The Porters' first child, a boy, died shortly after birth in 1888. A daughter, Margaret, was born the following year. Athol Porter never regained her health following the birth, which initiated a seven-year battle with tuberculosis.

Richard Hall's losing his bid for the governorship of Texas in 1890 cost Porter his job, but friends found employment for him as a teller at Austin's First National Bank. About this time Porter also began sending sketches, brief stories, and poems to local papers and magazines. He was encouraged in his writing by his wife, who shared his comparatively expensive tastes and found it difficult to live on his salary from the bank. At this point in Porter's career, however, he was better known as a cartoonist and artist than a writer, and was commissioned to illustrate J. K. Wilbarger's *Indian Depredations in Texas* (1889).

In 1894 Porter brought a long-standing dream to fruition when he and a partner, James P. Crane, purchased a small Austin monthly, the *Iconoclast*, and converted it into a satirical weekly paper called the *Rolling Stone*. Porter's lampoons, ethnic slurs, and college-level humor did nothing to ingratiate him with his audience or advertisers. The paper was in financial straits during the entire year of its existence despite a heavy subsidy from his in-laws. If this fugitive paper anticipated some of Porter's later themes and methods, it hardly was suggestive of future literary greatness.

Porter maintained his position at the bank while writing, editing, and publishing the *Rolling Stone*, and, as his financial frustrations mounted, he began altering accounts. Whatever his intentions or guilt might have been, a federal bank examiner discovered a fifty-five-hundred-dollar discrepancy in Porter's account books during an audit of the First National Bank in December

1894. Porter resigned, and his father-in-law and the bank's surety company agreed to make up three thousand dollars of the missing funds–a proposal that met with the approval of the directors of the bank–but Porter still was indicted on four counts of embezzlement.

A grand jury in July 1895 brought in a "no bill" judgment largely because of the testimony of Porter's friends and coworkers and the federal examiner's inability to establish a clear case of intent. A second hearing of the case was scheduled for February 1896, until which time Porter was allowed to remain free. In August 1895 he began a job as fill-in reporter for the *Houston Post*, created a daily humor and gossip column, and did most of the paper's editorial cartoons. Many of his free hours were spent caring for his wife, whose health had deteriorated noticeably. After he was arrested for nonappearance at the second hearing, Porter's trial was postponed until July 1896, so that he could spend time with his invalid wife and prepare an adequate defense.

For reasons that will never be clear, Porter decided that he was unable to face the trial. When July arrived, Porter boarded a train for Austin. En route, however, he switched trains and ended up in New Orleans. At the end of the summer he fled to Honduras. Legend has it that he did a short stint in New Orleans as a reporter for the *Picayune*. If so, he probably lived in the French Quarter, where he absorbed experiences he would later fictionalize in "Cherchez la Femme," "Whistling Dick's Christmas Stocking," and other New Orleans tales. Even less is known about Porter's experiences in Honduras than about his time in New Orleans. Perhaps he intended to remain in Honduras until the statute of limitations ran out and he could return to Texas as a free man. All that can be stated definitely is that Porter arrived in Honduras in August or September, that he continued to correspond with Athol Porter through trusted friends, that he absorbed enough of Central American life to write some twenty-five stories about it later, and that he returned to the United States and Austin in January 1897, when he received word that Athol Porter was dying.

The court granted Porter the privilege of a new bond and a continuance of the trial until after Athol Porter's death. She died in Austin, six months after Porter's homecoming, on 25 July 1897. Following his wife's death Porter and Margaret Porter moved to rooms above the grocery store owned by the Roaches.

Athol, Margaret, and William Sydney Porter

Porter's trial, in February 1898, was brief. He was indicted on two counts of flight to avoid prosecution as well as four counts of embezzlement and was sentenced to five years in the Ohio State Penitentiary–the lightest term possible under existing laws. Porter later identified himself with Joseph Conrad's Lord Jim, who ever after suffered the consequences of abandoning his ship and its passengers in a moment of panic; but as Gerald Langford has pointed out, "His handling of money throughout his life is a clear indication of how he was unable to change or grow" through his mistakes.

Porter entered the Ohio Penitentiary on 25 April 1898, as Prisoner 30664. He was profoundly ashamed of being a convict and for the rest of his life sought to keep his prison years a secret, even from his daughter. When fellow inmates encouraged him to "write up" the graphic and inhumane realities of their prison life, he responded, "I am not here as a reporter. . . . The prison and its shame are nothing to me." He added, "I will forget that I ever breathed behind these walls."

Porter's biographer C. Alphonso Smith, who uncovered the "shadow years," espoused the idea that Porter's literary talents blossomed while he was in prison–that Porter's sentence was an undeserved but providential trial by fire, refining and purifying a great modern talent. To some degree this attitude has been perpetuated by Gerald Langford, Richard O'Connor, and subsequent biographers. Eugene Current-García, for example, states that Porter "entered the Ohio Penitentiary an amateur, but he came out three years later as O. Henry, the professional literary artist." However, one should read of Porter's "prison renaissance" with a healthy skepticism. Only four stories were published while he was in prison–"The Miracle of Lava Canyon," "Whistling Dick's Christmas Stocking," "Georgia's Ruling," and "Money Maze"–and at most ten others were written, an average of some four stories for each year of his imprisonment. If any period in Porter's career is to be labeled a time of "blossoming," it almost certainly would have to be his two-year stint with the *New York Sunday World*, when he was obligated to produce a new story each week.

Following his release from prison on 24 July 1901, his sentence reduced by nearly two years for good behavior, Porter traveled to Pittsburgh, where his in-laws and daughter were now managing the Iron Front Hotel. Porter did free-lance writing for the *Pittsburgh Dispatch* and occasionally sent stories to magazines, for which he was paid about seventy-five dollars a story. One of the most popular of these earlier stories was "Holding Up a Train," which eventually appeared in *McClure's* (April 1904; collected in *Sixes and Sevens*, 1911) and was written in collaboration with Al Jennings, a convicted train robber Porter had first met in Honduras.

Early in 1902 the editors of *Ainslee's Magazine* advanced Porter two hundred dollars so that he might move to New York and be closer to his growing market. He finally arrived there in early April. Smith summarized Porter's relocation with this line: "If ever in American literature the place and the man met, they met when O. Henry strolled for the first time along the streets of New York." Porter was no less captivated by the teeming life of the city than another newspaperman, Walt Whitman, had been a half century before. New York held an *Arabian Nights* fascination for Porter; in every face he passed he saw a story worthy of Scheherazade. Although he spent time studying the better neighborhoods, with their elaborate restaurants and parks, he seemed to find the dark streets, obscure hotels, and disreputable bars of the down-and-out more intriguing and more satisfying to his writer's curiosity. His New York was not "the four hundred" of the social reg-

Porter in his teller's cage at the First National Bank in Austin, Texas

ister but "the four million." Between April and December Porter sold seventeen stories, most to *Ainslee's*. In August of that year *McClure's* purchased "Tobin's Palm" for one hundred dollars, the most the magazine had ever paid for a story by an "unknown."

Early in July 1903 Porter was hired by Joseph Pulitzer's *Sunday World*–then the largest newspaper in New York City–to write introductions for feature articles and by the fall was writing a short story for each Sunday edition of the *World*. At this point he dropped all his pen names (John Arbuthnott, Olivier Henry, James L. Bliss, S. H. Peters, Howard Clark, and T. B. Dowd), except that which has become famous: O. Henry.

Porter's income of one hundred dollars per week enabled him to relocate from his seedy accommodations near Madison Square to 55 Irving Place at Gramercy Park and to enroll Margaret in one of the South's most exclusive schools. He dined at fashionable restaurants, frequented the best theaters, and refreshed himself at posh bars, averaging two quarts of whiskey a day. He continually lived beyond his means, demanding larger advances for unwritten work and surviving on the fringes of bankruptcy.

In 1904, the most productive year of his career, Porter published sixty-six stories in the *World* and various magazines, and Witter Bynner of *McClure's* helped him to fashion a disjointed novel, *Cabbages and King,* out of eight previously published Central American tales and some new material. The book sold better abroad than in America, but reviews were favorable everywhere, and enough copies were sold to establish Porter as a safe author for book as well as periodical audiences.

In late 1905 Porter signed a by-the-word contract with *Munsey's.* In April 1906 twenty-five of his most popular stories from the files of the *Sunday World* were collected in *The Four Million,* a book that sold phenomenally well and made Porter's pseudonym a household name across America. Reviews of the collection compared Porter, advantageously, to a host of European writers. Two more collections were released in 1907–*The Trimmed Lamp* and *Heart of the West.* Although the latter received mixed reviews, it sold well, and Porter's price climbed to well over five hundred dollars per story. As his fees increased, however, his output fell drastically. He completed only eleven new stories for publication in 1907.

Porter had two affairs of the heart in the last decade of his life. His personal ad in the *New York Herald* (September 1905) for the "social acquaintance of . . . intelligent, attractive, and unconventional young ladies" led to a romantic correspondence for a time with Ethel Patterson. Beginning in 1905, Porter also corresponded with Sara Lindsay Coleman, a childhood sweetheart from Greensboro whom he had not seen for over twenty-five years. She visited him in New York during the summer of 1907, and they were married the following November. Porter apparently had grown accustomed to the bachelor life-style, however, and was restive in marriage. In 1908 Sara Porter moved to Asheville, North Carolina, where Porter visited her infrequently.

During 1908 Porter wrote twenty-nine new stories. Despite cash advances running to one thousand dollars per story and an income over fourteen thousand dollars for the year, he was still living on extended credit. Furthermore, he had grown dissatisfied with his work, seeing little in the stories that would endure. He accepted a substantial cash advance for a "more serious" work, a novel to be called "The Rat Trap." Nothing came of it, but the outline he presented to Harry Steger of Doubleday suggests that he intended an autobiographical novel built around his favorite themes of irony, destiny, and fate:

The "hero" of the story will be a man born and "raised" in a somnolent Southern town. . . . I'm going to take him through the main phases of life–wild adventure, city, society, something of the "underworld" and among many characteristic planes of the phases. I want him to acquire all the sophistication, that experience can give him, and always preserve his individual honest *human* view, and have him tell the *truth* about everything.
. . . I want this man to be a man of natural intelligence, of individual character, absolutely open and broad minded; and show how the Creator of the earth has got him in a rat trap–put him there "willy nilly" (you know the Omar phrase): and then I want to show what he does about it.

Porter also became obsessed with play writing about this time. A musical called *Lo!,* based on his story "To Him Who Waits" (*Collier's,* January 1909), died in the middle of a fourteen-week tour of the Middle West, and plans for a Broadway production were abandoned. Early in 1910 Porter took a $1000 advance for another play but was unable to deliver it. Ironically, Porter's stories have made the fortunes of other dramatists. When he resisted the blandishments of Broadway producer George Tyler for a stage version of "A Retrieved Reformation" and sold the rights for $250, Paul Armstrong was hired to write the script. Eventually Armstrong earned more than $100,000 as *Alias Jimmy Valentine* became one of the biggest hit plays of the early 1900s.

By the latter part of 1909 Porter was in poor health. He spent four or five months in Asheville and returned to New York in March 1910 a virtual invalid. On 3 June he suffered a complete collapse and was rushed to the Polyclinic Hospital. Porter died two days later, at age forty-seven, of cirrhosis of the liver and diabetes.

Porter's ninth collection of stories, *Strictly Business* (1910), appeared shortly before his death, and seven more volumes followed posthumously, from *Whirligigs* (1910) to *O. Henry Encore* (1936). He had written more than 230 stories, mainly in the meteoric last decade of his life, and by 1920 more than five million volumes of Porter's stories had been sold in the United States.

Porter often employed similar plots, themes, and characterizations. There are exceptional stories in his oeuvre, however, and his storytelling is competent.

William Sydney and Sara Porter

One of Porter's first efforts to write a full-length story was "The Miracle of Lava Canyon" (*McClure's Magazine*, September 1898). Though not written at the top of his form, it typifies strengths and weaknesses that remained throughout his career. The protagonists of the story are Texas sheriff Radcliff Conrad, a coward at heart who seeks out danger in an effort to prove his courage, and the independent and fearless Miss Boadicea Reed. Instead of developing his potentially fresh and engaging characters, however, Porter concentrates on a "happy" ending–and one that, by modern standards, is conspicuously chauvinistic. After Conrad vanquishes bad man Arizona Dan bare-handed, the sheriff and the lady exchange a lover's glance and trade personalities: "The soul of each had passed into the other." Characterization is subordinated to description, incident, and a superficial theme of masculinity and femininity. Too frequently in his subsequent work the wit, imagination, and style of Porter's stories would be overwhelmed by careless plot construction, unsubstantial thematic development, or inconsistencies in tone. This tale was later rewritten as "An Afternoon Miracle" (collected in *Heart of the West*).

"Whistling Dick's Christmas Stocking" (*McClure's Magazine*, December 1899; collected in *Roads of Destiny*, 1909), the first story written under the pen name O. Henry, features an honorable hobo who warns a wealthy family of an im-

pending attack on their home by the violent hobo gang that is holding him captive. Dick delivers his warning in the toe of a weighted silk stocking that he sends crashing through the dining-room window of the family's home on Christmas Eve. For his pains the family takes him in, feeds him Christmas dinner, and promises him a lifetime position of trust and responsibility on their plantation. True to Porter's recurring theme of "appearance versus reality," the "bum" turns out to be the noblest character in the tale.

Characterizations and settings are hastily drawn, the motivations that drive Dick are not accounted for, and the attempts to mimic German dialect are strained. But the conclusion of the story gives it interest and appeal. Whistling Dick elects not to stay on the plantation, instead "escaping" to "freedom" early Christmas morning before the family wakes up. Porter's hero stands in the tradition of James Fenimore Cooper's Natty Bumppo, who resists the influences of culture and society, and Twain's Huck Finn, who determinedly refuses to be "sivilized."

The protagonist of "A Blackjack Bargainer" (*Munsey's Magazine*, August 1901; collected in *Whirligigs*) is a disreputable lawyer named Yancey Goree, the last member of an aristocratic Southern family who has squandered his wealth in gambling and drink and lowers himself to selling the family estate and private cemetery to the "po' white trash" Pike Garvey. In the distant past Goree's ancestors had carried on a feud with the Coltranes. One afternoon the penniless Goree is visited by Pike, who has a strange request. He asks to "buy" Goree's share in the old Goree-Coltrane feud, believing it will give him respectability. Though disgusted by Pike's offer, Goree takes the two hundred dollars Pike offers him and immediately gambles it away. The following day Abner Coltrane, the last adult descendant of the Coltrane line, comes to rescue Goree from his life of temptation and degradation. On their way to the Coltrane home, they must pass by the old Goree estate. Goree, finally remembering the occurrences of the previous day, declares to Coltrane that he cannot ride past the family estate in rags, and begs for the use of Coltrane's coat and hat. Of course, Pike is lying in wait and shoots Goree, believing him to be Coltrane. Goree's final words to Coltrane are, "My friend."

The story is eminently readable but contrived and, finally, little more than a maudlin tale of deathbed repentance. Porter appears to be making symbolic use of names–"Abner" meaning "light from the Lord"; "Goree" for "gory"; "Bethel" (the town where the story occurs) signifying, ironically, "of God"–but the symbols go nowhere. Once again Porter is working with appearances and realities. Goree is *not* Abner Coltrane, as Pike thinks him to be; neither is he the detestable character he has seemed through most of the story. "A Blackjack Bargainer," written and published while Porter was in prison, seems to have been an act of vicarious penance. Like Goree, Porter was frequently drunk; more significantly, he felt that he had hopelessly damaged his family's name by ending up in prison.

The plot of "The Duplicity of Hargraves" (*Junior Munsey*, February 1902; collected in *Sixes and Sevens*) is simple. At their boardinghouse an aspiring actor becomes close friends with a man of "the old, old South," Maj. Pendleton Talbot, and spends many hours in his company. One evening Talbot happens to see a play in which the young actor has a part. He is livid when Hargraves appears on the stage as an old Southern gentleman, dressed as Talbot dresses, speaking as he does, and even telling his favorite stories. Hargraves offers compensation the next day, knowing that the elderly man is short of money, but Talbot orders him out of the room. By acting the role of an old black retainer who had borrowed the money on credit, Hargraves eventually succeeds in paying Talbot three hundred dollars.

"The Duplicity of Hargraves" is one of Porter's finest regional tales of the Old South and among the best stories he wrote. Besides the skillful characterization of Major Talbot, the witty description, and the generally snappy dialogue, the story brings up teasing questions about Northern and Southern hypocrisies, especially those centered on race relations. Porter does little more than suggest the hypocrisies, "duplicities," and ironies, but his suggestions have a surprising power and significance.

Perhaps the best of Porter's New Orleans tales, "The Renaissance at Charleroi" (*Era*, October 1902; collected in *Roads of Destiny*), begins with Adéle le Fauquier's refusal to marry her suitor, Grandmont Charles, until he learns the fate of her brother Victor, who disappeared ten years earlier following some family problems. Charles, believing Victor to have drowned, has little faith that he will be successful in meeting Adéle's request and so, in an effort to console himself, decides to use the money he has been saving for his marriage on a party at Charleroi, the old family mansion. Since the mansion has been de-

serted for years, recipients of Charles's invitations take them as a joke; no one materializes on the night of the party–except a passing tramp who has found a discarded invitation and seen the lighted windows. After the man has been washed and properly dressed, he joins Charles at the table. Predictably, he turns out to be Victor. All is forgiven, and a bright future is promised.

The story turns on Porter's favorite motif of appearances and reality. None of the central characters is entirely what he seems to be. Even though the story is essentially melodramatic, and its sense of mystery weakened thereby, it is thematically richer than much of Porter's work. The tale generates the ideas that humility is prerequisite to redemption, that a return to the past is necessary to expunge the wrongs of the past, and that redemption is not always purchasable–but is often granted or withheld according to the whims of fate.

"The Ghost of a Chance" (1903; collected in *Sixes and Sevens*) is perhaps Porter's closest approach to the excellence of a Saki tale and one of his comparatively few stories to deal with high society. The Kinsolvings, a newly monied New York family, have been embarrassed by the fabrications of one Mrs. Fischer-Suympkins, who has publicly claimed to have seen a hod-carrying ghost in the room in which she spent an evening at the Kinsolvings'. Mrs. Fischer-Suympkins's gossip is eventually put to rest when Mrs. Bellamy Bellmore, an even more highly respected member of the Kinsolvings' set, apparently sees the respectable ghost of a Colonial soldier during a weekend visit.

On the surface, there is not much story here. Mrs. Bellmore has accepted the Kinsolvings' invitation not so much out of kindness as curiosity. She has determined to find out for herself whether Terrence Kinsolving, the oldest son, is "shy" or "deep." Nor has Mrs. Bellmore fabricated her ghost. We learn that Terrence has donned a costume and entered Mrs. Bellmore's room during the night; once there, he has not only paraded about but has also awakened Mrs. Bellmore with a kiss. The subtlety and wit of the tale are very nearly spoiled in its last few paragraphs where Porter unnecessarily and elaborately reveals that Terrence was the ghost, a fact discerned by the reader long before. The balance of the story, however, is first-rate: its focus is on characterization rather than theme or conclusion; its central interest is the tension between characters rather than the trademark "twist." From

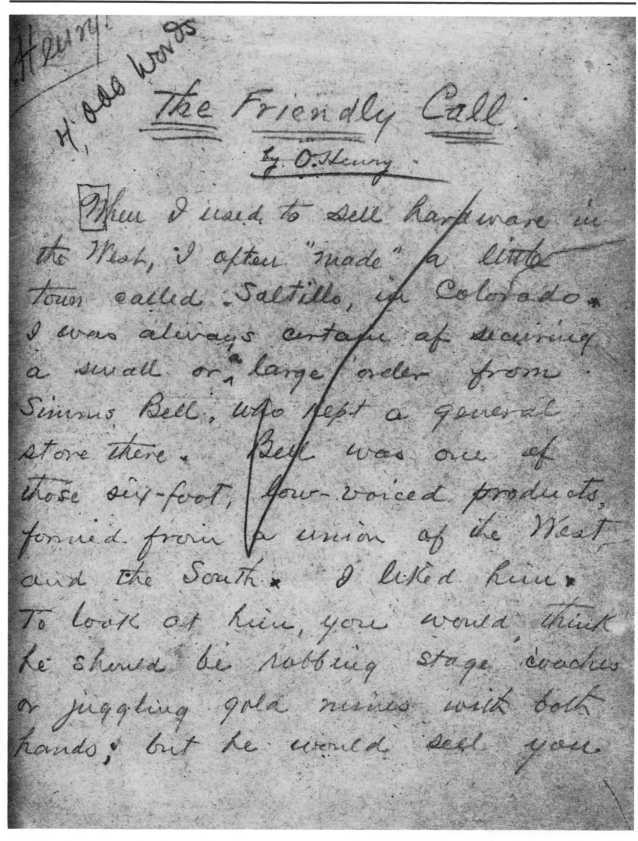

Pages from the manuscript for "The Friendly Call" (William Sydney Porter Collection [#6333], Clifton Waller Barrett Library, Special Collections Department, University of Virginia Library)

②

a paper of tacks or a spool of
thread, with ten times more patience
and courtesy than any saleslady
in a city department store.

I had a two-fold object in
my last visit to Saltillo. One was
to sell a bill of goods; the other,
to advise Bell of a chance that
I knew of, by which, I was certain,
he could make a small fortune.

In Mountain City, a town on
the Union Pacific, five times larger
than Saltillo, a mercantile firm was
about to go to the wall. It had
a lively and growing custom, but
was on the edge of dissolution
and ruin. Mismanagement, and
the gambling habit of one of the
partners, explained it. The condition

Mrs. Kinsolving's declamation, "Actually, a *hod!*"–which opens the story–to Mrs. Bellmore's explanation for deleting Terrence's name from a party list, "Too shy!"–which closes it–"The Ghost of a Chance" is charming, witty, and delightful storytelling.

Like "The Renaissance at Charleroi," "Cherchez la Femme" (1903; collected in *Roads of Destiny*) is a light mystery story. Robbins and Dumars, reporters for competing New Orleans papers, are determined to solve a case that has puzzled residents of the French Quarter for several months. One Gaspard Marin, a respected businessman and humanitarian, has passed away shortly after being entrusted with twenty thousand dollars by a former servant in his family, for whom he promised to invest the money. Working on the theory that the best of men are flawed and that one must "look for the woman" at the bottom of a strange situation, Robbins and Dumars research Marin's past. Instead of discovering juicy gossip, however, the reporters learn that Marin purchased gold bonds with his servant's inheritance and that she, not understanding what they were, has used them to paper up a crack in her restaurant wall.

The story is built almost entirely upon the tired joke of its title, and its primary interest today is its regionalism. Settings are deftly portrayed, characterizations are crisp if one-dimensional, and details of early-twentieth-century New Orleans life are skillfully captured.

"Roads of Destiny" (1903; collected in *Roads of Destiny*) has been called "the most carefully wrought out of O. Henry's longer stories"–having, according to C. Alphonso Smith, "an Alexandre Dumas exterior, a Poe structure, and an Omar Khayyam interior." The fairy tale depicts three possible conclusions to the life of David Mignot, a second-rate poet. All are the same: the collapse of Mignot's idealism and his subsequent death. The center of the tale concerns the collision of art, as represented by poetry and beauty, with the mechanics of reality, and man's inability "to order, shun or wield or mould" his own destiny. The story is overly long, its diction frequently heavy and cumbersome, and its characterizations superficial, but if read as a parable, with a core of oriental fatalism, it is arguably one of Porter's more successful stories.

Published the same month as "Roads of Destiny," "A Retrieved Reformation" (*Cosmopolitan*, April 1903; collected in *Roads of Destiny*) is among Porter's most sentimental and famous tales. Jimmy Valentine, a professional safecracker, jumps parole and adopts an alias but–after a salvific glance from the beautiful and genteel woman who agrees to marry him–abandons his life of crime and opens a respectable shoe store. Shortly before his wedding Valentine elects to blow his cover rather than to stand by as a small girl suffocates in an accidentally closed safe. He then turns himself in to a federal detective who happens to be standing by; the detective, impressed by Valentine's humanity, pretends not to know him.

"While the Auto Waits" (*Ainslee's*, May 1903; collected in *The Voice of the City*, 1908), one of Porter's best-known stories, represents the recurring theme of the impostor as well as what he called "turning the tables on Haroun al Raschid." It is the story of an apparently wealthy young woman who is courted by an apparently common young man in one of New York's busy parks. In actuality the young woman is a cashier in a garish restaurant near the park; the young man, who has claimed the restaurant as *his* place of employment, is the wealthy owner of the chauffeur-driven automobile the young woman has declared to be her own. The thematic significance of the tale seems to be that the young woman, in her pretensions to the empty and vain life of wealth, is a silly hypocrite. The young man, on the other hand, in his apparent desires for a life of more common substance, is worthy of sympathy and respect.

It is in his Western tales and his stories of the down-and-out that Porter is often hopelessly romantic and maudlin. Representative stories in each of these categories are "Jimmy Hayes and Muriel" (*Munsey's Magazine*, July 1903; collected in *Sixes and Sevens*) and, published almost exactly a year later, "The Furnished Room" (1904; collected in *The Four Million*).

Jimmy Hayes, a wet-behind-the-ears recruit of the Texas Rangers, is not fully accepted by his fellows because of his youth and his easygoing personality. His primary distinction is that he owns a pet horned frog named Muriel, who wears a bright red ribbon around her neck. When Hayes is missing after a brief skirmish with a band of Mexicans, it is believed by the other Rangers that he has fled in cowardice. Nearly a year later the leaders of the regiment come across "the scene of an unwritten tragedy": the skeletons of three Mexicans and, fifty yards away, that of a "solitary defender." From beneath "the weather-beaten rags" of the lone skeleton "wriggled out a horned frog with a faded red ribbon around its neck, and sat upon the shoulder of its long quiet master."

The plot of "The Furnished Room" may be stated more briefly: a young man, seeking his girlfriend and desperate because he cannot find her, commits suicide in the very room, as it turns out, where she committed suicide a week earlier.

Porter's attempts at tragedy are, from a latter-day perspective, unmoving. Pathos is upstaged by bathos; drama plays a secondary role to melodrama. The most telling weakness of either of these two stories is the superficiality of the sentiment. In the case of Hayes, the Ranger detachment really cares little about his fate. It is only concerned that he may have been "the first blot on its escutcheon." Porter tries to rescue "The Furnished Room" in the overtly ironic speech, delivered by the crusty landlady, which ends the story. But because the fate of the young man's girlfriend is also revealed in the landlady's final words, the speech intensifies the bathos of the situation rather than pointing up its ironies. While Leacock and other early critics considered "The Unfurnished Room" Porter's greatest story, by 1943 Cleanth Brooks and Robert Penn Warren had dismissed the surprise ending of the story as "a shabby trick."

The central character in "Witches' Loaves" (1904; collected in *Sixes and Sevens*) is a middle-aged spinster who runs a small bakery. Her romantic fantasies lead Miss Martha Meacham to believe that a favorite customer is a starving artist, and she longs to support him with home-cooked meals and her two-thousand-dollar bank account. During one visit Miss Martha covertly slips a slab of butter into each of his loaves. A short time later—when confronted by the now-irate customer—she learns that he is an architect and not an artist, that he has purchased stale bread because the crumbs are "better than India rubber" for erasing pencil lines, and that a prize architectural design has been spoiled because of the buttered loaves.

Though neither subtle nor profound, "Witches' Loaves" is an entertaining tale of initiation from sentimentality into reality. A twist on a familiar theme, the "appearances" are not generalized in the story but confined to Miss Martha's own perceptions. The reader has been led to suspect her delusions and is not tricked by the story's conclusion. Despite some contrivances, "Witches' Loaves" remains one of Porter's better efforts. It is fast moving and tightly constructed; its tone is nicely balanced between humor and pathos; the themes are more challenging than those Porter often dealt with; and Miss Martha is deftly characterized.

"A Matter of Mean Elevation" (1904; collected in *Whirligigs*) features the kidnapping by Venezuelan Indians of Mlle. Nina Giraud, star singer of the Alcazar Opera Company of New Orleans on tour in South America, and her eventual rescue by an American trader, Johnny Armstrong. Armstrong is initially awestruck before the goddesslike poise and beauty of Mlle. Giraud. But as Giraud and Armstrong descend from the mountains where she has been kept prisoner, a transformation takes place. The "goddess" acquires a sensuality as they reach the highlands; she becomes earthy as they travel through the lowlands; and by the time they reach the cities on the coast, she is coarse and vulgar.

The premise of the story—that an individual's character is determined by his or her environment—is the basis of many literary masterpieces. In comparison to such contemporary works as Joseph Conrad's *Heart of Darkness* (1902), Stephen Crane's *Maggie: A Girl of the Streets* (1893), or even Twain's *Puddn'head Wilson* (1894), however, "A Matter of Mean Elevation" is shallow indeed. The story has little more structure than a sketch (the loose introduction comprises nearly half its length), and the narrative lacks the philosophical and moral sophistication that would give its premise life and significance.

"The Caliph and the Cad" (1904; collected in *Sixes and Sevens*) explicitly transplants the *Arabian Nights' Entertainment* to Porter's beloved Bagdad-by-the-subway. His hero, the poor driver Corny Brannigan, reverses the habit of Haroun al Raschid, the Caliph of Bagdad, who disguised himself as a commoner so that he might associate with the poor. "After-hours" Corny likes to clothe himself in "the garb of the gentleman" and mingle with the rich and distinguished on Broadway. When he stands up to a gentleman who is mistreating the lady at his side, he "learned something about himself that he did not know before"—that despite his clothes and his breeding, he is more a "gentleman" than certain of the "swells" he has admired. While "The Caliph and the Cad" is an important example of Porter's "impostor" tales, its language and humor are mawkish, the conversation between the gentleman and the lady unconvincing, and the occasion for the "chivalric rescue" unclear.

"A Harlem Tragedy" (1904; collected in *The Trimmed Lamp*) is perhaps Porter's most bizarre tale. In the predominantly Irish Harlem of the early 1900s, Mrs. Fink is troubled to learn from Mrs. Cassidy, who lives in the flat one flight above, that Mrs. Cassidy's husband beats her–and then "repents" through expensive gifts and extravagant outings, instilling in his wife's countenance the "love light that shines in the eye of the Maori maid when she recovers consciousness in the hut of the wooer who has stunned and dragged her there." Mrs. Fink is overcome by a "rising, indignant jealousy" and determines that she will prompt her own glum, unromantic husband to "do his duty"–to "so far prove his manhood"–by inducing him to strike her. During the Labor Day holiday she sets upon him both verbally and physically, yearning for the return blow: "Mr. Fink sprang to his feet–Maggie caught him again on the jaw with a wide swing of her other hand. She closed her eyes in that fearful, blissful moment before his blow should come–she whispered his name to herself–she leaned to the expected shock, hungry for it." The story ends with Mrs. Fink sobbing on Mrs. Cassidy's shoulder, confessing that her outburst has had no other effect than to stir her husband to begin doing the laundry.

Potentially there is a powerful story here, both socially and psychologically. The dark sadomasochism, the proletarian characters, and the frustrated expectations suggest in various ways the stories of Edgar Allan Poe, Flannery O'Connor, or Frank Norris, especially *McTeague* (1899). Porter tells his story with economy, the characterizations are sharply set up, and specific details, such as the boxing imagery and the Labor Day motif, have greater than usual resonance. The story might have become an intriguing exploration of marriage expectations, the pathology of tenement life, or the real tragedies of wife-beating. Unfortunately, it is trivialized by its tone. Although the form of the story is ironic, there is sufficient tonal ambiguity to imply that Porter sympathized with the narrative's extreme chauvinism. In any case, it is difficult to see the story as a satire: wife-beating is treated as a simple fact of life, if not a joke.

"The Brief Début of Tildy" (1904; collected in *The Four Million*), published a couple months before, is thematically similar to "A Harlem Tragedy." A short, dumpy waitress in a small Eighth Avenue restaurant, Tildy thinks, "What bliss it must have been to have had a man follow one and black one's eye for love!" The strength of the story is its setting. In a few lines Porter

sketches a convincing turn-of-the-century café. But again he gets stranded in his sexual typing and sacrifices plot structure, theme, and characterization to background detail.

Written the same month as "A Harlem Tragedy," but standing in tonal contrast to it, "The Door of Unrest" (*Cosmopolitan*, May 1904; collected in *Sixes and Sevens*) attempts a movement from humor to tragedy. A small-town newspaper editor, new to his southern community, is determined to find out the truth about Mike O'Bader, one of the town's oldest residents. O'Bader suffers the delusion that he is Michob Ader, the Wandering Jew–the shoemaker who turned the cross-bearing Christ away from his doorstep. The editor eventually learns that O'Bader thirty years earlier had turned his profligate daughter away from his own door and into the hands of a mob, who then drove her out of town and on to suicide. The story has the bite of social criticism insofar as it makes a case against hard-line conservatism and cultural intractibility. But the force of the parable is blunted, as is often true of Porter, by a contrived plot and flat characterizations. The transition from humor to tragedy comes by fits and starts, and the tonal shifts consequently are distracting rather than chilling.

One of several Porter stories to dramatize man's tendency to relapse into old habits and the persistent influence of environment on mental habits is "The Pendulum" (1904; collected in *The Trimmed Lamp*). First published with the title "Katy, of the Frogmore Flats; or the Passing Repentance of John Perkins," this story of less than two thousand words has been compared to Guy de Maupassant's "An Artist" and cited as a possible cause for the psychologist William James's fondness for O. Henry. Protagonist John Perkins, a New York City flat dweller, is nearly overcome with loneliness when he arrives home from work one evening to discover that his wife unexpectedly has left to take care of her ailing mother. Recognizing his past inattentiveness to his wife's needs, Perkins resolves to be more sensitive to her and to spend more time at home, especially in the evenings. At that moment his wife returns: her mother was not so ill as she had imagined. Moments later Perkins is reaching for his hat. He can still get to the pool hall by 8:30 if he hurries.

"The Coming-Out of Maggie" (1904; collected in *The Four Million*) remains interesting for its period details of working-class entertainment in New York City and for its nonchalant ethnic prejudices. In the story Maggie, a rather unpopular girl, convinces Tony Spinelli to pose as an Irishman, Terry O'Sullivan, and to escort her to a weekly dance of the Give and Take Athletic Association, an Irish fisticuffs society. At the dance he gets into a row with the president of the association, Dempsey Donovan. Maggie prevents "Terry" from using his concealed stiletto on Dempsey ("Them Guineas always carries knives," she declares); he is shown down the backstairs; and Maggie is rewarded for her "courage" by a date with Dempsey for the following week. The morality of the story is suspect. Spinelli is condemned because of his clichéd nationality rather than his character. The proud and domineering Donovan certainly is no more honorable. And the narrative conveys no feeling that Maggie has been wrong to use Spinelli, rather that she has acted correctly in saving Donovan.

A novel by designation, *Cabbages and Kings* originated in Bynner's suggestion that Porter should take his Central American tales, supply them with new connective tissue, and produce a book that could be sold as a single work of fiction. The story "Money Maze," which had appeared in *Ainslee's* in May 1901, provided a rudimentary plot that, broken down and distributed, became the backbone of the novel. Porter drew together stories that had been published earlier in such other places as *McClure's, Smart Set,* and *Everybody's* and wrote several new pieces ("Fox-in-the-Morning," "The Vitagraphoscope," "The Remnants of the Code") to tie the narrative together. While some critics have argued that *Cabbages and Kings* is best described as a loosely related collection of short stories, the book, despite its multiplicity of subplots, has as much coherence as many popular works of the time.

The central story of the novel is recounted in the introduction and in seven of its eighteen chapters ("Fox-in-the-Morning," "Smith," "Caught," "Money Maze," "The Remnants of the Code," "Two Recalls," and "The Vitagraphoscope"). Miraflores, president of the "banana republic" of Anchuria (based on Honduras), is deposed in a revolution and replaced by the charismatic Losada. With his female companion Isabel Guilbert, an expatriate American opera singer, Miraflores escapes to Coralio, a small Anchurian village, from whence they hope to leave the country, taking a hundred thousand dollars that Miraflores has pilfered from the national treasury. Simultaneously, Churchill Wahrfield, the president of an American firm, the Republic Insurance Company, has skipped to Coralio with his daughter and a hundred thousand dollars stolen from company funds. Frank Goodwin, an American speculator who has located himself in Coralio, apprehends a man he believes to be the deposed Miraflores. Caught red-handed with a hundred thousand dollars, the man shoots himself. Goodwin marries the dead man's female companion, intending to keep the recovered loot for himself, but is blackmailed by an observant drunk who has witnessed Goodwin's recovery of the money. As it turns out, the real Miraflores and Isabel manage to escape to Nice. The suicide is Wahrfield, the woman Goodwin marries is Wahrfield's daughter, and the money Goodwin recovers is returned to the insurance firm. Ancillary tales in the novel describe Losada's fall from grace, portray various grafts and schemes of American speculators, and satirize the military bravado of Anchuria.

Beyond the relevance of embezzlement and flight to Central America to Porter's personal life, *Cabbages and Kings* is important for at least three reasons. First, it established Porter as a popular and aesthetically credible author who could sell books as well as short stories. The novel was greeted by eminent literary critics and provoked favorable comparisons between its author and such diverse figures as Kipling, de Maupassant, and Richard Harding Davis. Secondly, Porter's stories fixed in the American consciousness the notion of Latin America as a land of allure and romance, unpredictable and volatile, revolutionary but full of opportunity. Finally, the novel marks a stage in the portrayals of the "ugly American" from Mark Twain to Joan Didion.

The romantic landscapes of Latin America and Porter's poetic flourishes ("fragrant tropical flowers," "light-footed Caribs," "dark banana groves") took the fancy of his contemporaries but seem clichéd and formulaic today. The rapidity with which *Cabbages and Kings* was produced left a trail of mixed metaphors, vexing alliterations, careless diction, and verbosity. While many passages and even entire chapters are economically written and still make entertaining reading, Porter too often manifests the sentiments of his character Keogh, who declares: "The art of narrative consists in concealing from your audience everything it wants to know until after you expose your favorite opinions on topics foreign to the subject. A good story is like a bitter pill, with the sugar coating inside of it."

"An Unfinished Story" (*McClure's Magazine,* August 1905; collected in *The Four Million*) merits mention here as being, according to C. Alphonso Smith, "probably the most admired of all O. Henry's stories." This moral condemnation of the low wages paid to working girls by exploitive employers, however, is more a sermon than a tale. Its depiction of the "wage controversy" is simplistic. Its heroine, Dulcie, who starves for a little luxury in her joyless working life, is no match for Theodore Dreiser's Carrie Meeber.

Whatever superlatives have been applied to Porter's other tales, "The Gift of the Magi" unquestionably has been "the most widely known and best loved of all Porter's stories." This staple of high-school reading programs and inspiration for countless plays and skits was written in a three-hour burst under deadline pressure for the *New York Sunday World* of 10 December 1905 (collected in *The Four Million*). Assigned to provide a Christmas centerpiece for the *World* magazine section, Porter responded with the tale of a tender young couple, in a gray eight-dollar New York flat, who sacrifice their proudest possessions to buy an extravagant gift for each other. Della sells her rippling, cascading brown hair (which would have "depreciated" the Queen of Sheba) to purchase a platinum fob chain for her husband's watch. James Dillingham Young ("Jim") trades his ancestral gold watch (which King Solomon would have envied) for the jeweled combs Della has "worshipped" in a Broadway window. It would be churlish to criticize the sentimentality and rhetoric of this American classic, or to object that Porter's archetypal husband and wife are far removed from the complexities of married life that he well knew. "The Gift of the Magi" concludes in the tradition of an Eastern fable: "But in a last word to the wise of these days let it be said that of all who give gifts these two were the wisest."

"The Gift of the Magi" also illustrates Porter's tendency to recycle surefire characterizations and plot situations. The sacrifices of Della and Jim are foreshadowed in "A Service of Love," published in the *Sunday World* in January of the same year (1905; collected in *The Four Million*), where the newlywed artists Joe and Delia Larabee pretend to support each other through their respective talents (painting and music) but secretly hire themselves out to the same laundry.

"The Poet and the Peasant" (1905; collected in *Strictly Business*) is comprised of two tales. The first, which begins and ends the story, introduces a group of writers who are chagrined when a true-to-life pastoral poem is rejected by a city editor as "artificial" and, so, determine to set him up by submitting a clichéd and truly artificial "nature poem." The editor accepts the poem, commending its great immediacy and sense of reality. The second tale, which makes up the substance of the story, tells how a "hayseed" newly arrived in New York City is taken to be a con artist because he looks too "artificial." Only after he dons the fashion and bearing of a dandy do people suspect his country origins, and thieves steal his inheritance.

Porter's "put-offs"–his apologetic asides and philosophical detours–often are simply mannered. In this case, when he minimizes the importance of his frame tale ("But this has very little to do with the story"), he is able to achieve a stronger sense of irony, for the artificial pastoral poem *is* the story, or at least the point of it. Porter's themes of appearance and reality, artificiality and naturalness, materialism and idealism are nicely paralleled here and anticipate modern metafictions.

Porter's amusing tale "The Handbook of Hymen" (*Munsey's Magazine*, 1906; collected in *Heart of the West*) reflects his own infatuations with reference books and poetry, especially with *Webster's Unabridged Dictionary* and the poems of Tennyson. His protagonist, Sanderson Pratt, a crusty Montana prospector, wins the hand of the widow "Mrs. De Ormond Sampson, the queen of Rosa society," by impressing her with his rich knowledge of gee-whiz facts and figures he painstakingly gleaned from a small volume entitled *Herkimer's Handbook of Indispensable Information* while snowbound with his partner Idaho Green. Idaho had won his pick of the two books in their cabin and immersed himself in the poems of a Persian "wine agent" named "Homer K. M.," but he fails to seduce the commonsensical widow with the urgings of "Ruby Ott" to take "a jug of wine and a loaf of bread, and go singing and cavorting up and down under the trees." The story pokes gentle fun at both statistics and poetry and, despite the tall talk, demonstrates how charming Porter's narrative voice can be when he resists the temptation to sentimentalize his plots and characters or to philosophically reduce reality.

The story "'Girl'" (*American Magazine*, 1905; collected in *Whirligigs*) is little more than an extended joke. Hartley, the protagonist, appears to be taking a mistress but, at the punch line, is revealed to have done nothing more passionate or unorthodox than employ a cook. While the story is technically vapid, it is interesting for its sexual teasing. The dialogue and connecting narrative are frequently suggestive, and the characters are described in terms of their sexual appeal. " 'Girl' " is one of only a handful of Porter stories–notably the New Orleans French Quarter tales–that deal with anything but traditional and largely Puritanical men-women relationships. Porter affirms marital fidelity but in the process provides a generous dose of titillation for 1905 tastes. This was his last story to be published in the *World* magazine.

One of the few Porter characters actually to undergo change and mature is Nancy in "The Trimmed Lamp" (*McClure's Magazine*, August 1906; collected in *The Trimmed Lamp*). A New York "shop-girl" and professional man-hunter, she is determined to "bring down" the biggest "game." Her friend Lou, who makes twice Nancy's small salary, gradually becomes alienated from the commonplace through her increasing attraction to the exotic and worldly. Nancy, on the other hand, through the "education" provided by the shop where she works, learns an awareness of qualities apart from wealth, "such words as 'truth' and 'honour' and now and then just 'kindness.' " When Lou deserts her friends and past to marry a millionaire, Nancy falls in love and gets engaged to the faithful and practical man Lou has left behind, recognizing him as "the biggest catch in the world."

"The Trimmed Lamp" is weak thematically. Lou's motivations are undeveloped, and while we are told that Nancy changes, very little of the process is shown. However, the fashions, slang, values, recreation, and aspirations of working women in early-twentieth-century New York are nicely captured, as is their fascination for the dress and habits of the wealthy. While the story is an aesthetic disappointment, it is culturally interesting.

As the origin of the Cisco Kid, a character later glamorized in movies and on television, "The Caballero's Way" (*Everybody's Magazine*, July 1907; collected in *Heart of the West*) is perhaps the most famous of Porter's Western tales. The Cisco Kid appears as a renegade outlaw who arranges the death of Tonia, a woman who has betrayed him. The story thus institutionalizes several components of the Western: the heroic outlaw, the cool yet perpetually disappointed Ranger who stalks him, and the notion that betrayal is a greater crime than murder–that the betrayer is a target for "justified revenge." The story carries little weight aesthetically, but it has had cultural repercussions.

Of all Porter's tales, perhaps none wears quite so well as "The Ransom of Red Chief" (1907; collected in *Whirligigs*), which has been second only to "The Gift of the Magi" in popularity. The story tells how two amateur crooks, Sam and Bill, settle on a kidnapping as the means to earn the cash they need to set up a land scheme. After successfully kidnapping the redheaded son (who turns out to be more demon than human) of a prominent man from Summit, Illinois–and suffering the brat's company for a couple of days in the "wilderness" outside town–they withdraw their demand for ransom and *pay* the kid's father to take him off their hands.

The story is clearly derivative of the sketches of Twain and Ambrose Bierce; in turn, it has spawned a number of stories, films, and television programs that represent little more than variations on its central plot. Like the best sketches of America's earlier humorists, "The Ransom of Red Chief" has retained much of its original freshness and vitality. The first-person narrator, one of Porter's most satisfying characters, adds to the immediacy, humor, and zest of the tale. The "secret" or "twist" is out well before the concluding paragraphs, so there is almost no emphasis on rabbit-from-the-hat theatrics, but instead an impressive, controlled focus on plot, structure, and characterization.

"A Municipal Report" (1909; collected in *Strictly Business*) has been praised in terms that imply the flawlessness and excellence of a genuine masterpiece. True, its unusual characters, elements of mystery, and witty, conversational tone make it highly readable. Its ostensible concerns with the appropriate domain of fiction, especially with workable settings, give it more substance than many of Porter's tales, and its status as an original "Southern grotesque" makes it deserving of analysis. The narrative introduces such themes as the Old versus the New South and the role of the writer in the modern world.

The central plot, however, is cloying and sentimental. A city editor is sent to Nashville, Tennessee, to draw up a contract with one Azalea Adair, an antebellum relic with a flair for poetry. The editor learns that Miss Adair's drunken husband, Maj. Wentworth Caswell, has squandered all his wife's income, and that were it not for her black servant, Miss Adair long since would have starved. When Caswell robs his wife of the fifty-dollar advance that the editor makes on her poetry, he is murdered by Miss Adair's faithful servant. The identity of the murderer is known only to the editor, who quietly leaves town. The shallow plot is compounded by stereotyped characterizations: the wilting yet still noble Southern belle, the tyrannical and corrupted Southern "major," and the faithful Negro servant. And the Twainian humor of the long introduction does not prevent the story from becoming tedious. Porter supposedly wrote "A Municipal Report" to refute the quotation from Frank Norris that he uses to introduce the tale: "Fancy a novel about Chicago or Buffalo, let us say, or Nashville, Tennessee! There are just three big cities in the United States that are 'story cities'–New York, of course, New Orleans,. and, best of the lot, San Francisco."

"Adventures in Neurasthenia," published in *Cosmopolitan* for July 1910 and subsequently as "Let Me Feel Your Pulse" in *Sixes and Sevens*, was one of Porter's last completed works. It is noteworthy mainly for its autobiographical underpinnings and its lilting, uneven humor. The story centers on the experiences of its narrator, who, after finding no relief in "miracle drugs" for his numerous ailments, real and imagined, eventually accepts the fact that the time-honored prescription of exercise, balanced diet, and proper rest is the best remedy of all. The narrator's illnesses, together with his searchings for "cures," have their foundation in Porter's ill health during his last year of life. Although one of the few stories from Porter's later period to have a discernible biographical connection, this probably is the least "heavy" of his last works. The occasionally delightful wit is dulled by lapses into nostalgia and by Porter's apparent desire to turn his tale into something of a moral lesson.

The unfinished manuscript for a story called "The Dream" was discovered in Porter's rooms following his death. *Cosmopolitan*, which had ordered the story, published the manuscript with an explanatory note suggesting Porter's intentions for the story in September 1910 (collected in *Rolling Stones*, 1912). According to the note, Porter "planned to make this story different from his others." He is quoted as having said, "I want to show the public that I can write something new– new for me, I mean–a story without slang, a straightforward dramatic plot treated in a way that will come nearer my idea of real story-writing." What one gets, however, is much what one has come to expect from a Porter tale: sentimentalized language and situations, mediocre attempts at Spanish-American dialect, contrived

characters and events, and–in the projected ending for the story–the trademark "twist."

The story presents a criminal named Murray who faces execution for murdering his sweetheart. As he is taken into the execution chamber, he lapses into a kind of daydream: he sees a "little country cottage, bright, sun-lit, nestling in a bower of flowers." His wife and child are there, and when he talks to them, he discovers that "Some one has frightfully, irretrievably blundered," and that "the trial, the conviction, the sentence" are all a dream. "Then–at a sign from the prison warden the fatal current is turned on"– and the reader discovers that "Murray had dreamed the wrong dream."

Since the plot has been re-created by the *Cosmopolitan* editors, one cannot know Porter's precise intentions. It is clear, however, that his obsession with crime, prisons, guilt, and punishment–with his own past–remained intensely with him to the end. Though he wished it otherwise, Porter seems resigned to the fact that he had "dreamed the wrong dream" and that the idealized, romantic life he longed for was not to be. If there is a change in Porter's "style" in the story, it is simply that the last twist is tragic rather than optimistic.

Porter's literary reputation depends largely on his output from late 1903 to late 1905, when he completed 113 stories for the *Sunday World* and a dozen or so for other magazines. Nearly all these tales involve conflicts between the "aristocratic" and the "plebeian"–common human beings challenged by exotic characters or circumstances; exotic characters confronted by the perplexities of common life–a tension that Porter himself felt as long as he lived. Most of his tales explore themes of appearance and reality, the artist as a loner, the existence of beauty and significance in the mundane, or the role of fate in human affairs. Nearly all resolve in traditional values and morality.

The "O. Henry" paradigm was cemented in the stories for the *World* and imitated, and trivialized, by the host of writers who tried to duplicate Porter's success between 1910 and 1920. The stock elements of Porter's stories include: (1) a brisk opening that pulls the reader into the action with a surefire "hook"; (2) a confiding narrator who, nonetheless, withholds crucial information until the last possible moment; (3) a pleasant and worldly wise tone comprised of chitchat, wit, satire, philosophy, and swank; (4) liberal use of a "humane renegade"; (5) a healthy dose of coincidence, usually with a deus ex machina reversal in which everything is rescued and set right again; and (6) a "surprise ending."

The last three ingredients bear further comment. While Twain, William Dean Howells, Stephen Crane, and other "realists" tended to humanize their villains, Porter, as an idealistic romantic, pushes things further. He not only makes his villains sympathetic or "realistic"; he ennobles them, minimizing their sins and emphasizing their virtues. Porter's "humane renegades" and "gentle grafters" were anticipated in the prostitute-with-a-heart-of-gold motif employed by Bret Harte and his contemporaries. Porter moves the motif to the city and expands it to include a far wider panoply of the down-and-out and criminally inclined–thieves, drunkards, embezzlers, madames, kidnappers, bums. In arguing the humanity and even the nobility of people who previously had been portrayed as possessing neither, Porter affected not only American literary naturalism but socialism and reportage.

In his biographical essay on Porter, Carl Van Doren clarifies the fifth ingredient, the use of coincidence and reversal of fortune, common to his stories. "The episodes which touched his imagination enough to make him write stories about them were," Van Doren notes, "instances of the sort of irony which lets unexpected consequences follow familiar causes." If Porter's vision was ironic, however, it was not embittered. His stories show "little of the long memory of tragedy, which cherished one fatality after another until the lives of men are made to seem the playthings of blind, malicious forces." Almost without exception his coincidences work to romantic ends, glorifying traditional ideals and providing assurance that all things–given time and patience–will come out as they should.

Porter's sixth ingredient, the use of surprise endings, was a reason for his contemporary popularity as well as his subsequent fall from critical favor. Porter's love of the "twist" at the end was shared by his British contemporary H. H. Munro (Saki), whose stock, unlike Porter's, has risen over the years. In the work of Saki the central delight is the story itself–its well-rounded characters, its polished wit and dialogue, its charming tone and general effortlessness. In Porter, more often than not, everything–characterization, plot, dialogue, description, tone–seems to be skewed to accommodate the ending. Porter sacrifices too much for his punch lines.

Although Porter was suspicious of his abilities and described himself as a producer of "picayune goods," he took pride in his authorial role. He was deeply offended by requests to write stories from ready-made plot outlines. He had little tolerance for editors who published salacious material. He retained editorial control over his work, especially as he gained fame and influence, and he was particular about where his stories were published.

Only a handful of Porter's stories have retained their status as minor classics. The success of these few tales, furthermore, seems as often the product of luck or inspiration as of informed effort. His "classics" crop up sporadically. Two of his bravest efforts at serious fiction, "The Renaissance at Charleroi" and "A Municipal Report," appeared in 1902 and 1909 respectively, at the beginning and the end of his career. Their execution differs little from such other fine parables and satires as "The Roads of Destiny" (1903) or "The Poet and the Peasant" (1905). Porter's best humorous tales also occur at random–"The Ghost of a Chance," for example, in 1903, "The Handbook of Hymen" in 1906, "The Ransom of Red Chief" in 1907. Successful and inferior stories are scattered throughout Porter's career, which is not marked by any definable artistic periods.

Reasons should be offered for the lack of development and maturation across Porter's short career. Chief among these would be the pace of his work as week after week he produced his twenty-five hundred words to fill a page of the *Sunday World* or pay off other commissions. He had a seismic sensitivity to the taste of his turn-of-the-century audience but also became entrapped by it. He perhaps possessed more genius than talent, and he seems not fully to have understood when he was writing well and when he was not. The praise of Leacock and other early admirers sounds merely quaint today.

Nevertheless, if circumscribed, Porter still has grounds for positive attention. At his best he revealed a talent for humor approaching that of Bierce, Harte, and Twain. Even his least satisfying stories demonstrate an engaging wit, perceptiveness, and the knack for entertainment. Had he recognized his greater aptitude as a humorist than a writer of dramatic tales, he might have established a more enduring base for critical appeal. Unfortunately the tonal ambivalence between Porter's humor and his sentimentality often undercuts the "realities of common existence" and the "innate nobility of the human soul" for which he was initially lauded.

Porter will continue to be an important secondary author because of his contributions to the writing profession itself and to the culture at large. He has remained a popular writer over the years; many of his stories never have been out of print, and collections of his works continue to enjoy impressive sales. His immense reputation between 1904 and 1920 did a great deal to stimulate both the appeal and the critical acceptance of the American short-story form. Porter's public favor had a dramatic influence on the rates paid to writers, and he proved that it was possible to live well in America by writing stories.

Porter's works are documents of social and cultural as well as literary importance. The character types, class structures, emotions, vernacular styles, and scenic details of his stories, as much as their phenomenal reception, give them a significance both to social reportage and to the sociology of taste in America in the first decade of this century that can be claimed by few others. The stories of "O. Henry" are as vivid a record of his times as the columns of Finley Peter Dunne, the photojournalism of Jacob Riis, or the paintings of George Bellows. They offer excellent resources for exploring both our urban and regional folklore.

The veracity of Porter's Texas tales has been praised by the distinguished Western historian Walter P. Webb, and his contribution to the genre of the popular Western has been enduring, if less profound than that of a contemporary work, Owen Wister's *The Virginian* (1904). Hollywood immortalized The Cisco Kid and kept the cowboys, Rangers, and villains of Porter's Western tales alive through movies and television serials into the 1960s. *Cabbages and Kings*, furthermore, was in some respects a seminal depiction of North American interests in Central America.

For a time America's most popular and admired storyteller, Porter also has had a remarkable influence abroad. Early on, Current-García points out, his colloquialisms and his ability to create an "ingenious climax" were much admired by the Canadians and the British. His "dexterity in ordering and controlling his materials," his abounding *verve*," "intelligence armed with irony," and ability to dominate his characters "rather than suffering them" delighted the French. In the Soviet Union, Porter was praised especially for his "treatment of urban life, notably that of humble workers, and ... his ability to divert and amuse."

Some Soviets took his tales as "a bitter denunciation of the capitalist system," and even today, according to Deming Brown, they find him "magnificent railroad reading." The Russian formalist Boris Èjxenbaum expounded Porter's art of parody in a momentous essay, "O. Henry and the Theory of the Short Story," in 1925. He remains for foreign audiences today an important representative of American escape literature and a lens to the nation's colorful past.

It is conceivable that Porter's stock at home will rally in the coming years. As critical fashions change, the autonomous literary text and suspensions of disbelief so valued by the modern critics, and so seldom found in Porter's stories, have had to make room for new appreciations of the intrusive storytellers, narrative artifice, and verbal games at which Porter was a master. Recently Kent Bales has pointed to "suggested meanings" beneath the surfaces Porter showed to his audiences and has claimed that, through parody, he deconstructed a dying literary tradition and paved the way for reform. Taking as his example "A Municipal Report"–which a *New York Times* poll in 1914 chose as "the best American short story ever written"–Walter Evans has classified Porter as a "premodern master of Postmodern fiction" who simply "made the mistake of writing too innovatively half a century too soon." According to Evans, Porter's interest and delight for the contemporary reader pivot not on "bromides" like "appearance versus reality" but on his play with reality, his themes of illusion and imposture, his "pervasive self-consciousness, fondness for allusions, innovative structural pattern," and "metafictional references to storytelling."

Letters:

Letters to Lithopolis, from O. Henry to Mabel Wagnalls, edited by Mabel Wagnalls (Garden City, N.Y.: Doubleday, Page, 1922).

Bibliographies:

Paul S. Clarkson, *A Bibliography of William Sydney Porter* (Caldwell, Idaho: Caxton, 1938);
Richard C. Harris, *William Sydney Porter (O. Henry): A Reference Guide* (Boston: G. K. Hall, 1980).

Biographies:

Sara Lindsay Coleman, *Wind of Destiny* (New York: Doubleday, Page, 1916);
C. Alphonso Smith, *O. Henry Biography* (New York: Doubleday, Page, 1916); republished,

with an introduction by Warner Berthoff, in the American Men & Women of Letters Series (New York: Chelsea House, 1980);

Al Jennings, *Through the Shadows with O. Henry* (New York: Fly, 1921; London: Duckworth, 1923);

Frances G. Maltby, *The Dimity Sweetheart: O. Henry's Own Love Story* (Richmond, Va.: Dietz, 1930);

Robert H. Davis and Arthur B. Maurice, *The Caliph of Bagdad: Being Arabian Nights Flashes of the Life, Letters, and Work of O. Henry* (New York: Appleton, 1931);

William Wash Williams, *The Quiet Lodger of Irving Place* (New York: Dutton, 1936);

Lollie Cave Wilson, *Hard to Forget: The Young O. Henry* (Los Angeles: Lymanhouse, 1939);

E. Hudson Long, *O. Henry: The Man and His Work* (Philadelphia: University of Pennsylvania Press, 1949);

Dale Kramer, *The Heart of O. Henry* (New York: Rinehart, 1954);

Gerald Langford, *Alias O. Henry: A Biography of William Sydney Porter* (New York: Macmillan, 1957);

Ethel Stephens Arnett, *O. Henry from Polecat Creek* (Greensboro, N.C.: Piedmont, 1962);

Richard O'Connor, *O. Henry: The Legendary Life of William S. Porter* (Garden City, N.Y.: Doubleday, 1970).

References:

Cleanth Brooks, Jr., and Robert Penn Warren, *Understanding Fiction* (New York: Crofts, 1943);

Deming Brown, *Soviet Attitudes toward American Writing* (Princeton, N.J.: Princeton University Press, 1962), pp. 230-238;

B. M. Ejxenbaum, *O. Henry and the Theory of the Short Story*, translated, with notes and a postscript, by I. R. Titunik (Ann Arbor: University of Michigan Press, 1968);

Walter Evans, " 'A Municipal Report': O. Henry and Postmodernism," *Tennessee Studies in Literature*, 26 (1981): 101-116;

Joseph Gallegly, *From Alamo Plaza to Jack Harris's Saloon: O. Henry and the Southwest He Knew* (The Hague: Mouton, 1970);

Stephen Butler Leacock, *Essays and Literary Studies* (New York: John Lane, 1916), pp. 233-266;

H. L. Mencken, *Prejudices: Second Series* (New York: Knopf, 1920; London: Cape, 1921);

The Mentor, special O. Henry number, 11 (February 1923);

O. Henry Papers. Containing Some Sketches of His Life Together with an Alphabetical Index to His Complete Works (Garden City, N.Y.: Doubleday, Page, 1924);

Martin B. Ostrofsky, "O. Henry's Use of Stereotypes in His New York City Stories: An Example of the Utilization of Folklore in Literature," *New York Folklore Quarterly*, 7 (Summer 1981): 41-64;

Fred Lewis Pattee, *The Development of the American Short Story* (New York: Harper, 1923), pp. 357-379;

Upton Sinclair, *Bill Porter: A Drama of O. Henry in Prison* (Pasadena, Cal.: Privately printed, 1925).

Papers:

Manuscripts, first editions, reviews, letters, and other memorabilia concerning Porter can be found in the North Carolina Collection of the Greensboro Public Library, Greensboro, North Carolina. There are other important holdings of manuscripts, letters, and documents at the Alderman Library, University of Virginia; the Houghton Library, Harvard University; the Humanities Research Center, University of Texas at Austin; the William R. Perkins Library, Duke University; and The Huntington Library, San Marino, California.

Edith Wharton

(24 January 1862-11 August 1937)

Richard H. Lawson
University of North Carolina at Chapel Hill

See also the Wharton entries in *DLB 4: American Writers in Paris, 1920-1939; DLB 9: American Novelists, 1910-1945;* and *DLB 12: American Realists and Naturalists.*

BOOKS: *Verses,* anonymous (Newport, R.I.: C. E. Hammett, Jr., 1878);

The Decoration of Houses, by Wharton and Ogden Codman, Jr. (New York: Scribners, 1897; London: Batsford, 1898);

The Greater Inclination (New York: Scribners, 1899; London: John Lane/Bodley Head, 1899);

The Touchstone (New York: Scribners, 1900); republished as *A Gift from the Grave* (London: Murray, 1900);

Crucial Instances (New York: Scribners, 1901; London: Murray, 1901);

The Valley of Decision (2 volumes, New York: Scribners, 1902; 1 volume, London: Murray, 1902);

Sanctuary (New York: Scribners, 1903; London: Macmillan, 1903);

Italian Villas and Their Gardens (New York: Century, 1904; London: John Lane/Bodley Head, 1904);

The Descent of Man and Other Stories (New York: Scribners, 1904; enlarged edition, London & New York: Macmillan, 1904);

Italian Backgrounds (New York: Scribners, 1905; London: Macmillan, 1905);

The House of Mirth (New York: Scribners, 1905; London & New York: Macmillan, 1905);

Madame de Treymes (New York: Scribners, 1907; London: Macmillan, 1907);

The Fruit of the Tree (New York: Scribners, 1907; London: Macmillan, 1907);

The Hermit and the Wild Woman, and Other Stories (New York: Scribners, 1908; London: Macmillan, 1908);

A Motor-Flight Through France (New York: Scribners, 1908; London: Macmillan, 1908);

Artemis to Actaeon and Other Verse (New York: Scribners, 1909; London: Macmillan, 1909);

Edith Wharton (photograph by Gessford)

Tales of Men and Ghosts (New York: Scribners, 1910; London: Macmillan, 1910);

Ethan Frome (New York: Scribners, 1911; London: Macmillan, 1911);

The Reef (New York: Appleton, 1912; London: Macmillan, 1912);

The Custom of the Country (New York: Scribners, 1913; London: Macmillan, 1913);

Fighting France, from Dunkerque to Belfort (New York: Scribners, 1915; London: Macmillan, 1915);

Xingu and Other Stories (New York: Scribners, 1916; London: Macmillan, 1916);

Summer (New York: Appleton, 1917; London:
 Macmillan, 1917);

The Marne (New York: Appleton, 1918; London:
 Macmillan, 1918);

French Ways and Their Meaning (New York & London: Appleton, 1919; London: Macmillan,
 1919);

The Age of Innocence (New York & London: Appleton, 1920);

In Morocco (New York: Scribners, 1920; London:
 Macmillan, 1920);

The Glimpses of the Moon (New York & London: Appleton, 1922; London: Macmillan, 1923);

A Son at the Front (New York: Scribners, 1923; London: Macmillan, 1923);

*Old New York: False Dawn (The 'Forties), The Old
 Maid (The 'Fifties), The Spark (The 'Sixties),
 and New Year's Day (The 'Seventies)* (New York
 & London: Appleton, 1924);

The Mother's Recompense (New York & London: Appleton, 1925);

The Writing of Fiction (New York & London: Scribners, 1925);

Here and Beyond (New York & London: Appleton,
 1926);

Twelve Poems (London: Medici Society, 1926);

Twilight Sleep (New York & London: Appleton,
 1927);

The Children (New York & London: Appleton,
 1928); republished as *The Marriage Play-
 ground* (New York: Grosset & Dunlap,
 1930);

Hudson River Bracketed (New York & London: Appleton, 1929);

Certain People (New York & London: Appleton,
 1930);

The Gods Arrive (New York & London: Appleton,
 1932);

Human Nature (New York & London: Appleton,
 1933);

A Backward Glance (New York & London:
 Appleton-Century, 1934);

The World Over (New York & London: Appleton-
 Century, 1936);

Ghosts (New York & London: Appleton-Century,
 1937);

The Buccaneers (New York & London: Appleton-
 Century, 1938);

The Collected Short Stories of Edith Wharton, 2 volumes, edited by R. W. B. Lewis (New York:
 Scribners, 1968).

Although Edith Wharton is better known as
a novelist than a short-story writer, she was in
fact writing and publishing stories well before
her debut as a novelist in 1902. Her first published story was "Mrs. Manstey's View," in *Scribner's Magazine* of July 1891. From the perspective
of her boardinghouse window the elderly Mrs.
Manstey witnesses the preparations for building
onto the neighboring boardinghouse an addition
that will block her beloved view. Her un-
characteristic—because it is active—attempt at noc-
turnal arson fails, and the harsh night air brings
her pneumonia, which proves fatal. This first
story, somewhat contrived in that Mrs. Manstey is
primarily acted upon, contains in that very respect a prefiguration of what will emerge as the
chief theme of Wharton's stories: life is an entrapment, an imprisonment.

Wharton's imprisonment was the hereditary
society, even the family into which she was born,
which prized manners and conformity, that is, sup-
pression, above all, and which disdained artistic effort (or for that matter even commercial effort).
From the upper-class New York household of
her parents, George Frederic and Lucretia
Rhinelander Jones, who had their daughter educated at home by governesses, she entered, on 25
April 1885, into a disastrous marriage to Edward
Robbins (Teddy) Wharton—a union that reinforced her social imprisonment. The two were divorced in 1913. In Edith Wharton's fiction the
problem of marriage and divorce is a variant of
the imprisonment theme. Her concern with the
cultural scene finds expression in a large number
of artist stories—which, however, prove to be
aligned with the more fundamental theme of imprisonment, marriage, and divorce. Even in the
case of her dozen or so ghost stories, the flesh-and-
blood characters tend to have problematic orienta-
tions toward marriage, or divorce, or the role of
being a surviving spouse. The problem of marital
relationship continues after death in Wharton's
second published story, the allegory "The Fullness of Life," in *Scribner's Magazine* of December
1893. A deceased wife, deciding to forego the
yearned-for kindred spirit she meets in the after-
world, prefers to await her husband.

With "That Good May Come" (*Scribner's Magazine*, May 1894) Wharton returns to the real
world; not, however, to her own real world but
to the confined world of the lower-middle class.
The impoverished author Birkton sells his literary integrity in order to buy his younger sister a
confirmation dress. In an O. Henry-like pointe
he discovers that the gossip he has guiltily committed to print is, in fact, true. The relativistic na-

Edith Wharton during the early years of her marriage (Beinecke Rare Book and Manuscript Library, Yale University)

ture of Birkton's morality gives ample scope to Wharton's irony.

"The Lamp of Psyche" (*Scribner's Magazine,* October 1895), back in Wharton's native society, points to the effect on Delia's previously unqualified love for her husband, Corbett, when she discovers that he did not serve in the Civil War because of cowardice. In a marriage, like Delia's, like Wharton's own, a woman may be well advised to adapt to disillusionment. The reasoning may lie in its clear implication of her persistent subtheme that a woman without the protection of marriage is quite helpless in society. Some critics account "The Lamp of Psyche" among Wharton's best stories.

"The Valley of Childish Things, and Other Emblems" (*Century Magazine,* July 1896) is a curious gathering of ten parables, the shortest a mere eight lines in length, bound together chiefly by a whimsical and ironic contemplation of human relationships. These parables reflect, among other things, an adult beset by disturbing memories of a somewhat loveless childhood as well as a sense of feminine ambition being brutally suppressed.

Wharton's first published collection of short stories (plus a one-act play), *The Greater Inclination,* was brought out by Charles Scribner's Sons in 1899. The lead story, "The Muse's Tragedy" (*Scribner's Magazine,* January 1899), evoked critical comparison of Wharton to Henry James. An early example of a Wharton artist story, it is of interest for its treatment of Mary Anerton's conflicting roles of muse and lover. The artistic background is of less moment than the marital and nonmarital relationships that it conditions. The tragedy, for Wharton, lies in Mary Anerton's passive need to have an affair in the forlorn hope that someone may respond to her as a real person. Wharton does not appear to consider reversing the convention by which the woman inspires art that the man creates.

"A Journey" may also be interpreted as Wharton's fictional expression of the desire to escape the imprisonment of her marriage and her society. A nameless woman and her invalid husband undertake a train trip from Colorado to New York City. En route he dies. Terrified of being debarked with his corpse at some unknown outpost along the way, she manages to the end to maintain the fiction of his being alive, though very ill. At the final moment she collapses, striking her head against the dead man's berth—fatally, the reader is left to infer.

In "The Pelican" (*Scribner's Magazine,* January 1898) a young widow, Mrs. Amyot, is obliged to turn to lecturing in order to provide for her infant son, Lancelot. (It was once believed that pelicans fed their young with their own blood.) Much later, however, years after he has become successful on his own, Mrs. Amyot is still lecturing under the pretense that she is doing it "for the baby," insensitive to the pride of her son. On the other hand she has to do something; and society has given her nothing else to do.

Although like "The Pelican," "Souls Belated" is esteemed critically, it seems to suffer from an uncharacteristically heavy-handed irony. Lydia is in the process of obtaining a divorce, but as a rebel against social conformity she is unwilling to marry Gannett, the man she loves. She thus defies the conventions of the Anglo-American guests at a resort hotel in the Italian lake country. After social intercourse illustrates painfully to her the untenability of her rebellion, Lydia accepts convention. Wharton uses her favorite metaphor, that of the prison, to emphasize the plight of Lydia—who, incidentally, also serves as an ineffective muse to Gannett's futile efforts to follow up on a promising debut as a novelist. Wharton occasionally tends to allow characters in the context of irony to become caricatures; that surely happens with at least the secondary characters in "Souls Belated."

"A Coward" presents Mr. Carstyle, who failed to fulfill a trust in his youth and is now—doubtless by way of compensation—repaying the money his dead brother embezzled, insisting on a life-style far less grand than that his wife noisily proclaims as her social birthright. In the anecdotal and melodramatic "A Cup of Cold Water" Wharton combines social levels, the lower-middle class and her own patrician class (as she did in her 1907 novel, *The Fruit of the Tree*). This tale may be of primary interest for its early view of the larger social alignments that emerged in some of Wharton's novels beginning less than a decade later: the difficult mutualism of the lower stratum and the patricians against the despoilers, the factory owners.

"The Portrait" is that of Vard, a crooked and rapacious politician, painted by an accomplished artist, Lillo. So as not to undeceive Vard's worshipful daughter about her father, Lillo contrives to paint a portrait that will not reveal Vard's awful inner essence. The artist story is the platform on which is worked out the delicate psychological dynamism between the Vards, father and daughter. In the process Wharton gives vent to her scorn of the American political realities of her day and of figures, like Vard, who greedily exploit those realities.

The Greater Inclination is a remarkable effort for a first collection. As a whole the stories are characterized by complex and ambiguous personal relationships, generally well-tempered irony, and an elegant diction that only rarely succumbs to preciosity. They also give indication of her lifelong thematic concerns. The critics and Wharton's publishers were pleased. In at least three printings *The Greater Inclination* sold thirty-five hundred copies in the United States and Great Britain.

Wharton published three magazine stories in 1900. Two of them, in the *Youth's Companion*, are distinctly juvenile in theme (although not in style). "The Line of Least Resistance," in the October issue of *Lippincott's Magazine*, is quite another matter. Mindon, whose wife has been unfaithful, allows his friends to persuade him not to divorce her because of the children. Again Wharton wrestles with the problem of divorce vis-à-vis society. The hero and the milieu of "The Line of Least Re-

sistance" recur in her later novels, most specifically in *The Custom of the Country* (1913). Mindon is an aggressive businessman, quite without culture, whose commercial success has propelled him into a social world to whose concerns and niceties he remains a stranger.

Six stories and a "dialog"—a one-act play—are included in *Crucial Instances* (1901). In one way or another all of the stories connect thematically with the past, including the Italian past, a congenial topic with Wharton at this period and one doubtless brought to a focus by her research for her two-volume 1902 novel, *The Valley of Decision*. The lead story, "The Duchess at Prayer" (*Scribner's Magazine*, August 1900), is a story of the Italian past, of implicit sex, of forthright violence, and of the supernatural (the facial expression on a marble statue changes).

"The Angel at the Grave" (*Scribner's Magazine*, February 1901) provokes the question of how wise emotionally it might be for a young woman to immerse herself—and be immersed—in the role of curator of her grandfather's philosophical artifacts and reputation. By the time Paulina Anson is in her forties, her grandfather's scholarly reputation is on the verge of being revived by an attractive young male scholar, and her memories of her former sweetheart and the marriage she had given up are slightly restirred. The past, it seems, is not always linkable to the present except in such dilute measure.

One of Wharton's art stories, "The Recovery" (*Harper's Monthly*, February 1901), takes place at Hillbridge, often the setting for Wharton's examination of the cultural scene. The artistic recovery is that of Keniston, effected during a European sojourn. There is little indication that Keniston's artistic enlightenment is paralleled on the personal level. "The Rembrandt" (*Cosmopolitan*, August 1900) is not a Rembrandt at all, even though its owner, the aristocratic, aged, and impoverished Mrs. Fontage, thinks it is. Having acquired it on her long-past European honeymoon, she is now compelled to sell it, while still attempting to preserve her pride and her manner. Art is the medium, but the message is social: members of Wharton's elite society rally around one of their own who has been brought to a pitiful pass by the imperative of social dynamics.

"The Moving Finger" (*Harper's Monthly*, March 1901)—the allusion is to stanza 51 of the *Rubáiyát of Omar Khayyám*—is the guiding digit of one whom Wharton calls "the great Healer." Its agent is Claydon, a portrait painter, who yields to

Edith Wharton in 1898, at Land's End, the house in Newport, Rhode Island, that she bought in 1893
(Beinecke Rare Book and Manuscript Library, Yale University)

his friend Grancy's insistence that he age the portrait of Grancy's now dead wife. For Grancy avers that she is finding it increasingly difficult to relate to him now over a gap of five years during which Grancy himself has aged. Finally Claydon is charged to make the portrait of Mrs. Grancy reflect her knowledge that Grancy himself is soon fated to die. As usual in Wharton's fiction the artist situation is the background, perhaps even the catalyst for a personal, in this case (as in most) marital, interaction.

"The Moving Finger" is also an inchoate ghost story, accurately predicting Wharton's later work in this genre: with a minimum of ghostly trappings the dead do survive, and they are apt to be relentless. The "psychological complexities"–a phrase Wharton frequently used–are understated. It is just hinted that Claydon was in love with the living Mrs. Grancy, perhaps as much as her husband was. Claydon correspondingly shows signs of a guilty conscience. When Grancy calls on him to redo the portrait finally to depict Mrs. Grancy as *aware* of Grancy's impending death, he "miss[es] the mark" and paints her as *anticipating* Grancy's death (because he wishes his friend dead, the reader may infer).

The last story in *Crucial Instances*, "The Confessional," is an extended reflection of Wharton's profound fondness for Italy, a framed story depending heavily on melodrama. As a whole *Crucial Instances* embodies features of Wharton's later fiction, novels as well as short stories: psychological complexity, the theme of the deads' survival as ghosts, a pronounced distaste for pseudo-intellectualism, and the penetration into her hereditary society of those nouveaux riches whom she later called "the Invaders." Critics, probably with justice, ranked the stories in this collection as inferior to the more tightly drawn tales in *The Greater Inclination*.

Quite the contrary is true of her next collection, *The Descent of Man and Other Stories* (1904), which in all but one story treats American material, to which Wharton applies a discerningly ironic eye. "The Descent of Man" (*Scribner's Magazine*, March 1904) provides an ironic aperçu of American mass culture. A skeptical and deterministic entomologist, Professor Linyard of Hillbridge, writes "The Vital Thing," a satirical work on popular culture. Its adherents, failing to grasp the satire, make Linyard a culture hero. His fame, however, proves a difficult tiger from which to dismount. When Linyard, who has continued to pursue his scientific work, wants to write a "real book," in which to present his recent scientific discoveries, he learns that to obtain sufficient funds he must mortgage himself further to the pop crowd by writing a sequel to "The Vital Thing."

Jane's mission in "The Mission of Jane" (*Harper's Monthly*, December 1902) is to reconcile her adoptive parents. The thematic irony–others are abundant–lies in the fact that the reconciliation is effected only when, years later, they finally succeed in marrying Jane off. Only in being unburdened of her are Mr. and Mrs. Lethbury enabled to cast at least a tentative bridge over the abyss of their vast incompatibility. However unsuitable their marriage, implicit is that divorce would be even more unsuitable–another fictional reflection of Wharton's personal plight.

"The Other Two" (*Collier's*, 13 February 1904) is one of Wharton's most engaging stories. The title refers to the two previous husbands of the woman who is now Alice Waythorn: the unprepossessing Haskett and the affable Varick. Events reveal to her present husband, in a most disconcerting way, that Alice has had the faculty of adapting to each husband in turn, including him, by sacrificing a certain portion of her own self. As Waythorn phrases it, she is " 'as easy as an old shoe'–a shoe that too many feet had worn." This urbane tale of manners fittingly ends in the Waythorn library, whither each of the spouses, past and present, has repaired on one mission or another, only to find the others there. Alice Waythorn rises to the occasion in magisterially proffering tea to each. With a laugh Waythorn accepts the third cup.

It is divorce, of course, that has brought about this tense assemblage, adroitly put at ease by the adaptable Alice, so competent in dealing with the inevitable residue of divorces. Still, although Alice Waythorn prevails, it is at the cost of husbandly disillusionment and of her becoming something not quite human. Here Wharton is indeed a feminist.

"The Quicksand" (*Harper's Monthly*, June 1902) is about commercial success; what the quicksand swallows up is principle–not primarily that of Quentin the male entrepreneur but that of his wife, who over the course of time succumbs to the ease that money provides. The only refuge of her still lively conscience is frantic philanthropy. It is against falling into such a pattern that the widowed Mrs. Quentin warns Hope Fenno, the prospective bride of her son Alan. A secondary but

Wharton at the time she and Ogden Codman, Jr., wrote The Decoration of Houses *(1897)*

also well-developed thematic strand is the exceedingly finely tuned relationship between Mrs. Quentin and her son, Alan (which replicates that to be found in Wharton's 1903 novella, *Sanctuary*). The reader may be inclined to regard Mrs. Quentin's by no means emotionally disciplined advice to Hope Fenno as something less than pure altruism and to consider the possibility that she may wish, however subconsciously, to keep her son for herself–in short, the Oedipal situation, of which Wharton was thoroughly aware.

"The Dilettante" (*Harper's Monthly*, December 1903), the shortest tale in *The Descent of Man* and perhaps the most urbane, gradually reveals Thursdale's fiancée's distress that his long-prior relationship with Mrs. Vervain did not include lovemaking. More than urbanity, Ruth Gaynor's distress apparently reflects healthy self-interest (quite likely also Wharton's comment on her own largely sexless marriage).

"The Reckoning" (*Harper's Monthly*, August 1902) is the one meted Mrs. Clement Westall by her second husband when he announces that in accord with their enlightened marital agreement of a decade ago he now wishes his freedom. Unfortunately Julia has settled into the marriage and gradually acquired a conventional point of view. Deeply shocked at his sudden proclamation she is unable to grasp why Clement tired of their marriage. She forces a distraught visit on her first husband, whom she had left because she had become tired of him, while he could not understand. Now she tells him that at least she understands how he must have felt. In a somewhat schematic way–the resolution is at once melodramatic and intellectual–"The Reckoning" reflects Wharton's continued fictional involvement with the problems of marriage and divorce and the emotional cost of each.

In "Expiation" (*Cosmopolitan*, December 1903) Wharton's typical irony is laced with comedy. A bishop denounces from the pulpit his niece's just-barely scandalous novel, thus assuring its commercial success. She in turn becomes the chief contributor to the bishop's heart's desire, a stained-glass chantry window for the cathedral. "Expiation" gives a fair indication of Wharton's attitude toward religion: she does not denounce loudly, only by spoof and mild irony. The church reflects the society of which it is a form—with emphasis on the concept of form.

"The Lady's Maid's Bell" (*Scribner's Magazine*, November 1902) is a highly successful ghost story. Not only does Miss Hartley, the new lady's maid, respond to the bell of the kindly but ailing Mrs. Brympton, but also, it appears, does the ghost of Emma Saxon, who had been Mrs. Brympton's maid for twenty years. Related to the infrequent summonses of the bell are the infrequent visits of the master of the house, Mr. Brympton, "coarse, loud and pleasure-loving." The reader may divine that Emma Saxon had been in the habit of responding to the bell when Mrs. Brympton found her husband's advances unbearable. Sex and violence, or violent sex, is not infrequently thematic with Wharton. More unusual in "The Lady's Maid's Bell" is the narrative point of view: not that of the articulate upper-class male, nor the less frequent one of the upper-class woman, but rather that of an exceptionally articulate female servant.

The last story in *The Descent of Man*, "A Venetian Night's Entertainment" (*Scribner's Magazine*, December 1903), is essentially a spoof, a lightweight entry in an otherwise imposing collection. With this third collection Wharton reached maturity as a writer of short stories predominantly rooted in the experience of her own, limited American society. The stories are highly ironic in their revelations about that society, principally of how its members interact in the intimate circumstances of marriage and family. It is curious that Wharton's virtuoso concentration on her own society exposed her to criticism that seemed to suggest she ought to have been writing about something else.

Between *The Descent of Man* and *The Hermit and the Wild Woman, and Other Stories* (1908) Wharton produced four magazine stories that she did not include in her 1908 collection. None, it is fair to say, is on the level of those in *The Descent of Man*. "The Letter" (*Harper's Monthly*, April 1904) harks back to the Italian wars of independence in the first half of the nineteenth century. "The House of the Dead Hand" (*Atlantic Monthly*, August 1904), which takes place in contemporary Siena, is a tale of paternal cruelty, thwarted love, a painting by Leonardo, and failure by the romantic principals as well as the involved narrator to seize the moment. In fact the story is dominated by its milieu.

Only slightly more successful is "The Introducers" (*Ainslee's Magazine*, December 1905 and January 1906). The introducers are well-bred social secretaries, one male and one female, employed to smooth the social and romantic path for the new millionaires trying to crash Newport summer society (of which Wharton was a sometime member). Wharton wrote "Les Metteurs en scène" in French for the October 1908 issue of *Revue des Deux Mondes*. (An English translation appears in R. W. B. Lewis's edition of *The Collected Short Stories of Edith Wharton*, 1968.) The French term, meaning "theatrical producers," is here employed metaphorically. The function of *les metteurs* is similar to that of the introducers. The scene has shifted, along with the new millionaires, from Newport to Paris. The matchmaking has become more complicated, more stylized, perhaps more poignant (though contrivedly so). The character types in "Les Metteurs en scène," as well as their headquarters, the Nouveau Luxe Hotel, reappeared later, most prominently in Wharton's 1913 novel, *The Custom of the Country*.

The title story in *The Hermit and the Wild Woman, and Other Stories* is set in a mountainous eastern Mediterranean littoral, perhaps in the thirteenth century. A Christian hermit befriends a runaway nun, near whom he lives in an adjacent cave. The relationship is clearly sexless, but subconscious currents seem no less clearly at work.

Edith Wharton, 1900 (Beinecke Rare Book and Manuscript Library, Yale University)

One is tempted to regard this tale, which was first published in the February 1906 issue of *Scribner's Magazine*, as perhaps an elaborate–and by no means exact–emblem of Wharton's marital situation and dilemma.

"The Last Asset" (*Scribner's Magazine*, August 1904) in person is Sam Newell, discarded but not divorced husband of Mrs. Newell. As Mrs. Newell's position in European society shows signs of entering decline, she cleverly arranges for one final contribution by her long-lost husband: to present their daughter in marriage to the son of a rich French family; for the Trayases are prepared to renege on the contract if the American family is not able to come up with a father of the bride. Justifiably a critical favorite, "The Last Asset" includes among its themes the entrapment of marriage, rich Americans in European society, the family as clan (most tellingly the French family), and finally the stages of individual social decline, signaled by subtle, then more pronounced changes in the supporting social cast.

"In Trust" (*Appletons' Book Lovers' Magazine*, 7 April 1906) is a skillful lampoon on the no less devastating consequences of the climb *upward* in society. Mrs. Ned Halidon is the wife who surrenders to the social imperative, leading to the undoing and then the death of her pliant husband. Enjoying a more distinguished and lengthy social pedigree than Mrs. Sam Newell, Mrs. Halidon lacks that lady's chutzpah and insensate hypocrisy.

"The Pretext" (*Scribner's Magazine*, August 1908) continues in the illumination of the entrapments of unhappy human relationships. It is climactically revealed to the middle-aged wife of a New England college professor–never confident of her attractiveness–that she has served as a romantic pretext under cover of which a young English visitor has carried on an affair with another woman. Mrs. Robert Ransom, who has in any case lacked the courage for an affair with Guy Dawnish, must continue in the dull routine of her perfunctory marriage.

"The Verdict" (*Scribner's Magazine*, June 1908) probably a *conte à clef*, is a slight tale in which, characteristically for Wharton, art provides the means of illuminating human relationships. In this instance the relationship is between an artist of middling talent, who realizes his own insufficiency and gives up painting, and his wife, whose personal fortune enables him to switch to a life of Riviera ease. The irony is strengthened by the fact that art remains part of his existence but as an object of his well-developed discrimination, not his showy but spurious creativeness.

"The Pot-Boiler" (*Scribner's Magazine*, December 1904) is a story of art and artists in the lower-middle-class reaches of New York City. Shall an artist maintain his integrity or shall he adapt to popular taste and thereby prosper? It is both obvious and ironic that the untalented, for whom it is not a conscious decision, gravitate to the latter category. The characters do not engage the reader, and the tale is excessively spun out.

The title "The Best Man" (*Collier's*, 2 September 1905) refers to Gov. John Mornway's post-reelection desire to appoint to the office of attorney general the best man available, who happens to be the incumbent, Fleetwood. The reader gradually discovers, however, that two years earlier he had given Mrs. Mornway profitable tips on the stock market. Despite his opponents' threats of revelatory scandal, Mornway resolves to reappoint Fleetwood. Owing perhaps to her disdain for politics and politicians (all "bosses" and "immigrants," except Theodore Roosevelt), Wharton did not write a very convincing political tale. The refusal of Mornway–probably modeled on Roosevelt–to compromise reduces the story's persuasiveness, despite her care to portray him as a reform politician. Between her disdain and her overlay of naive idealism, Wharton may indeed have anticipated future political trends, but as literature her political story falls short.

The Hermit and the Wild Woman, a superior short-story collection if not necessarily Wharton's best–critics tended not to see its unevenness–sold about four thousand copies. For the author of the already celebrated novel *The House of Mirth* (1905), those sales figures seem quite small. Yet as to the effective, often subtle working out of her chief themes of familial and marital imprisonment, as to the development of the burgeoning social theme and subthemes, as to the telling use of irony–Wharton is with this collection a markedly more mature artist than she was a decade earlier.

In 1910, the year she decided to settle permanently in France, Wharton published *Tales of Men and Ghosts*. In stories of humans as well as ghosts Wharton became increasingly willing to delve into abnormal psychology, even while hewing to customary themes such as imprisonment and ex-

panding somewhat the theme of the double, not necessarily ghostly. The title of the consistently absorbing lead story, "The Bolted Door" (*Scribner's Magazine*, March 1909), metaphorically suggests the plight of its hero, Hurbert Granice. In effect Granice, the murderer whose confession no one takes seriously, is imprisoned in his own skin, unable to make effective–eventually indispensable–contact with his own society. Although "The Bolted Door" has been faulted for its melodrama, it in fact represents a psychologically masterful extension of her theme, accompanied at every stage of the way by a guiding and disciplined irony.

"His Father's Son" (*Scribner's Magazine*, June 1909) is more anecdotal, perhaps mainly interesting for its presumable evocations of Wharton's earlier doubts about her own legitimacy (there were rumors–almost certainly unfounded–that her older brothers' tutor was her father). How could the artistically sensitive Ronald Grew possibly be the offspring of the prosaic Mr. and Mrs. Grew? Do not certain letters indicate that his father was the celebrated pianist Fortuné Dolbrowski? No. The letters, as part of a modest prank, were actually composed by Mr. Grew, transcribed and signed by Mrs. Grew, and sent to Dolbrowski–who for six months responded. Along with the ironic treatment of illegitimacy the story engages in a bit of mild satire on the middle class as represented by the Grews.

"The Daunt Diana" (*Scribner's Magazine*, July 1909) refers to a sculpture owned initially by the insensitive collector Daunt, whose entire collection is bought by another collector, Neave. The overly sensitive Neave finds himself incapable of appreciating objects of art that have not individually established a rapport–note the direction–with him, and he accordingly disposes of Daunt's collection, only to repurchase its constituent members piece by piece, including the Diana, at prices that reduce him to penury. Art illuminates Neave's character, but what is illuminated seems hardly worth the candle, and the tale leaves the impression of being precious and overwrought.

"The Debt" (*Scribner's Magazine*, August 1909) is that owed by a young scientist to his preceptor. It is repaid not by suppressing new facts in favor of obsolescent dogma (that of his now dead preceptor) but by the allowance of new facts. A scant story, "The Debt" is nevertheless a persuasive indicator of Wharton's admiration of scientific method. "Full Circle" (*Scribner's Magazine*, October 1909) is something of a set piece, actually an extended anecdote dwelling, a bit too cleverly, on the psychological ramifications of the secretarial role played by a good, starving writer named Vyse to an inferior, prosperous writer named Betton. Another lesser effort is "The Legend" (*Scribner's Magazine*, March 1910), which depends for its effect on a bizarre instance of a live revenant. Pellerin, a distinguished writer of philosophy, returns after many years away to find his philosophy in the clutches of a celebrated bowdlerizer, who expounds his version of it to the likes of the Uplift Club. In this slender story Wharton directs her irony at the pretensions of both the intellectual and the social categories of society.

"The Eyes" (*Scribner's Magazine*, June 1910) is a truly brilliant tale, a gripping ghost story in which the human relationship is all. Andrew Culwin, an aged egotist of highly refined artistic sensitivity, tells his tale to the frame narrator and Phil Frenham, a youth much attracted to Culwin. In Culwin's younger days, upon sensibly breaking his engagement to his cousin Alice, he is confronted in the night by a pair of monstrous eyes. So awful is the sensation that he immediately flees to Europe. Three years later in Rome, upon finally breaking with his beautiful youthful protégé, Gilbert Noyes, he is once more confronted by the eyes. In breaking both relationships Culwin fancies that he has done something good, but the effect of his tale on his adoring current protégé, Frenham, is shatteringly revelatory. Homosexuality and its imputedly destructive emotional effect loom large in "The Eyes." If the reader has any doubts about what Wharton is suggesting by such an attribution as "our old friend 'liked 'em juicy,' " her unambiguous classical references resolve them. Culwin, abhorrent in manner as well as thought, is dominated by consuming egotism. Whether he and Frenham are actually having an affair, or whether that is the future suddenly revealed to Frenham, is narratively unimportant in comparison with Frenham's enlightenment, even if it consists only in the awareness that he has had a long-ago predecessor, of whom he is jealous.

"The Blond Beast" (*Scribner's Magazine*, September 1910), a tissue of ironies (both clear and ambiguous) on the Nietzschean concept, dwells on the would-be amoral adventuring of young Hugh Millner in the world of big business and big philanthropy. Millner, who theoretically believes "we're all born to prey on each other," is unable consistently to cast off such primitive forms

of egotism as pity, or even helpfulness. Wharton was well versed in the philosophy of Friedrich Nietzsche, among the vanguard of his American admirers and by 1908, as revealed in her correspondence, thoroughly immersed in his *Beyond Good and Evil* (1886). But perhaps she knew Nietzsche too well; "The Blond Beast," for all its irony and counterirony, is not one of her more successful stories.

In the ghost story "Afterward" (*Century*, January 1910) the revenant appears twice to Ned and Mary Boyne at their isolated house in the Dorsetshire downs—the house of which it is said that no one knows that its ghost is a ghost until long after one has seen it. On its second appearance the revenant fetches Ned Boyne, who disappears forever. The revenant, however, is not the premise for a complication and revelation of human relationships, but only for a melodramatic conclusion. "The Letters" (*Century*, August 1910) is a slight but extended tale, with somewhat forced irony, a reliance on coincidence and melodrama, and a clichéd picture of the middle-class American woman. These qualities anticipate Wharton's lesser magazine fiction of the 1920s. *Tales of Men and Ghosts*, in the critical view, fell short of the preceding collections. "The Eyes" is the only consentient masterpiece in the book. Even as critical voices were severe, sales were again in the neighborhood of 4,000. (By comparison *The House of Mirth* sold some 140,000 copies within months of publication.)

In *Xingu and Other Stories* (1916) the title story (*Scribner's Magazine*, December 1911) is an engaging satire on the fatuities of a Hillbridge ladies' lunch club, whose members "pursue Culture in bands, as though it were dangerous to meet alone." Mrs. Roby, the club's iconoclast, by her allusions to an otherwise unidentified "Xingu" cleverly induces the members to make fools of themselves in front of a guest of honor, the redoubtable authoress Osric Dane, whom the reader may take to embody Wharton's own attitude toward intellectual pretentiousness. Osric Dane has no more idea than the lunch club members what Xingu is, but she arranges to be privately enlightened by Mrs. Roby, who is promptly cashiered by the club. (Xingu is the name of a river in Brazil.)

"Coming Home" (*Scribner's Magazine*, December 1915) reflects the deep love for France that led Wharton to devote a major portion of her time to relief work during World War I. A young French lieutenant returns to his home in Lor-

Edith Wharton, Henry James, the Whartons' chauffeur, and Edward Wharton at the beginning of a 1907 trip through France in Edith Wharton's Panhard automobile

raine and makes the bitter discovery that his fiancée's receptiveness to the attentions of the local German commander has resulted in the unique sparing of his family's house. This war tale was esteemed by contemporary critics, but it is all but inaccessible to today's reader owing to Wharton's insistent application of a good-and-evil dichotomy to the contenders.

"Autres Temps . . ." has been generally acclaimed as brilliant. While its structure may well deserve such praise, the further passage of time may well have dulled the sensitivity of today's reader to its narrative conflict. Twenty years before the story begins, Mrs. Lidcote's divorce has caused her to be cut by New York City society. Now she apprehensively returns from Europe to New York to offer support to her daughter Leila, recently divorced and remarried. Mrs. Lidcote's antiquated social categories are thrown into confusion by her perception that Leila's divorce is accepted as a matter of course. Told that she need no longer worry about the sanctions imposed on her case so long ago, she senses otherwise, however, and events force her to the conclusion that the liberalization of views on divorce applies only to the present, not to the "other times," of which she must remain a victim.

"Autres Temps . . ." was first published under the title "Other Times, Other Manners" in the issues of *Century Magazine* for July and August 1911, that is, less than two years before Edith Wharton's own divorce became final, in April 1913. Mrs. Lidcote's burden is to some extent the burden of her creator, who also increasingly found Europe more of a home than the United States. The ironically selective changeability of social mores in "Autres Temps . . ." is presented quietly, thus perhaps all the more devastatingly. The problem for the reader lies in imagining that the consequences of divorce ever constituted such a social problem as to be, in Mrs. Lidcote's view, a form of imprisonment. "Autres Temps . . ." is the kernel of Wharton's later novel *The Mother's Recompense* (1925).

The revenants in the ghost story "Kerfol" (*Scribner's Magazine*, March 1916) are canine. Kerfol is a castle in Brittany presided over in the seventeenth century by the jealous Yves de Cornault, age sixty-two, and his second wife, Anne, evidently in her twenties. On a certain day each year ghost dogs are said still to reappear at Kerfol, where our twentieth-century narrator encounters them. Childlessness, later to become an important secondary theme in Wharton's fiction, is here specifically related to Anne's affection for her pets, slain by her husband. Most important and enduring thematically is, first, both metaphorical and literal imprisonment and, second, the rela-

318

tionship between eroticism–Anne's marital predicament and her husband's suspicion that a young male friend was her lover–and violence–the murder of her husband, whose body bears wounds that could have been inflicted by dogs, ghost dogs.

"The Long Run" (*Atlantic Monthly*, February 1912) is a moving and bitter story about the human result of socially induced romantic pusillanimity. Wharton returns a quietly savage indictment of the society–her New York City society of the turn of the century–whose forms triumph to turn the essentially humane bachelor, Halston Merrick, away from his unhappily married soul mate, Paulina Trant, when she very consciously throws herself at him. What Paulina has in mind is not for a night–a situation that Merrick could manage in the usual hypocritical way–but forever. This "forever," though, is not the same thing as "the long run" of the title, which refers to the assertion of the levelheaded if impassioned Paulina that "one way of finding out whether a risk is worth taking is *not* to take it, and then to see what one becomes in the long run, and draw one's inferences." In the long run the willing Paulina and the unwilling Merrick become something like zombies playing out their roles in a ritualized society. Merrick is an affecting, concentrated example of Wharton's typically ineffective, society-bound male heroes, who after minimal personal struggle are content to permit their women as well as themselves to be imprisoned in their society. Although modest by present standards, "The Long Run" seems to mark a new level of sexual frankness for Wharton.

"The Triumph of Night" (*Scribner's Magazine*, August 1914) is a ghost story set on a frigid New Hampshire winter night. The bitter cold is the instrument that causes the death of young Frank Rainer, tubercular heir to millions of dollars that his uncle embezzled to save himself from bankruptcy and investigation. The agent of Frank's death, ironically, is the young narrator Faxon, who flees into the arctic night after seeing a malevolent ghostly double standing behind the facade of the corporeal uncle. From this perhaps suicidal flight he is rescued by Frank Rainer, who then himself falls victim to the forces of the night. The uncle's double, however ghostly, is simply a double, presumably the vicious and avaricious alter ego behind the enigmatic social mask presented to the world. The basic irony of the tale lies in the narrator's inability to recognize that he could be Frank's savior and thereupon par-

adoxically serving the purposes of evil. There are indications that Faxon's crucial inaction and flight may spring from guilt over a latent homosexual attraction toward Frank Rainer.

"The Choice," originally published some eight years previously in the *Century Magazine* of November 1908, evokes with intense bitterness the theme of release from an intolerable marriage. Isabel Stilling wishes death for her drunken husband, Cobham. But when it comes to a showdown between Cobham and Austin Wrayford as both struggle against drowning, it is her husband who seizes the oar that Isabel thrusts into the dark waters beneath the boat house. Isabel's choice, being no choice, probably reflects Wharton's own tormented view that a miserable marriage may indeed be bearable.

By 1926, the year her next collection, *Here and Beyond*, appeared, Wharton's books had long been published with Appleton rather than Charles Scribner's Sons. Critics have judged her popular novels of the 1920s as inferior to her earlier work. This opinion is equally valid for the stories contained in *Here and Beyond*. They had previously appeared in slick magazines directed toward a readership that Wharton, in France, could scarcely have understood: the middle-class American housewife. Of the six generally undistinguished tales, "Miss Mary Pask" (*Pictorial Review*, April 1925) rises a bit above the general level. In this ghost story coincidence contrives to make the revenant a living person, dead to life and desperately in need of sympathy. But the egotistical and unsympathetic narrator cruelly resists Mary Pask's appeal that he stay longer. Possibly "Bewitched" (*Pictorial Review*, March 1925), a rural ghost story with undertones of witchery, also rises above mediocrity, although it lacks the restraint, and thus the effective irony, that illuminates Wharton's better stories.

The next collection, *Certain People* (1930), is excellent throughout. The first tale, "Atrophy" (*Ladies' Home Journal*, November 1927), dwells touchingly but also ironically on the awkward plight of Mrs. Nora Frenway when she tries to visit her lover, who lies dying under the jealous watchfulness of his sister. Thematically, as often in Wharton, love outside the bonds of marriage–even an awful marriage–yields bitter fruit.

"A Bottle of Perrier" (first published as "A Bottle of Evian" in the 27 March 1926 issue of the *Saturday Evening Post*) is a delightful ghost story without a ghost, only the suspicion of the presence of Henry Almodham, whose murdered

Edith Wharton at Pavillon Colombe, the house in St. Brice-sous-Forêt that she bought in 1918

body lies in the well and contaminates the water at his fortress-palace in the African desert. More accurately defined, the tale is a murder mystery, for neither the narrator Medford–a casually invited guest in Almodham's domain–nor the reader knows until the end–after a series of other possibilities have been eliminated–that the dead body of the mysteriously missing Almodham is in the well and that Almodham has been pushed into the well by his factotum Gosling, who resented the constant postponement of his promised vacation back in England. Medford early speculates that Almodham's gradual self-imprisonment in his own adventurous pose as desert lord might account for his odd mode of existence; Gosling's role as a de facto prisoner adds force to the irony. The reader is left to speculate on the psychological complexities inherent in the bizarre relationship between Almodham and Gosling. "A Bottle of Perrier" enjoys general, although not unanimous, critical esteem.

Also well received is "After Holbein" (*Saturday Evening Post*, 5 May 1928), based on Hans Holbein's paintings on the dance-of-death theme. The disciples of death in Wharton's story, set around 1900, are Evelina Jaspar, former grande dame of New York society but now dotty and re-

duced to charade, and Anson Warley, in his sixties, inveterate diner-out and epigone of that same society. Warley drops in one cold winter night on one of Mrs. Jaspar's fantasy-reenactments of the dinner parties she used to give when she was the reigning queen of society. He goes along with the macabre scene from a bygone era, as do Mrs. Jaspar's knowing caretakers. On complacently emerging into the frigid night Warley takes "a step forward, to where a moment before the pavement had been–and where there now was nothing"–one of Wharton's most effective endings, consonant with her irony throughout this savage tale. In "After Holbein" Wharton reestablished her connection with the long-gone New York of her youth, and the story is not an affectionate souvenir. The portrait of Evelina Jaspar, apparently modeled on Wharton's cousin once removed, Mrs. William Backhouse Astor, borders on vicious. The society represented by Jaspar and Warley was long dead, Wharton seems to be saying, even when it affected to be alive still. Perhaps nowhere else is her retrospective quite so astringent, so pitiless.

"Dieu d'Amour" (*Ladies' Home Journal*, October 1928) is set in Cyprus at the time of the Crusades. The princess Medea, descendant of the corrupt Lusignan ruling family, opts for entering a convent rather than flight with her sweetheart, the page Godfrey. The effect–reinforced by the title, which is the name of the Lusignan castle–is that of irony surpassing itself, for Godfrey had been concerned to separate the princess from the corruption before she should succumb to it.

"The Refugees" (*Saturday Evening Post*, 18 January 1919) is an unprepossessing story reflecting Wharton's own good works among World War 1 refugees and the ironic insights she gained. The final story in the collection, "Mr. Jones" (*Ladies' Home Journal*, April 1928), finds Wharton at the peak of her skill as a ghost-story writer. Mr. Jones is the invisible overseer of Bells, a beautiful and mysterious old place on the Sussex downs, recently inherited by Lady Jane Lynke. He is invisible, as it turns out, because he is long dead, but not so dead as to prevent his strangling of the housekeeper, Mrs. Clemm, because of her failure to keep certain family papers from the curious eyes of Lady Jane. The papers reveal that in 1817 a Miss Portallo, a deaf and dumb millionairess, was married off, with a large dowry, to a Lynke forbear, Viscount Thudeney of Bells; and that while squandering her fortune on travel, gambling, and women, the viscount kept her imprisoned at Bells for at least eleven years under the eye of her keeper, Mr. Jones, who was still alive then. "Mr. Jones" may well be Wharton's most gripping development of the theme of the imprisoned wife.

Her ninth volume of stories, *Human Nature*, was published by Appleton in 1933. The first story, "The Day of the Funeral" (first published as "In a Day" in the January 1933 issue of *Woman's Home Companion*), reverts to the theme of marital infidelity, or more precisely, the absence of viability in love outside of marriage. The funeral is that of poor Milly Trenham, who killed herself after her husband ignored her warnings to end his affair with Barbara Wake. When Barbara learns the reason for Milly's suicide, she breaks with Trenham. He takes a final small solace (so small as to be ironic) in the fact that at least his house and his housekeeper seem sensitive to his plight.

Two of the remaining three stories in *Human Nature* reveal too apparently their original function as commercial slick-magazine fiction, excessively dependent on coincidence as plot. "Joy in the House" (*Nash's Pall Mall Magazine*, December 1932), however, is a story of some distinction. Christine Ansley leaves her husband, a priggish

real-estate agent, for the Paris atelier of Jeff Lithgow, a talented and impecunious artist. Her husband Devons has made it clear, though, that within a six-month period Christine is free to return to their suburban home. When she announces that she is returning, Devons makes a welcome sign: "Joy in the House." After her departure from Paris, Jeff makes good his threat to kill himself, and Christine finds out that Devons knew of Jeff's suicide before he made the sign. She is once more within the imprisonment of marriage, made even worse by the fresh insight into the nature of her husband. On the other hand, in common with most Wharton heroines, she had failed to find the anticipated bliss in her extramarital relationship.

The World Over, published in 1936, is the last collection of Wharton stories to appear during her lifetime. Like its predecessor, it is uneven, containing some facile stories clearly aimed toward easy sale to magazines as well as some stories of the very first rank, among which is the ghost story, "Pomegranate Seed" (*Saturday Evening Post*, 25 April 1931), based on the myth of Persephone. It is not the shade of the late Elsie Ashby that returns to summon her widower to her new realm, but rather her letters in gray envelopes. They produce such an effect on Kenneth Ashby as to make his new wife, Charlotte, uncertain of her own relationship with, and attractiveness to, her husband. Finally the letters succeed in overwhelming Kenneth and causing him to disappear. One can profitably speculate on the psychological complexities of the former marital relationship between Kenneth and Elsie Ashby.

"Confession" (first published as "Unconfessed Crime" in the March 1936 issue of *Storyteller*) is also psychologically provocative. Kate Spain's acquittal of the murder of her brutal father, on the testimony of the servant girl Cassie Donovan, delivers Kate into psychological domination by Cassie, whose enjoyment of living well seems instrumental in her keeping suitors away from Kate. There is an indication that Cassie perjured herself at the trial and that Kate knows who murdered her father and is protecting that person. One may speculate about the details of the relationship between Ezra Spain and his daughter, perhaps even more about that between Ezra Spain and Cassie, and not least about that between Cassie and Kate. Wharton, not uncharacteristically for this final period of her creative life, allows hints to abound and contrives for certainty to be continually deflected.

"Roman Fever" (*Liberty*, 10 November 1934) is a short masterpiece, exquisitely constructed toward a devastatingly ironic climax, based on fact more than hint, but on fact carefully revealed. Two matrons visiting Rome in the 1920s reminisce about their girlhood visits to Rome, while their daughters pursue their romantic interests. Roman fever refers to the malaria to which the matrons' grandmothers' generation was exposed on their visits to Rome, but the term is used by Wharton in the metaphorical sense to refer to the perils of love in Rome. Although the dynamic Mrs. Slade taunts the quieter Mrs. Ansley about their romantic rivalry of twenty-five years ago, Mrs. Ansley in the very last line of the story reveals that her own daughter, the vivacious Barbara, is the daughter of the late Delphin Slade, who at the time of conception was engaged to marry the future Mrs. Slade.

"Duration" is an acerbic tale of two centenarians for whom a joint birthday ceremony is being rehearsed. Miss Martha Little, whose services to the family were counted on even as she was obliged to endure humiliation, rises to imperial heights as a centenarian. She obtains her most spectacular revenge on the system by tripping Syngleton Perch, sending her coeval rival sprawling. Although "Duration" does not entirely escape burlesque, it is on the whole neither good-natured nor sentimental; Martha Little has suffered too much in her family imprisonment for us to laugh freely at her belated emergence.

"All Souls'," which Wharton wrote several months before her death, is the lead story in *Ghosts*, published by Appleton in 1937 (the other stories in the book had been published in previous collections). Wharton's last story is one of her best, a ghost story that, as her narrator says, "isn't exactly a ghost-story." Early on the reader is alerted to the crucial role to be played by the all-too-reliable, long-in-the-family servants of the widow Sara Clayburn at her isolated–especially in winter–house in the Connecticut countryside. The reader also suspects the unfamiliar person Sara Clayburn sees nearby during a walk–on what chances to be All Souls' Eve–shortly before she breaks her ankle in an icy fall and is confined to bed on doctor's orders. Still, in a combination of physical pain and increasing fear of the silence and of the unknown, she does manage to drag herself around the house to confirm that for some inexplicable reason the five servants have decamped, apparently in an organized way, leaving her alone and almost helpless in a cold

house whose electricity and telephone have ceased to function. It appears that the mysterious female stranger, whether in the role of a fetch or of a living person inhabited by a witch, has summoned the servants to a witches' coven.

If the reader chooses to associate the coven on All Souls' Eve with visions of orgiastic sex, as some critics do, then the story may be interpreted as Wharton's familiar concatenation of sex and, if not violence, certainly the uncanny with implications of violence. Perhaps, however, a contrast would reflect the sense of "All Souls' " both more subtly and more effectively: between the presumed uninhibited revels at a coven and the aseptic emotional life of the servants at the estate, Whitegates, whose orderliness and cleanliness Wharton stresses, as well as that of Sara Clayburn, who flees, never to return, at the reappearance of the mysterious stranger just before All Souls' Eve the next year.

Edith Wharton's development as a short-story writer, while beginning several years before her debut as a novelist, followed somewhat the same course, once she made her own society her primary métier in about 1905. Before that point her stories often dealt with a lower-middle-class society. Although that is not a social stratum she could have known very well, she achieves an authenticity through her ability to depict psychological complication or, on a more personal level, by psychologically identifying with her fictional characters.

After having discovered the possibilities of her own society, Wharton did not promptly abandon all other milieus. She wrote stories of rural people, stories dwelling on the historical past, stories of Europeans as well as Americans, ghost stories, legends, and exile stories; but her most propitious ground was upper-class New York City around the turn of the century. Even her ghosts are usually seen, or possibly not seen, by members of that society or its exile extensions in England and France.

The situations and settings of Wharton's stories, even fictional proper names, tend to turn up later in her novels. Yet one needs to be cautious about regarding the stories as seeds of the novels, for sometimes the story is a byproduct of the novel-planning and novel-writing process–a byproduct that saw print before the novel. The often mediocre novels that Wharton wrote in the 1920s are anticipated and paralleled by similarly fragile stories about not always convincing members of a shallow bourgeoisie on the financial and social make. While the configuration is almost too pat, it is doubtless significant that her best late short stories, for example, "Roman Fever" and "All Souls'," mark her reconnection with her own now-past society as successfully as did her last and incomplete novel, *The Buccaneers* (1938).

Wharton can lay just claim to first rank as a story writer. She is not, however, an innovator, a fact that is evident from her consideration of short stories in her theoretical work, *The Writing of Fiction* (1925), as well as in her stories. She develops the straight-line or frame structure of the traditional story as far as genius can, endowing a clever–sometimes too coincidental–plot line with a remarkable complexity of human mind and character, but she does not change the mold of such admired models as Honoré de Balzac, Ivan Turgenev, and Gottfried Keller. Her style, above all her irony, from which her style is inseparable, is superb. For the most part her fictive narrators are male. She inhabits the male point of view convincingly, although such habitation probably incorporates a greater number of effectual aperçus of the woman's social or socially conditioned plight than a male's point of view would provide.

The modest sales of Wharton's short-story collections need to be evaluated not only in contrast to the huge printings of her best-selling novels but also in terms of the moderate-to-mass circulation of the magazines in which the stories first appeared. It serves little to compare Wharton's critical reception with those of Nathaniel Hawthorne or Henry James, for she has substantially less in common with those writers than an earlier generation of critics liked to imagine. She is anything but epigonal–chiefly by virtue of her focus on her own society and, above all, on the women in that society. Edith Wharton–quite aside from her reputation as a novelist–is among the most brilliant American short-story writers.

Letters:
The Letters of Edith Wharton, edited by R. W. B. Lewis and Nancy Lewis (New York: Scribners, 1988).

Bibliography:
Vito J. Brenni, *Edith Wharton: A Bibliography* (Morgantown: West Virginia University Library, 1966).

Biography:
R. W. B. Lewis, *Edith Wharton: A Biography* (New York, Evanston, San Francisco & London: Harper & Row, 1975).

References:
Louis Auchincloss, *Edith Wharton* (Minneapolis: University of Minnesota, 1961);

Auchincloss, *Edith Wharton: A Woman in Her Time* (New York: Viking, 1971);

Olivia Coolidge, *Edith Wharton, 1862-1937* (New York: Scribners, 1964);

Irving Howe, ed., *Edith Wharton: A Collection of Critical Essays* (Englewood Cliffs, N.J.: Prentice-Hall, 1962);

Grace Kellogg, *The Two Lives of Edith Wharton* (New York: Appleton-Century-Crofts, 1965);

Richard H. Lawson, *Edith Wharton* (New York: Ungar, 1977);

Robert M. Lovett, *Edith Wharton* (New York: McBride, 1925);

Percy Lubbock, *Portrait of Edith Wharton* (New York: Appleton-Century, 1947);

Margaret B. McDowell, *Edith Wharton* (Boston: Twayne, 1976);

McDowell, "Edith Wharton's Ghost Stories," *Criticism*, 12 (1970): 132-152;

Blake Nevius, *Edith Wharton* (Berkeley & Los Angeles: University of California Press, 1953);

Geoffrey Walton, *Edith Wharton: A Critical Interpretation* (Rutherford, N.J.: Fairleigh Dickinson University Press, 1970);

Cynthia Griffin Woolf, *A Feast of Words: The Triumph of Edith Wharton* (New York: Oxford University Press, 1977).

Papers:
The most important collection of Wharton's papers is in the Beinecke Library at Yale University. The Houghton Library at Harvard University and Princeton University also have large collections of Wharton's letters.

Owen Wister
(14 July 1860-21 July 1938)

Michael Butler
University of Kansas

See also the Wister entry in *DLB 9: American Novelists, 1910-1945*.

BOOKS: *The Lady of the Lake* (Cambridge, Mass.: Chorus Book, 1881);

The New Swiss Family Robinson: A Tale for Children of All Ages (Cambridge, Mass.: Charles W. Sever, University Bookstore, 1882);

The Dragon of Wantley: His Rise, His Voracity, & His Downfall: A Romance (Philadelphia: Lippincott, 1892);

Red Men and White (New York: Harper, 1896; London: Osgood, McIlvaine, 1896);

Lin McLean (New York & London: Harper, 1898);

The Jimmyjohn Boss and Other Stories (New York & London: Harper, 1900);

Ulysses S. Grant (Boston: Small, Maynard, 1900);

The Virginian: A Horseman of the Plains (New York & London: Macmillan, 1902);

Philosophy 4: A Story of Harvard University (New York & London: Macmillan, 1903);

Musk-ox, Bison, Sheep and Goat, by Wister, Caspar Whitney, and George Bird Grinnell (New York & London: Macmillan, 1904);

A Journey in Search of Christmas (New York & London: Harper, 1904);

Lady Baltimore (New York & London: Macmillan, 1906);

How Doth the Simple Spelling Bee (New York & London: Macmillan, 1907);

The Seven Ages of Washington: A Biography (New York: Macmillan, 1907);

Mother (New York: Dodd, Mead, 1907);

Padre Ignacio: or, The Song of Temptation (New York & London: Harper, 1911);

Members of the Family (New York & London: Macmillan, 1911);

The Pentecost of Calamity (New York & London: Macmillan, 1915);

A Straight Deal: or, The Ancient Grudge (New York & London: Macmillan, 1920);

Indispensable Information for Infants: or, Easy Entrance to Education (New York: Macmillan, 1921);

Owen Wister, age forty

Neighbors Henceforth (New York & London: Macmillan, 1922);

Watch Your Thirst: A Dry Opera in Three Acts (New York: Macmillan, 1923);

When West Was West (New York & London: Macmillan, 1928);

Roosevelt: The Story of a Friendship, 1880-1919 (New York: Macmillan, 1930); republished as *Theodore Roosevelt: The Story of a Friendship, 1880-1919* (London: Macmillan, 1930);

Two Appreciations of John Jay Chapman (New York: Privately printed, 1934).
Collection: *The Writings of Owen Wister*, 11 volumes (New York: Macmillan, 1928).

OTHER: "The Palace of the Closed Window," in *A Week Away From Time*, edited by Mrs. James Lodge (Boston: Roberts Brothers, 1887);
"Mother," in *A House Party* (Boston: Small, Maynard, 1901).

PERIODICAL PUBLICATION: "The Reprieve of Capitalist Clyve," *Lippincott's Magazine*, 52 (July 1893): 95-102.

Although best known for *The Virginian: A Horseman of the Plains* (1902), a novel often credited—if inaccurately—with being "the first Western," Owen Wister was in talent and predilection perhaps more a short-story writer than a novelist. He produced over sixty short stories, some of which provided the beginnings for his novels *Lin McLean* (1898) and *The Virginian*. All but a few of Wister's stories were about the American West, and, appearing in *Harper's New Monthly Magazine*, the *Saturday Evening Post, Collier's Weekly,* and *Cosmopolitan*, they helped to transform the region into a subject respectable enough for "quality" slick magazine fiction.

Wister was the only child of Sarah Butler and Owen Jones Wister. According to the writer's daughter, Fanny Wister, her grandparents' household in Germantown, Pennsylvania, was "intensely intellectual" and their relationship "temperamental." From a family of prosperous merchants, the father was a practical and hard-working country doctor known for his quick wit and temper. He once threw a beefsteak out the dining room window because it was not cooked to his liking. The writer's mother was the daughter of Fanny Kemble, a well-known actress and friend of such European celebrities as Sir Walter Scott, William Makepeace Thackeray, Robert Browning, and Felix Mendelssohn and of such Americans as historians William H. Prescott and John Lothrop Motley, naturalist Louis Agassiz, and writers Ralph Waldo Emerson, Oliver Wendell Holmes, James Russell Lowell, and Henry Wadsworth Longfellow. Sarah Butler was an intellectual who spoke several languages, played the piano well, translated the poetry of Alfred de Musset into English, and wrote unsigned articles for the *Atlantic Monthly*. She was, according to Fanny Wister, "very much aware . . . she was a personage." Owen Wister's mother was the great intellectual force in his life, but her strong personality tended to overshadow his own.

Wister received a patrician education which included short stints in Swiss, English, and Germantown private schools. At thirteen he entered St. Paul's in Concord, New Hampshire. While there he wrote his first published story, "Down in a Diving Bell," which appeared in the school magazine. In 1878, after five years at St. Paul's, Wister enrolled at Harvard, where he majored in music. During his university years he wrote both words and music for several college shows; had a burlesque novel, *The New Swiss Family Robinson* (1882), serialized in the *Harvard Lampoon;* and published a poem, "Beethoven," in the February 1882 *Atlantic Monthly*. He was elected Phi Beta Kappa and in 1882 graduated summa cum laude.

After spending the next year studying musical composition in Europe, where he was encouraged by Franz Liszt—a friend of his grandmother—Wister returned home to keep a promise to his father that he would safely establish himself in a sound profession. He went to work with Union Safe Deposit Vaults of Boston. There, he told his mother, he did three things: acted as a receiving teller, ran up stairs, and compounded interest. The life was, he said, "not difficult but exceedingly monotonous." Socially he fared better. In 1884 he helped form a number of "undomesticated young men" dedicated to jest, romp, and Chianti into the Tavern Club, the first president of which was William Dean Howells. He also collaborated with a distant cousin, Langdon Mitchell, on "A Wise Man's Son," a novel not submitted for publication on the advice of Howells, who judged it too racy for the American public.

During this period of his life Wister grew restless and dispirited. His health began to deteriorate. Throughout the winter of 1885 he was depressed and tended to withdraw into himself. That summer he took the advice of Dr. Silas Weir Mitchell, a novelist and also a kinsman, and went west. His body responded well and, just as important, so did his imagination. The opening entry in his first western journal reads: "One must come to the West to realize what one may have most probably believed all one's life long— that it is a very much bigger place than the East, and the future of America is just bubbling and seething in bare legs and pinafores here. I don't wonder a man never comes back [East] after he

Wister as a child (American Heritage Center,
University of Wyoming)

has once been here for a few years."

Wister did "come back," however; in October he enrolled at Harvard Law School, from which he graduated in 1888. He became a member of the Philadelphia bar in 1890. In the meantime he had continued his summer trips. For many years Wister followed a pattern of living in the East and taking holidays in the West. The notebooks he kept during those vacation jaunts reveal an increasing awareness of the literary possibilities of the regions he visited as well as a growing, and ever focusing, ambition to be the one to realize them. The moment at which dream became reality occurred one fall evening in 1891 as Wister was dining at his Philadelphia club with another young enthusiast fresh from the West. As he later wrote:

From oysters to coffee we compared experiences. Why wasn't some Kipling saving the sage-brush for American literature, before the sage-brush and all that it signified went the way of the California forty-niner, went the way of the Mississippi steam-boat, went the way of everything? . . .

What was fiction doing, fiction, the only thing that has always outlived fact? Must it be perpetual tea-cups? Was Alkali Ike in the comic papers the one figure which the jejune American imagination, always at full-cock to banter or to brag, could discern in that epic which was being lived at a gallop out in the sage-brush? "To hell with tea-cups and the great American laugh!" we two said, as we sat dining at the club. The claret had been excellent.

"Walter, I'm going to try it myself!" I exclaimed to Walter Furness. "I'm going to start this minute."

Wister walked upstairs to the club library and spent the night writing most of "Hank's Woman." Once again taking the advice of Dr. Silas Weir Mitchell, he sent it and another story, "How Lin McLean Went East," to Henry Mills Alden, former editor of *Harper's Weekly* and current editor of *Harper's Monthly*, who bought them both.

"Hank's Woman" (*Harper's Weekly*, 27 August 1892) is the story of an Austrian servant girl who, after being fired by her mistress at Yellowstone Park, makes the mistake of marrying a worthless American whose persecution of her for her religion drives her to murder. "How Lin McLean Went East" (*Harper's New Monthly Magazine*, December 1892) describes a young cowboy's disillusioning trip to his boyhood home in Massachusetts, where he discovers that his mean-spirited, petit bourgeois brother is embarrassed by his western appearance and behavior. Artistically and intellectually, Wister never drifted far from the marks set by those stories. Most of his later fiction deals with conflicts of various kinds between East and West or between the forces of purification and degeneration within the West itself. In form and style nearly all of Wister's short fiction conforms to contemporary models of the well-made magazine story. The controlling narrative voice is always a cultured personality superior to his subject in civilized qualities. In a few framed stories this character is told a tale by a more vernacular narrator; in some third-person narratives the personality is present only as the consciousness through which the action is filtered; in some first-person narratives he is a character in the story. Although less neatly structured than much contemporary periodical writing, Wister's stories are adequately plotted and proceed to fairly definite endings–whether those be neat resolutions, surprise twists in the manner of Frank Stockton or O. Henry, punch lines, or dramatically telling statements. More realistic in setting, situation, and characters than much rival fiction, Wister's work still tends toward the sentimental and, more frequently, the melodramatic. The latter was a characteristic he recognized: "Genteel critics in the East found these sketches 'melodramatic,'" he once wrote. "Poor Sketches, how could they help it and remain truthful?" Finally, despite some "risky" subjects, his stories lie comfortably within accepted bounds of decorum and convention. In spite of some grumbling, Wister never really challenged popular taste.

His early success gave Wister an artistic direction. He seriously set about becoming the "Kipling of the sage-brush." He read more studiously about the frontier; on his summer trips he hunted material with a vengeance. In 1893 Harper's proposed that he write them a series of western adventures, each "a thrilling story, having its ground in a real incident." Wister accepted. He then gave up his law practice and began the ten most productive years of his literary life. He wrote the stories which were to make up two collections, *Red Men and White* (1896) and *The Jimmyjohn Boss and Other Stories* (1900; retitled *Hank's Woman* as volume 3 of *The Writings of Owen Wister*, 1928), and those which he worked into the novels *Lin McLean* and *The Virginian*. He also produced an important essay, "The Evolution of the Cow-Puncher" (*Harper's New Monthly Magazine*, September 1895; collected as the preface to *Red Men and White* in *The Writings of Owen Wister*), which perhaps most clearly expresses the disquieting assumptions from which he evolved his version of the West. The cowboy was "not a new type," he wrote, "no product of the frontier but just the original kernel of the nut with the shell broken." The Wild West offered an opportunity for Anglo-Saxon blood to reinvigorate itself, for the manly spirit of adventure characteristic of earlier times to reawaken in modern men—that is, modern men of the proper racial stock. "No rood of modern ground," Wister said of America, "is more debased and mongrel with its hordes of encroaching alien vermin, that turn our cities to Babels and our citizenship to a hybrid farce, who degrade our commonwealth from a nation into something half pawn-shop, half broker's office. But to survive in the clean cattle country requires spirit of adventure, courage, and self-sufficiency; you will not find many Poles or Huns or Russian Jews in that district; but the Anglo-Saxon is still forever homesick for out-of-doors." Wister believed the tide of history ran against his ideal. The progress which had

brought the electric light and "the ignorance of Populist politics" had also doomed the Anglo-Saxon West. He thought that he was, from the beginning, a writer of historical fiction; by 1895 the day of the cowboy had passed.

Red Men and White collected eight stories which had appeared in *Harper's New Monthly Magazine* during the previous two years. In one way the volume was a significant success. Kipling liked it and sent Wister a brief poem celebrating Specimen Jones, a character in three of the stories. No doubt that pleased, or relieved, Wister; his volume definitely shows the influence of the British writer. The "Jones" stories–"Specimen Jones" (July 1894), "The General's Bluff" (September 1894), and "The Second Missouri Compromise" (March 1895)–deal, as does "Little Big Horn Medicine" (June 1894), with the difficulties encountered by the army in maintaining order on the far frontier. Wister's heroes are professional soldiers who struggle against renegade Indians, unreconstructed southerners, and the "Tommy Atkins Go Away" mentality of ignorant eastern bureaucrats. Three stories in the collection treat one of Wister's favorite subjects, women, who, with a few notable exceptions, appear most prominently in his work as either tramps or fools. In "The Serenade at Siskiyou" (August 1894) the ladies of a western town sentimentalize a young stage robber and murderer—an act of injustice which exasperates the men of the community into lynching him. In "Salvation Gap" (October 1894) a degraded miner slits the throat of a prostitute who had exploited his infatuation with her and then tries to do "the manly thing" by saving her lover when he is accused of the crime. In "La Tinaja Bonita" (May 1895) a young American delirious with thirst and suspicion stabs the Mexican girl who loves him and then dies himself. Populist democracy, another favorite subject, is the target of "A Pilgrim on the Gila" (November 1895), in which a dishonest Arizona lawyer-politician successfully defends a gang of Mormon highwaymen by bribing a jury. The underlying point of this tale is the contrast between territorial realities and the image of Arizona spun out in congress by William Jennings Bryan. *Lin McLean*, though ostensibly a novel, is actually a book composed of six previously published stories. Taken together, "How Lin McLean Went East," "The Winning of the Biscuit-Shooter" (*Harper's New Monthly Magazine*, December 1893), "Lin McLean's Honeymoon" (*Harper's New Monthly Magazine*, January 1895), "A Jour-

Bostonians George Norman and Copley Amory and guides George West and Jules Mason seated in front of Tigie, an Indian guide, and Owen Wister in Jackson Hole, Wyoming, 1887

ney in Search of Christmas" (*Harper's Weekly Magazine*, 14 December 1895), "Separ's Vigilante" (*Harper's New Monthly Magazine*, March 1897), and "Destiny at Drybone" (*Harper's New Monthly Magazine*, December 1897) loosely relate how after his return from Massachusetts Lin McLean, a Wyoming cowboy, woos and wins Katie Peck, discovers she is already married to a rainmaker's assistant, adopts her runaway son, woos but does not win "an American virgin" of inanely high moral standards who considers him married to Katie Peck, unsuccessfully tries to revive Katie after she has taken a lethal dose of laudanum, and finally weds the right girl. The book's structure is problematical, particularly since all of the episodes do not have the same narrative point of view. Wister persisted in claiming that the book *was* a novel: that its episodic structure was the best means of communicating the cowboy's picaresque existence. Readers persisted in calling it an anthology of stories. No doubt to remedy the situation, in a later edition Wister divided the six episodes into twenty chapters.

In 1898 Wister married Mary Channing Wister, a cousin he had known since childhood and a descendant of William Ellery Channing, one of the founders of Unitarianism. They had three

boys and three girls, and, according to Fanny Wister, Mary was the antithesis of Wister's mother: "Her house ran smoothly; her servants adored her. She kept her husband comfortable at all times, fending off annoyance and holding boring people at bay."

The years after this marriage were productive for Wister. His second collection, *The Jimmyjohn Boss and Other Stories*, appeared in 1900. Three of its eight stories—"Hank's Woman"; "The Promised Land" (*Harper's New Monthly Magazine*, April 1894), which describes a pioneer family's encounter with Wild Goose Jake, a renegade selling whiskey to Indians, and what turns out to be the retarded son he has brought west to protect from society; and "A Kinsman of Red Cloud" (*Harper's New Monthly Magazine*, May 1894), which portrays the cavalry's difficulties in capturing a murderous half-breed—had been written as part of the original contract with Harper's. Appearing in print for the first time were "The Jimmyjohn Boss" (retitled "The Boy and the Buccaroos" in volume 3 of *The Writings of Owen Wister*), which describes a nineteen-year-old foreman's proving himself as a handler of rebellious older hands, and "Napoleon Shave-tail," a mean-spirited story of an arrogant West Point graduate from "our Middle West where they encounter education too suddenly," whose adherence "to the book" results in the death of a veteran sergeant and an absurd military debacle. Much more interesting and successful are the three remaining stories in the collection. Two are satirical portraits of Sharon, a small southwestern town. "Sharon's Choice" (*Harper's New Monthly Magazine*, August 1897) describes an elocution contest in which two able performers–a girl who recites Charles Dickens's "Death of Paul Dombey" and a boy who does Mark Twain's "Blue Jay Yarn"–are defeated by an orphan raised by the patrons of a saloon. He captures the crowd's heart by rhythmically rattling through: "I love little pussy her coat is so warm/And if I don't hurt her she'll do me no harm. . . ." The conventional sentimentalism of the story is nicely undercut and given a political edge by last lines which ask what sort of citizen the orphan will grow up to be: "For whom will he vote? May he not himself come to sit in Washington and make laws for us? Universal suffrage holds so many possibilities." "Twenty Minutes for Refreshments" (*Harper's New Monthly Magazine*, January 1900) relates the adventures of Wister's eastern narrator at a baby contest in Sharon. It is most remarkable for a portrait of Mrs. Sedalia Preene, a cultivated and strong-willed woman whose character and relationship to the storyteller may well have been shaped by family memories. The most unusual story in the collection is "Padre Ignacio" (published as "Padre Ignazio," *Harper's New Monthly Magazine*, April 1900; published separately in 1911). It is, atypically, not about the cowboy West. Set in California in 1855, its title character is a highly cultivated Spanish priest whose encounter with a young Frenchman tempts him to leave his mission and return to Paris and the music he loves. In its celebration of things civilized, "Padre Ignacio" is more "European" than anything else in Wister's early stories. It also offers the first fully developed appearance of the civilized exile, a character prominent in his later work.

In 1901 Wister published two stories with eastern settings. "Philosophy 4" (*Lippincott's Magazine*, August 1901; published separately in 1903; collected in volume 8 of *The Writings of Owen Wister*), based on Wister's Harvard days, contrasts two rich, careless, and supposedly admirable students to their tutor, an impoverished, unimaginative, unattractive, and Jewish grind. "Mother" (first published in *A House Party*, 1901, a collection of stories by various authors; collected in vol-

ume 8 of *The Writings of Owen Wister*) is an account of stock-market speculation written in imitation of Frank Stockton. No doubt most of Wister's creative energy was at this time being directed toward *The Virginian*. *Harper's New Monthly Magazine* had previously published "Emily" (November 1893), the story about a hen who tried to hatch anything round; "Balaam and Pedro" (January 1894), the story of animal abuse which greatly upset Theodore Roosevelt, a friend since college; "Where Fancy Was Bred" (March 1896), the celebrated baby-switching episode; "Grandmother Stark" (June 1897), which dealt with the Virginian's wooing of Molly Wood; and "The Game and the Nation" (May 1900), the Virginian's tall tale of frog ranching. Like *Lin McLean*, the origins of *The Virginian* lay in short fiction. Wister was determined, however, that this time there would be no questions about the genre of his creation. He even turned to Gustave Flaubert's *Madame Bovary* (1856) as a model to work from. He succeeded in his efforts. The book was a popular and, to an extent, a critical success, although not with his mother, who wrote to tell him that *The Virginian* was piecemeal, its last chapter superfluous, its heroine a failure, its morality doubtful, and that, all in all, it reminded her of Ouida's popular adventure fiction.

In defending himself, Wister promised his mother that his next effort would be "a very big book indeed." But in the following year he published only "How the Energy Was Conserved" (*Collier's Weekly*, 21 February 1903), a cavalry story which describes the trouble caused by a secretary of war whose Populist rhetoric undermines the necessary–and natural–discipline of an army post. In 1906 *Lady Baltimore*, a "Jamesian" novel set in South Carolina, appeared. Nothing followed for two years; then the *Saturday Evening Post* printed two Western stories: "Timberline" (7 March 1908) and "The Gift Horse" (18 July 1908). The *Saturday Evening Post* published another Western, "Extra Dry," on 27 February 1909, and the *Century Magazine* published "With the Coin of Her Life" in their June issue. An imitation of Silas Weir Mitchell which detailed the physical and mental deterioration of a young girl of good family, this story was collected in volume 8 of *The Writings of Owen Wister*. In 1911 the *Saturday Evening Post* published two more Western stories, "The Drake Who Had Means of His Own" (11 March) and "Where It Was" (22 April). In that same year all of these pieces except "With the Coin of Her Life" were gathered together

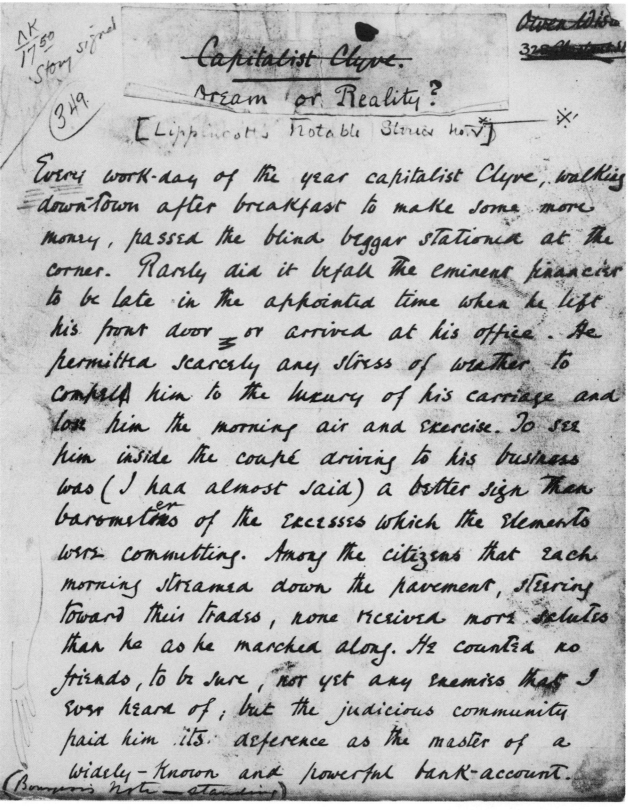

First and last pages from the manuscript for Wister's story that appeared as "The Reprieve of Capitalist Clyve" in the July 1893 issue of Lippincott's Magazine *(Owen Wister Collection [#6327], Clifton Waller Barrett Library, Special Collections Department, University of Virginia Library)*

19.

able for the first time to walk slowly downtown, he went through Independence Square and came upon the blind man. He paused, and then crossed the pavement to the patient figure.

"God bless you, sir!" said the beggar. "I've known your step these many years."

Owen Wister

with "Spit-Cat Creek" (first published as "The Vicious Circle," *Saturday Evening Post*, 13 December 1902) and "Happy Teeth" (first published as "The Patronage of High Bear," *Cosmopolitan*, January 1901) as *Members of the Family*. The soldier Specimen Jones reappears as a character in "How the Energy Was Conserved," which was retitled "In the Back." Scipio Le Moyne, a character in *The Virginian*, appears in all the rest. In some he might be called the hero; in others he is either an observer or the inside narrator of a framed story. Only three of the pieces in *Members of the Family* offer anything out of Wister's ordinary. "The Drake Who Had Means of His Own" slyly describes how a drake's arrogant behavior with two ducks teaches a henpecked husband the beneficial effect competition can have on a married man's situation. More interesting is "The Gift Horse." The subject of this story is lynching, which Wister had defended in several of his earlier works, most recently in *The Virginian*. In "The Gift Horse" the eastern narrative "I" so closely associated with Wister is threatened with hanging. Instead of a form of direct justice necessary in an unsettled country, the pending execution is here pictured as a terrifying farce motivated not by an Anglo-Saxon sense of the right but by the egotism of a rich rancher. "The Gift Horse" seems a retelling of some of Wister's earlier stories and perhaps suggests a reconsideration of old attitudes. The third notable work in the collection, "Where It Was," is a comic tale tinged with melancholy that reintroduces the exile. Here Wister portrayed a young easterner who because of intelligence, education, and maturity is out of place running a small store in the Northwest, and a pair of cranky old forty-niners bound together primarily by their common experiencing of an era long passed.

After the publication of *Members of the Family* Wister stopped writing fiction for about twelve years. In 1913 his wife died in childbirth. In 1914 he traveled to Europe. He was in Munich at the outbreak of World War I and spent the next years urging that the United States enter on the side of Britain and France. In 1915 he published *The Pentecost of Calamity*, a long essay advocating intervention. Following the armistice, Wister spent part of every year abroad. He took his children to see the great cathedrals. He made the acquaintanceship of such writers as Lord Dunsany, E. F. Benson, and Joseph Conrad. He became a connoisseur of French wines and began a book on the subject. But, according to his daughter, he

Wister at Yellowstone National Park, 1891 (American Heritage Center, University of Wyoming)

never talked about the West. In 1920 he published *A Straight Deal: or, The Ancient Grudge*, a defense of close Anglo-American relations, and in 1922, *Neighbors Henceforth*, an account of travels through France after its devastation in the war. Then in 1923 Wister began to write fiction again. In 1924 *Cosmopolitan* published "Sun Road" (July) and "Captain Quid" (September), a story of a cavalry officer, his irrational wife, and tobacco. In 1926 the same magazine printed "Once Round the Clock" (July) and "The Right Honorable the Strawberries" (November). In October 1927 *Harper's Magazine* published "Safe in the Arms of Croesus," a story set aboard an Atlantic liner which contrasts the nonprofiteering heroism of a self-effacing Charles Lindbergh to the egotistical, self-advertising materialism of most Americans. In 1928 *Cosmopolitan* published four more Western stories: "Moulting Pelican" (May), "Little Old Scaffold" (June), "Lone Fountain" (June), and "At the Sign of the Last Chance" (February). In the same year all of the *Cosmopolitan* stories plus one too bold for the magazines, "Skip to My Loo"–in which a black panderer is shot by a Texan whom he has led to an assignation with his own wife–were collected in *When West Was West*, a volume created for inclusion in *The Writings of Owen Wister*. "Safe in the Arms of Croesus" gave its name to the eighth volume of the collected writings, which brought together Wister's few non-Western stories.

With two exceptions, the pieces in *When West Was West* are not among Wister's best work, but they are interesting in that the figure of the exile is prominent. The most arresting character in "Once Round the Clock" and "Little Old Scaffold"–two stories set in a Texas county dominated by a woman, the quack healer Professor Salamanca–is Col. Steptoe McDee, a Mississippian forced west by the Civil War. McDee is too polite, too intelligent, and too civilized for the barbarism of his new home. "The Right Honorable the Strawberries," a story about "going native" perhaps influenced by Joseph Conrad, concerns an English remittance man banished to America for a gambling scandal. Some critics consider this one of Wister's best works; it is perhaps another example of his retelling an old story and consequently reassessing an old idea–in this case the Anglo-Saxon encounter with the frontier. "Absalom and Moulting Pelican" (originally titled "Moulting Pelican"), which revolves around an elaborate joke involving an imbecile clergyman's belief that American Indians descended from the lost tribes of Israel, has as its hero Hugh Lloyd, a graduate of St. Paul's School and Harvard sent west to a region he calls "a vacuum" in order to learn the practical business of running a ranch. Characters stranded in time play roles in some of these stories as well. By the end of "Absalom and Moulting Pelican," Hugh's only companion is, for all practical purposes, the last Apache in Arizona. Sun Road, the central character in "Bad Medicine" (originally titled "Sun Road"), is a graduate of Carlyle Indian School who tries to remain true to the old ways of his tribe but becomes infatuated with having his picture taken by tourists at Yellowstone Park. He is killed by a geyser and leaves his son an orphan only half educated in their heritage. In "Lone Fountain," a remarkably passionate Wyoming variation on Nathaniel Hawthorne's *The Marble Faun* (1860), Kenneth

Scott, a self-educated American "natural child," falls in love with Nina Schmidt, a sensual and pagan European who worships the old Greek gods. Nina ultimately gives herself to a deity who appears to her in a Wyoming geyser; Scott then lives out his life beside the crevices of Mount Etna. The melancholy sense of exile in space and time which haunts *When West Was West* is most successfully realized in "At the Sign of the Last Chance," a genuinely moving story in which some old men–Wister's alter ego eastern narrator among them–sit around talking about times past. Then in conformance with an English custom one of them has read about in an 1885 magazine, they go out and bury the sign of their ghost town's saloon. The piece comes close to trite sentimentalism, but Wister controls its emotion well. "At the Sign of the Last Chance" is one of Wister's best stories as well as a fitting farewell to his West.

After the publication of his collected writings in 1928, Wister wrote no more fiction. He died in 1938 of a cerebral hemorrhage. Aside from a growing melancholy and perhaps a greater openness, Wister's short fiction showed little development over the course of his career. The ideas–or prejudices–which informed his earliest stories informed the last. His racist theories did not change; his anti-Semitism did not abate; his political assumptions remained constant. His first volume of Western fiction contained one story about irrationally silly wives, one about a tramp. So did his last. He mocked the excesses of democratic society in *Red Men and White;* he did the same in "Safe in the Arms of Croesus." In terms of form and technique little distinguished his early work from late. Wister refined what he had begun with; he did not experiment. His notebooks make clear that as he wandered through the West looking for material, he did not seek to assimilate or understand the region as much as he sought out those striking characters and incidents which fit his conceptions of what literature was and life ought to be. His search was in a sense a voyage more of justification than of exploration. Consequently his fiction did not reveal the West as much as it illustrated one static version of it. Early in his career Wister took the advice of Henry James to pay more attention to the look of landscape in his work. Indeed one of the real strengths of his fiction is the way it translates the descriptive techniques of the painter into words. Unfortunately the debt seems to have stopped there; Wister's short stories do not suggest a writer trying, in James's words, "to be one of the people on whom nothing is lost." In fairness to Wister, however, it should be said that his stories are usually entertaining. His ideology never overwhelmed his art. He was a skillful and intelligent craftsman, and unlike most of his contemporaries who published in popular magazines, his work has stayed in print–an argument that it still has the power to please readers.

Today Wister is not considered a major figure in mainstream American literature. He would not be listed among important contributors to the development of the American short story. He is, however, still a writer to be reckoned with in Western American literature. Scholars in that field continue to try to fix the exact nature of his contribution and the extent of his influence. Taken together, two relatively modern statements perhaps accurately reflect the writer's current status. In 1960 Don D. Walker wrote: "Wister, I think it can be safely argued, was the first writer of seriousness and sophistication to use the cowboy imaginatively." In 1973 Richard W. Etulain declared: "Wister was a better yarn-spinner, a sketcher of episodes than a superb creator of character or a student of forms. He did not come to grips sufficiently with how a region could brand its unique ways into the hides of its natives. In several respects then ... Wister is a more important figure for the literary and cultural historians than he is for the student of American belles lettres."

Letters:
Owen Wister Out West: His Journals and Letters, edited by Fanny Kemble Wister (Chicago: University of Chicago Press, 1958);

That I May Tell You: Journals and Letters of the Owen Wister Family, edited by Fanny Kemble Wister (Wayne, Pa.: Haverford House, 1979).

Bibliographies:
N. Orwin Rush, "Fifty Years of *The Virginian*," *Papers of the Bibliographical Society of America*, 46 (Second Quarter 1952): 99-120;

Dean Sherman, "Owen Wister: An Annotated Bibliography," *Bulletin of Bibliography and Magazine Notes*, 28 (January-March 1971): 7-16;

Sanford E. Marovitz, "Owen Wister: An Annotated Bibliography of Secondary Material," *American Literary Realism 1870-1910*, 7 (Winter 1974): 1-110;

James T. Bratcher, "Guide to Dissertations on American Literary Figures, 1870-1910: Owen Wister," *American Literary Realism 1870-1910*, 8 (Autumn 1975): 341.

References:
Richard W. Etulain, *Owen Wister* (Boise, Idaho: Boise State College Western Writers Series, 1973);

Ben M. Vorpahl, "Henry James and Owen Wister," *Pennsylvania Magazine of History and Biography*, 95 (July 1971): 291-338;

Don D. Walker, "Wister, Roosevelt and James: A Note on the Western," *American Quarterly*, 12 (Fall 1960): 358-366.

Papers:
Collections of Wister's letters and manuscript materials are held by the Library of Congress, the New York Public Library, the University of Wyoming Library, and the Houghton Library of Harvard University.

Books for Further Reading

Canby, Henry S. *The Short Story in English*. New York: Holt, 1909.

Hicks, Granville. *The Great Tradition: An Interpretation of American Literature Since the Civil War*, revised edition. New York: Macmillan, 1968.

Hoffman, Daniel. *Form and Fable in American Fiction*. New York: Oxford University Press, 1961.

Kazin, Alfred. *On Native Grounds*. New York: Reynal & Hitchcock, 1942.

Klinkowitz, Jerome. *The Practice of Fiction in America: Writers from Hawthorne to the Present*. Ames: Iowa State University Press, 1980.

Matthews, Brander. *The Philosophy of the Short Story*. New York & London: Longmans, Green, 1901.

May, Charles E., ed. *Short Story Theories*. Athens: Ohio University Press, 1976.

Mott, Frank Luther. *A History of American Magazines*. 5 volumes. Cambridge, Mass.: Harvard University Press, 1938-1968.

O'Brien, Edward J. *The Advance of the American Short Story*, revised edition. New York: Dodd, Mead, 1931.

O'Connor, Frank. *The Lonely Voice: A Study of the Short Story*. Cambridge, Mass.: Harvard University Press, 1963.

Pattee, Fred Lewis. *The Development of the American Short Story: An Historical Survey*. New York & London: Harper, 1923.

Peden, William. *The American Short Story: Front Line in the National Defense of Literature*. Boston: Houghton Mifflin, 1964.

Thorp, Willard. *American Writing in the Twentieth Century*. Cambridge, Mass.: Harvard University Press, 1960.

Voss, Arthur. *The American Short Story: A Critical Survey*. Norman: University of Oklahoma Press, 1973.

West, Ray B., Jr. *The Short Story in America: 1900-1950*. Chicago: Regnery, 1952.

Contributors

Samuel I. Bellman ....*California State Polytechnic University, Pomona*
Martha G. Bower ....*University of New Hampshire*
Michael Butler ....*University of Kansas*
James R. Giles ....*Northern Illinois University*
Melody Graulich ....*University of New Hampshire*
Yoshinobu Hakutani ....*Kent State University*
Doty Hale ....*California State University, Los Angeles*
Rosalie Hewitt ....*Northern Illinois University*
Tonette Bond Inge ....*Washington, D.C.*
Glen M. Johnson ....*Catholic University of America*
David Kirby ....*Florida State University*
Earle Labor ....*Centenary College of Louisiana*
Deborah G. Lambert ....*Merrimack Valley College*
Keith Lawrence ....*University of Southern California*
Richard H. Lawson ....*University of North Carolina at Chapel Hill*
Luther S. Luedtke ....*University of Southern California*
Charlotte S. McClure ....*Georgia State University*
Joseph B. McCullough ....*University of Nevada at Las Vegas*
Albert J. Miles ....*Pennsylvania State University–Ogontz Campus*
John F. Moe ....*Ohio State University*
Sylvia Lyons Render ....*Alexandria, Virginia*
Kenneth A. Robb ....*Bowling Green State University*
B. A. St. Andrews ....*State University of New York, Health Science Center*
Kathryn L. Seidel ....*University of Central Florida*
James F. Smith, Jr. ....*Pennsylvania State University–Ogontz Campus*
Richard J. Thompson ....*Canisius College*
Arthur Waterman ....*Georgia State University*
Ritchie D. Watson ....*Randolph-Macon College*
Perry D. Westbrook ....*State University of New York at Albany*

Cumulative Index

Dictionary of Literary Biography, Volumes 1-78
Dictionary of Literary Biography Yearbook, 1980-1987
Dictionary of Literary Biography Documentary Series, Volumes 1-4

Cumulative Index

DLB before number: *Dictionary of Literary Biography*, Volumes 1-78
Y before number: *Dictionary of Literary Biography Yearbook*, 1980-1987
DS before number: *Dictionary of Literary Biography Documentary Series*, Volumes 1-4

A

E

F

Cumulative Index

H

I

Cumulative Index

N

P

Cumulative Index

Cumulative Index

Dictionary of Literary Biography